Ford Focus Diesel
Owners Workshop Manual

Martynn Randall

Models covered

(4807 - 7AR2 - 320)

Hatchback, Saloon & Estate models with diesel engines
1.6 litre (1560cc), 1.8 litre (1753cc) and 2.0 litre (1997cc)

Does not cover CVT, Powershift or automatic transmission
Does not cover features specific to C-Max or CC (Convertible) models

© Haynes Publishing 2013

ABCDE
FGHIJ
KLMNO

A book in the **Haynes Owners Workshop Manual Series**

ISBN **978 0 85733 700 9**

British Library Cataloguing in Publication Data
A catalogue record for this book is available from the British Library.

Printed in the USA

Haynes Publishing
Sparkford, Yeovil, Somerset BA22 7JJ, England

Haynes North America, Inc
861 Lawrence Drive, Newbury Park, California 91320, USA

Haynes Publishing Nordiska AB
Box 1504, 751 45 UPPSALA, Sverige

Contents

Contents

REPAIRS & OVERHAUL

REFERENCE

The vacuum servo-assisted brakes are disc at the front, and either disc or drum at the rear. An electronically-controlled Anti-lock Braking System (ABS) is fitted on all models, with Dynamic Stability and Traction Control System (DSTC) also available.

Electric power-assisted steering is standard on all models. Air conditioning is available, and all models have an ergonomically-designed passenger cabin with high levels of safety and comfort for all passengers.

Provided that regular servicing is carried out in accordance with the manufacturer's recommendations, the Focus should prove a reliable and economical car. The engine compartment is well-designed, and most of the items needing frequent attention are easily accessible.

Your Ford Focus manual

The aim of this manual is to help you get the best value from your vehicle. It can do so in several ways. It can help you decide what work must be done (even should you choose to get it done by a garage). It will also provide information on routine maintenance and servicing, and give a logical course of action and diagnosis when random faults occur. However, it is hoped that you will use the manual by tackling the work yourself. On simpler jobs it may even be quicker than booking the car into a garage and going there twice, to leave and collect it. Perhaps most important, a lot of money can be saved by avoiding the costs a garage must charge to cover its labour and overheads.

The manual has drawings and descriptions to show the function of the various components so that their layout can be understood. Tasks are described and photographed in a clear step-by-step sequence. The illustrations are numbered by the Section number and paragraph number to which they relate – if there is more than one illustration per paragraph, the sequence is denoted alphabetically.

References to the 'left' or 'right' of the vehicle are in the sense of a person in the driver's seat, facing forwards.

The original Focus model range was introduced to the UK in 1998. It was hailed as being innovative and stylish with excellent roadholding. The new range of Focus covered by this manual shares the attributes of its ancestor, but with improved refinement and performance, coupled with lower emissions. This new Focus shares a platform with other models from Ford's stable, most noticeably the Volvo S40 and V50 range.

Initially only available as a Hatchback or Estate, the range was expanded later by the addition of a 4-door Saloon model. Safety features include door side impact bars, airbags for the driver and front seat passenger, side airbags, head airbags, whiplash protection system (front seats), and an advanced seat belt system with pretensioners and load limiters. Vehicle security is enhanced, with an engine immobiliser, shielded locks, and security-coded audio equipment being fitted as standard, as well as double-locking doors on most models.

Three sizes of diesel engine are available, with the 1.6 and 2.0 litre models being shared by Citroën and Peugeot – a result of joint projects between Ford and PSA (Citroën/Peugeot's parent company), whilst the 1.8 litre unit is of Ford's own design, and is carried over from the previous Focus model. All of the engines are four cylinder turbo diesel units, and the 1.6 and 2.0 litre units are a 16-valve DOHC design. They incorporate the latest design of direct injection common rail fuel system, with a variable geometry turbocharger, intercooler, catalytic converter and exhaust particulate filter (certain markets only).

The transversely-mounted engines drive the front roadwheels through either a five- or six-speed manual transmission with a hydraulically-operated clutch.

The fully-independent suspension is by MacPherson struts and transverse lower arms at the front, with multilink independent suspension at the rear; anti-roll bars are fitted at front and rear.

Acknowledgements

Thanks are due to Draper Tools Limited, who provided some of the workshop tools, and to all those people at Sparkford who helped in the production of this manual.

We take great pride in the accuracy of information given in this manual, but vehicle manufacturers make alterations and design changes during the production run of a particular vehicle of which they do not inform us. No liability can be accepted by the authors or publishers for loss, damage or injury caused by any errors in, or omissions from, the information given.

Working on your car can be dangerous. This page shows just some of the potential risks and hazards, with the aim of creating a safety-conscious attitude.

General hazards

Scalding

• Don't remove the radiator or expansion tank cap while the engine is hot.
• Engine oil, automatic transmission fluid or power steering fluid may also be dangerously hot if the engine has recently been running.

Burning

• Beware of burns from the exhaust system and from any part of the engine. Brake discs and drums can also be extremely hot immediately after use.

Crushing

• When working under or near a raised vehicle, always supplement the jack with axle stands, or use drive-on ramps. *Never venture under a car which is only supported by a jack.*

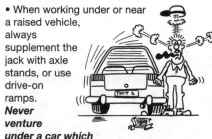

• Take care if loosening or tightening high-torque nuts when the vehicle is on stands. Initial loosening and final tightening should be done with the wheels on the ground.

Fire

• Fuel is highly flammable; fuel vapour is explosive.
• Don't let fuel spill onto a hot engine.
• Do not smoke or allow naked lights (including pilot lights) anywhere near a vehicle being worked on. Also beware of creating sparks (electrically or by use of tools).
• Fuel vapour is heavier than air, so don't work on the fuel system with the vehicle over an inspection pit.
• Another cause of fire is an electrical overload or short-circuit. Take care when repairing or modifying the vehicle wiring.
• Keep a fire extinguisher handy, of a type suitable for use on fuel and electrical fires.

Electric shock

• Ignition HT voltage can be dangerous, especially to people with heart problems or a pacemaker. Don't work on or near the ignition system with the engine running or the ignition switched on.

• Mains voltage is also dangerous. Make sure that any mains-operated equipment is correctly earthed. Mains power points should be protected by a residual current device (RCD) circuit breaker.

Fume or gas intoxication

• Exhaust fumes are poisonous; they often contain carbon monoxide, which is rapidly fatal if inhaled. Never run the engine in a confined space such as a garage with the doors shut.
• Fuel vapour is also poisonous, as are the vapours from some cleaning solvents and paint thinners.

Poisonous or irritant substances

• Avoid skin contact with battery acid and with any fuel, fluid or lubricant, especially antifreeze, brake hydraulic fluid and Diesel fuel. Don't syphon them by mouth. If such a substance is swallowed or gets into the eyes, seek medical advice.
• Prolonged contact with used engine oil can cause skin cancer. Wear gloves or use a barrier cream if necessary. Change out of oil-soaked clothes and do not keep oily rags in your pocket.
• Air conditioning refrigerant forms a poisonous gas if exposed to a naked flame (including a cigarette). It can also cause skin burns on contact.

Asbestos

• Asbestos dust can cause cancer if inhaled or swallowed. Asbestos may be found in gaskets and in brake and clutch linings. When dealing with such components it is safest to assume that they contain asbestos.

Special hazards

Hydrofluoric acid

• This extremely corrosive acid is formed when certain types of synthetic rubber, found in some O-rings, oil seals, fuel hoses etc, are exposed to temperatures above 400°C. The rubber changes into a charred or sticky substance containing the acid. *Once formed, the acid remains dangerous for years. If it gets onto the skin, it may be necessary to amputate the limb concerned.*
• When dealing with a vehicle which has suffered a fire, or with components salvaged from such a vehicle, wear protective gloves and discard them after use.

The battery

• Batteries contain sulphuric acid, which attacks clothing, eyes and skin. Take care when topping-up or carrying the battery.
• The hydrogen gas given off by the battery is highly explosive. Never cause a spark or allow a naked light nearby. Be careful when connecting and disconnecting battery chargers or jump leads.

Air bags

• Air bags can cause injury if they go off accidentally. Take care when removing the steering wheel and/or facia. Special storage instructions may apply.

Diesel injection equipment

• Diesel injection pumps supply fuel at very high pressure. Take care when working on the fuel injectors and fuel pipes.

⚠ *Warning: Never expose the hands, face or any other part of the body to injector spray; the fuel can penetrate the skin with potentially fatal results.*

Remember...

DO

• Do use eye protection when using power tools, and when working under the vehicle.

• Do wear gloves or use barrier cream to protect your hands when necessary.

• Do get someone to check periodically that all is well when working alone on the vehicle.

• Do keep loose clothing and long hair well out of the way of moving mechanical parts.

• Do remove rings, wristwatch etc, before working on the vehicle – especially the electrical system.

• Do ensure that any lifting or jacking equipment has a safe working load rating adequate for the job.

DON'T

• Don't attempt to lift a heavy component which may be beyond your capability – get assistance.

• Don't rush to finish a job, or take unverified short cuts.

• Don't use ill-fitting tools which may slip and cause injury.

• Don't leave tools or parts lying around where someone can trip over them. Mop up oil and fuel spills at once.

• Don't allow children or pets to play in or near a vehicle being worked on.

The following pages are intended to help in dealing with common roadside emergencies and breakdowns. You will find more detailed fault finding information at the back of the manual, and repair information in the main chapters.

If your car won't start and the starter motor doesn't turn

☐ Open the bonnet and make sure that the battery terminals are clean and tight (unclip the battery cover for access).
☐ Switch on the headlights and try to start the engine. If the headlights go very dim when you're trying to start, the battery is probably flat. Get out of trouble by jump starting (see next page) using a friend's car.

If your car won't start even though the starter motor turns as normal

☐ Is there fuel in the tank?
☐ Has the engine immobiliser been deactivated? This should happen automatically, on inserting the ignition key. However, if a replacement key has been obtained (other than from a Ford dealer), it may not contain the transponder chip necessary to deactivate the system. Even 'proper' replacement keys have to be coded to work properly – a procedure for this is outlined in the vehicle handbook.
☐ Is there moisture on electrical components under the bonnet? Switch off the ignition, then wipe off any obvious dampness with a dry cloth. Remove the plastic cover on the top of the engine (where applicable). Spray a water-repellent aerosol product (WD-40 or equivalent) on ignition and fuel system electrical connectors like those shown in the photos.

A Check the security and condition of the battery connections – unclip and lift the battery cover for access.

B Check the mass airflow sensor wiring plug.

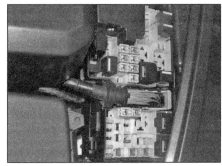

C Check that none of the engine compartment fuses have blown.

Check that all electrical connections are secure (with the ignition switched off). Spray the connector plugs with a water-dispersant spray like WD-40 if you suspect a problem due to damp. Diesel models do not usually suffer from damp starting problems, but check all visible connector plugs just in case.

Jump starting

When jump-starting a car using a booster battery, observe the following precautions:

✔ Before connecting the booster battery, make sure that the ignition is switched off.

✔ Ensure that all electrical equipment (lights, heater, wipers, etc) is switched off.

✔ Take note of any special precautions printed on the battery case.

✔ Make sure that the booster battery is the same voltage as the discharged one in the vehicle.

✔ If the battery is being jump-started from the battery in another vehicle, the two vehicles MUST NOT TOUCH each other.

✔ Make sure that the transmission is in neutral (or PARK, in the case of automatic transmission).

HAYNES HINT *Jump starting will get you out of trouble, but you must correct whatever made the battery go flat in the first place. There are three possibilities:*

1 *The battery has been drained by repeated attempts to start, or by leaving the lights on.*

2 *The charging system is not working properly (alternator drivebelt slack or broken, alternator wiring fault or alternator itself faulty).*

3 *The battery itself is at fault (electrolyte low, or battery worn out).*

1 Connect one end of the red jump lead to the positive (+) terminal of the flat battery

2 Connect the other end of the red lead to the positive (+) terminal of the booster battery.

3 Connect one end of the black jump lead to the negative (-) terminal of the booster battery

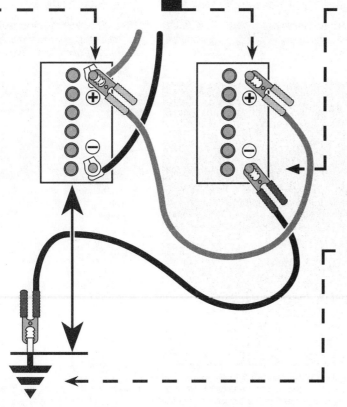

4 Connect the other end of the black lead to the to the earth terminal on the left-hand front suspension turret in the engine compartment.

5 Make sure that the jump leads will not come into contact with the fan, drive-belts or other moving parts of the engine.

6 Start the engine, then with the engine running at fast idle speed disconnect the jump leads in the reverse order of connection.

Wheel changing

 Warning: Do not change a wheel in a situation where you risk being hit by other traffic. On busy roads, try to stop in a lay-by or a gateway. Be wary of passing traffic while changing the wheel – it is easy to become distracted by the job in hand.

Preparation

☐ When a puncture occurs, stop as soon as it is safe to do so.

☐ Park on firm level ground, if possible, and well out of the way of other traffic.

☐ Use hazard warning lights if necessary.

☐ If you have one, use a warning triangle to alert other drivers of your presence.

☐ Apply the handbrake and engage first or reverse gear.

☐ Chock the wheel diagonally opposite the

one being removed – a couple of large stones will do for this.

☐ If the ground is soft, use a flat piece of wood to spread the load under the jack.

Changing the wheel

1 The spare wheel and tools are stored under the floor in the luggage compartment. Lift up the cover panel. Unscrew the retaining bolt, and lift the spare wheel out. The jack and wheel brace are located beneath the spare wheel. The screw-in towing eye is located alongside the spare wheel.

2 Where applicable, using the flat end of the wheel brace, prise off the wheel trim or centre cover for access to the wheel nuts. Models with alloy wheels may have special locking nuts – these are removed with a special tool, which should be provided with the wheel brace (or it may be in the glovebox).

3 Slacken each wheel nut by a half turn, using the wheel brace. If the nuts are too tight, DON'T stand on the wheel brace to undo them – call for assistance from one of the motoring organisations.

4 Two jacking points are provided on each side – use the one nearest the punctured wheel. Locate the jack head in the groove at the jacking point in the lower sill flange (don't jack the vehicle at any other point of the sill, nor on a plastic panel).

5 Turn the jack handle clockwise until the wheel is raised clear of the ground. Unscrew the wheel nuts, noting which way round they fit (tapered side inwards), and remove the wheel.

6 Fit the spare wheel, and screw on the nuts. Lightly tighten the nuts with the wheel brace, then lower the vehicle to the ground. Securely tighten the wheel nuts, then refit the wheel trim or centre cover, as applicable.

Finally . . .

☐ Remove the wheel chocks. Stow the punctured wheel and tools back in the luggage compartment, and secure them in position.

☐ Check the tyre pressure on the tyre just fitted. If it is low, or if you don't have a pressure gauge with you, drive slowly to the next garage and inflate the tyre to the correct pressure. In the case of the narrow 'space-saver' spare wheel this pressure is much higher than for a normal tyre.

☐ The wheel nuts should be slackened and retightened to the specified torque at the earliest possible opportunity.

☐ Have the punctured wheel repaired as soon as possible, or another puncture will leave you stranded.

Note: *Some models are supplied with a special lightweight 'space-saver' spare wheel, the tyre being narrower than standard. The 'space-saver' spare wheel is intended only for temporary use, and must be replaced with a standard wheel as soon as possible. Drive with particular care with this wheel fitted, especially through corners and when braking; do not exceed 50 mph.*

Identifying leaks

Puddles on the garage floor or drive, or obvious wetness under the car, suggest a leak that needs investigating. It can sometimes be difficult to decide where the leak is coming from, especially if the engine bay is very dirty already. Leaking oil or fluid can also be blown rearwards by the passage of air under the car, giving a false impression of where the problem lies.

 Warning: Most automotive oils and fluids are poisonous. Wash them off skin, and change out of contaminated clothing, without delay.

 The smell of a fluid leaking from the car may provide a clue to what's leaking. Some fluids are distinctively coloured. It may help to clean the car carefully and to park it over some clean paper overnight as an aid to locating the source of the leak.
Remember that some leaks may only occur while the engine is running.

Sump oil

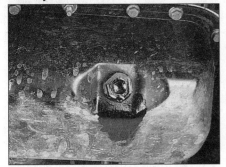

Engine oil may leak from the drain plug...

Oil from filter

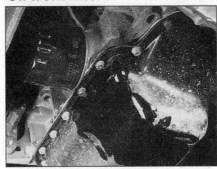

...or from the base of the oil filter.

Gearbox oil

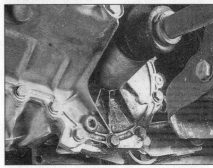

Gearbox oil can leak from the seals at the inboard ends of the driveshafts.

Antifreeze

Leaking antifreeze often leaves a crystalline deposit like this.

Brake fluid

A leak occurring at a wheel is almost certainly brake fluid.

Power steering fluid

Power steering fluid may leak from the pipe connectors on the steering rack.

Towing

When all else fails, you may find yourself having to get a tow home – or of course you may be helping somebody else. Long-distance recovery should only be done by a garage or breakdown service. For shorter distances, DIY towing using another car is easy enough, but observe the following points:

☐ Use a proper tow-rope – they are not expensive. The vehicle being towed must display an ON TOW sign in its rear window.

☐ Always turn the ignition key to the 'On' position when the vehicle is being towed, so that the steering lock is released, and the direction indicator and brake lights work.

☐ The towing eye is of the screw-in type, and is found in the spare wheel well. The towing eye screws into a threaded hole, accessible after prising out a cover on the right-hand side of the front or rear bumper – later models have a circular cover **(see illustration)**. **Note:** *The towing eye has a left-hand thread – rotate it anti-clockwise to install it.*

☐ Before being towed, release the handbrake and make sure the transmission is in neutral.

☐ Note that greater-than-usual pedal pressure will be required to operate the brakes, since the vacuum servo unit is only operational with the engine running.

☐ The driver of the car being towed must keep the tow-rope taut at all times to avoid snatching.

☐ Make sure that both drivers know the route before setting off.

☐ Only drive at moderate speeds and keep the distance towed to a minimum. Drive smoothly and allow plenty of time for slowing down at junctions.

Introduction

There are some very simple checks which need only take a few minutes to carry out, but which could save you a lot of inconvenience and expense.

These *Weekly checks* require no great skill or special tools, and the small amount of time they take to perform could prove to be very well spent, for example:

☐ Keeping an eye on tyre condition and pressures, will not only help to stop them wearing out prematurely, but could also save your life.

☐ Many breakdowns are caused by electrical problems. Battery-related faults are particularly common, and a quick check on a regular basis will often prevent the majority of these.

☐ If your car develops a brake fluid leak, the first time you might know about it is when your brakes don't work properly. Checking the level regularly will give advance warning of this kind of problem.

☐ If the oil or coolant levels run low, the cost of repairing any engine damage will be far greater than fixing the leak, for example.

Underbonnet check points

◀ 1.6 litre engine

A *Engine oil level dipstick*

B *Engine oil filler cap*

C *Coolant expansion tank*

D *Brake and clutch fluid reservoir*

E *Power steering fluid reservoir (underneath the headlight*

F *Screen washer fluid reservoir*

G *Battery*

◀ 2.0 litre engine

A *Engine oil level dipstick*

B *Engine oil filler cap*

C *Coolant expansion tank*

D *Brake and clutch fluid reservoir*

E *Power steering fluid reservoir (underneath the headlight*

F *Screen washer fluid reservoir*

G *Battery*

Engine oil level

Before you start
✔ Make sure that the car is on level ground.
✔ Check the oil level before the car is driven, or at least 5 minutes after the engine has been switched off.

 HAYNES HiNT *If the oil is checked immediately after driving the vehicle, some of the oil will remain in the upper engine components, resulting in an inaccurate reading on the dipstick.*

The correct oil
Modern engines place great demands on their oil. It is very important that the correct oil for your car is used (see *Lubricants and fluids*).

Car care
● If you have to add oil frequently, you should check whether you have any oil leaks. Place some clean paper under the car overnight, and check for stains in the morning. If there are no leaks, then the engine may be burning oil.
● Always maintain the level between the upper and lower dipstick marks (see photo 2). If the level is too low, severe engine damage may occur. Oil seal failure may result if the engine is overfilled by adding too much oil.

1 The dipstick is located at the front of the engine (see *Underbonnet check points* for exact location). Withdraw the dipstick. Using a clean rag or paper towel, remove all oil from the dipstick.

3 Oil is added through the filler cap. Unscrew the filler cap and top-up the level; a funnel may be useful in reducing spillage.

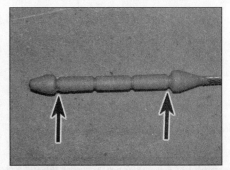

2 Insert the clean dipstick into the tube as far as it will go, then withdraw it again. Note the oil level on the end of the dipstick, which should be between the MAX and MIN marks. If the oil level is only just above, or below, the MIN mark, topping-up is required.

4 Add the oil slowly, checking the level on the dipstick often, and allowing time for the oil to run to the sump. Add oil until the level is just up to the MAX mark on the dipstick – don't overfill (see *Car care*)

Coolant level

 Warning: Do not attempt to remove the expansion tank pressure cap when the engine is hot, as there is a very great risk of scalding. Do not leave open containers of coolant about, as it is poisonous.

Car care
● With a sealed-type cooling system, adding coolant should not be necessary on a regular basis. If frequent topping-up is required, it is likely there is a leak. Check the radiator, all hoses and joint faces for signs of staining or wetness, and rectify as necessary.

● It is important that antifreeze is used in the cooling system all year round, not just during the winter months. Don't top up with water alone, as the antifreeze will become diluted.

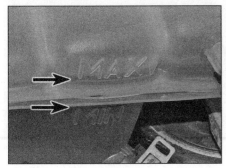

1 The coolant level varies with the temperature of the engine, and is visible through the expansion tank. When the engine is cold, the coolant level should be between the MAX and MIN marks on the front of the reservoir. When the engine is hot, the level may rise slightly above the MAX mark.

2 If topping-up is necessary, **wait until the engine is cold**. Slowly unscrew the expansion tank cap, to release any pressure present in the cooling system, and remove it.

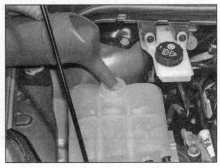

3 Add a mixture of water and antifreeze to the expansion tank until the coolant level is halfway between the level marks. Use only the specified antifreeze – if using Ford antifreeze, make sure it is the same type and colour as that already in the system. Refit the cap and tighten it securely.

Brake and clutch fluid level

Note: *All manual transmission models have a hydraulically-operated clutch, which uses the same fluid as the braking system.*

Warning:
• *Brake fluid can harm your eyes and damage painted surfaces, so use extreme caution when handling and pouring it.*
• *Do not use fluid that has been standing open for some time, as it absorbs moisture from the air, which can cause a dangerous loss of braking effectiveness.*

 HAYNES HiNT
• *Make sure that your car is on level ground.*

• *The fluid level in the reservoir will drop slightly as the brake pads wear down, but the fluid level must never be allowed to drop below the DANGER mark.*

Safety first!

● If the reservoir requires repeated topping-up this is an indication of a fluid leak somewhere in the system, which should be investigated immediately.
● If a leak is suspected, the car should not be driven until the braking system has been checked. Never take any risks where brakes are concerned

1 The brake fluid reservoir is located on the right-hand side of the engine compartment.

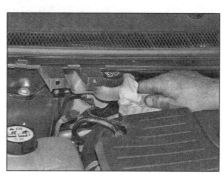

3 If topping-up is necessary, first wipe clean the area around the filler cap to prevent dirt entering the hydraulic system. Unscrew the reservoir cap and carefully lift it out of position, holding the wiring connector plug and taking care not to damage the level sender float. Inspect the reservoir; if the fluid is dirty, the hydraulic system should be drained and refilled (see Chapter 1).

2 The MAX and MIN marks are indicated on the front of the reservoir. The fluid level must be kept between the marks at all times.

4 Carefully add fluid, taking care not to spill it onto the surrounding components. Use only the specified fluid; mixing different types can cause damage to the system. After topping-up to the correct level, securely refit the cap and wipe off any spilt fluid.

Power steering fluid level

Note: *According to Ford, there is no requirement to check the fluid level. However, it may be prudent to check the level every few months or so.*

Before you start

✔ Park the vehicle on level ground.
✔ Set the steering wheel straight-ahead.
✔ The engine should be cold and turned off.

 HAYNES HiNT
For the check to be accurate, the steering must not be turned once the engine has been stopped.

Safety first!

● The need for frequent topping-up indicates a leak, which should be investigated immediately.

1 The reservoir is mounted under the right-hand headlight. Remove the headlight as described in Chapter 12. The fluid level can be viewed through the reservoir body, and should be between the MIN and MAX marks when the engine is cold. If the level is checked when the engine is running or hot, the level may rise slightly above the MAX mark.

2 If topping-up is necessary, use the specified type of fluid – do not overfill the reservoir. Undo the reservoir cap. Take care not to introduce dirt into the system when topping-up. When the level is correct, securely refit the cap.

Tyre condition and pressure

It is very important that tyres are in good condition, and at the correct pressure - having a tyre failure at any speed is highly dangerous. Tyre wear is influenced by driving style - harsh braking and acceleration, or fast cornering, will all produce more rapid tyre wear. As a general rule, the front tyres wear out faster than the rears. Interchanging the tyres from front to rear ("rotating" the tyres) may result in more even wear. However, if this is completely effective, you may have the expense of replacing all four tyres at once! Remove any nails or stones embedded in the tread before they penetrate the tyre to cause deflation. If removal of a nail does reveal that the tyre has been punctured, refit the nail so that its point of penetration is marked. Then immediately change the wheel, and have the tyre repaired by a tyre dealer.

Regularly check the tyres for damage in the form of cuts or bulges, especially in the sidewalls. Periodically remove the wheels, and clean any dirt or mud from the inside and outside surfaces. Examine the wheel rims for signs of rusting, corrosion or other damage. Light alloy wheels are easily damaged by "kerbing" whilst parking; steel wheels may also become dented or buckled. A new wheel is very often the only way to overcome severe damage.

New tyres should be balanced when they are fitted, but it may become necessary to re-balance them as they wear, or if the balance weights fitted to the wheel rim should fall off. Unbalanced tyres will wear more quickly, as will the steering and suspension components. Wheel imbalance is normally signified by vibration, particularly at a certain speed (typically around 50 mph). If this vibration is felt only through the steering, then it is likely that just the front wheels need balancing. If, however, the vibration is felt through the whole car, the rear wheels could be out of balance. Wheel balancing should be carried out by a tyre dealer or garage.

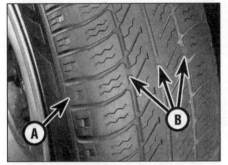

1 *Tread Depth - visual check*
   The original tyres have tread wear safety bands (B), which will appear when the tread depth reaches approximately 1.6 mm. The band positions are indicated by a triangular mark on the tyre sidewall (A).

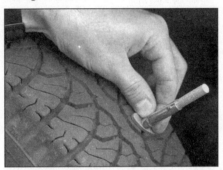

2 *Tread Depth - manual check*
   Alternatively, tread wear can be monitored with a simple, inexpensive device known as a tread depth indicator gauge.

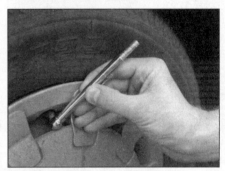

3 *Tyre Pressure Check*
   Check the tyre pressures regularly with the tyres cold. Do not adjust the tyre pressures immediately after the vehicle has been used, or an inaccurate setting will result.

Tyre tread wear patterns

Shoulder Wear

Underinflation (wear on both sides)
Under-inflation will cause overheating of the tyre, because the tyre will flex too much, and the tread will not sit correctly on the road surface. This will cause a loss of grip and excessive wear, not to mention the danger of sudden tyre failure due to heat build-up.
Check and adjust pressures
Incorrect wheel camber (wear on one side)
Repair or renew suspension parts
Hard cornering
Reduce speed!

Centre Wear

Overinflation
Over-inflation will cause rapid wear of the centre part of the tyre tread, coupled with reduced grip, harsher ride, and the danger of shock damage occurring in the tyre casing.
Check and adjust pressures

If you sometimes have to inflate your car's tyres to the higher pressures specified for maximum load or sustained high speed, don't forget to reduce the pressures to normal afterwards.

Uneven Wear

Front tyres may wear unevenly as a result of wheel misalignment. Most tyre dealers and garages can check and adjust the wheel alignment (or "tracking") for a modest charge.
Incorrect camber or castor
Repair or renew suspension parts
Malfunctioning suspension
Repair or renew suspension parts
Unbalanced wheel
Balance tyres
Incorrect toe setting
Adjust front wheel alignment
Note: *The feathered edge of the tread which typifies toe wear is best checked by feel.*

Washer fluid level

● The windscreen washer reservoir also supplies the tailgate washer jet, where applicable. On models so equipped, the same reservoir also serves the headlight washers.
● Screenwash additives not only keep the windscreen clean during bad weather, they also prevent the washer system freezing in cold weather – which is when you are likely to need it most. Don't top-up using plain water, as the screenwash will become diluted, and will freeze in cold weather.
Caution: On no account use engine coolant antifreeze in the screen washer system – this may damage the paintwork.

1 The washer fluid reservoir filler neck is located in the right-hand rear corner of the engine compartment. The washer level cannot easily be seen. Remove the filler cap, and look down the filler neck – if fluid is not visible, topping-up may be required.

2 When topping-up the reservoir, add a screenwash additive in the quantities recommended on the additive bottle.

Wiper blades

● Only fit good-quality wiper blades.
● When removing an old wiper blade, note how it is fitted. Fitting new blades can be a tricky exercise, and noting how the old blade came off can save time.
● While the wiper blade is removed, take care not to knock the wiper arm from its locked position, or it could strike the glass.

● Offer the new blade into position the same way round as the old one. Ensure that it clicks home securely, otherwise it may come off in use, damaging the glass.
Note: *Fitting details for wiper blades vary according to model, and according to whether genuine Ford wiper blades have been fitted. Use the procedures and illustrations shown as a guide for your car.*

HAYNES HiNT *If smearing is still a problem despite fitting new wiper blades, try cleaning the glass with neat screenwash additive or methylated spirit.*

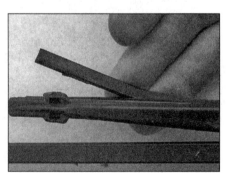

1 Check the condition of the wiper blades; if they are cracked or show any signs of deterioration, or if the glass swept area is smeared, renew them. Wiper blades should be renewed annually, regardless of their apparent condition.

2 To remove a windscreen wiper blade, pull the arm fully away from the glass until it locks. Position the blade at 90° to the arm and lift it from place.

3 To remove the tailgate blade, lift the arm, position the blade at 90° to the arm, and pull the blade from the arm.

Battery

Caution: Before carrying out any work on the vehicle battery, read the precautions given in 'Safety first!' at the start of this manual.

✔ Make sure that the battery tray is in good condition, and that the clamp is tight. Any 'white' corrosion on the terminals or surrounding area can be removed with a solution of water and baking soda; thoroughly rinse all cleaned areas with water. Any metal parts damaged by corrosion should be covered with a zinc-based primer, then painted.

✔ Periodically check the charge condition of the battery. On the original-equipment battery, the state of charge is shown by an indicator 'eye' in the top of the battery, which should be green – if the indicator is clear, or red, the battery may need charging or even renewal (see Chapter 5A).

✔ If the battery is flat, and you need to jump start your vehicle, see *Roadside Repairs*.

HAYNES HINT

Battery corrosion can be kept to a minimum by applying a layer of petroleum jelly to the clamps and terminals after they are reconnected.

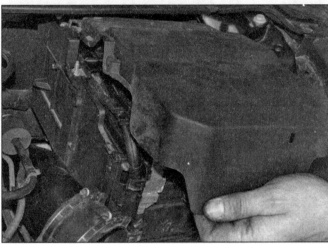

1 The battery is located in the left-hand rear corner of the engine compartment. Unclip and remove the battery cover to gain access. The exterior of the battery should be inspected periodically for damage such as a cracked case or cover.

2 Check the tightness of battery clamps to ensure good electrical connections. You should not be able to move them. Also check each cable for cracks and frayed conductors.

3 If corrosion (white, fluffy deposits) is evident, remove the cables from the battery terminals, clean them with a small wire brush, then refit them. Automotive stores sell a tool for cleaning the battery post . . .

4 . . . as well as the battery cable clamps

Bulbs and fuses

✔ Check all external lights and the horn. Refer to the appropriate Sections of Chapter 12 for details if any of the circuits are found to be inoperative.

✔ Visually check all accessible wiring connectors, harnesses and retaining clips for security, and for signs of chafing or damage.

HAYNES HINT *If you need to check your brake lights and indicators unaided, back up to a wall or garage door and operate the lights. The reflected light should show if they are working properly.*

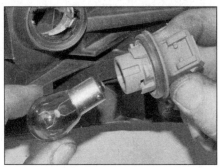

1 If a single indicator light, stop-light or headlight has failed, it is likely that a bulb has blown and will need to be renewed. Refer to Chapter 12 for details. If both stop-lights have failed, it is possible that the switch has failed (see Chapter 9).

2 If more than one indicator light or tail light has failed, it is likely that either a fuse has blown or that there is a fault in the circuit (see Chapter 12). The main fusebox is located below the glovebox on the passenger's side. To access the main fusebox, undo the 2 bolts and pull the trim panel downwards, then undo the two bolts and lower the fusebox from position. Pull the fusebox rearwards and lower it completely. The auxiliary fuse/relay box is located on the left-hand side of the engine compartment – unclip and remove the cover for access.

3 To renew a blown fuse, simply pull it out and fit a new fuse of the correct rating (see Chapter 12). Spare fuses, and a fuse removal tool, are provided on the inside of the auxiliary fusebox lid. If the fuse blows again, it is important that you find out why – a complete checking procedure is given in Chapter 12.

Lubricants and fluids

Engine . . . . Multigrade engine oil, viscosity SAE 5W/30 to
Ford specification WSS-M2C913-B

Cooling system. . . . . Motorcraft SuperPlus pink/red antifreeze to
Ford specification WSS-M97B44-D

Manual transmission . . . . SAE 75W/90 gear oil to Ford specification WSD-M2C200-C

Brake and clutch hydraulic system . . . . Hydraulic fluid to Ford specification ESD-M6C57-A,
Super DOT 4, paraffin-free

Power steering . . . . Ford or Motorcraft power steering fluid to
Ford specification WSS-M2C204-A2

Tyre pressures (cold)

The table below gives typical pressures. Check the sticker attached to the driver's door pillar for details specific to your model.

Tyre size:	Normal load		Full load	
	Front	Rear	Front	Rear
195/65 R 15	2.1 bar	2.3 bar	2.4 bar	2.8 bar
205/55 R 16	2.3 bar	2.3 bar	2.4 bar	2.8 bar
205/50 R 17	2.3 bar	2.3 bar	2.5 bar	2.8 bar
225/40 R 18	2.3 bar	2.3 bar	2.5 bar	2.8 bar

Chapter 1
Routine maintenance & servicing

Contents

Degrees of difficulty

Easy, suitable for novice with little experience	**Fairly easy,** suitable for beginner with some experience	**Fairly difficult,** suitable for competent DIY mechanic	**Difficult,** suitable for experienced DIY mechanic	**Very difficult,** suitable for expert DIY or professional

Lubricants and fluids. . . . . Refer to end of *Weekly checks* on page 0•17

Capacities

Engine oil (including filter)
1.6 litre engines . . . . 3.8 litres
1.8 litre engines . . . . 5.6 litres
2.0 litre engines . . . . 5.5 litres

Cooling system (approximate)
1.6 litre engines . . . . 7.3 litres
1.8 litre engines . . . . 8.1 litres
2.0 litre engines . . . . 8.4 litres

Washer fluid reservoir . . . . 3.3 litres

Fuel tank . . . . 53.0 litres

Cooling system
Antifreeze mixture:
50% antifreeze . . . . Protection down to –37°C
55% antifreeze . . . . Protection down to –45°C
Note: *Refer to antifreeze manufacturer for latest recommendations.*

Brakes
Friction material minimum thickness:
Brake pads . . . . 1.5 mm
Brake shoes . . . . 1.0 mm

Torque wrench settings

	Nm	lbf ft
Engine oil drain plug:		
1.6 litre engines	34	25
1.8 litre engines	36	27
2.0 litre engines	34	25
Engine oil filter housing cap:		
1.6 and 2.0 litre engines	24	18
1.8 litre engines	Not applicable	
Roadwheel nuts:		
Gold nuts for steel wheels	90	60
Silver nuts for steel wheels	130	96
One-piece alloy nuts for alloy wheels and 5-spoke steel wheels	130	96
Two-piece alloy nuts with conical washer	110	81

The maintenance intervals in this manual are provided with the assumption that you, not the dealer, will be carrying out the work. These are the minimum maintenance intervals recommended by us for vehicles driven daily. If you wish to keep your vehicle in peak condition at all times, you may wish to perform some of these procedures more often. We encourage frequent maintenance, because it enhances the efficiency, performance and resale value of your vehicle.

If the vehicle is driven in dusty areas, used to tow a trailer, or driven frequently at slow speeds (idling in traffic) or on short journeys, more frequent maintenance intervals are recommended.

When the vehicle is new, it should be serviced by a dealer service department (or other workshop recognised by the vehicle manufacturer as providing the same standard of service) in order to preserve the warranty. The vehicle manufacturer may reject warranty claims if you are unable to prove that servicing has been carried out as and when specified, using only original equipment parts or parts certified to be of equivalent quality.

Every 250 miles or weekly
☐ Refer to *Weekly checks*

Every 6000 miles or 6 months, whichever comes first
☐ Renew the engine oil and filter (Section 3)
Note: *Ford recommend that the engine oil and filter are changed every 12 500 miles or 12 months. However, oil and filter changes are good for the engine and we recommend that the oil and filter are renewed more frequently, especially if the vehicle is used on a lot of short journeys.*

Every 12 500 miles or 12 months, whichever comes first
In addition to the items listed above, carry out the following:
☐ Check the condition of the auxiliary drivebelt (Section 23)
☐ Check the operation of the lights and the horn (Section 4)
☐ Check under the bonnet for fluid leaks and hose condition (Section 5)
☐ Check the condition of the engine compartment wiring (Section 6)
☐ Check the condition of the seat belts (Section 7)
☐ Check the condition of the brake pads, shoes and discs (Section 8)
☐ Check the exhaust system (Section 9)
☐ Check the steering and suspension components for condition and security (Section 10)
☐ Check the condition of the driveshaft joints and gaiters (Section 11)
☐ Check the underbody and all fuel/brake lines (Section 12)
☐ Lubricate all hinges and locks (Section 13)
☐ Check roadwheel nut tightness (Section 14)
☐ Carry out a road test (Section 15)
☐ Renew the pollen filter (Section 16)*
☐ Check and if necessary adjust the handbrake (Section 17)
☐ Check the antifreeze/inhibitor strength (Section 26)
* Note: *If the vehicle is used in dusty conditions, the pollen filter should be renewed more frequently.*

Every 37 500 miles or 3 years, whichever comes first
In addition to the items listed above, carry out the following:
☐ Renew the fuel filter (Section 18)
☐ Renew the air filter (Section 19)*
☐ Refill the exhaust particulate filter additive tank (Section 20)
* Note: *If the vehicle is used in dusty conditions, the air filter should be renewed more frequently.*

Every 62 500 miles
In addition to the items listed above, carry out the following:
☐ Renew the timing belt and tensioner (Section 21)
Note: *The Ford interval for belt renewal is actually at a much higher mileage than this (100 000 miles or 8 years – 1.8 litre engines, 125 000 miles or 10 years – 1.6 and 2.0 litre engines). It is strongly recommended, however, that the interval is reduced to 62 500 miles, particularly on vehicles which are subjected to intensive use, ie, mainly short journeys or a lot of stop-start driving. The actual belt renewal interval is therefore very much up to the individual owner, but bear in mind that severe engine damage will result if the belt breaks.*

Every 75 000 miles
☐ Renew the exhaust particulate filter (Section 22)

Every 100 000 miles or 8 years, whichever comes first
☐ Renew the auxiliary belt (Section 23)

Every 2 years, regardless of mileage
☐ Renew the brake fluid (Section 24)
☐ Renew the remote control battery (Section 25)
☐ Renew the coolant (Section 26)*
☐ Check the transmission oil level (Section 27)
* Note: *If Ford pink/red antifreeze is used, the coolant can then be left indefinitely, providing the strength of the mixture is checked every year. If any antifreeze other than Ford's is to be used, the coolant must be renewed at regular intervals to provide an equivalent degree of protection; the conventional recommendation is to renew the coolant every two years.*

Underbonnet view of a 1.6 litre model

1 Engine oil level dipstick
2 Oil filler cap
3 Coolant expansion tank cap
4 Washer fluid reservoir cap
5 Brake/clutch fluid reservoir cap
6 Air filter element cover
7 Fuel filter
8 Battery cover
9 Fuse/relay box cover

Underbonnet view of a 2.0 litre model

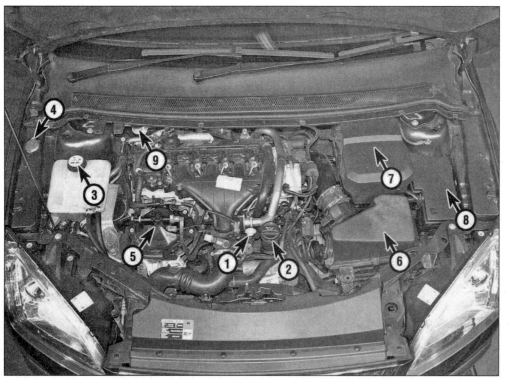

1 Engine oil level dipstick
2 Engine oil filler cap
3 Coolant expansion tank cap
4 Washer fluid reservoir cap
5 Fuel filter
6 Air filter cover
7 Battery cover
8 Fuse/relay box
9 Brake/clutch fluid reservoir cap

Front underbody view of a 1.6 litre model – others similar

1 Engine oil sump drain plug
2 Air conditioning compressor
3 Right-hand driveshaft intermediate bearing
4 Lower control arm
5 Track rod end
6 Front subframe
7 Catalytic converter
8 Front brake caliper

Rear underbody view

1 Anti-roll bar
2 Shock absorber
3 Fuel supply and return pipe connections
4 Handbrake cable
5 Hub carrier/lateral link
6 Lower control arm
7 Tie rod
8 Fuel tank

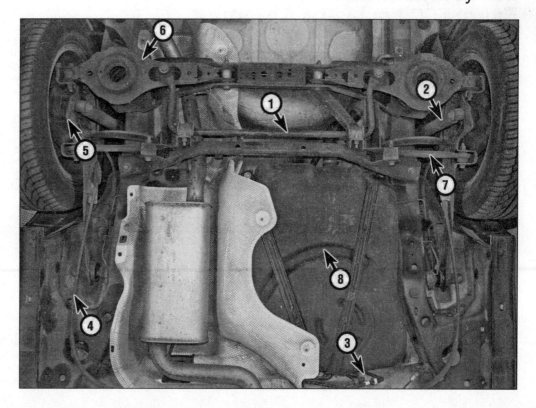

Maintenance procedures

1 General information

1 This Chapter is designed to help the home mechanic maintain his/her vehicle for safety, economy, long life and peak performance.

2 The Chapter contains a master maintenance schedule, followed by Sections dealing specifically with each task in the schedule. Visual checks, adjustments, component renewal and other helpful items are included. Refer to the accompanying illustrations of the engine compartment and the underside of the vehicle for the locations of the various components.

3 Servicing your vehicle in accordance with the mileage/time maintenance schedule and the following Sections will provide a planned maintenance programme, which should result in a long and reliable service life. This is a comprehensive plan, so maintaining some items but not others at the specified service intervals will not produce the same results.

4 As you service your vehicle, you will discover that many of the procedures can – and should – be grouped together, because of the particular procedure being performed, or because of the proximity of two otherwise-unrelated components to one another. For example, if the vehicle is raised for any reason, the exhaust can be inspected at the same time as the suspension and steering components.

5 The first step in this maintenance programme is to prepare yourself before the actual work begins. Read through all the Sections relevant to the work to be carried out, then make a list and gather all the parts and tools required. If a problem is encountered, seek advice from a parts specialist, or a dealer service department.

2 Regular maintenance

1 If, from the time the vehicle is new, the routine maintenance schedule is followed closely, and frequent checks are made of fluid levels and high-wear items, as suggested throughout this manual, the engine will be kept in relatively good running condition, and the need for additional work will be minimised.

2 It is possible that there will be times when the engine is running poorly due to the lack of regular maintenance. This is even more likely if a used vehicle, which has not received regular and frequent maintenance checks, is purchased. In such cases, additional work may need to be carried out, outside of the regular maintenance intervals.

3 If engine wear is suspected, a compression test or leakdown test (refer to the relevant part of Chapter 2) will provide valuable information regarding the overall performance of the main internal components. Such a test can be used as a basis to decide on the extent of the work to be carried out. If, for example, a compression or leakdown test indicates serious internal engine wear, conventional maintenance as described in this Chapter will not greatly improve the performance of the engine, and may prove a waste of time and money, unless extensive overhaul work is carried out first.

4 The following series of operations are those most often required to improve the performance of a generally poor-running engine:

Primary operations

a) Clean, inspect and test the battery (refer to 'Weekly checks').
b) Check all the engine-related fluids (refer to 'Weekly checks').
c) Check the condition and tension of the auxiliary drivebelt (Section 23).
d) Check the condition of the air filter, and renew if necessary (Section 19).
e) Renew the fuel filter (Section 18).
f) Check the condition of all hoses, and check for fluid leaks (Section 5).

5 If the above operations do not prove fully effective, carry out the following secondary operations:

Secondary operations

All items listed under *Primary operations*, plus the following:

a) Check the charging system (refer to Chapter 5).
b) Check the preheating system (refer to Chapter 5).
c) Check the fuel system (refer to Chapter 4A).

Every 6000 miles or 6 months

3 Engine oil and filter renewal

1 Frequent oil and filter changes are the most important preventative maintenance procedures which can be undertaken by the DIY owner. As engine oil ages, it becomes diluted and contaminated, which leads to premature engine wear.

2 Before starting this procedure, gather together all the necessary tools and materials. Also make sure that you have plenty of clean rags and newspapers handy, to mop-up any spills. Ideally, the engine oil should be warm, as it will drain more easily, and more built-up sludge will be removed with it. Take care not to touch the exhaust or any other hot parts of the engine when working under the vehicle. To avoid any possibility of scalding, and to protect yourself from possible skin irritants and other harmful contaminants in used engine oils, it is advisable to wear gloves when carrying out this work.

3 Remove the plastic cover on the top of the engine. Pull up the right-hand rear corner and the front edges, then pull the cover forwards to release it (see illustration).

1.6 litre engines

4 Remove the air cleaner assembly as described in Chapter 4A.

5 Using a socket on an extension bar, undo the oil filter housing cap. Lift the cap up, with the filter element inside it. Discard the filter and the O-ring seal around the circumference of the cap (see illustrations).

3.3 Remove the plastic cover by pulling it upwards starting at the front edge

3.5a The engine oil filter (arrowed) is located at the front, left-hand corner of the cylinder block

3.5b Unscrew the cap and remove it complete with filter element

3.7 The engine oil filter (arrowed) is located on the rear of the cylinder block, above the right-hand driveshaft

3.10a Disconnect the wiring plug, unclip the fuel pipe, then undo the 4 bolts (arrowed) . . .

3.10b . . . and Torx bolt on the side (arrowed)

Note that there may be another bolt securing the bracket

3.10c Lift up the fuel filter and move it to one side

3.11a Undo the oil filter cap (arrowed) . . .

1.8 litre engines

6 The canister-type oil filter is located on the rear of the engine block. Firmly apply the handbrake, then jack up the front of the vehicle and support it on axle stands (see *Jacking and vehicle support*). Undo the fasteners and remove the engine undershield (where fitted).

7 Move a container into position under the oil filter, then use an oil filter removal tool if necessary to slacken the filter cartridge initially, then unscrew it by hand the rest of the way **(see illustration)**. Empty the oil from the old filter into the container.

8 Use a clean rag to remove all oil, dirt and sludge from the filter sealing area on the engine.

9 Apply a light coating of clean engine oil to the sealing ring on the new filter, then screw the filter into position on the engine. Tighten the filter firmly by hand only – do not use any tools.

2.0 litre engines

10 Release the wiring harnesses from the cable ties on the fuel filter bracket, then disconnect the filter wiring plug, release the fuel pipe from the clip, undo the bolts at the top and the bolt(s) on the side, then lift up the filter with the bracket, and place it to one side **(see illustrations)**.

11 Using a 27 mm socket on an extension bar, undo the oil filter housing cap. Lift the cap up, with the oil filter inside it. Discard the filter and the O-ring around the circumference of the cap **(see illustrations)**.

All engines

12 If not already done so, firmly apply the handbrake, then jack up the front of the vehicle and support it on axle stands (see *Jacking and vehicle support*). Unscrew the fasteners and remove the plastic undershield below the engine **(see illustration)**.

13 Using a spanner, socket or Allen key as applicable, slacken the drain plug about half a

3.11b . . . then lift up the cap with the filter element . . .

3.11c . . . pull the element from the cap . . .

3.11d . . . and discard the O-ring seal

3.12 Undo the fasteners (arrowed) and remove the engine undershield

3.13a Engine oil sump drain plug (arrowed) – 1.6 litre engine . . .

3.13b . . . 1.8 litre engine (arrowed) . . .

3.13c . . . and 2.0 litre engine (arrowed)

turn **(see illustrations)**. Position the draining container under the drain plug, then remove the plug completely **(see Haynes Hint)**.

14 Allow some time for the oil to drain, noting that it may be necessary to reposition the container as the oil flow slows to a trickle.

15 After all the oil has drained, wipe the drain plug and the sealing washer (where fitted) with a clean rag. Examine the condition of the sealing washer, and renew it if it shows signs of scoring or other damage which may prevent an oil-tight seal (it is generally considered good

practice to fit a new washer every time). Clean the area around the drain plug opening, and refit the plug complete with the washer and tighten it to the specified torque **(see illustration)**.

16 Remove the old oil and all tools from under the vehicle, refit the undershield, then lower the vehicle to the ground.

1.6 litre engines

17 Ensure the oil filter housing and cap are clean, then fit a new O-ring seal to the cap.

18 Fit the new filter element into the cap, then fit the cap to the housing and tighten it to the specified torque.

2.0 litre engines

19 Ensure the oil filter housing and cap are clean, then fit a new O-ring seal to the cap.

20 Fit the new filter element into the cap, then fit the cap to the housing and tighten it to the specified torque.

21 Position the fuel filter and bracket, then refit the retaining bolts and tighten them securely. Refit the pipe into the clip, reconnect the wiring plug and secure the wiring harnesses to the bracket.

All engines

22 With the car on level ground, fill the engine, using the correct grade and type of oil (refer to *Weekly checks* for details of topping-up). An

oil can spout or funnel may help to reduce spillage. Pour in half the specified quantity of oil first, then wait a few minutes for the oil to run to the sump.

23 Continue adding oil a small quantity at a time until the level is up to the MIN mark on the dipstick. Adding around 1.0 litre of oil will now bring the level up to the MAX on the dipstick – do not worry if a little too much goes in, as some of the excess will be taken up in filling the oil filter. Refit the dipstick and the filler cap.

24 Start the engine and run it for a few minutes, while checking for leaks around the oil filter seal and the sump drain plug. Note that there may be a delay of a few seconds before the low oil pressure warning light goes out when the engine is first started, as the oil circulates through the new oil filter and the engine oil galleries before the pressure builds-up.

25 Stop the engine, and wait a few minutes for the oil to settle in the sump once more. With the new oil circulated and the filter now completely full, recheck the level on the dipstick, and add more oil as necessary.

26 Dispose of the used engine oil and the old oil filter safely, with reference to *General repair procedures* in the *Reference* section of this manual. Many local recycling points have containers for waste oil with oil filter disposal receptacles alongside.

HAYNES HINT

As the drain plug releases from the threads, move it away sharply so the stream of oil issuing from the sump runs into the container, not up your sleeve.

3.15 Renew the sump plug sealing washer

Every 12 500 miles or 12 months

4 Lights and horn operation check

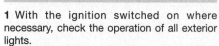

1 With the ignition switched on where necessary, check the operation of all exterior lights.
2 Check the brake lights with the help of an assistant, or by reversing up close to a reflective door. Make sure that all the rear lights are capable of operating independently, without affecting any of the other lights – for example, switch on as many rear lights as possible, then try the brake lights. If any unusual results are found, this is usually due to an earth fault or other poor connection at that rear light unit.
3 Again with the help of an assistant or using a reflective surface, check as far as possible that the headlights work on both main and dipped beam.
4 Renew any defective bulbs with reference to Chapter 12.

HAYNES HINT *Particularly on older vehicles, bulbs can stop working as a result of corrosion build-up on the bulb or its holder – fitting a new bulb may not cure the problem in this instance. When renewing any bulb, if you find any green or white-coloured powdery deposits, these should be cleaned off using emery cloth.*

5 Check the operation of all interior lights, including the glovebox and luggage area illumination lights. Switch on the ignition, and check that all relevant warning lights come on as expected – the vehicle handbook should give details of these. Now start the engine, and check that the appropriate lights go out. When you are next driving at night, check that all the instrument panel and facia lighting works correctly. If any problems are found, refer to Chapter 12.
6 Finally, choose an appropriate time of day to test the operation of the horn.

5 Underbonnet check for fluid leaks and hose condition

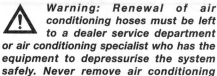

⚠ *Warning: Renewal of air conditioning hoses must be left to a dealer service department or air conditioning specialist who has the equipment to depressurise the system safely. Never remove air conditioning components or hoses until the system has been depressurised.*

1 Visually inspect the engine joint faces, gaskets and seals for any signs of water or oil leaks. Pay particular attention to the areas around the cylinder head cover, cylinder head, oil filter and sump joint faces. Bear in mind that, over a period of time, some very slight seepage from these areas is to be expected – what you are really looking for is any indication of a serious leak. Should a leak be found, renew the offending gasket or oil seal by referring to the appropriate Chapters in this manual.
2 High temperatures in the engine compartment can cause the deterioration of the rubber and plastic hoses used for engine, accessory and emission systems operation. Periodic inspection should be made for cracks, loose clamps, material hardening and leaks.
3 When checking the hoses, ensure that all the cable-ties or clips used to retain the hoses are in place, and in good condition. Clips which are broken or missing can lead to chafing of the hoses, pipes or wiring, which could cause more serious problems in the future.
4 Carefully check the large top and bottom radiator hoses, along with the other smaller-diameter cooling system hoses and metal pipes; do not forget the heater hoses/pipes which run from the engine to the bulkhead. Inspect each hose along its entire length, replacing any that is cracked, swollen or shows signs of deterioration. Cracks may become more apparent if the hose is squeezed, and may often be apparent at the hose ends.
5 Make sure that all hose connections are tight. If the large-diameter air hoses from the air cleaner are loose, they will leak air, and upset the engine idle quality. If the spring clamps that are used to secure many of the hoses appear to be slackening, they should be updated with worm-drive clips to prevent the possibility of leaks.
6 Some other hoses are secured to their fittings with clamps. Where clamps are used, check to be sure they haven't lost their tension, allowing the hose to leak. If clamps aren't used, make sure the hose has not expanded and/or hardened where it slips over the fitting, allowing it to leak.
7 Check all fluid reservoirs, filler caps, drain plugs and fittings, etc, looking for any signs of leakage of oil, transmission and/or brake hydraulic fluid, coolant and power steering fluid. Also check the clutch hydraulic fluid lines which lead from the fluid reservoir and slave cylinder (on the transmission).
8 If the vehicle is regularly parked in the same place, close inspection of the ground underneath it will soon show any leaks; ignore the puddle of water which will be left if the air conditioning system is in use. Place a clean piece of cardboard below the engine, and examine it for signs of contamination after the vehicle has been parked over it overnight.
9 Remember that some leaks will only occur with the engine running, or when the engine is hot or cold. With the handbrake firmly applied, start the engine from cold, and let the engine idle while you examine the underside of the engine compartment for signs of leakage.
10 If an unusual smell is noticed inside or around the car, especially when the engine is thoroughly hot, this may point to the presence of a leak.
11 As soon as a leak is detected, its source must be traced and rectified. Where oil has been leaking for some time, it is usually necessary to use a steam cleaner, pressure washer or similar to clean away the accumulated dirt, so that the exact source of the leak can be identified.

Vacuum hoses

12 It's quite common for vacuum hoses, especially those in the emissions system, to be colour-coded, or to be identified by coloured stripes moulded into them. Various systems require hoses with different wall thicknesses, collapse resistance and temperature resistance. When renewing hoses, be sure the new ones are made of the same material.
13 Often the only effective way to check a hose is to remove it completely from the vehicle. If more than one hose is removed, be sure to label the hoses and fittings to ensure correct installation.
14 When checking vacuum hoses, be sure to include any plastic T-fittings in the check. Inspect the fittings for cracks, and check the hose where it fits over the fitting for distortion, which could cause leakage.
15 A small piece of vacuum hose (quarter-inch inside diameter) can be used as a stethoscope to detect vacuum leaks. Hold one end of the hose to your ear, and probe around vacuum hoses and fittings, listening for the 'hissing' sound characteristic of a vacuum leak.

⚠ *Warning: When probing with the vacuum hose stethoscope, be very careful not to come into contact with moving engine components such as the auxiliary drivebelt, radiator electric cooling fan, etc.*

Fuel hoses

⚠ *Warning: There are certain precautions which must be taken when inspecting or servicing fuel system components. Work in a well-ventilated area, and do not allow open flames (cigarettes, appliance pilot lights, etc) or bare light bulbs near the work area. Mop-up any spills immediately, and do not store fuel-soaked rags where they could ignite.*

16 Check all fuel hoses for deterioration and chafing. Check especially for cracks in areas where the hose bends, and also just before fittings, such as where a hose attaches to the fuel filter.
17 It is not unusual for a high-mileage diesel engine to exhibit a 'film' of diesel fuel around the injectors, resulting in an oily appearance.

Unless there is clear evidence of a significant fuel leak, this is not normally a matter for concern. The best course of action would be to first clean the engine thoroughly; then, after several more miles have been covered, the source of the leak can be identified and its severity assessed.

18 High-quality fuel line, usually identified by the word 'Fluoroelastomer' printed on the hose, should be used for fuel line renewal. Never, under any circumstances, use non-reinforced vacuum line, clear plastic tubing or water hose as a substitute for fuel lines.

19 Spring-type clamps are commonly used on fuel lines. These clamps often lose their tension over a period of time, and can be 'sprung' during removal. Renew all spring-type clamps with proper petrol pipe clips whenever a hose is renewed.

Metal lines

20 Sections of metal piping are often used for fuel line between the fuel filter and the engine. Check carefully to be sure the piping has not been bent or crimped, and that cracks have not started in the line.

21 If a section of metal fuel line must be renewed, only seamless steel piping should be used, since copper and aluminium piping don't have the strength necessary to withstand normal engine vibration.

22 Check the metal lines where they enter the brake master cylinder, ABS hydraulic unit or clutch master/slave cylinders (as applicable) for cracks in the lines or loose fittings. Any sign of brake fluid leakage calls for an immediate and thorough inspection.

6 Engine compartment wiring check

1 With the vehicle parked on level ground, apply the handbrake firmly and open the bonnet. Using an inspection light or a small electric torch, check all visible wiring within and beneath the engine compartment. Make sure that the ignition is switched off – take out the key.

2 What you are looking for is wiring that is obviously damaged by chafing against sharp edges, or against moving suspension/

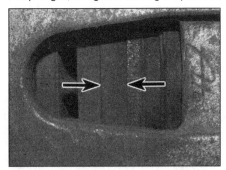

8.4 Check the brake pad friction material thickness (arrowed)

transmission components and/or the auxiliary drivebelt, by being trapped or crushed between carelessly-refitted components, or melted by being forced into contact with the hot engine castings, coolant pipes, etc. In almost all cases, damage of this sort is caused in the first instance by incorrect routing on reassembly after previous work has been carried out.

3 Depending on the extent of the problem, damaged wiring may be repaired by rejoining the break or splicing-in a new length of wire, using solder to ensure a good connection, and remaking the insulation with adhesive insulating tape or heat-shrink tubing, as appropriate. If the damage is extensive, given the implications for the vehicle's future reliability, the best long-term answer may well be to renew that entire section of the loom, however expensive this may appear.

4 When the actual damage has been repaired, ensure that the wiring loom is re-routed correctly, so that it is clear of other components, and not stretched or kinked, and is secured out of harm's way using the plastic clips, guides and ties provided.

5 Check all electrical connectors, ensuring that they are clean, securely fastened, and that each is locked by its plastic tabs or wire clip, as appropriate. If any connector shows external signs of corrosion (accumulations of white or green deposits, or streaks of 'rust'), or if any is thought to be dirty, it must be unplugged and cleaned using electrical contact cleaner. If the connector pins are severely corroded, the connector must be renewed; note that this may mean the renewal of that entire section of the loom – see your local Ford dealer for details.

6 If the cleaner completely removes the corrosion to leave the connector in a satisfactory condition, it would be wise to pack the connector with a suitable material which will exclude dirt and moisture, preventing the corrosion from occurring again; a Ford dealer may be able to recommend a suitable product.

7 Check the condition of the battery connections – remake the connections or renew the leads if a fault is found (see Chapter 5). Use the same techniques to ensure that all earth points in the engine compartment provide good electrical contact through clean, metal-to-metal joints, and that all are securely fastened.

8 Check the wiring to the glow plugs, referring to Chapter 5 if necessary.

7 Seat belt check

1 Check the seat belts for satisfactory operation and condition. Inspect the webbing for fraying and cuts. Check that they retract smoothly and without binding into their reels.

2 Check the seat belt mountings, ensuring that all the bolts are securely tightened.

8 Brake pads, shoes and discs check

1 The work described in this Section should be carried out at the specified intervals, or whenever a defect is suspected in the braking system. Any of the following symptoms could indicate a potential brake system defect:
  a) The vehicle pulls to one side when the brake pedal is depressed.
  b) The brakes make squealing, scraping or dragging noises when applied.
  c) Brake pedal travel is excessive, or pedal feel is poor.
  d) The brake fluid requires repeated topping-up. Note that, because the hydraulic clutch shares the same fluid as the braking system (see Chapter 6), this problem could be due to a leak in the clutch system.

Front disc brakes

2 Apply the handbrake, then loosen the front wheel nuts. Jack up the front of the vehicle, and support it on axle stands (see *Jacking and vehicle support*).

3 For better access to the brake calipers, remove the wheels.

4 Look through the inspection window in the caliper, and check that the thickness of the friction lining material on each of the pads is not less than the recommended minimum thickness given in the Specifications **(see illustration)**.

> **HAYNES HINT** *Bear in mind that the lining material is normally bonded to a metal backing plate. To differentiate between the metal and the lining material, it is helpful to turn the disc slowly at first – the edge of the disc can then be identified, with the lining material on each pad either side of it, and the backing plates behind.*

5 If it is difficult to determine the exact thickness of the pad linings, or if you are at all concerned about the condition of the pads, then remove them from the calipers for further inspection (refer to Chapter 9).

6 Check the other caliper in the same way.

7 If any one of the brake pads has worn down to, or below, the specified limit, *all four* pads at that end of the car must be renewed as a set. If the pads on one side are significantly more worn than the other, this may indicate that the caliper pistons have partially seized – refer to the brake pad renewal procedure in Chapter 9, and push the pistons back into the caliper to free them.

8 Measure the thickness of the discs with a micrometer, if available, to make sure that they still have service life remaining. Do not be fooled by the lip of rust which often forms on the outer edge of the disc, which may make the disc appear thicker than it really is – scrape off the loose rust if necessary, without scoring the disc friction (shiny) surface.

9 If any disc is thinner than the specified minimum thickness, renew it (refer to Chapter 9).

10 Check the general condition of the discs. Look for excessive scoring and discolouration caused by overheating. If these conditions exist, remove the relevant disc and have it resurfaced or renewed (refer to Chapter 9).

11 Make sure that the handbrake is firmly applied, then check that the transmission is in neutral. Spin the wheel, and check that the brake is not binding. Some drag is normal with a disc brake, but it should not require any great effort to turn the wheel – also, do not confuse brake drag with resistance from the transmission.

12 Before refitting the wheels, check all brake lines and hoses (refer to Chapter 9). In particular, check the flexible hoses in the vicinity of the calipers, where they are subjected to most movement **(see illustration)**. Bend them between the fingers (but do not actually bend them double, or the casing may be damaged) and check that this does not reveal previously-hidden cracks, cuts or splits.

13 On completion, refit the wheels and lower the car to the ground. Tighten the wheel nuts to the specified torque.

Rear disc brakes

14 Loosen the rear wheel nuts, then chock the front wheels. Jack up the rear of the car, and support it on axle stands. Release the handbrake and remove the rear wheels.

15 The procedure for checking the rear brakes is much the same as described in paragraphs 2 to 13 above. Check that the rear brakes are not binding, noting that transmission resistance is not a factor on the rear wheels. Abnormal effort may indicate that the handbrake needs adjusting – see Chapter 9.

Rear drum brakes

16 Loosen the rear wheel nuts, then chock the front wheels. Jack up the rear of the car, and support on axle stands (see *Jacking and vehicle support*). Release the handbrake and remove the rear wheels.

17 Spin the wheel to check that the brake is not binding. A small amount of resistance from the brake is acceptable, but no great effort should be required to turn the wheel hub. Abnormal effort may indicate that the handbrake needs adjusting – see Chapter 9.

18 To check the brake shoe lining thickness without removing the brake drums, prise the rubber plugs from the backplates, and use an electric torch to inspect the linings of the leading brake shoes. Check that the thickness of the lining material on the brake shoes is not less than the recommendation given in the Specifications.

19 If it is difficult to determine the exact thickness of the brake shoe linings, or if you are at all concerned about the condition of the

shoes, then remove the rear drums for a more comprehensive inspection (refer to Chapter 9).

20 With the drum removed, check the shoe return and hold-down springs for correct installation, and check the wheel cylinders for leakage of brake fluid. Apart from fluid being visible, a leaking wheel cylinder may be characterised by an excessive build-up of brake dust (stuck to the fluid which has leaked) at the cylinder seals.

21 Check the friction surface of the brake drums for scoring and discoloration. If excessive, the drum should be resurfaced or renewed.

22 Before refitting the wheels, check all brake lines and hoses (refer to Chapter 9). On completion, apply the handbrake and check that the rear wheels are locked. The handbrake can be adjusted as described in Chapter 9.

23 On completion, refit the wheels and lower the car to the ground. Tighten the wheel nuts to the specified torque.

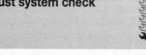

9 Exhaust system check

1 With the engine cold (at least three hours after the vehicle has been driven), check the complete exhaust system, from its starting point at the engine to the end of the tailpipe. Ideally, this should be done on a hoist, where unrestricted access is available; if a hoist is not available, raise and support the vehicle on axle stands.

2 Make sure that all brackets and rubber mountings are in good condition, and tight; if any of the mountings are to be renewed, ensure that the new ones are of the correct type – in the case of the rubber mountings, their colour is a good guide. Those nearest to the catalytic converter are more heat-resistant than the others.

3 Check the pipes and connections for evidence of leaks, severe corrosion, or damage. Leakage at any of the joints or in other parts of the system will usually show up as a black sooty stain in the vicinity of the leak. **Note:** *Exhaust sealants should not be used on any part of the exhaust system upstream of the catalytic converter (between the engine and the converter) – even if the sealant does not contain additives harmful to the converter,*

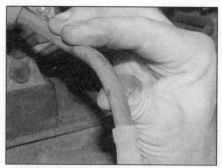

8.12 Bend the flexible hoses and check for cracks

pieces of it may break off and foul the element, causing local overheating.

4 At the same time, inspect the underside of the body for holes, corrosion, open seams, etc, which may allow exhaust gases to enter the passenger compartment. Seal all body openings with silicone or body putty.

5 Rattles and other noises can often be traced to the exhaust system, especially the rubber mountings **(see illustration)**. Try to move the system, silencer(s) and catalytic converter. If any components can touch the body or suspension parts, secure the exhaust system with new mountings.

10 Steering, suspension and roadwheel check

Front suspension and steering

1 Apply the handbrake, then raise the front of the vehicle and support it on axle stands.

2 Visually inspect the balljoint dust covers and the steering gear gaiters for splits, chafing or deterioration **(see illustration)**. Any wear of these components will cause loss of lubricant, together with dirt and water entry, resulting in rapid deterioration of the balljoints or steering gear.

3 Check the power-assisted steering fluid hoses for chafing or deterioration, and the pipe and hose unions for fluid leaks. Also check for signs of fluid leakage under pressure from the steering gear rubber gaiters, which would indicate failed fluid seals within the steering gear.

9.5 Check the condition of the rubber mountings

10.2 Check the condition of the steering rack gaiters

10.4 Grasp the roadwheel at the 12 o'clock and 6 o'clock positions, and try to rock it

4 Grasp the roadwheel at the 12 o'clock and 6 o'clock positions, and try to rock it **(see illustration)**. Very slight free play may be felt, but if the movement is appreciable, further investigation is necessary to determine the source. Continue rocking the wheel while an assistant depresses the footbrake. If the movement is now eliminated or significantly reduced, it is likely that the hub bearings are at fault. If the free play is still evident with the footbrake depressed, then there is wear in the suspension joints or mountings.

5 Now grasp the wheel at the 9 o'clock and 3 o'clock positions, and try to rock it as before. Any movement felt now may again be caused by wear in the hub bearings or the steering track rod balljoints. If the outer track rod balljoint is worn, the visual movement will be obvious. If the inner joint is suspect, it can be felt by placing a hand over the rack-and-pinion rubber gaiter, and gripping the track rod. If the wheel is now rocked, movement will be felt at the inner joint if wear has taken place.

6 Using a large screwdriver or flat bar, check for wear in the suspension mounting and subframe bushes by levering between the relevant suspension component and its attachment point. Some movement is to be expected as the mountings are made of rubber, but excessive wear should be obvious. Also check the condition of any visible rubber bushes, looking for splits, cracks or contamination of the rubber.

7 With the vehicle standing on its wheels, have an assistant turn the steering wheel back-and-forth, about an eighth of a turn each way. There should be very little, if any,

11.2 Check the condition of the driveshaft gaiters

lost movement between the steering wheel and roadwheels. If this is not the case, closely observe the joints and mountings previously described, but in addition, check the steering column joints for wear, and also check the rack-and-pinion steering gear itself.

Rear suspension

8 Chock the front wheels, then raise the rear of the vehicle and support it on axle stands.
9 Check the rear hub bearings for wear, using the method described for the front hub bearings (paragraph 4).
10 Using a large screwdriver or flat bar, check for wear in the suspension mounting bushes by levering between the relevant suspension component and its attachment point. Some movement is to be expected as the mountings are made of rubber, but excessive wear should be obvious.

Roadwheel check and balancing

11 Periodically remove the roadwheels, and clean any dirt or mud from the inside and outside surfaces. Examine the wheel rims for signs of rusting, corrosion or other damage. Light alloy wheels are easily damaged by 'kerbing' whilst parking, and similarly, steel wheels may become dented or buckled. Renewal of the wheel is very often the only course of remedial action possible.

12 The balance of each wheel and tyre assembly should be maintained, not only to avoid excessive tyre wear, but also to avoid wear in the steering and suspension components. Wheel imbalance is normally signified by vibration through the vehicle's bodyshell, although in many cases it is particularly noticeable through the steering wheel. Conversely, it should be noted that wear or damage in suspension or steering components may cause excessive tyre wear. Out-of-round or out-of-true tyres, damaged wheels and wheel bearing wear/maladjustment also fall into this category. Balancing will not usually cure vibration caused by such wear.

13 Wheel balancing may be carried out with the wheel either on or off the vehicle. If balanced on the vehicle, ensure that the wheel-to-hub relationship is marked in some way prior to subsequent wheel removal, so that it may be refitted in its original position.

12.5 Ensure the pipes are correctly supported in their clips

11 Driveshaft rubber gaiter and joint check

1 The driveshaft rubber gaiters are very important, because they prevent dirt, water and foreign material from entering and damaging the joints. External contamination can cause the gaiter material to deteriorate prematurely, so it's a good idea to wash the gaiters with soap and water occasionally.
2 With the vehicle raised and securely supported on axle stands, turn the steering onto full-lock, then slowly rotate each front wheel in turn. Inspect the condition of the outer constant velocity (CV) joint rubber gaiters, squeezing the gaiters to open out the folds. Check for signs of cracking, splits, or deterioration of the rubber, which may allow the escape of grease, and lead to the ingress of water and grit into the joint. Also check the security and condition of the retaining clips. Repeat these checks on the inner joints **(see illustration)**. If any damage or deterioration is found, the gaiters should be renewed as described in Chapter 8.
3 At the same time, check the general condition of the outer CV joints themselves, by first holding the driveshaft and attempting to rotate the wheels. Repeat this check on the inner joints, by holding the inner joint yoke and attempting to rotate the driveshaft.
4 Any appreciable movement in the joint indicates wear in the joint, wear in the driveshaft splines, or a loose driveshaft retaining bolt.

12 Underbody and fuel/brake line check

1 With the vehicle raised and supported on axle stands or over an inspection pit, thoroughly inspect the underbody and wheel arches for signs of damage and corrosion. In particular, examine the bottom of the side sills, and any concealed areas where mud can collect.
2 Where corrosion and rust is evident, press and tap firmly on the panel with a screwdriver, and check for any serious corrosion which would necessitate repairs.
3 If the panel is not seriously corroded, clean away the rust, and apply a new coating of underseal. Refer to Chapter 11 for more details of body repairs.
4 At the same time, inspect the lower body panels for stone damage and general condition.
5 Inspect all of the fuel and brake lines on the underbody for damage, rust, corrosion and leakage. Also make sure that they are correctly supported in their clips **(see illustration)**. Where applicable, check the PVC coating on the lines for damage.

13 Hinge and lock lubrication

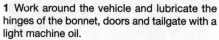

1 Work around the vehicle and lubricate the hinges of the bonnet, doors and tailgate with a light machine oil.

2 Check carefully the security and operation of all hinges, latches and locks, adjusting them where required. Check the operation of the central locking system (if fitted).

3 Where applicable, check the condition and operation of the tailgate struts, renewing them if either is leaking or no longer able to support the tailgate securely when raised.

14 Roadwheel nut tightness check

1 Checking the tightness of the wheel nuts is more relevant than you might think. Apart from the obvious safety aspect of ensuring they are sufficiently tight, this check will reveal whether they have been overtightened, as may have happened the last time new tyres were fitted, for example. If the car suffers a puncture, you may find that the wheel nuts cannot be loosened with the wheel brace.

2 Apply the handbrake, chock the wheels, and engage 1st gear.

3 Remove the wheel cover (or wheel centre cover), using the flat end of the wheel brace supplied in the tool kit.

4 Loosen the first wheel nut, using the wheel brace if possible. If the nut proves stubborn, use a close-fitting socket and a long extension bar.

⚠️ **Warning: Do not use makeshift means to loosen the wheel nuts if the proper tools are not available. If extra force is required, make sure that the tools fit properly, and are of good quality. Even so, consider the consequences of the tool slipping or breaking, and take precautions – wearing stout gloves is advisable to protect your hands. Do not be tempted to stand on the tools used – they are not designed for this, and there is a high risk of personal injury if the tool slips or breaks. If the wheel nuts are simply too tight, take the car to a garage equipped with suitable power tools.**

5 Once the nut has been loosened, remove it and check that the wheel stud threads are clean. Use a small wire brush to clean any rust or dirt from the threads, if necessary.

6 Refit the nut, with the tapered side facing inwards. Tighten it fully, using the wheel brace alone – no other tools. This will ensure that the wheel nuts can be loosened using the wheel brace if a puncture occurs. However, if a torque wrench is available, tighten the nut to the specified torque wrench setting.

7 Repeat the procedure for the remaining nuts, then refit the wheel cover or centre cover, as applicable.

8 Work around the car, checking and retightening the nuts for all four wheels.

15 Road test

Braking system

1 Make sure that the vehicle does not pull to one side when braking, and that the wheels do not lock when braking hard.

2 Check that there is no vibration through the steering when braking. On models equipped with ABS brakes, if vibration is felt through the pedal under heavy braking, this is a normal characteristic of the system operation, and is not a cause for concern.

3 Check that the handbrake operates correctly, without excessive movement of the lever, and that it holds the vehicle stationary on a slope, in both directions (facing up and down a slope).

4 With the engine switched off, test the operation of the brake servo unit as follows. Depress the footbrake four or five times to exhaust the vacuum, then start the engine. As the engine starts, there should be a noticeable 'give' in the brake pedal as vacuum builds-up. Allow the engine to run for at least two minutes, and then switch it off. If the brake pedal is now depressed again, it should be possible to detect a hiss from the servo as the pedal is depressed. After about four or five applications, no further hissing should be heard, and the pedal should feel considerably harder.

Steering and suspension

5 Check for any abnormalities in the steering, suspension, handling or road 'feel'.

6 Drive the vehicle, and check that there are no unusual vibrations or noises.

7 Check that the steering feels positive, with no excessive sloppiness or roughness, and check for any suspension noises when cornering and driving over bumps.

Drivetrain

8 Check the performance of the engine, transmission and driveshafts.

9 Check that the engine starts correctly, both when cold and when hot. Observe the glow plug warning light, and check that it comes on and goes off correctly.

10 Listen for any unusual noises from the engine and transmission.

11 Make sure that the engine runs smoothly when idling, and that there is no hesitation when accelerating.

12 Check that all gears can be engaged smoothly without noise, and that the gear lever action is smooth and not abnormally vague or 'notchy'.

13 Listen for a metallic clicking sound from the front of the vehicle as the vehicle is driven slowly in a circle with the steering on full-lock. Carry out this check in both directions. If a clicking noise is heard, this indicates wear in a driveshaft joint, in which case renew the joint if necessary.

Clutch

14 Check that the clutch pedal moves smoothly and easily through its full travel, and that the clutch itself functions correctly, with no trace of slip or drag.

15 If the clutch is slow to release, it is possible that the system requires bleeding (see Chapter 6). Also check the fluid pipes under the bonnet for signs of leakage.

16 Check the clutch as described in Chapter 6, Section 2.

Instruments and electrical equipment

17 Check the operation of all instruments and electrical equipment.

18 Make sure that all instruments read correctly, and switch on all electrical equipment in turn, to check that it functions properly.

16 Pollen filter renewal

1 Release the 2 fasteners and remove the trim panel above the passenger's side footwell (see illustration).

2 Remove the passenger's glovebox as described in Chapter 11.

3 Undo the 2 fasteners securing the fusebox/central junction box/GEM, then lift it from the mounting bracket on the bulkhead (see illustration). Move the fusebox/module to one side; there is no need to disconnect the wiring plugs.

4 Release the clips securing the wiring harness to the fusebox/module mounting bracket, then undo the 2 nuts and remove the bracket (see illustration).

5 On models with air conditioning, undo the retaining bolt and remove the cool air pipe from the heater housing to the side of the glovebox (see illustration).

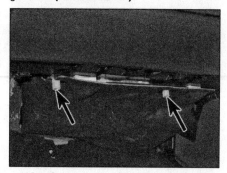

16.1 Squeeze together the sides and remove the two fasteners (arrowed)

16.3 Rotate the fasteners (arrowed) anti-clockwise and lift the fuse/junction box from the bracket

16.4 Undo the 2 nuts (arrowed) securing the bracket

16.5 Undo the bolt (arrowed) securing the glovebox cooling pipe

16.7a Undo the 3 bolts (arrowed), remove the cover . . .

16.7b . . . and pull the pollen filter from the housing

6 Disconnect the wiring plugs from the recirculation flap motor and heater blower motor resistor.

7 Undo the 3 bolts, remove the cover and pull the filter from the housing **(see illustrations)**.

8 Fit the new filter using a reversal of the removal procedure, ensuring that the filter is fitted with the airflow arrows pointing straight back into the cabin.

17 Handbrake check and adjustment

In service, the handbrake should be fully applied within 3 to 5 clicks of the handbrake lever ratchet. Should adjustment be necessary, refer to Chapter 9 for the full procedure description.

Every 37 500 miles or 3 years

18.3a Water draining nipple – 1.8 litre models . . .

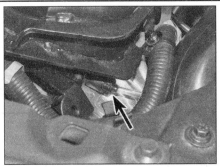

18.3b . . . and 2.0 litre models (arrowed)

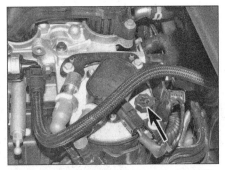

18.4a Slacken the bleed screw (arrowed) – 1.6 litre models . . .

18.4b . . . 1.8 litre models (arrowed) . . .

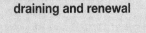

18 Fuel filter water draining and renewal

Water draining

1 The fuel filter is located at the front of the engine compartment on 2.0 litre models, and at the left-hand end of the cylinder head on 1.6 and 1.8 litre models. Remove the plastic cover on the top of the engine (where fitted).

2 To improve access on 1.8 litre models, remove the air filter assembly as described in Chapter 4A.

3 Position a container or cloth beneath the filter, then attach a length of plastic/rubber hose to the drain nipple, with the other end of the hose in a container **(see illustrations)**.

4 Slacken the drain nipple and the top bleed screw a few turns, and allow the fuel to drain until it appears clean and free from water droplets. Tighten the bleed screw and drain nipple **(see illustrations)**. Note that the bleed screw on the top of the filter on 1.6 litre models controls the flow through the drain nipple on its underside.

5 Remove the hose, and bleed the fuel system as described in Chapter 4A.

18.4c . . . and 2.0 litre models (arrowed)

18.7 Disconnect the sensor wiring plug

18.8 Undo the bolts and remove the metal shield

18.9 Depress the release buttons and disconnect the fuel pipes from the filter

18.11 Slide the fuel filter up from place

18.15 Undo the bolts (arrowed) and remove the metal shield

Filter renewal

6 Proceed as described in paragraphs 1 and 2 of this Section.

1.6 litre engine

7 Disconnect the wiring plug from the water sensor on the top of the filter **(see illustration)**.
8 Undo the bolts and remove the metal shield around the filter assembly **(see illustration)**.
9 Disconnect the fuel supply and return pipes from the filter **(see illustration)**. Plug the openings to prevent contamination.
10 Disconnect the fuel heater wiring plug from the side of the filter (where fitted).
11 Slide the filter assembly upwards from the bracket **(see illustration)**.
12 Slide the new filter into the bracket.
13 Reconnect the fuel supply and return pipes.
14 The remainder of fitting is a reversal of removal. Bleed the fuel system as described in Chapter 4A.

1.8 litre engine

15 Undo the bolts and remove the metal shield over the top of the filter **(see illustration)**.
16 Disconnect the wiring plug from the side of the filter housing.
17 Disconnect the fuel supply and return pipes **(see illustrations)**. Plug the openings to prevent contamination.
18 Slide the filter housing upwards from the mounting bracket.
19 Unscrew the collar and lift the filter cover and element from the housing **(see illustrations)**.
20 Discard the seal **(see illustration)**.

21 Position the new seal on the filter housing, and fit the new filter element to the cover.
22 Fit the new element and cover to the housing, ensuring the alignment arrows are

aligned correctly **(see illustration)**. Tighten the collar securely.
23 Refit the filter housing to the bracket, and reconnect the pipes/wiring plug.

18.17a Depress the release button and disconnect the fuel supply pipe

18.17b Prise out the locking catch (1), push in or pull out the clip (2), and disconnect the fuel return pipe

18.19a Unscrew the collar . . .

18.19b . . . then lift the cover and element from the filter housing

18.20 Renew the seal

18.22 Ensure the arrows align (arrowed)

18.26 Depress the release buttons and disconnect the fuel hoses from the filter head

18.27 Unscrew the filter head

18.29 Renew the filter element and the O-ring seal

24 The remainder of refitting is a reversal of removal. Bleed the fuel system as described in Chapter 4A.

2.0 litre engine

25 Release the wiring harnesses from the cable ties on the fuel filter bracket, then disconnect the filter wiring plug, release the fuel pipe from the clip, undo the bolts, then remove the bracket **(see illustrations 3.10a and 3.10b)**.

26 Depress the locking tabs and disconnect the fuel hoses from the filter head **(see illustration)**. Be prepared for fuel spillage. Use the plugs supplied in the filter kit to seal the hose openings.

27 Unscrew the filter head using a 27 mm socket or spanner, and lift it from place **(see illustration)**.

28 Remove the filter element, and discard the O-ring seal.

29 Fit the new filter element and O-ring seal to the filter head **(see illustration)**, then position the filter head and tighten it by rotating it clockwise until the stop on the filter housing abuts the stop on the filter head.

30 The remainder of refitting is a reversal of removal, but bleed the fuel system as described in Chapter 4A.

19 Air filter element renewal

Caution: Never drive the vehicle with the air cleaner filter element removed. Excessive engine wear could result, and backfiring could even cause a fire under the bonnet.

1 The air filter element is located in the air cleaner assembly on the left-hand side of the engine compartment.

2 Remove the plastic cover (where fitted) from the top of the engine.

3 On 1.8 and 2.0 litre models, disconnect the wiring plug from the mass airflow meter, and slacken the clamp securing the air outlet hose to the filter cover **(see illustration)**.

4 Undo the bolts, and lift the filter cover from place **(see illustrations)**.

5 Note which way round it's fitted, then lift the air filter element from the housing **(see illustrations)**

6 Wipe clean the inner surfaces of the cover and main housing, then locate the new element in the housing, making sure that the sealing lip is correctly engaged with the edge of the housing.

19.3 Slacken the clamp (arrowed) securing the air outlet hose to the filter cover

19.4a Filter cover bolts (arrowed) – 1.6 litre models . . .

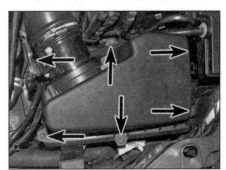

19.4b . . . 1.8 litre models (arrowed) . . .

19.4c . . . and 2.0 litre models (arrowed)

7 Refit the filter cover and tighten the bolts securely.

8 Reconnect the outlet hose and the wiring plug where applicable. Tighten the hose clamp securely, then refit the plastic cover over the engine.

20 Exhaust particulate filter additive tank refilling

Note: An exhaust particulate filter is only fitted to some 1.6 and 2.0 litre models. A particulate filter is not fitted to the 1.8 litre models.
Note: Although refilling the additive tank is straightforward, after topping it up the tank level counter in the control module must be reset in order for the system to function correctly. If the MIL (Malfunction Indicator Lamp) or PCL (Powertrain Control Light) are lit because of an empty or low fluid level in the additive tank, then system can only be reset with Ford test equipment. If you do not have access to this equipment, entrust this task to a Ford dealer or suitably-equipped specialist. If the MIL or PCL is not lit, then the system can be manually reset as described below.

1 Chock the front wheels, raise the rear of the vehicle and support it securely on axle stands (see *Jacking and vehicle support*). Remove the right-hand rear wheel.

Caution: Do not allow the additive to come into contact with skin, eyes or vehicle paintwork.

2 Release the locking tang and remove the additive tank overflow pipe quick release coupling blanking plug.

3 Fit the fuel additive refill kit overflow pipe – follow the manufacturer's information supplied with the kit.

4 Release the locking tang and remove the additive tank filler pipe quick-release coupling blanking cap **(see illustration)**.

5 Ensure the filling kit additive container valve is in the closed position, then connect the filling kit filler pipe to the tank filler pipe.

6 Attach the fuel additive tank filling kit hook, net and overflow container to the underside of the vehicle, then insert the additive tank overflow pipe into the container.

7 Using a transmission jack or suitable platform, with the refilling container in the horizontal position, raise the container until it's higher than the additive tank. Open the container valve until additive can be seen emerging from the overflow pipe, then close the valve.

8 Lower the filling container, and open the valve to allow the additive in the pipe to return to the container.

19.5a Lift the element from place – 1.6 litre models . . .

19.5b . . . 1.8 and 2.0 litre models

J46787

20.4 Remove the additive tank filler pipe coupling blanking plug (arrowed)

9 Disconnect the pipes, refit the blanking plugs/caps, refit the roadwheel and lower the vehicle to the ground.

10 With reference to the note at the beginning of this Section, the system must now be reset as follows:

11 Ensure the ignition switch is in position 0, and the fuel filler flap is closed. The following procedure must be completed within 60 seconds of the ignition switch being turned to position II:

> *Turn then ignition switch to position II.*
> *Open and close the fuel filler flap.*
> *Open and close the fuel filler flap.*
> *Turn the ignition switch to position 0.*
> *Turn the ignition switch to position II.*

12 The following sequence must be started within 60 seconds of the ignition switch being turned to position II in the last paragraph, and must be completed within 10 seconds after the fuel filler flap being opened as described in this paragraph:

> *Open and close the fuel filler flap.*
> *Open and close the fuel filler flap.*
> *Open and close the fuel filler flap.*

13 The following sequence must be started within 15 to 30 seconds after the fuel filler flap has be closed as described in the last paragraph, and completed within 10 seconds after the fuel filler flap has been opened as described in this paragraph:

> *Open and close the fuel filler flap.*
> *Open and close the fuel filler flap.*
> *Open and close the fuel filler flap.*

14 The following must be carried out within 60 seconds of the fuel filler flap being closed as described in the last paragraph. Ensure the vehicle is in neutral:

> *Start the engine and allow it to idle for a minimum of 20 seconds.*
> *After approximately 25 seconds the MIL or PCL should illuminate to indicate that resetting has been achieved.*
> *Turn the ignition to position 0.*
> *Turn the ignition to position II.*
> *Neither the MIL or PCL light should now be illuminated.*

15 If either the MIL or PCL are illuminated, repeat the procedure.

Every 62 500 miles

21 Timing belt renewal

The procedure is described in the relevant part of Chapter 2.

Every 75 000 miles

22 Exhaust particulate filter renewal

Note: *An exhaust particulate filter is only fitted to some 1.6 and 2.0 litre models. A particulate filter is not fitted to the 1.8 litre models.*

1 The renewal of the particulate filter is described with the exhaust/catalytic converter renewal procedure – refer to Chapter 4A.

Every 100 000 miles or 8 years

23 Auxiliary drivebelt check and renewal

Drivebelt check

1 A single auxiliary drivebelt is fitted at the right-hand side of the engine. An automatic adjuster is fitted, so checking the drivebelt tension is unnecessary.

2 Due to their function and material make-up, drivebelts are prone to failure after a long period of time, and should therefore be inspected regularly.

3 Since the drivebelt is located very close to the right-hand side of the engine compartment, it is possible to gain better access by raising the front of the vehicle, undoing the fasteners and removing the engine undershield **(see illustration 3.12)**.

4 With the engine stopped, inspect the full length of the drivebelt for cracks and separation of the belt plies. It will be necessary to turn the engine (using a spanner or socket and bar on the crankshaft pulley bolt) in order to move the belt from the pulleys so that the belt can be inspected thoroughly. Twist the belt between the pulleys so that both sides can be viewed. Also check for fraying, and glazing which gives the belt a shiny appearance. Check the pulleys for nicks, cracks, distortion and corrosion.

5 Note that it is not unusual for a ribbed belt to exhibit small cracks in the edges of the belt ribs, and unless these are extensive or very deep, belt renewal is not essential.

Drivebelt renewal

6 To remove the drivebelt, first raise the front of the vehicle and support on axle stands (see *Jacking and vehicle support*). Undo the fasteners and remove the engine undershield **(see illustration 3.12)**. Followed by the wheel arch liner.

7 Remove the plastic cover on the top of the engine (where fitted).

1.6 litre engines

8 Ford technicians use tool No 303-676 to rotate the belt tensioner. However, if the tool is not available, use a 15 mm spanner to rotate the tensioner, while an assistant lifts the belt from the pulleys **(see illustration)**.

9 Fit the tool or spanner to the tensioner arm and rotate the tensioner clockwise until the tensioner arm passes the hose in the housing, and a 5.0 mm drill bit can be inserted, locking the tensioner in position **(see illustration)**.

10 Note how the belt is routed, then remove the belt from the pulleys **(see illustrations)**.

11 Fit the new drivebelt onto the crankshaft, air conditioning compressor (where fitted), alternator and tensioner/idler pulleys. Fit the tool to the tensioner arm, hold the tensioner stationary with the tool and remove the locking drill bit. Slowly allow the tensioner arm to rotate and tension the belt. Remove the tool.

1.8 litre engines

12 Insert an M8 bolt, approximately 25 mm long into the bracket alongside the tensioner, and continue screwing in the bolt until the tension on the belt is relieved **(see illustrations)**.

13 Note how the belt is routed, then remove the belt from the pulleys **(see illustration 23.12a or 23.12b)**.

14 Fit the new belt to the pulleys, ensuring they are correctly seated in the pulley grooves.

15 Unscrew the bolt from the bracket and allow the tensioner to tension the belt.

2.0 litre engines

16 Using a spanner on the tensioner centre bolt, turn the tensioner anti-clockwise to release the drivebelt tension, then insert a 5 mm drill bit or rod through the holes in the arm/body when they align to lock the tensioner in this position **(see illustration)**.

23.8 Use a 15 mm open-ended spanner to rotate the tensioner clockwise

23.9 Insert a 5.0 mm drill bit/rod into the hole (arrowed) in the tensioner housing

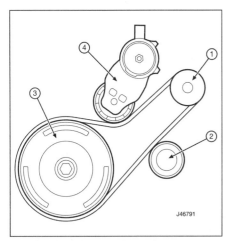

23.10a Auxiliary belt routing – 1.6 litre without air conditioning

1 *Alternator pulley*	3 *Crankshaft pulley*
2 *Idler pulley*	4 *Tensioner*

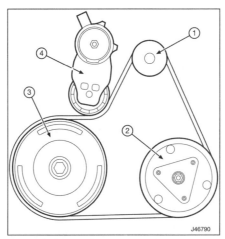

23.10b Auxiliary belt routing – 1.6 litre with air conditioning

1 *Alternator pulley*	3 *Crankshaft pulley*
2 *Air conditioning compressor*	4 *Tensioner*

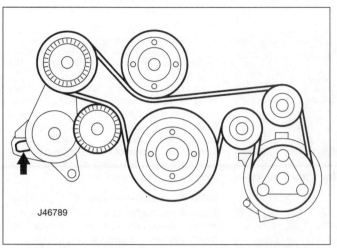

23.12a Insert the 8 x 25 mm bolt into the bracket (arrowed) alongside the tensioner – 1.8 litre with air conditioning . . .

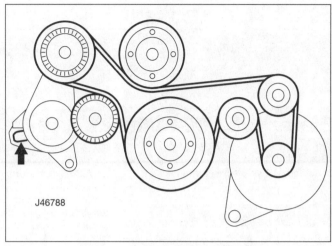

23.12b . . . and without air conditioning

23.16 Rotate the tensioner bolt anti-clockwise, then insert a 5 mm drill bit/rod through the locking holes once they align (arrowed)

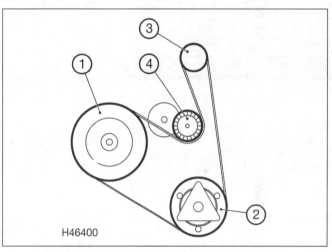

23.17 Auxiliary drivebelt routing – 2.0 litre models

1 Crankshaft pulley	3 Alternator
2 Air conditioning compressor	4 Tensioner

17 Note how the drivebelt is routed, then remove the belt from the pulleys **(see illustration)**.
18 Fit the new drivebelt onto the crankshaft, air conditioning compressor, alternator, and tensioner pulleys. Use a spanner to hold the tensioner arm, then remove the locking drill bit/rod, and allow the tensioner to rotate clockwise and gently tension the belt.

All engines

19 Refit the engine top cover and undershield, then lower the car to the ground.

Every 2 years, regardless of mileage

24 Brake fluid renewal

Warning: Brake hydraulic fluid can harm your eyes and damage painted surfaces, so use extreme caution when handling and pouring it. Do not use fluid that has been standing open for some time, as it absorbs moisture from the air. Excess moisture can cause a *dangerous loss of braking effectiveness. Brake fluid is also highly flammable – treat it with the same respect as petrol.*

1 The procedure is similar to that for the bleeding of the hydraulic system as described in Chapter 9.
2 Reduce the fluid level in the reservoir (by syphoning or using a poultry baster), but do not allow the fluid level to drop far enough to allow air into the system – if air enters the ABS hydraulic unit, the unit may need be bled using special Ford test equipment (see Chapter 9).

Warning: Do not syphon the fluid by mouth; it is poisonous.

3 Working as described in Chapter 9, open the first bleed screw in the sequence, and pump the brake pedal gently until nearly all the old fluid has been emptied from the master cylinder reservoir. Top-up to the MAX level with new fluid, and continue pumping until only the new fluid remains in the reservoir, and new fluid can be seen emerging from the bleed screw. Tighten the screw, and top the reservoir level

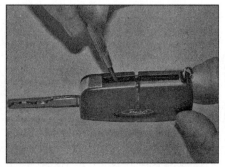

25.3a Insert a screwdriver into the slot . . .

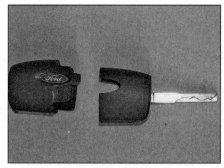

25.3b . . . and prise apart the 2 halves

25.4 Separate the 2 halves

25.5 The battery fits positive side down

up to the MAX level line. Old hydraulic fluid is invariably much darker in colour than the new, making it easy to distinguish the two.

4 Work through all the remaining bleed screws in the sequence until new fluid can be seen at all of them. Be careful to keep the master cylinder reservoir topped-up to above the MIN level at all times, or air may enter the system and greatly increase the length of the task.

5 When the operation is complete, check that all bleed screws are securely tightened, and that their dust caps are refitted. Wash off all traces of spilt fluid, and recheck the master cylinder reservoir fluid level.

6 Check the operation of the brakes before taking the car on the road.

7 Finally, check the operation of the clutch. Since the clutch shares the same fluid reservoir as the braking system, it may also be necessary to bleed the clutch as described in Chapter 6.

25 Remote control battery renewal

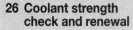

1 Although not in the Ford maintenance schedule, we recommend that the battery is changed every 2 years, regardless of the vehicle's mileage. However, if the door locks repeatedly fail to respond to signals from the remote control at the normal distance, change the battery in the remote control before attempting to troubleshoot any of the vehicle's other systems.

Type 1

2 Press the button to release the key blade. On passive type controls, remove the spare key.

3 On non-passive type controls, insert a small flat-bladed screwdriver into the slot provided,

push the screwdriver towards the key blade, and carefully prise the 2 halves of the control apart **(see illustrations)**.

4 On both types of control, insert a screwdriver as shown and separate the two halves **(see illustration)**.

5 Note the fitted position of the battery (positive side down), then prise the battery from place, and insert the new one **(see illustration)**. Avoid touching the battery or the terminals with bare fingers.

6 Snap the 2 halves of the control together.

7 Refit the key blade, and check for correct operation.

Type 2

8 Insert a small flat-bladed screwdriver into the slot provided and slide the transmitter unit from the key **(see illustration)**.

9 Use the screwdriver to release the clip each side and open the transmitter unit **(see illustration)**.

10 Note the fitted position of the battery (positive side up), then prise the battery from place, and insert the new one **(see illustration)**. Avoid touching the battery or the terminals with bare fingers.

11 Snap the 2 halves of the transmitter together, and re-attach it to the key.

26 Coolant strength check and renewal

⚠ *Warning: Do not allow antifreeze to come in contact with your skin or painted surfaces of the vehicle. Flush contaminated areas immediately with plenty of water. Don't store new coolant, or leave old coolant lying around, where it's accessible to children or pets – they're attracted by its sweet smell. Ingestion of even a small amount of coolant can be fatal. Wipe up garage-floor and drip-pan spills immediately. Keep antifreeze containers covered, and repair cooling system leaks as soon as they're noticed.*

⚠ *Warning: Never remove the expansion tank filler cap when the engine is running, or has just been switched off, as the cooling system will be*

25.8 Insert a screwdriver into the slot

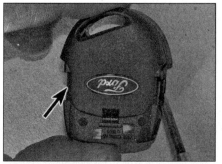

25.9 Release the clip each side (arrowed)

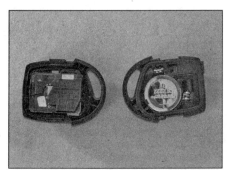

25.10 The battery fits positive side up

hot, and the consequent escaping steam and scalding coolant could cause serious injury.

⚠️ **Warning: Wait until the engine is cold before starting these procedures.**

Note: *If Ford pink/red antifreeze is used, the coolant can then be left indefinitely, providing the strength of the mixture is checked every year. If any antifreeze other than Ford's is to be used, the coolant must be renewed at regular intervals to provide an equivalent degree of protection; the conventional recommendation is to renew the coolant every two years.*

Strength check

1 Use a hydrometer to check the strength of the antifreeze. Follow the instructions provided with your hydrometer. The antifreeze strength should be approximately 50%. If it is significantly less than this, drain a little coolant from the radiator (see this Section), add antifreeze to the coolant expansion tank, then recheck the strength.

Coolant draining

2 To drain the system, first remove the expansion tank filler cap.
3 If the additional working clearance is required, raise the front of the vehicle and support it securely on axle stands (see *Jacking and vehicle support*). Undo the fasteners **(see illustration 3.12)** and remove the engine undershield.
4 Place a large drain tray underneath, and unscrew the radiator drain plug **(see illustration)**; direct as much of the escaping coolant as possible into the tray.
5 Once the coolant has stopped draining from the radiator, close the drain plug.

System flushing

6 With time, the cooling system may gradually lose its efficiency, as the radiator core becomes choked with rust, scale deposits from the water, and other sediment. To minimise this, as well as using only good-quality antifreeze and clean soft water, the system should be flushed as follows whenever any part of it is disturbed, and/or when the coolant is renewed.
7 With the coolant drained, refit the drain plug and refill the system with fresh water. Refit the expansion tank filler cap, start the engine and warm it up to normal operating temperature, then stop it and (after allowing it to cool down completely) drain the system again. Repeat as necessary until only clean water can be seen to emerge, then refill finally with the specified coolant mixture.
8 If only clean, soft water and good-quality antifreeze (even if not to Ford's specification) has been used, and the coolant has been renewed at the suggested intervals, the above procedure will be sufficient to keep clean the system for a considerable length of time. If, however, the system has been neglected, a more thorough operation will be required, as follows.

26.4 Undo the coolant drain plug at the left-hand lower corner of the radiator

9 First drain the coolant, then disconnect the radiator top and bottom hoses. Insert a garden hose into the radiator top hose connection, and allow water to circulate through the radiator until it runs clean from the bottom outlet.
10 To flush the engine, insert the garden hose into the radiator bottom hose, wrap a piece of rag around the garden hose to seal the connection, and allow water to circulate until it runs clear.
11 Try the effect of repeating this procedure in the top hose, although this may not be effective, since the thermostat will probably close and prevent the flow of water.
12 In severe cases of contamination, reverse-flushing of the radiator may be necessary. This may be achieved by inserting the garden hose into the bottom outlet, wrapping a piece of rag around the hose to seal the connection, then flushing the radiator until clear water emerges from the top hose outlet.
13 If the radiator is suspected of being severely choked, remove the radiator (Chapter 3), turn it upside-down, and repeat the procedure described in paragraph 12.
14 Flushing the heater matrix can be achieved using a similar procedure to that described in paragraph 12, once the heater inlet and outlet hoses have been identified. These two hoses will be of the same diameter, and pass through the engine compartment bulkhead (refer to the heater matrix removal procedure in Chapter 3 for more details).
15 The use of chemical cleaners is not recommended, and should be necessary only as a last resort; the scouring action of some chemical cleaners may lead to other cooling system problems. Normally, regular renewal of the coolant will prevent excessive contamination of the system.

Coolant filling

16 With the cooling system drained and flushed, ensure that all disturbed hose unions are correctly secured, and that the radiator/engine drain plug(s) is securely tightened. Refit the engine undershield. If it was raised, lower the vehicle to the ground.
17 Prepare a sufficient quantity of the specified coolant mixture (see below); allow for a surplus, so as to have a reserve supply for topping-up.
18 On 1.8 and 2.0 litre models, slacken the

26.18 Slacken the bleed screw (arrowed) on the EGR cooler hose

bleed screw located on the EGR cooler hose at the rear of the engine **(see illustration)**.
19 Slowly fill the system through the expansion tank. Since the tank is the highest point in the system, all the air in the system should be displaced into the tank by the rising liquid. Slow pouring reduces the possibility of air being trapped and forming airlocks.
20 As soon as a steady stream of bubble-free coolant emerges from the bleed screw on the EGR hose, tighten the screw.
21 Continue filling until the coolant level reaches the expansion tank MAX level line (see *Weekly checks*), then cover the filler opening to prevent coolant splashing out.
22 Start the engine and run it at idle speed, until it has warmed-up to normal operating temperature and the radiator electric cooling fan has cut in; watch the temperature gauge to check for signs of overheating. If the level in the expansion tank drops significantly, top-up to the MAX level line to minimise the amount of air circulating in the system.
23 Stop the engine, wash off any spilt coolant from the engine compartment and bodywork, then leave the car to cool down *completely* (overnight, if possible).
24 With the system cool, uncover the expansion tank filler opening, and top-up the tank to the MAX level line. Refit the filler cap, tightening it securely, and clean up any further spillage.
25 After refilling, always check carefully all components of the system (but especially any unions disturbed during draining and flushing) for signs of coolant leaks. Fresh antifreeze has a searching action, which will rapidly expose any weak points in the system.

Antifreeze type and mixture

Note: *Do not use engine antifreeze in the windscreen/tailgate washer system, as it will damage the vehicle's paintwork. A screenwash additive should be added to the washer system in its maker's recommended quantities.*
26 If the vehicle's history (and therefore the quality of the antifreeze in it) is unknown, owners are advised to drain and thoroughly reverse-flush the system, before refilling with fresh coolant mixture.
27 If the antifreeze used is to Ford's specification, the levels of protection it affords are indicated in the coolant packaging.

A leak in the cooling system will usually show up as white- or antifreeze-coloured deposits on the area adjoining the leak.

28 To give the recommended *standard* mixture ratio for antifreeze, 50% (by volume) of antifreeze must be mixed with 50% of clean, soft water; if you are using any other type of antifreeze, follow its manufacturer's instructions to achieve the correct ratio.

29 You are unlikely to fully drain the system at any one time (unless the engine is being completely stripped), and the capacities quoted in Specifications are therefore slightly academic for routine coolant renewal. As a guide, only two-thirds of the system's total capacity is likely to be needed for coolant renewal.

30 As the drained system will be partially filled with flushing water, in order to establish the recommended mixture ratio, measure out 50% of the system capacity in antifreeze and pour it into the expansion tank as described above, then top-up with water. Any topping-up while refilling the system should be done with water – for *Weekly checks* use a suitable mixture.

31 Before adding antifreeze, the cooling system should be drained, preferably flushed, and all hoses checked for condition and security. As noted earlier, fresh antifreeze will rapidly find any weaknesses in the system.

32 After filling with antifreeze, a label should be attached to the expansion tank, stating the type and concentration of antifreeze used, and the date installed. Any subsequent topping-up should be made with the same type and concentration of antifreeze.

General cooling system checks

33 The engine should be cold for the cooling system checks, so perform the following procedure before driving the vehicle, or after it has been shut off for at least three hours.

34 Remove the expansion tank filler cap, and clean it thoroughly inside and out with a rag. Also clean the filler neck on the expansion tank. The presence of rust or corrosion in the filler neck indicates that the coolant should be changed. The coolant inside the expansion tank should be relatively clean and transparent. If it is rust-coloured, drain and flush the system, and refill with a fresh coolant mixture.

35 Carefully check the radiator hoses and heater hoses along their entire length; renew any hose which is cracked, swollen or deteriorated (see Section 5).

36 Inspect all other cooling system components (joint faces, etc) for leaks. A leak in the cooling system will usually show up as white- or antifreeze-coloured deposits on the area adjoining the leak **(see Haynes Hint)**. Where any problems of this nature are found on system components, renew the component or gasket with reference to Chapter 3.

37 Clean the front of the radiator with a soft brush to remove all insects, leaves, etc, embedded in the radiator fins. Be careful not to damage the radiator fins, or cut your fingers on them. To do a more thorough job, remove the radiator grille as described in Chapter 11.

Airlocks

38 If, after draining and refilling the system, symptoms of overheating are found which did not occur previously, then the fault is almost certainly due to trapped air at some point in the system, causing an airlock and restricting the flow of coolant; usually, the air is trapped because the system was refilled too quickly.

39 If an airlock is suspected, first try gently squeezing all visible coolant hoses. A coolant hose which is full of air feels quite different to one full of coolant when squeezed. After refilling the system, most airlocks will clear once the system has cooled, and been topped-up.

40 While the engine is running at operating temperature, switch on the heater and heater fan, and check for heat output. Provided there is sufficient coolant in the system, lack of heat output could be due to an airlock in the system.

41 Airlocks can have more serious effects than simply reducing heater output – a severe airlock could reduce coolant flow around the engine. Check that the radiator top hose is hot when the engine is at operating temperature – a top hose which stays cold could be the result of an airlock (or a non-opening thermostat).

42 If the problem persists, stop the engine and allow it to cool down **completely** before unscrewing the expansion tank filler cap or loosening the hose clips and squeezing the hoses to bleed out the trapped air. In the worst case, the system will have to be at least partially drained (this time, the coolant can be saved for re-use) and flushed to clear the problem. If all else fails, have the system evacuated and vacuum filled by a suitably-equipped garage.

Expansion tank pressure cap check

43 Wait until the engine is completely cold – perform this check before the engine is started for the first time in the day.

44 Place a wad of cloth over the expansion tank cap, then unscrew it slowly and remove it.

45 Examine the condition of the rubber seal on the underside of the cap. If the rubber appears to have hardened, or cracks are visible in the seal edges, a new cap should be fitted.

46 If the car is several years old, or has covered a large mileage, consider renewing the cap regardless of its apparent condition – they are not expensive. If the pressure relief valve built into the cap fails, excess pressure in the system will lead to puzzling failures of hoses and other cooling system components.

27 Check the transmission oil level

1 Refer to Chapter 7, Section 6, paragraphs 6 to 8 (5-speed) or 9 to 11 (6-speed).

Chapter 2 Part A:
1.6 litre engine in-car repair procedures

Contents

Degrees of difficulty

Easy, suitable for novice with little experience	**Fairly easy,** suitable for beginner with some experience	**Fairly difficult,** suitable for competent DIY mechanic	**Difficult,** suitable for experienced DIY mechanic	**Very difficult,** suitable for expert DIY or professional

Specifications

General

Designation	Duratorq-TDCi (DV)
Engine codes*	G8DA, G8DB, G8DE, G8DF and GPDC
Capacity.	1560 cc
Bore	75.0 mm
Stroke.	88.3 mm
Direction of crankshaft rotation	Clockwise (viewed from the right-hand side of vehicle)
No 1 cylinder location.	At the transmission end of block
Maximum power output:	
All except GPDC.	80 kW @ 4000 rpm
GPDC	66 kW
Maximum torque output:	
All except GPDC.	230 Nm @ 2000 rpm
GPDC	215 Nm
Compression ratio	18.0 :1

* The engine code is stamped on a plate attached to the front of the cylinder block, next to the oil filter

Compression pressures (engine hot, at cranking speed)

Normal	20 ± 5 bar
Minimum.	15 bar
Maximum difference between any two cylinders.	5 bar

Camshaft

Drive.	Toothed belt

Lubrication system

Oil pump type.	Gear-type, driven directly by the right-hand end of the crankshaft, by two flats machined along the crankshaft journal.

Minimum oil pressure at 80°C:

Idle speed.	1.0 to 2.0 bar
2000 rpm	2.3 to 3.7 bar

Torque wrench settings

	Nm	lbf ft
Ancillary drivebelt tensioner roller	20	15
Big-end bolts:*		
Stage 1	10	7
Stage 2	Slacken 180°	
Stage 3	10	7
Stage 4	Angle-tighten a further 130°	
Camshaft bearing caps	10	7
Camshaft cover/bearing ladder:		
Studs	10	7
Bolts	10	7
Camshaft position sensor bolt	5	4
Camshaft sprocket	43	32
Coolant outlet housing bolts	8	6
Crankshaft position/speed sensor bolt	5	4
Crankshaft pulley/sprocket bolt:*		
Stage 1	35	26
Stage 2	Angle-tighten a further 180°	
Cylinder head bolts:*		
Stage 1	20	15
Stage 2	40	30
Stage 3	Angle-tighten a further 260°	
Cylinder head cover/manifold	10	7
EGR valve	10	7
Engine mountings:		
Right-hand mounting retaining bolts	90	66
Right-hand mounting bracket-to-engine bolts	56	41
Left-hand mounting nuts	48	35
Left-hand mounting bracket to transmission	80	59
Left-hand mounting centre bolt	148	109
Lower-rear torque rod bolts	80	59
Engine-to-transmission fixing bolts	47	35
Flywheel bolts:*		
Stage 1	30	22
Stage 2	Angle-tighten a further 90°	
Fuel pump sprocket	50	37
Main bearing ladder outer seam bolts:		
Stage 1	5	4
Stage 2	10	7
Main bearing ladder to cylinder block:		
Stage 1	10	7
Stage 2	Slacken 180°	
Stage 3	30	22
Stage 4	Angle-tighten a further 140°	
Piston oil jet spray tube bolt	20	15
Oil cooler retaining bolts	10	7
Oil filter cover	25	18
Oil pick-up pipe	10	7
Oil pressure switch	30	22
Oil pump to cylinder block	10	7
Sump drain plug	34	25
Sump bolts/nuts	10	7
Timing belt idler pulley	35	26
Timing belt tensioner pulley	30	22
Timing chain tensioner	10	7
Vacuum pump:		
Stage 1	18	13
Stage 2	Angle-tighten a further 5°	

* Do not re-use

1 General information

How to use this Chapter

This Part of Chapter 2 describes the repair procedures that can reasonably be carried out on the engine while it remains in the vehicle. If the engine has been removed from the vehicle and is being dismantled as described in Part D, any preliminary dismantling procedures can be ignored.

Note that, while it may be possible physically to overhaul items such as the piston/connecting rod assemblies while the engine is in the car, such tasks are not usually carried out as separate operations. Usually, several additional procedures are required (not to mention the cleaning of components and oilways); for this reason, all such tasks are classed as major overhaul procedures, and are described in Part D of this Chapter.

Part D describes the removal of the engine/ transmission from the car, and the full overhaul procedures that can then be carried out.

DV series engines

The 1.6 litre DV series engine is the result of development collaboration between Citroën/Peugeot and Ford. The engine is of double overhead camshaft (DOHC) 16-valve design. The direct injection, turbocharged, four-cylinder engine is mounted transversely, with the transmission mounted on the left-hand side.

A toothed timing belt drives the inlet camshaft, high-pressure fuel pump and coolant pump. The inlet camshaft drives the exhaust camshaft via a chain. The camshafts operate the inlet and exhaust valves via rocker arms which are supported at their pivot ends by hydraulic self-adjusting tappets. The camshafts are supported by bearings machined directly in the cylinder head and camshaft bearing housing.

The high-pressure fuel pump supplies fuel to the fuel rail, and subsequently to the electronically-controlled injectors which inject the fuel direct into the combustion chambers. This design differs from the previous type where an injection pump supplies the fuel at high pressure to each injector. The earlier, conventional type injection pump required fine calibration and timing, and these functions are now completed by the high-pressure pump, electronic injectors and engine management ECM.

The crankshaft runs in five main bearings of the usual shell type. Endfloat is controlled by thrustwashers either side of No 2 main bearing.

The pistons are selected to be of matching weight, and incorporate fully-floating gudgeon pins retained by circlips.

Repair operations precaution

The engine is a complex unit with numerous accessories and ancillary components. The design of the engine compartment is such that every conceivable space has been utilised, and access to virtually all of the engine components is extremely limited. In many cases, ancillary components will have to be removed, or moved to one side, and wiring, pipes and hoses will have to be disconnected or removed from various cable clips and support brackets.

When working on this engine, read through the entire procedure first, look at the car and engine at the same time, and establish whether you have the necessary tools, equipment, skill and patience to proceed. Allow considerable time for any operation, and be prepared for the unexpected.

Because of the limited access, many of the engine photographs appearing in this Chapter were, by necessity, taken with the engine removed from the vehicle.

⚠ **Warning: It is essential to observe strict precautions when working on the fuel system components of the engine, particularly the high-pressure side of the system. Before carrying out any engine operations that entail working on, or near, any part of the fuel system, refer to the special information given in Chapter 4A.**

Operations with engine in vehicle

a) Compression pressure – testing.
b) Cylinder head cover – removal and refitting.
c) Crankshaft pulley – removal and refitting.
d) Timing belt covers – removal and refitting.
e) Timing belt – removal, refitting and adjustment.
f) Timing belt tensioner and sprockets – removal and refitting.
g) Camshaft oil seal – renewal.
h) Camshaft, rocker arms and hydraulic tappets – removal, inspection and refitting.
i) Sump – removal and refitting.
j) Oil pump – removal and refitting.
k) Crankshaft oil seals – renewal.
l) Engine/transmission mountings – inspection and renewal.
m) Flywheel – removal, inspection and refitting.

2 Compression and leakdown tests – description and interpretation

Compression test

Note: *A compression tester specifically designed for diesel engines must be used for this test.*

1 When engine performance is down, or if misfiring occurs which cannot be attributed to the fuel system, a compression test can provide diagnostic clues as to the engine's condition. If the test is performed regularly, it can give warning of trouble before any other symptoms become apparent.

2 A compression tester specifically intended for diesel engines must be used, because of the higher pressures involved. The tester is connected to an adapter which screws into the glow plug or injector hole. On this engine, an adapter suitable for use in the glow plug holes will be required, so as not to disturb the fuel system components. It is unlikely to be worthwhile buying such a tester for occasional use, but it may be possible to borrow or hire one – if not, have the test performed by a garage.

3 Unless specific instructions to the contrary are supplied with the tester, observe the following points:

a) *The battery must be in a good state of charge, the air filter must be clean, and the engine should be at normal operating temperature.*
b) *All the glow plugs should be removed as described in Chapter 5 before starting the test.*
c) *Disconnect the fuel injector wiring plugs.*

4 The compression pressures measured are not so important as the balance between cylinders. Values are given in the Specifications.

5 The cause of poor compression is less easy to establish on a diesel engine than on a petrol one. The effect of introducing oil into the cylinders ('wet' testing) is not conclusive, because there is a risk that the oil will sit in the swirl chamber or in the recess on the piston crown instead of passing to the rings. However, the following can be used as a rough guide to diagnosis.

6 All cylinders should produce very similar pressures; any difference greater than that specified indicates the existence of a fault. Note that the compression should build-up quickly in a healthy engine; low compression on the first stroke, followed by gradually-increasing pressure on successive strokes, indicates worn piston rings. A low compression reading on the first stroke, which does not build-up during successive strokes, indicates leaking valves or a blown head gasket (a cracked head could also be the cause). Deposits on the undersides of the valve heads can also cause low compression.

7 A low reading from two adjacent cylinders is almost certainly due to the head gasket having blown between them; the presence of coolant in the engine oil will confirm this.

8 If the compression reading is unusually high, the cylinder head surfaces, valves and pistons are probably coated with carbon deposits. If this is the case, the cylinder head should be removed and decarbonised (see Part D). **Note:** *After performing this test, a fault code may be generated and stored in the PCM memory. Have the PCM self-diagnosis facility interrogated by a Ford dealer or suitably-equipped specialist, and the fault code erased.*

3.9 Insert a 5.0 mm drill bit/bolt through the round hole in the sprocket flange into the hole in the oil pump housing (lower timing belt removed for clarity)

3.10 Insert an 8.0 mm drill bit/bolt through the hole in the camshaft sprocket into the corresponding hole in the cylinder head

Leakdown test

9 A leakdown test measures the rate at which compressed air fed into the cylinder is lost. It is an alternative to a compression test, and in many ways it is better, since the escaping air provides easy identification of where pressure loss is occurring (piston rings, valves or head gasket).

10 The equipment needed for leakdown testing is unlikely to be available to the home mechanic. If poor compression is suspected, have the test performed by a suitably-equipped garage.

3 Engine assembly/ valve timing holes – general information and usage

Note: *Do not attempt to rotate the engine whilst the crankshaft and camshaft are locked in position. If the engine is to be left in this state for a long period of time, it is a good*

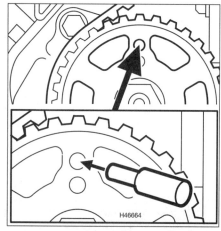

3.11 Insert Ford tool No 303-732 or a 5.0 mm drill bit through the hole in the fuel pump sprocket into the fuel pump mounting bracket

idea to place suitable warning notices inside the vehicle, and in the engine compartment. This will reduce the possibility of the engine being accidentally cranked on the starter motor, which is likely to cause damage with the locking pins in place.

1 Timing holes or slots are located only in the crankshaft pulley flange and camshaft sprocket hub. The holes/slots are used to position the pistons halfway up the cylinder bores. This will ensure that the valve timing is maintained during operations that require removal and refitting of the timing belt. When the holes/slots are aligned with their corresponding holes in the cylinder block and cylinder head, suitable diameter bolts/pins can be inserted to lock the crankshaft and camshaft in position, preventing rotation.

2 Note that the fuel system used on these engines does not have a conventional diesel injection pump, but instead uses a high-pressure fuel pump. However, the fuel pump sprocket must be pegged in position in a similar fashion to the camshaft sprocket.

3 To align the engine assembly/valve timing holes, proceed as follows.

4 Apply the handbrake, then jack up the front of the vehicle and support it on axle stands (see *Jacking and vehicle support*). Remove the right-hand front roadwheel.

5 To gain access to the crankshaft pulley, to enable the engine to be turned, the wheel arch plastic liner must be removed. The liner is secured by several plastic expanding rivets/ nut/bolts. To remove the rivets, push in the centre pins a little, then prise the clips from place. Remove the liner from under the front wing. The crankshaft can then be turned using a suitable socket and extension bar fitted to the pulley bolt.

6 Remove the upper and lower timing belt covers as described in Section 6.

7 Temporarily refit the crankshaft pulley bolt, remove the crankshaft locking tool, then turn the crankshaft until the timing hole in the

camshaft sprocket hub is aligned with the corresponding hole in the cylinder head. Note that the crankshaft must always be turned in a clockwise direction (viewed from the right-hand side of vehicle). Use a small mirror so that the position of the sprocket hub timing slot can be observed. When the slot is aligned with the corresponding hole in the cylinder head the camshaft is positioned correctly.

8 Remove the crankshaft drivebelt pulley as described in Section 5.

9 Insert a 5 mm diameter bolt, rod or drill through the hole in crankshaft sprocket flange and into the corresponding hole in the oil pump **(see illustration)**, if necessary, carefully turn the crankshaft either way until the rod enters the timing hole in the block.

10 Insert an 8 mm bolt, rod or drill through the hole in the camshaft sprocket hub and into engagement with the cylinder head **(see illustration)**.

11 When refitting the timing belt, insert Ford tool No 303-732 through the hole in the fuel pump sprocket and into the corresponding hole in the fuel pump mounting bracket **(see illustration)**. In the absence of this tool use a 5 mm bolt or drill bit.

12 The crankshaft and camshaft are now locked in position, preventing unnecessary rotation.

4 Cylinder head cover/manifold – removal and refitting

Removal

1 Disconnect the battery negative lead as described in Chapter 5.

2 Pull the plastic cover (where fitted) upwards from the top of the engine.

3 Remove the EGR cooler (where fitted) as described in Chapter 4B. On models without an EGR cooler, undo the bolts, release the clamp and remove the pipe from the EGR

4.3 Undo the Torx bolts (arrowed) securing the EGR pipe

4.4a Slacken the clamp (arrowed) and pull the inlet hose from the turbocharger . . .

4.4b . . . then release the clips and pull the breather hose from the manifold/cover

4.5a Depress the clip (arrowed) and disconnect the wiring plug from the injector

4.5b Undo the bolts (arrowed) and remove the wiring harness guide

valve to the cylinder head cover/manifold **(see illustration)**.

4 Release the clamps and disconnect the air filter outlet hose from the turbocharger, and the breather hose from the cover/manifold **(see illustrations)**.

5 Disconnect the wiring plugs from the top of each injector, undo the guide bolts, then make sure all wiring harnesses are freed from any retaining brackets on the cylinder head cover/ inlet manifold **(see illustrations)**. Disconnect any vacuum pipes as necessary, having first noted their fitted positions.

6 Depress the release buttons and disconnect the fuel feed and return hoses at the right-hand end of the cylinder head, then disconnect the fuel temperature sensor wiring plug, and move the pipe assembly to the rear **(see illustrations)**. Plug the openings to prevent contamination.

7 Prise out the retaining clips and disconnect the fuel return pipes from the injectors, then undo the unions and remove the high-pressure fuel pipes from the injectors and the common fuel rail at the rear of the cylinder head – counter-hold the unions with a second spanner **(see illustrations)**. Plug the openings to prevent dirt ingress.

8 Disconnect the wiring plug from the Manifold Absolute Pressure (MAP) sensor **(see illustration)**.

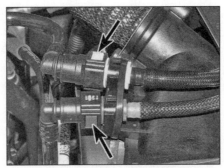

4.6a Depress the release buttons (arrowed) and disconnect the fuel hoses

4.6b Fuel temperature sensor (arrowed)

4.7a Prise out the clip and pull the return hose from the top of each injector

4.7b Use a second spanner to hold the injector port whilst slackening the fuel pipe unions

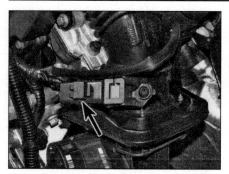

4.8 Disconnect the wiring plug from the MAP sensor (arrowed)

4.9a Remove the bolt (arrowed) . . .

4.9b . . . pull the tube from the mounting stud . . .

4.9c . . . then rotate the tube and disconnect it

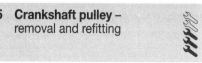

4.9d Slacken the clamp (arrowed) and disconnect the hose from the anti-shudder valve

9 Release the clamps, undo the bolts and remove the air ducting from the top of the turbocharger, and the anti-shudder valve attach to the manifold/cover. Make a note of their fitted positions, then disconnect any wiring plugs as the assembly is withdrawn **(see illustrations)**.

10 Undo the retaining bolts and remove the oil separator from the top of the cylinder head **(see illustration)**. Recover the rubber seal.

11 Undo the bolts securing the cylinder head cover/inlet manifold. Lift the assembly away **(see illustration)**. Recover the manifold rubber seals.

Refitting

12 Refitting is a reversal of removal, bearing in mind the following points:
 a) *Examine the seals for signs of damage and deterioration, and renew if necessary. Smear a little clean engine oil on the manifold seals.*
 b) *Renew the fuel injector high-pressure pipes – see Chapter 4A.*

5 Crankshaft pulley – removal and refitting

Removal

1 Remove the auxiliary drivebelt as described in Chapter 1.

2 To lock the crankshaft, working underneath the engine, insert Ford tool No 303-734 into the hole in the right-hand face of the engine block casting over the lower section of the flywheel. Rotate the crankshaft until the tool engages in the corresponding hole in the flywheel. In the absence of the Ford tool, insert a 12 mm rod or drill into the hole **(see illustration)**. Note: *The hole in the casting and the hole in the flywheel are provided purely to lock the crankshaft whilst the pulley bolt is undone, it does not position the crankshaft at TDC.*

3 Using a suitable socket and extension bar, unscrew the retaining bolt, remove the washer, then slide the pulley off the end of the crankshaft **(see illustration)**. If the pulley is tight fit, it can be drawn off the crankshaft using a suitable puller. If a puller is being used, refit the pulley retaining bolt without the washer, to avoid damaging the crankshaft as the puller is tightened.

Caution: Do not touch the outer magnetic sensor ring of the sprocket with your fingers, or allow metallic particles to come into contact with it.

4.10 Undo the bolts and remove the oil separator (arrowed)

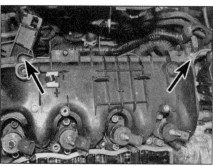
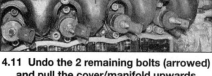

4.11 Undo the 2 remaining bolts (arrowed) and pull the cover/manifold upwards

5.2 The locking pin/bolt (arrowed) must locate in the hole in the flywheel (arrowed) to prevent rotation

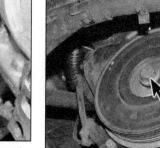

5.3 Undo the crankshaft pulley retaining bolt (arrowed)

Refitting

4 Refit the pulley to the end of the crankshaft.

5 Thoroughly clean the threads of the pulley retaining bolt, then apply a coat of locking compound to the bolt threads. Ford recommend the use of Loctite (available from your Ford dealer or automotive store); in the absence of this, any good-quality locking compound may be used.

6 Refit the crankshaft pulley retaining bolt and washer. Tighten the bolt to the specified torque, then through the specified angle, preventing the crankshaft from turning using the method employed on removal.

7 Refit and tension the auxiliary drivebelt as described in Chapter 1.

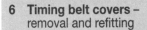

6 Timing belt covers –
removal and refitting

 Warning: Refer to the precautionary information contained in Section 1 before proceeding.

Removal

Upper cover

1 Remove the plastic cover from the top of the engine (where fitted).

2 Undo the 2 retaining bolts and move the brake master cylinder remote reservoir to one side (where fitted) **(see illustration)**.

3 Remove the wiper arms as described in Chapter 12.

4 Release the 5 clips and pull the windscreen cowl panel upwards from the moulding at the base of the windscreen **(see illustrations)**.

5 Undo the bolt at each end and pull the bulkhead extension panel forwards from the retaining clips **(see illustration)**.

6 Release the wiring harness and fuel pipes from the upper cover.

7 Undo the 5 bolts and remove the timing belt upper cover **(see illustration)**.

Lower cover

8 Remove the upper cover as described previously.

9 Drain the cooling system as described in Chapter 1.

10 Pull the coolant expansion tank upwards from its mountings, then release the clip and disconnect the supply hose from the coolant expansion tank **(see illustration)**.

11 Remove the crankshaft pulley as described in Section 5.

12 Position a trolley/workshop jack under the engine. Place a block of wood on the jack head, then take the weight of the engine.

13 Undo the nuts/bolts, and remove the right-hand engine mounting **(see illustration)**.

14 Undo the 4 bolts and remove the mounting bracket from the engine.

15 Undo the 5 bolts and remove the lower cover **(see illustration)**.

6.2 Undo the bolts securing the master cylinder remote reservoir (arrowed)

6.4b . . . and pull the scuttle cowl panel upwards from the moulding at the base of the windscreen

Refitting

16 Refitting of all the covers is a reversal of the relevant removal procedure, ensuring that each cover section is correctly located, and

6.4a Prise forwards the clips (arrowed) . . .

6.5 Undo the bolt (arrowed) at each end of the bulkhead extension panel

that the cover retaining bolts are securely tightened. Ensure that all disturbed hoses are reconnected and retained by their relevant clips.

6.7 Upper timing cover bolts (arrowed)

6.13 Remove the right-hand mounting assembly (arrowed)

6.10 Disconnect the coolant hose from the base of the expansion tank (arrowed)

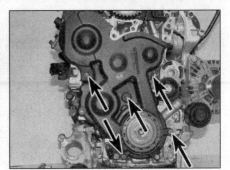

6.15 Lower timing belt cover bolts (arrowed)

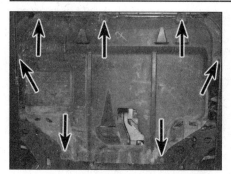

7.4 Undo the fasteners (arrowed) and remove the engine undershield

7.6 Undo the bolt (arrowed) and remove the crankshaft position sensor

7.7 Remove the timing belt protection bracket

7 Timing belt –
removal, inspection, refitting and tensioning

General

1 The timing belt drives the camshaft, high-pressure fuel pump, and coolant pump from a toothed sprocket on the end of the crankshaft. If the belt breaks or slips in service, the pistons are likely to hit the valve heads, resulting in expensive damage.

2 The timing belt should be renewed at the specified intervals, or earlier if it is contaminated with oil, or at all noisy in operation (a 'scraping' noise due to uneven wear).

3 If the timing belt is being removed, it is a wise precaution to check the condition of the coolant pump at the same time (check for signs of coolant leakage). This may avoid the need to remove the timing belt again at a later stage, should the coolant pump fail.

Removal

4 Apply the handbrake, then jack up the front of the vehicle and support it on axle stands (see *Jacking and vehicle support*). Remove the front right-hand roadwheel, wheel arch liner (to expose the crankshaft pulley), and the engine undershield. The wheel arch liner is secured by several bolts. The engine undershield is retained by several fasteners **(see illustration)**.

5 Remove the upper and lower timing belt covers, as described in Section 6.

6 Undo the bolt and remove the crankshaft position sensor adjacent to the crankshaft sprocket flange, and move it to one side **(see illustration)**.

7 Undo the retaining bolt and remove the timing belt protection bracket, again, adjacent to the crankshaft sprocket flange **(see illustration)**.

8 Lock the crankshaft and camshaft in the correct position as described in Section 3. If necessary, temporarily refit the crankshaft pulley bolt to enable the crankshaft to be rotated.

9 Insert a hexagon key into the belt tensioner pulley centre, slacken the pulley bolt, and allow the tensioner to rotate, relieving the belt tension **(see illustration)**. With belt slack, temporarily tighten the pulley bolt.

10 Note its routing, then remove the timing belt from the sprockets.

Inspection

11 Renew the belt as a matter of course, regardless of its apparent condition. The cost of a new belt is nothing compared with the cost of repairs should the belt break in service. If signs of oil contamination are found, trace the source of the oil leak and rectify it. Wash down the engine timing belt area and all related components, to remove all traces of oil. Check that the tensioner and idler pulleys rotate freely without any sign of roughness, and also check that the coolant pump pulley rotates freely. If necessary, renew these items.

Refitting and tensioning

12 Commence refitting by ensuring that the crankshaft, camshaft and fuel pump sprocket timing pins are in position as described in Section 3.

13 Locate the timing belt on the crankshaft sprocket, then keeping it taut, locate it around the idler pulley, camshaft sprocket, high-pressure pump sprocket, coolant pump sprocket, and the tensioner roller **(see illustration)**.

14 Refit the timing belt protection bracket and tighten the retaining bolt securely.

15 Slacken the tensioner pulley bolt, and using a hexagonal key, rotate the tensioner anti-clockwise, which moves the index arm clockwise, until the index arm is aligned as shown **(see illustration)**.

7.9 Slacken the bolt and allow the tensioner to rotate, relieving the tension on the belt

7.13 Timing belt routing

7.15 The index arm must align with the lug (arrowed)

16 Remove the camshaft, crankshaft and fuel pump sprocket (where applicable) timing pins and, using a socket on the crankshaft pulley bolt, rotate the crankshaft clockwise 10 complete revolutions. Refit the crankshaft and camshaft locking pins.

17 Check that the tensioner index arm is still aligned between the edges of the area shown **(see illustration 7.15)**. If it is not, remove and belt and begin the refitting process again, starting at Paragraph 12.

18 The remainder of refitting is a reversal of removal. Tighten all fasteners to the specified torque where given.

8 Timing belt sprockets and tensioner – removal and refitting

Camshaft sprocket

Removal

1 Remove the timing belt as described in Section 7.

2 Remove the locking tool from the camshaft sprocket/hub. Slacken the sprocket hub retaining bolt. To prevent the camshaft rotating as the bolt is slackened, a sprocket holding tool will be required. In the absence of the special Ford tool, an acceptable substitute can be fabricated at home **(see Tool Tip 1)**. *Do not* attempt to use the engine assembly/valve timing locking tool to prevent the sprocket from rotating whilst the bolt is slackened.

3 Remove the sprocket hub retaining bolt,

Tool Tip 1: A sprocket holding tool can be made from two lengths of steel strip bolted together to form a forked end. Drill holes and insert bolts in the ends of the fork to engage with the sprocket spokes.

and slide the sprocket and hub off the end of the camshaft.

4 Clean the camshaft sprocket thoroughly, and renew it if there are any signs of wear, damage or cracks.

Refitting

5 Refit the camshaft sprocket to the camshaft **(see illustration)**.

6 Refit the sprocket hub retaining bolt. Tighten the bolt to the specified torque, preventing the camshaft from turning as during removal.

7 Align the engine assembly/valve timing slot in the camshaft sprocket hub with the hole in the cylinder head and refit the timing pin to lock the camshaft in position.

8 Fit the timing belt around the pump sprocket and camshaft sprocket, and tension the timing belt as described in Section 7.

Crankshaft sprocket

Removal

9 Remove the timing belt as described in Section 7.

10 Check that the engine assembly/valve timing holes are still aligned as described in Section 3, and the camshaft sprocket and flywheel are locked in position.

11 Slide the sprocket off the end of the crankshaft and collect the Woodruff key **(see illustrations)**.

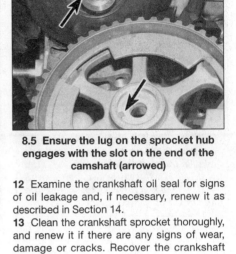

8.5 Ensure the lug on the sprocket hub engages with the slot on the end of the camshaft (arrowed)

12 Examine the crankshaft oil seal for signs of oil leakage and, if necessary, renew it as described in Section 14.

13 Clean the crankshaft sprocket thoroughly, and renew it if there are any signs of wear, damage or cracks. Recover the crankshaft locating key.

Refitting

14 Refit the key to the end of the crankshaft, then refit the crankshaft sprocket (with the flange facing the crankshaft pulley).

15 Fit the timing belt around the crankshaft sprocket, and tension the timing belt as described in Section 7.

Fuel pump sprocket

Removal

16 Remove the timing belt as described in Section 7.

17 Using a suitable socket, undo the pump sprocket retaining nut. The sprocket can be held stationary by inserting a suitably-sized locking pin, drill or rod through the hole in the sprocket, and into the corresponding hole in the backplate **(see illustration)**, or by using a suitable forked tool engaged with the holes in the sprocket **(see Tool Tip 1)**.

18 The pump sprocket is a taper fit on the pump shaft and it will be necessary to make up another tool to release it from the taper **(see Tool Tip 2 overleaf)**.

19 Partially unscrew the sprocket retaining nut, fit the home-made tool, and secure it to the sprocket with two suitable bolts. Prevent the sprocket from rotating as before, and

8.11a Slide the sprocket from the crankshaft . . .

8.11b . . . and recover the Woodruff key

8.17 Insert a suitable drill bit through the sprocket into the hole in the backplate

TOOL TIP

Tool Tip 2: Make a sprocket releasing tool from a short strip of steel. Drill two holes in the strip to correspond with the two holes in the sprocket. Drill a third hole just large enough to accept the flats of the sprocket retaining nut.

unscrew the sprocket retaining nut. The nut will bear against the tool as it is undone, forcing the sprocket off the shaft taper. Once the taper is released, remove the tool, unscrew the nut fully, and remove the sprocket from the pump shaft.

20 Clean the sprocket thoroughly, and renew it if there are any signs of wear, damage or cracks.

Refitting

21 Refit the pump sprocket and retaining nut, and tighten the nut to the specified torque. Prevent the sprocket rotating as the nut is tightened using the sprocket holding tool.

22 Refit the timing belt as described in Section 7.

9.5 Vacuum pump bolts (arrowed)

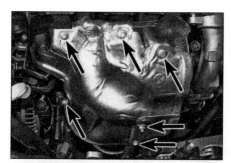

9.9a Undo the nut/bolts (arrowed) and remove the upper, outer section of the turbo heat shield . . .

8.31 Timing belt idler pulley retaining nut (arrowed)

Coolant pump sprocket

23 The coolant pump sprocket is integral with the pump, and cannot be removed. Coolant pump removal is described in Chapter 3.

Tensioner pulley

Removal

24 Remove the timing belt as described in Section 7.

25 Remove the tensioner pulley retaining bolt, and slide the pulley off its mounting stud.

26 Clean the tensioner pulley, but do not use any strong solvent which may enter the pulley bearings. Check that the pulley rotates freely, with no sign of stiffness or free play. Renew the pulley if there is any doubt about its condition, or if there are any obvious signs of wear or damage.

27 Examine the pulley mounting stud for signs of damage and if necessary, renew it.

9.7 Timing belt inner cover bolts (arrowed)

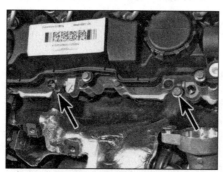

9.9b . . . followed by the inner section (bolts arrowed)

Refitting

28 Refit the tensioner pulley to its mounting stud, and fit the retaining bolt.

29 Refit the timing belt as described in Section 7.

Idler pulley

Removal

30 Remove the timing belt as described in Section 7.

31 Undo the retaining bolt/nut and withdraw the idler pulley from the engine (see illustration).

32 Clean the idler pulley, but do not use any strong solvent which may enter the bearings. Check that the pulley rotates freely, with no sign of stiffness or free play. Renew the idler pulley if there is any doubt about its condition, or if there are any obvious signs of wear or damage.

Refitting

33 Locate the idler pulley on the engine, and fit the retaining bolt/nut. Tighten the bolt/nut to the specified torque.

34 Refit the timing belt as described in Section 7.

9 Camshafts, rocker arms and hydraulic tappets – removal, inspection and refitting

Removal

1 Remove the cylinder head cover/manifold as described in Section 4.

2 Remove the injectors as described in Chapter 4A.

3 Remove the camshaft sprocket as described in Section 8.

4 Refit the right-hand engine mounting, but only tighten the bolts moderately; this will keep the engine supported during the camshaft removal.

5 Undo the bolts and remove the vacuum pump (see Chapter 9). Recover the pump O-ring seals (see illustration).

6 Remove the fuel filter (see Chapter 1), then undo the bolts and remove the fuel filter mounting bracket.

7 Release the wiring harness clips, then undo the 3 bolts and remove the timing belt inner, upper cover (see illustration).

8 Disconnect the wiring plug, unscrew the retaining bolt, and remove the camshaft position sensor from the camshaft cover/bearing ladder.

9 Undo the bolts/nut and remove the upper rear sections of the turbocharger heat shield, then working gradually and evenly, slacken and remove the bolts securing the camshaft cover/bearing ladder to the cylinder head in sequence (see illustrations). Lift the cover/ladder from position complete with the camshafts.

10 Undo the retaining bolts and remove the bearing caps. Note their fitted positions, as they must be refitted into their original positions **(see illustration)**. Note that the bearing caps are marked A for inlet, and E for exhaust, and 1 to 4 from the flywheel end of the cylinder head.

11 Undo the bolts securing the chain tensioner assembly to the camshaft cover/ bearing ladder, then lift the camshafts, chain and tensioner from place **(see illustrations)**. Discard the camshaft oil seal.

12 Obtain 16 small, clean plastic containers, and number them 1 to 8 inlet and 1 to 8 exhaust; alternatively, divide a larger container into 16 compartments.

13 Lift out each rocker arm. Place the rocker arms in their respective positions in the box or containers.

14 A compartmentalised container filled with engine oil is now required to retain the hydraulic tappets while they are removed from the cylinder head. Withdraw each hydraulic follower and place it in the container, keeping them each identified for correct refitting. The tappets must be totally submerged in the oil to prevent air entering them.

Inspection

15 Inspect the cam lobes and the camshaft bearing journals for scoring or other visible evidence of wear. Once the surface hardening of the cam lobes has been eroded, wear will occur at an accelerated rate. **Note:** *If these symptoms are visible on the tips of the camshaft lobes, check the corresponding rocker arm, as it will probably be worn as well.*

16 Examine the condition of the bearing surfaces in the cylinder head and camshaft bearing housing. If wear is evident, the cylinder head and bearing housing will both have to be renewed, as they are a matched assembly.

17 Inspect the rocker arms and tappets for scuffing, cracking or other damage and renew any components as necessary. Also check the condition of the tappet bores in the cylinder head. As with the camshafts, any wear in this area will necessitate cylinder head renewal.

Refitting

18 Thoroughly clean the sealant from the mating surfaces of the cylinder head and camshaft bearing housing. Use a suitable liquid gasket dissolving agent (available from

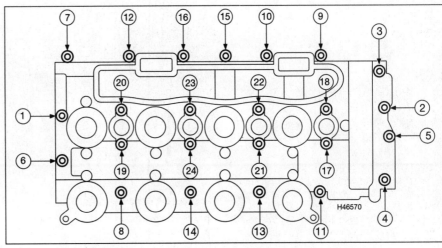

9.9c Camshaft cover/bearing ladder bolt slackening sequence

Ford dealers) together with a soft putty knife; do not use a metal scraper or the faces will be damaged. As there is no conventional gasket used, the cleanliness of the mating faces is of the utmost importance. Prise out the oil injector oil seals from the camshaft bearing housing.

19 Clean off any oil, dirt or grease from both components and dry with a clean lint-free cloth. Ensure that all the oilways are completely clean.

20 Liberally lubricate the hydraulic tappet bores in the cylinder head with clean engine oil.

21 Insert the hydraulic tappets into their original bores in the cylinder head unless they have been renewed **(see illustration)**.

22 Lubricate the rocker arms and place them over their respective tappets and valve stems **(see illustration)**.

23 Engage the timing chain around the camshaft sprockets, aligning the black-coloured links with the marked teeth on the camshaft sprockets **(see illustration)**. If the black colouring has been lost, there must be 12 chain link pins between the marks on the sprockets.

24 Fit the chain tensioner between the upper

9.10 The camshaft bearing caps are numbered 1 to 4 from the flywheel end – A for inlet, and E for exhaust (arrowed)

9.11a Undo the tensioner bolts (arrowed) . . .

9.11b . . . then lift the camshafts, chain and tensioner from place

9.21 Refit the hydraulic tappets . . .

9.22 . . . and rocker arms to their original locations

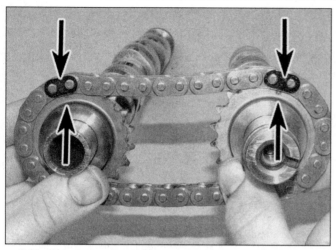

9.23 Align the marks on the sprockets with the centre of the black-coloured chain links (arrowed). There must be 12 link pins between the sprocket marks

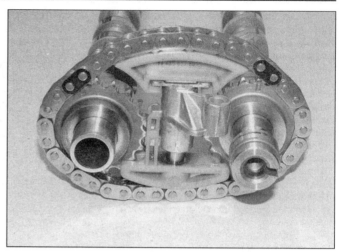

9.24a Assemble the chain tensioner between the upper and lower runs of the chain . . .

9.24b . . . and lower the camshaft, chain and tensioner into position

and lower runs of the chain, then lubricate the bearing surfaces with clean engine oil, and fit the camshafts into position on the underside of the camshaft cover/bearing ladder. Refit the bearing caps to their original positions and tighten the retaining bolts to the specified torque **(see illustrations)**. Tighten the tensioner retaining bolts to the specified torque.

25 Apply a thin bead of silicone sealant (Ford part No WSE-M4G323-A4) to the mating surface of the camshaft cover/bearing ladder as shown **(see illustration)**. Do not allow the sealant to obstruct the oil channels for the hydraulic chain tensioner.

26 Check that the black-coloured links on the chain are still aligned with the marks on the camshaft sprockets, then refit the camshaft cover/bearing ladder, and gradually and evenly tighten the retaining bolts until the cover/ladder is in contact with the cylinder head. Tighten the bolts to the specified torque in sequence **(see illustration)**. **Note:** *Ensure the cover/ladder is correctly located by checking the bores of the vacuum pump and camshaft oil seal at each end of the cover/ladder.*

27 Fit a new camshaft oil seal as described in Section 14.

28 Refit the camshaft sprocket, and tighten the retaining bolt finger-tight.

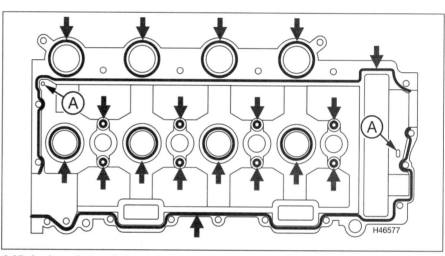

9.25 Apply sealant to the camshaft cover/bearing ladder as indicated by the heavy block lines. Ensure sealant does not enter the tensioner oil holes marked A

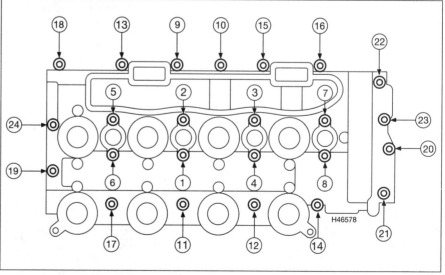

9.26 Camshaft cover/bearing ladder bolt tightening sequence

29 Using a spanner on the camshaft sprocket bolt, rotate the camshafts approximately 40 complete revolutions clockwise. Check the black-coloured links on the chain still align with the marks on the camshaft sprockets.

30 If the marks still align, refit the camshaft sprocket as described in Section 8.

31 Refit and adjust the camshaft position sensor as described in Chapter 4A.

32 Press the new oil seals into the bearing housing, using a tube/socket of approximately 20 mm outside diameter, ensuring the inner lip of the seal fits around the injector guide tube **(see illustrations)**. Refit the injectors as described in Chapter 4A.

33 Refit the cylinder head cover/manifold as described in Section 4.

10 Cylinder head – removal and refitting

Removal

1 Apply the handbrake, then jack up the front of the vehicle and support it on axle stands (see *Jacking and vehicle support*). Remove the front right-hand roadwheel, the engine undershield, and the front wheel arch liner. The undershield is secured by several fasteners, and the wheel arch liner is secured by several plastic expanding rivets/nuts/plastic clips. Push the centre pins in a little, then prise the rivet from place.

2 Disconnect the battery negative lead as described in Chapter 5.

9.32a Fit the new seal around a 20 mm outside diameter socket . . .

3 Drain the cooling system as described in Chapter 1.

4 Remove the camshafts, rocker arms and hydraulic tappets as described in Section 9.

5 Remove the turbocharger and exhaust manifold as described in Chapter 4A.

6 Remove the glow plugs as described in Chapter 5.

7 Undo the upper mounting bolts, and pivot the alternator away from the engine, undo the oil dipstick guide tube bolt, then undo the bolts securing the alternator mounting bracket to the cylinder head/block **(see illustration)**.

8 Undo the coolant outlet housing (left-hand end of the cylinder head) retaining bolts, slacken the two bolts securing the housing support bracket to the top of the transmission bellhousing, and move the outlet housing away from the cylinder head a little **(see illustration)**. There is no need to disconnect the hoses.

9.32b . . . and push it into place

9 Remove the brake vacuum pump as described in Chapter 9.

10 Disconnect the high-pressure fuel pipe from the common rail to the pump, and disconnect the fuel supply and return hoses. Remove the bracket at the rear of the pump, then undo the bolt/nut and remove the pump and mounting bracket as an assembly **(see illustrations)**. Note that a new high-pressure pipe must be fitted – see Chapter 4A.

11 Working in the **reverse** of the sequence shown **(see illustration 10.30)** undo the cylinder head bolts. Discard the bolts – new ones must be fitted.

12 Release the cylinder head from the cylinder block and location dowels by rocking it. The Ford tool for doing this consists simply of two metal rods with 90-degree angled ends **(see illustration)**. Do not prise between the mating faces of the cylinder head and block, as this may damage the gasket faces.

10.7 The engine oil level dipstick guide tube is secured to the alternator bracket by a Torx bolt (arrowed)

10.8 Undo the bolts (arrowed) and pull the coolant outlet housing from the left-hand end of the cylinder head

10.10a Remove the high-pressure pipe (arrowed) . . .

10.10b . . . and the bracket (arrowed)

10.10c Pump mounting bracket upper nut and lower mounting bolt (arrowed)

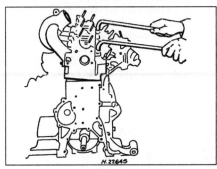

10.12 Free the cylinder head using angled rods

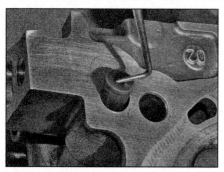

10.16a Pull the non-return valve from the cylinder head . . .

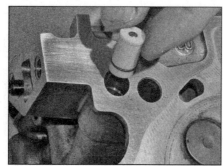

10.16b . . . and push a new one into place

10.21 Measure the piston protrusion using a DTI gauge

13 Lift the cylinder head from the block, and recover the gasket.

Preparation for refitting

14 The mating faces of the cylinder head and cylinder block must be perfectly clean before refitting the head. Ford recommend the use of a scouring agent for this purpose, but acceptable results can be achieved by using a hard plastic or wood scraper to remove all traces of gasket and carbon. The same method can be used to clean the piston crowns. Take particular care to avoid scoring or gouging the cylinder head/cylinder block mating surfaces during the cleaning operations, as aluminium alloy is easily damaged. Make sure that the carbon is not allowed to enter the oil and water passages – this is particularly important for the lubrication system, as carbon could block the oil supply to the engine's components. Using adhesive tape and paper, seal the water, oil and bolt holes in the cylinder block. To prevent carbon entering the gap between the pistons and bores, smear a little grease in the gap. After cleaning each piston, use a small brush

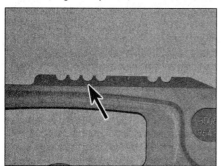

10.23 Cylinder head gasket thickness identification notches (arrowed)

to remove all traces of grease and carbon from the gap, then wipe away the remainder with a clean rag.

15 Check the mating surfaces of the cylinder block and the cylinder head for nicks, deep scratches and other damage. If slight, they may be removed carefully with a file, but if excessive, machining may be the only alternative to renewal. If warpage of the cylinder head gasket surface is suspected, use a straight-edge to check it for distortion. Refer to Part D of this Chapter if necessary.

16 Thoroughly clean the threads of the cylinder head bolt holes in the cylinder block. Ensure that the bolts run freely in their threads, and that all traces of oil and water are removed from each bolt hole. If required, pull the oil feed non-return valve from the cylinder head, and check the ball moves freely. Push a new valve into place if necessary **(see illustrations)**.

Gasket selection

17 The gasket thickness is indicated by notches/holes on the front edge of the gasket. If the crankshaft or pistons/connecting rods have

10.26 Ensure the gasket locates over the dowels (arrowed)

not been disturbed, fit a new gasket with the same number of notches/holes as the previous one. If the crankshaft/piston or connecting rods have been disturbed, it's necessary to work out the piston protrusion as follows:

18 Remove the crankshaft timing pin, then turn the crankshaft until pistons 1 and 4 are at TDC (Top Dead Centre). Position a dial test indicator (dial gauge) on the cylinder block adjacent to the rear of No 1 piston, and zero it on the block face. Transfer the probe to the crown of No 1 piston (10.0 mm in from the rear edge), then slowly turn the crankshaft back-and-forth past TDC, noting the highest reading on the indicator. Record this reading as protrusion A.

19 Repeat the check described in paragraph 18, this time 10.0 mm in from the front edge of the No 1 piston crown. Record this reading as protrusion B.

20 Add protrusion A to protrusion B, then divide the result by 2 to obtain an average reading for piston No 1.

21 Repeat the procedure described in paragraphs 18 to 21 on piston 4, then turn the crankshaft through 180° and carry out the procedure on the piston Nos 2 and 3 **(see illustration)**. Check that there is a maximum difference of 0.07 mm protrusion between any two pistons.

22 If a dial test indicator is not available, piston protrusion may be measured using a straight-edge and feeler blades or Vernier calipers. However, this is much less accurate, and cannot therefore be recommended.

23 Note the greatest piston protrusion measurement, and use this to determine the correct cylinder head gasket from the table below. The series of notches/holes on the side of the gasket are used for thickness identification **(see illustration)**.

Refitting

24 Turn the crankshaft and position Nos 1 and 4 pistons at TDC, then turn the crankshaft a quarter turn (90°) anti-clockwise.

25 Thoroughly clean the surfaces of the cylinder head and block.

26 Make sure that the locating dowels are in place, then fit the correct gasket the right way round on the cylinder block **(see illustration)**.

27 Carefully lower the cylinder head onto the gasket and block, making sure that it locates correctly onto the dowels.

Gasket selection table

Piston protrusion	Gasket identification	Gasket thickness
0.533 to 0.634 mm	2 notches	1.25 mm
0.634 to 0.684 mm	3 notches	1.30 mm
0.684 to 0.734 mm	1 notches	1.35 mm
0.734 to 0.784 mm	4 notches	1.40 mm
0.784 to 0.886 mm	5 notches	1.45 mm

28 Apply a smear of grease to the threads, and to the underside of the heads of the new cylinder head bolts.

29 Carefully insert the cylinder head bolts into their holes (*do not drop them in*) and initially finger-tighten them.

30 Working progressively and in sequence, tighten the cylinder head bolts to their Stage 1 torque setting, using a torque wrench and suitable socket **(see illustration)**.

31 Once all the bolts have been tightened to their Stage 1 torque setting, working again in the specified sequence, tighten each bolt to the specified Stage 2 setting. Finally, angle-tighten the bolts through the specified Stage 3 angle. It is recommended that an angle-measuring gauge is used during this stage of tightening, to ensure accuracy. **Note:** *Retightening of the cylinder head bolts after running the engine is not required.*

32 Refit the hydraulic tappets, rocker arms, and camshaft housing (complete with camshafts) as described in Section 9.

33 Refit the timing belt as described in Section 7.

34 The remainder of refitting is a reversal of removal, noting the following points.

a) *Use a new seal when refitting the coolant outlet housing.*

b) *When refitting a cylinder head, it is good practice to renew the thermostat.*

c) *Refit the camshaft position sensor and set the air gap with reference to Chapter 4A.*

d) *Tighten all fasteners to the specified torque where given.*

e) *Refill the cooling system as described in Chapter 1.*

f) *The engine may run erratically for the first few miles, until the engine management ECM relearns its stored values.*

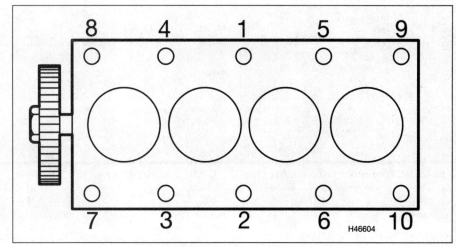

10.30 Cylinder head bolt tightening sequence

11 Sump –
removal and refitting

Removal

1 Drain the engine oil, then clean and refit the engine oil drain plug, tightening it securely. If the engine is nearing its service interval when the oil and filter are due for renewal, it is recommended that the filter is also removed, and a new one fitted. After reassembly, the engine can then be refilled with fresh oil. Refer to Chapter 1 for further information.

2 Apply the handbrake, then jack up the front of the vehicle and support it on axle stands (see *Jacking and vehicle support*). Undo the bolts and remove the engine undershield.

3 Remove the exhaust front pipe as described in Chapter 4A.

4 Where necessary, disconnect the wiring connector from the oil temperature sender unit, which is screwed into the sump.

5 Progressively slacken and remove all the sump retaining bolts/nuts. Since the sump bolts vary in length, remove each bolt in turn,

and store it in its correct fitted order by pushing it through a clearly-marked cardboard template. This will avoid the possibility of installing the bolts in the wrong locations on refitting.

6 Try to break the joint by striking the sump with the palm of your hand, then lower and withdraw the sump from under the car. If the sump is stuck (which is quite likely) use a putty knife or similar, carefully inserted between the sump and block. Ease the knife along the joint until the sump is released. While the sump is removed, take the opportunity to check the oil pump pick-up/strainer for signs of clogging or splitting. If necessary, remove the pump as described in Section 12, and clean or renew the strainer.

Refitting

7 Clean all traces of sealant from the mating surfaces of the cylinder block/crankcase and sump, then use a clean rag to wipe out the sump and the engine's interior.

8 On engines where the sump was fitted without a gasket, ensure that the sump mating surfaces are clean and dry, then apply a thin coating of silicone sealant (Ford part No WSE-M4G323-A4) to the sump or crankcase mating surface **(see illustration)**. Note that the sump must be installed within

10 minutes of applying the sealant, and the bolts tightened within a further 5 minutes.

9 Offer up the sump to the cylinder block/crankcase. Refit its retaining bolts/nuts, ensuring that each bolt is screwed into its original location. Tighten the bolts evenly and progressively to the specified torque setting **(see illustration)**.

10 Reconnect the wiring connector to the oil temperature sensor (where fitted).

11 Lower the vehicle to the ground, then refill the engine with oil as described in Chapter 1.

12 Oil pump –
removal, inspection and refitting

Removal

1 Remove the sump as described in Section 11.

2 Remove the crankshaft sprocket as described in Section 8. Recover the locating key from the crankshaft.

3 Disconnect the wiring plug, undo the bolts and remove the crankshaft position sensor, located on the right-hand end of the cylinder block.

11.8 Apply a bead of sealant to the sump or crankcase mating surface. Ensure the sealant is applied to the inside of the retaining bolt holes

11.9 Refit the sump and tighten the bolts

12.4 Oil pick-up tube bolts (arrowed)

12.5 Oil pump retaining bolts (arrowed)

4 Undo the three bolts and remove the oil pump pick-up tube from the pump/block **(see illustration)**. Discard the oil seal, a new one must be fitted.

5 Undo the 8 bolts, and remove the oil pump **(see illustration)**.

Inspection

6 Undo and remove the Torx bolts securing the cover to the oil pump **(see illustration)**. Examine the pump rotors and body for signs of wear and damage. If worn, the complete pump must be renewed.

7 Remove the circlip, and extract the cap, valve piston and spring, noting which way

around they are fitted **(see illustrations)**. The condition of the relief valve spring can only be measured by comparing it with a new one; if there is any doubt about its condition, it should also be renewed.

8 Refit the relief valve piston and spring, then secure them in place with the circlip.

9 Refit the cover to the oil pump, and tighten the Torx bolts securely.

Refitting

10 Remove all traces of sealant, and thoroughly clean the mating surfaces of the oil pump and cylinder block.

11 Apply a 4 mm wide bead of silicone

sealant to the mating face of the cylinder block **(see illustration)**. Ensure that no sealant enters any of the holes in the block.

12 With a new oil seal fitted, refit the oil pump over the end of the crankshaft, aligning the flats in the pump drive gear with the flats machined in the crankshaft **(see illustrations)**. Note that new oil pumps are supplied with the oil seal already fitted, and a seal protector sleeve. The sleeve fits over the end of the crankshaft to protect the seal as the pump is fitted.

13 Install the oil pump bolts and tighten them to the specified torque.

14 Refit the oil pick-up tube to the pump/

12.6 Undo the Torx bolts and remove the pump cover

12.7a Remove the circlip . . .

12.7b . . . cap . . .

12.7c . . . spring . . .

12.7d . . . and piston

12.11 Apply a bead of sealant to the cylinder block mating surface

12.12a Fit a new seal . . .

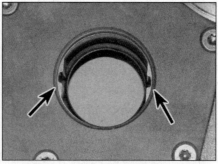

12.12b . . . align the pump gear flats (arrowed) . . .

12.12c . . . with those of the crankshaft (arrowed)

cylinder block using a new O-ring seal. Ensure the oil dipstick guide tube is correctly refitted.
15 Refit the woodruff key to the crankshaft, and slide the crankshaft sprocket into place.
16 The remainder of refitting is a reversal of removal.

13 Oil cooler – removal and refitting

Removal

1 Apply the handbrake, then jack up the front of the vehicle and support it on axle stands (see *Jacking and vehicle support*). Undo the fasteners and remove the engine undershield.
2 The oil cooler is fitted to the front of the oil filter housing. Drain the coolant as described in Chapter 1.
3 Drain the engine oil as described in Chapter 1, or be prepared for fluid spillage.
4 Undo the bolts/stud and remove the oil cooler. Recover the O-ring seals **(see illustrations)**.

Refitting

5 Fit new O-ring seals into the recesses in the oil filter housing, and refit the cooler. Tighten the bolts securely.
6 Refill or top-up the cooling system and engine oil level as described in Chapter 1 or *Weekly Checks* (as applicable). Start the engine, and check the oil cooler for signs of leakage.

14 Oil seals – renewal

Crankshaft

Right-hand oil seal

1 Remove the crankshaft sprocket and Woodruff key as described in Section 8.
2 Measure and note the fitted depth of the oil seal.
3 Pull the oil seal from the housing using a screwdriver. Alternatively, drill a small hole in the oil seal, and use a self-tapping screw and a pair of pliers to remove it **(see illustration)**.
4 Clean the oil seal housing and the crankshaft sealing surface.
5 The seal has a Teflon lip and must not be

13.4a Undo the oil cooler bolts/stud (arrowed)

oiled or marked. The new seal should be supplied with a protective sleeve, which fits over the end of the crankshaft to prevent any damage to the seal lip. With the sleeve in place, press the seal (open end first) into the pump to the previously-noted depth, using a suitable tube or socket **(see illustrations)**.
6 Where applicable, remove the plastic sleeve from the end of the crankshaft.
7 Refit the crankshaft sprocket as described in Section 8.

Left-hand oil seal

8 Remove the flywheel, as described in Section 16.
9 Measure and note the fitted depth of the oil seal.
10 Pull the oil seal from the housing using a screwdriver. Alternatively, drill a small hole in the oil seal, and use a self-tapping screw and a pair of pliers to remove it **(see illustration 14.3)**.

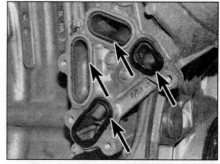

13.4b Renew the O-ring seals (arrowed)

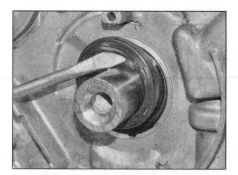

14.3 Take great care not to mark the crankshaft whilst levering out the oil seal

14.5a Slide the seal and protective sleeve over the end of the crankshaft . . .

14.5b . . . and press the seal into place

14.12 Slide the seal and protective sleeve over the left-hand end of the crankshaft

14.16 Drill a hole, insert a self-tapping screw, and pull the seal from place using pliers

14.18 Fit the protective sleeve and seal over the end of the camshaft

11 Clean the oil seal housing and the crank-shaft sealing surface.

12 The seal has a Teflon lip and must not be oiled or marked. The new seal should be supplied with a protective sleeve, which fits over the end of the crankshaft to prevent any damage to the seal lip **(see illustration)**. With the sleeve in place, press the seal (open end first) into the housing to the previously-noted depth, using a suitable tube or socket.

13 Where applicable, remove the plastic sleeve from the end of the crankshaft.

14 Refit the flywheel, as described in Section 16.

Camshaft

15 Remove the camshaft sprocket as described in Section 8. In principle there is no need to remove the timing belt completely, but remember that if the belt has been contaminated with oil, it must be renewed.

16 Pull the oil seal from the housing using a hooked instrument. Alternatively, drill a small hole in the oil seal and use a self-tapping screw and a pair of pliers to remove it **(see illustration)**.

17 Clean the oil seal housing and the camshaft sealing surface.

18 The seal has a Teflon lip and must not be oiled or marked. The new seal should be supplied with a protective sleeve. which fits over the end of the camshaft to prevent any damage to the seal lip **(see illustration)**. With the sleeve in place, press the seal (open end first) into the housing to the previously-noted

15.3 The oil pressure switch is located on the front face of the cylinder block (arrowed)

depth, using a suitable tube or socket which bears only of the outer edge of the seal.

19 Refit the camshaft sprocket as described in Section 8.

20 Where necessary, fit a new timing belt with reference to Section 7.

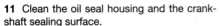

15 Oil pressure switch and level sensor – removal and refitting

Removal

Oil pressure switch

1 The oil pressure switch is located at the front of the cylinder block, adjacent to the oil dipstick guide tube. Note that on some models, access to the switch may be improved if the vehicle is jacked up and supported on axle stands, then undo the bolts and remove the engine undershield so that the switch can be reached from underneath (see *Jacking and vehicle support*).

2 Remove the protective sleeve from the wiring plug (where applicable), then disconnect the wiring from the switch.

3 Unscrew the switch from the cylinder block, and recover the sealing washer **(see illustration)**. Be prepared for oil spillage, and if the switch is to be left removed from the engine for any length of time, plug the hole in the cylinder block.

15.5 The oil level sensor is located on the rear face of the cylinder block (arrowed)

Oil level sensor

4 The oil level sensor is located at the rear of the cylinder block. Jack up the front of the vehicle and support it securely on axle stands (see *Jacking and vehicle support*). Undo the bolts and remove the engine undershield.

5 Reach up between the driveshaft and the cylinder block, and disconnect the sensor wiring plug **(see illustration)**.

6 Using an open-ended spanner, unscrew the sensor and withdraw it from position.

Refitting

Oil pressure switch

7 Examine the sealing washer for any signs of damage or deterioration, and if necessary renew.

8 Refit the switch, complete with washer, and tighten it to the specified torque where given.

9 Refit the engine undershield, and lower the vehicle to the ground.

Oil level sensor

10 Smear a little silicone sealant on the threads and refit the sensor to the cylinder block, tightening it securely.

11 Reconnect the sensor wiring plug.

12 Refit the engine undershield, and lower the vehicle to the ground.

16 Flywheel – removal, inspection and refitting

Removal

1 Remove the transmission as described in Chapter 7, then remove the clutch assembly as described in Chapter 6.

2 Prevent the flywheel from turning. *Do not* attempt to lock the flywheel in position using the crankshaft pulley locking tool described in Section 3. Insert a 12 mm diameter rod or drill bit through the hole in the flywheel cover casting, and into a slot in the flywheel **(see illustration 5.2)**

3 Make alignment marks between the flywheel and crankshaft to aid refitment. Slacken and remove the flywheel retaining bolts, and remove the flywheel from the end

16.9 Flywheel retaining Torx bolts

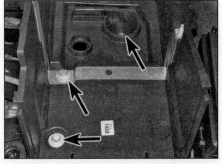

17.10 Undo the bolts (arrowed) and remove the battery tray

17.12 Left-hand mounting

of the crankshaft. Be careful not to drop it; it is heavy. If the flywheel locating dowel (where fitted) is a loose fit in the crankshaft end, remove it and store it with the flywheel for safe-keeping. Discard the flywheel bolts; new ones must be used on refitting.

Inspection

4 Examine the flywheel for scoring of the clutch face, and for wear or chipping of the ring gear teeth. If the clutch face is scored, the flywheel may be surface-ground, but renewal is preferable. Seek the advice of a Ford dealer or engine reconditioning specialist to see if machining is possible. If the ring gear is worn or damaged, the flywheel must be renewed, as it is not possible to renew the ring gear separately.

5 Note that on engines fitted with a dual-mass flywheel, the maximum travel of the primary mass in relation to the secondary must not exceed 15 teeth.

Refitting

6 Clean the mating surfaces of the flywheel and crankshaft. Remove any remaining locking compound from the threads of the crankshaft holes, using the correct size of tap, if available.

>
> *If a suitable tap is not available, cut two slots along the threads of one of the old flywheel bolts, and use the bolt to remove the locking compound from the threads.*

7 If the new flywheel retaining bolts are not supplied with their threads already pre-coated, apply a suitable thread-locking compound to the threads of each bolt.

8 Ensure that the locating dowel is in position. Offer up the flywheel, locating it on the dowel (where fitted), and fit the new retaining bolts. Where no locating dowel is fitted, align the previously-made marks to ensure the flywheel is refitted in its original position.

9 Lock the flywheel using the method

employed on dismantling, and tighten the retaining bolts to the specified torque **(see illustration)**.

10 Refit the clutch as described in Chapter 6. Remove the flywheel locking tool, and refit the transmission as described in Chapter 7.

17 Engine/transmission mountings – inspection and renewal

Inspection

1 If improved access is required, firmly apply the handbrake, then jack up the front of the car and support it on axle stands (see *Jacking and vehicle support*). Undo the bolts and remove the engine undershield.

2 Check the mounting rubbers to see if they are cracked, hardened or separated from the metal at any point; renew the mounting if any such damage or deterioration is evident.

3 Check that all the mountings' fasteners are securely tightened; use a torque wrench to check if possible.

4 Using a large screwdriver or a crowbar, check for wear in each mounting by carefully levering against it to check for free play. Where this is not possible, enlist the aid of an assistant to move the engine/transmission back-and-forth, or from side-to-side, while you watch the mounting. While some free play is to be expected even from new components, excessive wear should be obvious. If excessive free play is found, check first that the fasteners are correctly secured, then renew any worn components as described below.

Renewal

Right-hand mounting

5 Pull the coolant expansion tank upwards from its mountings, and move it to one side.

6 Undo the fasteners and remove the engine undershield, then place a jack beneath the engine, with a block of wood on the jack head.

Raise the jack until it is supporting the weight of the engine.

7 Undo the 2 bolts and 2 nuts and remove the mounting from place **(see illustration 6.13)**.

8 If required, undo the bolts/nuts securing the support bracket to the cylinder head/cylinder block.

9 Refitting is a reversal of removal, tightening all fittings to the specified torque where given.

Left-hand mounting

10 Remove the battery as described in Chapter 5, then undo the bolts and remove the battery tray **(see illustration)**.

11 Undo the fasteners and remove the engine undershield, then place a jack beneath the transmission, with a block of wood on the jack head. Raise the jack until it is supporting the weight of the transmission.

12 Undo the nuts/bolts and remove the mounting **(see illustration)**.

13 Check all components carefully for signs of wear or damage, and renew as necessary.

14 Refitting is a reversal of removal, tightening all fittings to the specified torque, where given.

Lower engine torque rod/ movement limiter link

15 If not already done, firmly apply the handbrake, then jack up the front of the vehicle and support it securely on axle stands (see *Jacking and vehicle support*). Undo the fasteners and remove the engine undershield.

16 Unscrew and remove the bolt securing the movement limiter link to the support bracket.

17 Remove the bolt securing the link to the subframe. Withdraw the link.

18 Check carefully for signs of wear or damage on all components, and renew them where necessary. The rubber bush fitted to the bearing housing is available as a separate item (at the time of writing), and can be pressed out and back into place.

19 Refit the movement limiter link, and tighten both its bolts to their specified torque settings. Refit the engine undershield.

20 Lower the vehicle to the ground.

Chapter 2 Part B:
1.8 litre engine in-car repair procedures

Contents

Degrees of difficulty

Easy, suitable for novice with little experience	**Fairly easy,** suitable for beginner with some experience	**Fairly difficult,** suitable for competent DIY mechanic	**Difficult,** suitable for experienced DIY mechanic	**Very difficult,** suitable for expert DIY or professional

Specifications

General

Engine type	Four-cylinder, in-line, single overhead camshaft, cast-iron cylinder head and engine block
Designation	DuraTorq-TDCi
Engine code	KKDA
Power output	85 kW @ 3700 rpm
Torque output	280 Nm @ 1900 rpm
Capacity	1753 cc
Bore	82.5 mm
Stroke	82.0 mm
Compression ratio	17.0:1
Firing order	1-3-4-2 (No 1 cylinder at timing belt end)
Direction of crankshaft rotation	Clockwise (seen from right-hand side of vehicle)

Camshaft

Camshaft bearing journal diameter	27.96 to 27.98 mm
Camshaft endfloat	0.100 to 0.240 mm

Valves

Valve clearances (cold):	
Inlet	0.30 to 0.40 mm
Exhaust	0.45 to 0.55 mm

Cylinder head

Camshaft bearing diameter (nominal)	30.500 to 30.525 mm
Maximum permissible gasket surface distortion	0.6 mm

Lubrication

Oil pressure – minimum (engine at operating temperature):
- At idle . . . . 0.75 bars
- At 2000 rpm . . . . 1.50 bars

Oil pump clearance (inner-to-outer rotors). . . . . 0.23 mm

Torque wrench settings

	Nm	lbf ft
Air conditioning compressor	25	18
Alternator bracket to block:		
M10 bolts	23	17
M8 bolts	15	11
Nuts	15	11
Auxiliary drivebelt idler pulley bolt	48	35
Auxiliary drivebelt tensioner mounting bolts	23	17
Auxiliary shaft oil seal carrier	23	17
Big-end bearing cap bolts:*		
Stage 1	27	20
Stage 2	Angle-tighten a further 60°	
Stage 3	Angle-tighten a further 20°	
Camshaft bearing cap	20	15
Camshaft oil baffle	20	15
Camshaft sprocket bolt	50	37
Coolant pump pulley bolts	23	17
Crankcase ventilation oil separator	25	18
Crankshaft oil seal carrier.	20	15
Crankshaft position sensor bracket	10	7
Crankshaft pulley bolt:*		
Stage 1	100	74
Stage 2	Angle-tighten a further 180°	
Cylinder head bolts:*		
Stage 1	20	15
Stage 2	54	40
Stage 3	Angle-tighten a further 90°	
Stage 4:		
Short bolts	Angle-tighten a further 70°	
Long bolts.	Angle-tighten a further 90°	
Cylinder head cover bolts	5	4
Engine mountings:		
Right-hand mounting retaining bolts	90	66
Right-hand mounting bracket-to-engine bolts.	56	41
Left-hand mounting nuts	48	35
Left-hand mounting bracket to transmission	80	59
Left-hand mounting centre bolt	148	109
Lower-rear torque rod bolts	80	59
Engine oil drain plug.	36	27
Flywheel bolts:*		
Stage 1	35	26
Stage 2	Angle-tighten a further 45°	
Fuel injection pump sprocket.	42	31
Lower crankcase to cylinder block.	11	8
Main bearing cap bolts:		
Stage 1	45	33
Stage 2	70	52
Stage 2	Angle-tighten a further 60°	
Oil baffle plate nuts	20	15
Oil inlet pipe bracket to block	10	7
Oil pressure switch.	20	15
Oil pump bolts/studs:		
Stage 1	10	7
Stage 2	23	17
Roadwheel nuts	Refer to Chapter 1	
Sump bolts.	11	8
TDC setting plug cover.	24	18
Timing belt inner cover bolts:		
M6.	10	7
M8.	24	18
Timing belt outer covers.	7	5
Timing belt tensioner bolt.	50	37

Torque wrench settings (continued)

	Nm	lbf ft
Timing belt tensioner to cylinder head	50	37
Timing chain guide retaining bolts	23	17
Timing chain housing:		
M6	10	7
M8	23	17
Timing chain tensioner	63	46
Transmission-to-engine bolts	48	35

* Do not re-use

1 General information

How to use this Chapter

This Part of Chapter 2 is devoted to repair procedures possible while the engine is still installed in the vehicle. Since these procedures are based on the assumption that the engine is installed in the vehicle, if the engine has been removed from the vehicle and mounted on a stand, some of the preliminary dismantling steps outlined will not apply.

Information concerning engine/transmission removal and refitting and engine overhaul, can be found in Part D of this Chapter.

Engine description

The DuraTorq-TDCi engine is a further development of the Endura-Di unit, and both units featured in previous Focus models. The engine is an eight-valve, single overhead camshaft (SOHC), four-cylinder, in-line type, mounted transversely at the front of the vehicle, with the transmission on its left-hand end. It is only available in 1.8 litre form.

All major engine castings are of cast-iron; the engine has a lower crankcase which is bolted to the underside of the cylinder block/crankcase, with a sump bolted under that. This arrangement offers greater rigidity than the normal sump arrangement, and helps to reduce engine vibration.

The crankshaft runs in five main bearings, the centre main bearing's upper half incorporating thrustwashers to control crankshaft endfloat. The connecting rods rotate on horizontally-split bearing shells at their big-ends. The pistons are attached to the connecting rods by gudgeon pins which are a floating fit in the connecting rod small-end eyes, secured by circlips. The aluminium alloy pistons are fitted with three piston rings: two compression rings and an oil control ring. After manufacture, the cylinder bores and piston skirts are measured and classified into two grades, which must be carefully matched together to ensure the correct piston/cylinder clearance; no oversizes are available to permit reboring.

The inlet and exhaust valves are each closed by coil springs; they operate in guides which are shrink-fitted into the cylinder head, as are the valve seat inserts.

These engines are unusual in that the fuel injection pump/high-pressure pump is driven by an offset double-row ('gemini') chain from a sprocket on the crankshaft, with the camshaft being driven from the injection pump sprocket by a conventional toothed timing belt.

The camshaft operates the eight valves via conventional cam followers with shims. The camshaft rotates in five bearings that are line-bored directly in the cylinder head and the (bolted-on) bearing caps; this means that the bearing caps are not available separately from the cylinder head, and must not be interchanged with caps from another engine.

The vacuum pump (used for the brake servo and other vacuum actuators) is driven by a pushrod operated directly by a special lobe on the camshaft.

The coolant pump is bolted to the right-hand end of the cylinder block, and is driven with the steering pump and alternator by a multi-ribbed auxiliary drivebelt from the crankshaft pulley.

When working on this engine, note that Torx-type (both male and female heads) and hexagon socket (Allen head) fasteners are widely used; a good selection of bits, with the necessary adapters, will be required so that these can be unscrewed without damage and, on reassembly, tightened to the torque wrench settings specified.

Lubrication system

Lubrication is by means of a G-rotor pump, which is mounted on the crankshaft right-hand end, and draws oil through a strainer located in the sump. The pump forces oil through an externally-mounted full-flow cartridge-type filter. From the filter, the oil is pumped into a main gallery in the cylinder block/crankcase, from where it is distributed to the crankshaft (main bearings) and cylinder head. An oil cooler is fitted next to the oil filter, at the rear of the block. The cooler is supplied with coolant from the engine cooling system.

While the crankshaft and camshaft bearings receive a pressurised supply, the camshaft lobes and valves are lubricated by splash, as are all other engine components. The undersides of the pistons are cooled by oil, sprayed from nozzles fitted above the upper main bearing shells. The turbocharger receives its own pressurised oil supply.

Operations with engine in car

The following major repair operations can be accomplished without removing the engine from the vehicle. However, owners should note that any operation involving the removal of the sump requires careful forethought, depending on the level of skill and the tools and facilities available; refer to the relevant text for details.

a) Compression pressure – testing.
b) Cylinder head cover – removal and refitting.
c) Timing belt cover – removal and refitting.
d) Timing belt – renewal.
e) Timing belt tensioner and sprockets – removal and refitting.
f) Camshaft oil seals – renewal.
g) Camshaft and cam followers – removal and refitting.
h) Cylinder head – removal, overhaul and refitting.
i) Cylinder head and pistons – decarbonising.
j) Sump – removal and refitting.
k) Crankshaft oil seals – renewal.
l) Oil pump – removal and refitting.
m) Piston/connecting rod assemblies – removal and refitting (but see note below).
n) Flywheel – removal and refitting.
o) Engine/transmission mountings – removal and refitting.

Note: It is possible to remove the pistons and connecting rods (after removing the cylinder head and sump) without removing the engine, however, this is not recommended. Work of this nature is more easily and thoroughly completed with the engine on the bench, as described in Chapter 2D.

Clean the engine compartment and the exterior of the engine with some type of degreaser before any work is done (and/or clean the engine using a steam cleaner). It will make the job easier and will help to keep dirt out of the internal areas of the engine.

Depending on the components involved, it may be helpful to remove the bonnet, to improve access to the engine as repairs are performed (refer to Chapter 11 if necessary). Cover the wings to prevent damage to the paint; special covers are available, but an old bedspread or blanket will also work.

2 Compression and leakdown tests – description and interpretation

Compression test

Note: *A compression tester suitable for use with diesel engines will be required for this test.*

1 When engine performance is down, or if misfiring occurs which cannot be attributed to the fuel or emissions systems, a compression test can provide diagnostic clues as to the engine's condition. If the test is performed regularly, it can give warning of trouble before any other symptoms become apparent.

2 The engine must be fully warmed-up to normal operating temperature, the battery must be fully-charged and the glow plugs must be removed. The aid of an assistant will be required.

3 Make sure that the ignition is switched off (take out the key). Remove the plastic cover on the top of the engine, then disconnect the wiring plugs from the injectors.

4 Remove the glow plug relay **(see illustration)** from the central junction box/fusebox under the passenger's side of the facia (see Chapter 12).

5 Remove the glow plugs as described in Chapter 5.

6 Fit a compression tester to the No 1 cylinder glow plug hole. The type of tester which screws into the plug thread is preferred.

7 Crank the engine for several seconds on the starter motor. After one or two revolutions, the compression pressure should build-up to a maximum figure and then stabilise. Record the highest reading obtained.

8 Repeat the test on the remaining cylinders, recording the pressure in each.

9 The cause of poor compression is less easy to establish on a diesel engine than on a petrol engine. The effect of introducing oil into the cylinders (wet testing) is not conclusive, because there is a risk that the oil will sit in the recess on the piston crown, instead of passing to the rings. However, the following

2.4 Glow plug relay (arrowed)

can be used as a rough guide to diagnosis.

10 All cylinders should produce very similar pressures. Any great difference indicates the existence of a fault. Note that the compression should build-up quickly in a healthy engine. Low compression on the first stroke, followed by gradually increasing pressure on successive strokes, indicates worn piston rings. A low compression reading on the first stroke, which does not build-up during successive strokes, indicates leaking valves or a blown head gasket (a cracked head could also be the cause).

11 A low reading from two adjacent cylinders is almost certainly due to the head gasket having blown between them and the presence of coolant in the engine oil will confirm this.

12 On completion, remove the compression tester, and refit the glow plugs, with reference to Chapter 5.

13 Take out the ignition key, then reconnect the injection pump wiring connector.

Leakdown test

14 A leakdown test measures the rate at which compressed air fed into the cylinder is lost. It is an alternative to a compression test, and in many ways it is better, since the escaping air provides easy identification of where pressure loss is occurring (piston rings, valves or head gasket).

15 The equipment required for leakdown testing is unlikely to be available to the home mechanic. If poor compression is suspected,

have the test performed by a suitably-equipped garage.

3 Setting the engine to Top Dead Centre (TDC) on No 1 cylinder

General information

1 TDC is the highest point in the cylinder that each piston reaches as it travels up and down when the crankshaft turns. Each piston reaches TDC at the end of the compression stroke and again at the end of the exhaust stroke, but TDC generally refers to piston position on the compression stroke. No 1 piston is at the timing belt end of the engine.

2 Positioning No 1 piston at TDC is an essential part of many procedures, such as timing belt removal and camshaft removal.

3 The design of the engines covered in this Chapter is such that piston-to-valve contact may occur if the camshaft or crankshaft is turned with the timing belt removed. For this reason, it is important to ensure that the camshaft and crankshaft do not move in relation to each other once the timing belt has been removed from the engine.

Setting TDC on No 1 cylinder

Note: *Suitable tools will be required to lock the camshaft and the fuel injection pump sprocket in position during this procedure – see text.*

4 Disconnect the battery negative (earth) lead (refer to Chapter 5).

5 Remove the cylinder head cover as described in Section 4.

6 Remove the fuel filter as described in Chapter 1, then undo the bolts and remove the fuel filter mounting bracket **(see illustration)**.

7 Loosen the right-hand front wheel nuts, then firmly apply the handbrake. Jack up the front of the car, and support on axle stands (see *Jacking and vehicle support*). Remove the right-hand front wheel.

8 Undo the fasteners and remove the engine undershield **(see illustration)**.

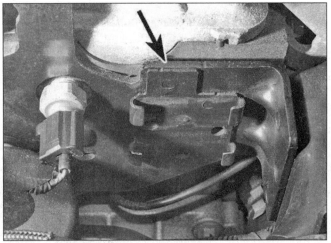

3.6 Remove the fuel filter bracket (arrowed)

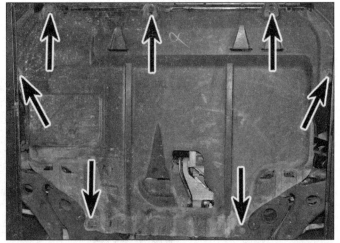

3.8 Undo the fasteners (arrowed) and remove the engine undershield

3.9a Offset slot in the camshaft aligned with the cylinder head

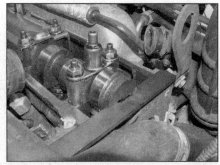

3.9b Flat bar engaged with the slot in the camshaft

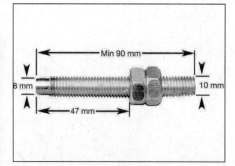

3.11a Tool fabricated to locate the crankshaft at TDC . . .

3.11b . . . screw the tool into the cylinder block to locate with the crankshaft

3.13a Unscrew the blanking plug . . .

3.13b . . . and insert the timing pin

9 When No 1 cylinder is set to TDC on compression, an offset slot in the left-hand end of the camshaft (left as seen from the driver's seat) should align with the top surface of the cylinder head, to allow a special tool (Ford No 303-376) to be fitted. This tool can be substituted by a suitable piece of flat bar **(see illustrations)**. There is no need to fit this tool at this stage, but check that the slot comes into the required alignment while setting TDC – if the slot is above the level of the head, No 1 cylinder could be on the exhaust stroke.

10 If required, further confirmation that No 1 cylinder is on the compression stroke can be inferred from the positions of the camshaft lobes for No 1 cylinder. When the cylinder is on compression, the inlet and exhaust lobes should be pointing upwards (ie, not depressing the cam followers). The camshaft lobes are only visible once the oil baffle plate is removed, and the securing nuts also retain two of the camshaft bearing caps – for more information, refer to Section 9.

11 A TDC timing hole is provided on the front of the cylinder block, to permit the crankshaft to be located more accurately at TDC. A timing pin (Ford service tool 303-193, obtainable from Ford dealers or a tool supplier) screws into the hole, and the crankshaft is then turned so that it contacts the end of the tool. A tool can be fabricated to set the timing at TDC, using a piece of threaded rod **(see illustrations)**. The fabricated tool has the following dimensions:
Thread diameter = 10 mm.
Length from 1st nut face to the point = 47 mm.
Point ground down to 8 mm.

12 To gain access to the blanking plug fitted

over the timing pin hole, remove the auxiliary drivebelt as described in Chapter 1, then unbolt and remove the alternator coupling, as described in the alternator removal procedure in Chapter 5.

13 Remove the camshaft setting tool from the slot, and turn the engine back slightly from the TDC position. Unscrew the timing pin blanking plug (which is located in a deeply-recessed hole), and screw in the timing pin **(see illustrations)**. Now carefully turn the crankshaft forwards until it contacts the timing pin (it should be possible to feel this point – the crankshaft cannot then be turned any further forward).

14 Once No 1 cylinder has been positioned at TDC on the compression stroke, TDC for any of the other cylinders can then be located by rotating the crankshaft clockwise 180° at a time and following the firing order (see Specifications).

15 Before rotating the crankshaft again,

make sure that the timing pin and camshaft setting bar are removed. When operations are complete, do not forget to refit the timing pin blanking plug.

---

4 Cylinder head cover – removal and refitting

Removal

1 Pull the plastic cover on the top of the engine upwards to release the retaining clips **(see illustration)**.

2 Undo the 2 bolts and detach the Manifold Absolute Pressure (MAP) sensor from the cylinder head cover. Move the sensor to one side **(see illustration)**.

3 Noting their positions carefully for refitting, release the hose clips and detach the crankcase ventilation hoses from the cylinder

4.1 Pull the engine cover upwards

4.2 Undo the bolts and move the MAP sensor to one side (arrowed)

4.3a Disconnect the ventilation hoses (1), and the camshaft position sensor (2) . . .

4.3b . . . then disconnect the ventilation hose at the rear (arrowed)

4.5a Unscrew the securing bolts . . .

4.5b . . . and lift away the cylinder head cover

head cover **(see illustrations)**. There are two hoses at the front, and one at the rear. Move the hoses aside as far as possible.

4 Disconnect the camshaft position sensor wiring plug **(see illustration 4.3a)**.

5 Unscrew the three securing bolts, and lift the cylinder head cover off the engine **(see illustrations)**. Discard the gasket – a new one must be fitted.

6 If required, the baffle plate fitted below the cover can be removed by unscrewing the nuts and taking off the spacer plates and sleeves – note, however, that these nuts also secure Nos 2 and 4 camshaft bearing caps. Note the positions of all components carefully for refitting.

Refitting

7 Clean the sealing surfaces of the cover and the head, and check the condition of the rubber seals fitted to the cover bolts.

8 Before refitting the cover, check that the

crankcase ventilation holes are clear. The connection at the rear of the cover leads to the ventilation valve – if this appears to be blocked, use a suitable degreaser to wash out the valve (it is not advisable to use petrol, as this may damage the valve itself).

9 Lightly lubricate the surfaces of the gasket with fresh oil, then fit the gasket to the cover, making sure it is correctly located.

10 Lower the cover into position, ensuring that the gasket is not disturbed, then fit the three bolts and tighten them a little at a time, so that the cover is drawn down evenly to make a good seal.

11 Further refitting is a reversal of removal. Ensure that the pipes are routed as noted on removal, and that the ventilation hoses are correctly and securely reconnected.

12 When the engine has been run for some time, check for signs of oil leakage from the gasket joint.

5 Valve clearances – checking and adjustment

Checking

1 Remove the cylinder head cover as described in Section 4.

2 Remove the baffle plate fitted below the cover by unscrewing the four nuts and taking off the spacer plates and sleeves. Note, however, that these nuts also secure Nos 2 and 4 camshaft bearing caps – refit the nuts temporarily, once the baffle plate has been removed **(see illustrations)**. Note the positions of all components carefully for refitting.

3 During the following procedure, the crankshaft must be turned in order to position the peaks of the camshaft lobes away from the valves. To do this, either turn the crankshaft on the pulley bolt or alternatively raise the front right-hand corner of the vehicle, engage 5th gear, and turn the front roadwheel. Access to the pulley bolt is gained by jacking up the front of the vehicle and supporting on axle stands, then removing the auxiliary drivebelt lower cover.

4 If desired, to enable the crankshaft to be turned more easily, remove the glow plugs as described in Chapter 5.

5 Draw the valve positions on a piece of paper, numbering them 1 to 8 from the timing belt end of the engine. Identify them as inlet or exhaust (ie, 1I, 2E, 3I, 4E, 5I, 6E, 7I, 8E).

6 Turn the crankshaft until the valves of No 4 cylinder (flywheel end) are 'rocking' – the exhaust valve will be closing and the inlet valve will be opening. The piston of No 1 cylinder will be at the top of its compression stroke, with both valves fully closed. The clearances for both valves of No 1 cylinder may be checked at the same time.

7 Use feeler blade(s) to measure the exact clearance between the heel of the camshaft lobe and the shim on the cam follower; the feeler blades should be a firm sliding fit **(see illustration)**. Record the measured clearance on the drawing. From this clearance it will be possible to calculate the thickness of the new shim to be fitted, where necessary. Note

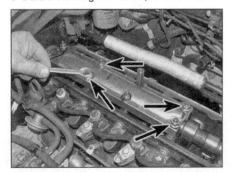

5.2a Unscrew the 4 nuts (arrowed) . . .

5.2b . . . and lift off the baffle plate . . .

5.2c . . . then refit the camshaft bearing cap nuts temporarily

that the inlet and exhaust valve clearances are different, so it is important that you know which valve clearance you are checking.

8 With No 1 cylinder valve clearances checked, turn the engine through half a turn so that No 2 valves are 'rocking', then measure the valve clearances of No 3 cylinder in the same way. Similarly check the valve clearances of No 4 cylinder with No 1 valves 'rocking' and No 2 cylinder with No 3 valves 'rocking'. Compare the measured clearances with the values give in the Specifications – any which fall within the range do not require adjustment.

Adjustment

9 If adjustment is required, turn the engine in the normal direction of rotation through approximately 90°, to bring the pistons to mid-stroke. If this is not done, the pistons at TDC will prevent the cam followers being depressed, and valve damage may result. Depress the cam followers and then either shim can be withdrawn if the peak of the cam does not prevent access. The Ford tools for this operation are Nos 303-195 and 303-196, but with care and patience a C-spanner or screwdriver can be used to depress the cam follower and the shim can be flicked out with a small screwdriver.

10 If the valve clearance was too small, a thinner shim must be fitted. If the clearance was too large, a thicker shim must be fitted. The thickness of the shim (in mm) is engraved on the side facing away from the camshaft. If the marking is missing or illegible, a micrometer will be needed to establish shim thickness.

11 When the shim thickness and the valve clearance are known, the required thickness of the new shim can be calculated as follows (all measurements in mm):

Sample calculation

Desired clearance (A)	= 0.50
Measured clearance (B)	= 0.35
Shim thickness found (C)	= 3.95
Shim thickness required (D)	= C+B-A = 3.80

12 With the correct shim fitted, release the cam follower depressing tool. Turn the engine back so that the cam lobes are again pointing upwards and check that the clearance is now correct.

13 Repeat the process for the remaining valves, turning the engine each time to bring a pair of cam lobes upwards.

14 It will be helpful for future adjustment if a record is kept of the thickness of shim fitted at each position. The shims required can be purchased in advance once the clearances and the existing shim thicknesses are known.

15 It is permissible to interchange shims between cam followers to achieve the correct clearances but it is not advisable to turn the camshaft with any shims removed, since there is a risk that the cam lobe will jam in the empty cam follower.

16 When all the clearances are correct, refit the glow plugs (Chapter 5), then refit the

5.7 Use feeler gauges to measure the exact clearance

oil baffle plate and tighten the nuts to the specified torque. Refit the cylinder head cover as described in Section 4.

6 Crankshaft pulley – removal and refitting

Removal

1 Disconnect the battery negative lead as described in Chapter 5.

2 Loosen the right-hand front roadwheel nuts, then raise the front of the vehicle, and support securely on axle stands (see *Jacking and vehicle support*). Remove the roadwheel.

3 Undo the fasteners and withdraw the engine undershield from under the car **(see illustration 3.8)**.

4 Remove the auxiliary drivebelt, as described in Chapter 1.

5 The centre bolt which secures the crankshaft pulley must now be slackened. This bolt is tightened to a very high torque, and it is first of all essential to ensure that the car is adequately supported, as considerable effort will be needed.

6 Ford technicians use a special holding tool (205-072) which locates in the outer holes of the pulley and prevents it from turning **(see illustration)**. If this is not available, select a gear, and have an assistant firmly apply the handbrake and footbrake as the bolt is loosened. If this method is unsuccessful, remove the starter motor as described in Chapter 5, and jam

6.6 Special tool used to stop the crankshaft from turning

the flywheel ring gear, using a suitable tool, to prevent the crankshaft from rotating.

7 Unscrew the bolt securing the pulley to the crankshaft, and remove the pulley. It is essential to obtain a new bolt for reassembly **(see illustration)**.

8 With the pulley removed, it is advisable to check the crankshaft oil seal for signs of oil leakage. If necessary, fit a new seal as described in Section 16.

Refitting

9 Refit the pulley to the crankshaft sprocket, then fit the new pulley securing bolt and tighten it as far as possible before the crankshaft starts to rotate.

10 Holding the pulley against rotation as for removal, first tighten the bolt to the specified Stage 1 torque.

11 Stage 2 involves tightening the bolt though an angle, rather than to a torque. The bolt must be rotated through the specified angle – special angle gauges are available from tool outlets. As a guide, a 180° angle is equivalent to a half-turn, and this is easily judged by assessing the start and end positions of the socket handle or torque wrench.

12 Refit and tension the auxiliary drivebelt as described in Chapter 1.

13 Refit the engine undershield.

14 Refit the roadwheel, lower the vehicle to the ground, and reconnect the battery negative lead as described in Chapter 5. Tighten the wheel nuts to the specified torque.

7 Timing belt – removal and refitting

Removal

1 Disconnect the battery negative lead as described in Chapter 5.

2 Remove the cylinder head cover as described in Section 4.

3 Referring to the information in Section 3, set the engine to TDC on No 1 cylinder. The timing pin described must be used, to ensure accuracy.

4 Remove the coolant expansion tank by pulling it up from its mountings, and move it to one side without disconnecting the hoses.

6.7 Renew the crankshaft pulley bolt when reassembling

7.5a Unclip the fuel pipes from the timing belt cover

7.5b Intercooler hose-to-throttle body clamp (arrowed)

7.9 Engine mounting nuts and bolts (arrowed)

5 Unclip the fuel pipes, then undo the nut, slacken the clamps and remove the intercooler outlet pipe from the right-hand end of the engine **(see illustrations)**.

6 Ford recommend that the engine is further prevented from turning by fitting another special tool, to lock the flywheel ring gear (this prevents the injection pump sprocket from moving). This tool (Ford No 303-393) is also available from Ford dealers, and is quite simple. With the starter motor removed, as described in Chapter 5, the tool bolts across the starter motor aperture in the bellhousing, and a peg on the back of the tool engages and locks the flywheel ring gear. A substitute for this tool could be made, or the ring gear jammed using another suitable tool.

7 Before unbolting the engine mounting, it is recommended that the right-hand wheel is refitted, and the car lowered to the ground

(assuming the car has been raised as part of setting the engine to TDC).

8 The engine must now be supported before the right-hand mounting is removed. Ford technicians use an engine support bar, which locates in the channels at the top of each inner wing, and a further beam attached to this, which rests on the front crossmember. If such an arrangement is not available, use an engine crane; either way, use a suitable length of chain and hooks to attach the lifting gear to the engine lifting eye. If the engine must be supported from below (and this is not recommended), use a large piece of wood on a trolley jack to spread the load and reduce the chance of damage to the sump.

9 With the weight of the engine supported, unscrew the two nuts and two bolts securing the top half of the engine right-hand mounting, and lift the mounting off the two studs **(see illustration)**.

10 Before the timing belt outer cover can be removed, the stud fitted to the front of the engine mounting must be unscrewed and removed. This can be achieved using a socket on the Torx end fitting provided **(see illustrations)**.

11 Unscrew the three bolts (and one stud/bolt at the top), and remove the timing belt outer cover **(see illustration)**.

12 If the timing belt is not being fitted straight away (or if the belt is being removed as part of another procedure, such as cylinder head removal), temporarily refit the engine right-hand mounting and tighten the bolts securely.

13 Before proceeding further, check once more that the engine is positioned at TDC on No 1 cylinder, as described in Section 3.

14 Slacken the timing belt tensioner bolt, and remove the tensioner completely. Slip the timing belt from the sprockets, and remove it **(see illustrations)**.

15 The camshaft sprocket must be removed – this is necessary as part of setting up the new timing belt, to ensure that the correct valve timing is preserved. Not only will a method for holding the sprocket stationary be required, but the sprocket itself is mounted on a taper, so a puller will be needed to free it from the camshaft. Due to its design, the sprocket cannot readily be removed using an ordinary puller, so either the Ford tool (303-651) must be obtained, or a suitable alternative fabricated.

16 Holding the camshaft sprocket using a suitable tool, loosen the sprocket bolt **(see**

7.10a Using a suitable socket on the Torx end fitting . . .

7.10b . . . unscrew and remove the engine mounting front stud

7.11 Remove the timing belt outer cover

7.14a Slacken the tensioner bolt . . .

7.14b . . . and slip the timing belt from its sprockets

7.16 Using a forked holding tool, unscrew the camshaft sprocket bolt

7.17a Fit Ford tool 303-651 to the camshaft sprocket

7.17b Using the special Ford pulley, free the sprocket from its taper . . .

illustration). **Note:** *Do not rely on the TDC setting bar engaged in the slot at the opposite end of the camshaft to hold it stationary – not only is this dangerous, it could well result in damage to the camshaft.*

17 Using a suitable puller, release the camshaft sprocket from the taper, and remove it **(see illustrations)**.

18 Do not be tempted to re-use the old timing belt under any circumstances – even if it is known to have covered less mileage than the renewal interval indicated in Chapter 1. Ford state that, once a new timing belt has been run on the engine, it is considered worn, and should be discarded. In any case, given the potential expense involved should the belt fail in service, re-using an old belt would be a false economy.

19 Before disposing of the old belt, however, examine it for evidence of contamination by coolant or lubricant. If there are any signs of contamination, find the source of the contamination before progressing any further. If an oil leak is evident, this will most likely be from the camshaft seal. Cure the problem, then wash down the whole area (including the sprockets) with degreaser and allow to dry before fitting the new belt.

20 Spin the tensioner pulley, and check for signs of sticking or roughness, indicating bearing wear. Many professional mechanics will fit a new tensioner as a matter of course when fitting a new timing belt. This should be considered a good idea, especially if the engine has completed a large mileage.

Refitting

21 Ensure that the crankshaft and camshaft are still set to TDC on No 1 cylinder, as described in Section 3.

22 Refit the camshaft sprocket to the camshaft, tightening the bolt by hand only **(see illustration)**. The sprocket must be able to rotate independently of the camshaft.

23 Fit the timing belt tensioner into position, noting that the adjustment arm must be set pointing as shown **(see illustration)**. Fit the retaining bolt, tightening it finger-tight only at this stage.

24 Fit the new timing belt over the sprockets and above the tensioner pulley, ensuring that the injection pump sprocket does not move

7.17c . . . then remove the sprocket bolt and washer . . .

(the camshaft sprocket must be free to turn – remember that the camshaft itself is locked by the tool fitted to its slotted end). Where applicable, ensure the arrow on the back of the belt points in the direction of engine rotation.

25 Using an Allen key in the adjuster arm,

7.22 Refit the camshaft sprocket bolt, hand-tight at first

7.25a Rotate the tensioner arm anti-clockwise . . .

7.17d . . . and finally remove the camshaft sprocket

maintain the tensioner's position whilst the retaining bolt is slackened, then rotate the adjuster arm anti-clockwise until the pointer is positioned between the sides of the adjustment 'window' **(see illustrations)**. Fully tighten the tensioner retaining bolt.

7.23 Note that the adjustment arm (arrowed) must be approximately pointing as shown

7.25b . . . until the pointer is between the sides of the 'window' (arrowed)

26 Hold the camshaft sprocket against rotation, and tighten the sprocket retaining bolt.

27 Remove the locking tools from the engine, so that it can be turned; these may include the timing pin, the plate fitted into the camshaft slot, and the tool used to lock the flywheel.

28 Mark the TDC position of the crankshaft pulley, using paint or typist's correction fluid, to give a rough indication of TDC, and so that the number of turns can be counted.

29 Using a spanner or socket on the crankshaft pulley centre bolt, turn the engine forwards (clockwise, viewed from the timing belt end) through six full turns, bringing the engine almost up to the TDC position on completion.

30 Using the information in Section 3, set the engine to TDC on No 1 cylinder. Make sure that the timing pin and camshaft locking tools are refitted – also lock the flywheel against rotation, using the same method used previously (see paragraph 6). If the special tools cannot be refitted, go back to paragraph 21 and repeat the setting procedure.

31 Check the position of the timing belt automatic tensioner pointer. If the pointer is still within the two sides of the 'window', proceed to next paragraph. If the pointer is outside the 'window', repeat the tensioning procedure.

32 Remove the locking tools from the engine; these may include the timing pin, the plate fitted into the camshaft slot, and the tool used to lock the flywheel.

33 If the engine right-hand mounting had been temporarily refitted as described in paragraph 12, support the engine once more, and remove the mounting.

34 Refit the timing belt outer cover, and tighten the retaining bolts securely.

35 Refit the front stud to the engine mounting, and tighten it securely, using a similar method to that used for the stud's removal.

36 Refit the top half of the engine right-hand mounting, and tighten the nuts and bolts to the specified torque's.

37 With the engine securely supported by its mounting once more, the engine supporting tools can be carefully removed.

38 Refit the cylinder head cover as described in Section 4.

9.6 Remove the camshaft bearing shells

39 Refit the coolant expansion tank to the inner wing.

40 Refit the intercooler outlet pipe and reclip the fuel pipes.

41 Reconnect the battery negative lead as described in Chapter 5.

8 Timing belt tensioner and sprockets – removal, inspection and refitting

Timing belt tensioner

1 The timing belt tensioner is removed as part of the timing belt renewal procedure, in Section 7.

Camshaft sprocket

2 The camshaft sprocket is removed as part of the timing belt renewal procedure, in Section 7.

Fuel injection pump sprocket

3 Removal of the injection pump sprocket is described as part of the injection pump removal procedure, in Chapter 4A. Note that the sprocket is sealed to the pump using two types of sealant/locking compound.

9 Camshaft and cam followers – removal, inspection and refitting

Note: A new camshaft oil seal will be required on refitting.

Removal

1 Remove the timing belt and camshaft sprocket as described in Section 7.

2 Remove the camshaft oil seal. The seal is quite deeply recessed – Ford dealers have a special seal extractor for this (tool No 303-293). In the absence of this tool, do not use any removal method which might damage the sealing surfaces, or a leak will result when the new seal is fitted.

> **HAYNES HINT** *One of the best ways to remove an oil seal is to carefully drill or punch two holes through the seal, opposite each other (taking care not to damage the surface behind the seal as this is done). Two self-tapping screws are then screwed into the holes; by pulling on the screw heads alternately with a pair of pliers, the seal can be extracted.*

3 Unscrew and remove the nuts securing the oil baffle plate to the top of the engine, noting that these nuts also secure Nos 2 and 4 camshaft bearing caps. Lift off the baffle plate, and recover the bearing caps – if no identification numbers are evident on the caps, mark them for position, as they must be refitted to the correct locations.

4 Progressively unscrew (by half a turn at a time) the nuts securing the remaining bearing caps (Nos 1, 3 and 5) until the camshaft is free.

5 Lift off each bearing cap and bearing shell in turn, and mark it for position if necessary – all the caps must be refitted in their original positions.

6 Carefully lift out the camshaft, and place it somewhere safe – the lobes must not be scratched. Remove the lower part of the bearing shells in turn, and mark them for position **(see illustration)**.

7 Before lifting out the cam followers and shims, give some thought to how they will be stored while they are removed. Unless new components are being fitted, the cam followers and shims must be identified for position. The best way to do this is to take a box, and divide it into eight compartments, each with a clearly-marked number; taking No 1 cam follower and shim as being that nearest the timing belt end of the engine, lift out each cam follower and shim, and place it in the box. Alternatively, keep the cam follower/shim assemblies in line, in fitted order, as they are removed – mark No 1 to avoid confusion.

Inspection

8 With the camshaft removed, examine the bearing caps and the bearing locations in the cylinder head for signs of obvious wear or pitting. If evident, a new cylinder head will probably be required. Also check that the oil supply holes in the cylinder head are free from obstructions. (New bearing shells should be used on reassembly.)

9 Visually inspect the camshaft for evidence of wear on the surfaces of the lobes and journals. Normally their surfaces should be smooth and have a dull shine; look for scoring, erosion or pitting and areas that appear highly polished, indicating excessive wear. Accelerated wear will occur once the hardened exterior of the camshaft has been damaged, so always renew worn items. **Note:** *If these symptoms are visible on the tips of the camshaft lobes, check the corresponding cam follower/shim, as it will probably be worn as well.*

10 If suitable precision measuring equipment (such as a micrometer) is available, the camshaft bearing journals can be checked for wear, by comparing the values measured with those specified.

11 If the machined surfaces of the camshaft appear discoloured or blued, it is likely that it has been overheated at some point, probably due to inadequate lubrication. This may have distorted the shaft, in which case the runout should be checked; Ford do not quote a runout tolerance, so if this kind of damage is suspected, an engine reconditioning specialist should be consulted. In the case of inadequate lubrication, distortion is unlikely to be the only damage which has occurred, and a new camshaft will probably be needed.

12 To measure the camshaft endfloat, temporarily refit the camshaft to the cylinder head, then fit Nos 1 and 5 bearing caps and tighten the retaining nuts to the specified torque setting. Anchor a DTI gauge to the timing belt end of the cylinder head. Push the camshaft to one end of the cylinder head as far as it will travel, then rest the DTI gauge probe on the end face of the camshaft, and zero the gauge. Push the camshaft as far as it will go to the other end of the cylinder head, and record the gauge reading. Verify the reading by pushing the camshaft back to its original position and checking that the gauge indicates zero again. **Note:** *The cam followers must **not** be fitted whilst this measurement is being taken.*

13 Check that the camshaft endfloat measurement is within the limit listed in the Specifications. If the measurement is outside the specified limit, wear is unlikely to be confined to any one component, so renewal of the camshaft, cylinder head and bearing caps must be considered.

14 Inspect the cam followers and shims for obvious signs of wear or damage, and renew if necessary.

Refitting

15 Make sure that the top surfaces of the cylinder head, and in particular the camshaft bearings and the mating surfaces for the camshaft bearing caps, are completely clean.

16 Smear some clean engine oil onto the sides of the cam followers, and offer each one into position in their original bores in the cylinder head, together with its respective shim **(see illustration)**. Push them down until they contact the valves, then lubricate the top surface of each shim.

17 Lubricate the camshaft and cylinder head bearing journals with clean engine oil. If the pushrod which operates the brake vacuum pump has been removed from the cylinder head **(see illustration)**, refit it now – once the camshaft is in position, the pushrod cannot be refitted.

18 Carefully lower the camshaft into position in the cylinder head, making sure that the cam lobes for No 1 cylinder are pointing upwards. Also use the position of the locking tool slot at the end of the camshaft as a guide to correct alignment when refitting – the slot should be flush to the top surface of the cylinder head (the larger 'semi-circle' created by the offset slot should be uppermost).

19 Prior to refitting the No 1 camshaft bearing cap, the front halves of the flat sealing surface must be coated with a smear of suitable sealant, as shown **(see illustration)**.

20 Lubricate Nos 1, 3 and 5 bearing caps and shells with clean oil (taking care not to get any on the sealant-coated surfaces of No 1 cap), then place them into their correct positions. Refit the bearing cap nuts, and tighten them progressively to the specified torque wrench setting.

21 The outer edges of No 1 bearing cap must now be sealed to the cylinder head surface with a thin bead of suitable sealant.

22 Clean out the oil seal housing and the sealing surface of the camshaft by wiping it with a lint-free cloth. Remove any swarf or burrs that may cause the seal to leak.

9.16 Lubricate the cam followers before refitting

23 Apply a little oil to the new camshaft oil seal, and fit it over the end of the camshaft, lips facing inwards. To avoid damaging the seal lips, wrap a little tape over the end of the camshaft. Ford dealers have a special tool (No 303-199) for fitting the seal, but if this is not available, a deep socket of suitable size can be used. It is important that the seal is fitted square to the shaft, and is fully-seated.

24 Refit the camshaft sprocket and timing belt as described in Section 7.

25 Check the valve clearances as described in Section 5.

26 Oil the bearing surfaces of Nos 2 and 4 bearing caps, then refit them and the oil baffle

9.17 Refit the brake vacuum pump pushrod before refitting the camshaft

plate to the engine. Tighten the bearing cap nuts to the specified torque.

27 Refit the cylinder head cover as described in Section 4.

28 Further refitting is a reversal of removal.

10 Camshaft oil seal – renewal

1 Remove the timing belt and camshaft sprocket as described in Section 7. Access to the seal is hampered by the presence of the timing belt backplate, but this can only be removed after taking off the injection pump

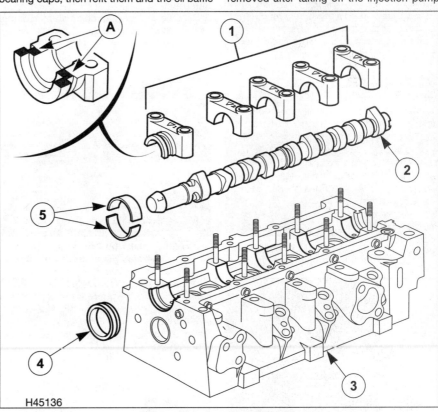

H45136

9.19 Camshaft refitting details

1 *Bearing caps (1 to 5)*
2 *Camshaft*
3 *Cylinder head*
4 *Camshaft oil seal*
5 *Bearing shells*
A *Sealant application areas on No 1 bearing cap*

10.4a Lubricate the oil seal before fitting over the camshaft . . .

10.4b . . . and use a suitable socket to tap the seal in squarely

sprocket; it should not prove necessary to remove the backplate in practice.

2 Remove the camshaft oil seal. The seal is quite deeply recessed – Ford dealers have a special seal extractor for this (tool No 303-293). In the absence of this tool, do not use any removal method which might damage the sealing surfaces, or a leak will result when the new seal is fitted **(see Haynes Hint)**.

HAYNES HINT *One of the best ways to remove an oil seal is to carefully drill or punch two holes through the seal, opposite each other (taking care not to damage the surface behind the seal as this is done). Two self-tapping screws are then screwed into the holes; by pulling on the screw heads alternately with a pair of pliers, the seal can be extracted.*

3 Clean out the seal housing and the sealing surface of the camshaft by wiping it with a lint-free cloth. Remove any swarf or burrs that may cause the seal to leak.

4 Apply a little oil to the new camshaft oil seal, and fit it over the end of the camshaft, lips facing inwards. To avoid damaging the seal lips, wrap a little tape over the end of the camshaft. Ford dealers have a special tool (No 303-199) for fitting the seal, but if this is not available, a deep socket of suitable size can be used. **Note:** *Select a socket that bears only on the hard outer surface of the seal, not the inner lip which can easily be damaged.* It is important that the seal is fitted square to the shaft, and is fully-seated **(see illustrations)**.

5 Refit the camshaft sprocket and timing belt as described in Section 7.

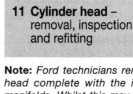

11 Cylinder head – removal, inspection and refitting

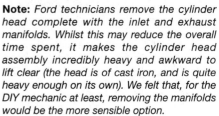

Note: *Ford technicians remove the cylinder head complete with the inlet and exhaust manifolds. Whilst this may reduce the overall time spent, it makes the cylinder head assembly incredibly heavy and awkward to lift clear (the head is of cast iron, and is quite heavy enough on its own). We felt that, for the DIY mechanic at least, removing the manifolds would be the more sensible option.*

Removal

1 Remove the battery as described in Chapter 5, then unscrew the three bolts securing the battery tray, and remove the tray from the engine compartment.

2 Remove the air cleaner housing, as described in Chapter 4A.

3 Remove the cylinder head cover as described in Section 4.

4 Using the information in Section 3, bring the engine round to just before the TDC position on No 1 cylinder. Do not insert any of the locking tools at this stage.

5 Apply the handbrake, then jack up the front of the car and support it on axle stands (see *Jacking and vehicle support*).

6 Drain the cooling system as described in Chapter 1.

7 Remove the turbocharger/exhaust manifold and the inlet manifold as described in Chapter 4A.

8 Remove the timing belt as described in Section 7.

9 Remove the bolt securing the timing belt backplate to the cylinder head, and the seven nuts around the injection pump sprocket **(see illustrations)**. While this does not allow the backplate to be removed, it makes it possible to bend the plate enough for the camshaft's tapered end to pass as the head is lifted. If the backplate is to be removed completely, this requires that the injection pump sprocket and its oil seal housing are also removed, as described in Chapter 4A.

10 Disconnect the glow plug supply lead in front of the dipstick tube, and move the wiring harness to one side **(see illustration)**.

11 Release the clips from the crankcase ventilation hoses as necessary, and disconnect the wiring plug from the oil pressure switch, then unbolt and remove the oil separator from the left-hand end of the cylinder head **(see illustrations)**.

12 Unclip and disconnect the wiring plug for the cylinder head temperature sensor, next to the brake vacuum pump **(see illustration)**.

13 Disconnect the vacuum hose and the oil return pipe from the vacuum pump at the left-hand end of the cylinder head (left as seen from the driver's seat). Unscrew the top mounting bolt, and loosen the lower bolt – the lower mounting is slotted, to make removal easier – and lift off the pump. Recover the

11.9a Remove the timing belt backplate bolt from the cylinder head . . .

11.9b . . . and the 7 nuts around the injection pump sprocket

11.10 Unscrew the nut securing the glow plug supply lead

11.11a Disconnect the breather hoses . . .

11.11b ... unscrew the mounting bolt ...

11.11c ... disconnect the oil pressure warning light switch ...

11.11d ... and remove the oil separator from the end of the cylinder head

large O-ring seal – a new one must be used on reassembly **(see illustrations)**.

14 Remove the screw securing the glow plug supply lead to the thermostat housing. Remove the two bolts securing the thermostat housing to the front of the head, then pull the housing forwards and rest it clear of the head without disconnecting any further pipework **(see illustrations)**. Note that a new thermostat housing gasket will be needed for reassembly.

15 Clean the area around the high-pressure fuel injection pipes from the pump to the supply manifold (common rail), and the from injectors to the supply manifold.

16 Disconnect the fuel return pipes from the injectors (see Chapter 4A). Cover, or plug the openings to prevent dirt ingress.

17 Disconnect the wiring plugs from each injector.

18 Make a note of their exact fitted positions,

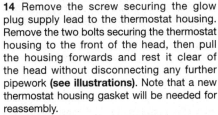

11.12 Disconnect the cylinder head temperature sensor wiring plug

then remove the high-pressure pipe clamps **(see illustration)**.

19 Disconnect the wiring plug from the pressure sensor on the fuel supply manifold **(see illustration)**.

11.13a Unscrew the vacuum hose union ...

20 Unscrew the union nuts and remove the high-pressure fuel injection pipes from the fuel supply manifold to the injectors. When unscrewing the unions, counter-hold the adapters with one spanner, and loosen the

11.13b ... release the hose clip and disconnect the oil return pipe ...

11.13c ... then unbolt ...

11.14a Remove the glow plug supply lead securing bolt

11.14b Unscrew the thermostat housing bolts

11.13d ... and remove the vacuum pump – recover the O-ring

11.18 Note their positions, then remove the pipe clamps

11.19 Disconnect the pressure sensor wiring plug

11.20a Use a second spanner to counter-hold the adapters whilst undoing the union nuts at the injectors . . .

11.20b . . . and at the fuel supply manifold (common rail)

unions with another. Cover over the end fittings on the supply manifold and on the injectors, to keep the dirt out **(see illustrations)**. Ford insist that the fuel injection delivery pipes are not re-used – discard the pipes.

21 Undo the bolt/nut and remove the bracket supporting the high-pressure fuel pipe from the pump to the supply manifold **(see illustration)**.

22 Unscrew the union nuts and remove the high-pressure fuel pipe from the pump to the supply manifold – again, counter-hold the adapters with a second spanner. Note its fitted position, then remove the clamp from the pipe, Cover or plug the openings to prevent dirt ingress. Ford insist that the pipe is not re-used – discard it.

23 Remove the three bolts securing the fuel supply manifold bracket to the engine, and withdraw the supply manifold complete with the bracket.

24 If not already done, it is recommended before removing the cylinder head that the engine right-hand mounting is refitted, and the engine supporting tools removed. This will improve working room if a hoist or engine support bar was used, and avoids the risk of the engine slipping if it was supported from below.

25 Remove the four nuts securing the oil baffle plate, and carefully lift the plate off the engine. Note that these nuts are also used to secure Nos 2 and 4 camshaft bearing caps, which will then be loose. Once the plate is removed, refit the nuts by hand, to keep the caps in place.

26 Check around the head and the engine bay that there is nothing still attached to the cylinder head, nor anything which would prevent it from being lifted away.

27 Working in the **reverse** order of the tightening sequence **(see illustration 11.53)**,

loosen the cylinder head bolts by half a turn at a time, until they are all loose. Remove the head bolts, and discard them – Ford state that they must not be re-used, even if they appear to be serviceable **(see illustrations)**. Note the fitted positions of the two shorter bolts, which should be the two nearest the timing belt end of the engine.

28 Bend the timing belt backplate gently away from the head sufficiently for the camshaft stub to clear it. Lift the cylinder head away; use assistance if possible, as it is a very heavy assembly.

29 If the head is stuck (as is possible), be careful how you choose to free it. Striking the head with tools carries the risk of damage, and the head is located on two dowels, so its movement will be limited. Do not, under any circumstances, lever the head between the mating surfaces, as this will certainly damage the sealing surfaces for the gasket, leading to leaks.

30 Once the head has been removed, recover the gasket from the two dowels. The gasket is manufactured from laminated steel, and cannot be re-used, but see paragraph 32.

Inspection

31 If required, dismantling and inspection of the cylinder head is covered in Part D of this Chapter.

Cylinder head gasket selection

32 Examine the old cylinder head gasket for manufacturer's identification markings. These will be in the form of notches (two to seven) on the front edge of the gasket, which indicate the gasket's thickness **(see illustration 11.49)**.

33 Unless new components have been fitted, or the cylinder head has been machined (skimmed), the new cylinder head gasket must be of the same type as the old one. Purchase the required gasket, and proceed to paragraph 40.

34 If the head has been machined, or if new pistons have been fitted, it is likely that a head gasket of different thickness to the original will be needed. Gasket selection is made on the basis of the measured piston protrusion above the cylinder head gasket surface. If the head has not been machined, and the pistons,

11.21 Remove the pipe support bracket (arrowed)

11.27a Working in the reverse of the tightening sequence, unscrew . . .

11.27b . . . and remove the cylinder head bolts

11.35 Measure piston projection with a dial test indicator (DTI)

connecting rods, and crankshaft have not been disturbed, use a new head gasket with the same number of notches as the old one.

35 To measure the piston protrusion, anchor a dial test indicator (DTI) to the top face (cylinder head gasket mating face) of the cylinder block, and zero the gauge on the gasket mating face **(see illustration)**.

36 Rest the gauge probe above No 1 piston crown, and turn the crankshaft slowly by hand until the piston reaches TDC (its maximum height). Measure and record the maximum piston projection at TDC.

37 Repeat the measurement for the remaining pistons, and record the results.

38 If the measurements differ from piston to piston, take the highest figure, and use this to determine the thickness of the head gasket required.

39 Note the greatest piston protrusion measurement, and use this to determine the correct cylinder head gasket from the table (right). The series of notches/holes on the side of the gasket are used for thickness identification **(see illustration 11.49)**.

Preparation for refitting

40 The mating faces of the cylinder head and cylinder block must be perfectly clean before refitting the head. Use a hard plastic or wooden scraper to remove all traces of gasket and carbon; also clean the piston crowns. **Note:** *The new head gasket has rubber-coated surfaces, which could be damaged from sharp edges or debris left by a metal scraper.*

41 Take particular care when cleaning the piston crowns, as the soft aluminium alloy is easily damaged.

42 Make sure that the carbon is not allowed to enter the oil and water passages – this is particularly important for the lubrication system, as carbon could block the oil supply to the engine's components. Using adhesive tape and paper, seal the water, oil and bolt holes in the cylinder block.

43 To prevent carbon entering the gap between the pistons and bores, smear a little grease in the gap. After cleaning each piston, use a small brush to remove all traces of grease and carbon from the gap, then wipe away the remainder with a clean rag. Clean all the pistons in the same way.

44 Check the mating surfaces of the cylinder block and the cylinder head for nicks, deep scratches and other damage (refer to the Note in paragraph 40). If slight, they may be removed carefully with a file, but if excessive, machining may be the only alternative to renewal.

45 If warpage of the cylinder head gasket surface is suspected, use a straight-edge to check it for distortion. Refer to Part D of this Chapter if necessary.

46 Ensure that the cylinder head bolt holes in the crankcase are clean and free of oil. Syringe or soak up any oil left in the bolt holes. This is most important in order that the correct

bolt tightening torque can be applied, and to prevent the possibility of the block being cracked by hydraulic pressure when the bolts are tightened.

Refitting

47 Turn the crankshaft anti-clockwise all the pistons at an equal height, approximately halfway down their bores from the TDC position (see Section 3). This will eliminate any risk of piston-to-valve contact as the cylinder head is refitted.

48 To guide the cylinder head into position, screw two long studs (or old cylinder head bolts with the heads cut off, and slots cut in the ends to enable the bolts to be unscrewed) into the end cylinder head bolt locations on the manifold side of the cylinder block.

49 Ensure that the cylinder head locating dowels are in place at the front corners of

the cylinder block, then fit the new cylinder head gasket over the dowels, ensuring that the OBEN/TOP marking is uppermost, and the notches are at the front (there is a further cut-out at the timing belt end of the gasket) **(see illustration)**. Take care to avoid damaging the gasket's rubber coating.

50 Lower the cylinder head into position on the gasket, ensuring that it engages correctly over the guide studs and dowels.

51 Fit the new cylinder head bolts to the eight remaining bolt locations, (remember that the two shorter bolts are fitted at the timing belt end of the engine) and screw them in as far as possible by hand. Do not apply oil to the bolts.

52 Unscrew the two guide studs from the exhaust side of the cylinder block, then screw in the two remaining new cylinder head bolts as far as possible by hand.

Gasket selection table

Piston protrusion	Gasket identification	Gasket thickness
0.550 to 0.600 mm	*2 notches*	*1.27 mm*
0.601 to 0.650 mm	*3 notches*	*1.32 mm*
0.651 to 0.700 mm	*4 notches*	*1.37 mm*
0.701 to 0.750 mm	*5 notches*	*1.42 mm*
0.751 to 0.800 mm	*6 notches*	*1.47 mm*
0.801 to 0.850 mm	*7 notches*	*1.52 mm*

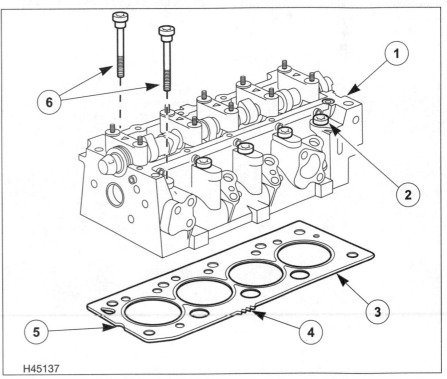

H45137

11.49 Cylinder head bolt positions and gasket details

1 *Cylinder head*
2 *Longer bolts (eight, 177 mm long)*
3 *Cylinder head gasket*
4 *Thickness markings (notches)*
5 *Position marking (cut-out)*
6 *Shorter bolts (two, 137 mm long)*

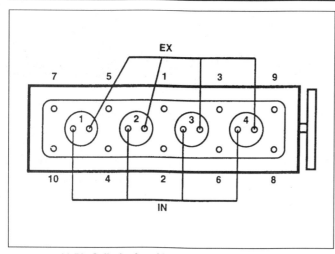

11.53 Cylinder head bolt tightening sequence

11.55 The 2 shorter bolts are tightened through less of an angle than the longer bolts

53 Working in sequence **(see illustration)**, tighten all the cylinder head bolts to the specified Stage 1 torque.

54 Again working in sequence, tighten all the cylinder head bolts to the specified Stage 2 torque.

55 Stages 3 and 4 involve tightening the bolts though an angle, rather than to a torque **(see illustration)**. Each bolt in sequence must be rotated through the specified angle – special angle gauges are available from tool outlets. As a guide, a 90° angle is equivalent to a quarter-turn, and this is easily judged by assessing the start and end positions of the socket handle or torque wrench. **Note:** *The*

two shorter bolts at the timing belt end of the engine are tightened through a smaller angle than the remaining eight bolts – do not get confused when following the tightening sequence.

56 After finally tightening the cylinder head bolts, turn the crankshaft forwards to bring No 1 piston up to TDC, so that the crankshaft contacts the timing pin (see Section 3).

57 The remainder of the refitting procedure is a reversal of the removal procedure, bearing in mind the following points:

a) *Refit the timing belt with reference to Section 7.*

b) *Reconnect the exhaust front section to the exhaust manifold with reference to Chapter 4A.*

c) *Refit the fuel supply manifold and new high-pressure fuel delivery pipes as described in Chapter 4A.*

d) *Refit the cylinder head cover with reference to Section 4.*

e) *Refit the air cleaner and intercooler as described in Chapter 4A.*

f) *Refill the cooling system as described in Chapter 1.*

g) *Check and if necessary top up the engine oil level and power steering fluid level as described in ëWeekly checksí.*

h) *Before starting the engine, read through the section on engine restarting after overhaul, at the end of Chapter 2D.*

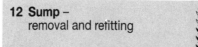

12 Sump –
removal and refitting

Note: *The full procedure outlined below must be followed so that the mating surfaces can be cleaned and prepared to achieve an oil-tight joint on reassembly.*

Removal

1 Apply the handbrake, then jack up the front of the vehicle and support it on axle stands (see *Jacking and vehicle support*).

2 Referring to Chapter 1 if necessary, drain the engine oil, then clean and refit the engine oil drain plug, tightening it to the specified torque wrench setting. Although not strictly necessary as part of the dismantling procedure, owners are advised to remove and discard the oil filter, so that it can be renewed with the oil.

3 A conventional sump gasket is not used, and sealant is used instead.

4 Progressively unscrew the sump retaining bolts, and the two retaining nuts (the bolts are of different lengths, but it will be obvious where they fit on reassembly). Break the joint by striking the sump with the palm of the hand, then lower the sump away, turning it as necessary.

5 Unfortunately, the use of sealant can make removal of the sump more difficult. If care is taken not to damage the surfaces, the sealant can be cut around using a sharp knife. On no account lever between the mating faces, as this will almost certainly damage them, resulting in leaks when finished. Ford technicians have a tool comprising a metal rod which is inserted through the sump drain hole, and a handle to pull the sump downwards.

> **HAYNES HINT** *If the sump is particularly difficult to remove, extracting the two studs may prove useful – thread two nuts onto the stud, tightening them against each other, then use a spanner on the inner nut to unscrew the stud. Note the locations of the studs for refitting.*

Refitting

6 On reassembly, thoroughly clean and degrease the mating surfaces of the cylinder block/crankcase and sump, removing all traces of sealant, then use a clean rag to wipe out the sump and the engine's interior.

7 If the two studs have been removed, they must be refitted before the sump is offered up, to ensure that it is aligned correctly. If this is not done, some of the sealant may enter the

12.8 Sump bolt tightening sequence and sealant application details

Dotted line – 2.5 mm diameter bead of sealant

H45202

13.8 Undo the retaining bolts and remove the rotor cover

13.9 Check the condition of the pressure relief valve and clean out the oilways

13.10 Check the clearance between the inner and outer rotor

blind holes for the sump bolts, preventing the bolts from being fully fitted.

8 Referring to the accompanying illustration, apply silicone sealant (Ford part No WSE-M4G323-A4) to the sump flange. Do not allow sealant to enter the bolts holes. Ford specify that the sealant must be applied in a bead of 2.5 mm diameter **(see illustration)**. **Note:** *The sump must be refitted within 10 minutes of applying the sealant.*

9 Fit the sump over the studs, and insert the sump bolts and two nuts, tightening them by hand only at this stage.

10 Tighten all the bolts and nuts in the sequence shown **(see illustration 12.8)**.

11 Lower the car to the ground. Wait at least 1 hour for the sealant to cure (or whatever time is indicated by the sealant manufacturer) before refilling the engine with oil. If removed, fit a new oil filter with reference to Chapter 1.

---

13 Oil pump –
removal, inspection
and refitting

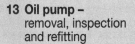

Removal

1 Remove the crankshaft pulley as described in Section 6.

2 Unbolt the auxiliary drivebelt idler pulley in front of the crank pulley location.

3 Remove the timing belt and camshaft sprocket as described in Section 7.

4 Remove the injection pump sprocket and oil seal housing as described in Chapter 4A.

5 Unbolt and remove the timing belt backplate from the engine.

6 The oil pump is secured by 7 studs and 12 bolts – note their positions carefully for refitting. The studs can be unscrewed using a spanner on the hex provided.

7 Once all the fasteners have been removed, carefully lift the pump from its location. Recover the main gasket, and the smaller spacer ring from below the injection pump. Neither gasket may be re-used – obtain new ones for reassembly.

Inspection

8 Undo the retaining screws and remove the cover from the oil pump **(see illustration)**. Note the location of the identification marks on the inner and outer rotors for refitting.

9 Unscrew the plug and remove the pressure relief valve, spring and plunger, clean out and check condition of components **(see illustration)**.

10 The clearance between the inner and outer rotors can be checked using feeler blades, and compared with the value given in the Specifications **(see illustration)**.

11 Check the general condition of the oil pump, and in particular, its mating face to the cylinder block. If the mating face is damaged significantly, this may lead to oil loss (and a resulting drop in oil pressure).

12 Inspect the rotors for obvious signs of wear or damage; it is not clear at the time of writing whether individual components are available separately. Lubricate the rotors with fresh engine oil and refit them into the body, making sure that the identification marks are positioned as noted on removal **(see illustration)**.

13 If the oil pump has been removed as part of a major engine overhaul, it is assumed that the engine will have completed a substantial mileage. In this case, it is often considered good practice to fit a new (or reconditioned) pump as a matter of course. In other words, if the rest of the engine is being rebuilt, the engine has completed a large mileage, or there is any question as to the old pump's condition, it is preferable to fit a new oil pump.

Refitting

14 Before fitting the oil pump, ensure that the mating faces on the pump and the engine block are completely clean.

15 Lay the main metal gasket and a new spacer ring in position on the engine – in the case of the spacer ring, 'stick' it in position with a little oil or grease if required **(see illustration)**.

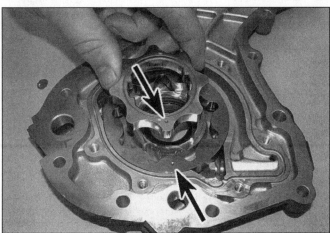

13.12 Align the dots on the 2 rotors (arrowed)

13.15 Fit a new metal gasket and spacer ring (arrowed) in position

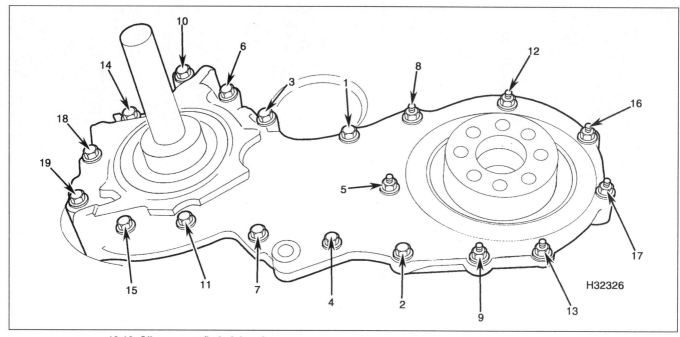

13.16 Oil pump nut/bolt tightening sequence – note special tool 303-652 used to align the pump

16 Offer the pump into position, and secure it with the studs and bolts, tightened only loosely at this stage **(see illustration)**.

17 Ford technicians use a special tool (303-652) to align the oil pump as it is being fitted and tightened **(see illustration)**. The tool is basically a circular socket, which fits over the end of the crankshaft, and ensures that the corresponding hole in the oil pump is centrally located over the end of the crankshaft. In the absence of the tool, this alignment could be confirmed visually, or a large socket/piece of tubing (perhaps wrapped with tape) could be used instead.

18 Ensuring that the correct alignment of the pump is maintained, tighten the pump securing studs and bolts to the specified Stage 1 torque, in sequence **(see illustration 13.16)**.

19 When all the fasteners have been tightened to the Stage 1 torque, go around again in the sequence, and tighten them all to the specified Stage 2 torque.

20 Refit the timing belt backplate to the engine.

21 Refit the injection pump sprocket and oil seal housing as described in Chapter 4A.

22 Refit the timing belt and camshaft sprocket as described in Section 7.

23 Refit the auxiliary drivebelt idler pulley, and tighten the bolt to the specified torque.

24 Refit the crankshaft pulley as described in Section 6.

25 When the engine is next started, check for correct oil pump operation (at least, as indicated by the oil pressure warning light going out).

14 Oil pressure warning light switch – removal and refitting

Removal

1 The switch is screwed into the left-hand (flywheel) end of the cylinder head, behind the vacuum pump.

2 Open the bonnet and disconnect the battery negative (earth) lead as described in Chapter 5.

3 To improve access to the switch, it will be necessary to remove (or partially remove)

the air cleaner inlet duct and the intercooler right-hand air duct, using the information in Chapter 4A. It will also be helpful to release the hoses and remove the crankcase ventilation system oil separator from the left-hand end of the cylinder head.

4 Unplug the wiring from the switch and unscrew it; be prepared for some oil loss **(see illustration)**.

Refitting

5 Refitting is the reverse of the removal procedure; apply a thin smear of suitable sealant to the switch threads, and tighten it to the specified torque wrench setting.

6 Refit all components removed for access to the switch.

7 Check the engine oil level and top-up as necessary (see *Weekly checks*).

8 Check for correct warning light operation, and for signs of oil leaks, once the engine has been restarted and warmed-up to normal operating temperature.

15 Oil cooler – removal and refitting

Note: *New sealing rings will be required on refitting.*

Removal

1 The oil cooler is mounted next to the oil filter on the rear of the cylinder block. Access to the oil cooler is best obtained from below – apply the handbrake, then jack up the front of the car and support it on axle stands. Undo the screws and remove the engine undershield.

2 Position a container beneath the oil filter to

13.17 Tool used to align the oil pump before tightening the bolts fully

14.4 Disconnect the wiring from the oil pressure warning switch

15.4 Disconnect the turbocharger oil supply union bolt (arrowed)

catch escaping oil and coolant. To improve access to the coolant hoses, unscrew and remove the oil filter, making sure that the filter sealing ring is removed with the filter cartridge – anticipate a small loss of engine oil as the filter is removed. Provided the filter is not due for renewal, it can be refitted on completion.

3 Clamp the oil cooler coolant hoses to minimise spillage, then remove the clips, and disconnect the hoses from the oil cooler. Be prepared for coolant spillage.

4 Loosen the turbocharger oil supply union bolt at the top of the cooler **(see illustration)**, and separate the pipe (be prepared for oil spillage). Recover the copper washers from the union – new ones must be used on reassembly.

5 Unscrew the four bolts securing the oil cooler, noting their positions, as they are of different lengths. Remove the oil cooler from the engine, and recover the gasket (a new gasket must be used on refitting).

Refitting

6 Refitting is a reversal of removal, bearing in mind the following points:

 a) *Use a new gasket (see illustration).*
 b) *Fit the oil cooler mounting bolts to the positions noted on removal, and tighten them securely. Refit the oil filter*

if removed – apply a little oil to the filter sealing ring, and tighten the filter securely by hand (do not use any tools).
 c) *Use new copper washers when reconnecting the oil supply union at the top of the cooler, and tighten the union bolt securely.*
 d) *On completion, lower the car to the ground. Check and if necessary top-up the oil and coolant levels, then start the engine and check for signs of oil or coolant leakage.*

16 Crankshaft oil seals – renewal

Timing belt end seal

1 Remove the crankshaft pulley (see Section 6).

2 Note the fitted depth of the oil seal as a guide for fitting the new one.

3 Using a screwdriver or similar tool, carefully prise the oil seal from its location. Take care not to damage the oil seal contact surfaces or the oil seal seating. An alternative method of removing the seals is to drill a small hole in the seal (taking care not to drill any deeper than necessary), then insert a self-tapping screw and use pliers to pull out the seal.

4 Wipe clean the oil seal contact surfaces and seating, and clean up any sharp edges or burrs which might damage the new seal as it is fitted, or which might cause the seal to leak once in place.

5 The new oil seal should be supplied fitted with a locating sleeve, which must **not** be removed prior to fitting. No oil should be applied to the oil seal, which is made of PTFE.

6 Ford technicians use a special seal-fitting tool (303-652), but an adequate substitute can be achieved using a large socket or piece of

15.6 Renew the oil cooler gasket

tubing of sufficient size to bear on the outer edge of the new seal.

7 Locate the new seal (lips facing inwards) over the end of the crankshaft, using the tool **(see illustration)**, socket, or tubing to press the seal squarely and fully into position, to the previously-noted depth. Once the seal is fully fitted, remove the locating sleeve, if necessary.

8 The remainder of reassembly is the reverse of the removal procedure, referring to the relevant text for details where required. Check for signs of oil leakage when the engine is restarted.

Flywheel end seal

9 Remove the transmission as described in Chapter 7, and the clutch assembly as described in Chapter 6.

10 Unbolt the flywheel (see Section 17).

11 Unbolt and remove the oil seal carrier; the seal is renewed complete with the carrier, and is not available separately. A complete set of new carrier retaining bolts should also be obtained for reassembly **(see illustration)**.

12 Clean the end of the crankshaft, polishing off any burrs or raised edges, which may have caused the seal to fail in the first place. Clean also the seal carrier mating face on the engine block, using a suitable solvent for degreasing if necessary.

16.7 Use a locating tool to press the seal in squarely (locating sleeve not required when using this tool)

16.11 The oil seal is renewed complete with the carrier

16.14a Fit the new seal assembly, complete with guide sleeve over the end of the crankshaft . . .

16.14b . . . then remove the guide sleeve

17.12 Align the bolts holes in the crankshaft – they will only line up in one position

17.13 Tool (arrowed) fabricated to lock the flywheel

13 The new oil seal is supplied fitted with a locating sleeve, which must **not** be removed prior to fitting (it will drop out on its own when the carrier is bolted into position). No oil should be applied to the oil seal, which is made of PTFE.

14 Offer up the carrier into position, feeding the locating sleeve over the end of the crankshaft. Insert the new seal carrier retaining bolts, and tighten them all by hand **(see illustrations)**.

15 Ford technicians use a special tool (308-204) to centre the oil seal carrier around the end of the crankshaft. In the absence of the tool, this alignment could be confirmed visually, or a large socket/piece of tubing (perhaps wrapped with tape) could be used instead.

16 Ensuring that the correct alignment of the carrier is maintained, tighten the retaining bolts to the specified torque. If the seal locating sleeve is still in position, remove it now.

17 The remainder of the reassembly procedure is the reverse of dismantling, referring to the relevant text for details where required. Check for signs of oil leakage when the engine is restarted.

17 Flywheel – removal, inspection and refitting

Removal

1 Remove the transmission as described in Chapter 7. Now is a good time to check components such as oil seals and renew them if necessary.

2 Remove the clutch as described in Chapter 6. Now is a good time to check or renew the clutch components and release bearing.

3 Use a centre-punch or paint to make alignment marks on the flywheel and crankshaft, to ensure correct alignment during refitting.

4 Prevent the flywheel from turning by locking the ring gear teeth, or by bolting a strap between the flywheel and the cylinder block/crankcase. Slacken the bolts evenly until all are free.

5 Remove each bolt in turn and ensure that new ones are obtained for reassembly; these bolts are subjected to severe stresses and so must be renewed, regardless of their apparent condition, whenever they are disturbed.

6 Withdraw the flywheel, remembering that it is very heavy – do not drop it.

Inspection

7 Clean the flywheel to remove grease and oil. Inspect the surface for cracks, rivet grooves, burned areas and score marks. Light scoring can be removed with emery cloth. Check for cracked and broken ring gear teeth. Lay the flywheel on a flat surface and use a straight-edge to check for warpage.

8 Clean and inspect the mating surfaces of the flywheel and the crankshaft. If the crankshaft seal is leaking, renew it (see Section 16) before refitting the flywheel. If the engine has covered a high mileage, it may be worth fitting a new seal as a matter if course, given the amount of work needed to access it.

9 While the flywheel is removed, clean carefully its inboard (right-hand) face, particularly the recesses which serve as the reference points for the crankshaft speed/position sensor. Clean the sensor's tip and check that the sensor is securely fastened.

10 Thoroughly clean the threaded bolt holes in the crankshaft, removing all traces of locking compound.

11 Note that on models fitted with a dual-mass flywheel, the maximum travel of the primary mass in relation to the secondary must not exceed 15 teeth.

Refitting

12 Fit the flywheel to the crankshaft so that all bolt holes align – it will fit only one way – check this using the marks made on removal **(see illustration)**. Apply suitable locking compound to the threads of the new bolts, then insert them.

13 Lock the flywheel by the method used on dismantling **(see illustration)**. Working in a diagonal sequence, tighten the bolts to the specified Stage 1 torque wrench setting.

14 Stage 2 involves tightening the bolts though an angle, rather than to a torque. Each bolt must be rotated through the specified angle – special angle gauges are available from tool outlets.

15 The remainder of reassembly is the reverse of the removal procedure, referring to the relevant text for details where required.

18 Engine/transmission mountings – inspection and renewal

Refer to Chapter 2A, Section 17, but note the different torque wrench settings given at the beginning of this Chapter.

Chapter 2 Part C:
2.0 litre engine in-car repair procedures

Contents

Degrees of difficulty

Easy, suitable for novice with little experience		**Fairly easy,** suitable for beginner with some experience	**Fairly difficult,** suitable for competent DIY mechanic	**Difficult,** suitable for experienced DIY mechanic	**Very difficult,** suitable for expert DIY or professional	

Specifications

General

Engine type.	Four-cylinder, in-line, double overhead camshaft, aluminium cylinder head and cast iron engine block with turbocharger
Designation	2.0 litre Duratorq-TDCi
Engine code	G6DA and G6DB
Power output	100 kW @ 4000 rpm
Torque output	320 Nm @ 1750 rpm
Capacity	1998 cc
Bore	85.0 mm
Stroke	88.0 mm
Compression ratio	18:1
Firing order	1-3-4-2 (No 1 cylinder at transmission end)
Direction of crankshaft rotation	Clockwise (seen from right-hand side of vehicle)

Valves

Valve clearances.	Hydraulic adjusters – no adjustment necessary

Lubrication

Oil pressure – minimum (engine at operating temperature):

At 2000 rpm	2.0 bar
At 4000 rpm	4.0 bar

Torque wrench settings

	Nm	lbf ft
Air conditioning compressor	28	21
Big-end bearing cap bolts:*		
Stage 1	20	15
Stage 2	Angle-tighten a further 70°	
Camshaft bearing housing:		
Stage 1	5	4
Stage 2	10	7
Camshaft sprocket bolt:		
Stage 1	20	15
Stage 2	Angle-tighten a further 60°	
Camshaft position sensor	10	7
Crankshaft oil seal carrier	14	10
Crankshaft pulley bolt:*		
Stage 1	70	52
Stage 2	Angle-tighten a further 60°	
Cylinder head lower section-to-block bolts:*		
Stage 1	60	44
Stage 2	Angle-tighten a further 220°	
Cylinder head upper section-to-lower section bolts:		
Stage 1	5	4
Stage 2	10	7
Cylinder head cover/inlet manifold:		
Stage 1	5	4
Stage 2	10	7
Engine mountings:		
Right-hand mounting retaining bolts	90	66
Right-hand mounting bracket-to-engine bolts	56	41
Left-hand mounting nuts	48	35
Left-hand mounting bracket to transmission	80	59
Left-hand mounting centre bolt	148	109
Lower-rear torque rod bolts	80	59
Engine oil drain plug	34	25
Engine-to-transmission bolts	48	35
Flywheel bolts*	48	35
Fuel high-pressure pump mounting bolts	20	15
Fuel high-pressure pipe unions	30	22
Fuel injector mounting studs	10	7
Main bearing bolts:		
Stage 1	25	18
Stage 2	Angle-tighten a further 60°	
Oil pressure switch	35	26
Oil pump bolts	16	12
Oil pump pick-up tube bolts	12	9
Piston cooling jet	10	7
Roadwheel nuts	Refer to Chapter 1	
Subframe mounting bolts:*		
Front	120	89
Rear	280	207
Subframe rear mounting brackets to body	25	18
Sump bolts	16	12
Thermostat housing to cylinder head	18	13
Timing belt tensioner	21	15
Timing chain tensioner	6	4

Do not re-use

1 General information

How to use this Chapter

This Part of Chapter 2 is devoted to repair procedures possible while the engine is still installed in the vehicle. Since these procedures are based on the assumption that the engine is installed in the vehicle, if the engine has been removed from the vehicle and mounted on a stand, some of the preliminary dismantling steps outlined will not apply.

Information concerning engine/transmission removal and refitting and engine overhaul, can be found in Part D of this Chapter.

Engine description

The engine is a result of a joint venture between Ford and Peugeot. This DOHC (Double Overhead Camshaft) 16-valve engine features common rail direct injection, and a VNT (Variable Nozzle Turbine) turbocharger.

All major components are made from aluminium, apart from the cast-iron cylinder block – no liners are fitted, the cylinders are bored directly into the block. An aluminium main bearing ladder is fitted. This arrangement offers greater rigidity than the normal sump arrangement, and helps to reduce engine vibration.

The crankshaft runs in five main bearings, thrustwashers are fitting either side of the No 1 cylinder main bearings to control crankshaft endfloat. The connecting rods rotate on horizontally-split bearing shells at their big-ends. The pistons are attached to the connecting rods by gudgeon pins which are a floating fit in the connecting rod small-end eyes, secured by circlips. The aluminium alloy pistons are fitted with three piston rings: two compression rings and an oil control ring. After manufacture, the cylinder bores and piston skirts are measured and classified into four weight grades, which must be carefully matched together to ensure the correct piston/cylinder clearance; no oversizes are available to permit reboring.

The inlet and exhaust valves are each closed by coil springs; they operate in guides which are shrink-fitted into the cylinder head, as are the valve seat inserts.

A rubber toothed-belt driven by the crankshaft sprocket rotates the coolant pump and the exhaust camshaft sprocket. The inlet camshaft is driven by a short timing chain from the exhaust sprocket.

The camshafts operate the 16 valves via roller-rocker arms with hydraulic clearance adjusters. The camshafts rotate in five bearings that are line-bored directly into the two sections of the cylinder head.

The vacuum pump (used for the brake servo and other vacuum actuators) is driven from the end of the inlet camshaft, whilst the fuel pump is driven from the end of the exhaust camshaft.

When working on this engine, note that Torx-type (both male and female heads) and hexagon socket (Allen head) fasteners are widely used; a good selection of bits, with the necessary adapters, will be required so that these can be unscrewed without damage and, on reassembly, tightened to the torque wrench settings specified.

Lubrication system

The oil pump is mounted under the cylinder block, and is chain driven from a crankshaft sprocket. The pump forces oil through an externally-mounted full-flow cartridge-type filter. From the filter, the oil is pumped into a main gallery in the cylinder block/crankcase, from where it is distributed to the crankshaft (main bearings) and cylinder head. An oil cooler is fitted next to the oil filter, at the rear of the block. The cooler is supplied with coolant from the engine cooling system.

While the crankshaft and camshaft bearings receive a pressurised supply, the camshaft lobes and valves are lubricated by splash, as are all other engine components. The undersides of the pistons are cooled by oil, sprayed from nozzles fitted above the upper main bearing shells. The turbocharger receives its own pressurised oil supply.

Operations with engine in car

The following major repair operations can be accomplished without removing the engine from the vehicle. However, owners should note that any operation involving the removal of the sump requires careful forethought, depending on the level of skill and the tools and facilities available; refer to the relevant text for details.

a) *Compression pressure – testing.*
b) *Cylinder head cover – removal and refitting.*
c) *Timing belt cover – removal and refitting.*
d) *Timing belt/chain – renewal.*
e) *Timing belt tensioner and sprockets – removal and refitting.*
f) *Camshaft oil seal – renewal.*
g) *Camshaft and cam followers – removal and refitting.*
h) *Cylinder head – removal, overhaul and refitting.*
i) *Cylinder head and pistons – decarbonising.*
j) *Sump – removal and refitting.*
k) *Crankshaft oil seals – renewal.*
l) *Oil pump – removal and refitting.*
m) *Piston/connecting rod assemblies – removal and refitting (but see note below).*
n) *Flywheel – removal and refitting.*
o) *Engine/transmission mountings – removal and refitting.*

Note: *It is possible to remove the pistons and connecting rods (after removing the cylinder head and sump) without removing the engine, however, this is not recommended. Work of this nature is more easily and thoroughly completed with the engine on the bench, as described in Chapter 2D.*

Clean the engine compartment and the exterior of the engine with some type of degreaser before any work is done (and/or clean the engine using a steam cleaner). It will make the job easier and will help to keep dirt out of the internal areas of the engine.

Depending on the components involved, it may be helpful to remove the bonnet, to improve access to the engine as repairs are performed (refer to Chapter 11 if necessary). Cover the wings to prevent damage to the paint; special covers are available, but an old bedspread or blanket will also work.

2 Compression and leakdown tests – description and interpretation

Compression test

Note: *A compression tester suitable for use with diesel engines will be required for this test.*

1 When engine performance is down, or if misfiring occurs which cannot be attributed to the fuel or emissions systems, a compression test can provide diagnostic clues as to the engine's condition. If the test is performed regularly, it can give warning of trouble before any other symptoms become apparent.

2 The engine must be fully warmed-up to normal operating temperature, the battery must be fully-charged and the glow plugs must be removed. The aid of an assistant will be required.

3 Pull the plastic cover on the top of the engine upwards to release it from its mountings.

4 Disconnect the wiring plugs from the injectors.

5 Remove the glow plugs as described in Chapter 5.

6 Raise the front of the vehicle and support it securely on axle stands (see *Jacking and vehicle support*).

7 Undo the fasteners and remove the engine undershield, then remove the splash shield under the radiator.

8 At the left-hand side of the radiator lower support bracket, unplug the glow plug relay.

9 Fit a compression tester to the No 1 cylinder glow plug hole. The type of tester which screws into the plug thread is preferred.

10 Crank the engine for several seconds on the starter motor. After one or two revolutions, the compression pressure should build-up to a maximum figure and then stabilise. Record the highest reading obtained.

11 Repeat the test on the remaining cylinders, recording the pressure in each.

12 The cause of poor compression is less easy to establish on a diesel engine than on a petrol engine. The effect of introducing oil into the cylinders (wet testing) is not conclusive, because there is a risk that the oil will sit in the recess on the piston crown, instead of passing to the rings. However, the following can be used as a rough guide to diagnosis.

13 All cylinders should produce very similar pressures. Any great difference indicates the existence of a fault. Note that the compression should build-up quickly in a healthy engine. Low compression on the first stroke, followed by gradually increasing pressure on successive strokes, indicates worn piston rings. A low compression reading on the first stroke, which does not build-up during successive strokes, indicates leaking valves or a blown head gasket (a cracked head could also be the cause).

14 A low reading from two adjacent cylinders is almost certainly due to the head gasket having blown between them and the presence of coolant in the engine oil will confirm this.

15 On completion, remove the compression tester, and refit the glow plugs.

16 Reconnect the injector wiring plugs, refit the glow plug relay and the engine/radiator undershields.

Leakdown test

17 A leakdown test measures the rate at which compressed air fed into the cylinder is lost. It is an alternative to a compression test, and in many ways it is better, since the escaping air provides easy identification of where pressure loss is occurring (piston rings, valves or head gasket).

18 The equipment required for leakdown testing is unlikely to be available to the home mechanic. If poor compression is suspected, have the test performed by a suitably-equipped garage.

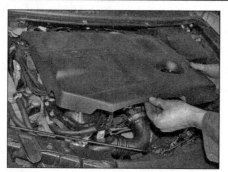

3.1 Pull up at the front and remove the engine cover

3.4a Prise forwards the clips (arrowed) . . .

3.4b . . . then pull the scuttle cowling panel upwards from the base of the windscreen

3 Cylinder head cover – removal and refitting

Removal

1 The cylinder head cover is integral with the inlet manifold. Begin by removing the plastic cover from the top of the engine by pulling it straight up from its mountings at the right-hand rear corner, right-hand front corner and left-hand front corner, then sliding it forwards **(see illustration)**.
2 Undo the 2 bolts securing the brake fluid remote reservoir (where fitted) to the engine compartment bulkhead.
3 Remove the wiper arms as described in Chapter 12.

4 Release the 5 clips and remove the wind-screen cowl panel, then undo the 2 bolts and remove the bulkhead extension panel **(see illustrations)**.
5 Disconnect the battery negative lead as described in Chapter 5A.
6 Disconnect the crankcase ventilation hoses from the inlet manifold/cover, then release the clamp and disconnect the EGR pipe from the inlet manifold **(see illustrations)**.
7 Undo the bolts and remove the throttle body/anti-shudder valve and retaining bracket **(see illustration)**.
8 Undo the remaining bolts and remove the EGR pipe.
9 Release the clips and detach the wiring harness and fuel pipes from the timing belt upper cover.
10 Undo the bolt and remove the wiring

bracket from the right-hand rear corner of the cylinder head.
11 Disconnect the wiring plug, undo the retaining bolt and remove the camshaft position sensor **(see illustration)**.
12 Undo the bolts, slacken the nut, then remove the timing belt upper cover.
13 Disconnect the injector wiring plugs, then detach the harness duct from the inlet manifold/cover and position it to one side **(see illustration)**.
14 Release the glow plugs wiring harness from the 2 clips on the manifold.
15 Unclip the fuel temperature sensor (located on underside the inlet manifold).
16 Undo the manifold/cover retaining bolts in the **reverse** of the sequence shown **(see illustration 3.18)**. Discard the gaskets, new ones must be fitted.

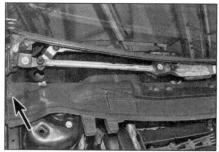

3.4c Undo the bolt at each end (right-hand one arrowed) and pull the bulkhead extension panel forwards

3.6a Release the clamps and disconnect the breather hose (arrowed) from the cylinder head cover . . .

3.6b . . . the EGR pipe (arrowed) from the inlet manifold . . .

3.6c . . . then depress the clip and disconnect the breather hose from the rear of the cylinder head cover

3.7 Anti-shudder valve/throttle body bolts (arrowed)

3.11 Undo the bolt (arrowed) and remove the camshaft position sensor

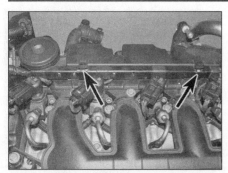

3.13 Release the clips (arrowed) and detach the injector wiring harness duct

Refitting

17 Clean the sealing surfaces of the manifold/cover and the head.

18 Fit the new seals to the inlet manifold/cover, then fit it to the cylinder head. Use a little petroleum jelly on the manifold O-rings to ease assembly. Tighten the bolts to the specified torque in sequence (see illustration).

19 The remainder of refitting is a reversal of removal, noting the following points:

a) Tighten all fasteners to their specified torque where given.

b) The camshaft position sensor must be refitted in accordance with the instructions given in Chapter 4A, otherwise it will not function correctly.

4 Crankshaft pulley – removal and refitting

Removal

1 Loosen the right-hand front roadwheel nuts, then raise the front of the vehicle, and support securely on axle stands (see *Jacking and vehicle support*). Remove the roadwheel. Access is greatly improved once the wheel arch liner has been removed.

2 Release the fasteners and withdraw the engine undershield from under the car (see illustration).

3 Remove the auxiliary drivebelt as described in Chapter 1.

4 The centre bolt which secures the crankshaft pulley must now be slackened. This bolt

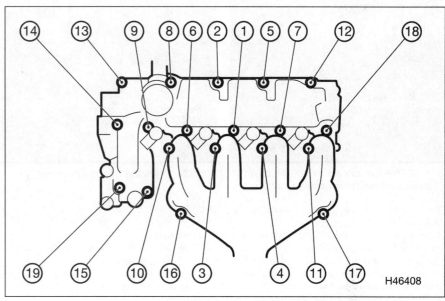

3.18 Inlet manifold/cylinder head cover bolt tightening sequence

Note that the 55 mm bolt is fitted to position 14, and 70 mm bolts are fitted to positions 16 and 17

is tightened to a very high torque, and it is first of all essential to ensure that the car is adequately supported, as considerable effort will be needed.

5 Ford technicians use a special holding tool (303-393/303-393-01) which bolts to the transmission housing and engages with the starter ring gear teeth once the starter motor has been removed. If this is not available, select a gear, and have an assistant firmly apply the handbrake and footbrake as the bolt is loosened.

6 Unscrew the bolt securing the pulley to the crankshaft, and remove the pulley. It is essential to obtain a new bolt for reassembly (see illustrations). If required, remove the sensor ring/spacer. **Note:** *Do not touch the outer sensor ring.*

7 With the pulley removed, it is advisable to check the crankshaft oil seal for signs of oil leakage. If necessary, fit a new seal as described in Section 14.

Refitting

8 Refit the pulley to the crankshaft sprocket,

then fit the new pulley securing bolt and tighten it as far as possible before the crankshaft starts to rotate.

9 Holding the pulley against rotation as for removal, first tighten the bolt to the specified Stage 1 torque.

10 Stage 2 involves tightening the bolt though an angle, rather than to a torque. The bolt must be rotated through the specified angle – special angle gauges are available from tool outlets.

11 The remainder of refitting is a reversal of removal.

5 Timing belt and tensioner – removal and refitting

Removal

1 Disconnect the battery negative lead as described in Chapter 5A.

2 Undo the 2 bolts securing the brake fluid remote reservoir (where fitted) to the engine compartment bulkhead.

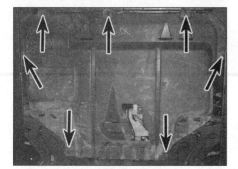

4.2 Undo the fasteners (arrowed) and remove the engine undershield

4.6a Undo the bolt and remove the crankshaft pulley . . .

4.6b . . . followed by the TDC sensor ring/spacer

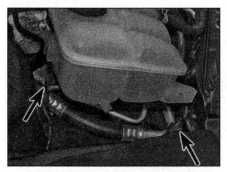

5.7 Pull the coolant expansion tank upwards from its mountings (arrowed)

5.9a Undo the 2 bolts (arrowed) . . .

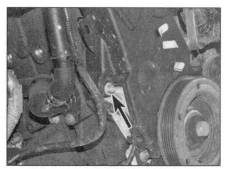

5.9b . . . and slacken the nut (arrowed)

3 Remove the wiper arms as described in Chapter 12.

4 Release the 5 clips and remove the windscreen cowl panel, then undo the bolt at each end and pull the bulkhead extension panel forwards and remove it **(see illustration 3.4a, 3.4b and 3.4c)**

5 Pull the plastic cover on top of the engine straight up from its mountings at the right-hand rear corner, right-hand front corner and left-hand front corner, then slide it forwards.

6 Remove the auxiliary drivebelt as described in Chapter 1.

7 Pull the coolant expansion tank up from its position, and move the tank to one side without disconnecting the hoses **(see illustration)**.

8 Release the wiring harness from the timing belt cover, then unclip the fuel pipes.

9 Undo the 2 bolts, slacken the nut, and remove the upper timing belt cover **(see illustrations)**.

10 Slacken the front right-hand roadwheel bolts, then jack up the front of the vehicle and support it securely on axle stands (see *Jacking and vehicle support*). Remove the roadwheel.

11 Release the fasteners and remove the engine undershield **(see illustration 4.2)**.

12 The engine must now be supported before the right-hand mounting is removed. Ford technicians use an engine support bar, which locates in the channels at the top of each inner wing, and a further beam attached to this, which rests on the front crossmember. If such an arrangement is not available, use an engine crane; either way, use a suitable length of chain and hooks to attach the lifting gear to the engine lifting eye. If the engine

must be supported from below (and this is not recommended), use a large piece of wood on a trolley jack to spread the load and reduce the chance of damage to the sump.

13 With the weight of the engine supported, unscrew the bolts/nuts, and remove the right-hand engine mounting **(see illustration)**.

14 Slacken the crankshaft pulley bolt as described in Section 4. Do not discard the old bolt yet – it is used during reassembly.

15 Two special tools are now required to set the engine at TDC (Top Dead Centre) for No1 cylinder (at the transmission end). Ford tool No 303-105 locates through a hole in the rear flange of the cylinder block into a corresponding hole in the rear of the flywheel, whilst tool No 303-735 locates through a hole in the exhaust camshaft sprocket into a hole in the cylinder head casting. In the absence of these tools, use an 8 mm drill bit to lock the camshaft sprocket, and an 8 mm rod to lock the flywheel. **Note:** *The flywheel locking bolt must be flat (not tapered at all) at the end.*

16 Undo the starter motor bolts and position the motor to one side, to expose the crankshaft setting tool hole in the cylinder block flange. Refer to Chapter 5A if necessary.

17 Using a spanner or socket on the crankshaft pulley bolt, rotate the engine in a clockwise direction (viewed from the timing belt end of the engine) until the hole in the camshaft sprocket begins to align with the corresponding hole in the cylinder head.

18 Insert the crankshaft setting tool though the hole in the cylinder block flange and press it against the back of the flywheel. Have an assistant very slowly rotate the crankshaft clockwise, and the tool should slide into the flywheel as the holes align **(see illustrations)**.

19 It should now be possible to insert the camshaft locking tool (303-735) or equivalent through the hole in the camshaft sprocket into the hole in the cylinder head **(see illustration)**. Note that it may be necessary to rotate the camshaft sprocket backwards or forwards very slightly to be able to insert the tool.

20 At this point, Ford technicians use the tool described in paragraph 5 of Section 4 to lock the crankshaft in this position. The use of this tool, or an equivalent is strongly recommended.

21 Disconnect the crankshaft position sensor

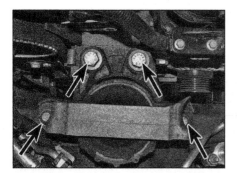

5.13 Undo the bolts (arrowed) and remove the right-hand engine mounting

5.18a The tool fits through the hole in the cylinder block flange . . .

5.18b . . . and into a hole in the rear of the flywheel

5.19 The tool fits through the hole in the exhaust camshaft sprocket, into the timing hole in the cylinder head

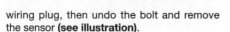

5.21 Crankshaft position sensor bolt (arrowed)

5.23 Timing belt lower cover bolts (arrowed)

5.24 Slacken the tensioner pulley bolt (arrowed)

wiring plug, then undo the bolt and remove the sensor **(see illustration)**.

22 Remove the crankshaft pulley, followed by the sensor ring/spacer **(see illustration 4.6a and 4.6b)**. **Note:** *Do not touch the outer sensor ring.*

23 Undo the bolts/nut and remove the lower timing belt cover **(see illustration)**.

24 Raise the engine slightly, then relieve the timing belt tension by slackening the bolt in the centre of the tensioning pulley **(see illustration)**.

25 Remove the timing belt from the sprockets. Note that the belt must not be re-used.

26 Slacken the bolts a few turns, remove the engine mounting bracket and the idler pulley, then undo the tensioner bolt **(see illustration)**. Discard both the tensioner and idler pulleys – new ones must be fitted.

27 If a new timing belt is not being fitted straight away (or if the belt is being removed as

part of another procedure, such as cylinder head removal), temporarily refit the engine right-hand mounting and tighten the bolts securely.

Refitting

28 Ensure that the crankshaft and camshaft are still set to TDC on No 1 cylinder.

29 Position the new idler pulley and insert the retaining bolt **(see illustration)**.

30 Refit the engine mounting bracket, then tighten the retaining bolts (including the idler pulley bolt) to the specified torque, where given.

31 Fit the new timing belt tensioner into position, but tighten the retaining finger-tight only at this stage.

32 Fit the new timing belt over the various sprockets in the following order: crankshaft, idler pulley, camshaft, tensioner and coolant pump **(see illustrations)**. Pay attention to any arrows on the belt indicating direction of rotation.

33 Using an Allen key in the tensioner arm, rotate the arm anti-clockwise until the pointer is positioned between the sides of the adjustment 'window' **(see illustrations)**. Fully tighten the tensioner retaining bolt.

34 Refit the timing belt lower cover and tighten the bolts securely.

35 Refit the sensor ring/spacer and the crankshaft pulley, then tighten the old pulley bolt to 50 Nm (37 lbf ft).

36 Remove the crankshaft and camshaft setting/locking tools, then rotate the crankshaft 2 complete revolutions clockwise, until the crankshaft setting tool can be re-inserted. Check that the camshaft locking tool can be inserted.

37 Check position of the tensioner pointer, and if necessary slacken the retaining bolt and use the Allen key to align the pointer in the centre of the adjustment 'window'. Tighten the retaining bolt securely.

5.26 Slacken the engine mounting bracket bolts and remove the idler pulley

5.29 Fit the new idler pulley

5.32a Timing belt routing

5.32b The arrows on the belt must point in the direction of rotation

5.33a Use an Allen key in the tensioner arm hole (arrowed)

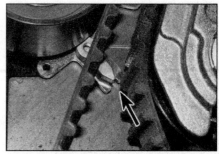

5.33b Rotate the arm anti-clockwise until the pointer is between the sides of the adjustment 'window' (arrowed)

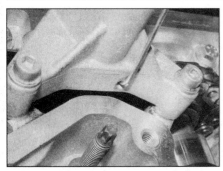

6.3 Lift up the chain upper guide rail and insert a 2.0 mm diameter rod/drill bit into the hole in the tensioner housing

38 Remove the old crankshaft pulley bolt, and fit the new one. Tighten the bolt to the specified torque, using the method employed during removal to prevent the crankshaft from rotating.

39 Remove the crankshaft and camshaft locking tools.

40 The remainder of refitting is a reversal of removal, remembering to tighten all fasteners to their specified torque where given.

6 Timing chain and tensioner – removal and refitting

Timing chain

1 Removal of the timing chain is included in the camshaft removal and refitment procedure, as described in Section 7.

7.4a Depress the release tab (arrowed) and disconnect the servo hose from the pump

7.5 Undo the unions (arrowed) and remove the high-pressure fuel pipe between the fuel rail and pump

6.4 Undo the tensioner retaining bolts (arrowed)

Tensioner

2 Remove the cylinder head cover as described in Section 3.

3 Press the tensioner upper guide rail upwards into the housing, then insert a 2.0 mm locking pin/drill bit to secure the rail in position **(see illustration)**.

4 Undo the 2 retaining bolts and withdrawn the tensioner **(see illustration)**.

5 Begin refitting by ensuring the tensioner and cylinder head mating faces are clean and free of debris.

6 Install the tensioner and tighten the retaining bolts to the specified torque.

7 Press the tensioner upper guide rail into the housing, pull out the locking pin/drill bit, then slowly release the guide rail.

8 Refit the cylinder head cover as described in Section 3.

7.4b Undo the nut (arrowed) securing the EGR pipe and fuel hose

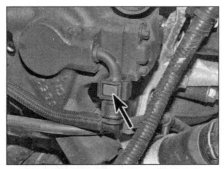

7.6a Depress the release tab (arrowed) and disconnect the fuel return hose . . .

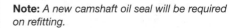

7 Camshaft, rocker arms and hydraulic adjusters – removal, inspection and refitting

Note: *A new camshaft oil seal will be required on refitting.*

Removal

1 Remove the timing belt as described in Section 5.

2 Remove the timing chain tensioner as described in Section 6.

3 Remove the air cleaner assembly as described in Chapter 4A.

4 Working at the left-hand end of the cylinder head, depress the release tab and disconnect the hose from the vacuum pump, undo the nut securing the EGR pipe and fuel supply hose, then undo the 3 Allen bolts and remove the pump from the cylinder head **(see illustrations)**. Check the condition of the pump O-ring seals and renew if necessary.

5 Undo the unions and remove the high-pressure fuel pipe between the fuel rail and the high-pressure pump located at the left-hand end of the cylinder head **(see illustration)**. Discard the pipe, a new one must be fitted. Plug or seal the openings to prevent contamination.

6 Slide off the retaining clip/depress the release tab and disconnect the fuel supply and return hoses from the high-pressure pump **(see illustrations)**. Plug or seal the openings to prevent contamination.

7.4c Vacuum pump securing bolts (arrowed)

7.6b . . . and the fuel supply hose (arrowed)

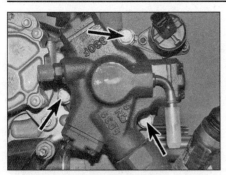

7.8 High-pressure fuel pump retaining bolts (arrowed)

7 Note their fitted positions, and disconnect the wiring plug(s) from the high-pressure fuel pump.

8 Undo the 3 retaining bolts and pull the high-pressure fuel pump out from the cylinder head **(see illustration)**. Be prepared for fuel spillage.

9 Remove the injectors as described in Chapter 4A.

10 Undo the retaining bolt and pull the sprocket from the exhaust camshaft. Use a tool to prevent the camshaft and sprocket from rotating whilst the nut is released **(see Tool Tip)**.

11 Undo the bolts and remove the engine mounting bracket from the right-hand end of the cylinder head/block.

12 Undo the bolts securing the timing belt inner cover to the cylinder head **(see illustration)**.

13 Undo the 2 bolts and remove the EGR pipe from over the left-hand end of the cylinder head.

14 Unscrew the injector mounting studs using a Torx socket, in sequence **(see illustration)**.

15 Working in the **reverse** of the sequence given **(see illustration 7.28)**, gradually and evenly remove the bolts securing the upper section of the cylinder head.

16 Carefully tap around the edge of the cylinder head upper section and lift it from position. Note that the cover will probably be

To make a camshaft sprocket holding tool, obtain two lengths of steel strip about 6 mm thick by 30 mm wide or similar, one 600 mm long, the other 200 mm long (all dimensions are approximate). Bolt the two strips together to form a forked end, leaving the bolt slack so that the shorter strip can pivot freely. Drill holes and insert bolts of a suitable size in the ends of the fork to engage in the sprocket spokes. Hold the bolts at the ends firmly in place by using a nut on the other side of the steel strip.

reluctant to lift due to the sealant used, and possible corrosion around the two locating dowels at the front edge.

17 Lift the camshafts from position, disengage the timing chain from the sprockets, and remove the exhaust camshaft seal.

18 Have ready a box divided into 16 segments, or some containers or other means of storing and identifying the rockers arms and hydraulic adjusters after removal. It's essential that if they are to be refitted, they return to their original positions. Mark the segments in the box or the containers with the cylinder number for each rocker arm/adjuster, and left or right, for the particular cylinder.

19 Lift out the rockers arms and hydraulic

7.12 Remove the bolts (arrowed) securing the belt inner cover

adjusters, Keep them identified for position, and place them in their respective positions in the box or container **(see illustration)**.

Inspection

20 With the camshaft removed, examine the bearing surfaces in the upper and lower sections of the cylinder head for signs of obvious wear or pitting. If evident, a new cylinder head will probably be required. Also check that the oil supply holes in the cylinder head are free from obstructions.

21 Visually inspect the camshaft for evidence of wear on the surfaces of the lobes and journals. Normally their surfaces should be smooth and have a dull shine; look for scoring, erosion or pitting and areas that appear highly polished, indicating excessive wear. Accelerated wear will occur once the hardened exterior of the camshaft has been damaged, so always renew worn items. **Note:** *If these symptoms are visible on the tips of the camshaft lobes, check the rocker arm, as it will probably be worn as well.*

22 If any doubt exists as to the condition of the camshafts or cylinder head, have them examined at a Ford dealer workshop or suitably-equipped automotive repair facility.

23 Inspect the rocker arms and hydraulic adjusters for obvious signs of wear or damage, and renew if necessary.

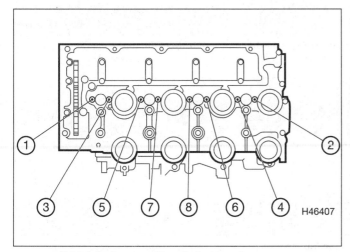

7.14 Injector mounting stud removal sequence

7.19 Lift out the rocker arms and hydraulic adjusters

7.24 Fit the secondary timing chain lower guide rail

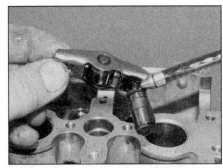

7.25a Apply clean oil to the hydraulic adjusters . . .

7.25b . . . and refit them to their original positions

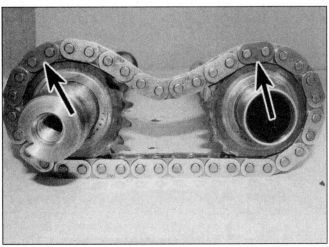

7.26a Align the coloured links on the chain (arrowed) with the marks on the camshaft sprockets . . .

7.26b . . . the mark on the sprockets is a dot, and a line . . .

Refitting

24 Make sure that the top surfaces of the cylinder head, and in particular the camshaft bearings and the mating surfaces are completely clean. Ensure the secondary timing chain lower guide rail is in place **(see illustration)**.

25 Smear some clean engine oil onto the sides of the hydraulic adjusters, and offer each one into position in their original bores in the cylinder head, together with its rocker arm **(see illustrations)**.

26 Locate the timing chain on the camshaft sprockets, aligning the two coloured chain links

7.26c . . . then fit the camshafts with the mark on the inlet camshaft (arrowed) in the 12 o'clock position

with the marks on the camshaft sprockets, then lubricate the camshaft and cylinder head bearing journals with clean engine oil, and lower the camshafts into position **(see illustrations)**. The mark on the inlet camshaft must be in the 12 o'clock position.

27 Apply a thin bead of silicone sealant (Ford part No WSE-M4G323-A4) to the mating surface of the cylinder head. Take great care to ensure the chain tensioner oil supply hole is free from sealant **(see illustrations)**.

28 Lower the upper section of the cylinder head into place, and tighten the retaining bolts to the specified torque in sequence **(see illustration)**.

29 Refit the fuel injector mounting studs and tighten them to the specified torque.

30 Refit the camshaft timing chain tensioner assembly, and tighten the retaining bolts to the specified torque. Press the tensioner guide rail up into the housing and pull out the locking pin/drill bit. Slowly release the guide rail to tension the chain.

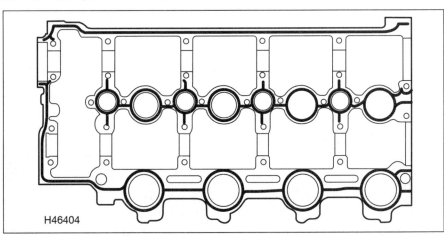

H46404

7.27a Apply a thin bead of sealant as indicated by the heavy black line

7.27b We inserted a tapered rod (arrowed) into the tensioner oil supply hole to prevent any sealant from entering

31 Fit a new exhaust camshaft oil seal as described in Section 8.

32 Refit the 2 bolts securing the timing belt inner cover to the cylinder head, and the single bolt to the cylinder block, then tighten the bolts securely.

33 Slide the exhaust camshaft sprocket into place, aligning the integral key with the camshaft and fit the camshaft sprocket locking tool (**see illustration 5.19**).

34 Fit the sprocket retaining bolt and tighten it to the specified torque, preventing the sprocket from turning using the tool used during removal.

35 Refit the engine mounting bracket to the right-hand end of the cylinder head/block, and tighten the bolts to the specified torque.

36 The remainder of refitting is a reversal of removal, noting the following points:

a) Refit the injectors as described in Chapter 4A.
b) Fit the new timing belt, tensioner and idler pulley as described in Section 5.
c) Tighten all fasteners to their specified torque, where given.
d) Check the engine oil and coolant levels as described in 'Weekly checks'.

8 Camshaft oil seal – renewal

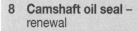

1 Remove the timing belt as described in Section 5, and the camshaft sprocket as described in paragraph 10 of the previous

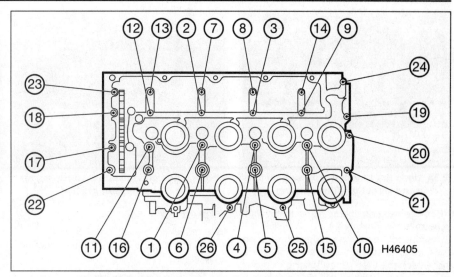

7.28 Cylinder head upper section bolt tightening sequence

Section. Recover the sprocket locating key from the end of the camshaft.

2 Carefully prise or pull the seal from position.

> **HAYNES HINT** One of the best ways to remove an oil seal is to carefully drill or punch two holes through the seal, opposite each other (taking care not to damage the surface behind the seal as this is done). Two self-tapping screws are then screwed into the holes; by pulling on the screw heads alternately with a pair of pliers, the seal can be extracted.

3 Clean out the seal housing and the sealing surface of the camshaft by wiping it with a lint-free cloth. Remove any swarf or burrs that may cause the seal to leak.

4 Apply a little oil to the new camshaft oil seal, and fit it over the end of the camshaft, lips facing inwards. To avoid damaging the seal lips, wrap a little tape over the end of the camshaft. Ford dealers have a special tool (No 303-684/1) for fitting the seal, but if this is not available, a deep socket of suitable size can be used. **Note:** Select a socket that

bears only on the hard outer surface of the seal, not the inner lip which can easily be damaged. It is important that the seal is fitted square to the shaft, and is fully-seated (**see illustrations**).

5 Refit the camshaft sprocket (and key – Section 7) and timing belt as described in Section 5.

9 Cylinder head – removal, inspection and refitting

Removal

1 Remove the battery as described in Chapter 5, then unscrew the three bolts securing the battery tray, and remove the tray from the engine compartment.

2 Drain the coolant as described in Chapter 1.

3 Remove the camshafts, rocker arms and hydraulic adjusters as described in Section 7.

4 Undo the bolts, and remove the bracket over the fuel filter.

5 Undo the Torx bolt, lift out the filter housing, then undo the bolts and remove the fuel filter bracket. Refit the bolt securing the lifting bracket to the cylinder head (**see illustrations**).

8.4a Apply a little clean oil to the oil seal inner lip . . .

8.4b . . . then use a socket (or similar) to drive the seal into place . . .

8.4c . . . until the seal is flush with the casing surface

9.5a Undo the Torx bolt (arrowed) on the side and lift out the filter housing . . .

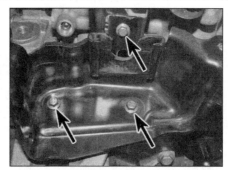

9.5b . . . then undo the bolts (arrowed) and remove the filter bracket

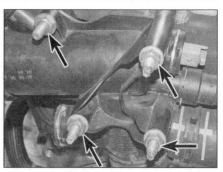

9.7 Thermostat housing studs (arrowed)

6 Remove the turbocharger/exhaust manifold as described in Chapter 4A.

7 Disconnect the wiring plugs, then undo the 4 nuts, unscrew the 4 mounting studs and detach the thermostat housing from the left-hand of the cylinder head. Be prepared for coolant spillage (see illustration).

8 Disconnect the wiring plug from the pressure sensor on the underside of the common fuel rail at the front of the cylinder head.

9 Undo the retaining bolt, and remove the oil filler pipe support bracket.

10 Working in the **reverse** of the sequence shown in paragraph 34, gradually and evenly slacken and remove the cylinder head bolts. Discard the bolts, new ones must be fitted.

11 Lift the cylinder head away; use assistance if possible, as it is a very heavy assembly. Do not place the cylinder head flat on its sealing surface, as the ends of the glow plugs may be damaged – support the ends of the cylinder head on wooden blocks.

12 If the head is stuck (as is possible), be careful how you choose to free it. Striking the head with tools carries the risk of damage, and the head is located on two dowels, so its movement will be limited. Do not, under any circumstances, lever the head between the mating surfaces, as this will certainly damage the sealing surfaces for the gasket, leading to leaks.

13 Once the head has been removed, recover the gasket from the two dowels.

14 Do not discard the gasket at this stage – it will be needed for correct identification of the new gasket.

9.20 Zero the DTI on the gasket face

Inspection

15 If required, dismantling and inspection of the cylinder head is covered in Part D of this Chapter.

Cylinder head gasket selection

16 Examine the old cylinder head gasket for manufacturer's identification markings. These will be in the form of holes on the front edge of the gasket, which indicate the gasket's thickness.

17 Unless new components have been fitted, or the cylinder head has been machined (skimmed), the new cylinder head gasket must be of the same type as the old one. Purchase the required gasket, and proceed to paragraph 24.

18 If the head has been machined, or if new pistons have been fitted, it is likely that a head gasket of different thickness to the original will be needed.

19 Gasket selection is made on the basis of the measured piston protrusion above the cylinder head gasket surface.

20 To measure the piston protrusion, anchor a dial test indicator (DTI) to the top face (cylinder head gasket mating face) of the cylinder block, and zero the gauge on the gasket mating face (see illustration).

21 Rest the gauge probe above No 1 piston crown, and turn the crankshaft slowly by hand until the piston reaches TDC (its maximum height). Measure and record the maximum piston projection at TDC.

22 Repeat the measurement for the remaining pistons, and record the results.

23 If the measurements differ from piston to piston, take the highest figure, and use this to determine the thickness of the head gasket required (see table below).

Preparation for refitting

24 The mating faces of the cylinder head and cylinder block must be perfectly clean before refitting the head. Use a hard plastic or wooden scraper to remove all traces of gasket and carbon; also clean the piston crowns. **Note:** *The new head gasket has rubber-coated surfaces, which could be damaged from sharp edges or debris left by a metal scraper.* Take particular care when cleaning the piston crowns, as the soft aluminium alloy is easily damaged.

25 Make sure that the carbon is not allowed to enter the oil and water passages – this is particularly important for the lubrication system, as carbon could block the oil supply to the engine's components. Using adhesive tape and paper, seal the water, oil and bolt holes in the cylinder block.

26 To prevent carbon entering the gap between the pistons and bores, smear a little grease in the gap.

27 After cleaning each piston, use a small brush to remove all traces of grease and carbon from the gap, then wipe away the remainder with a clean rag. Clean all the pistons in the same way.

28 Check the mating surfaces of the cylinder block and the cylinder head for nicks, deep scratches and other damage (refer to the Note in paragraph 24). If slight, they may be removed carefully with a file, but if excessive, machining may be the only alternative to renewal.

29 If warpage of the cylinder head gasket surface is suspected, use a straight-edge to check it for distortion. Refer to Part D of this Chapter if necessary.

30 Ensure that the cylinder head bolt holes in the crankcase are clean and free of oil.

Cylinder head gasket selection

Piston protrusion	Gasket identification	Gasket thickness
0.55 to 0.60 mm	1 notch/hole	1.25 ± 0.04 mm
0.61 to 0.65 mm	2 notches/hole	1.30 ± 0.04 mm
0.66 to 0.70 mm	3 notches/hole	1.35 ± 0.04 mm
0.71 to 0.75 mm	4 notches/hole	1.40 ± 0.04 mm

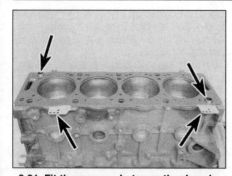

9.31 Fit the new gasket over the dowels, with the thickness identification holes at the front (arrowed)

Syringe or soak up any oil left in the bolt holes. This is most important in order that the correct bolt tightening torque can be applied, and to prevent the possibility of the block being cracked by hydraulic pressure when the bolts are tightened.

Refitting

31 Ensure that the cylinder head locating dowels are in place at the corners of the cylinder block, then fit the new cylinder head gasket over the dowels, ensuring that the identification holes are at the front **(see illustration)**. Take care to avoid damaging the gasket's rubber coating.

32 Lower the cylinder head into position on the gasket, ensuring that it engages correctly over the dowels.

33 Fit the new cylinder head bolts and screw them in as far as possible by hand.

34 Working in sequence **(see illustration)**, tighten all the cylinder head bolts to the specified Stage 1 torque using an E14 Torx socket.

35 Stage 2 involves tightening the bolts though an angle, rather than to a torque **(see illustration)**. Each bolt in sequence must be rotated through the specified angle – special angle gauges are available from tool outlets.

36 The remainder of the refitting procedure is a reversal of the removal procedure, bearing in mind the following points:

a) Refit the camshafts, rocker arms and hydraulic adjusters as described in Section 7.

b) Reconnect the exhaust front section to the exhaust manifold with reference to Chapter 4A.

c) Fit new high-pressure fuel delivery pipes as described in Chapter 4A.

d) Refit the inlet manifold/cylinder head cover with reference to Section 3.

e) Refit the air cleaner as described in Chapter 4A.

f) Refill the cooling system as described in Chapter 1.

g) Check and if necessary top-up the engine oil level and power steering fluid level as described in 'Weekly checks'.

h) Before starting the engine, read through the section on engine restarting after overhaul, at the end of Chapter 2D.

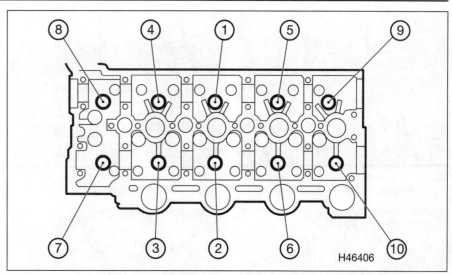

9.34 Cylinder head lower section bolt tightening sequence

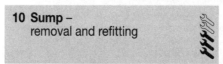

10 Sump –
removal and refitting

Note: *The full procedure outlined below must be followed so that the mating surfaces can be cleaned and prepared to achieve an oil-tight joint on reassembly.*

Removal

1 Apply the handbrake, then jack up the front of the vehicle and support it on axle stands (see *Jacking and vehicle support*). Undo the fasteners and remove the engine undershield **(see illustration 4.2)**.

2 Referring to Chapter 1 if necessary, drain the engine oil, then clean and refit the engine oil drain plug, tightening it to the specified torque wrench setting. We strongly advise renewing the oil filter element, also described in Chapter 1.

3 Pull the plastic cover on the top of the engine upwards from its mountings.

4 Slacken the hose clamps, undo the bracket bolt and remove the charge air pipe from the underside of the engine **(see illustration)**.

5 Remove the air conditioning compressor drivebelt as described in Chapter 1, then undo

9.35 Use an angle gauge for the Stage 2 torque setting

the mounting bolts and move the compressor to one side without disconnecting the refrigerant pipes. Suspend the compressor from the radiator crossmember using wires or straps.

6 Progressively unscrew the sump retaining bolts, including the 2 bolts securing the sump to the transmission housing. Don't forget the 4 bolts at the left-hand end accessed through the holes. Break the joint by carefully inserting a putty knife (or similar) between the sump and cylinder block **(see illustrations)**. Take care not to damage the sealing surfaces.

10.4 Undo the charge air pipe bracket bolt (arrowed)

10.6a Undo the 2 bolts securing the sump to the transmission (arrowed) . . .

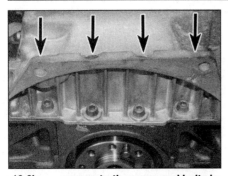

10.6b . . . access to the sump end bolts is through the holes (arrowed)

10.8 Apply sealant around the inside of the bolt holes

11.1a Slide off the crankshaft sprocket . . .

11.1b . . . and recover the crankshaft key

Refitting

7 On reassembly, thoroughly clean and degrease the mating surfaces of the cylinder block/crankcase and sump, removing all traces of sealant, then use a clean rag to

11.4 Oil level pipe bracket bolt (arrowed)

11.5b . . . undo the oil pump mounting bolts (arrowed), slide the assembly from the crankshaft . . .

wipe out the sump and the engine's interior.

8 Apply a 3 mm thick bead of sealant (Ford part No WSE-M4G323-A4) to the sump flange, making sure the bead is around the inside

11.5a Remove the sprocket key . . .

11.5c . . . and recover the O-ring between the sprocket and crankshaft (arrowed)

edge of the bolt holes. Do not allow the sealant to enter the bolt holes **(see illustration)**. **Note:** *The sump must be refitted within 4 minutes of applying the sealant.*

9 Refit the sump and fit the retaining bolts, tightening them by hand only at this stage.

10 Tighten the 2 bolts securing the sump to the transmission casing to the specified torque, then tighten the remaining bolts, gradually and evenly to the specified torque.

11 Lower the car to the ground. Wait at least 1 hour for the sealant to cure (or whatever time is indicated by the sealant manufacturer) before refilling the engine with oil. If removed, fit a new oil filter with reference to Chapter 1.

11 Oil pump – removal, inspection and refitting

Removal

1 Remove the timing belt as described in Section 5, then slide off the crankshaft sprocket **(see illustrations)**.

2 Remove the sump as described in Section 10.

3 Undo the retaining bolts and remove the cover and crankshaft seal. Note the original locations of the cover bolts – they are of different lengths.

4 Undo the bolt securing the oil level pipe **(see illustration)**.

5 Pull out the key from the crankshaft sprocket, then undo the pump mounting bolts, slide the pump, chain, and crankshaft sprocket from the end of the engine **(see illustrations)**. Recover the O-ring between the sprocket and crankshaft.

Inspection

6 Undo the retaining bolts and remove the cover from the oil pump **(see illustration)**. Note the location of any identification marks on the inner and outer rotors for refitting.

7 Unscrew the plug and remove the pressure relief valve, spring and plunger, clean out and check condition of components **(see illustration)**.

8 No specifications for the pump internal components are given by Ford.

9 Check the general condition of the oil

11.6 Oil pump cover bolts

pump, and in particular, its mating face to the cylinder block. If the mating face is damaged significantly, this may lead to oil loss (and a resulting drop in available oil pressure).

10 Inspect the rotors for obvious signs of wear or damage; at the time of writing, no new parts are available. If the pump is faulty, it must be renewed as a complete unit. Lubricate the rotors with fresh engine oil and refit them into the body, making sure that the identification marks are positioned as noted on removal.

11 If the oil pump has been removed as part of a major engine overhaul, it is assumed that the engine will have completed a substantial mileage. In this case, it is often considered good practice to fit a new (or reconditioned) pump as a matter of course. In other words, if the rest of the engine is being rebuilt, the engine has completed a large mileage, or there is any question as to the old pump's condition, it is preferable to fit a new oil pump.

Refitting

12 Before fitting the oil pump, ensure that the mating faces on the pump and the engine block are completely clean.

13 Fit the O-ring to the end of the crankshaft **(see illustration)**.

14 Engage the drive chain with the oil pump and crankshaft sprockets, then slide the crankshaft sprocket into place (aligning the slot in the sprocket with the keyway in the crankshaft) as the pump is refitted. Refit the crankshaft key.

15 Refit the mounting bolts and tighten them to the specified torque. Note that the front, left-hand bolt is slightly longer than the others.

16 Apply a 3 mm wide bead of silicone sealant (Ford part No WSE-M4G323-A4) to the oil seal carrier flange. Refit the cover and tighten the bolts to the specified torque. Note that the bolts must be tightened within 4 minutes of the sealant being applied.

17 Fit a new oil seal to the cover as described in Section 14.

18 Refit the bolt securing the oil level pipe.

19 The remainder of refitting is a reversal of removal, remembering to fit a new oil filter element, and replenish the engine oil.

12 Oil pressure warning light switch – removal and refitting

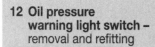

Removal

1 The switch is screwed into the oil filter housing **(see illustration)**. Access is from under the vehicle. Undo the fasteners and remove the engine undershield. To further improve access, undo the mounting bolts and move the air conditioning compressor to one side. Suspend the compressor from the radiator crossmember using wire or straps. There is no need to disconnect the refrigerant pipes.

11.7 Oil pressure relief valve plug

2 Disconnect the switch wiring plug.

3 Unscrew the switch from the housing; be prepared for some oil loss.

Refitting

4 Refitting is the reverse of the removal procedure; fit a new pressure switch sealing washer, and tighten the switch to the specified torque wrench setting.

5 Reconnect the switch wiring plug.

6 Refit all components removed for access to the switch.

7 Check the engine oil level and top-up as necessary (see *Weekly checks*).

8 Check for correct warning light operation, and for signs of oil leaks, once the engine has been restarted and warmed-up to normal operating temperature.

13 Oil cooler – removal and refitting

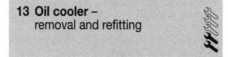

Note: *New sealing rings will be required on refitting – check for availability prior to commencing work.*

Removal

1 The cooler is fitted to the oil filter housing on the front of the cylinder block. Access is from under the vehicle. Undo the fasteners and remove the engine undershield. To further improve access, undo the mounting bolts and move the air conditioning compressor to one side. Suspend the compressor from the radiator crossmember using wire or straps.

12.1 Oil pressure warning switch (arrowed)

11.13 Fit the O-ring to the end of the crankshaft

There is no need to disconnect the refrigerant pipes.

2 Undo the 4 retaining bolts and detach the cooler from the housing **(see illustration)**. Recover the sealing rings and be prepared for oil/coolant spillage.

Refitting

3 Refitting is a reversal of removal, bearing in mind the following points:

 a) *Use new sealing rings.*

 b) *Tighten the cooler mounting bolts securely.*

 c) *On completion, lower the car to the ground. Check and if necessary top-up the oil and coolant levels, then start the engine and check for signs of oil or coolant leakage.*

14 Crankshaft oil seals – renewal

Timing belt end seal

1 Remove the timing belt as described in Section 5.

2 Slide the belt sprocket from the crankshaft, and recover the locating key from the groove on the crankshaft **(see illustrations 11.1a and 11.1b)**.

3 Note the fitted depth of the oil seal as a guide for fitting the new one.

4 Using a screwdriver or similar tool, carefully prise the oil seal from its location. Take care not to damage the oil seal contact surfaces

13.2 Oil cooler retaining bolts (arrowed)

14.4a Drill a small hole in the seal . . .

14.4b . . . insert a self-tapping screw and pull out the seal

14.7a Locate the new seal and guide over the end of the crankshaft . . .

14.7b . . . then drive the seal home until it's flush with the cover

14.11a Drill a hole in the seal . . .

14.11b . . . then insert a self-tapping screw and pull out the seal

or crankshaft. Alternatively, drill a small hole in the seal (taking care not to drill any deeper than necessary), then insert a self-tapping screw and use pliers to pull out the seal **(see illustrations)**.

5 Wipe clean the oil seal contact surfaces and seating, and clean up any sharp edges or burrs which might damage the new seal as it is fitted, or which might cause the seal to leak once in place.

6 No oil should be applied to the oil seal, which is made of PTFE. Ford technicians use a special seal-fitting tool (303-255/303-395), but an adequate substitute can be achieved using a large socket or piece of tubing of sufficient size to bear on the outer edge of the new seal. Note that the new seal is supplied with a guide which fits over the end of the crankshaft.

7 Locate the new seal (with guide still fitted) over the end of the crankshaft, using the tool

(see illustrations), socket, or tubing to press the seal squarely and fully into position, to the previously-noted depth. Remove the guide from the end of the crankshaft.

8 The remainder of reassembly is the reverse of the removal procedure, referring to the relevant text for details where required. Check for signs of oil leakage when the engine is restarted.

Flywheel end seal

9 Remove the transmission as described in Chapter 7, and the clutch assembly as described in Chapter 6.

10 Unbolt the flywheel (see Section 15).

11 Using a screwdriver or similar, carefully prise the oil seal from place. Take great care not to damage the seal seating area or the crankshaft sealing surface. Alternatively, punch or drill two small holes opposite each other in the oil seal, then screw a self-tapping

screw into each hole, and pull the screws with pliers to extract the seal **(see illustrations)**.

12 Clean the end of the crankshaft, polishing off any burrs or raised edges, which may have caused the seal to fail in the first place. Clean also the seal mating face on the engine block, using a suitable solvent for degreasing if necessary.

13 The new oil seal is supplied fitted with a locating sleeve, which must **not** be removed prior to fitting (it will drop out on its own when the seal is fitted). Do not lubricate the seal.

14 Offer the new seal into position, feeding the locating sleeve over the end of the crankshaft **(see illustration)**.

15 Ford technicians use a special tool (205-307) to pull the seal into position. In the absence of the tool, use a large socket/piece of tubing which bears only on the hard outer edge of the seal, and carefully tap the seal into position **(see illustration)**.

16 If the seal locating sleeve is still in position, remove it now.

17 The remainder of the reassembly procedure is the reverse of dismantling, referring to the relevant text for details where required. Check for signs of oil leakage when the engine is restarted.

15 Flywheel – removal, inspection and refitting

14.14 Locate the seal and locating sleeve over the end of the crankshaft

14.15 Press the seal in until it's flush with the surface

Removal

1 Remove the transmission as described

15.5 Flywheel retaining bolts

15.10 Note the locating dowel and corresponding hole (arrowed)

15.11 A simple home-made tool to lock the flywheel

in Chapter 7. Now is a good time to check components such as oil seals and renew them if necessary.

2 Remove the clutch as described in Chapter 6. Now is a good time to check or renew the clutch components and release bearing.

3 Use a centre-punch or paint to make alignment marks on the flywheel and crankshaft, to ensure correct alignment during refitting.

4 Prevent the flywheel from turning by locking the ring gear teeth, or by bolting a strap between the flywheel and the cylinder block/ crankcase. Slacken the Torx bolts evenly until all are free.

5 Remove each bolt in turn and ensure that new ones are obtained for reassembly; these bolts are subjected to severe stresses and so must be renewed, regardless of their apparent condition, whenever they are disturbed **(see illustration)**.

6 Withdraw the flywheel, remembering that it is very heavy – do not drop it.

Inspection

7 Clean the flywheel to remove grease and oil. Inspect the surface for cracks, rivet grooves, burned areas and score marks. Light scoring can be removed with emery cloth. Check for cracked and broken ring gear teeth. Lay the flywheel on a flat surface and use a straight-edge to check for warpage.

8 Clean and inspect the mating surfaces of the flywheel and the crankshaft. If the crankshaft seal is leaking, renew it (see Section 14) before refitting the flywheel. If the engine has covered a high mileage, it may be worth fitting a new seal as a matter if course, given the amount of work needed to access it.

9 Thoroughly clean the threaded bolt holes in the crankshaft, removing all traces of locking compound.

Refitting

10 Fit the flywheel to the crankshaft ensuring the dowel aligns with the hole in the crankshaft – it will fit only one way **(see illustration)**. Insert the new bolts.

11 Lock the flywheel by the method used on dismantling **(see illustration)**. Working in a diagonal sequence, tighten the bolts to the specified torque wrench setting.

12 Refit the clutch (Chapter 6) and the transmission (Chapter 7).

16 Engine/transmission mcuntings – inspection and renewal

Refer to Chapter 2A, Section 17, but use the torque wrench settings in this Chapter.

Chapter 2 Part D:
Engine removal and overhaul procedures

Contents

Degrees of difficulty

Easy, suitable for novice with little experience	**Fairly easy,** suitable for beginner with some experience	**Fairly difficult,** suitable for competent DIY mechanic	**Difficult,** suitable for experienced DIY mechanic	**Very difficult,** suitable for expert DIY or professional

Specifications

Note: *At the time of writing, some specifications for certain engines were not available. Where the relevant specifications are not given here, refer to your Ford dealer for further information.*

Cylinder head
Maximum gasket face distortion:
    1.6 litre engines . . . . 0.05 mm
    1.8 litre engines . . . . 0.06 mm
    2.0 litre engines . . . . 0.03 mm

Valves

	Inlet	Exhaust
Valve stem diameter:		
1.6 litre engines	5.485 +0.0, -0.015 mm	5.475 +0.0, -0.015 mm
1.8 litre engines	Not available	
2.0 litre engines	5.978 ± 0.009 mm	5.968 ± 0.009 mm

Cylinder block
Cylinder bore diameter (nominal):
    1.6 litre engines . . . . 75.00 mm
    1.8 litre engines . . . . 82.50 mm
    2.0 litre engines . . . . 85.00 mm

Piston rings
End gaps:
    1.6 litre engines:
        Top compression ring. . . . . 0.20 to 0.35 mm
        Second compression ring. . . . . 0.20 to 0.40 mm
        Oil control ring . . . . 0.80 to 1.00 mm
    1.8 litre engines:
        Top compression ring. . . . . 0.31 to 0.50 mm
        Second compression ring. . . . . 0.31 to 0.50 mm
        Oil control ring . . . . 0.25 to 0.58 mm
    2.0 litre engines:
        Top compression ring. . . . . 0.20 to 0.35 mm
        Second compression ring. . . . . 0.80 to 1.00 mm
        Oil control ring . . . . 0.25 to 0.50 mm

Crankshaft
Endfloat:
1.6 litre engines thrustwasher thickness . . . . 2.4 ± 0.05 mm
1.8 litre engines . . . . 0.11 to 0.37 mm
2.0 litre engines . . . . 0.07 to 0.32 mm
Maximum bearing journal out-of-round (all engines) . . . . 0.007 mm

1 General information

Included in this Part of Chapter 2 are details of removing the engine/transmission from the car and general overhaul procedures for the cylinder head, cylinder block/crankcase and all other engine internal components.

The information given ranges from advice concerning preparation for an overhaul and the purchase of parts, to detailed step-by-step procedures covering removal, inspection, renovation and refitting of engine internal components.

After Section 8, all instructions are based on the assumption that the engine has been removed from the car. For information concerning in-car engine repair, as well as the removal and refitting of those external components necessary for full overhaul, refer to Part A, B or C of this Chapter (as applicable) and to Section 5. Ignore any preliminary dismantling operations described in Part A, B or C that are no longer relevant once the engine has been removed from the car.

Apart from torque wrench settings, which are given at the beginning of Part A, B or C (as applicable), all specifications relating to engine overhaul are at the beginning of this Part of Chapter 2.

2 Engine overhaul – general information

It is not always easy to determine when, or if, an engine should be completely overhauled, as a number of factors must be considered.

High mileage is not necessarily an indication that an overhaul is needed, while low mileage does not preclude the need for an overhaul. Frequency of servicing is probably the most important consideration. An engine which has had regular and frequent oil and filter changes, as well as other required maintenance, should give many thousands of miles of reliable service. Conversely, a neglected engine may require an overhaul very early in its life.

Excessive oil consumption is an indication that piston rings, valve seals and/or valve guides are in need of attention. Make sure that oil leaks are not responsible before deciding that the rings and/or guides are worn. Perform a compression test, as described in Part A, B

or C of this Chapter, to determine the likely cause of the problem.

Check the oil pressure with a gauge fitted in place of the oil pressure switch, and compare it with that specified. If it is extremely low, the main and big-end bearings, and/or the oil pump, are probably worn out.

Loss of power, rough running, knocking or metallic engine noises, excessive valve gear noise, and high fuel consumption may also point to the need for an overhaul, especially if they are all present at the same time. If a complete service does not cure the situation, major mechanical work is the only solution.

An engine overhaul involves restoring all internal parts to the specification of a new engine. During an overhaul, the pistons and the piston rings are renewed. New main and big-end bearings are generally fitted; if necessary, the crankshaft may be renewed to restore the journals. The valves are also serviced as well, since they are usually in less-than-perfect condition at this point. While the engine is being overhauled, other components, such as the distributor, starter and alternator, can be overhauled as well. The end result should be an as-new engine that will give many trouble-free miles.

Note: *Critical cooling system components such as the hoses, thermostat and coolant pump should be renewed when an engine is overhauled. The radiator should be checked carefully, to ensure that it is not clogged or leaking. Also, it is a good idea to renew the oil pump whenever the engine is overhauled.*

Before beginning the engine overhaul, read through the entire procedure, to familiarise yourself with the scope and requirements of the job. Overhauling an engine is not difficult if you follow carefully all of the instructions, have the necessary tools and equipment, and pay close attention to all specifications. It can, however, be time-consuming. Plan on the car being off the road for a minimum of two weeks, especially if parts must be taken to an engineering works for repair or reconditioning. Check on the availability of parts and make sure that any necessary special tools and equipment are obtained in advance. Most work can be done with typical hand tools, although a number of precision measuring tools are required for inspecting parts to determine if they must be renewed. Often the engineering works will handle the inspection of parts and offer advice concerning reconditioning and renewal.

Always wait until the engine has been completely dismantled, and until all

components (especially the cylinder block/crankcase and the crankshaft) have been inspected, before deciding what service and repair operations must be performed by an engineering works. The condition of these components will be the major factor to consider when determining whether to overhaul the original engine, or to buy a reconditioned unit. Do not, therefore, purchase parts or have overhaul work done on other components until they have been thoroughly inspected. As a general rule, time is the primary cost of an overhaul, so it does not pay to fit worn or sub-standard parts.

As a final note, to ensure maximum life and minimum trouble from a reconditioned engine, everything must be assembled with care, in a spotlessly-clean environment.

3 Engine/transmission removal – methods and precautions

If you have decided that the engine must be removed for overhaul or major repair work, several preliminary steps should be taken.

Engine/transmission removal is extremely complicated and involved on these vehicles. It must be stated, that unless the vehicle can be positioned on a ramp, or raised and supported on axle stands over an inspection pit, it will be very difficult to carry out the work involved.

Cleaning the engine compartment and engine/transmission before beginning the removal procedure will help keep tools clean and organised.

An engine hoist will also be necessary. Make sure the equipment is rated in excess of the combined weight of the engine and transmission. Safety is of primary importance, considering the potential hazards involved in removing the engine/transmission from the car.

The help of an assistant is essential. Apart from the safety aspects involved, there are many instances when one person cannot simultaneously perform all of the operations required during engine/transmission removal.

Plan the operation ahead of time. Before starting work, arrange for the hire of or obtain all of the tools and equipment you will need. Some of the equipment necessary to perform engine/transmission removal and installation safely (in addition to an engine hoist) is as follows: a heavy duty trolley jack, complete sets of spanners and sockets as described in the rear of this manual, wooden blocks, and plenty of rags and cleaning solvent for

4.4a Prise forwards the clips (arrowed) . . .

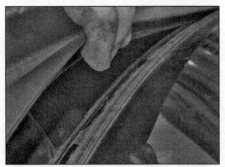

4.4b . . . then pull the scuttle cowling panel upwards from the base of the windscreen

4.4c Undo the bolt at each end (right-hand one arrowed) and pull the bulkhead extension panel forwards

mopping-up spilled oil, coolant and fuel. If the hoist must be hired, make sure that you arrange for it in advance, and perform all of the operations possible without it beforehand. This will save you money and time.

Plan for the car to be out of use for quite a while. An engineering machine shop or engine reconditioning specialist will be required to perform some of the work which cannot be accomplished without special equipment. These places often have a busy schedule, so it would be a good idea to consult them before removing the engine, in order to accurately estimate the amount of time required to rebuild or repair components that may need work.

During the engine/transmission removal procedure, it is advisable to make notes of the locations of all brackets, cable ties, earthing points, etc, as well as how the wiring harnesses, hoses and electrical connections are attached and routed around the engine and engine compartment. An effective way of doing this is to take a series of photographs of the various components before they are disconnected or removed; the resulting photographs will prove invaluable when the engine/transmission is refitted.

Always be extremely careful when removing and refitting the engine/transmission. Serious injury can result from careless actions. Plan ahead and take your time, and a job of this nature, although major, can be accomplished successfully.

On all Focus models, the engine must be removed complete with the transmission as an assembly. There is insufficient clearance in the engine compartment to remove the engine leaving the transmission in the vehicle. The assembly is removed by raising the front of the vehicle, and lowering the assembly from the engine compartment.
Note: *Such is the complexity of the power unit arrangement on these vehicles, and the variations that may be encountered according to model and optional equipment fitted, that the following should be regarded as a guide to the work involved, rather than a step-by-step procedure. Where differences are encountered, or additional component disconnection or removal is necessary, make notes of the work involved as an aid to refitting.*

4 Engine and transmission – removal, separation and refitting

Removal

1 Remove the battery (see Chapter 5), then undo the bolts and remove the battery tray.
2 Undo the 2 bolts securing the brake fluid remote reservoir (where fitted) to the engine compartment bulkhead.
3 Remove the wiper arms as described in Chapter 12.
4 Release the 5 clips and remove the windscreen cowl panel, then undo the bolt at each end, release the 2 clips and remove the bulkhead extension panel **(see illustrations)**.
5 Apply the handbrake, then jack up the front of the vehicle and support it on axle stands (see *Jacking and vehicle support*). Remove both front roadwheels and wheel arch liners. Also remove the undershield from beneath the engine and transmission where fitted.
6 Remove the engine top cover. To improve access, remove the bonnet as described in Chapter 11.
7 Drain the cooling system with reference to Chapter 1.
8 Drain the transmission oil as described in Chapter 7. Refit the drain plug, and tighten it to the specified torque setting.
9 If the engine is to be dismantled, drain the engine oil and remove the oil filter as described in Chapter 1. Clean and refit the drain plug, tightening it to the specified torque.

10 Refer to Chapter 8 and remove both front driveshafts.
11 Remove the air cleaner assembly as described in Chapter 4A (if not already done so).
12 Remove the intercooler as described in Chapter 4A.
13 Remove the radiator as described in Chapter 3.
14 Refer to Chapter 1 and remove the auxiliary drivebelt.
15 Release the clamp and disconnect the coolant supply hose from the expansion tank.
16 Disconnect the fuel supply pipe(s) at the right-hand side of the engine compartment **(see illustrations)**. Plug/cover the openings to prevent contamination.
17 On 1.8 litre engines, release the clamps, undo the retaining bolt, disconnect the MAP sensor wiring plug, then remove the intercooler outlet pipe.
18 Remove the engine management PCM as described in Chapter 4A. Note their fitted positions, then disconnect the engine/transmission harness wiring plugs and earth connections from the fusebox on the right-hand side of the engine compartment. Make a note of the harness routing. Also trace the wiring connectors back to the transmission and disconnect all engine related wiring and earth leads in this area, including the earth lead on the left-hand suspension turret, and the earth connections on the left-hand chassis member. Check that all the relevant connectors have been disconnected, and that the harness is

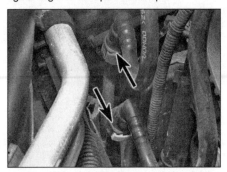

4.16a The fuel pipes (arrowed) are at the right-hand side of the engine compartment

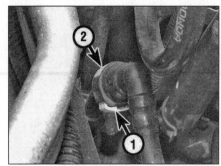

4.16b Prise out the clip (1) and depress the release tab (2) to disconnect the hose

4.19a Rotate the collar (arrowed) 30° anti-clockwise . . .

4.19b . . . and pull the hose from the connection

released from all the clips or ties. Move the harness to one side.

19 Rotate the collars approximately 30° anti-clockwise and disconnect the heater coolant hoses at the engine compartment bulkhead **(see illustrations)**. Note that when refitting the hoses, rotate the collars to the 'locked' position, then push the hoses onto the pipe stubs.

20 Release the clamps and remove the throttle body inlet pipe, the release the clamp, undo the mounting bolt and nut, then remove the turbocharger outlet pipe.

21 With reference to Chapter 4A, remove the front section of the exhaust pipe. On 2.0 litre models, undo the mounting nuts and remove the catalytic converter support bracket.

22 On 1.8 litre engines, undo the bolts, and remove the 'crash box' (where fitted) from the subframe behind the right-hand driveshaft location.

4.25 Depress the release tab (arrowed) and disconnect the vacuum pipe

4.29 Attach a hoist to the engine lifting eyes

23 Undo the bolts and remove the engine rear lower torque rod/movement limiter.

24 Disconnect the wiring plug, undo the retaining bolts and move the air conditioning compressor to one side (where fitted). There is no need to disconnect the refrigerant pipes. Suspend the compressor from the vehicle body using cable ties/straps to prevent any strain on the pipes.

25 Depress the release button and disconnect the vacuum pipe from the brake vacuum pump **(see illustration)**. Disconnect the vacuum feed pipe from the servo hose.

26 Disconnect the fluid supply pipe from the clutch slave cylinder as described in Chapter 6. Remove the clip and detach the pipe/hose from the retaining bracket **(see illustration)**. Plug the opening to prevent contamination.

27 Disconnect the selector cable(s) as described in Chapter 7.

28 Note their fitted positions and routing, then

4.26 Prise out the clip (arrowed) at the base of the pipe connection

4.31 Undo the left-hand mounting centre bolt (arrowed)

disconnect the various coolant hoses from the engine. Be prepared for fluid spillage.

29 Raise the front of the vehicle sufficiently high enough to be able to remove the engine/transmission assembly from underneath it. Position a workshop trolley jack under the engine/transmission, or attach an engine lifting hoist. Take the weight of the engine **(see illustration)**.

30 Refer to Chapter 2A and unbolt the right-hand engine mounting.

31 Unscrew and remove the left-hand engine/transmission mountings central bolt **(see illustration)**.

32 Make a final check that any components which would prevent the removal of the engine/transmission from the car have been removed or disconnected. Ensure that components such as the gearchange selector cables are secured so that they cannot be damaged on removal.

33 Carefully lower the assembly to the ground, making sure it clears the surrounding engine compartment components.

Separation

34 Remove the starter motor.

35 Remove the bolts securing the transmission to the engine.

36 With the aid of an assistant, draw the transmission off the engine. Once it is clear of the dowels, do not allow it to hang on the input shaft.

Refitting

37 Make sure that the clutch is correctly centred and that the clutch release components are fitted to the bellhousing. Do not apply any grease to the transmission input shaft, the guide sleeve, or the release bearing itself, as these components have a friction-reducing coating which does not require lubrication.

38 Manoeuvre the transmission squarely into position, and engage it with the engine dowels. Refit the bolts securing the transmission to the engine, and tighten them to the specified torque. Refit the starter motor.

39 The remainder of refitting is essentially a reversal of removal, noting the following points:

a) Tighten all fastenings to the specified torque and, where applicable, torque angle. Refer to the relevant Chapters of this manual for torque wrench settings not directly related to the engine.

b) Reconnect and if necessary, adjust the manual transmission selector cables as described in Chapter 7.

c) Refit the air cleaner assembly as described in Chapter 4A.

d) Refit the auxiliary drivebelt(s), then refill the engine with coolant and oil as described in Chapter 1.

e) Refill the transmission with lubricant if necessary as described in Chapter 7.

f) Refer to Section 20 before starting the engine.

5 Engine overhaul – dismantling sequence

1 It is much easier to dismantle and work on the engine if it is mounted on a portable engine stand. These stands can often be hired from a tool hire shop. Before the engine is mounted on a stand, the flywheel/driveplate should be removed, so that the stand bolts can be tightened into the end of the cylinder block/crankcase.

2 If a stand is not available, it is possible to dismantle the engine with it blocked up on a sturdy workbench, or on the floor. Be extra careful not to tip or drop the engine when working without a stand.

3 If you are going to obtain a reconditioned engine, all the external components must be removed first, to be transferred to the new engine (just as they will if you are doing a complete engine overhaul yourself). These components include the following:

a) Engine wiring harness and support brackets.
b) Alternator, power steering pump and air conditioning compressor mounting brackets (as applicable).
c) Coolant inlet and outlet housings.
d) Dipstick tube.
e) Fuel system components.
f) All electrical switches and sensors.
g) Inlet and exhaust manifolds and, where fitted, the turbocharger.
h) Oil filter and oil cooler.
i) Flywheel.

Note: When removing the external components from the engine, pay close attention to details that may be helpful or important during refitting. Note the fitted position of gaskets, seals, spacers, pins, washers, bolts, and other small items.

4 If you are obtaining a 'short' engine (which consists of the engine cylinder block/crankcase, crankshaft, pistons and connecting rods all assembled), then the cylinder head, sump, oil pump, and timing belt will have to be removed also.

5 If you are planning a complete overhaul, the engine can be dismantled, and the internal components removed, in the order given below, referring to Part A, B or C of this Chapter unless otherwise stated.

a) Inlet and exhaust manifolds (Chapter 4A).
b) Timing belt, sprockets and tensioner.
c) Coolant pump (Chapter 3).
d) Cylinder head.
e) Flywheel.
f) Sump.
g) Oil pump.
h) Pistons/connecting rods (Section 10 of this Chapter).
i) Crankshaft (Section 11 of this Chapter).

6 Before beginning the dismantling and overhaul procedures, make sure that you have all of the correct tools necessary. See *Tools and working facilities* for further information.

6 Cylinder head – dismantling

Note: New and reconditioned cylinder heads are available from the manufacturer, and from engine overhaul specialists. Be aware that some specialist tools are required for the dismantling and inspection procedures, and new components may not be readily available. It may therefore be more practical and economical for the home mechanic to purchase a reconditioned head, rather than dismantle, inspect and recondition the original head.

1 Remove the cylinder head as described in Part A, B or C of this Chapter (as applicable).

2 If not already done, remove the inlet and exhaust manifolds with reference to Chapter 4A.

Remove any remaining brackets or housings as required.

3 Remove the camshaft(s), tappets and rockers (as applicable) as described in Part A, B or C of this Chapter. On the DOHC engines, remove the camshaft drive chain guide from the cylinder head **(see illustration)**.

4 If not already done so, remove the glow plugs as described in Chapter 5.

5 On all models, using a valve spring compressor, compress each valve spring in turn until the split collets can be removed. Release the compressor, and lift off the spring retainer, spring and, where fitted, the spring seat. Using a pair of pliers, carefully extract the valve stem oil seal from the top of the guide. On 16-valve engines, the valve stem oil seal also forms the spring seat and is deeply recessed in the cylinder head. It is also a tight fit on the valve guide making it difficult to remove with pliers or a conventional valve stem oil seal removal tool. It can be easily removed, however, using a self-locking nut of suitable diameter screwed onto the end of a bolt and locked with a second nut. Push the nut down onto the top of the seal; the locking portion of the nut will grip the seal allowing it to be withdrawn from the top of the valve guide. Access to the valves is limited, and it may be necessary to make up an adapter out of metal tube – cut out a 'window' so that the valve collets can be removed **(see illustrations)**.

6 If, when the valve spring compressor is screwed down, the spring retainer refuses to free and expose the split collets, gently tap

6.3 Remove the camshaft drive chain guide – DOHC engines

6.5a Compress the valve spring using a spring compressor . . .

6.5b . . . then extract the collets and release the spring compressor

6.5c Remove the spring retainer . . .

6.5d . . . followed by the valve spring . . .

6.5e ... and the spring seat (not all models)

6.5f Remove the valve stem oil seal using a pair of pliers

6.5g Metal tube adapter for access to the valve collets

6.5h Secure a self-locking nut of suitable diameter to a long bolt, then use the tool to remove the valve stem oil seal

6.8 Place each valve and its associated components in a labelled bag

the top of the tool, directly over the retainer, with a light hammer. This will free the retainer.

7 Withdraw the valve from the combustion chamber. Remove the valve stem oil seal from the top of the guide, then lift out the spring seat where fitted.

8 It is essential that each valve is stored together with its collets, retainer, spring, and spring seat. The valves should also be kept in their correct sequence, unless they are so badly worn that they are to be renewed. If they are going to be kept and used again, place each valve assembly in a labelled polythene bag or similar small container **(see illustration)**. Note that No 1 valve is nearest to the transmission (flywheel) end on the 1.6 and 2.0 litre engines.

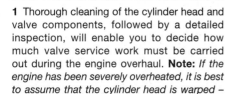

7 Cylinder head and valves – cleaning and inspection

1 Thorough cleaning of the cylinder head and valve components, followed by a detailed inspection, will enable you to decide how much valve service work must be carried out during the engine overhaul. **Note:** *If the engine has been severely overheated, it is best to assume that the cylinder head is warped – check carefully for signs of this.*

Cleaning

2 Scrape away all traces of old gasket material from the cylinder head.

3 Scrape away the carbon from the

combustion chambers and ports, then wash the cylinder head thoroughly with paraffin or a suitable solvent.

4 Scrape off any heavy carbon deposits that may have formed on the valves, then use a power-operated wire brush to remove deposits from the valve heads and stems.

Inspection

Note: *Be sure to perform all the following inspection procedures before concluding that the services of a machine shop or engine overhaul specialist are required. Make a list of all items that require attention.*

Cylinder head

5 Inspect the head very carefully for cracks, evidence of coolant leakage, and other damage. If cracks are found, a new cylinder head should be obtained. Use a straight-edge and feeler blade to check that the cylinder

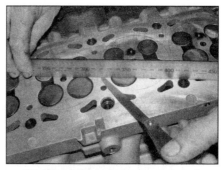

7.5 Check the cylinder head gasket surface for distortion

head gasket surface is not distorted **(see illustration)**. If it is, it may be possible to have it machined, provided that the cylinder head height is not significantly reduced.

6 Examine the valve seats in each of the combustion chambers. If they are severely pitted, cracked, or burned, they will need to be renewed or recut by an engine overhaul specialist. If they are only slightly pitted, this can be removed by grinding-in the valve heads and seats with fine valve-grinding compound, as described below. If in any doubt, have the cylinder head inspected by an engine overhaul specialist.

7 Check the valve guides for wear by inserting the relevant valve, and checking for side-to-side motion of the valve. A very small amount of movement is acceptable. If the movement seems excessive, remove the valve. Measure the valve stem diameter (see below), and renew the valve if it is worn. If the valve stem is not worn, the wear must be in the valve guide, and the guide must be renewed. The renewal of valve guides is best carried out by a Ford dealer or engine overhaul specialist, who will have the necessary tools available. Where no valve stem diameter is specified, seek the advice of a Ford dealer on the best course of action.

8 If renewing the valve guides, the valve seats should be recut or reground only *after* the guides have been fitted.

9 Examine the camshaft oil supply non-return valve (where fitted) in the oil feed bore at the timing belt end of the cylinder head. Check that the valve is not loose in the cylinder head and that the ball is free to move within the valve body. If the valve is a loose fit in its bore, or if there is any doubt about its condition, it should be renewed. The non-return valve can be removed (assuming it is not loose), using compressed air, such as that generated by a tyre foot pump. Place the pump nozzle over the oil feed bore of the camshaft bearing journal and seal the corresponding oil feed bore with a rag. Apply the compressed air and the valve will be forced out of its location in the underside of the cylinder head **(see illustrations)**. Fit the new non-return valve to its bore on the underside of the head ensuring it is fitted the correct way. Oil should be able to pass upwards through the valve to the camshafts, but the ball in the valve should prevent the oil from returning back to the cylinder block. Use a thin socket or similar to push the valve fully into position.

Valves

10 Examine the head of each valve for pitting, burning, cracks, and general wear. Check the valve stem for scoring and wear ridges. Rotate the valve, and check for any obvious indication that it is bent. Look for pits or excessive wear on the tip of each valve stem. Renew any valve that shows any such signs of wear or damage.

11 If the valve appears satisfactory at this stage, measure the valve stem diameter at several points using a micrometer **(see illustration)**. Any significant difference in the readings obtained indicates wear of the valve stem. Should any of these conditions be apparent, the valve must be renewed.

12 If the valves are in satisfactory condition, they should be ground (lapped) into their respective seats, to ensure a smooth, gas-tight seal. If the seat is only lightly pitted, or if it has been recut, fine grinding compound *only* should be used to produce the required finish. Coarse valve-grinding compound should *not* be used, unless a seat is badly burned or deeply pitted. If this is the case, the cylinder head and valves should be inspected by an expert, to decide whether seat recutting, or even the renewal of the valve or seat insert (where possible) is required.

13 Valve grinding is carried out as follows. Place the cylinder head upside-down on a bench.

14 Smear a trace of (the appropriate grade of) valve-grinding compound on the seat face, and press a suction grinding tool onto the valve head **(see illustration)**. With a semi-rotary action, grind the valve head to its seat, lifting the valve occasionally to redistribute the grinding compound. A light spring placed under the valve head will greatly ease this operation.

15 If coarse grinding compound is being used, work only until a dull, matt even surface is produced on both the valve seat and the valve, then wipe off the used compound, and repeat the process with fine compound. When a smooth unbroken ring of light grey matt finish is produced on both the valve and seat,

7.9a Apply compressed air to the oil feed bore of the inlet camshaft; seal the bore in the exhaust camshaft with a rag . . .

7.11 Measure the valve stem diameter with a micrometer

the grinding operation is complete. *Do not* grind-in the valves any further than absolutely necessary, or the seat will be prematurely sunk into the cylinder head.

16 When all the valves have been ground-in, carefully wash off *all* traces of grinding compound using paraffin or a suitable solvent, before reassembling the cylinder head.

Valve components

17 Examine the valve springs for signs of damage and discoloration. No minimum free length is specified by Ford, so the only way of judging valve spring wear is by comparison with a new component.

18 Stand each spring on a flat surface, and check it for squareness. If any of the springs are damaged, distorted or have lost their tension, obtain a complete new set of springs. It is normal to renew the valve springs as a matter of course if a major overhaul is being carried out.

7.9b . . . and the camshaft oil supply non-return valve will be ejected from the underside of the cylinder head

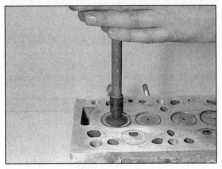

7.14 Grinding-in a valve

19 Renew the valve stem oil seals regardless of their apparent condition.

8 Cylinder head – reassembly

1 Working on the first valve assembly, refit the spring seat then dip the new valve stem oil seal in fresh engine oil. Locate the seal on the valve guide and press the seal firmly onto the guide using a suitable socket **(see illustrations)**.

2 Lubricate the stem of the first valve, and insert it in the guide **(see illustration)**.

3 Locate the valve spring on top of its seat, then refit the spring retainer.

4 Compress the valve spring, and locate the split collets in the recess in the valve stem. Release the compressor, then repeat the

8.1a Locate the valve stem oil seal (arrowed) on the valve guide . . .

8.1b . . . and press the seal firmly onto the guide using a suitable socket

8.1c On some engines, the valve stem oil seal is integral with the spring seat

8.2 Lubricate the stem of the valve and insert it into the guide

procedure on the remaining valves. Ensure that each valve is inserted into its original location. If new valves are being fitted, insert them into the locations to which they have been ground.

> **HAYNES HINT** Use a little dab of grease to hold the collets in position on the valve stem while the spring compressor is released.

5 With all the valves installed, support the cylinder head and, using a hammer and interposed block of wood, tap the end of each valve stem to settle the components.
6 Refit the camshafts, tappets and rocker arms (as applicable) as described in Part A, B or C of this Chapter.
7 Refit any remaining components using the

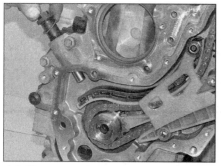

9.3 Unscrew the chain tensioner from the housing

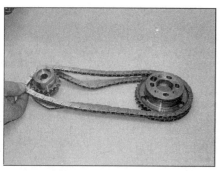

9.8 Two chains ('gemini') which run next to one another, offset by half a link

reverse of the removal sequence and with new seals or gaskets as necessary.
8 The cylinder head can then be refitted as described in Part A, B or C of this Chapter.

9 Fuel injection pump drive chain (1.8 litre models) – removal, inspection and refitting

Removal

1 With the engine removed from the vehicle, proceed as follows.
2 Remove the oil pump as described in Chapter 2B.
3 At the rear of the engine block, locate the drive chain hydraulic tensioner (below and behind the coolant pump). Using the hex in the top of the tensioner body, unscrew and extract the tensioner from the block (see illustration). Be prepared for a small amount of oil spillage as this is done.
4 Unscrew the two bolts securing the chain guides, then carefully slide the two sprockets simultaneously from their locations, and remove the complete chain, guide and sprocket assembly from the engine.

Inspection

5 Examine the guides for scoring or wear ridges, and for chipping or wear of the sprocket teeth (see illustration).
6 Check the chains for wear, which will be evident in the form of excess play between the links. If the chains can be lifted at either

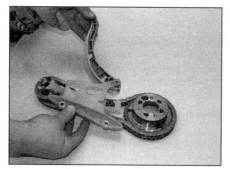

9.5 Examine the chain guides for wear

9.9 Tighten the chain guide retaining bolts

'end' of their run so that the sprocket teeth are visible, they have stretched excessively.
7 Check the chain tensioner for signs of wear, and renew if required.
8 At the time of writing, only the chain tensioner is available separately; if the chains or sprockets are worn, the complete assembly of sprockets, guides and chains must be purchased (see illustration). If possible, compare the old items with new components, or seek the advice of an engineering works, before concluding that renewal is necessary.

Refitting

9 Refitting is a reversal of removal, noting the following points:
  a) Tighten the chain guide retaining bolts securely to the specified torque (see illustration).
  b) Especially if a new chain and sprocket assembly has been fitted, lubricate it thoroughly with fresh engine oil.
  c) Refit the chain tensioner, and tighten it to the specified torque.
  d) Refit the oil pump as described in Chapter 2B.

10 Piston/connecting rod assembly – removal

1 Remove the cylinder head, sump and oil pump as described in Part A, B or C.
2 If there is a pronounced wear ridge at the top of any bore, it may be necessary to remove it with a scraper or ridge reamer, to avoid piston damage during removal. Such a ridge indicates excessive wear of the cylinder bore.
3 Using quick-drying paint, mark each connecting rod and big-end bearing cap with its respective cylinder number on the flat machined surface provided; if the engine has been dismantled before, note carefully any identifying marks made previously (see illustration).
4 Turn the crankshaft to bring pistons 1 and 4 to BDC (bottom dead centre).
5 Unscrew the nuts or bolts, as applicable from No 1 piston big-end bearing cap. Take off the cap, and recover the bottom half bearing shell (see illustration). If the bearing shells are to be re-used, tape the cap and the shell together.

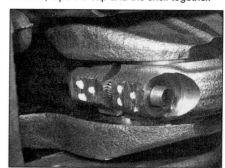

10.3 Connecting rod and big-end bearing cap identification marks (No 3 shown)

6 Where applicable, to prevent the possibility of damage to the crankshaft bearing journals, tape over the connecting rod stud threads **(see illustration)**.

7 Using a hammer handle, push the piston up through the bore, and remove it from the top of the cylinder block. Recover the bearing shell, and tape it to the connecting rod for safe-keeping.

8 Loosely refit the big-end cap to the connecting rod, and secure with the nuts/bolts – this will help to keep the components in their correct order.

9 Remove No 4 piston assembly in the same way.

10 Turn the crankshaft through 180° to bring pistons 2 and 3 to BDC (bottom dead centre), and remove them in the same way.

11 Crankshaft – removal

1 Remove the crankshaft sprocket and the oil pump as described in Part A, B or C of this Chapter (as applicable).

2 Remove the pistons and connecting rods, as described in Section 10. If no work is to be done on the pistons and connecting rods, there is no need to remove the cylinder head, or to push the pistons out of the cylinder bores. The pistons should just be pushed far enough up the bores so that they are positioned clear of the crankshaft journals.

3 Check the crankshaft endfloat as described in Section 14, then proceed as follows.

1.6 litre engines

4 Working around the inner periphery of the crankcase, unscrew the small bolts securing the crankshaft bearing cap housing to the base of the cylinder block. Note the correct fitted depth of the left-hand crankshaft oil seal in the cylinder block/bearing cap housing.

5 Working in the **reverse** of the tightening sequence, evenly and progressively slacken the ten large bearing cap housing retaining bolts by a turn at a time. Once all the bolts are loose, remove them from the housing. **Note:** *Prise up the two caps at the flywheel end of the housing to expose the two end main bearing bolts* **(see illustration)**.

6 With all the retaining bolts removed, tap around the outer periphery of the bearing cap housing using a soft-faced mallet to break the seal between the housing and cylinder block. Once the seal is released and the housing is clear of the locating dowels, lift it up and off the crankshaft and cylinder block **(see illustration)**. Recover the lower main bearing shells, and tape them to their respective locations in the housing. If the two locating dowels are a loose fit, remove them and store them with the housing for safe-keeping.

7 Lift out the crankshaft, and collect the left-hand oil seal.

8 Recover the upper main bearing shells,

10.5 Remove the big-end bearing shell and cap

10.6 To protect the crankshaft journals, tape over the connecting rod stud threads

and store them along with the relevant lower bearing shell. Also recover the two thrustwashers (one fitted either side of No 2 main bearing) from the cylinder block.

1.8 litre engines

9 Check the main bearing caps, to see if they are marked to indicate their locations. They should be numbered consecutively from the timing belt end of the engine – if not, mark them with number-stamping dies or a centre-punch. The caps will also have an embossed arrow pointing to the timing belt end of the engine **(see illustration)**. Noting, where applicable, the different fasteners (for the oil baffle nuts) used on caps 2 and 4, slacken the cap bolts a quarter-turn at a time each, starting with the left- and right-hand end caps and working toward the centre, until they can be removed by hand.

10 Gently tap the caps with a soft-faced hammer, then separate them from the cylinder

11.5 Prise up the two caps to expose the main bearing bolts at the flywheel end

11.9 Main bearing caps are marked with cylinder number and arrowhead

block/crankcase. If necessary, use the bolts as levers to remove the caps. Try not to drop the bearing shells if they come out with the caps.

11 Carefully lift the crankshaft out of the engine. It may be a good idea to have an assistant available, since the crankshaft is quite heavy. With the bearing shells in place in the cylinder block/crankcase and main bearing caps, return the caps to their respective locations on the block, or refit the lower crankcase, and tighten the bolts finger-tight. Leaving the old shells in place until reassembly will help prevent the bearing recesses from being accidentally nicked or gouged. New shells should be used on reassembly.

2.0 litre engines

12 Slacken and remove the retaining bolts, and remove the oil seal carrier from the timing belt end of the cylinder block, along with its gasket (where fitted) **(see illustration)**.

11.6 Remove the crankshaft bearing cap housing

11.12 Remove the oil seal housing from the right-hand end of the cylinder block

11.13a Remove the oil pump drive chain . . .

11.13b . . . then slide off the drive sprocket . . .

11.13c . . . and remove the Woodruff key from the crankshaft

13 Remove the oil pump drive chain, and slide the drive sprocket and spacer (where fitted) off the end of the crankshaft. Remove the Woodruff key, and store it with the sprocket for safe-keeping **(see illustrations)**.

14 The main bearing caps should be numbered 1 to 5, starting from the transmission (flywheel) end of the engine **(see illustration)**. If not, mark them accordingly using quick-drying paint. Also note the correct

fitted depth of the crankshaft oil seal in the bearing cap.
15 Slacken and remove the main bearing cap retaining bolts/nuts, and lift off each bearing cap. Recover the lower bearing shells, and tape them to their respective caps for safe-keeping. Also recover the lower thrust -washer halves from the side of No 2 main bearing cap **(see illustration)**. Remove the rubber sealing strips from the sides of No 1 main bearing cap, and discard them.
16 Lift out the crankshaft, and discard the oil seal **(see illustration)**.
17 Recover the upper bearing shells from the cylinder block, and tape them to their respective caps for safe-keeping **(see illustration)**. Remove the upper thrustwasher halves from the side of No 2 main bearing, and store them with the lower halves.

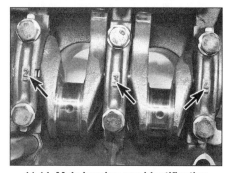

11.14 Main bearing cap identification markings (arrowed)

11.15 Note the thrustwasher (arrowed) fitted to the No 2 main bearing cap

12 Cylinder block/crankcase – cleaning and inspection

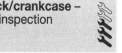

Cleaning

1 Remove all external components and electrical switches/sensors from the block. For complete cleaning, the core plugs should ideally be removed **(see illustrations)**. Drill a small hole in the plugs, then insert a self-tapping screw into the hole. Pull out the plugs by pulling on the screw with a pair of grips, or by using a slide hammer.
2 Where applicable, undo the retaining bolts

11.16 Lift out the crankshaft

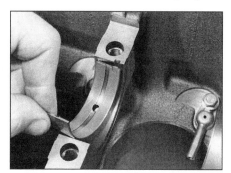

11.17 Remove the upper main bearing shells

12.1a Cylinder block core plugs (arrowed)

12.1b Remove the air conditioning compressor bracket

12.1c Remove the cylinder block ventilation/oil separator box

and remove the piston oil jet spray tubes from inside the cylinder block **(see illustration)**.

3 Scrape all traces of gasket from the cylinder block/crankcase, and from the main bearing ladder (where fitted), taking care not to damage the gasket/sealing surfaces.

4 Remove all oil gallery plugs (where fitted). The plugs are usually very tight – they may have to be drilled out, and the holes retapped. Use new plugs when reassembling.

5 If any of the castings are extremely dirty, all should be steam-cleaned.

6 After the castings are returned, clean all oil holes and oil galleries one more time. Flush all internal passages with warm water until the water runs clear. Dry thoroughly, and apply a light film of oil to all mating surfaces, to prevent rusting. On cast-iron block engines, also oil the cylinder bores. If you have access to compressed air, use it to speed up the drying process, and to blow out all the oil holes and galleries.

 Warning: Wear eye protection when using compressed air.

7 If the castings are not very dirty, you can do an adequate cleaning job with hot (as hot as you can stand), soapy water and a stiff brush. Take plenty of time, and do a thorough job. Regardless of the cleaning method used, be sure to clean all oil holes and galleries very thoroughly, and to dry all components well. On cast-iron block engines, protect the cylinder bores as described above, to prevent rusting.

8 All threaded holes must be clean, to ensure accurate torque readings during reassembly. To clean the threads, run the correct-size tap into each of the holes to remove rust, corrosion, thread sealant or sludge, and to restore damaged threads. If possible, use compressed air to clear the holes of debris produced by this operation.

9 Apply suitable sealant to the new oil gallery plugs, and insert them into the holes in the block. Tighten them securely. Apply suitable sealant to the new core plugs, and insert them into the holes in the block. Tap them into place with a close-fitting tube or socket.

10 Where applicable, clean the threads of the piston oil jet retaining bolt, and apply a drop of thread-locking compound to the bolt threads. Refit the piston oil jet spray tube to the cylinder block, and tighten its retaining bolt to the specified torque setting.

11 If the engine is not going to be reassembled right away, cover it with a large plastic bag to keep it clean; protect all mating surfaces and the cylinder bores as described above, to prevent rusting.

Inspection

12 Visually check the castings for cracks and corrosion. Look for stripped threads in the threaded holes. If there has been any history of internal water leakage, it may be worthwhile having an engine overhaul specialist check the cylinder block/crankcase with special

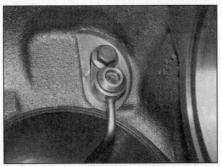

12.2 Piston cooling jets may be fitted to the base of each cylinder bore

equipment. If defects are found, have them repaired if possible, or renew the assembly.

13 Check each cylinder bore for scuffing and scoring. Check for signs of a wear ridge at the top of the cylinder, indicating that the bore is excessively worn.

14 If wear is suspected, have the cylinder bores measured by an automotive engineering workshop, who will be able to carry out the reboring, and supply suitable pistons/rings, etc, as applicable.

15 At the time of writing, it was not clear whether oversize pistons were available for all models. Consult your Ford dealer for the latest information on piston availability. If oversize pistons are available, then it may be possible to have the cylinder bores rebored and oversize pistons fitted. If oversize pistons are not available, and the bores are worn, renewal of the block is the only option.

13 Piston/connecting rod assembly – inspection

1 Before the inspection process can begin, the piston/connecting rod assemblies must be cleaned, and the original piston rings removed from the pistons.

2 Carefully expand the old rings over the top of the pistons. The use of two or three old feeler blades will be helpful in preventing the rings dropping into empty grooves **(see illustration)**. Be careful not to scratch the piston with the ends of the ring. The rings are brittle, and will snap if they are spread too

13.2 Remove the piston rings with the aid of feeler gauges

far. They are also very sharp – protect your hands and fingers. Note that the third ring incorporates an expander. Always remove the rings from the top of the piston.

3 Scrape away all traces of carbon from the top of the piston. A hand-held wire brush (or a piece of fine emery cloth) can be used, once the majority of the deposits have been scraped away.

4 Remove the carbon from the ring grooves in the piston, using an old ring. Break the ring in half to do this. Be careful to remove only the carbon deposits – do not remove any metal, and do not nick or scratch the sides of the ring grooves.

5 Once the deposits have been removed, clean the piston/connecting rod assembly with paraffin or a suitable solvent, and dry thoroughly. Make sure that the oil return holes in the ring grooves are clear.

6 If the pistons and cylinder bores are not damaged or worn excessively, and if the cylinder block does not need to be rebored, the original pistons can be refitted. Normal piston wear shows up as even vertical wear on the piston thrust surfaces, and slight looseness of the top ring in its groove. New piston rings should always be used when the engine is reassembled.

7 Carefully inspect each piston for cracks around the skirt, around the gudgeon pin holes, and at the piston ring 'lands' (between the ring grooves).

8 Look for scoring and scuffing on the piston skirt, holes in the piston crown, and burned areas at the edge of the crown. If the skirt is scored or scuffed, the engine may have been suffering from overheating, and/or abnormal combustion which caused excessively high operating temperatures. The cooling and lubrication systems should be checked thoroughly. Scorch marks on the sides of the pistons show that blow-by has occurred. A hole in the piston crown, or burned areas at the edge of the piston crown, indicates that abnormal combustion (pre-ignition, knocking, or detonation) has been occurring. If any of the above problems exist, the causes must be investigated and corrected, or the damage will occur again.

9 Corrosion of the piston, in the form of pitting, indicates that coolant has been leaking into the combustion chamber and/or the crankcase. Again, the cause must be corrected, or the problem may persist in the rebuilt engine.

10 On aluminium-block engines with wet liners, it is not possible to renew the pistons separately; pistons are only supplied with piston rings and a liner, as a part of a matched assembly. On iron-block engines, pistons can be purchased from a Ford dealer.

11 Examine each connecting rod carefully for signs of damage, such as cracks around the big-end and small-end bearings. Check that the rod is not bent or distorted. Damage is highly unlikely, unless the engine has been seized or badly overheated. Detailed checking

13.15a Prise out the circlip . . .

13.15b . . . and withdraw the gudgeon pin

of the connecting rod assembly can only be carried out by a Ford dealer or engine repair specialist with the necessary equipment.

12 The big-end cap bolts/nuts must be renewed as a complete set prior to refitting. This should be done after the big-end bearing running clearance check has been carried out.

13 The gudgeon pins are of the floating type, secured in position by two circlips. The pistons and connecting rods can be separated as described in the following paragraphs.

14 Before separating the piston and connecting rod, check the position of the valve recesses or markings on the piston crown in relation to the connecting rod big-end bearing shell cut-outs and make a note of the orientation.

15 Using a small flat-bladed screwdriver, prise out the circlips, and push out the gudgeon pin **(see illustrations)**. Hand pressure should be sufficient to remove the pin. Identify the piston and rod to ensure correct reassembly. Discard the circlips – new ones *must* be used on refitting.

16 Examine the gudgeon pin and connecting rod small-end bearing for signs of wear or damage. Wear can be cured by renewing both the pin and bush. Bush renewal, however, is a specialist job – press facilities are required, and the new bush must be reamed accurately.

17 The connecting rods themselves should not be in need of renewal, unless seizure or some other major mechanical failure has occurred. Check the alignment of the

connecting rods visually, and if the rods are not straight, take them to an engine overhaul specialist for a more detailed check.

18 Examine all components, and obtain any new parts from your Ford dealer. If new pistons are purchased, they will be supplied complete with gudgeon pins and circlips. Circlips can also be purchased individually.

19 Position the piston in relation to the connecting rod big-end bearing shell cut-outs as noted during separation.

20 Apply a smear of clean engine oil to the gudgeon pin and slide it into the piston and through the connecting rod small-end. Check that the piston pivots freely on the rod, then secure the gudgeon pin in position with two new circlips. Ensure that each circlip is correctly located in its groove in the piston.

14 Crankshaft – inspection

Checking endfloat

1 If the crankshaft endfloat is to be checked, this must be done when the crankshaft is installed in the cylinder block/crankcase, but is free to move.

2 Check the endfloat using a dial gauge in contact with the end of the crankshaft. Push the crankshaft fully one way, and then zero the gauge. Push the crankshaft fully the other way, and check the endfloat. The

result can be compared with the specified amount, and will give an indication as to whether new thrustwashers are required **(see illustration)**.

3 If a dial gauge is not available, feeler gauges can be used. First push the crankshaft fully towards the flywheel end of the engine, then use feeler gauges to measure the gap between the web and the thrustwasher **(see illustration)**.

Inspection

4 Clean the crankshaft using paraffin or a suitable solvent, and dry it, preferably with compressed air if available. Be sure to clean the oil holes with a pipe cleaner or similar probe, to ensure that they are not obstructed.

⚠️ **Warning: Wear eye protection when using compressed air.**

5 Check the main and big-end bearing journals for uneven wear, scoring, pitting and cracking.

6 Big-end bearing wear is accompanied by distinct metallic knocking when the engine is running (particularly noticeable when the engine is pulling from low speed) and by some loss of oil pressure.

7 Main bearing wear is accompanied by severe engine vibration and rumble – getting progressively worse as engine speed increases – and again by loss of oil pressure.

8 Check the bearing journal for roughness by running a finger lightly over the bearing surface. Any roughness (which will be accompanied by obvious bearing wear) indicates that the crankshaft requires regrinding (where possible) or renewal.

9 If the crankshaft has been reground, check for burrs around the crankshaft oil holes (the holes are usually chamfered, so burrs should not be a problem unless regrinding has been carried out carelessly). Remove any burrs with a fine file or scraper, and thoroughly clean the oil holes as described previously.

10 Have the crankshaft inspected and measured by an automotive engineering workshop, who will be able to carry out any necessary repairs, and supply relevant parts.

11 Check the oil seal contact surfaces at each end of the crankshaft for wear and damage. If the seal has worn a deep groove in the surface of the crankshaft, consult an engine overhaul specialist; repair may be possible, but otherwise a new crankshaft will be required.

12 Ford produce a set of undersize bearing shells for both the main and big-end bearings on most engines. Where the crankshaft journals have not already been reground, it may be possible to have the crankshaft reconditioned, and to fit undersize shells. If no undersize shells are available and the crankshaft has worn beyond the specified limits, the crankshaft will have to be renewed. Consult your Ford dealer or engine specialist for further information on parts availability.

14.2 Check the crankshaft endfloat using a DTI gauge . . .

14.3 . . . or with feeler gauges

15 Main and big-end bearings – inspection

1 Even though the main and big-end bearings should be renewed during the engine overhaul, the old bearings should be retained for close examination, as they may reveal valuable information about the condition of the engine. The bearing shells are graded by thickness, the grade of each shell being indicated by the colour code marked on it.

2 Bearing failure can occur due to lack of lubrication, the presence of dirt or other foreign particles, overloading the engine, or corrosion (**see illustration**). Regardless of the cause of bearing failure, the cause must be corrected (where applicable) before the engine is reassembled, to prevent it from happening again.

3 When examining the bearing shells, remove them from the cylinder block/crankcase, the main bearing ladder/caps (as appropriate), the connecting rods and the connecting rod big-end bearing caps. Lay them out on a clean surface in the same general position as their location in the engine. This will enable you to match any bearing problems with the corresponding crankshaft journal. *Do not* touch any shell's bearing surface with your fingers while checking it, or the delicate surface may be scratched.

4 Dirt and other foreign matter gets into the engine in a variety of ways. It may be left in the engine during assembly, or it may pass through filters or the crankcase ventilation system. It may get into the oil, and from there into the bearings. Metal chips from machining operations and normal engine wear are often present. Abrasives are sometimes left in engine components after reconditioning, especially when parts are not thoroughly cleaned using the proper cleaning methods. Whatever the source, these foreign objects often end up embedded in the soft bearing material, and are easily recognised. Large particles will not embed in the bearing, and will score or gouge the bearing and journal. The best prevention for this cause of bearing failure is to clean all parts thoroughly, and keep everything spotlessly-clean during engine assembly. Frequent and regular engine oil and filter changes are also recommended.

5 Lack of lubrication (or lubrication breakdown) has a number of interrelated causes. Excessive heat (which thins the oil), overloading (which squeezes the oil from the bearing face) and oil leakage (from excessive bearing clearances, worn oil pump or high engine speeds) all contribute to lubrication breakdown. Blocked oil passages, which usually are the result of misaligned oil holes in a bearing shell, will also oil-starve a bearing, and destroy it. When lack of lubrication is the cause of bearing failure, the bearing material is wiped or extruded from the steel backing of the bearing. Temperatures may increase to the point where the steel backing turns blue from overheating.

6 Driving habits can have a definite effect on bearing life. Full-throttle, low-speed operation (labouring the engine) puts very high loads on bearings, tending to squeeze out the oil film. These loads cause the bearings to flex, which produces fine cracks in the bearing face (fatigue failure). Eventually, the bearing material will loosen in pieces, and tear away from the steel backing.

7 Short-distance driving leads to corrosion of bearings, because insufficient engine heat is produced to drive off the condensed water and corrosive gases. These products collect in the engine oil, forming acid and sludge. As the oil is carried to the engine bearings, the acid attacks and corrodes the bearing material.

8 Incorrect bearing installation during engine assembly will lead to bearing failure as well. Tight-fitting bearings leave insufficient bearing running clearance, and will result in oil starvation. Dirt or foreign particles trapped behind a bearing shell result in high spots on the bearing, which lead to failure.

9 *Do not* touch any shell's bearing surface with your fingers during reassembly; there is a risk of scratching the delicate surface, or of depositing particles of dirt on it.

10 As mentioned at the beginning of this Section, the bearing shells should be renewed as a matter of course during engine overhaul; to do otherwise is false economy.

16 Engine overhaul – reassembly sequence

1 Before reassembly begins, ensure that all new parts have been obtained, and that all necessary tools are available. Read through the entire procedure to familiarise yourself with the work involved, and to ensure that all items necessary for reassembly of the engine are at hand. In addition to all normal tools and materials, thread-locking compound will be needed. A suitable tube of liquid sealant will also be required for the joint faces that are fitted without gaskets. It is recommended that Ford's own products are used, which are specially formulated for this purpose; the relevant product names are quoted in the text of each Section where they are required.

2 In order to save time and avoid problems, engine reassembly can be carried out in the following order:

a) *Crankshaft (Section 18).*
b) *Piston/connecting rod assemblies (Section 19).*
c) *Oil pump (see Part A, B or C – as applicable).*
d) *Sump (see Part A, B or C – as applicable).*
e) *Flywheel (see Part A, B or C – as applicable).*
f) *Cylinder head (see Part A, B or C – as applicable).*
g) *Timing belt tensioner and sprockets,*

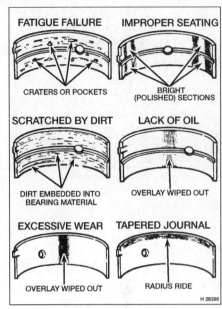

15.2 Typical bearing failures

and timing belt (see Part A, B or C – as applicable).
h) *Engine external components.*

3 At this stage, all engine components should be absolutely clean and dry, with all faults repaired. The components should be laid out (or in individual containers) on a completely clean work surface.

17 Piston rings – refitting

1 Before fitting new piston rings, the ring end gaps must be checked as follows.

2 Lay out the piston/connecting rod assemblies and the new piston ring sets, so that the ring sets will be matched with the same piston and cylinder during the end gap measurement and subsequent engine reassembly.

3 Insert the top ring into the first cylinder, and push it down the bore using the top of the piston. This will ensure that the ring remains square with the cylinder walls. Position the ring near the bottom of the cylinder bore, at the lower limit of ring travel. Note that the top and second compression rings are different. The second ring is easily identified by the step on its lower surface, and by the fact that its outer face is tapered.

4 Measure the end gap using feeler gauges.

5 Repeat the procedure with the ring at the top of the cylinder bore, at the upper limit of its travel, and compare the measurements with the figures given in the Specifications (**see illustration**). Where no figures are given, seek the advice of a Ford dealer or engine reconditioning specialist.

6 If the gap is too small (unlikely if genuine Ford parts are used), it must be enlarged, or

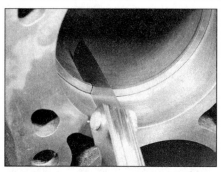

17.5 Measure the piston ring end gap with feeler gauges

the ring ends may contact each other during engine operation, causing serious damage. Ideally, new piston rings providing the correct end gap should be fitted. As a last resort, the end gap can be increased by filing the ring ends very carefully with a fine file. Mount the file in a vice equipped with soft jaws, slip the ring over the file with the ends contacting the file face, and slowly move the ring to remove material from the ends. Take care, as piston rings are sharp, and are easily broken.

7 With new piston rings, it is unlikely that the end gap will be too large. If the gaps are too large, check that you have the correct rings for your engine and for the particular cylinder bore size.

8 Repeat the checking procedure for each ring in the first cylinder, and then for the rings in the remaining cylinders. Remember to keep rings, pistons and cylinders matched up.

9 Once the ring end gaps have been checked and if necessary corrected, the rings can be fitted to the pistons.

10 Fit the piston rings using the same technique as for removal. Fit the bottom (oil control) ring first, and work up. When fitting the oil control ring, first insert the expander (where fitted), then fit the ring with its gap positioned 180° from the expander gap. Ensure that the second compression ring is fitted the correct way up, with its identification mark (either a dot of paint or the word TOP stamped on the ring surface) at the top, and the stepped surface at the bottom **(see illustration)**. Arrange the gaps of the top and second compression rings 120° either side of the oil control ring gap. **Note:** *Always follow any instructions supplied with the new piston ring sets – different manufacturers may specify different procedures. Do not mix up the top and second compression rings, as they have different cross-sections.*

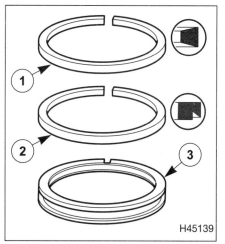

17.10 Piston ring details (typical)

1 *Top compression ring*
2 *2nd compression ring*
3 *Oil scraper ring assembly*

18.7 Place the thrustwashers each side of the No 2 bearing upper location

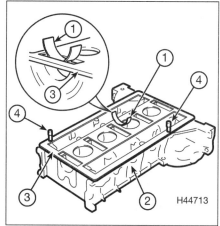

18.5 Main bearing shell fitment – 1.6 litre engine

1 *Bearing shell*
2 *Main bearing ladder*
3 *Ford tool No 303-245*
4 *Aligning pins*

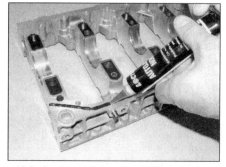

18.8 Apply a thin bead of RTV sealant to the bearing cap housing mating surface

18 Crankshaft – refitting

New main bearing shells

1 To ensure that the main bearing running clearance is correct, the bearing shells are supplied in various thicknesses or grades. The grades are indicated by a colour-coding marked on the edge of each shell. The grade of the new bearing shells required (either standard size or undersize) is selected using the reference marks on the cylinder block and on the crankshaft. The cylinder block marks identify the diameter of the bearing bores in the block, and the crankshaft marks identify the diameter of the crankshaft journals.

2 Note that on the engines described in this Manual, the upper shells are all of the same size, and the running clearance is controlled by fitting a lower bearing shell of the required thickness.

3 Numerous grades of standard and oversize bearing shells are available, depending on the engine type, year of manufacture, and country of export. Using the cylinder block and crankshaft reference marks together with the crankshaft journal diameter, a Ford dealer or engine overhaul specialist will be able to supply the correct bearing shells to give the required bearing running clearance for each journal.

Final crankshaft refitting

4 Crankshaft refitting is the first major step in engine reassembly. It is assumed at this point that the cylinder block/crankcase and crankshaft have been cleaned, inspected and repaired or reconditioned as necessary. Position the engine upside-down.

1.6 litre engines

5 Place the bearing shells in their locations. If new shells are being fitted, ensure that all traces of protective grease are cleaned off using paraffin. Wipe dry the shells with a lint-free cloth. The upper bearing shells all have a grooved surface, whereas the lower shells have a plain surface. It's essential that the lower bearing shells are centrally located in the bearing cap housing/ladder. To ensure this use a Ford tool (No 303-245) positioned over the housing/ladder, and insert the bearing shells through the slots in the tool **(see illustration)**.

6 Liberally lubricate each bearing shell in the cylinder block with clean engine oil then lower the crankshaft into position.

7 Insert the thrustwashers to either side of No 2 main bearing upper location and push them around the bearing journal until their edges are horizontal **(see illustration)**. Ensure that the oilway grooves on each thrustwasher face outwards (away from the bearing journal).

8 Thoroughly degrease the mating surfaces of the cylinder block and the crankshaft bearing

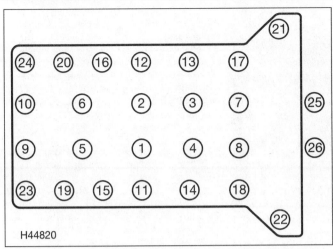

18.11 Main bearing cap housing/ladder retaining bolt tightening sequence

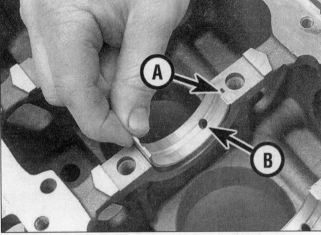

18.18a Ensure the tab (A) and oil hole (B) are correctly aligned when refitting the shells

cap housing. Apply a thin bead of silicone sealant (Ford part No WSE-M4G323-A4) to the bearing cap housing mating surface **(see illustration)**.

9 Lubricate the lower bearing shells with clean engine oil, then refit the bearing cap housing, ensuring that the shells are not displaced, and that the locating dowels engage correctly.

10 Install the ten large diameter, and sixteen smaller diameter crankshaft bearing cap housing retaining bolts, and screw them in until they are just making contact with the housing.

11 Working in sequence, tighten the bolts to the torque settings given in the Specifications **(see illustration)**.

12 With the bearing cap housing in place, check that the crankshaft rotates freely.

13 Refit the piston/connecting rod assemblies to the crankshaft as described in Section 19.

14 Refit the oil pump and sump.

15 Fit a new crankshaft left-hand oil seal, then refit the flywheel.

16 Where removed, refit the cylinder head, crankshaft sprocket and timing belt.

1.8 litre engines

17 If they're still in place, remove the old bearing shells from the block and the main bearing caps. Wipe the bearing recesses with a clean, lint-free cloth. They must be kept spotlessly clean.

18 Clean the backs of the new main bearing shells. Fit the shells with an oil groove in each main bearing location in the block. Note the thrustwashers integral with the No 3 (centre) upper main bearing shell, or the thrustwasher halves fitted either side of No 3 upper main bearing location. Fit the other shell from each bearing set in the corresponding main bearing cap. Make sure the tab on each bearing shell fits into the notch in the block or cap/lower crankcase. Also, the oil holes in the block must line up with the oil holes in the bearing shell **(see illustrations)**. Don't hammer the shells into place, and don't nick or gouge the bearing faces.

19 Clean the bearing surfaces of the shells in the block, then apply a thin, uniform layer of clean molybdenum disulphide-based grease, engine assembly lubricant, or clean engine oil to each surface **(see illustration)**. Coat the thrustwasher surfaces as well.

20 Lubricate the crankshaft oil seal journals with molybdenum disulphide-based grease, engine assembly lubricant, or clean engine oil.

21 Make sure the crankshaft journals are clean, then lay the crankshaft back in place in the block **(see illustration)**.

22 Refit and tighten the main bearing caps as follows:

18.18b Note the thrustwashers fitted to the No 3 main bearing shell

18.19 Oil the bearing shells before fitting the crankshaft

a) Clean the bearing surfaces of the shells in the caps, then lubricate them. Refit the caps in their respective positions, with the arrows pointing to the timing belt end of the engine.

b) Working on one cap at a time, from the centre main bearing outwards (and ensuring that each cap is tightened down squarely and evenly onto the block), tighten the main bearing cap bolts to the specified torque wrench setting **(see illustration)**.

23 Rotate the crankshaft a number of times by hand, to check for any obvious binding.

24 Check the crankshaft endfloat (see Sec-

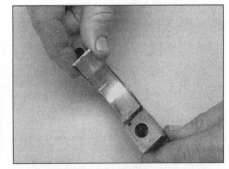

18.18c Make sure the tab on the cap bearing shell engages correctly

18.21 Lower the crankshaft gently into place

18.22 Tighten the main bearing cap bolts

18.31 Apply sealant to the No 1 main bearing cap mating face on the cylinder block, around the sealing strip holes in the corners

tion 14). It should be correct if the crankshaft thrustwashers/thrust control bearing(s) aren't worn or damaged, or have been renewed.

25 Refit the crankshaft left-hand oil seal carrier and install a new seal (Chapter 2B).

18.33 Use 2 metal strips (arrowed) to hold the sealing strips in place as the bearing cap is fitted

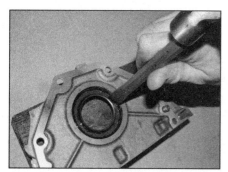

18.38a Drive out the old oil seal . . .

18.26 Ensure the oil grooves on each thrustwasher are facing outwards from the No 2 main bearing location

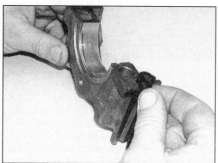

18.32 Fit the sealing strips to the No 1 main bearing cap

2.0 litre engines

26 Using a little grease, stick the upper thrustwashers to each side of the No 2 main bearing upper location. Ensure that the

18.34 Trim off the ends of the bearing cap sealing strips, so that they protrude by approximately 1.0 mm

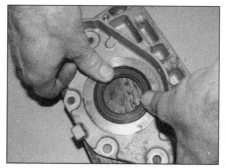

18.38b . . . then press in the new one to the previously-noted depth

oilway grooves on each thrustwasher face outwards (away from the cylinder block) **(see illustration)**.

27 Place the bearing shells in their locations. If new shells are being fitted, ensure that all traces of protective grease are cleaned off using paraffin. Wipe dry the shells and connecting rods with a lint-free cloth. Liberally lubricate each bearing shell in the cylinder block/crankcase and cap with clean engine oil.

28 Lower the crankshaft into position so that Nos 2 and 3 cylinder crankpins are at TDC; Nos 1 and 4 cylinder crankpins will be at BDC, ready for fitting No 1 piston. Check the crankshaft endfloat, referring to Section 14.

29 Lubricate the lower bearing shells in the main bearing caps with clean engine oil. Make sure that the locating lugs on the shells engage with the corresponding recesses in the caps.

30 Fit main bearing caps Nos 2 to 5 to their correct locations, ensuring that they are fitted the correct way round (the bearing shell tab recesses in the block and caps must be on the same side). Insert the bolts/nuts, tightening them only loosely at this stage.

31 Apply a small amount of sealant to the No 1 main bearing cap mating face on the cylinder block, around the sealing strip holes **(see illustration)**.

32 Locate the tab of each sealing strip over the pins on the base of No 1 bearing cap, and press the strips into the bearing cap grooves. It is now necessary to obtain two thin metal strips, of 0.25 mm thickness or less, in order to prevent the strips moving when the cap is being fitted. Ford garages use the tool shown, which acts as a clamp. Metal strips (such as old feeler blades) can be used, provided all burrs which may damage the sealing strips are first removed **(see illustration)**.

33 Where applicable, oil both sides of the metal strips, and hold them on the sealing strips. Fit the No 1 main bearing cap, insert the bolts loosely, then carefully pull out the metal strips in a horizontal direction, using a pair of pliers **(see illustration)**.

34 Tighten all the main bearing cap bolts/nuts evenly to the specified torque. Using a sharp knife, trim off the ends of the No 1 bearing cap sealing strips, so that they protrude above the cylinder block/crankcase mating surface by approximately 1.0 mm **(see illustration)**.

35 Fit a new crankshaft left-hand oil seal as described in Part C of this Chapter.

36 Refit the piston/connecting rod assemblies to the crankshaft as described in Section 19.

37 Refit the Woodruff key, then slide on the oil pump drive sprocket and spacer (where fitted), and locate the drive chain on the sprocket.

38 Ensure that the mating surfaces of the right-hand oil seal carrier and cylinder block are clean and dry. Note the correct fitted depth of the oil seal then, lever or drive out the old seal from the housing. If preferred, a new oil seal can be pressed into the housing at this stage **(see illustrations)**.

39 Apply a smear of suitable silicone sealant (Ford part No WSE-M4G323-A4) to the oil seal carrier mating surface. Ensure that the locating dowels are in position, then slide the carrier over the end of the crankshaft and into position on the cylinder block (**see illustrations**). Tighten the carrier retaining bolts to the specified torque.

40 If not already done, fit a new crankshaft right-hand oil seal as described in Part C of this Chapter.

41 Ensuring that the drive chain is correctly located on the sprocket, refit the oil pump and sump as described in Part C of this Chapter.

42 Where removed, refit the cylinder head as described in Part C of this Chapter.

19 Pistons/connecting rods – refitting

Note: *New big-end cap nuts/bolts must be used on refitting.*

1 Note that the following procedure assumes that the crankshaft and main bearing ladder/caps are in place.

2 Clean the backs of the bearing shells, and the bearing locations in both the connecting rod and bearing cap.

All engines except 1.6 litre

3 Press the bearing shells into their locations, ensuring that the tab on each shell engages in the notch in the connecting rod and cap. Take care not to touch any shell's bearing surface with your fingers (**see illustration**).

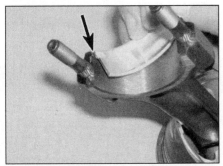

19.3 Ensure the bearing shell tab (arrowed) locates correctly in the cut-out

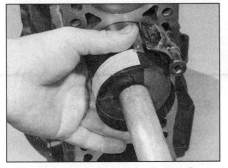

19.7 Tap the piston into the bore using a hammer handle

18.39a Apply the sealant . . .

All engines

4 Lubricate the cylinder bores, the pistons, and piston rings, then lay out each piston/connecting rod assembly in its respective position.

5 Start with assembly No 1. Make sure that the piston rings are still spaced as described in Section 17, then clamp them in position with a piston ring compressor.

6 Insert the piston/connecting rod assembly into the top of cylinder/liner No 1, ensuring the piston is correctly positioned as follows.

a) On 1.6 and 1.8 litre engines, ensure that the DIST mark or arrow on the piston crown is towards the timing belt end of the engine.

b) On 2.0 litre diesel engines, ensure that the valve recesses on the piston crown are towards the rear of the cylinder block.

7 Once the piston is correctly positioned, using a block of wood or hammer handle against the piston crown, tap the assembly into the cylinder/liner until the piston crown is flush with the top of the cylinder/liner (**see illustration**).

All engines except 1.6 litre

8 Ensure that the bearing shell is still correctly installed. Liberally lubricate the crankpin and both bearing shells. Taking care not to mark the cylinder/liner bores, pull the piston/connecting rod assembly down the bore and onto the crankpin. Refit the big-end bearing cap and fit the new nuts, tightening them finger-tight at first (**see illustration**). Note that the faces with the identification marks must match (which means that the bearing shell locating tabs abut each other).

19.8 Fit the big-end bearing cap, ensuring it is fitted the right-way around, and fit the new nuts

18.39b . . . and refit the oil seal housing

9 Tighten the bearing cap retaining nuts evenly and progressively to the specified torque setting.

1.6 litre engines

10 On these engines, then connecting rod is made in one piece, then the big-end bearing cap is 'cracked' off. This ensures that the cap fits onto the connecting rod only in one position, and with maximum rigidity. Consequently, there are no locating notches for the bearing shells to fit into.

11 To ensure that the big-end bearing shells are centrally located in the connecting rod and cap, two special tools are available from Ford (part No 303-736). These half-moon shaped tools are pressed in from either side of the rod/cap and locate the shell exactly in the centre (**see illustration**). Fit the shells into the connecting rods and big-end caps and lubricate them with plenty of clean engine oil.

12 Pull the connecting rods and pistons down the bores and onto the crankshaft journals. Fit the big-end caps – they will only fit properly one way round (see paragraph 10), and insert the new bolts.

13 Tighten the bolts to the specified torque settings.

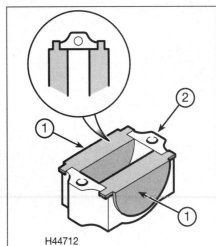

H44712

19.11 Big-end bearing shell positioning – 1.6 litre engine

1 Ford tool No 303-736
2 Bearing shell in the cap

All engines

14 Once the bearing cap retaining nuts have been correctly tightened, rotate the crankshaft. Check that it turns freely; some stiffness is to be expected if new components have been fitted, but there should be no signs of binding or tight spots.

15 Refit the cylinder head and oil pump as described in Part A, B or C of this Chapter (as applicable).

20 Engine – initial start-up after overhaul

1 With the engine refitted in the vehicle, double-check the engine oil and coolant levels. Make a final check that everything has been reconnected, and that there are no tools or rags left in the engine compartment.

2 Prime the fuel system (refer to Chapter 4A). Although the system is self-priming, it will help if the ignition is switched on and off several times before attempting to start the engine in order to purge air from the system.

3 Turn the engine on the starter until the oil pressure warning light goes out.

4 Fully depress the accelerator pedal, turn the ignition key to position M, and wait for the preheating warning light to go out.

5 Start the engine, noting that this may take a little longer than usual, due to the fuel system components having been disturbed.

6 While the engine is idling, check for fuel, water and oil leaks. Don't be alarmed if there are some odd smells and smoke from parts getting hot and burning off oil deposits.

7 Assuming all is well, keep the engine idling until hot water is felt circulating through the top hose, then switch off the engine.

8 After a few minutes, recheck the oil and coolant levels as described in *Weekly Checks*, and top-up as necessary.

9 Note that there is no need to retighten the cylinder head bolts once the engine has first run after reassembly.

10 If new pistons, rings or crankshaft bearings have been fitted, the engine must be treated as new, and run-in for the first 500 miles. Do not operate the engine at full-throttle, or allow it to labour at low engine speeds in any gear. It is recommended that the oil and filter be changed at the end of this period.

Chapter 3
Cooling, heating and air conditioning systems

Contents

Degrees of difficulty

Easy, suitable for novice with little experience	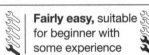	**Fairly easy,** suitable for beginner with some experience	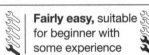	**Fairly difficult,** suitable for competent DIY mechanic	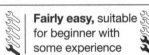	**Difficult,** suitable for experienced DIY mechanic		**Very difficult,** suitable for expert DIY or professional	

Specifications

System pressure

Pressure test .... 1.3 to 1.5 bars approximately – see cap for actual value

Expansion tank filler cap

Pressure rating .... 1.3 to 1.5 bars approximately – see cap for actual value

Thermostat

1.6 litre engine .... 88°C
1.8 litre and 2.0 litre:
    Starts to open....................................... 92°C
    Fully-open.. 99°C

Air conditioning system

Refrigerant R134a
Refrigerant quantity .... 600 g
Refrigerant oil.. Ford WSH-M1C231-B
Refrigerant oil capacity:
    When refilling .... 200 ml
    When renewing the condenser........................... 30 ml
    When renewing the evaporator .... 30 ml
    When renewing the accumulator/dehydrator................. 90 ml
    When renewing the compressor:
        If the oil drained from the faulty compressor is less than 150 ml.. 150 ml
        If the oil drained from the faulty compressor is more than 150 ml. 200 ml
    When renewing the refrigerant pipes .... 200 ml

Torque wrench settings

	Nm	lbf ft
Air conditioning compressor mounting bolts	24	18
Air conditioning high pressure cut-off switch	10	7
Coolant by-pass pipe retaining bolts:		
1.8 litre engine	48	35
2.0 litre engine	18	13
Coolant by-pass valve bolts (2.0 litre engine only).	6	4
Coolant outlet connector	20	15
Coolant pump bolts:		
1.6 litre engine	10	7
1.8 litre engine:		
Lower bolt	23	17
Upper bolts	10	7
2.0 litre engine	16	12
Coolant pump pulley bolts	24	18
Cylinder head temperature sensor (1.8 litre engine only)	20	15
Door check strap bolts	23	17
Door hinge bolts	15	11
Facia crossmember bolts:		
Inner	20	15
Outer	25	18
Side bolts	80	59
Radiator mounting bracket-to-subframe bolts	25	18
Refrigerant line connection	8	6
Refrigerant line to compressor	20	15
Refrigerant line to evaporator	25	18
Thermostat cover bolts:		
1.8 litre engine	9	7
2.0 litre engine	6	4
Thermostat housing bolts/nuts:		
1.6 litre engine:		
Front bolts	4	3
Rear bolts	7	5
1.8 litre engine	23	17
2.0 litre engine	10	7

1 General information

⚠ Warning: DO NOT attempt to remove the expansion tank filler cap, or to disturb any part of the cooling system, while it or the engine is hot, as there is a very great risk of scalding. If the expansion tank filler cap must be removed before the engine and radiator have fully cooled down (even though this is not recommended) the pressure in the cooling system must first be released. Cover the cap with a thick layer of cloth, to avoid scalding, and slowly unscrew the filler cap until a hissing sound can be heard. When the hissing has stopped, showing that pressure is released, slowly unscrew the filler cap further until it can be removed; if more hissing sounds are heard, wait until they have stopped before unscrewing the cap completely. At all times, keep well away from the filler opening.

⚠ Warning: Do not allow coolant to come in contact with your skin, or with the painted surfaces of the vehicle. Rinse off spills immediately with plenty of water. Never leave coolant lying around in an open container, or in a puddle in the driveway or on the garage floor.

Children and pets are attracted by its sweet smell, but coolant is fatal if ingested.

⚠ Warning: If the engine is hot, the electric cooling fan may start rotating even if the engine is not running, so be careful to keep hands, hair and loose clothing well clear when working in the engine compartment.

The cooling system is of pressurised semi-sealed type with the inclusion of an expansion tank to accept coolant displaced from the system when hot and to return it when the system cools.

Water-based coolant is circulated around the cylinder block and head by the coolant pump which is driven by the engine timing belt. As the coolant circulates around the engine it absorbs heat as it flows then, when hot, it travels out into the radiator to pass across the matrix. As the coolant flows across the radiator matrix, air flow created by the forward motion of the vehicle cools it, and it returns to the cylinder block. Airflow through the radiator matrix is assisted by a two-speed electric fan, which is controlled by the engine management system ECM.

A thermostat is fitted to control coolant flow through the radiator. When the engine is cold, the thermostat valve remains closed so that the coolant flow which occurs at normal operating temperatures through the radiator matrix is interrupted.

As the coolant warms up, the thermostat valve starts to open and allows the coolant flow through the radiator to resume.

The engine temperature will always be maintained at a constant level (according to the thermostat rating) whatever the ambient air temperature.

Most models have an oil cooler mounted on the sump/cylinder block – this is basically a heat exchanger with a coolant supply, to take heat away from the oil in the sump.

The vehicle interior heater operates by means of coolant from the engine cooling system. Coolant flow through the heater matrix is constant; temperature control being achieved by blending cool air from outside the vehicle with the warm air from the heater matrix, in the desired ratio.

Air entering the passenger compartment is filtered by a pleated paper filter element, sometimes known as a pollen filter. Also available instead of a pollen filer is a multifilter, which is a carbon impregnated filter which absorbs incoming smells, etc. With this system a pollution sensor monitors the quality of the incoming air, and opens and closes the recirculation flaps accordingly.

The standard climate control (air conditioning) systems are described in detail in Section 11.

Available as options are additional electric and fuel-fired cabin and engine block heaters. These can be remotely operated, or programmed to operate for a suitable period before the vehicle is required.

2 Engine coolant (antifreeze) – general information

![warning triangle] **Warning: Engine coolant (antifreeze) contains monoethylene glycol and other constituents, which are toxic if taken internally. They can also be absorbed into the skin after prolonged contact.**

Note: *Refer to Chapter 1 for further information on coolant renewal.*

The cooling system should be filled with a water/monoethylene glycol-based coolant solution, of a strength which will prevent freezing down to at least –25°C, or lower if the local climate requires it. Coolant also provides protection against corrosion, and increases the boiling point.

The cooling system should be maintained according to the schedule described in Chapter 1. If the engine coolant used is old or contaminated it is likely to cause damage, and encourage the formation of corrosion and scale in the system. Use coolant which is to Ford's specification and to the correct concentration.

Before adding the coolant, check all hoses and hose connections, because coolant tends to leak through very small openings. Engines don't normally consume coolant, so if the level goes down, find the cause and correct it.

The engine coolant concentration should be between 40% and 55%. If the concentration drops below 40% there will be insufficient protection, this must then be brought back to specification. Hydrometers are available at most automotive accessory shops to test the coolant concentration.

3 Cooling system hoses – disconnection and renewal

Note: *Refer to the warnings given in Section 1 of this Chapter before starting work.*

3.3 You can buy special tools specifically designed to release spring type hose clamps

1 If the checks described in Chapter 1 reveal a faulty hose, it must be renewed as follows.
2 First drain the cooling system (see Chapter 1); if the coolant is not due for renewal, the drained coolant may be re-used, if it is collected in a clean container.
3 To disconnect any hose, use a pair of pliers to release the spring clamps (or a screwdriver to slacken screw-type clamps), then move them along the hose clear of the union. Carefully work the hose off its stubs **(see illustration)**. The hoses can be removed with relative ease when new – on an older car, they may have stuck.
4 If a hose proves stubborn, try to release it by rotating it on its unions before attempting to work it off. Gently prise the end of the hose with a blunt instrument (such as a flat-bladed screwdriver), but do not apply too much force, and take care not to damage the pipe stubs or hoses. Note in particular that the radiator hose unions are fragile; do not use excessive force when attempting to remove the hoses. If all else fails, cut the hose with a sharp knife, then slit it so that it can be peeled off in two pieces. While expensive, this is preferable to buying a new radiator. Check first, however, that a new hose is readily available.
5 When refitting a hose, first slide the clamps onto the hose, then work the hose onto its unions. If the hose is stiff, use soap (or washing-up liquid) as a lubricant, or soften it by soaking it in boiling water, but take care to prevent scalding.
6 Work each hose end fully onto its union,

then check that the hose is settled correctly and is properly routed. Slide each clip along the hose until it is behind the union flared end, before tightening it securely.
7 Refill the system with coolant (see Chapter 1).
8 Check carefully for leaks as soon as possible after disturbing any part of the cooling system.

4 Thermostat – removal, testing and refitting

Note: *Refer to the warnings given in Section 1 of this Chapter before starting work.*

Removal

1 Drain the cooling system (see Chapter 1). If the coolant is relatively new or in good condition, drain it into a clean container and re-use it.

1.6 litre engines

2 Remove the air cleaner assembly as described in Chapter 4A.
3 The thermostat housing is located at the left-hand end of the cylinder head. Release the clips and disconnect the coolant hoses from the thermostat housing **(see illustration)**.
4 Disconnect the wiring plug from the engine coolant temperature sensor.
5 Undo the coolant bypass pipe retaining bolt.
6 Undo the 4 retaining bolts and remove the thermostat housing **(see illustration)**. Note that the thermostat is integral with the housing. If the thermostat is faulty, the housing must be renewed.

1.8 litre engines

7 Remove the plastic cover from the top of the engine **(see illustration)**.
8 The thermostat cover is located at the front of the engine cylinder block. Undo the 3 retaining bolts and move the cover to one side **(see illustration)**.
9 Note the position of the air bleed valve (where fitted), and how the thermostat is installed (ie, which end is facing outwards), then pull the thermostat and rubber seal from

4.3 Release the clips and disconnect the coolant hoses from the housing

4.6 Undo the bolts (arrowed) and detach the thermostat housing

4.7 Pull the plastic cover upwards to release it

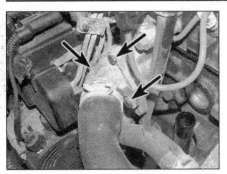

4.8 Undo the thermostat cover bolts (arrowed)

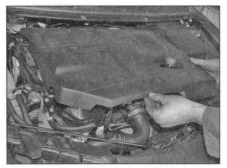

4.10 Pull the plastic cover upwards to release it

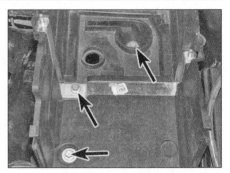

4.11 Undo the 3 bolts (arrowed) and remove the battery tray

place. Discard the rubber seal – a new one must be fitted.

2.0 litre engines

10 Remove the plastic cover from the top of the engine **(see illustration)**. The thermostat housing is located at the left-hand end of the cylinder head.
11 Remove the battery as described in Chapter 5, then undo the bolts and remove the battery tray **(see illustration)**.
12 Undo the retaining nuts and remove the support bracket at the left-hand end of the thermostat housing **(see illustration)**.
13 Release the clamps and disconnect the hoses from the thermostat housing.
14 Disconnect the wiring plug(s) from the thermostat housing.
15 Undo the 4 retaining nuts and remove the housing **(see illustrations)**. Examine the rubber seal and renew if necessary. Note that the thermostat is integral with the housing – if faulty the complete assembly must be renewed.

Testing

General

16 Before assuming the thermostat is to blame for a cooling system problem, check the coolant level (see *Weekly checks*), the auxiliary drivebelt tension and condition (see Chapter 1) and the temperature gauge operation.
17 If the engine seems to be taking a long time to warm up (based on heater output or temperature gauge operation), the thermostat may be stuck open.

18 If the engine runs hot, use your hand to check the temperature of the radiator top hose. If the hose isn't hot, but the engine is, the thermostat is probably stuck closed, preventing the coolant inside the engine from escaping to the radiator.
19 If the radiator top hose is hot, it means that the coolant is flowing and the thermostat is open. Consult the *Fault finding* Section at the end of this manual to assist in tracing possible cooling system faults.

Thermostat test

Note: *The following only applies to the 1.8 litre engine with a traditional thermostat.*
Note: *Frankly, if there is any question about the operation of the thermostat, it's best to renew it – they are not usually expensive items. Testing involves heating in, or over, an open pan of boiling water, which carries with it the risk of scalding. A thermostat which has seen more than five years' service may well be past its best already.*
20 If the thermostat remains in the open position at room temperature, it is faulty, and must be renewed as a matter of course.
21 To test it fully, suspend the (closed) thermostat on a length of string in a container of cold water, with a thermometer beside it; ensure that neither touches the side of the container.
22 Heat the water, and check the temperature at which the thermostat begins to open; compare this value with that specified. Checking the fully-open temperature may not be possible in an open container, if it is higher than the boiling point of water at atmospheric

pressure. Remove the thermostat and allow it to cool down; check that it closes fully.
23 If the thermostat does not open and close as described, if it sticks in either position, or if it does not open at the specified temperature, it must be renewed.

Refitting

24 Refitting is the reverse of the removal procedure, noting the following points:
 a) *Clean the mating surfaces carefully, and renew the thermostat's sealing ring/ gasket.*
 b) *Fit the thermostat in the same position as noted on removal.*
 c) *Tighten the thermostat cover/housing bolts/nuts to the specified torque wrench setting.*
 d) *Remake all the coolant hose connections, then refill the cooling system as described in Chapter 1.*
 e) *Start the engine and allow it to reach normal operating temperature, then check for leaks and proper thermostat operation.*

---

5 Radiator electric cooling fan
 – testing, removal and refitting

Note: *Refer to the warnings given in Section 1 of this Chapter before starting work.*

Testing

1 The radiator cooling fan is controlled by the engine management system's ECM, acting on the information received from the cylinder

4.12 Undo the nuts and move the support bracket to one side

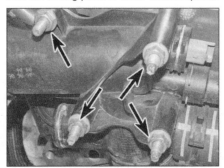

4.15a Thermostat housing retaining nuts (arrowed)

4.15b Renew the thermostat housing sealing ring

5.8a Undo the bolt and prise out the 4 scrivets . . .

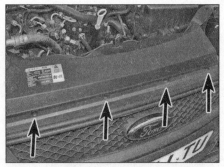

5.8b . . . located at the front edge of the air deflector panel (arrowed)

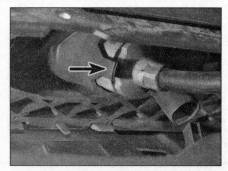

5.9a Release the clip each side of the lock cylinder (arrowed)

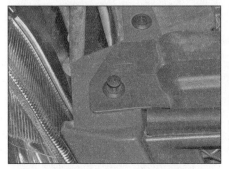

5.9b Undo the scrivet each side of the radiator grille

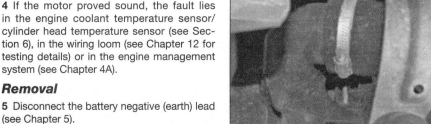

5.11a Undo the fasteners (arrowed) and remove the engine undershield

5.11b Undo the bolts (left-side bolts arrowed) and remove the radiator shield

head temperature sensor and engine coolant temperature sensor.

2 First, check the relevant fuses and relays (see Chapter 12).

3 To test the fan motor, unplug the electrical connector, and use fused jumper wires to connect the fan directly to the battery. If the fan still does not work, renew the motor.

4 If the motor proved sound, the fault lies in the engine coolant temperature sensor/ cylinder head temperature sensor (see Section 6), in the wiring loom (see Chapter 12 for testing details) or in the engine management system (see Chapter 4A).

Removal

5 Disconnect the battery negative (earth) lead (see Chapter 5).

1.6 litre engines

6 Remove the radiator as described in Section 7.

7 Disconnect the wiring plug, then depress the clips and detach the cooling fan and shroud from the radiator.

1.8 and 2.0 litre engines

8 Undo the bolts and prise out the 4 scrivets, release the 2 clips, then detach the air deflector panel from above the radiator grille **(see illustrations)**.

9 Release the clips and detach the lock cylinder from the radiator grille, then undo the scrivet each side, and remove the radiator grille **(see illustrations)**.

10 Raise the front of the vehicle and support it securely on axle stands (see *Jacking and vehicle support*).

11 Undo the fasteners and remove the engine undershield, followed by the shield under the radiator **(see illustrations)**.

12 Slacken the clamps and remove the inlet hose from the intercooler **(see illustration)**.

13 Release the radiator lower coolant hose

5.12 Slacken the clamp and disconnect the inlet hose from the intercooler – viewed from under the left-hand side of the vehicle

5.14a Radiator support bracket bolts (arrowed)

from the clip on the cooling fan shroud **(see illustration)**.

14 Undo the radiator support bracket front retaining bolts, and substitute them with M8 x 30 mm bolts, leaving at least 15 mm of thread exposed **(see illustrations)**.

5.13 Release the hose from the cooling fan shroud clip

5.14b Substitute the front mounting bolts with M8 x 30 mm ones

5.17 Undo the intercooler outlet hose bolt (arrowed) – viewed through the right-hand headlight aperture

15 Remove the radiator support bracket rear retaining bolts.

16 Unplug the cooling fan electrical connector, and release the connector from the fan shroud.

17 Remove the right-hand headlight as described in Chapter 12, then undo the bolt securing the intercooler outlet hose to the radiator **(see illustration)**.

18 Slacken the clamps and remove the outlet hose from the intercooler.

19 Depress the clip each side, lift the cooling fan and shroud upwards from the retaining brackets and manoeuvre it rearwards and downwards from place **(see illustration)**.

Refitting

20 Refitting is the reverse of the removal procedure, noting the following points:

a) Ensure the intercooler hoses are clean on

6.2 Unbolt and remove the crankcase vent

6.5 Disconnect the wiring plug and remove the sensor (arrowed)

5.19 Depress the clip each side (arrowed), and lift the cooling fan shroud upwards

the inside. If they are greasy/oily, they will not grip the intercooler/pipes.

b) Ensure that the shroud is settled correctly at all four mounting points before finally clipping into position.

---

6 Coolant system electronic components – removal and refitting

Cylinder head temperature sensor

Note: *Only the 1.8 litre engine is fitted with this sensor.*

1 Remove the plastic cover from the top of the engine **(see illustration 4.7)**.

2 Disconnect the hoses, then undo the retaining bolt and remove the crankcase vent oil separator from the end of the cylinder head **(see illustration)**.

6.9 Slide out the clip (arrowed) and remove the coolant temperature sensor – 1.6 litre engines

3 Undo the 2 retaining bolts and remove the crash shield above the fuel filter **(see illustration)**.

4 Disconnect the fuel filter wiring plug, then release the clips securing the fuel hoses and move the fuel filter to one side.

5 Disconnect the wiring plug, unclip the plug from the bracket, then unscrew the cylinder head temperature sensor from place **(see illustration)**.

6 Refitting is a reversal of removal. Tighten the sensor to the specified torque.

Coolant temperature sensor

Note: *Refer to the warnings given in Section 1 of this Chapter before starting work.*

7 Drain the cooling system (see Chapter 1). If the coolant is relatively new or in good condition, drain it into a clean container and re-use it.

1.6 litre engines

8 Remove the air cleaner assembly as described in Chapter 4A.

9 The sensor is fitted to the thermostat housing at the left-hand end of the cylinder head. Disconnect the sensor wiring plug, pull out the retaining clip, and remove the sensor **(see illustration)**. Renew the sensor seal if necessary.

10 Refitting is a reversal of removal.

2.0 litre engines

11 Remove the battery as described in Chapter 5, then undo the bolts and remove the battery tray **(see illustration 4.11)**.

12 Prise out the retaining clip, and disconnect the coolant hose from the heater to the thermostat housing.

13 Disconnect the sensor wiring plug, pull out the retaining clip, and remove the engine coolant temperature sensor **(see illustration)**. Renew the sensor seal if necessary.

14 Refitting is a reversal of removal.

Coolant shut-off valve

Note: *This valve is only fitted to 2.0 litre engines*

15 The coolant shut-off valve is controlled by the engine management ECM, and limits coolant flow to the coolant expansion tank during the engine warm-up phase. It's located in the feed pipe from the thermostat housing to the tank.

6.13 Slide out the clip (arrowed) and remove the coolant temperature sensor – 2.0 litre engines

7.9 Intercooler mounting bolt (right-hand side bolt arrowed)

7.10a Radiator lower hose (arrowed) . . .

7.10b . . . and upper hose (viewed through the left-hand headlight aperture)

16 To remove the valve, begin by draining the cooling system as described in Chapter 1, or be prepared for coolant spillage as the hoses are disconnected.

17 Disconnect the valve wiring plug, then release the clips and disconnect the hoses from the valve.

18 Undo the retaining bolts and remove the valve.

19 Refitting is the reversal of removal.

Coolant by-pass valve

Note: *This valve is only fitted to 2.0 litre engines*

20 The coolant by-pass valve is controlled by the engine management ECM, and limits the coolant flow to the coolant pump during the engine warm-up phase. It's located on the top of the thermostat housing.

21 To remove the valve, begin by draining the cooling system as described in Chapter 1.

22 Remove the brake vacuum pump as described in Chapter 9.

23 Disconnect the wiring plug, then undo the 2 retaining bolts and remove the by-pass valve. Renew the valve O-ring seals if necessary.

24 Refitting is a reversal of removal.

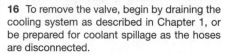

| 7 | Radiator and expansion tank – removal, inspection and refitting |

Note: *Refer to the warnings given in Section 1 of this Chapter before starting work.*

Radiator

Note: *If leakage is the reason for removing the radiator, bear in mind that minor leaks can often be cured using a radiator sealant added to the coolant with the radiator in situ.*

Removal

1 Drain the coolant system as described in Chapter 1.

2 To provide greater clearance for the radiator to be lowered and removed, ensure that the handbrake is firmly applied, then raise and support the front of the car on axle stands (see *Jacking and vehicle support*). Remove the splash shield under the radiator **(see illustration 5.11b)**.

3 Undo the 4 bolts, prise out the scrivets, then release the clips and detach the air

deflector panel from above the radiator grille **(see illustration 5.8a and 5.8b)**.

4 Release the clips and detach the lock cylinder from the radiator grille **(see illustration 5.9a)**. Undo the 2 scrivets, release the clips and remove the radiator grille.

5 On models with air conditioning, depress the lower clips securing the condenser to the radiator, then lift the condenser slightly and secure it to the bonnet slam panel with cables ties/string.

6 Remove the headlights as described in Chapter 12.

7 Undo and remove the intercooler outlet pipe support bracket retaining bolt **(see illustration 5.17)**.

8 Slacken the clamps and remove the intercooler outlet and inlet hoses. Note that the clips are moulded into the hose. Do not attempt to separate them.

9 Undo the 2 retaining bolts, lift the intercooler upwards from the mounting brackets and remove it downwards **(see illustration)**.

10 Slacken the clamps and disconnect the radiator upper and lower coolant hoses **(see illustrations)**. Unclip the hoses from the cooling fan shroud.

11 Release the clamp and disconnect the hose from the radiator to the expansion tank **(see illustration)**. To improve access to the hose, remove the left-hand headlight as described in Chapter 12.

12 Disconnect the cooling fan motor wiring plug.

13 Undo the 4 retaining bolts and remove the radiator lower support bracket **(see**

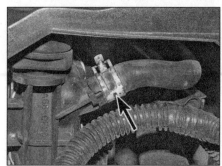

7.11 Expansion tank hose (arrowed)

illustration 5.14a). Disconnect the relay wiring plug (if fitted).

14 Carefully lower the radiator from place, complete with the cooling fan shroud. Take care not to damage the condenser or radiator cooling fins.

15 If required, depress the clip each side, and lift the cooling fan shroud from the radiator **(see illustration 5.19)**.

Inspection

16 With the radiator removed, it can be inspected for leaks and damage. If it needs repair, have a radiator specialist or dealer service department perform the work, as special techniques are required.

17 Insects and dirt can be removed from the radiator with a garden hose or a soft brush. Take care not to damage the cooling fins as this is being done.

Refitting

18 Refitting is the reverse of the removal procedure, noting the following points:

a) *Be sure the mounting rubbers are seated properly at the base of the radiator.*

b) *After refitting, refill the cooling system with the recommended coolant (see Chapter 1).*

c) *Start the engine, and check for leaks. Allow the engine to reach normal operating temperature, indicated by the radiator top hose becoming hot. Once the engine has cooled (ideally, leave overnight), recheck the coolant level, and add more if required.*

Expansion tank

19 With the engine completely cool, remove the expansion tank filler cap to release any pressure, then refit the cap.

20 Disconnect the hoses from the tank, upper hose first. As each hose is disconnected, drain the tank's contents into a clean container. If the coolant is not due for renewal, the drained coolant may be re-used, if it is kept clean.

21 Pull the tank upwards from the mountings on the inner wing **(see illustration)**.

22 Wash out the tank, and inspect it for cracks and chafing – renew it if damaged.

23 Refitting is the reverse of the removal procedure. Refill the cooling system with the recommended coolant (see Chapter 1), then

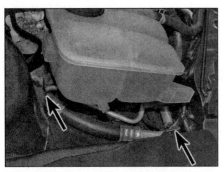

7.21 Pull the expansion tank upwards from its mountings (arrowed)

start the engine and allow it to reach normal operating temperature, indicated by the radiator top hose becoming hot. Recheck the coolant level and add more if required, then check for leaks.

8	Coolant pump –
	checking, removal and refitting

Note: *Refer to the warnings given in Section 1 of this Chapter before starting work.*

Checking

1 A failure in the coolant pump can cause serious engine damage due to overheating.
2 There are three ways to check the operation of the coolant pump while it's installed on the engine. If the pump is defective, fit a new or rebuilt unit.
3 With the engine running at normal operating

8.9a Undo the bolts (arrowed) and remove the coolant pump

8.15 Remove the coolant pump from the cylinder block

temperature, squeeze the radiator top hose. If the coolant pump is working properly, a pressure surge should be felt as the hose is released.

 Warning: Keep your hands away from the radiator electric cooling fan blades.

4 Coolant pumps are equipped with weep or vent holes. If a failure occurs in the pump seal, coolant will leak from the hole. In most cases you'll need an electric torch to find the hole on the coolant pump from underneath to check for leaks.
5 If the coolant pump shaft bearings fail, there may be a howling sound at the drivebelt end of the engine while it's running. Shaft wear can be felt if the coolant pump pulley is rocked up and down.
6 Don't mistake drivebelt slippage, which causes a squealing sound, for coolant pump bearing failure.

Removal

7 Drain the cooling system (see Chapter 1).

1.6 litre engines

8 Remove the upper timing belt as described in Chapter 2A.
9 Undo the bolts and remove the coolant pump **(see illustrations)**.

1.8 litre engines

10 Disconnect the battery negative lead with reference to Chapter 5.
11 Slacken the coolant pump pulley bolts, then remove the auxiliary drivebelt as described in Chapter 1.
12 Unbolt the coolant pump pulley and remove.

8.9b Renew the coolant pump gasket

8.17a Coolant pump retaining bolts (arrowed)

13 Remove the timing belt cover and engine mounting as described in Chapter 2B. The engine must be supported as the engine front mounting is disconnected; support the engine from above with a hoist or engine support bar, if available. If the engine is supported from below with a trolley jack, use a wide block of wood between the jack head and the sump, to spread the load.
14 Remove the four bolts securing the engine front mounting bracket to the block, then lift the engine up by approximately 20 mm.
15 Unscrew the seven coolant pump securing bolts and withdraw the pump **(see illustration)**. Recover the gasket. **Note:** *Take care not to damage or contaminate the timing belt as the pump is removed. Place some stiff cardboard around the belt in the pump area.*

2.0 litre engines

16 Remove the timing belt as described in Chapter 2C.
17 Undo the retaining bolts and remove the coolant pump **(see illustrations)**. Recover the gasket.

Refitting

18 Clean the pump mating surfaces carefully; the gasket/O-ring must be renewed whenever it is disturbed. Refit the pump and tighten the bolts evenly to the specified torque wrench setting.
19 The remainder of the refitting procedure is the reverse of dismantling, noting the following points:
   a) Tighten all fixings to the specified torque wrench settings (where given).
   b) Where applicable, check the timing belt for contamination and renew if required, as described in the relevant part of Chapter 2.
   c) On completion, refill the cooling system as described in Chapter 1.

9	Heater/ventilation
	components –
	removal and refitting

Heater blower motor

Note: *This is a difficult procedure requiring patience and dexterity to release the blower*

8.17b Renew the coolant pump gasket

motor retaining clip. It's much easier if the facia is removed as described in Chapter 11.

1 Disconnect the battery negative lead as described in Chapter 5.

2 Release the fasteners securing the lower passenger side footwell trim **(see illustration)**, then withdraw the panel from the vehicle.

3 Remove the passenger's glovebox as described in Chapter 11.

4 Disconnect the support strut, then remove the glovebox lid **(see illustration)**.

5 Undo the 2 fasteners and pivot the central junction box/fusebox downwards, then lift it from place. Disconnect the engine wiring harness from the junction/fusebox, and move it to one side **(see illustrations)**.

6 Undo the 2 nuts securing the junction/fusebox bracket **(see illustration)**. Disconnect the additional heater element wiring harness from the bracket (where fitted).

7 Disconnect the flap wiring plug, then undo the 3 bolts and remove the air recirculation flap housing **(see illustration)**.

8 On RHD models with air conditioning, remove the clutch pedal assembly as described in Chapter 6.

9 Disconnect the blower motor wiring plug, then depress the release clip, and rotate the blower motor clockwise (RHD) or anticlockwise (LHD) and pull the motor from the housing **(see illustrations)**. Take great care not to damage the motor fan – it's extremely delicate. Do not pull on the fan, or allow the motor to rest on the fan.

10 Refitting is the reverse of the removal procedure.

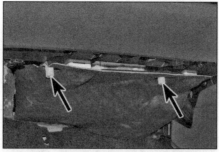

9.2 Squeeze together the side of the fasteners (arrowed) and pull them downwards

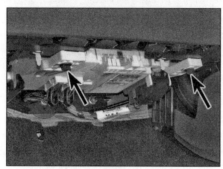

9.5a Rotate the fasteners (arrowed) anticlockwise . . .

Blower motor resistor

11 Proceed as described in Paragraphs 1 to 5 in this Section.

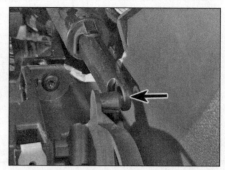

9.4 Push the support strut (arrowed) from the lug on the glovebox lid

9.5b . . . and lower the junction box/ fusebox

12 Disconnect the wiring plug, undo the 2 bolts, and pull the resistor from the housing **(see illustration)**.

13 Refitting is a reversal of removal.

9.6 Undo the 2 nuts (arrowed) and remove the bracket

9.9b Depress the clip, rotate the housing (see text) . . .

9.7 Recirculation flap housing bolts (arrowed)

9.9c . . . and gently pull the motor from the other side of the housing

9.9a The motor retaining clip is at the front edge of the housing (arrowed)

9.12 Heater blower motor resistor (arrowed)

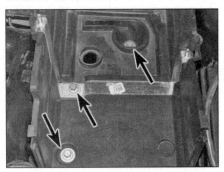

9.15 Battery tray bolts (arrowed)

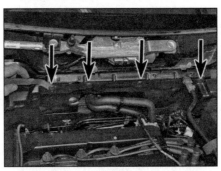

9.16a Prise out the 4 clips (arrowed)

9.16b Undo the 2 inner bolts, slacken the outer bolt, remove the nuts and pivot the cross-stay away from the bulkhead

9.16c Remove the plastic panel

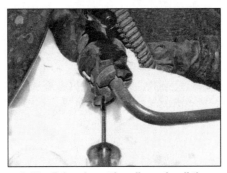

9.19a Prise down the clip and pull the pressure pipe from the clutch master cylinder

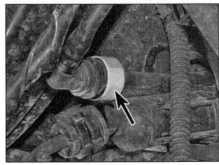

9.19b Pull back the collar (arrowed) and disconnect the fluid supply pipe

Heater matrix removal

14 Disconnect the battery negative (earth) lead (see Chapter 5).

Models with a plastic panel in front of the brake master cylinder

15 Remove the battery as described in Chapter 5A, then undo the 3 bolts and slide the battery tray forward a little (see illustration).
16 Prise out the 4 plastic clips securing the plastic panel to the engine compartment bulkhead, then undo the inner 2 retaining bolts on the suspension turret, slacken the outer bolt, remove the nuts and pivot the cross-stay each side away from the bulkhead. Lift the plastic panel from place (see illustrations). Refit the bolts to secure the tops of the suspension struts to the vehicle body.

All models

17 Jack up the front of the vehicle and support it securely on axle stands. Undo the fasteners and remove the engine undershield.
18 Drain the cooling system (see Chapter 1).
19 Pull back the collar/prise out the clip and disconnect the pressure pipe from the clutch master cylinder connection at the engine compartment bulkhead, then disconnect the fluid supply hose from the master cylinder (see illustrations). Be prepared for fluid spillage – wipe up any spills immediately – the fluid could damage paintwork, etc.
20 Remove the plastic cover from the top of the engine, where fitted.
21 Rotate the collars anti-clockwise 30° and detach the heater hoses from the connections

at the engine compartment bulkhead (see illustrations).
22 Working inside the passenger compartment, remove the facia as described in Chapter 11.
23 Remove the clutch pedal assembly as described in Chapter 6.
24 Unclip the wiring harness, then undo the nuts and remove the support bracket from the right-hand side of the heater housing (see illustration).
25 Remove the rear vent tube, then undo the 6 bolts and remove the heater matrix upper cover (see illustrations).
26 Undo the 2 bolts and remove the bulkhead aperture cover and spacer around the heater matrix pipes (see illustrations).
27 On models up to 10/2004, release the clamps securing the two halves of the matrix

9.21a Rotate the collar (arrowed) 30° anti-clockwise . . .

9.21b . . . and pull the hose from the connection

9.24 Note the earth connection (arrowed) at the top of the bracket

9.25a Remove the rear vent tube

9.25b Undo the heater matrix upper cover bolts (left-hand side ones arrowed) . . .

9.25c . . . and remove the upper cover

pipes, and remove the matrix from the housing. On models after this date, cut through the matrix pipes as shown, and remove the matrix. In production, these later models were fitted with one-piece pipes, whereas new matrices are supplied with two-piece pipes and suitable clamps (see illustrations). Be prepared for fluid spillage.

Heater matrix refitting

28 Refitting is the reverse of the removal procedure. Note that new matrices are supplied with two-piece pipes and suitable clamps. Push the pipes into the aperture in the bulkhead, before installing the matrix in the housing, then use the clamps and seals supplied to join the pipes.

29 Refill the cooling system with the recommended coolant (see Chapter 1). Start the engine and allow it to reach normal operating temperature, indicated by the radiator top hose becoming hot. Recheck the coolant level and add more if required, then check for leaks. Check the operation of the heater.

Pollen filter

30 Refer to Chapter 1.

10 Heater/air conditioning controls – removal and refitting

Heater control panel

1 Disconnect the battery negative (earth) lead (see Chapter 5).

9.26a Undo the 2 bolts (arrowed) and remove the cover . . .

9.27a Cut through the heater matrix pipes with a hacksaw (see text)

2 Remove the facia-mounted audio unit as described in Chapter 12.

Manual temperature control

3 On models up to 03/2007, undo the 2 bolts

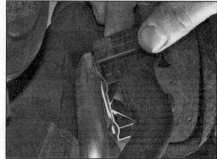

9.26b . . . followed by the spacer

9.27b Lift the matrix from the housing

and unclip the heater control panel trim (see illustrations).

4 Undo the 2 retaining bolts and manoeuvre the control panel away from the facia a little (see illustration).

10.3a Undo the panel retaining bolts (arrowed)

10.3b Release the clips (arrowed)

10.4 Heater control panel retaining bolts (arrowed)

10.5 Squeeze together the sides of the clip (arrowed) and pull the outer cable fitting from the panel

5 Taking careful note of all their locations, disconnect the various wiring connectors from the rear of the panel and unclip the heater operating cables from the temperature and direction controls **(see illustration)**.
6 Make sure that nothing remains attached to the panel, then withdraw it from the facia.

Automatic temperature control

7 On models up to 03/2007, undo the 2 bolts and unclip the heater control panel trim **(see illustrations 10.3a and 10.3b)**.
8 Undo the 2 retaining bolts and manoeuvre the control panel away from the facia a little **(see illustration 10.4)**.
9 Taking careful note of all their locations, disconnect the various wiring connectors from the rear of the panel.
10 Make sure that nothing remains attached to the panel, then withdraw it from the facia

DVD navigation system

11 The climate control function is built-into the DVD navigation touch screen. Removal of the screen assembly is described in Chapter 12.
12 Undo the bolt each side and remove the climate control module from the unit.

Blower motor switch – manual control only

13 Remove the heater control panel as described above.
14 Ensure the switch control knob is in position I during removal and refitting. Pull the control knob from the switch.
15 Cut through the retaining tabs and remove

11.3 Air conditioning refrigerant circuit high- and low-pressure service ports (arrowed)

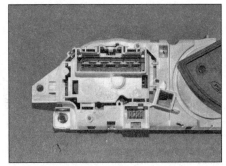

10.15 Cut through the retaining tabs and remove the switch

the switch cover from the rear of the panel **(see illustration)**.
16 Pull the switch from place.
17 Refitting is the reverse of the removal procedure. Note that new switches are supplied with a cover that is retained by 2 bolts (also supplied). Check the operation of the controls on completion.

11 Air conditioning system – general information and precautions

General information

The air conditioning system consists of a condenser mounted in front of the radiator, an evaporator mounted adjacent to the heater matrix, a compressor driven by an auxiliary drivebelt, an accumulator/dehydrator, and the plumbing connecting all of the above components – this contains a choke (or 'venturi') mounted in the inlet to the evaporator, which creates the drop in pressure required to produce the cooling effect.

A blower fan forces the warmer air of the passenger compartment through the evaporator core (rather like a radiator in reverse), transferring the heat from the air to the refrigerant. The liquid refrigerant boils off into low-pressure vapour, taking the heat with it when it leaves the evaporator.

The refrigerant circuit high- and low-pressure service ports are located on the right-hand side of the engine compartment **(see illustration)**.

Precautions

> ⚠ **Warning: The air conditioning system is under high pressure. Do not loosen any fittings or remove any components until after the system has been discharged. Air conditioning refrigerant should be properly discharged at a dealer service department or an automotive air conditioning repair facility capable of handling R134a refrigerant. Always wear eye protection when disconnecting air conditioning system fittings.**

When an air conditioning system is fitted, it is necessary to observe the following special

precautions whenever dealing with any part of the system, its associated components, and any items which necessitate disconnection of the system:
a) While the refrigerant used is less damaging to the environment than the previously-used R12, it is still a very dangerous substance. It must not be allowed into contact with the skin or eyes, or there is a risk of frostbite. It must also not be discharged in an enclosed space – while it is not toxic, there is a risk of suffocation. The refrigerant is heavier than air, and so must never be discharged over a pit.
b) The refrigerant must not be allowed to come in contact with a naked flame, otherwise a poisonous gas will be created – under certain circumstances, this can form an explosive mixture with air. For similar reasons, smoking in the presence of refrigerant is highly dangerous, particularly if the vapour is inhaled through a lighted cigarette.
c) Never discharge the system to the atmosphere – R134a is not an ozone-depleting ChloroFluoroCarbon (CFC) like R12, but is instead a hydrofluorocarbon, which causes environmental damage by contributing to the 'greenhouse effect' if released into the atmosphere.
d) R134a refrigerant must not be mixed with R12; the system uses different seals (now green-coloured, previously black) and has different fittings requiring different tools, so that there is no chance of the two types of refrigerant becoming mixed accidentally.
e) If for any reason the system must be discharged, entrust this task to your Ford dealer or an air conditioning specialist.
f) It is essential that the system be professionally discharged prior to using any form of heat – welding, soldering, brazing, etc – in the vicinity of the system, before having the vehicle oven-dried at a temperature exceeding 70°C after repainting, and before disconnecting any part of the system.

12 Air conditioning system components – removal and refitting

> ⚠ **Warning: The air conditioning system is under high pressure. Do not loosen any fittings or remove any components until after the system has been discharged. Air conditioning refrigerant should be properly discharged into an approved type of container at a dealer service department or an automotive air conditioning repair facility capable of handling R134a refrigerant. Cap or plug the pipe lines as soon as they are disconnected to prevent the entry of moisture. Always wear eye protection when disconnecting air conditioning system fittings.**

Note: *This Section refers to the components of the air conditioning system itself – refer to Sections 9 and 10 for details of components common to the heating/ ventilation system.*

Condenser

1 Have the refrigerant discharged at a dealer service department or an automotive air conditioning repair facility.
2 Disconnect the battery negative (earth) lead (see Chapter 5).
3 Apply the handbrake, then raise the front of the vehicle and support on axle stands.
4 Remove the intercooler as described in Chapter 4A.
5 Disconnect the refrigerant lines from the condenser. Immediately cap the open fittings, to prevent the entry of dirt and moisture.
6 Undo the nuts securing the power steering fluid cooler to the radiator crossmember.
7 Remove the two bolts from each side of the radiator support bracket (note that the condenser is also mounted on the brackets in front of the radiator), have a jack or pair of axle stands ready to support the weight.
8 Unclip the lower mountings, then lift the condenser upwards to disengage the condenser upper mountings, and lower it from under the vehicle **(see illustration)**. Store it upright, to prevent fluid loss. Take care not to damage the condenser fins.
9 Refitting is the reverse of removal. Renew the O-rings and lubricate with refrigerant oil.
10 Have the system evacuated, charged and leak-tested by the specialist who discharged it.

Evaporator

11 The evaporator is mounted inside the heater housing with the heater matrix. In order to remove the evaporator, the complete heater housing must be removed.
12 Have the refrigerant discharged at a dealer service department or an automotive air conditioning repair facility.
13 Disconnect the battery negative (earth) lead (see Chapter 5).
14 Drain the cooling system as described in Chapter 1.
15 Remove the facia as described in Chapter 11.

12.8 Depress the clip each side (arrowed) and lift the condenser upwards

16 Remove both front doors as described in Chapter 11.
17 Prise out the grommet then undo the bolt each end securing the facia crossmember to the door pillars **(see illustration)**.
18 Remove the front wiper motor and linkage as described in Chapter 12.
19 Remove the plastic cover from the top of the engine, where fitted.

Models with a plastic panel in front of the brake master cylinder

20 Remove the battery as described in Chapter 5A, then undo the 3 bolts and slide the battery tray forward a little.
21 Prise out the 4 plastic clips securing the plastic panel to the engine compartment bulkhead, then undo the inner 2 retaining bolts, slacken the outer bolt, remove the nuts and pivot the cross-stay each side away from the bulkhead. Lift the plastic panel from place **(see illustrations 9.16a, 9.16b and 9.16c)**. Refit the bolts to secure the tops of the suspension struts to the vehicle body.

All models

22 Rotate the collars anti-clockwise 30° approximately, and detach the heater hoses from the connections at the engine compartment bulkhead **(see illustration 9.21a and 9.21b)**.
23 Undo the bolt and detach the refrigerant pipes at the engine compartment bulkhead **(see illustration)**. Plug or cover the openings to prevent contamination. Renew the O-ring seals.

12.17 Unscrew the bolt securing each end of the facia crossmember to the door pillars

24 Working in the footwell, unscrew and remove the steering column universal joint pinch-bolt **(see illustration)**. Discard the bolt, a new one must be fitted.
25 Disconnect the wiring plugs, undo the 4 mounting bolts, and remove the steering column – refer to Chapter 10 if necessary.
26 Undo the bolt and remove the footwell air duct each side **(see illustration)**.
27 Undo the bolt each side securing the heater/evaporator housing to the support brackets, then undo the nuts and remove the support bracket each side. Note the routing, then release any wiring harnesses from their clips as the brackets are withdrawn **(see illustration 9.24)**.
28 Unclip and remove the rear footwell air duct **(see illustration 9.25a)**, then undo the 6 bolts and remove the heater matrix upper cover **(see illustration 9.25b and 9.25c)**.
29 Pull away the rubber weatherstrips from the door aperture adjacent to the A-pillar on each side, then remove both A-pillar trim panels as described in Chapter 11.
30 Pull up the door sill trim each side, then pull the footwell kick panel away from the A-pillar to release the retaining clips **(see illustrations)**.
31 Note their fitted positions, and the harness routing, then unplug all electrical connectors that would prevent the facia crossmember assembly being removed.
32 Undo the 2 bolts securing the cross-member to the heater housing in the centre **(see illustration)**.

12.23 Undo the bolt (arrowed) and pull the refrigerant pipes from the bulkhead

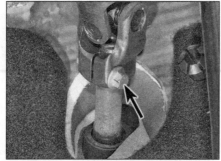

12.24 Undo the steering column UJ pinch-bolt (arrowed)

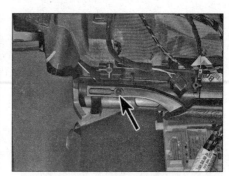

12.26 Undo the bolt (arrowed) and remove the footwell air duct each side

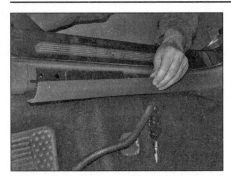

12.30a Pull the door sill trim upwards . . .

12.30b . . . then pull the footwell kick panel away from the pillar

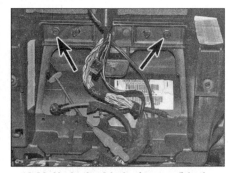

12.32 Undo the 2 bolts (arrowed) in the centre aperture

12.33a Undo the 2 bolts accessible from the engine compartment (arrowed) . . .

12.33b . . . and the 2 at each end of the facia crossmember (arrowed)

12.34 Disconnect the drain tube (arrowed) as the heater is withdrawn

33 Mark the position of the facia crossmember in relation to the door pillars, then undo the 2 inner bolts and the 4 outer bolts, pull the crossmember rearwards and lift it from place. The help of an assistant during this procedure is absolutely essential **(see illustrations)**.

34 Ensure all relevant electrical connectors are disconnected then lift the heater housing from position. Disconnect the evaporator drain tube as the housing is removed **(see illustration)**.

35 Undo the bolts securing the bulkhead aperture cover around the heater matrix and evaporator pipes **(see illustration 9.26a and 9.26b)**.

36 Undo the retaining bolts and remove the evaporator cover **(see illustration)**.

37 Withdraw the heater matrix and evaporator from the heater housing at the same time **(see illustration)**.

38 Refitting is the reverse of removal, noting the following points:

a) *Align the crossmember with the previously-made marks, then refit and tighten the four bolts securing it to the A-pillar before inserting the bolt each end from the sides.*

b) *Tighten all fasteners to the specified torque where given.*

c) *Have the system evacuated, charged and leak-tested by the specialist who discharged it.*

Compressor

39 Have the refrigerant discharged at a dealer service department or an automotive air conditioning repair facility.

40 Disconnect the battery negative (earth) lead (see Chapter 5).

41 Apply the handbrake, then raise the front of the vehicle and support on axle stands. Remove the right-hand front roadwheel.

42 Remove the right-hand front wheel arch liner, and engine undershield.

43 Remove the auxiliary drivebelt as described in Chapter 1.

44 Unscrew the clamping bolt to disconnect the refrigerant lines from the compressor. Plug the line connections to prevent entry of any dirt or moisture **(see illustration)**. Discard the O-ring seals, new ones must be fitted.

45 Unbolt the compressor from the cylinder block/crankcase, unplug its electrical connector, then withdraw the compressor from the vehicle. **Note:** *Keep the compressor level during handling and storage. If the compressor has seized, or if you find metal particles in the refrigerant lines, the system must be flushed out by an air conditioning technician, and the accumulator/dehydrator must be renewed.*

12.36 Undo the evaporator cover bolts (arrowed)

12.37 Withdraw the heater matrix at the same time as the evaporator

12.44 Compressor refrigerant lines clamp bolts (arrowed)

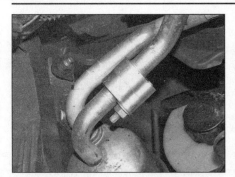

12.54 Disconnect the refrigerant pipes from the accumulator/dehydrator

12.55 The rear mounting bolt (arrowed) is accessible through the wheel arch

12.62a Prise forwards the clips (arrowed) . . .

46 Prior to installation, turn the compressor clutch centre six times, to disperse any oil that has collected in the head.

47 Refit the compressor in the reverse order of removal; renew all seals disturbed.

48 If you are installing a new compressor, refer to the compressor manufacturer's instructions for adding refrigerant oil to the system.

49 Have the system evacuated, charged and leak-tested by the specialist that discharged it.

Accumulator/dehydrator

50 Have the refrigerant discharged at a dealer service department or an automotive air conditioning repair facility.

51 Apply the handbrake, then raise the front of the vehicle and support on axle stands.

52 Remove the right-hand front wheel. Unscrew the inner wheel arch liner and remove from the vehicle.

53 Remove the right-hand headlight as described in Chapter 12.

54 Undo the retaining nuts and detach the refrigerant pipes from the accumulator/ dehydrator **(see illustration)**. Immediately cap the open fittings, to prevent the entry of dirt and moisture.

55 Undo the 3 mounting bolts/nuts (the rear one is accessible through the wheel arch) and withdraw the accumulator/dehydrator **(see illustration)**.

56 Refit the accumulator/dehydrator in the reverse order of removal; renew all seals disturbed.

57 If you are installing a new accumulator/ dehydrator, top-up with new oil to the volume removed, plus 90 cc of extra refrigerant oil.

58 Refit the headlight and wheel arch liner.

59 Have the system evacuated, charged and leak-tested by the specialist that discharged it.

High-pressure and low-pressure cut-off switches

60 Have the refrigerant discharged at a dealer service department or an automotive air conditioning repair facility.

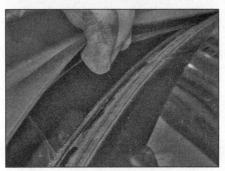

12.62b . . . then pull the scuttle cowling panel upwards from the base of the windscreen

61 Remove the wiper arms as described in Chapter 12.

62 Release the clips and remove the scuttle panel grille **(see illustrations)**.

63 Undo the bolts securing the brake fluid reservoir (where fitted) to the bulkhead extension, then undo the bolts at each end and remove the extension **(see illustration)**.

64 Unplug the relevant switch electrical connector, and unscrew the switch **(see illustrations)**. Plug the openings to prevent contamination.

65 Refitting is the reverse of the removal procedure. Renew the O-rings and lubricate with refrigerant oil.

66 Have the system evacuated, charged and leak-tested by the specialist that discharged it. Check the operation of the air conditioning system.

12.64a One pressure switch is located at the engine compartment bulkhead . . .

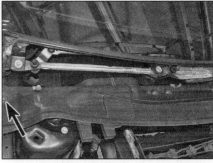

12.63 Undo the bolt at each end (right-hand one arrowed) and pull the bulkhead extension panel forwards

13 Electric booster heater –
general information,
removal and refitting

General information

1 Because diesel engines give off low residual heat, an electric booster heating element is fitted into the heater housing. At engine coolant temperatures of less than 60°C and ambient temperatures of less then 10°C, when the high temperature setting is selected, the GEM (see Chapter 12), provides power to the heating element. Power is cut to the element when the engine coolant temperature exceeds 70°C or the ambient temperature exceeds 20°C.

12.64b . . . whilst the other is behind the right-hand headlight (arrowed)

13.4a Undo the bolts (arrowed) . . .

13.4b . . . and slide out the booster heater element

Removal

2 Remove the facia as described in Chapter 11.

3 Release the wiring harness retaining clips, then undo the bolts and remove the support bracket from the right-hand side of the heater housing **(see illustration 9.24)**.

4 Disconnect the booster heater wiring plug and undo the bolts and slide the booster heater element from the heater housing **(see illustrations)**.

Refitting

5 Refitting is a reversal of removal.

Chapter 4 Part A:
Fuel and exhaust systems

Contents

Degrees of difficulty

| Easy, suitable for novice with little experience | | Fairly easy, suitable for beginner with some experience | | Fairly difficult, suitable for competent DIY mechanic | | Difficult, suitable for experienced DIY mechanic | | Very difficult, suitable for expert DIY or professional | |

Specifications

General

System type:

1.6 litre engines	Bosch direct injection common rail, with timing belt driven high-pressure delivery pump, variable nozzle turbocharger, and intercooler
1.8 litre engines	Siemens direct injection common rail with a chain-driven high-pressure delivery pump, variable nozzle turbocharger and intercooler
2.0 litre engines	Siemens direct injection common rail with a camshaft-driven high-pressure delivery pump, variable nozzle turbocharger, and intercooler

Torque wrench settings	Nm	lbf ft
Camshaft position sensor:		
1.6 litre engines	10	7
1.8 litre engines	10	7
Common rail mounting bolts:		
1.6 litre engines	22	16
1.8 litre engines	24	18
2.0 litre engines	22	16
Crankshaft position sensor:		
1.6 litre engines	8	6
1.8 litre engines	6	4
2.0 litre engines	8	6
Exhaust manifold to cylinder head:		
1.6 litre engines	25	18
1.8 litre engines	25	18
2.0 litre engines	30	22
Fuel high-pressure pipe union nuts:*		
To fuel rail:		
1.6 litre engines.	25	18
1.8 litre engines.	38	28
2.0 litre engines.	23	17
To fuel pump:		
1.6 litre engines.	25	18
1.8 litre engines.	25	18
2.0 litre engines.	23	17
To fuel injectors:		
1.6 litre engines.	25	18
1.8 litre engines.	25	18
2.0 litre engines.	23	17
Fuel injector clamp nuts/bolts:		
1.6 litre engines:		
Stage 1	4	3
Stage 2	Angle-tighten a further 45°	
1.8 litre engines:		
Stage 1	5	4
Stage 2	Angle-tighten a further 90°	
2.0 litre engines:		
Stage 1	4	3
Stage 2	Angle-tighten a further 45°	
Fuel injection pump mounting bolts:		
1.6 litre engines	22	16
1.8 litre engines	20	15
2.0 litre engines	20	15
Fuel tank sender unit collar	85	63
Throttle body bolts:		
1.6 litre engines	8	6
Turbocharger oil supply banjo bolt:		
1.6 litre engines	30	22
1.8 litre engines	18	13
2.0 litre engines:		
To engine block.	40	30
To turbocharger	28	21
Turbocharger support bracket bolt:		
1.6 litre engines	25	18
1.8 litre engines	45	33
2.0 litre engines	15	11
Turbocharger to exhaust manifold:		
1.6 litre engines	25	18
1.8 litre engines	10	7
2.0 litre engines	25	18
Turbocharger-to-turbocharger support bracket bolt:		
1.8 litre engines	25	18
2.0 litre engines	30	22

* Do not re-use

2.2a Slacken the clamp (arrowed) and pull the air outlet hose from the turbocharger

2.2b Release the clips and disconnect the breather hose

1 General information and precautions

General information

The operation of the fuel injection system is described in more detail in Section 5.

Fuel is drawn from a tank under the rear of the vehicle by a tank-immersed electric pump, and then forced through a filter to the injection pump.

The camshaft-driven injection pump is a tandem pump – a low pressure vane-type pump which supplies the high-pressure pump with fuel at a constant pressure, and a high-pressure piston-type pump which supplies fuel to the common fuel rail at variable pressure.

Fuel is supplied from the common fuel rail to the injectors. Also inside the injection pump assembly is a pressure control valve which regulates the pressure of fuel from the high-pressure pump, and a fuel volume control valve which regulates the fuel flow to the high-pressure side of the pump. The injectors are operated by solenoids controlled by the PCM, based on information supplied by various sensors. The engine PCM also controls the preheating side of the system – refer to Chapter 5 for more details.

The engine management system fitted, incorporates a 'drive-by-wire' system, where the traditional accelerator cable is replaced by an accelerator pedal position sensor. The position and rate-of-change of the accelerator pedal is reported by the position sensor to the PCM, which then adjusts the fuel injectors and fuel pressure to deliver the required amount of fuel and optimum combustion efficiency.

The exhaust system incorporates a turbocharger and an EGR system. Further detail of the emission control systems can be found in Chapter 4B.

Precautions

• When working on diesel fuel system components, scrupulous cleanliness must be observed, and care must be taken not to introduce any foreign matter into fuel lines or components.

• After carrying out any work involving disconnection of fuel lines, it is advisable to check the connections for leaks; pressurise the system by cranking the engine several times.

• Electronic control units are very sensitive components, and certain precautions must be taken to avoid damage to these units.

• When carrying out welding operations on the vehicle using electric welding equipment, the battery and alternator should be disconnected.

• Although the underbonnet-mounted modules will tolerate normal underbonnet conditions, they can be adversely affected by excess heat or moisture. If using welding equipment or pressure-washing equipment in the vicinity of an electronic module, take care not to direct heat, or jets of water or steam, at the module. If this cannot be avoided, remove the module from the vehicle, and protect its wiring plug with a plastic bag.

• Before disconnecting any wiring, or removing components, always ensure that the ignition is switched off.

• Do not attempt to improvise PCM fault diagnosis procedures using a test lamp or multimeter, as irreparable damage could be caused to the module.

• After working on fuel injection/engine management system components, ensure that all wiring is correctly reconnected before reconnecting the battery or switching on the ignition.

2 Air cleaner assembly – removal and refitting

Removal

1.6 litre engines

1 Pull the plastic cover (where fitted) on the top of the engine upwards from its mountings.
2 Slacken the clamps and remove the air cleaner outlet hose. Disconnect the engine breather hose at the same time **(see illustrations)**.
3 Slide up the red locking clip, then disconnect the mass airflow sensor wiring plug.
4 Release the rubber retaining strap and pull the air cleaner assembly upwards from place. Disconnect the inlet hose and vacuum hose as the assembly is removed **(see illustrations)**.

2.4a Release the rubber strap . . .

2.4b . . . disconnect the vacuum hose . . .

2.4c . . . and the inlet hose

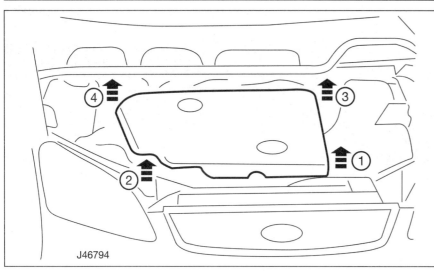

2.5 Pull the engine cover upwards to release the clips in the order shown – 1.8 litre models

1.8 litre engines

5 Pull the plastic cover on the top of the engine upwards to release its mountings in the order shown **(see illustration)**. Take care to manoeuvre the cover around the MAP sensor.
6 Disconnect the mass airflow meter wiring plug, release the harness clip, slacken the clamp and disconnect the outlet hose from the mass airflow meter **(see illustration)**.
7 Release the rubber retaining strap at the front of the housing **(see illustration)**.
8 Pull the housing upwards sharply to release it from the mounting grommets.

2.0 litre engines

9 Disconnect the mass airflow sensor wiring plug.
10 Slacken the clamp and disconnect the outlet hose from the mass airflow sensor **(see illustration)**.
11 Release the rubber retaining strap at the front of the housing **(see illustration)**.
12 Pull the housing upwards sharply to release it from the mounting grommets.

Refitting

13 Refitting is a reversal of removal.

2.6 Slacken the clamp (arrowed) and disconnect the hose from the airflow meter

2.7 Release the rubber strap at the front of the air filter housing

2.10 Slacken the clamp (arrowed) and disconnect the outlet hose

2.11 Release the strap at the front of the air filter housing

3 Fuel tank – removal and refitting

Note: *Observe the precautions in Section 1 before working on any component in the fuel system.*

Removal

1 Run the fuel level as low as possible prior to removing the tank. There is no drain plug fitted (and syphoning may prove difficult). It is preferable to keep as much fuel in the pipes as possible, to reduce the need for bleeding the system when restarting the engine.
2 Equalise tank pressure by removing the fuel filler cap.
3 Disconnect the battery negative (earth) lead (see Chapter 5).
4 Chock the front wheels, then jack up the rear of the car and support it on axle stands (see *Jacking and vehicle support*). Remove the rear roadwheels.
5 Unhook the exhaust system mounting rubbers from the centre and rear hangers, and allow the exhaust system to rest on the rear suspension crossmember.
6 Undo the nuts securing the flange of the exhaust system rear section, then manoeuvre the rear section to one side, and secure it in place using cable ties/wire/string.
7 Undo the fasteners and remove the left-hand side rear air deflector shield **(see illustration)**.
8 Undo the fasteners and remove the exhaust centre and rear section heat shields from the vehicle underside **(see illustration)**.
9 Release the clips and disconnect the fuel tank filler and vent pipes at the rear of the tank. Do not use any sharp-edged tools to release the pipes from their stubs, as the pipes are easily damaged. If crimp-type clips are fitted, discard the pipe clips and obtain some worm-type/Jubilee clips for refitting. **Note:** *It's important to note the fitted positions of the original clips, and fit the new clips in exactly the same place/orientation.*
10 On models equipped with a particulate filter, depress the release buttons, and disconnect the additive pipes from the rear of the fuel tank.

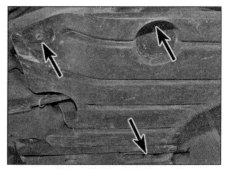

3.7 Undo the bolts and remove the air deflector panel (arrowed)

11 Disconnect the fuel supply and return hoses at the front of the tank **(see illustration)**.
12 Support the tank using a trolley jack and a large sheet of wood to spread the load.
13 Note exactly how the fuel tank retaining straps are arranged, to make refitting easier. In particular, note their fitted order under the retaining bolt heads, where applicable.
14 Unbolt and remove the fuel tank retaining straps **(see illustrations)**.
15 Partially lower the tank on the jack, taking care that no strain is placed on any fuel lines or wiring. As soon as the wiring connector for the fuel pump/gauge sender on top of the tank is accessible, reach in and disconnect it.
16 Lower the fuel tank to the ground, checking all the way down that no pipes or wiring are under any strain. Remove the tank from under the car.

Inspection

17 Whilst removed, the fuel tank can be inspected for damage or deterioration. Removal of the fuel pump/fuel gauge sender unit (see Section 7) will allow a partial inspection of the interior. If the tank is contaminated with sediment or water, swill it out with clean fuel. Do not under any circumstances undertake any repairs on a leaking or damaged fuel tank; this work must be carried out by a professional who has experience in this critical and potentially-dangerous work.
18 Whilst the fuel tank is removed from the car, it should be placed in a safe area where sparks or open flames cannot ignite the fumes coming out of the tank. Be especially careful inside garages where a natural-gas type appliance is located, because the pilot light could cause an explosion.
19 Check the condition of the lower filler pipe and renew it if necessary.

Refitting

20 Refitting is a reversal of the removal procedure, noting the following points:
  a) *Ensure that all pipe and wiring connections are securely fitted.*
  b) *When refitting the quick-release couplings, press them together until the locking lugs snap into their groove.*
  c) *Tighten the tank strap retaining bolts securely.*
  d) *If evidence of contamination was found, do not return any previously-drained fuel to the tank unless it is carefully filtered.*

4 Accelerator pedal – removal and refitting

Removal

1 Remove the driver's side facia lower panel, as described in Chapter 11.
2 Disconnect the battery negative lead as described in Chapter 5.

3.8 Remove the heat shield under the fuel tank

3.14a Fuel tank strap rear bolts (arrowed) . . .

3 Disconnect the wiring plug from the throttle position sensor, then unscrew the 3 mounting nuts and remove the pedal/sensor assembly from the bulkhead studs **(see illustration)**. Note that the sensor is not available separately from the pedal assembly. **Note:** *Ford insist that the sensor wiring plug can only be disconnected 10 times before is becomes irreversibly damaged. Use a marker pen to record each disconnection on the side of the connector. Only disconnect the plug if it's absolutely necessary.*

Refitting

4 Refit in the reverse order of removal. On completion, check the action of the pedal to ensure that the throttle has full unrestricted movement, and fully returns when released.
5 Reconnect the battery as described in Chapter 5.

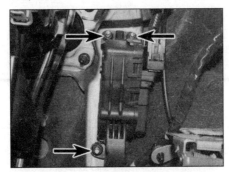
4.3 Accelerator pedal assembly retaining nuts (arrowed)

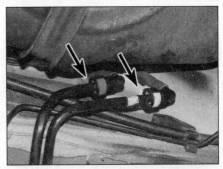
3.11 Prise up the catches (arrowed), depress the buttons on the other side and disconnect the fuel supply and return hoses

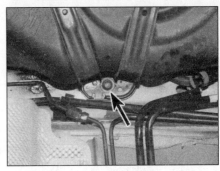
3.14b . . . and front bolt (arrowed)

5 Fuel injection system – general information

The system is under the overall control of the engine management PCM (Powertrain Control Module), which also controls the preheating system (see Chapter 5).

Fuel is supplied from the rear-mounted fuel tank, via an electrically-powered lift pump and the fuel filter, to the fuel injection pump. The fuel injection pump supplies fuel under high pressure to the common fuel rail. The fuel rail provides a reservoir of fuel under pressure ready for the injectors to deliver direct to the combustion chamber. The individual fuel injectors incorporate piezoelectrical/electromagnetic elements, which when operated, allow the high-pressure fuel to be injected. The elements are controlled by the PCM. The fuel injection pump purely provides high-pressure fuel. The timing and duration of the injection is controlled by the PCM based, on the information received from the various sensors. In order to increase combustion efficiency and reduce combustion noise (diesel 'knock'), a small amount of fuel is injected before the main injection takes place – this is known as Pre- or Pilot-injection. The fuel filter incorporates a heater element.

Additionally, the engine management PCM activates the preheating system (Chapter 5), and the exhaust gas recirculation (EGR) system (see Chapter 4B).

5.9 The diagnostic connector is below the driver's side of the facia (arrowed)

The system uses the following sensors.

a) *Crankshaft sensor – informs the PCM of the crankshaft speed and position.*

b) *Coolant/cylinder head temperature sensor – informs the PCM of engine temperature.*

c) *Mass airflow sensor – informs the PCM of the mass air entering the inlet tract.*

d) *Wheel speed sensor – informs the PCM of the vehicle speed.*

e) *Accelerator pedal position sensor – informs the PCM of throttle position, and the rate of throttle opening/closing.*

f) *Fuel high-pressure sensor – informs the PCM of the pressure of the fuel in the common rail.*

g) *Camshaft position sensor – informs the PCM of the camshaft position so that the engine firing sequence can be established.*

h) *Stop-light switch – informs the PCM when the brakes are being applied*

i) *Boost pressure sensor – informs the PCM*

of the boost pressure generated by the turbocharger.

j) *Air conditioning pressure sensor – informs the PCM of the high-pressure side of the air conditioning circuit, in case a raised idle speed is required to compensate for compressor load.*

k) *Inlet air temperature sensor – informs the PCM of the inlet air temperature.*

l) *Clutch pedal switch – informs the PCM of the clutch pedal position.*

m) *Turbocharger position sensor – informs the PCM of the position of the variable in take nozzle guide rails.*

On all models, a 'drive-by-wire' throttle control system is used. The accelerator pedal is not physically connected to the fuel injection pump with a traditional cable, but instead is monitored by a dual potentiometer mounted on the pedal assembly, which provides the powertrain control module (PCM) with a signal relating to accelerator pedal movement.

The signals from the various sensors are processed by the PCM, and the optimum fuel quantity and injection timing settings are selected for the prevailing engine operating conditions.

Catalytic converters and an exhaust gas recirculation (EGR) system are fitted, to reduce harmful exhaust gas emissions. Details of this and other emissions control system equipment are given in Chapter 4B.

If there is an abnormality in any of the readings obtained from any sensor, the PCM enters its back-up mode. In this event, the PCM ignores the abnormal sensor signal, and

assumes a preprogrammed value which will allow the engine to continue running (albeit at reduced efficiency). If the PCM enters this back-up mode, the warning light on the instrument panel will come on, and the relevant fault code will be stored in the PCM memory.

If the warning light comes on, the vehicle should be taken to a Ford dealer or specialist at the earliest opportunity. A complete test of the system can then be carried out, using a special electronic test unit which is simply plugged into the system's diagnostic connector. The connector is located below the driver's side of the facia above the pedals **(see illustration)**.

**6   Fuel system –
priming and bleeding**

1 After disturbing the fuel system before the high-pressure fuel injection pump, the system must be bled. To do this, Ford technicians use a hand pump (No 310-110) that sucks fuel from the tank, and forces it through the filter. In the absence of this tool, use a hand-held vacuum pump.

2 Remove the plastic cover on the top of the engine.

Using the Ford pump

3 Disconnect the fuel supply pipe quick-release connector from the high-pressure fuel injection pump, and place the end of the pipe in a suitable container to catch the emerging fuel.

4 Disconnect the fuel supply hose to the fuel filter, and connect the hand pump (or equivalent) between the hose and the filter. Ensure the arrow on the pump is pointing towards the fuel filter.

5 Operate the pump until there is a continuous flow of fuel into the container. Squeeze and hold the hand pump for 10 seconds.

6 Release the pump, then squeeze and hold the pump for a further 10 seconds.

7 Reattach the pipe to the high-pressure pump, then operate the pump until strong resistance is felt.

8 Operate the starter motor and run the engine until it reaches normal operating temperature. *Caution: Do not operate the starter motor for more than 10 seconds, then wait 30 seconds before trying again.*

9 Stop the engine, and remove the hand pump. Wipe up any fuel spillage, and refit the engine cover.

Using a hand-held vacuum pump

10 Depress the release tab(s) and disconnect the fuel outlet hose from the fuel filter **(see illustrations)**.

11 Connect the vacuum pump pipe to the outlet on the filter, and continue to pull a vacuum until bubble-free fuel emerges from the hose **(see illustration)**.

12 Reconnect the fuel hose.

6.10a Depress the button and disconnect the fuel outlet hose – 1.6 litre models . . .

6.10c . . . and depress the clip (arrowed) on 2.0 litre models

6.10b . . . prise out the clip on 1.8 litre models . . .

6.11 Attach the hand-held vacuum pump hose to the filter outlet, and continue to pull a vacuum until bubble-free fuel emerges

13 Operate the starter motor and run the engine until it reaches normal operating temperature.
Caution: Do not operate the starter motor for more than 10 seconds, then wait 30 seconds before trying again.
14 Stop the engine. Wipe up any fuel spillage, and refit the engine cover.

7 Fuel gauge sender unit – removal and refitting

Note: Observe the precautions in Section 1 before working on any component in the fuel system.

Removal

1 Remove the fuel tank as described in Section 3.
2 Depress the release buttons, and disconnect the fuel supply and return hoses from the sender unit **(see illustration)**.
3 Unscrew the sender unit plastic retaining collar using a pair of large, crossed-screwdrivers, or improvise a tool **(see illustration)**.
4 Lift the sender unit from the tank **(see illustrations)**. Discard the O-ring seal, a new one must be fitted. Note that on models with a fuel-fired auxiliary heater, undo the plug for the suction pipe on the underside of the level sensor, and transfer the pipe to the new sensor (if renewed). No separate parts are available.
5 If required, attach the leads from a multimeter to the sender unit wires, and measure the resistance at full float deflection and zero deflection. The resistance of the unit we tested was 200 ohms at full deflection, and 10 ohms at zero deflection **(see illustration)**.

Refitting

6 Refitting is a reversal of removal, bearing in mind the following points:
  a) Use a new O-ring seal smeared with petroleum jelly.
  b) Position the sender unit so the arrow on the cover aligns with the marks on the fuel tank align **(see illustration)**.
  c) Tighten the sender unit retaining collar to the specified torque, where tools permit.

8 Fuel injection system – testing and adjustment

Testing

1 If a fault appears in the fuel injection system, first ensure that all the system wiring connectors are securely connected and free from corrosion. Ensure that the fault is not due to poor maintenance; ie, check that the air cleaner filter element is clean, that the cylinder compression pressures are correct (see Chapter 2A, 2B or 2C), and that the engine breather hoses are clear and undamaged (see Chapter 4B).

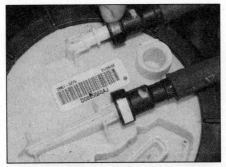

7.2 Depress the locking collars and disconnect the supply and return hoses from the tank sender unit

7.4a Lift the sender unit from the tank . . .

2 If the engine will not start, check the condition of the glow plugs (see Chapter 5).
3 If these checks fail to reveal the cause of the problem, the vehicle should be taken to a Ford dealer or specialist for testing using special electronic equipment which is plugged into the diagnostic connector (see Section 5). The tester should locate the fault quickly and simply, avoiding the need to test all the system components individually, which is time-consuming, and also carries a risk of damaging the PCM.

Adjustment

4 The engine idle speed, maximum speed and fuel injection pump timing are all controlled by the PCM. Whilst in theory it is possible to check the settings, if they are found to be in need of adjustment, the car will have to

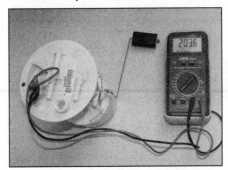

7.5 Use a multimeter to measure the sender unit resistance at full and zero float arm deflection

7.3 We used a home-made tool to unscrew the sender unit plastic collar

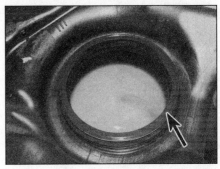

7.4b . . . discard the seal (arrowed) a new one must be fitted

be taken to a suitably-equipped Ford dealer or specialist. They will have access to the necessary diagnostic equipment required to test and (where possible) adjust the settings.

9 Fuel injection pump – removal and refitting

Caution: Cleanliness is essential. Be careful not to allow dirt into the injection pump or injector pipes during this procedure.
Note: Any rigid high-pressure fuel pipes disturbed must be renewed.

1.6 litre engines

Note: A new fuel pump-to-accumulator (common) rail high-pressure fuel pipe will be required for refitting.

7.6 The arrow on the sender cover must align with the marks on the fuel tank (arrowed)

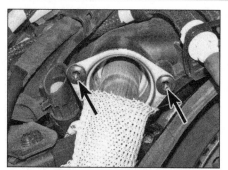

9.3a Undo the 2 bolts (arrowed) securing the EGR pipe to the manifold/cover . . .

9.3b . . . then the bolt (arrowed) securing the pipe to the head . . .

9.3c . . . then release the clamp (arrowed) and remove the EGR pipe

Tool Tip 1: A sprocket holding tool can be made from two lengths of steel strip bolted together to form a forked end. Bend the ends of the strip through 90° to form the 'prongs'.

TOOL TiP

Tool Tip 2: Make a sprocket releasing tool from a short strip of steel. Drill two holes in the strip to correspond with the two holes in the sprocket. Drill a third hole just large enough to accept the flats of the sprocket retaining nut.

Removal

1 Disconnect the battery (see Chapter 5) and remove the timing belt as described in Chapter 2A. After removal of the timing belt, temporarily refit the right-hand engine mounting but do not fully tighten the bolts.

2 Remove the air filter assembly as described in Section 2.

3 Remove the EGR cooler as described in Chapter 4B, or on models without a cooler, undo the bolts, release the clamps and remove the EGR pipe **(see illustrations)**.

4 Undo the bolts/nuts and remove the support brackets above the fuel common rail and the high-pressure pump.

5 Undo the union nuts and remove the high-pressure fuel pipe between the fuel common rail and the high-pressure pump. Plug the openings to prevent contamination.

6 Disconnect the wiring plug from the high-pressure fuel pump.

7 Depress the release buttons and disconnect the fuel supply and return hoses from the pump. Note that the hoses may have a release button on each side of the fitting. Plug the openings to prevent contamination.

8 Hold the pump sprocket stationary, and loosen the centre nut securing it to the pump shaft **(see Tool Tip 1)**.

9 The fuel pump sprocket is a taper fit on the pump shaft and it will be necessary to make up a tool to release it from the taper **(see Tool Tip 2)**. Partially unscrew the sprocket retaining nut, fit the home-made tool, and secure it to the sprocket with two 7.0 mm bolts and nuts. Prevent the sprocket from rotating as before, and screw down the nuts, forcing the sprocket off the shaft taper.

10 Once the taper is released, remove the tool, unscrew the nut fully, and remove the sprocket from the pump shaft.

11 Undo the three bolts, and remove the pump from the mounting bracket.

Caution: The high-pressure fuel pump is manufactured to extremely close

9.16 Remove the seal housing retaining nuts

tolerances and must not be dismantled in any way. Do not unscrew the fuel pipe male union on the rear of the pump, or attempt to remove the sensor, piston de-activator switch, or the seal on the pump shaft. No parts for the pump are available separately and if the unit is in any way suspect, it must be renewed.

Refitting

12 Refitting is a reversal of removal, noting the following points:

a) *Always renew the pump-to-common rail high-pressure pipe.*

b) *With everything reassembled and reconnected, and observing the precautions listed in Section 1, start the engine and allow it to idle. Check for leaks at the high-pressure fuel pipe unions with the engine idling. If satisfactory, increase the engine speed to 3000 rpm and check again for leaks.*

c) *Take the car for a short road test and check for leaks once again on return. If any leaks are detected, obtain and fit another new high-pressure fuel pipe. Do not attempt to cure even the slightest leak by further tightening of the pipe unions.*

1.8 litre engines

Removal

13 Disconnect the battery negative lead as described in Chapter 5.

14 Remove the timing belt as described in Chapter 2B.

15 Slacken the three bolts securing the injection pump timing belt sprocket, and remove the sprocket from the pump. The sprocket may need to be prevented from turning as this is done – it should prove sufficient to select a gear and apply the handbrake, but it may be necessary to jam the flywheel ring gear as described in Chapter 2B, Section 6. The sprocket is sealed to the inner pulley using RTV sealant, and may need to be prised free; recover the metal gasket.

16 Remove the 7 nuts which secure the injection pump oil seal housing, and withdraw the seal housing from around the pump inner pulley **(see illustration)**. Withdraw the timing belt backplate from the oil pump housing studs, noting which way round it fits.

9.17 Undo the support bracket bolts (arrowed)

9.18 Place the spanner on the thickest section of the union nut (arrowed)

9.20 Remove the support bracket bolts at the rear of the pump (arrowed)

9.21 Depress the clip and disconnect the fuel return pipe

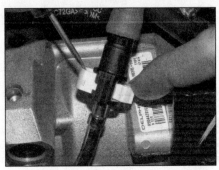

9.22 Prise out the locking catch, then prise out the clip and disconnect the fuel supply pipe

17 Undo the bolt/nut and remove the high-pressure fuel supply pipe support bracket from the pump (see illustration). Note: *Place rags over the alternator to prevent fuel damaging the unit.*

18 Ensure the area around fuel pipes connections on the pump and supply manifold are absolutely clean, place rags over the top of the alternator to protect it from fuel spillage. Slacken the unions and the clamp bolt, clean the pipes once the unions nuts have been moved along the pipe, then remove the pump-to-supply manifold rigid metal fuel pipe (see illustration). Plug or cap the openings to prevent dirt ingress. Make a note of the exact position of the pipe clamp, to enable it to be fitted in exactly the same place on the new pipe.

19 Note their fitted positions, then disconnect all wiring plugs from the pump.

20 Undo the 2 bolts securing the support bracket to the rear of the pump (see illustration).

21 Depress the locking tabs and disconnect the fuel return pipe from the pump (see illustration). Plug or cap the opening to prevent dirt ingress.

22 Prise out the locking catch, then using a small screwdriver, prise out the clip and disconnect the fuel supply pipe from the pump (see illustration). Plug or cap the opening to prevent dirt ingress.

23 Unscrew and remove the 4 bolts securing the drive chain sprocket to the injection pump. As with removal of its timing belt sprocket, it may be necessary to prevent the pulley from turning as the bolts are loosened.

24 Undo the 3 bolts securing the pump to the engine casing. It may not be possible to remove the bolts completely.

25 Manoeuvre the pump from the engine.

Refitting

26 Align the hole in the fuel pump drive flange with the etched mark on the pump body (see illustration).

27 With a new gasket and seal, refit the pump to the front engine casing, and tighten the bolts to the specified torque.

28 Refit the 4 chain sprocket bolts and tighten them to the specified torque.

29 Before reconnecting the return and supply pipes, the injection pump should be primed with fuel, to reduce the length of time spent cranking the engine at start-up. If a new pump has been fitted (or the old pump has been off the engine for some time), priming with fuel is essential, as the fuel lubricates the pump internals, which may otherwise be dry. Follow the procedures in Section 6. If a vacuum pump is not available, a new pump can be partially primed by pouring in clean fuel via the fuel supply and return connections – take precautions against fuel spillage on delicate components by covering the surrounding area with clean rags, and be very careful not to introduce dirt into the pump.

30 Remove the blanking plugs/cap (if not already done so), and reconnect the fuel return and supply pipes to the pump.

31 If removed, refit the fuel pump rear support bracket to the pump, and tighten the bolts securely.

32 Reconnect the wiring plugs to the pump.

33 Fit the clamp to the new rigid pump-to-supply manifold metal pipe in exactly the same position as it was fitted to the original.

34 Spray the threads of the pump and supply manifold unions with a lubricant (eg, WD40, etc), then remove the blanking plugs and fit the pipe in place, but only finger-tighten the unions at this stage.

35 Refit the pump rear support bracket, and tighten the bolts securely.

36 Using a crow's-foot spanner, tighten the rigid metal pipe unions to the specified torque, starting at the supply manifold first. Ensure the spanner acts upon the part of the union where there is the most metal, to avoid damage to the union (see illustration 9.18).

37 Refit the support bracket to the ridged metal pipe at the pump, and tighten the bolt/nut securely.

38 Fit a new metal gasket to the pump drive chain sprocket. Apply a coating of Loctite RTV 5910 sealant to the sprocket (avoiding the three sprocket bolt holes). The three bolts should be cleaned, then lightly coated with Loctite 518 locking fluid. Offer up the timing belt sprocket, aligning the bolt holes carefully, then fit the three bolts and tighten to the specified torque.

39 Refit the timing belt as described in Chapter 2B.

40 Start the engine, and let it idle, noting that it may take a while before a stable idle speed is achieved, as the engine management module (PCM) may have to relearn some of

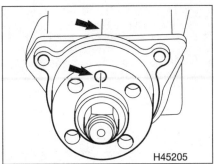

9.26 Align the hole in the drive flange with the mark on the pump body (arrowed)

9.43 Remove the pipe (arrowed) between the high-pressure pump and the fuel rail

9.44a Depress the release tabs (arrowed) and disconnect the fuel supply . . .

9.44b . . . and return hoses from the pump (arrowed)

9.46 Undo the 3 bolts and remove the pump (arrowed)

9.48 Ensure the pump drive dog (arrowed) is aligned with the slot in the end of the camshaft

between the pump and common rail, then tighten to the specified torque, using a crow's-foot adapter.

51 The remainder of refitting is a reversal of removal, bearing in mind the following points:

a) *Bleed the fuel system as described in Section 6.*

b) *Once the engine has started, thoroughly check for fuel leaks from the disturbed pipes/hoses.*

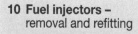

10 Fuel injectors – removal and refitting

Caution: Be careful not to allow dirt into the injection pump or injector pipes during this procedure.

Removal

1.6 litre engines

the 'adaptive' values. As the engine warms-up, check for signs of leakage from the fuel unions. If no leakage is evident, take the car for a short journey (of at least 5 miles) to allow the PCM to complete its 'learning' process.

2.0 litre engines

Removal

41 Remove the plastic cover from the top of the engine, by pulling it straight up from its mountings at the front and right-hand edges, then pull it forwards.

42 Remove the air cleaner assembly as described in Section 2.

43 Undo the unions and remove the high-pressure fuel pipe between the pump and the fuel rail **(see illustration)**. Discard the pipe, a new one must be fitted.

44 Note their fitted positions, depress the release tabs, and disconnect the fuel

supply and return pipes from the pump **(see illustrations)**. Be prepared for fuel spillage. Plug the openings to prevent contamination.

45 Note their fitted positions, and disconnect the wiring plugs from the pump.

46 Undo the 3 retaining bolts and pull the pump from the cylinder head **(see illustration)**. Discard the gasket.

Refitting

47 Ensure that the mating surfaces of the pump and cylinder head are clean and dry, and fit the new gasket.

48 Ensure the slot in the end of the camshaft and the pump drive dog are aligned, then refit the pump, tightening the mounting bolts to the specified torque **(see illustration)**.

49 Reconnect the fuel supply and return pipes to the pump, and the wiring plugs.

50 Fit the new high-pressure fuel pipe

1 Disconnect the battery negative lead as described in Chapter 5.

2 Pull the plastic cover (where fitted) on the top of the engine upwards to release it from the mountings.

3 Undo the 2 retaining bolts and move the brake master cylinder remote reservoir (where fitted) to one side **(see illustration)**.

4 Remove the wiper arms as described in Chapter 12.

5 Release the 5 clips and remove the windscreen cowl panel by pulling it up from the base of the windscreen **(see illustrations)**.

6 Undo the bolt at each end, release the 2 clips

10.3 Undo the bolts (arrowed) and move the remote reservoir to one side

10.5a Prise forwards the clips (arrowed) on each side . . .

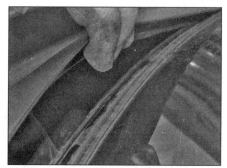

10.5b . . . and pull the windscreen cowl panel upwards from the base of the windscreen

10.6 Undo the bolt at each end (arrowed) and pull the bulkhead extension panel forwards

10.7a Undo the injector wiring guide bolts (arrowed)

10.7b Depress the clip and disconnect the wiring plugs from the injectors

and remove the bulkhead extension panel **(see illustration)**.

7 Undo the 3 bolts, lift the injector wiring guide from place, then disconnect the wiring plugs from the top of each injector **(see illustrations)**.

8 Extract the retaining circlip and disconnect the leak-off pipe from each fuel injector **(see illustration)**.

9 Clean the area around the high-pressure fuel pipes between the injectors and the common rail, then unscrew the pipe unions. Use a second spanner to counter-hold the union screwed into the injector body **(see illustration)**. The injectors screwed-in unions must not be allowed to move. Remove the bracket above the common rail unions, then remove the pipes. Plug the openings in the common rail and injectors to prevent dirt ingress.

10 Unscrew the injector retaining bolts, and carefully pull or lever the injector from place. If necessary, use an open-ended spanner and twist the injector to free it from position **(see illustrations)**. Do not lever against or pull on the solenoid housing at the top of the injector. Note down the injector's position – if the injectors are to be refitted, they must be refitted to their original locations. If improved access is required, undo the bolts and remove the oil separator housing from the front of the cylinder head cover.

11 Remove the copper washer and the upper seal from each injector, or from the cylinder head if they remained in place during injector removal. New copper washers and upper

seals will be required for refitting. Cover the injector hole in the cylinder head to prevent dirt ingress.

12 Examine each injector visually for any signs of obvious damage or deterioration. If any defects are apparent, renew the injector(s).

Caution: The injectors are manufactured to extremely close tolerances and must not be dismantled in any way. Do not unscrew the fuel pipe union on the side of the injector, or separate any parts of the injector body. Do not attempt to clean carbon deposits from the injector nozzle or carry out any form of ultrasonic or pressure testing.

1.8 litre engines

13 Remove the plastic cover on the top of the engine **(see illustration 2.5)**. Take care to manoeuvre the cover around the MAP sensor.

14 Disconnect the battery negative lead as described in Chapter 5.

15 Release the clamps and disconnect the breather hoses from the cylinder head cover **(see illustration)**.

16 Disconnect the wiring plugs from the high-pressure fuel pump and the common rail.

17 Disconnect the wiring plug from the fuel temperature sensor, then disconnect the wiring plug from each injector **(see illustrations)**. Move the wiring harness to one side.

18 Ensure the areas around the injection pipes and unions is absolutely clean. If possible, use a vacuum cleaner to remove all debris from the vicinity.

19 Slacken and unscrew the pipe unions at the injectors and the fuel supply manifold (common rail), but keep the metal pipes in contact with the injectors and manifold until the unions have been moved along the pipe and the areas at the ends of the pipes cleaned.

10.8 Prise out the clip and pull the return pipe from each injector

10.9 Use a second spanner to counter-hold the high-pressure pipe union nuts

10.10a Injector retaining bolts (arrowed)

10.10b Use a spanner to twist the injector and free it from position

10.15 Disconnect the breather hoses (arrowed) from the cylinder head cover

10.17a Disconnect the fuel temperature sensor wiring plug (arrowed)

10.17b Depress the clip (arrowed) and disconnect the injector wiring plugs

10.22a Slacken the injector clamp bolts . . .

10.22b . . . and pull the injectors from place

10.26a Prise down the lower edge of the retaining clip (shown with the return hose disconnected for clarity) . . .

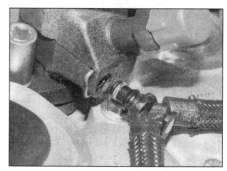

10.26b . . . then pull the return hoses from the injectors

Use a second spanner to counter-hold the unions at the injectors. Be prepared for fuel spillage.

20 With any dirt/debris removed, detach the pipes from the injectors and manifold, then plug the openings to prevent dirt ingress. Discard the pipes – Ford insist that new ones must be fitted.

21 Ensure the area around the injectors is absolutely clean and free from debris. If possible, use a vacuum cleaner to remove any dirt.

22 Slacken the injector clamps retaining bolts, and pull the injectors from place **(see illustrations)**. Discard the clamp bolts – new ones must be fitted. If the original injectors are to be refitted, it is absolutely essential that they are refitted in to their original positions.

23 Discard the injectors sealing washers – new ones must be fitted.

2.0 litre engines

24 Remove the cylinder head cover/inlet manifold as described in Chapter 2C.

25 Make sure the areas around the high-pressure fuel pipe unions from the fuel rail to the injectors is scrupulously clean and free from debris, etc. If possible, use a vacuum cleaner and a degreaser to clean the area.

26 Carefully prise down the lower edge of the retaining clips, then disconnect the fuel return hoses from the injectors **(see illustrations)**. Take care not to drop the retaining clips as they are removed, and check the condition of the O-ring seals – renew if necessary.

27 Undo the unions, then remove the high-pressure fuel pipes from the fuel rail to the injectors. Discard the fuel pipes, new ones must be fitted. Use a second open-ended spanner on the injector port to counter-hold when slackening the pipe union **(see**

illustration). Be prepared for fuel spillage and plug/cover the ports in the injectors and fuel rail to prevent dirt ingress.

28 Unscrew the two bolts securing each injector clamp, and carefully remove the injectors. Slide the copper sealing washer from the end of each injector. Discard the sealing washers – new ones must be fitted **(see illustration)**.

Refitting

29 Locate a new upper seal (1.6 and 2.0 litre) on the body of each injector, and place a new copper washer on the injector nozzle **(see illustration)**.

30 Refit the injector clamp locating dowels (where fitted) to the cylinder head.

1.6 litre engines

31 Ensure the injector clamps are in place over their respective circlips on the injector

10.27 Use a second spanner to counter-hold the injector port when slackening the union nut

10.28 Injector clamp bolts (arrowed)

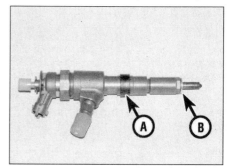

10.29 Upper seal (A) and copper washer (B)

10.31 Fit the injectors into their original locations

10.33 Note the injector classification number

10.34 Take note of the identification numbers of the new injectors, these need to be uploaded into the PCM

bodies, then fit the injectors into place in the cylinder head. If the original injectors are being refitted, ensure they are fitted into their original positions **(see illustration)**.

32 Fit the injector retaining bolts/nuts, but only finger-tighten them at this stage. When tightening the nuts/bolts, ensure the clamps stay horizontal.

33 If new injectors have been fitted, note down the new 8-digit injector classification number – this will be need to be entered into the PCM memory using dedicated Ford test equipment **(see illustration)**.

1.8 litre engines

34 If new injectors are being fitted, take of note of the identification numbers **(see illustration)**. These need to be uploaded into the PCM on completion of the work.

35 Fit a new sealing washer onto each injector **(see illustration)**.

36 Fit the injectors and clamps into the cylinder head, then tighten the new clamps bolts finger-tight only at this stage.

2.0 litre engines

37 Place the injector clamp in the slot on each injector body and refit the injectors to the cylinder head. Guide the clamp over the mounting stud and onto the locating dowel as each injector is inserted. Ensure the upper injector seals are correctly located in the cylinder head.

38 Fit the washer and a new injector clamp retaining nut to each mounting stud. Tighten the nuts finger-tight only at this stage.

All engines

39 Working on one fuel injector at a time, remove the blanking plugs from the fuel pipe unions on the common rail and the relevant injector. Locate a new high-pressure fuel pipe over the unions and screw on the union nuts. Take care not to cross-thread the nuts or strain the fuel pipes as they are fitted. Once the union nut threads have started, finger-tighten the nuts only at this stage, to the ends of the threads.

40 When all the fuel pipes are in place, tighten the injector clamp retaining nuts/bolts to the specified torque and angle.

41 Using an open-ended spanner, hold each fuel pipe union in turn and tighten the

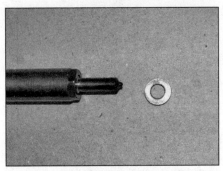

10.35 Fit a new sealing washer onto each injector

union nut to the specified torque using a torque wrench and crow's-foot adapter **(see illustration)**. Tighten all the disturbed union nuts in the same way.

42 If new injectors have been fitted, their classification numbers must be programmed into the engine management PCM using dedicated diagnostic equipment/scanner. If this equipment is not available, entrust this task to a Ford dealer or suitably-equipped repairer. Note that it should be possible to drive the vehicle, albeit with reduced performance/increased emissions, to a repairer for the numbers to be programmed.

43 The remainder of refitting is a reversal of removal, noting the following points:
a) *Ensure all wiring connectors and harnesses are correctly refitting and secured.*
b) *Reconnect the battery as described in Chapter 5.*

11.3 Crankshaft position sensor (arrowed) – 1.6 litre

10.41 Tighten the high-pressure pipe union nuts using a 'crow's-foot' adapter

c) *Observing the precautions listed in Section 1, start the engine and allow it to idle. Check for leaks at the high-pressure fuel pipe unions with the engine idling. If satisfactory, increase the engine speed to 3000 rpm and check again for leaks. Take the car for a short road test and check for leaks once again on return. If any leaks are detected, obtain and fit additional new high-pressure fuel pipes as required. **Do not** attempt to cure even the slightest leak by further tightening of the pipe unions.*

11 Engine management system components – removal and refitting

Crankshaft position/speed sensor

1.6 litre engines

1 The crankshaft position sensor is located adjacent to the crankshaft pulley on the right-hand end of the engine. Slacken the right-hand front roadwheel bolts, then jack the front of the vehicle up and support it on axle stands (see *Jacking and vehicle support*). Remove the right-hand front roadwheel.

2 Release the fasteners and remove the right-hand front wheel arch liner.

3 Disconnect the sensor wiring plug **(see illustration)**.

4 Undo the bolt and remove the sensor.

5 Refitting is a reversal of removal, tightening the sensor retaining bolt to the specified torque.

11.7 Crankshaft position sensor – 1.8 litre

11.9 Undo the bolt (arrowed), then slide the sensor from place

11.15 Slide up the red locking clip (arrowed) and disconnect the mass airflow sensor

1.8 litre engines

6 Before removing the sensor, set the crankshaft at TDC on No 1 cylinder, as described in Chapter 2B.

7 The sensor is located at the flywheel end of the engine, low down at the rear **(see illustration)**. For improved access, apply the handbrake then jack up the front of the vehicle and support it on axle stands (see *Jacking and vehicle support*).

8 Disconnect the wiring plug from the sensor.

9 Unscrew the mounting bolt, then slide the sensor to towards the timing belt end of the engine and withdraw it **(see illustration)**.

10 Refitting is a reversal of removal, but ensure that the sensor and the block mounting face is clean and free from debris, and tighten the bolt to the specified torque.

2.0 litre engines

11 Remove the crankshaft pulley as described in Chapter 2C.

12 The sensor is located adjacent to the crankshaft pulley. Disconnect the sensor wiring plug.

13 Slacken and remove the retaining bolt and carefully remove the sensor.

14 Refitting is the reverse of removal, tightening the retaining bolt to the specified torque.

Mass airflow sensor

1.6 and 1.8 litre engines

15 On these engines, a combined Inlet Air Temperature (IAT) and Mass AirFlow (MAF) sensor is fitted to the air cleaner cover outlet.

Slacken the clamp and disconnect the air outlet hose from the sensor **(see illustration)**.

16 Disconnect the sensor wiring plug.

17 Undo the bolts then remove the airflow sensor from the air cleaner housing, along with its sealing ring.

18 Refitting is the reverse of removal, lubricating the sealing ring.

2.0 litre engines

19 Disconnect the sensor wiring plug.

20 Slacken the clamp and disconnect the air outlet hose from the sensor **(see illustration 2.10)**.

21 Undo the bolts then remove the airflow sensor from the air cleaner housing, along with its sealing ring.

22 Refitting is the reverse of removal, lubricating the sealing ring.

Coolant temperature sensor

23 Refer to Chapter 3 for removal and refitting details.

Accelerator pedal position sensor

24 The sensor is secured to the accelerator pedal. Refer to Section 4 of this Chapter for pedal removal. Note that at the time of writing, the sensor was not available separately from the pedal assembly.

Manifold absolute pressure (MAP) sensor

Note: *No MAP sensor is fitted to the 1.8 litre engine*

25 The sensor is mounted on the inlet manifold/throttle body **(see illustrations)**.

26 Pull the plastic cover (where fitted) on the top of the engine straight up from its mountings at the front and right-hand edges, then pull it forwards.

27 Ensure the ignition is switched off then disconnect the wiring connector from the sensor.

28 Slacken and remove the retaining bolt and remove the sensor from the vehicle.

29 Refitting is the reverse of removal, tightening the sensor retaining securely.

Stop-light switch

30 The powertrain control module receives a signal from the stop-light switch which indicates when the brakes are being applied. Stop-light switch removal and refitting details can be found in Chapter 9.

Powertrain control module (PCM)

Note: *If a new control module is fitted, it must be programmed using dedicated Ford test equipment. Entrust this task to a Ford dealer or suitably-equipped specialist.*

31 Disconnect the battery negative lead (see Chapter 5), then wait at least 2 minutes before commencing work, to allow any stored electrical energy to dissipate.

32 Slacken the left-hand front roadwheel nuts, then raise the front of the vehicle and support it securely on axle stands (see *Jacking and vehicle support*). Remove the roadwheel.

33 Remove the bolts and remove the left-front wheel arch liner **(see illustrations)**.

11.25a MAP sensor (arrowed) – 1.6 litre . . .

11.25b . . . and 2.0 litre (arrowed)

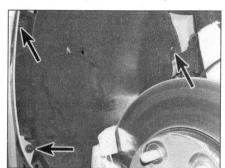

11.33a Undo the bolts at the front of the wheel arch liner (arrowed) . . .

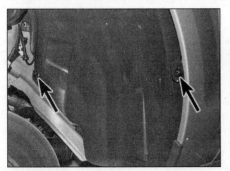

11.33b ...and the rear (arrowed)

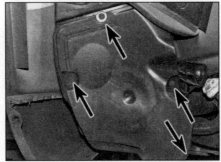

11.34 PCM cover bolts (arrowed)

11.35 Pull the PCM to release the clips

34 Undo the 4 Torx bolts and remove the PCM cover **(see illustration)**.

35 Pull the PCM from place to release the retaining clips **(see illustration)**.

36 On models fitted with a security bracket over the PCM, drill a hole in the end and remove the shear bolt **(see illustration)**. Slide the bracket from the PCM.

37 Pivot over the locking catches, and disconnect the 3 wiring plugs from the PCM **(see illustration)**.

38 Refitting is a reversal of removal, ensuring the cover's rubber seal (where fitted) is correctly positioned in the groove.

Inlet air temperature sensor

1.8 and 2.0 litre engines only

39 Remove the plastic cover from over the top of the engine by pulling it straight up from its mountings at the front and right-hand edges, then pull it forwards.

40 Disconnect the sensor wiring plug **(see illustrations)**.

41 Undo the retaining bolt and pull the sensor from position.

42 Apply a little petroleum jelly to ease the sensor in to place, then tighten the retaining bolt securely.

43 Reconnect the sensor wiring plug and refit the engine cover.

Fuel pressure sensor

44 It is not possible to replace the sensor separately from the fuel rail. Ford advise that no attempt should be made to remove it. If the sensor is faulty, renew the fuel rail as described in this Section.

Fuel (common) rail

Removal – 1.6 litre engines

45 Remove the cylinder head cover/inlet manifold as described in Chapter 2A.

46 Drain the cooling system as described in Chapter 1.

47 Remove the EGR cooler or pipe as described in Chapter 4B.

48 Undo the mounting bolts, slacken the clamps, and move aside the coolant pump outlet assembly **(see illustration)**.

49 Clean around the pipe, then undo the

11.36 Drill out the shear bolt (arrowed)

11.37 Pivot over the locking catches and disconnect the wiring plugs

unions and remove the high-pressure pipe from the common rail to the high-pressure pump. Plug the openings to prevent contamination.

11.40a Inlet air temperature sensor –
1.8 litre . . .

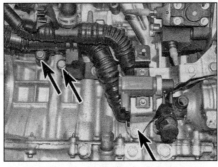

11.48 Undo the bolts (arrowed) and move aside the coolant outlet assembly

50 Disconnect the pressure sensor wiring plug from the common rail **(see illustration)**.

51 Unscrew the two rail mounting bolts and manoeuvre it from place **(see illustration)**.

11.40b ...and 2.0 litre (arrowed)

11.50 The pressure sensor is located at the end of the common rail (arrowed)

11.51 Common rail mounting bolt/stud (arrowed)

11.57 Undo the two bolts (arrowed) and remove the supply manifold

11.60 Undo the 3 bolts (arrowed) and remove the fuel filter bracket

Note: Ford insist that the fuel pressure sensor on the common rail must not be removed.
Caution: Do not attempt to remove the four high-pressure fuel pipe male unions from the common rail. These parts are not available separately and if disturbed are likely to result in fuel leakage on reassembly.

Removal – 1.8 litre engines

52 Disconnect the high-pressure fuel pipes from the common rail as described in Section 10. Discard the pipes, new ones must be fitted.
53 Ensure the area around the pump-to-fuel supply manifold pipe is absolutely clean. If possible, use a vacuum cleaner to remove any debris.
54 Slacken the nut/bolt securing the pipe support bracket to the pump. Make a note of the fitted position of the clamp on the pipe – it will need to be transferred to the new pipe.
55 Slacken and undo the pump-to-supply manifold pipe unions, then clean the area at the ends of the pipe before removing and discarding it. Plug or cover the openings in the pump and manifold to prevent dirt ingress.
56 Disconnect the wiring plug from the fuel pressure sensor on the supply manifold.
57 Undo the two bolts and remove the fuel supply manifold **(see illustration)**.
58 No further dismantling of the manifold is advised, no parts are available separately.

Removal – 2.0 litre engines

59 Remove the inlet manifold/cylinder head cover as described in Chapter 2C.

60 Remove the fuel filter as described in Chapter 1, then undo the bolts and remove the fuel filter bracket **(see illustration)**.
61 Make sure the areas around the high-pressure fuel pipe unions from the fuel rail to the injectors, and the high-pressure pump is scrupulously clean and free from debris, etc. If possible, use a vacuum cleaner and a degreaser to clean the area.
62 Undo the unions, then remove the high-pressure fuel pipes from the fuel rail to the injectors, and from the fuel rail to the high-pressure pump. Discard the fuel pipes, new ones must be fitted. Use a second open-ended spanner on the ports to counter-hold when slackening the pipe union **(see illustration 10.27)**. Be prepared for fuel spillage and plug/cover the ports in the injectors, high-pressure pump and fuel rail to prevent dirt ingress.
63 Disconnect the fuel pressure sensor wiring plug **(see illustration)**.
64 Undo the nuts and remove the fuel rail.

Refitting – all engines

65 Locate the common rail in position, refit and finger-tighten the mounting bolts/nuts.
66 Reconnect the common rail wiring plug(s).
67 Fit the new pump-to-rail high-pressure pipe, and only finger-tighten the unions at first, then tighten the unions to the Stage 1 torque setting, followed by the Stage 2 torque setting. Use a second spanner to counter-hold the union screwed into the pump body.

68 Fit the new set of rail-to-injector high-pressure pipes, and finger-tighten the unions. If it's not possible to fit the new pipes to the injector unions, remove and refit the injectors as described in Section 10, and try again.
69 Tighten the common rail mounting bolts/nuts to the specified torque.
70 Tighten the rail-to-injector pipe unions to the Stage 1 torque setting, followed by the Stage 2 setting. Use a second spanner to counter-hold the injector unions. Use a crow's-foot adapter to tighten the union nuts **(see illustration)**.
71 The remainder of refitting is a reversal of removal, noting the following points:
  a) *Ensure all wiring connectors and harnesses are correctly refitting and secured.*
  b) *Reconnect the battery as described in Chapter 5.*
  c) *Observing the precautions listed in Section 1, start the engine and allow it to idle. Check for leaks at the high-pressure fuel pipe unions with the engine idling. If satisfactory, increase the engine speed to 3000 rpm and check again for leaks. Take the car for a short road test and check for leaks once again on return. If any leaks are detected, obtain and fit additional new high-pressure fuel pipes as required. **Do not** attempt to cure even the slightest leak by further tightening of the pipe unions.*

Camshaft position sensor

1.6 and 2.0 litre engines

72 The camshaft position sensor is mounted on the right-hand end of the cylinder head cover, directly behind the camshaft sprocket.
73 Remove the upper timing belt cover, as described in Chapter 2A or 2C as applicable.
74 Unplug the sensor wiring connector.
75 Undo the bolt and pull the sensor from position **(see illustrations)**.
76 Upon refitting, position the sensor so that the nipple of the sensor is just in contact with the camshaft signal wheel. Tighten the sensor retaining bolt to the specified torque.
77 The remainder of refitting is a reversal of removal.

11.63 The fuel pressure sensor (arrowed) is located on the underside of the common fuel rail

11.70 Use a 'crow's-foot' adapter to tighten the union nuts

11.75a Camshaft position sensor bolt (arrowed) – 1.6 litre

11.75b Camshaft position sensor (arrowed) – 2.0 litre

11.79 Camshaft position sensor – 1.8 litre

1.8 litre engines

78 Carefully pull the plastic cover on the top of the engine upwards from place.

79 The sensor is located on the cylinder head cover. Disconnect the sensor wiring plug **(see illustration)**.

80 Undo the bolt and pull the sensor from position.

81 Refitting is a reversal of removal.

Turbocharger boost pressure regulator valve

1.6 and 2.0 litre engines only

82 Remove the plastic cover (where fitted) from over the top of the engine

83 Disconnect the wiring plug, then undo the 2 regulator retaining nuts **(see illustrations)**.

84 Note their fitted locations and disconnect the vacuum hoses as the regulator is withdrawn.

85 Refitting is a reversal of removal.

Fuel pressure control valve and fuel volume control valve

86 These valves are fitted to the high-pressure injection pump. They are not available as separate items, and can only be renewed along with the pump. Ford advise that no attempt should be made to remove the valves.

Anti-shudder control valve

87 On some engines, an anti-shudder valve is fitted to the inlet manifold to reduce vibration when the engine is turned off. It achieves this by closing the inlet port, preventing any air from being drawn into the cylinders. The valve body is fitted between the inlet manifold and the intercooler. Remove the plastic cover from the top of the engine.

88 To remove the valve body, note their fitted positions, and disconnect wiring plugs from the various sensors/motors fitted to the valve body **(see illustration)**.

89 Slacken the clamps, and disconnect the air inlet hoses from the valve body.

90 Undo the mounting bolts and remove the valve body **(see illustration)**.

91 Refitting is a reversal of removal.

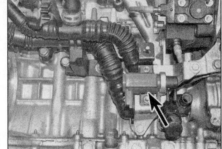

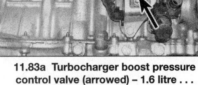

11.83a Turbocharger boost pressure control valve (arrowed) – 1.6 litre . . .

12 Turbocharger – description and precautions

Description

A turbocharger increases engine efficiency by raising the pressure in the inlet manifold above atmospheric pressure. Instead of the air simply being sucked into the cylinders, it is forced in. Additional fuel is supplied by the injection pump in proportion to the increased air inlet.

Energy for the operation of the turbocharger comes from the exhaust gas. The gas flows through a specially-shaped housing (the turbine housing) and in so doing, spins the turbine wheel. The turbine wheel is attached to a shaft, at the end of which is another vaned wheel known as the compressor wheel. The

11.88 Anti-shudder valve (arrowed) – 1.6 litre

11.83b . . . and at the left-hand end of the cylinder head on the 2.0 litre (arrowed)

compressor wheel spins in its own housing and compresses the inducted air on the way to the inlet manifold.

The compressed air passes through an intercooler. This is an air-to-air heat exchanger, mounted with the radiator at the front of the vehicle. The purpose of the intercooler is to remove from the inducted air some of the heat gained in being compressed. Because cooler air is denser, removal of this heat further increases engine efficiency.

The turbocharger has adjustable guide vanes controlling the flow of exhaust gas into the turbine. On 1.6 and 2.0 litre engines, the vanes are swivelled by a vacuum unit on the turbocharger, controlled by the boost pressure regulator valve, controlled in turn by the engine management PCM. On 1.8 litre engines, the position of the vanes is controlled by an electric motor attached to the turbocharger, again, controlled by the PCM. At lower

11.90 Anti-shudder valve bolts (arrowed) – 2.0 litre

13.3a Slacken the clamp (arrowed) and disconnect the turbocharger inlet hose

13.3b Slacken the clamp (arrowed) and disconnect the outlet hose

13.3c Undo the outlet pipe bolt (arrowed) . . .

13.3d . . . pull the pipe up from the mounting stud (arrowed) . . .

13.3e . . . and rotate it to remove it

13 Turbocharger – removal and refitting

engine speeds, the vanes close together, giving a smaller exhaust gas entry port, and therefore higher gas speed, which increases boost pressure at low engine speed. At high engine speed, the vanes are turned to give a larger exhaust gas entry port, and therefore lower gas speed, effectively maintaining a reasonably constant boost pressure over the engine rev range. This is known as a Variable Nozzle Turbocharger (VNT).

The turbo shaft is pressure-lubricated by an oil feed pipe from the main oil gallery. The shaft 'floats' on a cushion of oil. A drain pipe returns the oil to the sump.

Precautions

The turbocharger operates at extremely high speeds and temperatures. Certain precautions must be observed to avoid premature failure of the turbo or injury to the operator.

• **Do not** operate the turbo with any parts exposed. Foreign objects falling onto the rotating vanes could cause excessive damage and (if ejected) personal injury.
• **Do not** race the engine immediately after start-up, especially if it is cold. Give the oil a few seconds to circulate.
• **Always** allow the engine to return to idle speed before switching it off – do not blip the throttle and switch off, as this will leave the turbo spinning without lubrication.
• Allow the engine to idle for several minutes before switching off after a high-speed run.
• Observe the recommended intervals for oil and filter changing, and use a reputable oil of the specified quality (see *Lubricants and fluids*). Neglect of oil changing, or use of inferior oil, can cause carbon formation on the turbo shaft and subsequent failure.

1.6 litre engines

Removal

1 Apply the handbrake, then jack up the front of the vehicle and support it on axle stands (see *Jacking and vehicle support*). Undo the bolts and remove the engine undershield.
2 Place a sheet of thick cardboard over the rear of the radiator to protect it from accidental damage.
3 Slacken the clamps, undo the bolts, and remove the air ducts to and from the turbocharger and air filter assembly **(see illustrations)**. Note their fitted positions and disconnect the various wiring plugs as the assembly is withdrawn.
4 Slacken the clamps, undo the bolts and remove the intercooler inlet pipe **(see illustrations)**.
5 Undo the mounting bolts **(see illustration)**, and remove the heat shield from above turbocharger/catalytic converter.
6 Undo the 2 bolts and remove the heat shield above the exhaust manifold.
7 Disconnect the vacuum hose from the turbocharger wastegate control assembly **(see illustration)**.
8 Undo the oil supply pipe banjo bolts and recover the sealing washers **(see illustration)**. **Note:** *Ford insist that any strainer fitted to the*

13.4a Intercooler inlet pipe bolt on the transmission housing (arrowed) . . .

13.4b . . . and above the oil filter (arrowed)

13.5 Undo the bolts and remove the heat shield above the turbocharger

banjo bolt at the lower end of the oil supply pipe must be removed, using pliers, and discarded.

9 Slacken the retaining clip and disconnect the oil return pipe from the turbocharger and cylinder block.

10 Make a note of its fitted position, then slacken the clamp securing the catalytic converter to the turbocharger **(see illustration)**.

11 Unscrew the four nuts, and the nut securing the support bracket, then remove the turbocharger from the exhaust manifold **(see illustration)**.

Inspection

12 With the turbocharger removed, inspect the housing for cracks or other visible damage.

13 Spin the turbine or the compressor wheel, to verify that the shaft is intact and to feel for excessive shake or roughness. Some play is normal, since in use, the shaft is 'floating' on a film of oil. Check that the wheel vanes are undamaged.

14 If oil contamination of the exhaust or induction passages is apparent, it is likely that turbo shaft oil seals have failed.

15 No DIY repair of the turbo is possible and none of the internal or external parts are available separately. If the turbocharger is suspect in any way a complete new unit must be obtained.

Refitting

16 Refitting is a reverse of the removal procedure, bearing in mind the following points:

a) *Renew the turbocharger retaining nuts and gaskets.*

b) *When refitting the oil supply pipe, it's absolutely essential that the banjo bolts are tightened without placing the pipe under stress.*

c) *If a new turbocharger is being fitted, change the engine oil and filter.*

d) *Prime the turbocharger by injecting clean engine oil through the oil feed pipe union before reconnecting the union.*

1.8 litre engines

Removal

17 The turbocharger should only be removed with the engine completely cool. Disconnect the battery negative lead (see Chapter 5).

18 Remove the catalytic converter as described in Section 17.

19 Remove the air cleaner and inlet duct as described in Section 2.

20 Remove the EGR tube or cooler, as described in Chapter 4B.

21 Using the information in Section 15 if necessary, disconnect the intercooler air ducts from the turbocharger and inlet manifold, and remove them from the top of the engine – there is no need to remove the intercooler itself.

22 Undo the nuts and remove the turbocharger to exhaust manifold retaining clamp.

23 Disconnect the turbocharger wastegate actuator wiring plug **(see illustration)**.

13.7 Disconnect the vacuum hose (arrowed)

13.10 Slacken the clamp (arrowed) securing the catalytic converter to the turbocharger

24 Undo the nut securing the turbocharger oil supply pipe support bracket, then undo the banjo bolt and disconnect the oil supply pipe from the cylinder block. Note that the banjo bolt cannot be removed from the pipe.

25 Slacken the 3 nuts securing the turbocharger support bracket to the cylinder block.

26 Undo the bolts and remove the oil return pipe from the underside of the turbocharger. Discard the gaskets.

27 Undo the 2 bolts securing the turbocharger to the support bracket, and manoeuvre it from position.

28 No further dismantling of the turbocharger is recommended. Interfering with the wastegate setting may lead to a reduction in performance, or could result in engine damage. No parts appear to be available separately for the turbocharger.

29 If on inspection there are any signs of internal oil contamination on the turbine or

13.23 Turbocharger wastegate actuator wiring plug (arrowed)

13.8 Turbocharger oil supply and return pipes (arrowed)

13.11 Turbocharger upper retaining nuts (arrowed)

compressor wheels, this indicates failure of the turbocharger oil seals. Renewing these seals is a job best left to a turbocharger specialist. In the event of any problem with the turbocharger, one of these specialists will usually be able to rebuild a defective unit, or offer a rebuilt unit on an exchange basis, either of which will prove cheaper than a new unit.

Refitting

30 Refitting is a reversal of removal, noting the following points:

a) *Clean the mating surfaces, use a new exhaust manifold gasket, and tighten the manifold bolts to the specified torque.*

b) *Refit and tighten the engine rear mounting bolt to the specified torque.*

c) *Use new gaskets for the turbocharger oil return connections.*

d) *When refitting the EGR tube/cooler, offer it into position, and hand-tighten the*

13.39 Turbocharger inlet hose support bracket bolt (arrowed)

13.43 Undo the bolts/nuts and remove the bracket under the turbocharger (arrowed)

13.44 Turbocharger van position sensor/ actuator wiring plug and vacuum hose (arrowed)

13.45 Undo the two bolts (arrowed) securing the inlet hose

bolts. Position the new clamp as noted on removal, tighten the clamp nut/bolt to the specified torque, then tighten the remaining bolts.

e) *Refer to Section 17 when refitting the catalytic converter.*

f) *On models with the EGR cooler, top-up the cooling system as necessary (see 'Weekly checks').*

2.0 litre engines

Removal

31 Drain the cooling system as described in Chapter 1.

32 Remove the plastic cover from the top of the engine, then undo the bolts securing the brake master cylinder remote reservoir to the engine compartment bulkhead (where fitted).

33 Remove the wiper arms as described in Chapter 12.

34 Release the clips and remove the windscreen cowl panel **(see illustrations 10.5a and 10.5b)**.

35 Undo the bolt at each end, release the clips and remove the bulkhead extension panel **(see illustration 10.6)**.

36 Depress the release button and disconnect the engine breather hose from the inlet manifold.

37 Remove the right-hand driveshaft as described in Chapter 8.

38 Undo the 2 bolts securing the right-hand engine mounting to the inner wing.

39 Undo the bolt securing the turbocharger inlet hose support bracket **(see illustration)**.

40 Slacken the clamp and disconnect the outlet pipe from the turbocharger.

41 Remove the catalytic converter as described in Section 17.

42 Remove the catalytic converter support bracket.

43 Undo the nuts/bolts and remove the support bracket from the underside of the turbocharger **(see illustration)**.

44 Note their fitted positions, then disconnect the vacuum hose and wiring plug from the wastegate control assembly **(see illustration)**.

45 Undo the bolts and detach the inlet hose from the turbocharger. Depress the release clip and detach the pipe from the cylinder head cover **(see illustration)**.

46 Release the clamp and disconnect the heater core-to-bypass coolant hose.

47 Slacken the clamp, remove the support bracket bolt, undo the connection bolts and remove the bypass hose **(see illustration)**. Recover the O-ring seal, and renew if necessary.

48 Undo the banjo bolts and securing the oil supply pipe to the cylinder block. Renew the sealing washers. Note that a small filter is fitted into the banjo bolt – renew it **(see illustration)**.

49 Undo the 2 bolts securing the oil return hose to the underside of the turbocharger **(see illustration)**. Renew the gasket.

50 Undo the nuts and separate the turbocharger from the manifold **(see illustration)**.

51 If required, undo the banjo bolt and detach the oil supply pipe from the turbocharger. Renew the seals.

Refitting

52 Refitting is a reversal of removal, noting the following points:

a) *Ensure all mating surfaces are clean and dry.*

b) *Renew all O-rings, seals and gaskets.*

c) *Tighten all fasteners to the specified torque where available.*

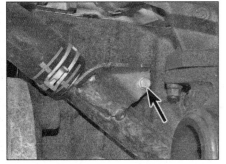

13.47 Coolant bypass pipe bolt (arrowed)

13.48 The oil feed banjo bolt incorporates a filter

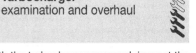

14 Turbocharger – examination and overhaul

With the turbocharger removed, inspect the housing for cracks or other visible damage.

Spin the turbine or the compressor wheel to verify that the shaft is intact and to feel for excessive shake or roughness. Some play is normal since in use the shaft is 'floating' on a film of oil. Check that the wheel vanes are undamaged.

13.49 Turbocharger oil return hose retaining bolts (arrowed)

13.50 Undo the nuts (arrowed) securing the turbocharger to the manifold

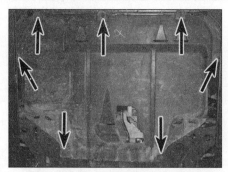

15.2a Engine undershield fasteners (arrowed)

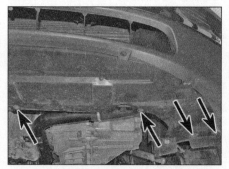

15.2b Radiator splash shield left-hand bolts (arrowed)

15.3 The intercooler outlet pipe bolt (arrowed) is accessed through the right-hand headlight aperture

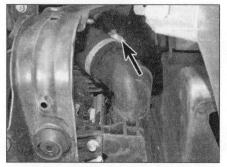

15.4a Slacken the intercooler inlet hose clamp (arrowed) . . .

15.4b . . . and the outlet hose clamp (arrowed)

15.5 Undo the retaining bolt (arrowed) each side

The wastegate and actuator are integral with the turbocharger, and cannot be checked or renewed separately. Consult a Ford dealer or other specialist if it is thought that the wastegate may be faulty.

If the exhaust or induction passages are oil-contaminated, the turbo shaft oil seals have probably failed. (On the induction side, this will also have contaminated the intercooler, where applicable, which if necessary should be flushed with a suitable solvent.)

No DIY repair of the turbo is possible. A new unit may be available on an exchange basis.

15 Intercooler – removal and refitting

Removal

1 Raise the front of the vehicle and support it securely on axle stands (see *Jacking and vehicle support*).
2 Undo the fasteners and remove the engine undershield, followed by the splash shield under the radiator **(see illustrations)**.
3 Remove the right-hand headlight as described in Chapter 12, then undo the Torx bolt securing the intercooler outlet pipe to the radiator fan shroud **(see illustration)**
4 Slacken the clamps and disconnect the inlet and outlet hoses from the intercooler **(see illustrations)**. Note that the clamps are integral with the hoses.
5 Undo the 2 retaining bolts, lift the intercooler upwards to disengage the upper mounting

lugs, and lower the intercooler from position **(see illustration)**.

Refitting

6 Refitting is a reversal of removal. Ensure the inside of the inlet and outlet hoses is clean where they attach to the intercooler.

16 Manifolds – removal and refitting

Inlet manifold

1.6 litre engines

1 The inlet manifold is integral with the cylinder head cover – refer to Chapter 2A.

1.8 litre engines

2 The manifold is integral with the EGR valve – refer to Chapter 4B.

2.0 litre engines

3 The manifold is integral with the cylinder head cover – refer to Chapter 2C.

Exhaust manifold

Removal

4 Remove the turbocharger as described in Section 13.
5 On 2.0 litre models, pull the manifold heat shield upwards to release the 2 retaining clips.
6 Undo the nuts securing the exhaust manifold to the cylinder head, and recover the spacers **(see illustration)**. Pull the manifold from the mounting studs. If the manifold is

being removed to renew the gasket, no further dismantling is required. Remove the gasket.

Refitting

7 Examine the studs for signs of damage and corrosion; remove traces of corrosion, and repair or renew any damaged studs.
8 Ensure the mating surfaces of the exhaust manifold and cylinder head are clean and dry. Position the new gasket, and refit the exhaust manifold to the cylinder head. Tighten the nuts to the specified torque.
9 The remainder of refitting is a reversal of removal, noting the following points:
   a) Tighten all fasteners to their specified torque where available.
   b) Apply a little high-temperature anti-seize grease (Copperslip) to the manifold studs.
   c) Top-up the coolant system as described in 'Weekly checks'.
   d) Check and, if necessary, top-up the oil level as described in Chapter 7.

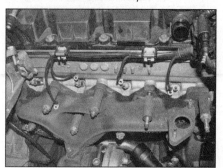

16.6 Undo the nuts and recover the manifold spacers – 2.0 litre

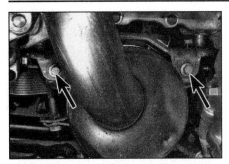

17.11 Undo the bolts (arrowed) securing the catalytic converter to the bracket – viewed from underneath

17.14a Unscrew the pressure take-off union from the side of the catalyst/filter . . .

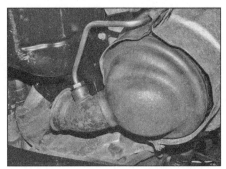

17.14b . . . and the one at the base

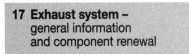

17 Exhaust system – general information and component renewal

1 The exhaust system consists of several sections: the front pipe with the catalytic converter(s), and the rear section with the intermediate and rear silencers. A particulate filter is available as standard or optional fitment on 1.6 and 2.0 litre models, depending on the market the vehicle is sold in. If required, the rear silencer can be renewed independently of the remainder of the system, by cutting the old silencer from the pipe, and slipping the new one over the cut end – details are given in this Section.

2 The exhaust system is joined together by a mixture of flanged, or sliding joints. Apply plenty of penetrating fluid to the fasteners prior to removal, undo the fasteners, unhook the rubber mountings, and manoeuvre the system from under the vehicle.

3 Each section is refitted by reversing the removal sequence, noting the following points:

a) *Ensure that all traces of corrosion have been removed from the flanges and renew all gaskets.*

b) *Inspect the rubber mountings for signs of damage or deterioration, and renew as necessary.*

c) *Prior to tightening the exhaust system fasteners to the specified torque, ensure that all rubber mountings are correctly located, and that is adequate*

clearance between the exhaust system and vehicle underbody.

Catalytic converter – 1.6 litre engines

4 Remove the plastic cover from the top of the engine (where fitted).

5 Raise the front of the vehicle and support it securely on axle stands (see *Jacking and vehicle support*).

6 Remove the cooling fan and shroud as described in Chapter 3.

7 Undo the bolt securing the intercooler inlet pipe bracket to the cylinder block.

8 Slacken the clamps and remove the intercooler inlet pipe assembly.

9 Attach wooden 'splints' each side of the exhaust flexible section using cable ties. This is to prevent excessive bending of the section as it's disconnected. Undo the 2 nuts securing the flexible section to the catalytic converter/particulate filter.

10 On models without a particulate filter, undo the bolts and remove the heat shield **(see illustration 13.5)**

11 Undo the 2 nuts securing the catalytic converter to the support bracket, and the bolts securing the support bracket to the cylinder block **(see illustration)**.

12 Undo the nut securing the catalytic converter bracket to the transmission casing.

Models with a particulate filter

13 Disconnect the wiring plug, and unscrew the temperature sensor from the catalytic converter/particulate filter.

14 Note their fitted positions, and

disconnect the pressure take-off hoses from the catalytic converter/particulate filter **(see illustrations)**.

15 Undo the bolts and remove the heat shield over the catalytic converter.

All models

16 Slacken the clamp securing the catalytic converter to the turbocharger. Note its fitted position to aid refitment.

17 Remove the heat shield bracket.

18 Manoeuvre the catalytic converter from place.

19 If required, note its fitted position, then slacken the clamp and detach the particulate filter from the base of the catalytic converter **(see illustration)**.

Catalytic converter – 1.8 litre engines

20 Raise the front of the vehicle and support it securely on axle stands (see *Jacking and vehicle support*).

21 Undo the fasteners and remove the engine undershield.

22 Undo the bolts and remove the underfloor brace adjacent to the front exhaust mounting **(see illustration)**.

23 Attach wooden 'splints' each side of the exhaust flexible section using cable ties. This is to prevent excessive bending of the section as it's disconnected. Undo the nuts securing the flexible section to the intermediate section.

24 Undo the nuts securing the catalytic converter to the turbocharger **(see illustration)**.

25 Undo the catalytic converter support

17.19 Undo the clamp (arrowed) and slide the particulate filter from the catalytic converter

17.22 Undo the bolts and remove the underfloor brace (arrowed)

17.24 Catalytic converter-to-turbocharger nuts (arrowed)

bracket nuts, release the mounting rubbers, and manoeuvre the catalytic converter from position.

Catalytic converter – 2.0 litre engines

26 Raise the front of the vehicle and support it securely on axle stands (see *Jacking and vehicle support*).

27 Undo the fasteners and remove the engine undershield.

28 Undo the bolts and remove the underfloor brace adjacent to the front exhaust mounting **(see illustration 17.22)**.

29 Attach wooden 'splints' each side of the exhaust flexible section using cable ties. This is to prevent excessive bending of the section as it's disconnected. Undo the nuts securing the flexible section to the intermediate section. Pull the intermediate section rearwards, and allow the exhaust to hang down.

30 Disconnect the wiring plug, then unscrew the temperature sensor (where fitted) from the front section of the catalytic converter.

31 Slacken the clamp securing the catalytic converter to the turbocharger **(see illustration)**.

32 Undo the catalytic converter support bracket nuts, release the mounting rubbers, and manoeuvre the catalytic converter from position **(see illustration)**.

Particulate filter

1.6 litre engines

33 Remove the catalytic converter as described in this Section, then slacken the clamp and detach the filter from the base of the catalytic converter **(see illustration 17.19)**.

2.0 litre engines

34 Raise the front of the vehicle and support

17.31 Catalytic converter-to-turbocharger clamp (arrowed)

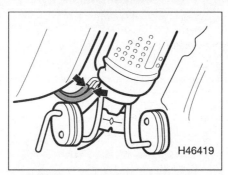

17.36 Disconnect the pressure sensor hoses (arrowed) from the particulate filter

17.32 Undo the support bracket nuts

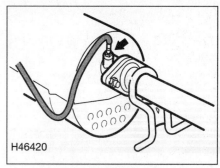

17.37 Exhaust temperature sensor (arrowed)

it securely on axle stands (see *Jacking and vehicle support*).

35 Attach wooden 'splints' each side of the exhaust flexible section using cable ties. This is to prevent excessive bending of the section as it's disconnected. Undo the nuts securing the flexible section to the particulate filter.

36 Note their fitted positions, and disconnect the pressure pipes from the front of the particulate filter **(see illustration)**.

37 Unscrew the temperature sensor from the front of the filter **(see illustration)**.

38 Undo the nuts securing the rear exhaust section to the particulate filter, and manoeuvre the filter from position.

Rear silencer

39 Slacken the various clamps securing the exhaust pipe/silencer, then release it from the rubber mountings.

Notes

Chapter 4 Part B:
Emission control systems

Contents

Degrees of difficulty

Easy, suitable for novice with little experience	Fairly easy, suitable for beginner with some experience	Fairly difficult, suitable for competent DIY mechanic	Difficult, suitable for experienced DIY mechanic	Very difficult, suitable for expert DIY or professional

1 General information

All models covered by this manual have various features built into the fuel and exhaust systems to help minimise harmful emissions. These features fall broadly into two categories; crankcase emission control and exhaust emission control. The main features of these systems are as follows.

Crankcase emission control

To reduce the emission of unburned hydrocarbons from the crankcase into the atmosphere, the engine is sealed and the blow-by gases and oil vapour are drawn from inside the crankcase, through a wire mesh oil separator, into the inlet tract to be burned by the engine during normal combustion.

Under all conditions, the gases are forced out of the crankcase by the (relatively) higher crankcase pressure. All diesel engines have a ventilation valve in the camshaft cover, to control the flow of gases from the crankcase.

Exhaust emission control

EGR system

An oxidation catalyst is fitted in the exhaust system of all diesel-engined models. This has the effect of removing a large proportion of the gaseous hydrocarbons, carbon monoxide and particulates present in the exhaust gas.

An Exhaust Gas Recirculation (EGR) system is fitted to all diesel-engined models. This reduces the level of nitrogen oxides produced during combustion by introducing a proportion of the exhaust gas back into the inlet manifold, under certain engine operating conditions, via a plunger valve. The system is controlled electronically by the engine management system. On some models, a cooler is fitted to the EGR, through which engine coolant is passed. This lowers the temperature of the recirculated gas, thus reducing the formation of NOx (oxides of nitrogen) in the exhaust gases.

Particulate filter

A particulate filter is also available as standard or as an option on 1.6 and 2.0 litre models, depending on the vehicle's country market.

This device is designed to trap carbon particulates produced by the combustion process. In order for the particulate filter to function correctly, and not to block up, an additive is injected into the fuel tank. As this additive passes through the combustion process, it reacts with the elements of the particulate filter, causing them to heat up and burn off the particles. The additive is automatically added to the tank whenever more than 5 litres of fuel is added. The whole process is controlled by an additive system module (ASM), which also informs the driver when the additive level is low. Replenishing the additive can only be performed by a dealer or specialist, as the ASM must be reset using specialist equipment. The consumption of additive is such that refilling should only be necessary every 3 years/37 500 miles approximately.

Note: *The particulate filter may block up prematurely on vehicles used mainly for short runs. Occasional longer runs (20 minutes or more) at motorway speeds will assist the regeneration process.*

Catalytic converters

Catalytic converters are fitted to all diesel models. The catalytic converter is fitted between the turbocharger and the particulate filter.

2 Catalytic converter – general information and precautions

An oxidation catalytic converter is fitted downstream from the turbocharger.

The catalytic converter is a reliable and simple device, which needs no maintenance in itself, but there are some facts of which an owner should be aware if the converter is to function properly for its full service life.

a) *DO NOT use fuel or engine oil additives – these may contain substances harmful to the catalytic converter.*

b) *DO NOT continue to use the vehicle if the engine burns oil to the extent of leaving a visible trail of blue smoke.*

c) *Remember that the catalytic converter operates at very high temperatures. DO NOT, therefore, park the vehicle in dry undergrowth, over long grass or piles of dead leaves, after a long run.*

d) *Remember that the catalytic converter is FRAGILE. Do not strike it with tools during servicing work.*

e) *The catalytic converter used on a well-maintained and well-driven vehicle should last for between 50 000 and 100 000 miles. If the converter is no longer effective, it must be renewed.*

3.5a Unscrew the mounting bolts . . .

3.5b . . . and remove the separator from the engine

3 Crankcase emission control system – checking and component renewal

Checking

1 The components of this system require no attention other than to check that the hoses are clear and undamaged.

Oil separator

1.6 litre engines

2 The oil separator is integral with the cylinder head cover/inlet manifold – refer to Chapter 2A.

1.8 litre engines

3 The oil separator is located at the left-hand end of the cylinder head. Pull the plastic cover on the top of the engine upwards from its

mountings at the front and right-hand edges, then pull it forwards.
4 Release the clamps and disconnect the breather hoses from the separator.
5 Undo the retaining bolts and remove the oil separator **(see illustrations)**.
6 Refitting is a reversal of removal.

2.0 litre engines

7 The oil separator is integral with the cylinder head cover/inlet manifold – refer to Chapter 2C.

4 Exhaust emission control systems – checking and component renewal

Checking

1 Checking of the system as a whole entails a close visual inspection of all hoses, pipes and connections for condition and security.

Apart from this, any known or suspected faults should be attended to by a Ford dealer or suitably-equipped specialist.

Catalytic converter

2 Removal of the catalytic converter is described in Chapter 4A – Exhaust system.

EGR solenoid/valve

1.6 litre engines

3 Disconnect the battery negative lead as described in Chapter 5.
4 Remove the plastic cover from the top of the engine (where fitted) by pulling it upwards at the right-hand and front edges, then pull it forwards.
5 Remove the wiper arms as described in Chapter 12, then undo the 2 bolts and move the remote brake fluid reservoir (where fitted) to one side **(see illustration)**.
6 Release the clips and remove the windscreen cowl panel by pulling it upwards from the moulding at the base of the windscreen **(see illustrations)**.
7 Undo the bolt at each end, then release the clips and remove the bulkhead extension panel from the engine compartment **(see illustration)**.
8 Disconnect the EGR valve wiring plug.
9 Make a note of its fitted position, then remove the clamp securing the pipe to the EGR valve **(see illustration)**.
10 Undo the 2 bolts and remove the valve. Note that if a new valve is fitted, the base setting must be programmed using Ford specialist diagnostic equipment (WDS).
11 Refitting is a reversal of removal.

1.8 litre engines

12 Proceed as described in Paragraphs 3 to 7 in this Section.
13 Remove the exhaust manifold as described in Chapter 4A.
14 Disconnect the vacuum hose from the MAP sensor on the inlet manifold.
15 Note their fitted positions, then disconnect the various wiring plugs from the EGR valve/inlet manifold **(see illustration)**.
16 Unclip the EGR cooler coolant hose from the support bracket.
17 Slacken the clamp and disconnect the air hose from the inlet manifold **(see illustration)**.
18 Undo the retaining nuts/bolts and remove

4.5 Undo the bolts (arrowed) and move the remote reservoir to one side

4.6a Prise forwards the clips (right-hand clips arrowed) . . .

4.6b . . . and pull the windscreen cowl panel upwards from the base of the windscreen

4.7 Undo the bolt (arrowed) at each end of the bulkhead extension panel

4.9 Release the EGR pipe clamp (arrowed)

4.15 Disconnect the wiring plug from the EGR valve (arrowed)

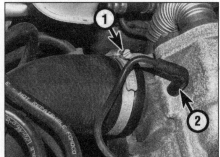

4.17 Air inlet hose clamp (1) and MAP sensor vacuum hose (2)

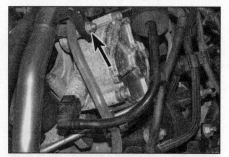

4.21 Undo the nut (arrowed) and remove the stud securing the EGR pipe support bracket

4.22a Release the EGR pipe clamp (arrowed) . . .

4.22b . . . and undo the 2 bolts securing the pipe to the valve

4.24 EGR cooler-to-valve bolts (arrowed)

the inlet manifold. Note that the EGR valve is integral with the manifold.

19 Refitting is a reversal of removal.

2.0 litre engines

20 Proceed as described in Paragraphs 3 to 7 in this Section.

21 Undo the EGR pipe support bracket retaining nut (see illustration).

22 Release the clamp securing the EGR pipe to the inlet manifold, and the 2 bolts securing the pipe to the EGR valve (see illustrations).

23 Disconnect the wiring plug from the EGR valve.

24 Undo the bolts securing the EGR cooler to the valve (see illustration).

25 Slacken the EGR valve lower retaining bolt

26 Undo the 2 remaining retaining bolts and remove the valve. Note that if a new valve is fitted, the base setting must be programmed using Ford specialist diagnostic equipment (WDS).

27 Refitting is a reversal of removal.

EGR cooler

28 Drain the cooling system as described in Chapter 1.

1.6 litre engines

29 Proceed as described in Paragraphs 3 to 7 in this Section.

30 Disconnect the injector wiring plugs, then undo the bolts and move the injector wiring harness guide to one side (see illustration).

31 Release the clamps and disconnect the coolant hoses from the EGR cooler (see illustration).

32 Release the clamp securing the EGR pipe to the cooler, then undo the 2 bolts securing the pipe to the inlet manifold (see illustration). Remove the pipe.

33 Release the clamp securing the EGR cooler to the EGR valve, then undo the nut/bolt and remove the cooler (see illustration).

34 Refitting is a reversal of removal.

4.30 Injector wiring harness bolts (arrowed)

4.31 Release the EGR cooler hose clamps (arrowed)

4.32 EGR pipe-to-manifold bolts (arrowed)

4.33 Release the clamp (arrowed) securing the EGR cooler to the valve

4.45 EGR cooler pipe clamp and coolant hose clamps (arrowed)

1.8 litre engines

35 Proceed as described in Paragraphs 3 to 7 in this Section.

36 Release the clamps and disconnect the coolant hoses from the EGR cooler.

37 Undo the bolts securing the cooler to the exhaust manifold and inlet manifold, then manoeuvre it from position.

38 Refitting is a reversal of removal.

2.0 litre engines

39 Proceed as described in Paragraphs 3 to 7 in this Section.

40 Pull the coolant expansion tank upwards to release its mountings. Move it to one side.

4.47 EGR 'elbow'-to-manifold nuts (arrowed)

41 Raise the front of the vehicle and support it securely on axle stands (see *Jacking and vehicle support*). Remove the engine undershield.

42 Position a trolley jack under the engine, with a block of wood between the jack head and take the weight of the engine.

43 Undo the bolts securing the right-hand engine mounting to the inner wing, then carefully pull the engine forwards a little.

44 Release the clamp and disconnect the turbocharger inlet pipe breather hose.

45 Prise out the wire clip and disconnect the heater-to-EGR cooler hose, then release the clamp and disconnect the coolant bypass-to-EGR cooler hose **(see illustration)**.

46 Undo the nuts and remove the EGR tube heat shield.

47 Release the clamp, undo the 2 retaining nuts, and remove the EGR cooler 'elbow' connecting pipe **(see illustration)**. Renew the gasket.

48 Undo the 2 retaining bolts, and remove the EGR cooler.

Particulate filter

49 Particulate filter renewal is described in Chapter 4A, Exhaust system.

Particulate filter additive system module (ASM)

50 Disconnect the battery negative lead (see Chapter 5), then remove the rear seat as described in Chapter 11.

51 Remove the rear right-hand side door sill trim as described in Chapter 11.

52 Lift up the carpet on the right-hand side under the seat, undo the 2 nuts and remove the ASM. Disconnect the ASM wiring plug as the unit is withdrawn.

53 Refitting is a reversal of removal. Note that if the ASM has been renewed, the new unit must be programmed using software downloaded from Ford. Consult a Ford dealer or specialist.

Chapter 5
Starting and charging systems

Contents

Degrees of difficulty

Easy, suitable for novice with little experience 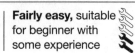	**Fairly easy,** suitable for beginner with some experience	**Fairly difficult,** suitable for competent DIY mechanic	**Difficult,** suitable for experienced DIY mechanic	**Very difficult,** suitable for expert DIY or professional

Specifications

System type .... 12 volt, negative earth

Battery

Type	Silver-calcium (marked Ca), low-maintenance or maintenance-free sealed for life
Capacity	60, 70 or 80 Ah (depending on model)

Charge condition:
Poor	12.5 volts
Normal	12.6 volts
Good	12.7 volts

Alternator

Output .... 120 or 150 A

Torque wrench settings	Nm	lbf ft
Alternator mounting bolts:		
1.6 litre models	45	33
1.8 litre models	27	20
2.0 litre models	45	33
Glow plugs:		
1.6 litre models	8	6
1.8 litre models	15	11
2.0 litre models	10	7
Starter motor mounting bolts:		
1.6 litre models	25	18
1.8 litre models	Not available	
2.0 litre models	35	26

1 General information and precautions

General information

The engine electrical system consists mainly of the charging, starting, and diesel preheating systems. Because of their engine-related functions, these components are covered separately from the body electrical devices such as the lights, instruments, etc (which are covered in Chapter 12).

The electrical system is of the 12 volt negative earth type.

The battery is of the low-maintenance or maintenance-free (sealed for life) type, and is charged by the alternator, which is belt-driven from the crankshaft pulley.

The starter motor is of the pre-engaged type, incorporating an integral solenoid. On starting, the solenoid moves the drive pinion into engagement with the flywheel ring gear before the starter motor is energised. Once the engine has started, a one-way clutch prevents the motor armature being driven by the engine until the pinion disengages from the flywheel.

Further details of the various systems are given in the relevant Sections of this Chapter. While some repair procedures are given, the usual course of action is to renew the component concerned.

Precautions

⚠️ **Warning: It is necessary to take extra care when working on the electrical system to avoid damage to semi-conductor devices (diodes and transistors), and to avoid the risk of personal injury. In addition to the precautions given in Safety first!, observe the following when working on the system:**

• **Always remove rings, watches, etc before working on the electrical system.** Even with the battery disconnected, capacitive discharge could occur if a component's live terminal is earthed through a metal object. This could cause a shock or nasty burn.

• **Do not reverse the battery connections.** Components such as the alternator, electronic control units, or any components having semi-conductor circuitry could be irreparably damaged.

• Never disconnect the battery terminals, the alternator, any electrical wiring or any test instruments when the engine is running.

• Do not allow the engine to turn the alternator when the alternator is not connected.

• Never test for alternator output by 'flashing' the output lead to earth.

• Always ensure that the battery negative lead is disconnected when working on the electrical system.

• If the engine is being started using jump leads and a slave battery, connect the batteries *positive-to-positive* and *negative-to-negative* (see *Jump starting*). This also applies when connecting a battery charger.

• **Never** use an ohmmeter of the type incorporating a hand-cranked generator for circuit or continuity testing.

• Before using electric-arc welding equipment on the car, *disconnect the battery, alternator and components such as the electronic control units* (where applicable) to protect them from the risk of damage.

2 Battery – testing and charging

Testing

Standard and low-maintenance battery

1 If the vehicle covers a small annual mileage, it is worthwhile checking the specific gravity of the electrolyte every three months to determine the state of charge of the battery. Use a hydrometer to make the check, and compare the results with the following table. Note that the specific gravity readings assume an electrolyte temperature of 15°C; for every 10°C below 15°C subtract 0.007. For every 10°C above 15°C add 0.007.

	Ambient temperature	
	Above 25°C	Below 25°C
Fully-charged	1.210 to 1.230	1.270 to 1.290
70% charged	1.170 to 1.190	1.230 to 1.250
Discharged	1.050 to 1.070	1.110 to 1.130

2 If the battery condition is suspect, first check the specific gravity of electrolyte in each cell. A variation of 0.040 or more between any cells indicates loss of electrolyte or deterioration of the internal plates.

3 If the specific gravity variation is 0.040 or more, the battery should be renewed. If the cell variation is satisfactory but the battery is discharged, it should be charged as described later in this Section.

Maintenance-free battery

4 In cases where a sealed for life maintenance-free battery is fitted, topping-up and testing of the electrolyte in each cell may not be possible (see Chapter 1). The condition of the battery can therefore only be tested using a battery condition indicator or a voltmeter.

5 Certain models my be fitted with a maintenance-free battery, with a built-in charge condition indicator. The indicator is located in the top of the battery casing, and indicates the condition of the battery from its colour. The charge conditions denoted by the colour of the indicator should be printed on a label attached to the battery – if not, consult a Ford dealer or automotive electrician for advice.

6 If testing the battery using a voltmeter, connect the voltmeter across the battery and note the voltage. The test is only accurate if the battery has not been subjected to any kind of charge for the previous six hours. If this is not the case, switch on the headlights for 30 seconds, then wait four to five minutes before testing the battery after switching off the headlights. All other electrical circuits must be switched off, so check that the doors and tailgate are fully shut when making the test.

7 If the voltage reading is less than 12.2 volts, then the battery is discharged, whilst a reading of 12.2 to 12.4 volts indicates a partially-discharged condition.

8 If the battery is to be charged, remove it from the vehicle and charge it as described later in this Section.

Charging

Note: *The following is intended as a guide only. Always refer to the manufacturer's recommendations (often printed on a label attached to the battery) before charging a battery.*

Standard and low-maintenance battery

9 Charge the battery at a rate equivalent to 10% of the battery capacity (eg, for a 45 Ah battery charge at 4.5 A) and continue to charge the battery at this rate until no further rise in specific gravity is noted over a four-hour period.

10 Alternatively, a trickle charger charging at the rate of 1.5 amps can safely be used overnight.

11 Specially rapid boost charges which are claimed to restore the power of the battery in 1 to 2 hours are not recommended, as they can cause serious damage to the battery plates through overheating. If the battery is completely flat, recharging should take at least 24 hours.

12 While charging the battery, note that the temperature of the electrolyte should never exceed 38°C.

Maintenance-free battery

13 This battery type takes considerably longer to fully recharge than the standard type, the time taken being dependent on the extent of discharge, but it can take anything up to three days.

14 A constant voltage type charger is required, to be set, when connected, to 13.9 to 14.9 volts with a charger current below 25 amps. Using this method, the battery should be useable within three hours, giving a voltage reading of 12.5 volts, but this is for a partially-discharged battery and, as mentioned, full charging can take far longer.

15 If the battery is to be charged from a fully-discharged state (condition reading less than 12.2 volts), have it recharged by your Ford dealer or local automotive electrician, as the charge rate is higher, and constant supervision during charging is necessary.

3.1a Lift the battery cover from place . . .

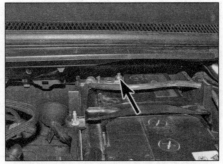

3.1b . . . then slacken the nut (arrowed) and disconnect the negative terminal

3.5 Slacken the nut and disconnect the positive terminal

3 Battery –
disconnection, removal and refitting

Caution: Wait at least 5 minutes after turning off the ignition switch before disconnect the battery. This is to allow sufficient time for the various control modules to store information.

Caution: If a Ford 'Keycode' audio unit is fitted, the unit will not function again on reconnection until the correct security code is entered. Details of this procedure, which varies according to the unit and model year, are given in the 'Ford Audio Systems Operating Guide' supplied with the car when new, with the code itself being given in a 'Radio Passport' and/or a 'Keycode label' at the same time. Ensure you have the correct code before you disconnect the battery. For obvious security reasons, the procedure is not given in this manual. If you do not have the code or detail of the correct procedure, the car's selling dealer may be able to help.

Disconnection

1 The battery is located on the left-hand side of the engine compartment. If all is needed is for the negative lead to be disconnected, release the clip, remove the battery cover, slacken the clamp nut and pull the terminal upwards from the battery post **(see illustrations)**. Position the terminal to one side, and secure it in place to prevent accidental reconnection. When reconnecting, refer to paragraph 15.

Removal

2 To remove the battery, begin by removing the air cleaner as described in Chapter 4A.
3 Unclip and remove the plastic cover over the top of the battery.
4 Slacken the clamp nut and disconnect the battery negative lead terminal **(see illustration 3.1b)**.
5 Slacken the clamp nut and disconnect the battery positive lead terminal **(see illustration)**.
6 Release the clips securing the cables to the front of the battery box, then pull up and

release the front wall of the battery box **(see illustrations)**.
7 Unscrew the nuts and remove the battery retaining clamp **(see illustration)**.
8 Lift the battery out of the engine compartment **(see illustration)**.

Refitting

9 Position the battery in the battery box.
10 Refit the retaining clamp and tighten the retaining nut securely.
11 Refit the front section of the battery box.
12 Ensure no-one is inside the vehicle as the battery is reconnected. Reconnect the battery positive lead, and tighten the clamp nut securely. Repeat this with the negative lead. Smear a little petroleum jelly on the terminals.
13 Secure the cables with the clips at the front of the battery box, then refit the cover over the cables.

14 Refit the battery cover, followed by the air cleaner assembly.
15 After reconnecting the battery, the engine may run erratically until it's been driven for a few minutes to allow the PCM to relearn. Also the electric windows may need to be re-initialised as follows:
  a) Press and hold the window control close button until the window is fully closed.
  b) Release the button, then press it again for 3 seconds.
  c) Briefly press the open button to the second detent, then release it. The window should open automatically.
  d) Briefly press the close button to the second detent, then release it. If the window does not close automatically, repeat the complete procedure.
  e) Repeat this procedure on each window.

3.6a Release the clip (where applicable) . . .

3.6b . . . and slide up the cover at the front

3.7 Undo the clamp nuts (arrowed)

3.8 Lift the battery from place

5.3 Slacken the inlet hose clamp (arrowed)

5.4 Anti-shudder valve bolts (arrowed)

5.5 Disconnect the alternator wiring connections (arrowed)

4 Charging system – testing

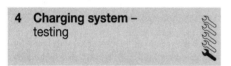

Note: *Refer to the warnings given in Safety first! and in Section 1 of this Chapter before starting work.*

1 If the ignition/no-charge warning light fails to illuminate when the ignition is switched on, first check the alternator wiring connections for security. If all is satisfactory, the alternator maybe at fault and should be renewed or taken to an auto-electrician for testing and repair.

2 If the ignition warning light illuminates when the engine is running, stop the engine and check that the drivebelt is correctly tensioned (see Chapter 1) and that the alternator connections are secure. If all is so

far satisfactory, have the alternator checked by an auto-electrician for testing and repair.

3 If the alternator output is suspect even though the warning light functions correctly, the regulated voltage may be checked as follows.

4 Connect a voltmeter across the battery terminals and start the engine.

5 Increase the engine speed until the voltmeter reading remains steady; the reading should be between 13.5 and 14.8 volts.

6 Switch on as many electrical accessories (eg, the headlights, heated rear window and heater blower) as possible, and check that the alternator maintains the regulated voltage between 13.5 and 14.8 volts.

7 If the regulated voltage is not as stated, the fault may be due to worn brushes, weak brush springs, a faulty voltage regulator, a faulty diode, a severed phase winding, or worn or damaged slip-rings. The brushes and

slip-rings may be checked (see Section 6), but if the fault persists the alternator should be renewed or taken to an auto-electrician for testing and repair.

5 Alternator – removal and refitting

Removal

1 Disconnect the battery negative lead (see Section 3).

2 Remove the auxiliary drivebelt as described in Chapter 1.

1.6 litre engines

3 Slacken the clamp and disconnect the air inlet hose from the air inlet tube above the alternator (see illustration).

4 Disconnect the sensor(s) wiring plug(s), then undo the retaining bolts and remove the air inlet tube/anti-shudder valve (see illustration). Recover the O-ring seal, and renew if necessary.

5 Disconnect the wiring plug from the alternator, then prise up the rubber cap, undo the nut and disconnect the battery cable from the alternator (see illustration).

6 Undo the retaining bolts and remove the auxiliary drivebelt tensioner (see illustration).

7 Remove the alternator upper rear and front retaining bolts.

8 On models with air conditioning, disconnect the wiring plug, undo the 4 bolts and lower the air conditioning compressor from place. Use string or wire to suspend the compressor from the vehicle bodywork. There's no need to disconnect the refrigerant pipes.

9 Remove the lower retaining bolt and lower the alternator from position.

1.8 litre models with air conditioning

10 Remove the plastic cover, unscrew the nut and disconnect the wiring from the alternator (see illustration).

11 Undo the four bolts from the air conditioning compressor and remove to one side. *Caution: Do not disconnect the refrigerant pipes.*

12 Undo the pulley bracket bolts, then slacken the three generator coupling bolts and remove the coupling (see illustrations).

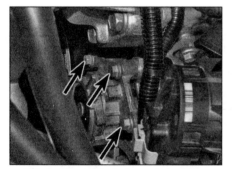

5.6 Auxiliary drivebelt tensioner bolts (arrowed)

5.10 Prise up the plastic cover (arrowed) then disconnect the alternator wiring

5.12a Undo the two pulley bolts . . .

5.12b . . . slacken the three coupling bolts . . .

5.12c ... and remove the coupling from the alternator

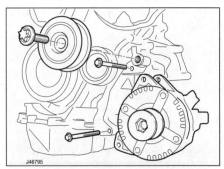

5.15 Alternator mounting bolts and idler pulley bolt

5.17 Alternator lower bolt (arrowed) – engine removed for clarity

Unscrew the alternator mounting bolts and carefully lift the alternator from the engine

1.8 litre models without air conditioning

13 Remove the plastic cover, unscrew the nut and disconnect the wiring from the alternator **(see illustration 5.10)**.

14 Undo the Torx bolt, and remove the auxiliary drivebelt idler pulley from above the alternator.

15 Undo the 2 retaining bolts and remove the alternator **(see illustration)**.

2.0 litre models

16 Undo the retaining bolts and remove the auxiliary drivebelt tensioner.

17 Undo and remove the alternator lower retaining bolt **(see illustration)**.

18 Slacken the clamp and disconnect the intercooler outlet pipe from the anti-shudder valve **(see illustration)**.

19 Undo the bolts and remove the crash shield over the fuel filter **(see illustration)**.

20 Note their fitted positions, then disconnect the various wiring plugs from the fuel filter assembly.

21 Undo the retaining bolt, then lift the fuel filter upwards from the bracket and position it to one side **(see illustration)**. There's no need to disconnect the fuel pipes, but release them from the various retaining clips.

22 Undo the 3 retaining bolts and remove the fuel filter bracket **(see illustration)**.

23 Disconnect the wiring plug, then undo the nut and disconnect the cable from the alternator.

24 Slacken the alternator lower mounting

clamp bolt, then undo the upper mounting bolts, slide the alternator to the right, and manoeuvre it from place **(see illustration)**.

Refitting

25 Refitting is a reversal of removal. Remembering to tighten the various fasteners to their specified torque where given.

6 Alternator – brush holder renewal

At the time of writing, the alternators are only available as complete units. However, consult your Ford dealer or parts/auto-electrical specialist before obtaining a new unit. Internal parts may be available at some stage in the future.

7 Starting system – testing

Note: *Refer to the precautions given in Safety first! and in Section 1 of this Chapter before starting work.*

1 If the starter motor fails to operate when the ignition key is turned to the appropriate position, the following possible causes may be to blame:
  a) *The battery is faulty.*
  b) *The electrical connections between the switch, solenoid, battery and starter motor are somewhere failing to pass the necessary current from the battery through the starter to earth.*
  c) *The solenoid is faulty.*

5.18 Slacken the air pipe clamp (arrowed)

5.19 Undo the bolts (arrowed) and remove the crash shield

5.21 Unscrew the bolt (arrowed) on the right-hand side of the filter

5.22 Fuel filter bracket bolts (arrowed)

5.24 Undo the upper bolts, and slacken the lower Allen bolt (arrowed)

8.1 Battery tray bolts (arrowed)

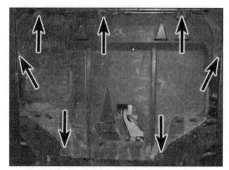

8.9 Undo the fasteners and remove the engine undershield (arrowed)

8.10 Remove the wiring connectors from the starter motor

d) The starter motor is mechanically or electrically defective.

2 To check the battery, switch on the headlights. If they dim after a few seconds, this indicates that the battery is discharged – recharge (see Section 2) or renew the battery. If the headlights glow brightly, operate the ignition switch and observe the lights. If they dim, then this indicates that current is reaching the starter motor, therefore the fault must lie in the starter motor. If the lights continue to glow brightly (and no clicking sound can be heard from the starter motor solenoid), this indicates that there is a fault in the circuit or solenoid – see following paragraphs. If the starter motor turns slowly when operated, but the battery is in good condition, then this indicates that either the starter motor is faulty, or there is considerable resistance somewhere in the circuit.

3 If a fault in the circuit is suspected, disconnect the battery leads (including the earth connection to the body), the starter/solenoid wiring and the engine/transmission earth strap. Thoroughly clean the connections, and reconnect the leads and wiring, then use a voltmeter or test light to check that full battery voltage is available at the battery positive lead connection to the solenoid, and that the earth is sound. Smear petroleum jelly around the battery terminals to prevent corrosion – corroded connections are amongst the most frequent causes of electrical system faults.

4 If the battery and all connections are in good condition, check the circuit by disconnecting the wire from the solenoid blade terminal. Connect a voltmeter or test light between the wire end and a good earth (such as the battery

negative terminal), and check that the wire is live when the ignition switch is turned to the start position. If it is, then the circuit is sound – if not, the circuit wiring can be checked as described in Chapter 12.

5 The solenoid contacts can be checked by connecting a voltmeter or test light between the battery positive feed connection on the starter side of the solenoid, and earth. When the ignition switch is turned to the start position, there should be a reading or lighted bulb, as applicable. If there is no reading or lighted bulb, the solenoid is faulty and should be renewed.

6 If the circuit and solenoid are proved sound, the fault must lie in the starter motor. In this event, it may be possible to have the starter motor overhauled by a specialist, but check on the cost of spares before proceeding, as it may prove more economical to obtain a new or exchange motor.

8 Starter motor – removal and refitting

Removal

1.6 litre engines

1 Remove the battery as described in Section 3, then undo the 3 bolts and remove the battery tray **(see illustration)**.

2 Note their fitted positions, then disconnect the wiring connections from the starter motor, which is located on the rear of the cylinder block.

3 Raise the front of the vehicle and support it securely on axle stands (see *Jacking and vehicle support*). Undo the bolts and remove the engine undershield.

4 Undo the starter motor lower mounting bolt from underneath.

5 Remove the upper mounting bolts, and remove the starter motor.

1.8 litre engines

6 Disconnect the battery negative lead as described in Section 3.

7 Remove the air cleaner assembly as described in Chapter 4A.

8 Undo the upper starter motor retaining bolts.

9 Raise the front of the vehicle and support it securely on axle stands (see *Jacking and vehicle support*). Undo the fasteners and remove the engine undershield **(see illustration)**.

10 Undo the nuts, and disconnect the wiring connections from the starter motor **(see illustration)**.

11 Undo the mounting bolt and remove the starter downwards.

2.0 litre engines

12 Disconnect the battery negative lead as described in Section 3.

13 Pull the plastic cover on the top of the engine upwards to release its mountings.

14 Undo the nuts and disconnect the wiring from the starter motor solenoid **(see illustration)**.

15 Undo the 3 mounting bolts, and remove the starter motor **(see illustration)**. Check the locating dowel is still in place in the starter motor mounting face.

Refitting

16 Refitting is a reversal of removal. Tighten all fasteners to their specified torque where given.

9 Starter motor – testing and overhaul

If the starter motor is thought to be suspect, it should be removed from the vehicle and taken to an auto-electrician for testing. Most auto-electricians will be able to supply and fit

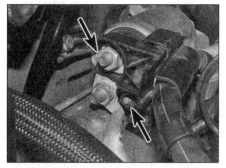

8.14 Undo the nuts (arrowed) and disconnect the wiring

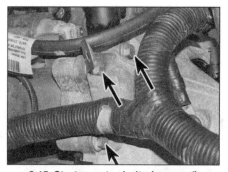

8.15 Starter motor bolts (arrowed)

brushes at a reasonable cost. However, check on the cost of repairs before proceeding, as it may prove more economical to obtain a new or exchange motor.

10 Preheating system – general information

To assist cold starting, diesel engine models are fitted with a preheating system, which comprises a relay, and four glow plugs. The system is controlled by the engine management PCM (Powertrain Control Module), using information provided by the coolant temperature sensor (see Chapter 3).

The glow plugs are miniature electric heating elements, encapsulated in a metal case with a probe at one end, and an electrical connection at the other. The combustion chambers have a glow plug threaded into it. When the glow plug is energised, it heats up rapidly causing the temperature of the air charge drawn into each of the combustion chambers to rise. Each glow plug probe is positioned directly in line with the incoming spray of fuel from the injector. Hence the fuel passing over the glow plug probe is also heated, allowing its optimum combustion temperature to be achieved more readily.

The duration of the preheating period is governed by the engine management Powertrain control module (PCM), using information provided by the coolant temperature sensor (see Chapter 3). The PCM alters the preheating time (the length for which the glow plugs are supplied with current) to suit the prevailing conditions.

A warning light informs the driver that preheating is taking place. The lamp extinguishes when sufficient preheating has taken place to allow the engine to be started, but power will still be supplied to the glow plugs for a further period, known as post-heating, to reduce exhaust emissions. If no attempt is made to start the engine, the power supply to the glow plugs is switched off to prevent battery drain and glow plug burn-out.

11 Preheating system – testing

1 Full testing of the system can only be carried out using specialist diagnostic equipment which is connected to the engine management system diagnostic wiring connector (see Chapter 4A). If the preheating system is thought to be faulty, some preliminary checks of the glow plug operation may be made as described in the following paragraphs.
2 Connect a voltmeter or 12 volt test lamp between the glow plug supply cable, and a good earth point on the engine. *Caution: Make sure that the live connection is kept well clear of the engine and bodywork.*

12.3 Undo the remote reservoir bolts (arrowed)

12.5b ... then pull the windscreen cowl panel upwards from the base of the windscreen

3 Have an assistant activate the preheating system by turning the ignition key to the second position, and check that battery voltage is applied to the glow plug electrical connection. **Note:** *The supply voltage will be less than battery voltage initially, but will rise and settle as the glow plug heats up. It will then drop to zero when the preheating period ends and the safety cut-out operates.*
4 If no supply voltage can be detected at the glow plug, then the glow plug relay or the supply cable may be faulty.
5 To locate a faulty glow plug, measure the electrical resistance between the glow plug terminal and the engine earth, and compare it with the resistance of the other glow plugs, or known working example. If the reading is significantly different, the glow plug is probably defective.
6 If no problems are found, take the vehicle to

12.7 Pull the electrical connector from each glow plug

12.5a Prise forwards the clips (right-hand side clips arrowed) . . .

12.6 Undo the bolt (arrowed) at each end of the bulkhead extension panel

a Ford dealer or specialist for testing using the appropriate diagnostic equipment.

12 Glow plugs – removal, inspection and refitting

Removal

1 Disconnect the battery negative lead as described in Section 3.

1.6 litre engines

2 Pull the plastic cover (where fitted) on the top of the engine upwards to release it from the mountings.
3 Undo the 2 bolts and move the brake fluid remote reservoir (where fitted) to one side **(see illustration)**.
4 Remove the wiper arms as described in Chapter 12.
5 Prise forwards the 5 retaining clips, then pull the windscreen cowl panel upwards from the base of the windscreen **(see illustrations)**.
6 Undo the bolt at each end, then release the clips and remove the bulkhead extension panel from the engine compartment **(see illustration)**.
7 Reach down the back of the engine, pull the electrical connector from each glow plug, and move the supply cable to one side **(see illustration)**. Access to No 1 glow plug is extremely limited – if improved access is required, remove the EGR cooler as described in Chapter 4B.

12.12 Undo the nuts (right-hand side glow plugs arrowed) and disconnect the supply cable

12.15 Undo the nuts (arrowed) securing the electrical connections to the glow plugs

12.16 Unscrew the glow plugs from the cylinder head

8 Using a deep socket, carefully unscrew each glow plug from the cylinder head.

1.8 litre engines

9 Pull the plastic cover on the top of the engine upwards to release it from the mountings.
10 Release the clamps and disconnect the 2 engine breather hoses from the front of the cylinder head cover.
11 Undo the bolt securing the engine oil level dipstick guide tube.
12 Undo the nuts and disconnect the electrical supply cable from the top of each glow plug **(see illustration)**.
13 Using a deep socket, carefully unscrew each glow plug from the cylinder head.

2.0 litre engines

14 Remove the EGR valve and cooler as described in Chapter 4B.
15 Undo the nuts (1 per plug) and disconnect the wiring harness from the glow plugs **(see illustration)**.

16 Unscrew each glow plug from the cylinder head using a deep socket **(see illustration)**.

Inspection

17 Inspect the glow plugs for signs of damage. Burt or eroded glow plug tips can be caused by a bad injector spray pattern. Have the injectors checked if this sort of damage is found.
18 If the glow plugs are in good condition, check them electrically, as described in Section 11.
19 The glow plugs can be energised by applying 12 volts to them to verify that they heat up evenly and in the required time. Observe the following precautions:

a) *Support the glow plug by clamping it carefully in a vice or self-locking pliers. Remember it will be red hot.*
b) *Make sure that the power supply or test lead incorporates a fuse or overload trip*

to protect against damage from a short-circuit.
c) *After testing, allow the glow plug to cool for several minutes before attempting to handle it.*

20 A glow plug in good condition will start to glow red at the tip after drawing current for 5 seconds or so. Any plug which takes much longer to start glowing, or which starts glowing in the middle instead of at the tip, is probably defective.

Refitting

21 Thoroughly clean the glow plugs, and the glow plug seating areas in the cylinder head.
22 Apply a smear of anti-seize compound to the glow plug threads, then refit the glow plug and tighten it to the specified torque.
23 Reconnect the wiring to the glow plug and tighten the nut securely.
24 The remainder of refitting is a reversal of removal.

Chapter 6
Clutch

Contents

Degrees of difficulty

Easy, suitable for novice with little experience	Fairly easy, suitable for beginner with some experience	Fairly difficult, suitable for competent DIY mechanic	Difficult, suitable for experienced DIY mechanic	Very difficult, suitable for expert DIY or professional 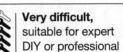

Specifications

Clutch

Driven plate diameter	228 mm
Pedal travel (not adjustable)	135 ± 3 mm

Torque wrench settings	Nm	lbf ft
Clutch cover/pressure plate to flywheel*	29	21
Clutch master cylinder mounting	10	7
Clutch pedal bracket nuts	25	18
Clutch slave cylinder mounting*	10	7

Do not re-use

1 General information

All manual transmission models are equipped with a single dry plate diaphragm spring clutch assembly. The pressure plate assembly consists of a steel cover (doweled and bolted to the flywheel face), the pressure plate, and a diaphragm spring.

The driven plate is free to slide along the splines of the transmission input shaft, and is held in position between the flywheel and the pressure plate by the pressure of the diaphragm spring. Friction lining material is riveted to the driven plate (friction disc), which on some models, has a spring-cushioned hub, to absorb transmission shocks and help ensure a smooth take-up of the drive. On other models, a dual-mass flywheel is fitted, where the flywheel is split into to masses – a primary mass (incorporating the starter ring gear) secured to the engine crankshaft, and secondary mass which is the driving surface mated to the clutch driven plate. Between these two masses are rubber/spring elements which absorb the power pulses from the engine as well as the transmission shocks.

The clutch release bearing contacts the fingers of the diaphragm spring. Depressing the clutch pedal pushes the release bearing against the diaphragm fingers, so moving the centre of the diaphragm spring inwards. As the centre of the spring is pushed inwards, the outside of the spring pivots outwards, so moving the pressure plate backwards and disengaging its grip on the driven plate.

When the pedal is released, the diaphragm spring forces the pressure plate back into contact with the friction linings on the driven plate. The plate is now firmly held between the pressure plate and the flywheel, thus transmitting engine power to the transmission. On some models, a self-adjusting clutch (SAC) is fitted, where an adjustment ring rotates in the pressure plate assembly, adjusting the diaphragm spring fingers pivot points as the driven plate wears. This maintains the clutch pedal 'bite point'.

All Focus models have a hydraulically-operated clutch. A master cylinder is mounted below the clutch pedal, and takes its hydraulic fluid supply from a separate chamber in the brake fluid reservoir. Depressing the clutch pedal operates the master cylinder pushrod, and the fluid pressure is transferred along the fluid lines to a slave cylinder mounted inside the bellhousing. The slave cylinder is incorporated into the release bearing – when the slave cylinder operates, the release bearing moves against the diaphragm spring fingers and disengages the clutch.

The hydraulic clutch offers several advantages over a cable-operated clutch – it is completely self-adjusting, requires less pedal effort, and is less subject to wear problems.

Since many of the procedures covered in this Chapter involve working under the vehicle, make sure that it is securely supported on axle stands placed on a firm, level floor (see *Jacking and vehicle support*).

> **Warning: The hydraulic fluid used in the system is brake fluid, which is poisonous. Take care to keep it off bare skin, and in particular out of your eyes. The fluid also attacks paintwork, and may discolour carpets, etc – keep spillages to a minimum, and wash any off immediately with cold water. Finally, brake fluid is highly inflammable, and should be handled with the same care as petrol.**

2 Clutch pedal – removal and refitting

Note: *Renewal of the clutch pedal return spring supposedly involves removal of the pedal assembly as described here. However, some owners report that it can be renewed in situ, although it is difficult to get at. The spring can be seen in illustration 2.8, top right.*

> **Warning: Hydraulic fluid is poisonous; wash off immediately and thoroughly in the case of skin contact, and seek immediate medical advice if any fluid is swallowed or gets into the eyes. Certain types of hydraulic fluid are inflammable, and may ignite when allowed into contact with hot components; when**

2.2 Battery tray retaining bolts (arrowed)

2.3a Prise out the 4 clips (arrowed)

2.3b Undo the 2 inner bolts, slacken the outer bolt, undo the 2 nuts and pivot the cross-stay (arrowed) each side away . . .

and ensure that it comes from a freshly-opened sealed container.

2.3c . . . so the plastic panel in front of the master cylinder can be removed

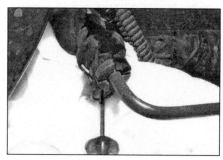

2.4a Prise down the clip and pull the pressure pipe from the clutch master cylinder

Removal

1 Remove the facia as described in Chapter 11, then remove the steering column as described in Chapter 10.

Later models with a plastic panel in front of the brake master cylinder

2 Remove the battery as described in Chapter 5, then undo the 3 bolts and slide the battery tray forward a little **(see illustration)**.

3 Prise out the 4 plastic clips securing the plastic panel to the engine compartment bulkhead, then undo the inner 2 retaining bolts, slacken the outer bolt, remove the nuts and pivot the cross-stay each side away from the bulkhead. Lift the plastic panel (where fitted) from place **(see illustrations)**. Refit the bolts to secure the tops of the suspension struts to the vehicle body.

All models

4 Depress the release buttons/prise out the clip and disconnect the pressure pipe from the clutch master cylinder connection at the engine compartment bulkhead, then disconnect the fluid supply hose from the master cylinder **(see illustrations)**. Be prepared for fluid spillage – wipe up any spills immediately – the fluid could damage paintwork, etc.

5 Disconnect the clutch pedal position sensor wiring plug **(see illustration)**.

6 Undo the retaining nuts and manoeuvre the clutch pedal complete with the bracket and master cylinder from place **(see illustration)**.

7 To separate the master cylinder from the pedal bracket, begin by squeezing the sides

servicing any hydraulic system, it is safest to assume that the fluid IS inflammable, and to take precautions against the risk of fire as though it is petrol that is being handled. Hydraulic fluid is also an effective paint stripper, and will attack plastics; if any is spilt,

it should be washed off immediately, using copious quantities of clean water. Finally, it is hygroscopic (it absorbs moisture from the air) – old fluid may be contaminated and unfit for further use. When topping-up or renewing the fluid, always use the recommended type,

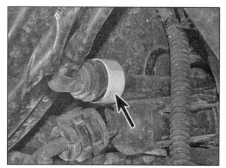

2.4b Pull back the collar (arrowed) and disconnect the fluid supply pipe

2.5 Disconnect the wiring plug (arrowed) from the clutch pedal position sensor

2.6 Undo the nuts (arrowed) and remove the pedal/master cylinder assembly

2.7 Squeeze the sides of the clip (arrowed) and pull the pushrod from the pedal

2.8 Rotate the master cylinder 60° clockwise and pull it from the bracket

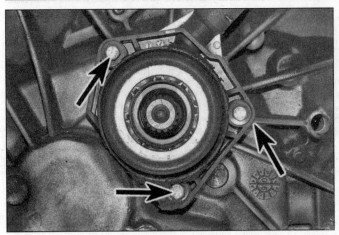

4.3 Slave cylinder mounting bolts (arrowed)

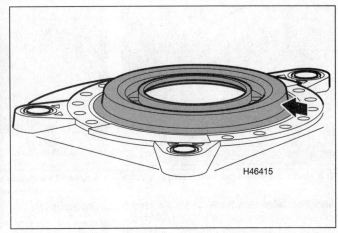

4.4 Apply a bead of sealant to the slave cylinder around the edge (arrowed)

of the retaining clip and pull the pushrod from the pedal (see illustration).

8 Rotate the master cylinder 60° clockwise and pull it from the bracket (see illustration).

Refitting

9 Refit by reversing the removal operations. Note the following points:
a) Tighten all fasteners securely.
b) Renew the seal between the master cylinder and the bulkhead if necessary.
c) Bleed the clutch hydraulic system as described in Section 5.
d) Check the operation of the clutch before refitting the lower facia panel.

3 Clutch master cylinder – removal and refitting

Note: At the time of writing, it would appear that master cylinder internal components are not available separately, and therefore no repair or overhaul of the cylinder is possible. In the event of a hydraulic system fault, or any sign of visible fluid leakage on or around the master cylinder or clutch pedal, the unit should be renewed – consult a Ford dealer or specialist.

1 Removal and refitting of the master cylinder is included in the pedal removal and refitting procedure described previously.

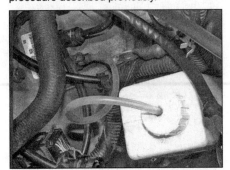

5.3 Connect the hose to the bleed nipple on the top of the transmission housing

4 Clutch slave cylinder and release bearing – removal and refitting

Note 1: Slave cylinder internal components are not available separately, and no repair or overhaul of the cylinder is possible. In the event of a hydraulic system fault, or any sign of fluid leakage, the unit should be renewed.

Note 2: Refer to the warning at the beginning of Section 2 before proceeding.

Removal

1 Remove the transmission as described in Chapter 7. The internal slave cylinder cannot be removed with the transmission in place.

2 Release the rubber seal from the transmission.

3 Remove the mounting bolts securing the cylinder and release bearing assembly to the transmission, and remove the assembly, feeding the fluid pipe in through the transmission aperture (see illustration).

Refitting

4 Ensure the release bearing/slave cylinder and transmission casing mating surfaces are clean. Apply a bead of sealant (Ford No ESK-M4G269-A) to the bearing/cylinder as shown (see illustration).

5 Lubricate the inner lips of the seal with a little grease, then position the release bearing/slave cylinder on the input shaft, and tighten the bolts to the specified torque. Take care not to damage the seal lips with the input shaft splines – wrap adhesive tape around the splines prior to fitting the cylinder.

6 Refit the rubber seal around the pipes, ensuring it is correctly positioned.

7 The remainder of refitting is a reversal of removal, noting the following points:
a) Remove the adhesive tape from the input shaft splines.
b) Refit the transmission as described in Chapter 7.
c) Bleed the clutch hydraulic system on completion (Section 5).

5 Clutch hydraulic system – bleeding

Note: Refer to the warning at the beginning of Section 2 before proceeding.

1 Top-up the hydraulic fluid reservoir on the brake master cylinder with fresh clean fluid of the specified type (see Weekly checks).

2 Remove the air cleaner assembly as described in Chapter 4A.

3 Remove the dust cover, and fit a length of clear hose over the bleed nipple on the slave cylinder (see illustration). Place the other end of the hose in a jar containing a small amount of hydraulic fluid.

4 Slacken the bleed nipple half a turn, then have an assistant depress the clutch pedal. Tighten the bleed screw when the pedal is depressed. Have the assistant release the pedal, then slacken the bleed screw again.

5 Repeat the process until clean fluid, free of air bubbles, emerges from the bleed nipple. Tighten the nipple at the end of a pedal downstroke, and remove the hose and jar. Refit the dust cover.

6 Top-up the hydraulic fluid reservoir.

7 Pressure bleeding equipment may be used if preferred – refer to the information in Chapter 9, Section 14.

6 Clutch components – removal, inspection and refitting

⚠️ **Warning:** Dust created by clutch wear and deposited on the clutch components may contain asbestos, which is a health hazard. DO NOT blow it out with compressed air, and do not inhale any of it. DO NOT use petrol or petroleum-based solvents to clean off the dust. Brake system cleaner or methylated spirit should be used to flush the dust

6.3 Undo the pressure plate retaining bolts

into a suitable receptacle. After the clutch components are wiped clean with rags, dispose of the contaminated rags and cleaner in a sealed, marked container.

Removal

1 Access to the clutch may be gained in one of two ways. The engine/transmission unit can be removed, as described in Chapter 2D, and the transmission separated from the engine on the bench. Alternatively, the engine may be left in the vehicle and the transmission removed independently, as described in Chapter 7.

2 Having separated the transmission from the engine, check if there are any marks identifying the relation of the clutch pressure plate to the flywheel. If not, make your own marks using a dab of paint or a scriber. These marks will be used if the original pressure plate is refitted, and will help to maintain the balance of the unit. A new pressure plate may be fitted in any position allowed by the locating dowels.

3 Unscrew the six clutch pressure plate retaining bolts, working in a diagonal sequence, and slackening the bolts only a turn at a time **(see illustration)**. If necessary, the flywheel may be held stationary using a wide-bladed screwdriver, inserted in the teeth of the starter ring gear and resting against part of the cylinder block. Ford state that new pressure plate bolts must be used when refitting.

4 Ease the clutch pressure plate off its locating dowels. Be prepared to catch the clutch driven plate, which will drop out as the pressure plate is removed. Note which way round the driven plate is fitted.

6.12b Position the driven plate using a clutch aligning tool

6.12a The clutch driven plate should be marked to indicate which side faces the transmission or flywheel

Inspection

Note: *On models equipped with a self-adjusting clutch, Ford insist that if a new driven plate is fitted, the pressure plate must also be renewed.*

5 The most common problem which occurs in the clutch is wear of the clutch driven plate (friction disc). However, all the clutch components should be inspected at this time, particularly if the engine has covered a high mileage. Unless the clutch components are known to be virtually new, it is worth renewing them all as a set (driven plate, pressure plate and release bearing). Renewing a worn driven plate by itself is not always satisfactory, especially if the old one was slipping and causing the pressure plate to overheat.

6 Examine the linings of the driven plate for wear and loose rivets, and the plate hub and rim for distortion, cracks, broken torsion springs, and worn splines (where applicable). The surface of the friction linings may be highly glazed, but as long as the friction material pattern can be clearly seen, and the rivet heads are at least 1 mm below the lining surface, this is satisfactory. The plate must be renewed if the lining thickness has worn down to, or just above, the level of the rivet heads.

7 If there is any sign of oil contamination, indicated by shiny black discoloration, the driven plate must be renewed, and the source of the contamination traced and rectified. This will be a leaking crankshaft oil seal or transmission input shaft oil seal. The renewal procedure for the former is given in the relevant Part of Chapter 2. Renewal of the transmission input shaft oil seal should

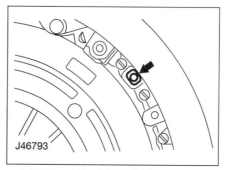

6.17 Check the 'stop-pin' (arrowed) is moveable as the bolts are tightened

be entrusted to a Ford dealer, as it involves dismantling the transmission, and (where applicable) the renewal of the clutch release bearing guide tube, using a press.

8 Check the machined faces of the flywheel and pressure plate. If either is grooved, or heavily scored, renewal is necessary. The pressure plate must also be renewed if any cracks are apparent, or if the diaphragm spring is damaged or its pressure suspect. Pay particular attention to the tips of the spring fingers, where the release bearing acts upon them.

9 With the transmission removed, it is also advisable to check the condition of the release bearing, although having got this far, it is almost certainly worth renewing it. Note that the release bearing is integral with the slave cylinder – the two must be renewed together; however, given that access to the slave cylinder is only possible with the transmission removed, not to renew it at this time is probably a false economy.

Refitting

10 It is important that no oil or grease is allowed to come into contact with the friction material of the driven plate or the pressure plate and flywheel faces. To ensure this, it is advisable to refit the clutch assembly with clean hands, and to wipe down the pressure plate and flywheel faces with a clean dry rag before assembly begins.

11 Ford technicians use a special tool for centralising the driven plate at this stage. The tool holds the driven plate centrally on the pressure plate, and locates in the middle of the diaphragm spring fingers. If the tool is not available, it will be necessary to centralise the driven plate after assembling the pressure plate loosely on the flywheel, as described in the following paragraphs.

12 Place the driven plate against the flywheel, ensuring that it is the right way round **(see illustrations)**. It may be marked FLYWHEEL SIDE, but if not, position it so that the raised hub with the cushion springs is facing away from the flywheel.

13 Place the clutch pressure plate over the dowels. Fit the new retaining bolts, and tighten them finger-tight so that the driven plate is gripped lightly, but can still be moved.

14 The driven plate must now be centralised so that, when the engine and transmission are mated, the splines of the gearbox input shaft will pass through the splines in the centre of the driven plate hub.

15 Centralisation can be carried out by inserting a round bar through the hole in the centre of the driven plate, so that the end of the bar rests in the hole in the rear end of the crankshaft. Move the bar sideways or up-and-down, to move the driven plate in whichever direction is necessary to achieve centralisation. Centralisation can then be checked by removing the bar and viewing the driven plate hub in relation to the diaphragm spring fingers, or by viewing through the side apertures of the pressure plate, and checking that the disc is central in relation to the outer edge of the pressure plate.

16 An alternative and more accurate method of centralisation is to use a commercially-available clutch-aligning tool, obtainable from most accessory shops **(see illustration 6.12b)**.

17 Once the clutch is centralised, progressively tighten the pressure plate bolts in a diagonal sequence to the torque setting given in the Specifications. **Note:** *On models with a self-adjusting clutch, Check that the 'stop-pin' is moveable during the tightening of the bolts* **(see illustration)**.

18 Ensure that the input shaft splines and driven plate splines are clean. Apply a thin smear of high melting-point grease to the input shaft splines – do not apply excessively, however, or it may end up on the driven plate, causing the new clutch to slip.

19 Refit the transmission to the engine.

Chapter 7
Manual transmission

Contents

Degrees of difficulty

Easy, suitable for novice with little experience	Fairly easy, suitable for beginner with some experience	Fairly difficult, suitable for competent DIY mechanic	Difficult, suitable for experienced DIY mechanic	Very difficult, suitable for expert DIY or professional

Specifications

General

Transmission type. . . . . Five or six forward gears and one reverse. Synchromesh on all gears
Designation:
    1.6 and 1.8 litre models (5-speed) MTX75
    2.0 litre models (6-speed). MMT6

Lubricant capacity

MTX75 . . . . 1.9 litres
MMT6 . . . . 1.75 litres

Gear ratios

1.6 litre models

1st. 3.667:1
2nd. 2.048:1
3rd 1.345:1
4th 0.921:1
5th 0.705:1
Reverse 3.727:1
Final drive. 3.412:1

1.8 litre models

1st. 3.800:1
2nd. 2.048:1
3rd 1.345:1
4th 1.921:1
5th 0.705:1
Reverse 3.727:1
Final drive. 3.410:1

2.0 litre models

1st. 3.077:1
2nd. 1.864:1
3rd 1.241:1
4th 0.842:1
5th 0.886:1
6th 0.711:1
Reverse 1.360:1

Torque wrench settings

	Nm	lbf ft
Engine/transmission mountings.	See Chapter 2A, 2B or 2C Specifications	
Oil filler/drain plugs.	35	26
Reversing light switch	25	18
Roadwheel nuts	Refer to Chapter 1	
Transmission-to-engine bolts.	48	35

1 General information

The 5-speed manual transmission and final drive are housed in an aluminium casing, bolted directly to the left-hand side of the engine. Gear selection is by a remotely-sited lever assembly, operating the transmission selector mechanism via cables.

The Ford transmission code is MTX 75. MT standing for Manual Transmission, X for transaxle (front-wheel drive), and 75 being the distance between the input and output shafts in mm **(see illustration)**. On 2.0 litre models a 6-speed transmission is fitted, with the designation MMT6. Synchromesh is fitted to all gears.

Because of the complexity, possible unavailability of parts and special tools necessary, internal repair procedures for the manual transmission are not included for the home mechanic. For readers who wish to tackle a transmission rebuild, brief notes on overhaul are provided in Section 8. The bulk of the information in this Chapter is devoted to removal and refitting procedures.

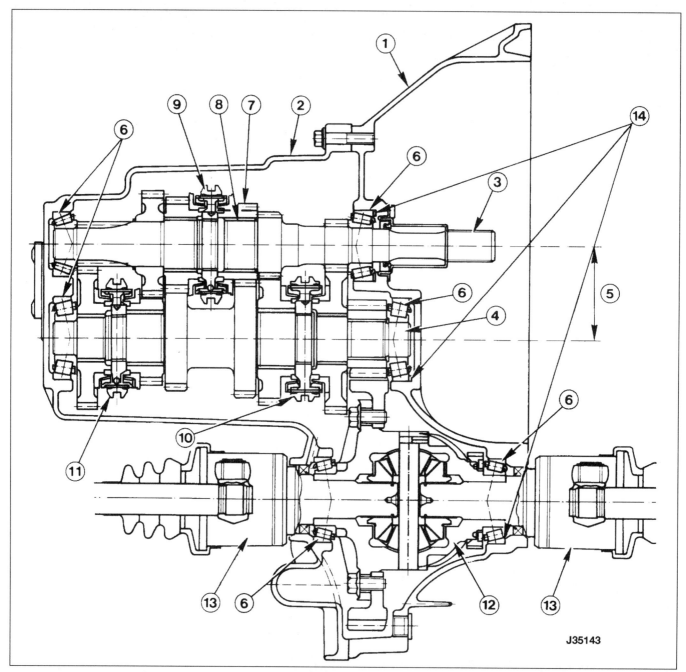

J35143

1.2 MTX 75 transmission

1 Clutch housing
2 Transmission housing
3 Input shaft
4 Output shaft
5 Distance between shaft centres = 75 mm
6 Taper roller bearings
7 4th gear
8 Needle roller bearings
9 3rd/4th gear synchro
10 1st/2nd gear synchro
11 5th/reverse gear synchro
12 Differential
13 Driveshafts
14 Shims

2 Gear lever housing – removal and refitting

Removal

1 Remove the centre console as described in Chapter 11.

2 Undo the bolts and remove the bracket between the floor and the facia central support brackets each side of the heater housing **(see illustration)**.

3 Unscrew the knob from the gear lever, and remove it along with the gaiter.

4 Prise off the selector inner cable socket ends from the balljoints on the levers, then rotate the collars anti-clockwise/squeeze together the clips/pull the collar forwards (as applicable) and disengage the outer cables from the brackets on the housing **(see illustrations)**.

5 Undo the 4 bolts securing the housing assembly to the floor **(see illustration)**.

Refitting

6 Refit by reversing the removal operations. Tighten the 4 bolts securely.

3 Selector cables – removal, refitting and adjustment

Removal

1 Remove the air cleaner assembly as described in Chapter 4A.

5-speed transmission

2 Depress the release button and pull the end of the selector cable from the transmission lever balljoint **(see illustration)**. Repeat this procedure with the shift cable.

3 Rotate the collars anti-clockwise and detach the selector and shift outer cables from the bracket on the transmission **(see illustration)**.

6-speed transmission

4 Depress the release button and pull the end of the selector cable from the transmission lever balljoint, then carefully prise the end of

2.2 Remove the bracket (arrowed) between the floor and the support bracket each side

2.4b Rotate this collar (arrowed) anti-clockwise and lift it from place

the gearchange cable from the balljoint on the transmission lever **(see illustrations)**.

5 Squeeze together the locking clips, and lift the outer cable end fittings from the bracket on the transmission **(see illustration)**.

3.2 Depress the release button (arrowed) and pull the cable from the balljoint

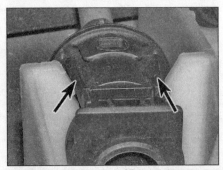

2.4a Squeeze together the clips (arrowed) and lift this type of collar from the bracket

2.5 Undo the 4 bolts (arrowed) and remove the gear lever housing

All models

6 Jack up the front of the vehicle and support it securely on axle stands (see *Jacking and vehicle support*).

7 Undo the 4 fasteners, and slide the heat

3.3 Rotate the collar (arrowed) anti-clockwise

3.4a Depress the release button (arrowed) and detach the selector cable

3.4b Prise the gearchange cable from the balljoint

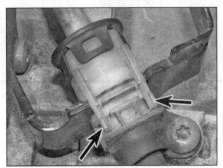

3.5 Squeeze together the locking clips (arrowed)

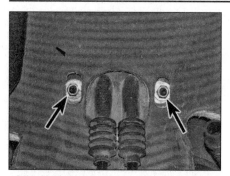

3.11 Undo the 2 nuts (arrowed) securing the cable grommet to the floor

3.21 Insert a 3 mm drill bit (arrowed) into the gear lever base mechanism

3.22 Prise up the lock button (arrowed)

3.26 Prise out the locking catch on the side of the selector cable

3.27 Insert a 2.5 mm drill bit, set the vertical height of the drill bit to 25 mm by pulling or pushing the preload sleeve, then rotate it to the position shown

3.29a Fit the plate/tool around the gear lever to hold it in 4th gear

shield above the intermediate section of the exhaust pipe rearwards.

8 Release the cables from the retaining clips on the underside of the floor.

9 Disconnect the selector cables from the gear lever as described in Section 2.

10 Fold back the carpet each side of the centre console area, and carefully cut away the sound insulation around the cable grommet, located just in front of the heater housing. Remove the sound insulation.

11 Undo the 2 nuts securing the cable

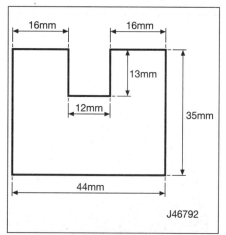

3.29b Fabricate a gear lever holding tool from aluminium plate to the dimensions shown
Not to scale

grommet to the floor, and lift the grommet from the mounting studs **(see illustration)**.

12 Manoeuvre the cable assembly into the passenger cabin, then out of the vehicle.

Refitting

13 Manoeuvre the cable assembly into position, through the hole in the floor, up to the transmission, then fit the grommet over the mounting studs and tighten the retaining nuts securely.

14 Reposition the sound insulation around the grommet, and tape over the cuts.

15 Reconnect the selector cables to the gear lever as described in Section 2.

16 Reclip the cables to the underside of the floor.

17 Refit the heat shield above the exhaust system.

18 Adjust the selector cable as described in this Section.

Adjustment

19 If not already done so, remove the centre air cleaner assembly as described in Chapter 4A.

20 If the centre console is still in place, carefully prise up the gear lever gaiter from the console.

5-speed transmission

21 Using a 3.0 mm drill bit, lock the gear lever in the 4th gear position **(see illustration)**.

22 Pull out the lock button on the side of the left-hand inner (selector) cable fitting at the selector lever on the transmission **(see illustration)**.

23 Check that the selector lever on the transmission is in the 4th gear position.

24 Press in the lock button on the side of the inner cable at the selector lever on the transmission, and check that the gear positions are readily obtainable.

25 Refit the air cleaner assembly, and centre console/gaiter using a reversal of the removal procedure.

6-speed transmission

26 Disconnect both gearchange cables from the levers on the transmission as described earlier in this Section, then prise up the locking catch on the end fitting of the selector cable **(see illustration)**.

27 Insert a 2.5 mm drill bit into the centre of the roll-pin securing the selector mechanism preload sleeve, set the vertical distance of 25 mm, and turn the selector arm to engage 4th gear as shown **(see illustration)**.

28 If the centre console is still in place, carefully prise up the gear lever gaiter from the console.

29 Ford technicians now use a special tool to hold the gearchange lever in the 4th gear position. For models up to 10/2005 tool No 308-154 is specified, and tool No 308-666 for models after this date. In the absence of these tools, make a tool from thin aluminium plate to the dimensions shown **(see illustrations)**. If none of the tools are available, the only option is to have an assistant attempt to hold the gearchange lever in the 4th gear position.

30 Re-attach the selector lever cable to the

balljoint, and press down the locking catch. Re-attach the shift cable end fitting.

31 Remove the drill bit and special tools (where applicable) and check the operation of the gearchange mechanism. If all appears satisfactory, refit the air cleaner assembly, and centre console/gaiter.

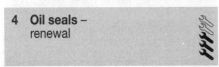

4 Oil seals – renewal

Driveshaft seals

1 Remove the left- or right-hand driveshaft (as appropriate) with reference to Chapter 8.
2 Drain the transmission oil as described in Section 6.
3 Using a large screwdriver or suitable lever, carefully prise the oil seal out of the trans- mission casing, taking care not to damage the casing **(see illustration)**.
4 Wipe clean the oil seal seating in the trans- mission casing.
5 Apply a small amount of general purpose grease to the new seal lips, then press it a little way into the casing by hand, making sure that it is square to its seating.
6 Using suitable tubing or a large socket, carefully drive the oil seal fully into position until it is flush with the casing edge **(see illustration)**.
7 Refit the driveshaft(s) as described in Chapter 8.
8 Replenish the transmission oil as described in Section 6.

Input shaft oil seal

5-speed transmission

9 The input shaft seal is integral with the clutch slave cylinder/release bearing. Renew the cylinder/bearing as described in Chapter 6.

6-speed transmission

10 Remove the clutch release bearing/slave cylinder as described in Chapter 6.
11 Note its fitted depth, then drill a small hole in the hard outer surface of the seal, insert a self-tapping screw, and use pliers to extract the seal **(see illustration)**.
12 Lubricate the new seal with grease and fit it to the bellhousing, lips pointing to the gearbox side. Use a deep socket or suitable tubing to seat it **(see illustration)**.
13 Refit the release bearing/slave cylinder using a reversal of removal.

5 Reversing light switch – removal and refitting

Removal

5-speed transmission

1 Remove the air cleaner assembly as described in Chapter 4A.

4.3 Prise the driveshaft oil seal from place

4.11 Insert a self-tapping screw and pull the seal from place

2 Disconnect the wiring plug, then unscrew the switch from the top of the transmission casing **(see illustration)**.

6-speed transmission

3 The reversing light switch is located on the upper face of the transmission, between the two gear selector levers. Remove the air cleaner assembly as described in Chapter 4A.
4 Clean around the switch, disconnect the wiring connector **(see illustration)** and unscrew the switch.

Refitting

5 Refit by reversing the removal operations.

6 Manual transmission oil – draining and refilling

Note: Renewal of the transmission oil is not a

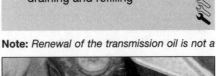

5.2 Reversing light switch (arrowed) – 5-speed transmission

4.6 Drive the new oil seal into place using a socket which bears only on the hard, outer edge of the seal

4.12 Drive the new seal squarely into place to its original depth

service requirement and will normally only be necessary if the unit is removed for overhaul or renewal. However, if the car has completed a high mileage, or is used under arduous conditions (eg, extensive towing or taxi work), it would be advisable to change the oil as a precaution, especially if the gearchange quality has deteriorated.

Draining

1 Slacken the left-hand front roadwheel bolts, then jack up the front of the vehicle and support it securely on axle stands (see *Jacking and vehicle support*). Remove the roadwheel.
2 Release the fasteners and remove the engine undershield (where fitted), then position a suitable container beneath the transmission.

5-speed transmission

3 On the right-hand side of the transmission casing, you will see the drain plug. Unscrew

5.4 Reversing light switch (arrowed) – 6-speed transmission

6.3 Transmission drain plug – 5-speed transmission

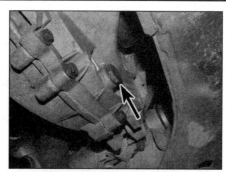

6.4 Transmission drain plug (arrowed) – 6-speed transmission

6.6 Oil filler/level plug (arrowed) – 5-speed transmission

6.9 Oil filler/level plug (arrowed) – 6-speed transmission

and remove the drain plug and allow the oil to drain into the container **(see illustration)**. Check the condition of the drain plug sealing washer, and renew if necessary.

6-speed transmission

4 The drain plug is located on the left-hand side of the transmission. Unscrew and remove the drain plug and allow the oil to drain into the container **(see illustration)**. Check the condition of the drain plug sealing washer (where fitted), and renew if necessary.

All models

5 When all the oil has drained, refit the drain plug and tighten it to the specified torque.

Refilling

Note: *For the level check to be accurate, the car must be completely level. If the front of the car has been jacked up, the rear should be jacked up also.*

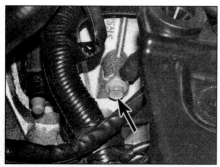

7.9 Note the earth connection on the top of the transmission housing (arrowed)

5-speed transmission

6 Unscrew the level/filler plug located on the front of the transmission casing **(see illustration)**. Discard the sealing washer, a new one must be fitted.

7 Add oil of the correct specification (see *Lubricants and fluids*) until oil begins to trickle out of the filler/level plug.

8 Fit a new sealing washer to the filler plug and tighten it to the specified torque.

6-speed transmission

9 Wipe clean the area around the filler/level plug, and unscrew the plug from the casing **(see illustration)**.

10 Fill the transmission through the filler plug orifice with the correct type of oil (see *Lubricants and fluids*) until the oil begins to run out of the orifice.

11 Refit the filler/level plug with a new seal

7.14 Remove the catalytic converter support bracket (arrowed)

(where fitted), and tighten it to the specified torque.

All models

12 Dispose of the old oil safely in accordance with environmental regulations. Refit the undershield (where applicable) and the road-wheel, then lower the vehicle to the ground.

7 Manual transmission – removal and refitting

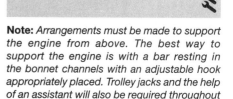

Note: *Arrangements must be made to support the engine from above. The best way to support the engine is with a bar resting in the bonnet channels with an adjustable hook appropriately placed. Trolley jacks and the help of an assistant will also be required throughout the procedure.*

Removal

1 Remove the plastic cover from the top of the engine.

2 Remove the battery as described in Chapter 5, then undo the 3 bolts and remove the battery tray.

3 Remove the air cleaner assembly as described in Chapter 4A, and all relevant inlet ducting around the left-hand side of the engine.

4 Remove both headlamps as described in Chapter 12.

5 Slacken the clamps, disconnect and remove the intercooler outlet pipe.

6 Disconnect the gearchange cables as described in Section 3.

7 Remove both driveshafts as described in Chapter 8.

8 Prise out the retaining clip and disconnect the clutch hydraulic fluid pipe from the junction at the transmission bellhousing, then pull the pipe's rubber bush upwards from the bracket on the transmission. Plug or seal the openings to prevent contamination.

9 Note the fitted position of any earth lead on the top/front of the transmission (where fitted), then disconnect the lead, along with the reversing light switch wiring plug **(see illustration)**.

10 Undo the fasteners and remove the splash shield under the radiator.

11 Slacken the bolt, undo the clamp and remove the intercooler intake pipe/hose.

12 Undo the 3 bolts and remove the 'crashbox' from the front of the subframe (where fitted), under the right-hand driveshaft location.

13 Undo the bolts and remove the engine lower torque rod/movement limiter link (see Chapter 2A, 2B or 2C as applicable).

14 Remove the catalytic converter as described in Chapter 4A, then undo the bolts and remove the support bracket **(see illustration)**.

15 Support the engine from above (see the note at the start of this Section), then undo the nuts/bolts and remove the left-hand engine/ transmission mounting and bracket **(see illustration)**.

16 Undo the bolts and remove the left-hand mounting bracket from the top of the transmission.

17 Remove the starter motor as described in Chapter 5.

18 On 2.0 litre models, remove the clutch housing cover at the rear of the engine adjacent to the right-hand driveshaft aperture.

19 Undo the upper bolts securing the transmission to the engine.

20 Lower the engine and transmission by approximately 10 mm.

21 Securely and safely support the transmission from below on a trolley jack.

22 Undo the remaining bolts securing the transmission to the engine. Withdraw the transmission squarely off the engine dowels, taking care not to allow the weight of the transmission to hang on the input shaft. Lower the engine slightly as the transmission is withdrawn to clear the chassis sidemember.

23 Lower the jack and remove the unit from under the car.

Refitting

24 Ensure the transmission input shaft is clean and free of rust or grease, then apply a little grease (Ford part No SA-M1C9107-A) to the splines of the input shaft – wipe off any excess grease. Check to make sure all locating dowels are in good condition and fitted correctly.

25 Manoeuvre the transmission squarely into position, and engage it with the engine dowels. Refit the lower bolts securing the transmission to the engine, and tighten them to the specified torque.

26 Raise the engine to its approximate fitted position. Refit the left-hand engine mounting bracket and torque rod, and secure with the bolts tightened to the specified torque.

27 The remainder of refitting is a reversal of removal, noting the following points:
  a) *Tighten all fasteners to their specified torque where given.*
  b) *Top-up the gearbox oil as described in Section 6 of this Chapter.*
  c) *Adjust the selector lever cables as described in Section 3.*
  d) *Bleed the clutch hydraulic system as described in Chapter 6.*
  e) *Reconnect the battery negative lead as described in Chapter 5.*

8 Manual transmission overhaul – general information

Overhauling a manual transmission is a difficult job for the do-it-yourselfer. It involves the dismantling and reassembly of many small parts. Numerous clearances must be precisely measured and, if necessary, changed with selected spacers and circlips. As a result, if transmission problems arise, while the unit can be removed and refitted by a competent do-it-yourselfer, overhaul should be left to a transmission specialist. Rebuilt transmissions may be available – check with your dealer parts department, motor factors, or transmission specialists. At any rate, the time and money involved in an overhaul is almost sure to exceed the cost of a rebuilt unit.

Nevertheless, it's not impossible for an experienced mechanic to rebuild a transmission, providing the special tools

7.15 Undo the bolts/nuts and remove the left-hand transmission mounting and bracket

are available, and the job is done in a deliberate step-by-step manner, so nothing is overlooked.

The tools necessary for an overhaul include: internal and external circlip pliers, a bearing puller, a slide hammer, a set of pin punches, a dial test indicator, and possibly a hydraulic press. In addition, a large, sturdy workbench and a vice or transmission stand will be required.

During dismantling of the transmission, make careful notes of how each part comes off, where it fits in relation to other parts, and what holds it in place.

Before taking the transmission apart for repair, it will help if you have some idea what area of the transmission is malfunctioning. Certain problems can be closely tied to specific areas in the transmission, which can make component examination and renewal easier. Refer to the *Fault finding* section at the rear of this manual for information regarding possible sources of trouble.

Chapter 8
Driveshafts

Contents

Degrees of difficulty

Easy, suitable for novice with little experience		Fairly easy, suitable for beginner with some experience		Fairly difficult, suitable for competent DIY mechanic		Difficult, suitable for experienced DIY mechanic		Very difficult, suitable for expert DIY or professional	

Specifications

General

Driveshaft type . . . . Equal-length solid-steel shafts, splined to inner and outer constant velocity joints. Intermediate shaft incorporated in right-hand driveshaft assembly

Outer constant velocity joint type. . . . . Ball-and-cage

Inner constant velocity joint type . . . . Tripod

Lubrication

Lubricant type . . . . Special grease supplied in repair kit, or suitable molybdenum disulphide grease – consult a Ford dealer or parts specialist

CV joint grease capacity (approximate):	Outboard joint	Inboard joint
1.6 and 1.8 litre models	100 g	150 g
2.0 litre models.	140 g	170 g

Torque wrench settings

	Nm	lbf ft
Crash box bolts	40	30
Driveshaft bolt:*		
Stage 1.	45	33
Stage 2.	Angle-tighten a further 90°	
Headlight levelling sensor bracket-to-lower arm	8	6
Lower arm balljoint-to-hub carrier*	70	52
Right-hand driveshaft support bearing cap nuts*	25	18
Roadwheel nuts	Refer to Chapter 1	

Do not re-use

---

1 General information

Drive is transmitted from the differential to the front wheels by means of two solid-steel, equal-length driveshafts equipped with constant velocity (CV) joints at their inner and outer ends. Due to the position of the transmission, an intermediate shaft and support bearing are incorporated into the right-hand driveshaft assembly.

A ball-and-cage type CV joint is fitted to the outer end of each driveshaft. The joint has an outer member, which is splined at its outer end to accept the wheel hub, and is threaded so that it can be fastened to the hub by a large bolt. The joint contains six balls within a cage, which engage with the inner member. The complete assembly is protected by a flexible gaiter secured to the driveshaft and joint outer member.

At the inner end, the driveshaft is splined to engage a tripod type CV joint, containing needle roller bearings and cups. On the left-hand side, the driveshaft inner CV joint engages directly with the differential sun wheel. On the right-hand side, the inner joint is integral with the intermediate shaft, the inner end of which engages with the differential sun wheel. As on the outer joints, a flexible gaiter secured to the driveshaft and CV joint outer member protects the complete assembly.

2.3a Slacken the driveshaft retaining bolt (arrowed)

2.3b On some models, prise out the centre cap and slacken the bolt

2.4 Undo the bolts (arrowed) and remove the engine undershield

2 Driveshafts – removal and refitting

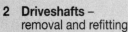

Removal

1 Firmly apply the handbrake and chock the rear wheels. When the driveshaft bolt is to be loosened (or tightened), it is preferable to do so with the car resting on its wheels. If the car is jacked up, this places a high load on the jack, and the car could slip off.

2 If the car has steel wheels, remove the wheel trim on the side being worked on – the driveshaft bolt can then be loosened with the wheel on the ground. On models with alloy wheels, the safest option is to remove the wheel on the side being worked on, and to fit the temporary spare (see *Wheel changing* at

the front of this Manual) – this wheel allows access to the driveshaft bolt.

3 With an assistant firmly depressing the brake pedal, slacken the driveshaft retaining bolt using a socket and a long extension bar **(see illustrations)**. Note that this bolt is extremely tight – ensure that the tools used to loosen it are of good quality, and a good fit.

4 Loosen the front wheel nuts, then jack up the front of the car and support it on axle stands (see *Jacking and vehicle support*). Remove the appropriate front roadwheel, then undo the fasteners and remove the engine undershield (where fitted) **(see illustration)**.

5 Remove the previously-slackened driveshaft retaining bolt. Discard the bolt – a new one must be fitted.

6 Tap the end of the driveshaft approximately 15 to 20 mm into the wheel hub.

7 Undo the bolt/nut and detach the headlight

levelling sensor bracket from the lower arm (where applicable).

8 Undo the bolts and remove the crash box from the subframe (where fitted).

9 Slacken the lower control arm balljoint nut until the end of the balljoint shank is level with the top of the nut.

10 Detach the lower control arm balljoint from the hub carrier using a balljoint separator tool **(see illustration)**.

11 Push down on the suspension arm using a stout bar to release the balljoint shank from the hub carrier. Take care not to damage the balljoint dust cover during and after disconnection.

12 Swivel the suspension strut and hub carrier assembly outwards, and withdraw the driveshaft CV joint from the hub flange **(see illustration)**.

13 If removing the left-hand driveshaft, free the inner CV joint from the transmission by levering between the edge of the joint and the transmission casing with a large screwdriver or similar tool. Take care not to damage the transmission oil seal or the inner CV joint gaiter. Withdraw the driveshaft from under the wheel arch.

14 If removing the right-hand driveshaft, undo the two nuts and remove the cap from the intermediate shaft support bearing **(see illustration)**. Pull the intermediate shaft out of the transmission, and remove the driveshaft assembly from under the wheel arch. **Note:** *Do not pull the outer shaft from the intermediate shaft – the coupling will separate.*

Refitting

15 Refitting is a reversal of removal, but observe the following points.

a) *Prior to refitting, remove all traces, rust, oil and dirt from the splines of the outer CV joint, and lubricate the splines of the inner joint with wheel bearing grease.*

b) *Apply a little grease to the driveshaft seal lips in the transmission casing.*

c) *If working on the left-hand driveshaft, ensure that the inner CV joint is pushed fully into the transmission, so that the retaining circlip locks into place in the differential gear.*

d) *Always use a new driveshaft-to-hub retaining bolt (see illustration).*

2.10 Use a balljoint separator tool to detach the balljoint from the hub carrier

2.12 Push the lower control arm downwards, pull the hub carrier outwards, and withdraw the driveshaft

2.14 Undo the 2 nuts (arrowed) and remove the intermediate bearing cap

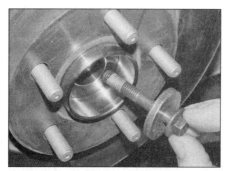

2.15 Always renew the driveshaft retaining bolt

3.2 Cut the gaiter retaining clips

3.6 Pack the outer CV joint with about half the grease supplied

3.9a Locate the outer clip on the gaiter . . .

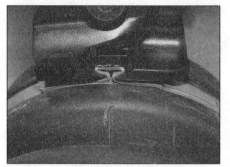

3.9b . . . then using a special pair of pliers . . .

3.9c . . . remove any slack in the clip

3.10 Lift the inner edge of the gaiter to equalise the air pressure

e) *Fit the same wheel as was used for loosening the driveshaft bolt, and lower the car to the ground.*
f) *Tighten all nuts and bolts to the specified torque (see Chapters 9 and 10 for brake and suspension component torque settings). When tightening the driveshaft bolt, tighten first using a torque wrench, then further, through the specified angle, using an angle-tightening gauge.*
g) *Ford insist that when refitting the right-hand driveshaft the intermediate shaft bearing cap nuts must be renewed.*
h) *Where applicable, refit the alloy wheel on completion. Tighten the roadwheel nuts to the specified torque.*

3 Outer constant velocity joint gaiter – renewal

1 Dismantle the inner constant velocity joint as described in Section 4.
2 Cut off the gaiter retaining clips, then slide the gaiter down the shaft to expose the outer constant velocity joint **(see illustration)**.
Caution: Do not disassemble the outer CV joint.
3 Scoop out as much grease as possible from the joint.
4 Inspect the ball tracks on the inner and outer members. If the tracks have widened, the balls will no longer be a tight fit. At the same time, check the ball cage windows for wear or cracking between the windows. If the

joints appear worn, complete renewal may be the only option – check with a Ford dealer or specialist.
5 If the joint is in satisfactory condition, obtain a repair kit from your Ford dealer, consisting of a new gaiter, retaining clips, driveshaft bolt, circlip and grease.
6 Pack the joint with the half of the grease supplied, working it well into the ball tracks, and into the driveshaft opening in the inner member **(see illustration)**.
7 Slide the rubber gaiter onto the shaft.
8 Apply the remaining grease to the joint and the inside of the gaiter.
9 Locate the outer lip of the gaiter in the groove on the joint outer member, then fit the retaining clip. Remove any slack in the clips by carefully compressing the raised section using a special pair of pincers **(see illustrations)**. **Note:** *Ensure no grease is on the surfaces between the gaiter and the joint housing.*
10 Use a small screwdriver to lift the inner lip of the gaiter, allowing the air pressure inside the gaiter to equalise, then fit the inner clip to the gaiter **(see illustration)**.
11 Reassembly the inner constant velocity joint as described in Section 4.

4 Inner constant velocity joint gaiter – renewal

1 Remove the driveshaft(s) as described in Section 2.

2 Cut through the metal clips, and slide the gaiter from the inner CV joint.
3 Clean out some of the grease from the joint, then make alignment marks between the housing and the shaft, to aid reassembly **(see illustration)**.
4 Carefully pull the housing from the tripod, twisting the housing so the tripod rollers come out one at a time. If necessary, use a soft-faced hammer or mallet to tap the housing off.
5 Clean the grease from the tripod and housing.
6 Remove the circlip, and carefully drive the tripod from the end of the shaft **(see illustrations)**. Discard the circlip, a new one (supplied in the repair kit) must be fitted. Remove the gaiter if still on the shaft.
7 Slide the new gaiter onto the shaft along with the smaller clip **(see illustration)**.

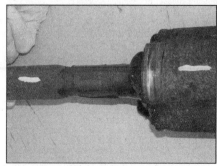

4.3 Make alignment marks between the shaft and housing

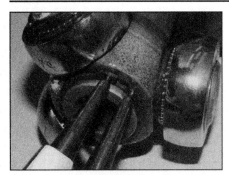

4.6a Remove the circlip from the end of the shaft ...

4.6b ... then carefully drive the tripod from the shaft

4.7 Slide the new gaiter and smaller diameter clip onto the shaft

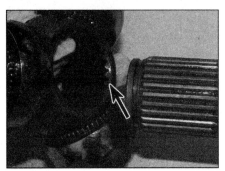

4.8a Fit the tripod with the bevelled edge (arrowed) towards the shaft ...

4.8b ... then fit the new circlip

8 Refit the tripod with the bevelled edge towards the driveshaft, and drive it fully into place, until the new circlip can be installed **(see illustrations)**.

9 Lubricate the tripod rollers with some of the grease supplied in the gaiter kit, then fill the housing and gaiter with the remainder.

10 Refit the housing to the tripod, tapping it gently into place using a soft-hammer or mallet if necessary.

11 Slide the new gaiter into place ensuring the smaller diameter of the gaiter locates over the grooves in the shaft **(see illustration)**.

12 Fit the new retaining clips **(see illustration)**.

13 Fit the new circlip to the end of the shaft **(see illustration)**.

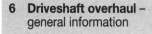

5 Right-hand driveshaft support bearing – removal and refitting

Note: *At the time of writing, it would appear the support bearing was not available as a separate part. If the bearing is worn of*

damaged, the complete driveshaft must be renewed. Exchange driveshafts may be available – check with a Ford dealer or specialist.

6 Driveshaft overhaul – general information

Road test the car, and listen for a metallic clicking from the front as the car is driven slowly in a circle with the steering on full-lock. Repeat the check on full-left and full-right lock. This noise may also be apparent when pulling away from a standstill with lock applied. If a clicking noise is heard, this indicates wear in the outer constant velocity joints.

If vibration, consistent with roadspeed, is felt through the car when accelerating, there is a possibility of wear in the inner constant velocity joints.

If the joints are worn or damaged, it would appear at the time of writing that no parts are available, other then boot kits, and the complete driveshaft must be renewed. Exchange driveshafts may be available – check with a Ford dealer or specialist.

4.11 The smaller diameter of the gaiter must locate over the groove in the shaft (arrowed)

4.12 Equalise the air pressure before tightening the gaiter clip

4.13 The circlip on the end of the shaft must be renewed

Chapter 9
Braking system

Contents

Degrees of difficulty

Easy, suitable for novice with little experience 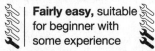	Fairly easy, suitable for beginner with some experience	Fairly difficult, suitable for competent DIY mechanic	Difficult, suitable for experienced DIY mechanic	Very difficult, suitable for expert DIY or professional

Specifications

Front brakes

Type	Ventilated disc, with single sliding piston caliper
Disc diameter:	
1.6 and 1.8 litre models	278 or 300 mm
2.0 litre models	300 mm
Disc thickness:	
New	25.0 mm
Minimum	23.0 mm
Maximum disc thickness variation	0.020 mm
Maximum disc/hub run-out (installed)	0.050 mm
Caliper piston diameter	54.0 mm
Brake pad friction material minimum thickness	1.5 mm

Rear drum brakes

Type	Leading and trailing shoes, with automatic adjusters
Drum diameter:	
New	228.3 mm
Maximum	230.2 mm
Shoe width	38.0 mm
Brake shoe friction material minimum thickness	1.0 mm

Rear disc brakes

Type	Solid disc, with single-piston floating caliper
Disc diameter:	
All models	280 mm
Disc thickness:	
New	11.0 mm
Minimum	9.0 mm
Maximum disc thickness variation	0.020 mm
Maximum disc/hub runout (installed)	0.050 mm
Brake pad friction material minimum thickness	1.5 mm

Torque wrench settings

	Nm	lbf ft
ABS wheel sensor securing bolts	5	4
Brake pipe to hydraulic control unit	11	8
Brake pipe to master cylinder	17	13
Brake pipe unions	15	11
Front caliper guide bolts	28	21
Front caliper mounting bracket bolts	120	89
Handbrake lever mountings	35	26
Master cylinder to servo mountings	25	18
Pedal bracket to servo mountings	23	17
Rear caliper bracket	70	52
Rear caliper guide bolts	35	26
Rear wheel cylinder bolts	10	7
Roadwheel nuts	Refer to Chapter 1	
Vacuum pump:		
1.6 litre models	18	13
1.8 and 2.0 litre models	22	16
Yaw rate sensor bracket to body	5	4

1 General information

The braking system is of diagonally-split, dual-circuit design, with ventilated discs at the front, and drum or disc brakes (according to model) at the rear. The front calipers are of single sliding piston design, and (where fitted) the rear calipers are of a single-piston floating design, using asbestos-free pads. The rear drum brakes are of the leading and trailing shoe type, and are self-adjusting during footbrake operation. The rear brake shoe linings are of different thicknesses, in order to allow for the different proportional rates of wear.

The servo unit uses vacuum generated from the camshaft-driven vacuum pump to boost the effort applied by the driver at the brake pedal and transmits this increased effort to the master cylinder pistons.

The handbrake is cable-operated, and acts on the rear brakes. On rear drum brake models, the cables operate on the rear trailing brake shoe operating levers; on rear disc brake models, they operate on levers on the rear calipers. The handbrake lever incorporates an automatic adjuster, which will adjust the cable when the handbrake is operated several times.

The anti-lock braking system (ABS) uses the basic conventional brake system, together with an ABS hydraulic unit fitted between the master cylinder and the four brake units at each wheel. The hydraulic unit consists of a hydraulic actuator, an ABS brake pressure pump, and an ABS module. Braking at each of the four wheels is controlled by separate solenoid valves in the hydraulic actuator. If wheel lock-up is detected by one of the wheel sensors, when the vehicle speed is above 3 mph, the valve opens releasing pressure to the relevant brake until the wheel regains a rotational speed corresponding to the speed of the vehicle. The cycle can be repeated many times a second. In the event of a fault in the ABS system, the conventional braking system is not affected. Diagnosis of a fault in the ABS system requires the use of special equipment, and this work should therefore be left to a Ford dealer or suitably-equipped specialist. The wheel speed sensor signal rings are built-into the oil seals of the wheel bearings.

Where fitted, the traction control systems are integrated with the ABS, and use the same wheel sensors. The hydraulic control unit has additional solenoid valves incorporated to enable control of the wheel brake pressure. The system is only active at speeds up to 53 mph – when the system is active the warning light on the instrument panel illuminates to warn the driver. This uses controlled braking of the spinning driving wheel when the grip at the driven wheels are different. The spinning wheel is braked by the ABS system, transferring a greater proportion of the engine torque through the differential to the other wheel, which increases the use of the available traction control.

On several models in the range, there is an Electronic Stability Program (ESP) available. This system supports the vehicle's stability and steering through a combination of ABS and traction control operations. There is a switch on the centre console, so that if required the system can be switched off. This will then illuminate the warning light on the instrument panel, to inform the driver that the ESP is not in operation. The stability of the vehicle is measured by Yaw rate and Accelerometer sensors, which sense the movement of the vehicle about its vertical axis, and also lateral acceleration.

Note: *When servicing any part of the system, work carefully and methodically; also observe scrupulous cleanliness when overhauling any part of the hydraulic system. Always renew components (in axle sets, where applicable) if in doubt about their condition, and use only genuine Ford parts, or at least those of known good quality. Note the warnings given in 'Safety first!' and at relevant points in this Chapter concerning the dangers of asbestos dust and hydraulic fluid.*

2 Front brake pads – renewal

Warning: Renew both sets of front brake pads at the same time – never renew the pads on only one wheel, as uneven braking may result. Note that the dust created by wear of the pads may contain asbestos, which is a health hazard. Never blow it out with compressed air, and don't inhale any of it. An approved filtering mask should be worn when working on the brakes. DO NOT use petrol or petroleum-based solvents to clean brake parts; use brake cleaner or methylated spirit only.

1 Apply the handbrake, then slacken the front roadwheel nuts. Jack up the front of the vehicle and support it on axle stands. Remove both front roadwheels.

2 Follow the accompanying photos **(illustrations 2.2a to 2.2p)** for the actual pad renewal procedure. Be sure to stay in order and read the caption under each illustration, and note the following points:

a) *New pads may have an adhesive foil on the backplates. Remove this foil prior to installation.*

b) *Thoroughly clean the caliper guide surfaces, and apply a little brake assembly (polycarbamide) grease.*

c) *When pushing the caliper piston back to accommodate new pads, keep a close eye on the fluid lever in the reservoir.*

Caution: Pushing back the piston causes a reverse-flow of brake fluid, which has been known to 'flip' the master cylinder rubber seals, resulting in a total loss of braking. To avoid this, clamp the caliper flexible hose and open the bleed screw – as the piston is pushed back, the fluid can be directed into a suitable container using a hose attached to the bleed screw. Close the screw just before the piston is pushed fully back, to ensure no air enters the system.

2.2a Use a flat-bladed screwdriver to carefully prise off the caliper retaining spring

2.2b Prise out the rubber caps . . .

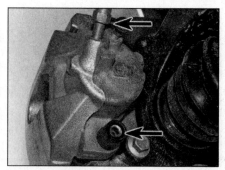

2.2c . . . and use an Allen key to undo the caliper guide bolts (arrowed)

2.2d Slide the caliper and inner pad from the disc

2.2e Pull the inner brake pad from the caliper piston . . .

2.2f . . . and lift the outer pad from the caliper bracket

2.2g If you're fitting new pads, push the piston back into the caliper using a piston retraction tool or G-clamp

2.2h Clean the pad mounting surfaces with a wire brush

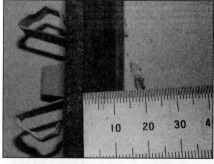

2.2i Measure the thickness of the pad's friction material. If it's 1.5 mm or less, renew all the front pads

2.2j Fit the outer pad to the caliper mounting bracket . . .

2.2k . . . then fit the inner pad to the caliper piston

2.2l Slide the caliper with the inner panel fitted over the disc and outer pad

2.2m Refit the caliper guide bolts and tighten them to the specified torque

2.2n Press the rubber caps into position

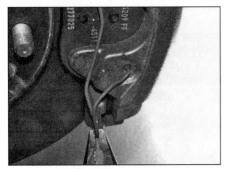

2.2o Use a pair of pliers . . .

2.2p . . . to refit the caliper retaining spring

3 Depress the brake pedal repeatedly, until the pads are pressed into firm contact with the brake disc, and normal (non-assisted) pedal pressure is restored.

4 Repeat the above procedure on the remaining front brake caliper.

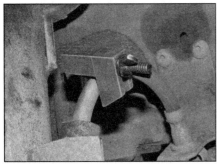

3.2 Use a hose clamp on the flexible hoses

3.3 Slacken the flexible hose union (arrowed)

5 Refit the roadwheels, then lower the vehicle to the ground and tighten the roadwheel nuts to the specified torque.

6 Check the hydraulic fluid level as described in *Weekly checks*.
Caution: New pads will not give full braking efficiency until they have bedded-in. Be prepared for this, and avoid hard braking as far as possible for the first hundred miles or so after pad renewal.

> **3 Front brake caliper –**
> removal, overhaul and refitting

Note: *Refer to the warning at the beginning of the previous Section before proceeding.*

Removal

1 Apply the handbrake. Loosen the front wheel nuts, then jack up the front of the

3.6 Caliper bracket bolts (arrowed)

vehicle and support it on axle stands. Remove the appropriate front wheel.

2 Fit a brake hose clamp to the flexible hose leading to the caliper **(see illustration)**. This will minimise brake fluid loss during subsequent operations.

3 Loosen the union on the caliper end of the flexible brake hose **(see illustration)**. Once loosened, do not try to unscrew the hose at this stage.

4 Remove the brake pads as described in Section 2.

5 Support the caliper in one hand, and prevent the hydraulic hose from turning with the other hand. Unscrew the caliper from the hose, making sure that the hose is not twisted unduly or strained. Once the caliper is detached, plug the open hydraulic unions in the caliper and hose, to keep out dust and dirt.

6 If required, the caliper bracket can be unbolted from the hub carrier **(see illustration)**.

Overhaul

Note: *Before starting work, check on the availability of parts (caliper overhaul kit/seals).*
7 With the caliper on the bench, brush away all traces of dust and dirt, but take care not to inhale any dust, as it may be harmful to your health.

8 Pull the dust cover rubber seal from the end of the piston.

9 Apply low air pressure to the fluid inlet union, to eject the piston. Only low air pressure is required for this, such as is produced by a foot-operated tyre pump.
Caution: The piston may be ejected with some force. Position a thin piece of wood between the piston and the caliper body to prevent damage to the end face of the piston in the event of it being ejected suddenly.

10 Using a suitable blunt instrument, prise the piston seal from the groove in the cylinder bore. Take care not to scratch the surface of the bore.

11 Clean the piston and caliper body with methylated spirit, and allow to dry. Examine the surfaces of the piston and cylinder bore for wear, damage and corrosion. If the piston alone is unserviceable, a new piston must be obtained, along with seals. If the cylinder bore is unserviceable, the complete caliper must be renewed. The seals must be renewed, regardless of the condition of the other components.

12 Coat the piston and seals with clean brake fluid, then manipulate the piston seal into the groove in the cylinder bore.

13 Push the piston squarely into its bore, taking care not to damage the seal.

14 Fit the dust cover rubber seal onto the piston and caliper, then depress the piston fully.

Refitting

15 Refit the caliper by reversing the removal

4.2 Suspend the caliper from the spring using wire or string

4.4 Measure the thickness of the disc using a micrometer

4.10 Lift the brake disc from the studs

operations. Make sure that the flexible brake hose is not twisted. Tighten the mounting bolts and wheel nuts to the specified torque.

16 Bleed the brake circuit according to the procedure given in Section 14, remembering to remove the brake hose clamp from the flexible hose. Make sure there are no leaks from the hose connections. Test the brakes carefully before returning the vehicle to normal service.

4 Front brake disc – inspection, removal and refitting

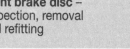

Note: *To prevent uneven braking, BOTH front brake discs should be renewed or reground at the same time.*

Inspection

1 Apply the handbrake. Loosen the relevant wheel nuts, jack up the front of the vehicle and support it on axle stands. Remove the appropriate front wheel.

2 Remove the front brake caliper from the disc with reference to Section 3, and undo the two caliper bracket securing bolts. Do not disconnect the flexible hose. Support the caliper on an axle stand, or suspend it out of the way with a piece of wire, taking care to avoid straining the flexible hose **(see illustration)**.

3 Temporarily refit two of the wheel nuts to diagonally-opposite studs, with the flat sides of the nuts against the disc. Tighten the nuts progressively, to hold the disc firmly.

4 Scrape any corrosion from the disc. Rotate the disc, and examine it for deep scoring, grooving or cracks. Using a micrometer, measure the thickness of the disc in several places **(see illustration)**. The minimum thickness is stamped on the disc hub. Light wear and scoring is normal, but if excessive, the disc should be removed, and either reground by a specialist, or renewed. If regrinding is undertaken, the minimum thickness must be maintained. Obviously, if the disc is cracked, it must be renewed.

5 Using a dial gauge or a flat metal block and feeler gauges, check that the disc run-out 10 mm from the outer edge does not

exceed the limit given in the Specifications. To do this, fix the measuring equipment, and rotate the disc, noting the variation in measurement as the disc is rotated. The difference between the minimum and maximum measurements recorded is the disc run-out.

6 If the run-out is greater than the specified amount, check for variations of the disc thickness as follows. Mark the disc at eight positions 45° apart then, using a micrometer, measure the disc thickness at the eight positions, 15 mm in from the outer edge. If the variation between the minimum and maximum readings is greater than the specified amount, the disc should be renewed.

7 The hub face run-out can also be checked in a similar way. First remove the disc as described later in this Section, fix the measuring equipment, then slowly rotate the hub, and check that the run-out does not exceed the amount given in the Specifications. If the hub face run-out is excessive, this should be corrected (by renewing the hub bearings – see Chapter 10) before rechecking the disc run-out.

Removal

8 With the wheel, caliper and bracket removed, remove the wheel nuts which were temporarily refitted in paragraph 3.

9 Mark the disc in relation to the hub, if it is to be refitted.

10 Remove the washer/retaining clip(s) (where fitted), and withdraw the disc over the wheel studs **(see illustration)**.

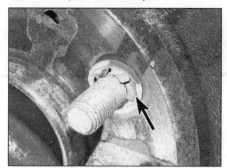

5.2a Prise off the clip (arrowed)

Refitting

11 Make sure that the disc and hub mating surfaces are clean, then locate the disc on the wheel studs. Align the previously-made marks if the original disc is being refitted.

12 Refit the washer/retaining clip(s), where fitted.

13 Refit the brake caliper and bracket with reference to Section 2.

14 Refit the wheel, and lower the vehicle to the ground. Tighten wheel nuts to their specified torque.

15 Test the brakes carefully before returning the vehicle to normal service.

5 Rear brake drum – removal, inspection and refitting

Note: *Refer to the warning at the beginning of Section 6 before proceeding.*
Note: *To prevent uneven braking, BOTH rear brake drums should be renewed at the same time.*

Removal

1 Chock the front wheels, release the handbrake and engage 1st gear. Loosen the relevant wheel nuts, jack up the rear of the vehicle and support it on axle stands. Remove the appropriate rear wheel.

2 Prise off the spring clip (where fitted), and pull the drum from place. If the drum is reluctant to move, use two 8.0 mm bolts screwed into the threaded holes provided, and draw the drum from place **(see illustrations)**.

5.2b Use 2 x 8 mm bolts to force the drum from place

6.3 Clean the components with brake cleaner

6.4 Depress the hold-down spring, and slide it from under the head of the pin

6.5 Pull the top end of the shoe assembly outwards from the wheel cylinder

6.7a Pull the bottom end of the shoes from the anchor . . .

6.7b . . . then pivot the whole brake shoe assembly outwards

3 With the brake drum removed, clean the dust from the drum, brake shoes, wheel cylinder and backplate, using brake cleaner or methylated spirit. Take care not to inhale the dust, as it may contain asbestos.

Inspection

4 Clean the inside surfaces of the brake drum, then examine the internal friction surface for signs of scoring or cracks. If it is cracked, deeply scored, or has worn to a diameter greater than the maximum given in the Specifications, then it should be renewed, together with the drum on the other side.

5 Regrinding of the brake drum is not recommended.

Refitting

6 Refitting is a reversal of removal, tightening relevant bolts to their specified torque. Where necessary, adjust the handbrake as described in Section 22.

6.8 Pull the spring back and disengage the handbrake lever cable end fitting from the lever on the shoe

7 Test the brakes carefully before returning the vehicle to normal service.

6 Rear brake shoes – renewal

⚠️ *Warning: Drum brake shoes must be renewed on BOTH rear wheels at the same time – never renew the shoes on only one wheel, as uneven braking may result. Also, the dust created by wear of the shoes may contain asbestos, which is a health hazard. Never blow it out with compressed air, and don't inhale any of it. An approved filtering mask should be worn when working on the brakes. DO NOT use petroleum-based solvents to clean brake parts; use brake cleaner or methylated spirit only.*

1 Chock the front wheels, release the

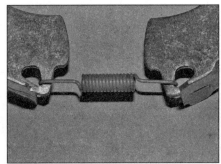

6.9 Unhook the lower return spring

handbrake and engage 1st gear. Loosen the relevant wheel nuts, jack up the rear of the vehicle and support it on axle stands. Remove the rear wheels. Work on one brake assembly at a time, using the assembled brake for reference if necessary.

2 Remove the rear brake drum as described in Section 5.

3 Note the fitted position of the springs and the brake shoes, then clean the components with brake cleaner, and allow to dry **(see illustration)**; position a tray beneath the backplate, to catch the cleaner and residue.

4 Remove the two shoe hold-down springs, use a pair of pliers to depress the ends so that they can be withdrawn off the pins. If required, remove the hold-down pins from the backplate **(see illustration)**. Note that on some models, it's not possible to remove the rearmost hold-down pin with the backplate in place.

5 Disconnect the top ends of the shoes from the wheel cylinder, taking care not to damage the rubber boots **(see illustration)**.

6 To prevent the wheel cylinder pistons from being accidentally ejected, fit a suitable elastic band or wire lengthways over the cylinder/pistons. DO NOT press the brake pedal while the shoes are removed.

7 Pull the bottom end of the brake shoes from the bottom anchor **(see illustrations)** using pliers or an adjustable spanner over the edge of the shoe to lever it away, if required.

8 Pull the handbrake cable spring back from the operating lever on the rear of the trailing shoe. Unhook the cable end from the cut-out in the lever, and remove the brake shoes **(see illustration)**.

9 Working on a clean bench, move the bottom ends of the brake shoes together, and unhook the lower return spring from the shoes, noting the location holes **(see illustration)**.

10 Pull the leading shoe from the strut and brake shoe adjuster **(see illustration)**.

11 Pull the adjustment strut to release it from the trailing brake shoe, then unhook the upper return spring from the shoes, noting the location holes **(see illustrations)**. Ford insist that the upper return spring is renewed.

12 If the wheel cylinder shows signs of fluid

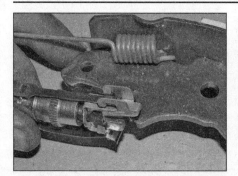

6.10 Pull the shoe from the strut and brake shoe adjuster

6.11a Pull the adjustment strut from the trailing shoe . . .

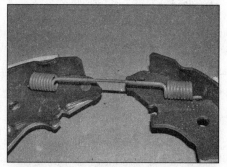

6.11b . . . then unhook the upper return spring

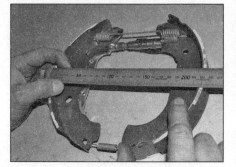

6.15a Set the adjustment strut so the diameter of the shoe assembly is 228 mm

6.15b When reassembled, the top of the assembly should look like this . . .

6.15c . . . and the lower end should look like this

leakage, or if there is any reason to suspect it of being defective, inspect it now, as described in the next Section.

13 Clean the backplate, and apply small amounts of high melting-point brake grease to the brake shoe contact points. Be careful not to get grease on any friction surfaces.

14 Lubricate the sliding components of the brake shoe adjuster with a little high melting-point brake grease.

15 Fit the new brake shoes using a reversal of the removal procedure, but set the adjustment strut so the diameter of the shoe assembly is 228 mm **(see illustrations)**.

16 Before refitting the brake drum, it should be inspected as described in Section 5.

17 With the drum in position and all the securing bolts and nuts tightened to their specified torque, refit the wheel, then carry out the renewal procedure on the remaining rear brake.

18 Lower the vehicle to the ground, and tighten the wheel nuts to the specified torque.

19 Depress the brake pedal several times, in order to operate the self-adjusting mechanism and set the shoes at their normal operating position.

20 Make several forward and reverse stops, and operate the handbrake fully two or three times (adjust the handbrake as required). Give the vehicle a road test, to make sure that the brakes are functioning correctly, and to bed-in the new shoes to the contours of the drum. Remember that the new shoes will not give full braking efficiency until they have bedded-in.

7 Rear wheel cylinder –
removal, overhaul and refitting

Note: *Before starting work, check on the availability of parts (wheel cylinder or overhaul kit/seals). Also bear in mind that if the brake shoes have been contaminated by fluid leaking from the wheel cylinder, they must be renewed. The shoes on BOTH sides of the vehicle must be renewed, even if they are only contaminated on one side.*

Removal

1 Remove the brake drum as described in Section 5

2 Minimise fluid loss either by removing the master cylinder reservoir cap, and then tightening it down onto a piece of polythene to obtain an airtight seal, or by using a brake hose clamp, a G-clamp, or similar tool, to clamp the flexible hose at the nearest convenient point to the wheel cylinder.

3 Pull the brake shoes apart at their top ends, so that they are just clear of the wheel cylinder. The automatic adjuster will hold the shoes in this position, so that the cylinder can be withdrawn.

4 Wipe away all traces of dirt around the hydraulic union at the rear of the wheel cylinder, then undo the union nut.

5 Unscrew the two bolts securing the wheel cylinder to the backplate **(see illustration)**.

6 Withdraw the wheel cylinder from the backplate so that it is clear of the brake shoes.

Plug the open hydraulic unions, to prevent the entry of dirt, and to minimise further fluid loss whilst the cylinder is detached.

Overhaul

7 No overhaul procedures or parts were available at the time of writing, check availability of spares before dismantling. Renewing a wheel cylinder as a unit is recommended.

Refitting

8 Wipe clean the backplate and remove the plug from the end of the hydraulic pipe. Fit the cylinder onto the backplate and screw in the hydraulic union nut by hand, being careful not to cross-thread it.

9 Tighten the mounting bolts, then fully tighten the hydraulic union nut.

10 Retract the automatic brake adjuster mechanism, so that the brake shoes engage

7.5 Undo the 2 bolts (arrowed) and remove the wheel cylinder

with the pistons of the wheel cylinder. To do this, prise the shoes apart slightly, turn the automatic adjuster to its minimum position, and release the shoes.

11 Remove the clamp from the flexible brake hose, or the polythene from the master cylinder (as applicable).

12 Refit the brake drum with reference to Section 5.

13 Bleed the hydraulic system as described in Section 14. Providing suitable precautions were taken to minimise loss of fluid, it should only be necessary to bleed the relevant rear brake.

14 Test the brakes carefully before returning the vehicle to normal service.

8.2a **Prise away the retaining spring**

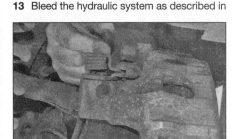

8.2b **Pull out the rubber caps . . .**

8 Rear brake pads – renewal

⚠ *Warning: Renew both sets of rear brake pads at the same time – never renew the pads on only one wheel, as uneven braking may result. Note that the dust created by wear of the pads may contain asbestos, which is a health hazard. Never blow it out with compressed air, and don't inhale any of it. An approved filtering mask should be worn when working on the brakes. DO NOT use petrol or petroleum-based solvents to clean brake parts; use brake cleaner or methylated spirit only.*

1 Chock the front wheels, slacken the rear road-wheel nuts, then jack up the rear of the vehicle and support it on axle stands (see *Jacking and vehicle support*). Remove the rear wheels.

2 With the handbrake lever fully released, follow the accompanying photos **(see illustrations 8.2a to 8.2u)** for the actual pad renewal procedure. Be sure to stay in order and read the caption under each illustration, and note the following points:

  a) *If re-installing the original pads, ensure they are fitted to their original position.*

  b) *Thoroughly clean the caliper guide surfaces and guide bolts.*

  c) *If new pads are to be fitted, use a piston retraction tool to push the piston back and twist it clockwise at the same time – keep an eye on the fluid level in the reservoir whilst retracting the piston.*

Caution: Pushing back the piston causes a reverse-flow of brake fluid, which has been known to 'flip' the master cylinder rubber seals, resulting in a total loss of braking. To avoid this, clamp the caliper flexible hose and open the bleed screw – as the piston is pushed back, the fluid can be directed into a suitable container using a hose attached to the bleed screw. Close the screw just before the piston is pushed fully back, to ensure no air enters the system.

8.2c **. . . and use a 7 mm Allen key or bit to unscrew the guide bolts**

8.2d **Unclip the brake hose from the bracket**

8.2e **Lift away the caliper . . .**

8.2f **. . . and suspend it from the suspension using cable ties/string**

8.2g **Remove the outer brake pad . . .**

8.2h **. . . and the inner pad**

8.2i **Measure the thickness of the pad friction material**

8.2j Use a wire brush to clean the pad mounting bracket

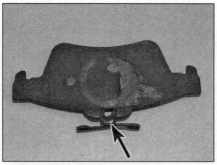

8.2k Note that the inner pad has an anti-rattle spring (arrowed)

8.2l Apply a little high-temperature anti-seize grease (Copperslip) to the rear of the pad . . .

8.2m . . . and the areas where the pad backing plate contacts the mounting bracket

8.2n Fit the inner pad – friction material side against the disc . . .

8.2o . . . followed by the outer pad

8.2p If new pads have been fitted, use a retraction tool to rotate the caliper piston clockwise, at the same time as pushing it into the caliper

8.2q Refit the caliper over the pads . . .

8.2r . . . then refit and tighten the guide bolts to the specified torque

8.2s Refit the rubber caps

8.2t Clip the brake hose back into the bracket

8.2u Use pliers to refit the caliper retaining spring

9.4 Unclip the cable end fitting (arrowed) from the caliper lever

3 Depress the brake pedal repeatedly, until the pads are pressed into firm contact with the brake disc, and normal (non-assisted) pedal pressure is restored.
4 Repeat the above procedure on the remaining brake caliper.
5 If necessary, adjust the handbrake as described in Section 22.
6 Refit the roadwheels, then lower the vehicle to the ground and tighten the roadwheel nuts to the specified torque.
7 Check the hydraulic fluid level as described in *Weekly checks*.
Caution: New pads will not give full braking efficiency until they have bedded-in. Be prepared for this, and avoid hard braking as far as possible for the first hundred miles or so after pad renewal.

9 Rear brake caliper – removal, overhaul and refitting

Removal

1 Chock the front wheels, and engage 1st gear. Loosen the rear wheel nuts, jack up the rear of the vehicle and support it on axle stands. Remove the appropriate rear wheel.
2 Fit a brake hose clamp to the flexible hose leading to the caliper **(see illustration 3.2).** This will minimise brake fluid loss during subsequent operations.
3 Slacken (but do not completely unscrew)

10.3 Pull the rear brake disc over the wheel studs

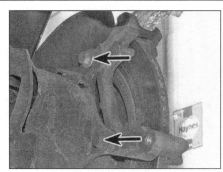

9.6 Undo the caliper mounting bracket bolts (arrowed)

the union on the caliper end of the flexible hose.
4 Unclip the handbrake inner cable fitting from the lever on the caliper, then detach the outer cable from the bracket **(see illustration).**
5 Unscrew the caliper from the hydraulic brake hose, making sure that the hose is not twisted or strained unduly. Plug the open hydraulic unions to keep dust and dirt out.
6 If necessary, unbolt the caliper bracket from the hub carrier **(see illustration).**

Overhaul

7 No overhaul procedures, or parts, were available at the time of writing. Check the availability of spares before dismantling the caliper. Do not attempt to dismantle the handbrake mechanism inside the caliper; if the mechanism is faulty, the complete caliper assembly must be renewed.

Refitting

8 Refit the caliper, and where applicable the bracket, by reversing the removal operations. Refer to the points made in Section 22 when reconnecting the handbrake cable. Tighten the mounting bolts and wheel nuts to the specified torque, and do not forget to remove the brake hose clamp from the flexible brake hose.
9 Bleed the brake circuit according to the procedure given in Section 14. Make sure there are no leaks from the hose connections. Test the brakes carefully before returning the vehicle to normal service.

11.4 Battery tray retaining bolts (arrowed)

10 Rear brake disc – inspection, removal and refitting

Removal

1 Remove the rear caliper and pads as described in Section 8.
2 Unbolt the caliper bracket from the hub **(see illustration 9.6)**, then mark the disc in relation to the hub, if it is to be refitted.
3 Remove the retaining clip from the wheel stud (where fitted), and withdraw the disc over the wheel studs **(see illustration)**.
4 Procedures for inspection of the rear brake discs are the same as the front brake discs as described in Section 4.

Refitting

5 Refitting is a reversal of removal, as described in the relevant Sections. Apply a little thread locking compound to the caliper bracket-to-hub carrier bolts.

11 Master cylinder – removal and refitting

⚠ *Warning: Brake fluid is poisonous. Take care to keep it off bare skin, and in particular not to get splashes in your eyes. The fluid also attacks paintwork and plastics – wash off spillages immediately with cold water. Finally, brake fluid is highly inflammable, and should be handled with the same care as petrol.*

Removal

1 Exhaust the vacuum in the servo by pressing the brake pedal a few times, with the engine switched off.
2 Disconnect the battery negative lead. Note: *Before disconnecting the battery, refer to Chapter 5 for precautions.*

⚠ *Warning: Do not syphon the fluid by mouth; it is poisonous. Any brake fluid spilt on paintwork should be washed off with clean water, without delay – brake fluid is also a highly-effective paint-stripper.*

3 Where fitted, undo the 2 nuts securing the brake fluid reservoir extension to the bulkhead extension panel, then depress the release button and detach the reservoir extension hose from the reservoir above the master cylinder.

Later models with a plastic panel in front of the brake master cylinder

4 Remove the battery as described in Chapter 5, then undo the 3 bolts and slide the battery tray forward a little **(see illustration)**.
5 Prise out the 4 plastic clips securing the plastic panel to the engine compartment bulkhead, then undo the inner 2 retaining bolts, slacken the outer bolt, remove the nuts

11.5a Prise out the 4 clips (arrowed)

11.5b Undo the 2 inner bolts, slacken the outer bolt, undo the 2 nuts and pivot the cross-stay (arrowed) each side away from the engine compartment bulkhead . . .

11.5c . . . so the plastic panel in front of the master cylinder can be removed

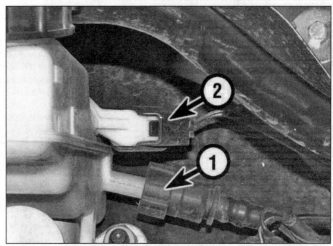

11.7 Depress the release button (on the reverse of the connector (1)), and disconnect the clutch fluid supply hose, then disconnect the level warning sensor wiring plug (2)

and pivot the cross-stay each side away from the bulkhead. Lift the plastic panel (where fitted) from place (see illustrations). Refit the bolts to secure the tops of the suspension struts to the vehicle body.

All models

6 Raise the vehicle and remove the wheels. Slacken the front bleed nipples, attach a rubber hose to the nipple, and place the other end of the hose in a suitable container. Operate the brake pedal until the fluid level is down to the base of the reservoir.

7 Depress the release button and detach the clutch master cylinder fluid supply hose from the side of the brake fluid reservoir (see illustration). Plug the openings to prevent contamination.

8 Disconnect the wiring plug from the fluid level sensor on the side of the reservoir (see illustration 11.7).

9 Identify the locations of each brake pipe on the master cylinder, then place rags beneath

the master cylinder to catch spilt hydraulic fluid.

10 Clean around the hydraulic union nuts. Unscrew the nuts, and disconnect the hydraulic lines from the master cylinder. If the nuts are tight, a split ring spanner should be used in preference to an open-ended spanner (see illustration).

11.10 Undo the brake pipe unions (arrowed)

Cap the end of the pipes and the master cylinder to prevent any dirt contamination.

11 Undo the master cylinder securing nuts, and withdraw the master cylinder from the studs on the servo unit (see illustration).

12 Recover the gasket/seal from the master cylinder.

11.11 Master cylinder retaining nuts (arrowed)

11.17 Pull out the reservoir retaining pin (arrowed – viewed from underneath)

13 If the master cylinder is faulty, it must be renewed. At the time of writing, no overhaul kits were available.

Refitting

14 Refitting is a reversal of the removal procedure, noting the following points:
 a) *Clean the contact surfaces of the master cylinder and servo, and locate a new gasket on the master cylinder.*
 b) *Refit and tighten the nuts to the specified torque.*
 c) *Carefully insert the brake pipes in the apertures in the master cylinder, then tighten the union nuts. Make sure that the nuts enter their threads correctly.*
 d) *Fill the reservoir with fresh brake fluid.*
 e) *Bleed the brake hydraulic system as described in Section 14.*
 f) *Test the brakes carefully before returning the vehicle to normal service.*

12.4 Disconnect the wiring plugs from the brake pedal switches

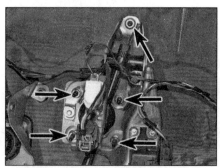

12.6 Brake pedal bracket assembly retaining nuts (arrowed)

Brake fluid reservoir

15 Carry out the procedure described in Paragraph 3 to 7 of this Section.
16 Disconnect the wiring plug from the fluid level sensor on the side of the reservoir.
17 Remove the retaining pin and detach the reservoir from the master cylinder **(see illustration)**.

12 Brake pedal – removal and refitting

Removal

1 Working inside the vehicle, move the driver's seat fully to the rear, to allow maximum working area.
2 Remove the driver's side lower facia panel as described in Chapter 11.
3 Remove the accelerator pedal as described in Chapter 4A.
4 Disconnect the electrical connectors to the brake pedal switches. Remove the switches by turning them, then pulling them out of the pedal bracket **(see illustration)**.
5 Prise out the pin securing the servo pushrod to the pedal **(see illustration)**. Discard the pin – a new one must be fitted.
6 Slacken the 5 retaining nuts on the pedal bracket assembly **(see illustration)**.
7 Manoeuvre the pedal assembly rearwards, and down from under the facia. No further dismantling of the assembly is recommended – it would appear that only the complete assembly is available.

12.5 Prise out and discard the servo pushrod pin

13.7 Use a brake pipe spanner to slacken the union nuts

Refitting

8 Refitting is a reversal of the removal procedure.
9 Refit the brake pedal switches as described in Section 21.

13 Hydraulic pipes and hoses – inspection, removal and refitting

Note: *Refer to the warning at the start of Section 14 concerning the dangers of brake fluid.*

Inspection

1 Jack up the front and rear of the vehicle, and support on axle stands (see *Jacking and vehicle support*). Making sure the vehicle is safely supported on a level surface.
2 Check for signs of leakage at the pipe unions, then examine the flexible hoses for signs of cracking, chafing and fraying.
3 The brake pipes should be examined carefully for signs of dents, corrosion or other damage. Corrosion should be scraped off, and if the depth of pitting is significant, the pipes renewed. This is particularly likely in those areas underneath the vehicle body where the pipes are exposed and unprotected.
4 Renew any defective brake pipes and/or hoses.

Removal

5 If a section of pipe or hose is to be removed, loss of brake fluid can be reduced by unscrewing the filler cap, and completely sealing the top of the reservoir with cling film or adhesive tape. Alternatively, the reservoir can be emptied (see Section 11).
6 To remove a section of pipe, hold the adjoining hose union nut with a spanner to prevent it from turning, then unscrew the union nut at the end of the pipe, and release it. Repeat the procedure at the other end of the pipe, then release the pipe by pulling out the clips attaching it to the body.
7 Where the union nuts are exposed to the full force of the weather, they can sometimes be quite tight. If an open-ended spanner is used, burring of the flats on the nuts is not uncommon, and for this reason, it is preferable to use a split ring (brake) spanner **(see illustration)**, which will engage all the flats. If such a spanner is not available, self-locking grips may be used as a last resort; these may well damage the nuts, but if the pipe is to be renewed, this does not matter.
8 To further minimise the loss of fluid when disconnecting a flexible brake line from a rigid pipe, clamp the hose as near as possible to the pipe to be detached, using a brake hose clamp or a pair of self-locking grips with protected jaws.
9 To remove a flexible hose, first clean the ends of the hose and the surrounding area, then unscrew the union nuts from the hose ends. Remove the spring clip, and withdraw

the hose from the serrated mounting in the support bracket. Where applicable, unscrew the hose from the caliper.

10 Brake pipes supplied with flared ends and union nuts can be obtained individually or in sets from Ford dealers or accessory shops. The pipe is then bent to shape, using the old pipe as a guide, and is ready for fitting. Be careful not to kink or crimp the pipe when bending it; ideally, a proper pipe-bending tool should be used.

Refitting

11 Refitting of the pipes and hoses is a reversal of removal. Make sure that all brake pipes are securely supported in their clips, and ensure that the hoses are not kinked. Check also that the hoses are clear of all suspension components and underbody fittings, and will remain clear during movement of the suspension and steering.

12 On completion, bleed the hydraulic system as described in Section 14.

14 Hydraulic system – bleeding

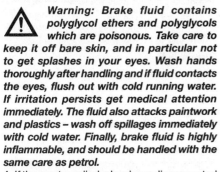

⚠️ **Warning: Brake fluid contains polyglycol ethers and polyglycols which are poisonous. Take care to keep it off bare skin, and in particular not to get splashes in your eyes. Wash hands thoroughly after handling and if fluid contacts the eyes, flush out with cold running water. If irritation persists get medical attention immediately. The fluid also attacks paintwork and plastics – wash off spillages immediately with cold water. Finally, brake fluid is highly inflammable, and should be handled with the same care as petrol.**

1 If the master cylinder has been disconnected and reconnected, then the complete system (all circuits) must be bled of air. If a component of one circuit has been disturbed, then only that particular circuit need be bled.

2 Bleeding should commence on the furthest bleed nipple from the master cylinder, followed by the next one until the bleed nipple remaining nearest to the master cylinder is bled last.

3 There are a variety of do-it-yourself 'one-man' brake bleeding kits available from motor accessory shops, and it is recommended that one of these kits be used wherever possible, as they greatly simplify the brake bleeding operation. Follow the kit manufacturer's instructions in conjunction with the following procedure. If a pressure-bleeding kit is obtained, then it will not be necessary to depress the brake pedal in the following procedure.

4 During the bleeding operation, do not allow the brake fluid level in the reservoir to drop below the minimum mark. If the level is allowed to fall so far that air is drawn in, the whole procedure will have to be started

14.7a Prise off the dust cap from the bleed screw (arrowed)

again from scratch. Only use new fluid for topping-up, preferably from a freshly-opened container. Never re-use fluid bled from the system.

5 Before starting, check that all rigid pipes and flexible hoses are in good condition, and that all hydraulic unions are tight. Take great care not to allow hydraulic fluid to come into contact with the vehicle paintwork, otherwise the finish will be seriously damaged. Wash off any spilt fluid immediately with cold water.

6 If a brake bleeding kit is not being used, gather together a clean jar, a length of plastic or rubber tubing which is a tight fit over the bleed screw, and a new container of the specified brake fluid (see *Lubricants and fluids*). The help of an assistant will also be required.

7 Clean the area around the bleed screw on the rear brake unit to be bled (it is important that no dirt be allowed to enter the hydraulic system), and remove the dust cap. Connect one end of the tubing to the bleed screw, and immerse the other end in the jar **(see illustrations)**. The jar should be filled with sufficient brake fluid to keep the end of the tube submerged.

8 Open the bleed screw by half a turn, and have the assistant depress the brake pedal to the floor. Tighten the bleed screw at the end of the downstroke, then have the assistant release the pedal. Continue this procedure until clean brake fluid, free from air bubbles, can be seen flowing into the jar. Finally tighten the bleed screw with the pedal in the fully-depressed position.

9 Remove the tube, and refit the dust cap. Top-up the master cylinder reservoir if necessary, then repeat the procedure on the opposite rear brake.

10 Repeat the procedure on the front brake furthest from the master cylinder, followed by the brake nearest to the master cylinder.

11 Check the feel of the brake pedal – It should be firm. If it is spongy, there is still some air in the system, and the bleeding procedure should be repeated.

12 When bleeding is complete, top-up the master cylinder reservoir and refit the cap.

13 On models with manual transmission, check the clutch operation on completion; it may be necessary to bleed the clutch hydraulic system as described in Chapter 6.

14.7b Connect the kit and open the bleed screw

15 Vacuum servo unit – testing, removal and refitting

Testing

1 To test the operation of the servo unit, depress the footbrake four or five times to dissipate the vacuum, then start the engine while keeping the footbrake depressed. As the engine starts, there should be a noticeable give in the brake pedal as vacuum builds-up. Allow the engine to run for at least two minutes, and then switch it off. If the brake pedal is now depressed again, it should be possible to hear a hiss from the servo when the pedal is depressed. After four or five applications, no further hissing should be heard, and the pedal should feel harder.

2 Before assuming that a problem exists in the servo unit itself, inspect the non-return valve as described in the next Section.

Removal

RHD models

3 On models with air conditioning, have the refrigerant circuit evacuated as described in Chapter 3. When disconnecting the air conditioning pipes, cap the ends to prevent any contamination.

4 Refer to Section 11 and remove the master cylinder.

5 Remove the right-hand headlight assembly as described in Chapter 12.

6 Detach the coolant expansion tank from the right-hand side inner wing and move it to one side.

7 Disconnect the wiring plugs from the high- and low-pressure cut-off switches in the refrigerant pipes, then undo the bolt securing the pipes to the connection at the engine compartment bulkhead **(see illustrations)**. Discard the O-ring seals – new ones must be fitted.

8 Undo the bolts securing the refrigerant pipes to the connections at the condenser and accumulator/dehydrator, and unclip the pipes from the inner wing. Discard the O-ring seals – new ones must be fitted. Plug the openings to prevent contamination.

15.7a Undo the bolt securing the refrigerant pipes (arrowed)

9 Carefully prise the vacuum non-return valve from the servo **(see illustration 16.3)**.
10 Remove the driver's side lower facia panel as described in Chapter 11.
11 Disconnect their wiring plugs, then remove the brake pedal position switch (coloured blue/white) and brake light switch (coloured black) from the bracket. Rotate the position switch anti-clockwise, and the light switch clockwise. Do not move the brake pedal during this procedure.
12 Carefully prise the pin from the servo actuator rod **(see illustration 12.5)**. Discard the pin – a new one must be fitted
13 Undo the 4 nuts securing the servo to the bulkhead/pedal bracket and manoeuvre it from the engine compartment.
14 Note that the servo unit cannot be dismantled for repair or overhaul and, if faulty, must be renewed.

LHD models

15 Remove the brake master cylinder as described in Section 11.
16 Undo the brake pipes to the hydraulic control unit. Cap the end of the pipes and the hydraulic unit to prevent any dirt contamination.
17 Disconnect the vacuum pipe from the servo.
18 Remove the driver's side lower facia panel as described in Chapter 11.
19 Disconnect their wiring plugs, then remove the brake pedal position switch (coloured blue/white) and brake light switch (coloured black) from the bracket. Rotate the position switch anti-clockwise, and the light switch clockwise.

16.3 Servo non-return valve (arrowed)

15.7b Renew the refrigerant pipe O-ring seals (arrowed)

Do not move the brake pedal during this procedure.
20 Carefully prise the pin from the servo actuator rod **(see illustration 12.5)**. Discard the pin – a new one must be fitted
21 Undo the 4 nuts securing the servo to the bulkhead/pedal bracket and manoeuvre it from the engine compartment.
22 Note that the servo unit cannot be dismantled for repair or overhaul and, if faulty, must be renewed.

Refitting

23 Refitting is a reversal of the removal procedure, noting the following points:
  a) Refer to the relevant Sections/ Chapters for details of refitting the other components removed.
  b) Compress the actuator rod into the brake servo, before refitting.
  c) Make sure the gasket is correctly positioned on the servo.
  d) Test the brakes carefully before returning the vehicle to normal service.

16 Vacuum servo unit vacuum hose and non-return valve – removal, testing and refitting

Removal

1 With the engine switched off, depress the brake pedal four or five times, to dissipate any remaining vacuum from the servo unit.
2 Disconnect the vacuum hose adapter at the servo unit, by pulling it free from the rubber

17.3 Release the clips (arrowed) and disconnect the ABS unit wiring plug

grommet. If it is reluctant to move, prise it free, using a screwdriver with its blade inserted under the flange.
3 Detach the vacuum hose from the vacuum pump connection. The non-return valve is located in the vacuum hose **(see illustration)**.
4 If the hose or the fixings are damaged or in poor condition, they must be renewed.

Testing

5 Examine the non-return valve for damage and signs of deterioration, and renew it if necessary. The valve may be tested by blowing through its connecting hoses in both directions. It should only be possible to blow from the servo end towards the inlet manifold.

Refitting

6 Refitting is a reversal of the removal procedure. If fitting a new non-return valve, ensure that it is fitted the correct way round.

17 ABS hydraulic unit – removal and refitting

Note: *At the time of writing, no parts for the ABS hydraulic unit were available, and it must therefore be renewed as an assembly. Refer to the warning at the start of Section 14 concerning the dangers of brake fluid.*

Removal

1 Remove the battery (see Chapter 5) and the PCM (Chapter 4A), then undo the bolts and remove the battery tray **(see illustration 11.4)**.
2 Raise the vehicle and remove the wheels. Slacken the front bleed nipples, attach a rubber hose to the nipple, and place the other end of the hose in a suitable container. Operate the brake pedal until the fluid level is down to the base of the reservoir.

⚠ *Warning: Do not syphon the fluid by mouth; it is poisonous. Any brake fluid spilt on paintwork should be washed off with clean water, without delay – brake fluid is also a highly-effective paint-stripper.*

3 Depress the retaining clips, release the retainer and disconnect the wring plug from the ABS control unit **(see illustration)**. Cover the disconnected plug and socket to prevent contamination.
4 Undo the six brake pipes to the hydraulic control unit. Cap the end of the pipes and the hydraulic unit to prevent any dirt contamination. Unclip the brake lines from the retaining clips.
5 Undo the securing bolts from the brake hydraulic unit, and withdraw from the bulkhead. Remove it from the engine compartment, taking care not to damage any other components.

Refitting

6 Refitting is a reversal of removal. Ensure

that the multiplug is securely connected, and that the brake pipe unions are tightened to the specified torque. On completion, bleed the hydraulic system as described in Section 14.

18 ABS wheel sensor – testing, removal and refitting

Testing

1 Checking of the sensors is done either by substitution with a known good unit, or interrogating the ABS ECU for stored fault codes, using dedicated test equipment found at Ford dealers or suitably-equipped specialists.

Removal

Front wheel sensor

2 Apply the handbrake and loosen the relevant front wheel nuts. Jack up the front of the vehicle and support it on axle stands. Remove the wheel.
3 Disconnect the sensor wiring plug.
4 Unscrew the sensor mounting bolt from the hub carrier and withdraw the sensor (see illustration). Withdraw the O-ring seal.

Rear wheel sensor

5 Chock the front wheels, and engage 1st gear. Jack up the rear of the vehicle and support it on axle stands. Remove the relevant wheel.
6 Disconnect the sensor wiring plug.
7 Unscrew the sensor mounting bolt, and withdraw the sensor (see illustration). Withdraw the O-ring seal.

Refitting

8 Refitting is a reversal of the removal procedure. Fit a new O-ring seal to the hub carrier – not the sensor.

19 Electronic stability control components – removal and refitting

Note: This system uses the same components as the ABS and Traction control system. The only additional components are the 'yaw rate' sensor and 'accelerometer sensor', which are mounted on the same bracket on the floor crossmember, and the steering wheel rotation sensor.

Yaw rate and accelerometer sensor

Removal

1 Remove the driver's side front seat as described in Chapter 11.
2 Open the relevant door, then pull the trim upwards from along the sill.
3 Remove the driver's side B-pillar trim panel as described in Chapter 11.

18.4 Front ABS sensor mounting bolt (arrowed)

4 Pull the carpet back to gain access to the sensors.
5 Disconnect the sensor wiring plug.
6 Undo the two retaining bolts and remove the sensor and bracket.

Refitting

7 Refitting is a reversal of the removal procedure. Ensure the sensor and bracket is correctly positioned.

Steering wheel rotation sensor

8 The steering wheel rotation sensor is integral with the driver's airbag contact unit, beneath the steering wheel. Removal of the unit is described in Chapter 12.

20 Traction control system – general information

1 The Traction control system is an expanded version of the ABS system. It is integrated with the ABS, and uses the same wheel sensors. It also uses the hydraulic control unit, which incorporates additional internal solenoid valves.
2 To remove the hydraulic unit or wheel sensors, carry out the procedures as described in Sections 17 and 18.

21 Brake switches – removal, refitting and adjustment

Removal

Brake pedal position switch

1 Disconnect the battery negative (earth) lead (see Chapter 5).
2 Remove the driver's side lower facia panel as described in Chapter 11.
3 Disconnect the wiring connector from the brake pedal position switch. This is the upper of the two switches, and is coloured blue and white (see illustration 12.4).
4 Rotate the switch anti-clockwise by a quarter-turn, and withdraw it from the pedal bracket. Do not depress the brake pedal during the removal or refitting procedure – the pedal must be 'at rest'.

18.7 Rear ABS sensor retaining bolt (arrowed) – disc brake model

Brake light switch

5 Proceed as described in Paragraphs 1 and 2 in this Section.
6 Disconnect the wiring connector from the brake light switch. This is the lower of the two switches, and is coloured black (see illustration 12.4).
7 Rotate the switch clockwise by a quarter-turn, and withdraw it from the pedal bracket (see illustration). Do not depress the brake pedal during the removal or refitting procedure – the pedal must be 'at rest'.

Refitting and adjustment

8 Refitting is a reversal of the removal procedure. Note: If both switches have been removed, the brake pedal position switch must be installed before the light switch.
9 Both switches are automatically adjusted/calibrated by the vehicle system.

22 Handbrake lever – removal and refitting

Removal

1 Chock the front wheels, and engage 1st gear.
2 Remove the centre console as described in Chapter 11.
3 Disconnect the electrical connector from the handbrake switch (see illustration).
4 Slacken the locknut, then undo the handbrake adjusting nut (see illustration).

21.7 Rotate the brake light switch clockwise to remove it

22.3 Disconnect the handbrake warning light switch (arrowed)

22.4 Handbrake adjusting locknut (arrowed)

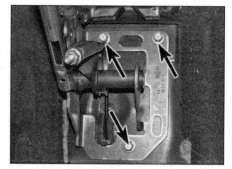

22.5 Handbrake lever bracket bolts (arrowed)

22.11 Insert a 0.7 mm feeler gauge between the caliper lever and the abutment (stop)

5 Unscrew the mounting bolts securing the handbrake lever to the floor **(see illustration)**.

6 Withdraw the handbrake from inside the vehicle.

Refitting

7 Refitting is a reversal of removal, ensuring the cable retaining tab is positioned away from the cable.

8 When refitting the lever, it will be necessary to adjust the mechanism, as follows. **Note:** *The handbrake should only be adjusted when the brakes are cool.*

9 Tighten the cable adjustment nut finger-tight, then raise the handbrake lever 12 notches.

10 Fully release the handbrake, then slacken the adjustment nut to the end of the threads.

Disc brake models

11 Working on one rear calipers, insert a

23.4 Remove the air deflector panel each side (arrowed)

22.15 Insert a 2.0 mm feeler gauge between the lever end stop and the side of the shoe

0.7 mm feeler gauge between the handbrake lever and the caliper abutment on both sides **(see illustration)**.

12 With the help of an assistant, tighten the adjustment nut until movement is observed on one of the caliper handbrake levers.

13 Remove the feeler gauges from both sides, then check the wheels rotate freely with no excess friction or drag caused by the brake. Tighten the adjustment locknut.

Drum brake models

14 Remove the brake drums as described in Section 5.

15 Ensure the handbrake lever is fully released, then insert a 2.0 mm feeler gauge between the handbrake lever end stop and the rear brake shoe on each side **(see illustration)**.

16 With the help of an assistant, tighten the cable adjustment nut until movement is observed on one of the handbrake levers.

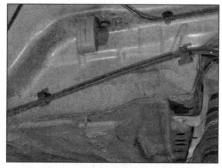

23.7 Release the handbrake cable from the retaining clips

17 Remove the feeler gauges, and refit the drum brakes as described in Section 5.

18 Check the wheels rotate freely with no excess friction or drag caused by the brake. Tighten the adjustment locknut.

23 Handbrake cables – removal and refitting

Removal

1 Unclip the gaiter from around the handbrake lever, and remove it.

2 Slacken the handbrake adjustment nut to the end of the threads.

3 Chock the front wheels, and engage 1st gear. Loosen the wheel nuts on the relevant rear wheel, then jack up the rear of the vehicle and support it on axle stands. Fully release the handbrake lever.

4 Release the fasteners and remove the air deflector panel on each side **(see illustration)**.

5 Remove the exhaust system as described in Chapter 4A.

6 Undo the fasteners and remove the exhaust front and centre heat shields.

7 Remove the relevant rear wheel and unclip the handbrake outer cable from its retaining clips **(see illustration)**.

Disc brake models

8 Unbolt the cable guide from the arm on both side **(see illustration)**.

9 Use a pair of pliers to detach the handbrake

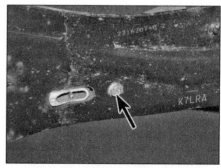

23.8 Undo the bolt (arrowed) securing the cable guide to the tie-bar

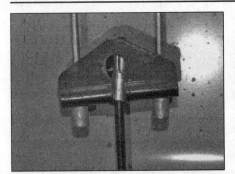

23.10a Disconnect the cables from the equaliser bracket

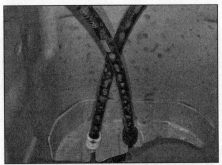

23.10b Note that the cables cross over when fitted correctly

23.11 Undo the bolt (arrowed) securing the handbrake cable to the tie-bar

cable inner fitting from the lever on each caliper **(see illustration 9.4)**.

10 Detach each outer cable from the bracket on the vehicle underbody, then disengage them from the equaliser bracket **(see illustrations)**. Note that the left-hand cable has a black sleeve, and the right-hand cable has a white sleeve.

Drum brake models

11 Unbolt the outer cable guide from the tie-bar on both sides **(see illustration)**.

12 Unclip the handbrake cable from the both sides. Pull the cable through the tie-bar on both sides.

13 Unclip the cable from the support hangers. Note that there are marks on the cable outer sleeve to indicate the clip positions.

14 Rotate each cable through 90° and detach them from the equaliser, then depress the clips and pull the outer cables from the bracket **(see illustrations 23.10a and 23.10b)**. Withdraw the cables from beneath the vehicle. Note that the left-hand cable has a black sleeve, whilst the right-hand cable has a white sleeve.

Refitting

15 Refitting is a reversal of the removal procedure, noting the following points:
 a) *Adjust the cable as described in Section 22.*
 b) *Make sure that the cable end fittings are correctly located*
 c) *Check the operation of the handbrake. Make sure that both wheels are locked, then free to turn, as the handbrake is operated.*

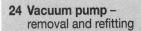

24 Vacuum pump –
   removal and refitting

Removal

1.6 litre models

1 Remove the plastic cover from the top of the engine (where fitted).

2 Undo the bolt and remove the crash shield around the fuel filter (where fitted).

3 Disconnect the hose from the vacuum pump **(see illustration)**.

4 Undo the 2 retaining bolts and remove the

vacuum pump Discard the O-ring seals, new ones must be fitted.

1.8 litre models

5 Remove the plastic cover from the top of the engine.

6 Unscrew the union nut and disconnect the vacuum line from the top of the pump **(see illustration)**.

7 Release the retaining clips and disconnect the oil separator/return hose(s) from the cylinder head cover.

8 Unbolt the air inlet hoses from the top of the cylinder head cover, and detach the breather hoses.

9 Unbolt and remove the cylinder head cover.

10 Using a suitable socket or spanner on the crankshaft pulley bolt, turn the crankshaft until the vacuum pump pushrod (operated by the eccentric on the camshaft end) is fully retracted into the cylinder head.

24.3 Depress the button (arrowed) and pull the hose from the vacuum pump

24.13 Slacken the bolts evenly, then remove the top bolt

11 Disconnect the electrical connectors from the heater/glow plug, the engine temperature sensor and the oil pressure switch.

12 Release the retaining clips and disconnect the oil separator/return hose(s) from the pump. Be prepared for some oil spillage as the hose is disconnected and mop-up any spilt oil.

13 Evenly and progressively slacken the bolts securing the pump to the front of the cylinder head **(see illustration)**. Note that there is no need to remove the lower bolt completely, as the lower end of the pump is slotted.

14 Remove the pump from the engine compartment, along with its sealing ring **(see illustration)**. Discard the sealing ring, a new one should be used on refitting.

2.0 litre models

15 Remove the plastic cover from the top of the engine.

24.6 Undo the vacuum line from the top of the pump

24.14 Renew the sealing ring when refitting the brake vacuum pump

24.18 Vacuum pump retaining bolts (arrowed)

24.19a Renew the pump O-ring seals (arrowed)

24.19b Ensure the drive lugs engage with the slot in the end of the camshaft (arrowed)

16 Unclip the fuel pipe from the support bracket above the vacuum pump – located at the left-hand end of the cylinder head.

17 Undo the stud/nut and detach the EGR pipe from the pump.

18 Undo the bolts/nut and remove the vacuum pump **(see illustration)**. Discard the O-ring seals, new ones must be fitted.

Refitting

19 Refitting is a reversal of removal, noting the following points:
 a) *Ensure the pump and cylinder head mating surfaces are clean and dry. Fit the new sealing ring to the pump recess.*
 b) *On 1.6 and 2.0 litre models, ensure the*

drive coupling is aligned with the slot in the camshaft **(see illustrations)**.
 c) *Start the engine and check for correct operation of the pump (check brakes have servo action) as described in Section 15.*
 d) *Make sure all the hose connections are secure, and check for leaks.*

25 Vacuum pump – testing and overhaul

Note: *A vacuum gauge will be required for this check.*

1 The operation of the braking system vacuum

pump can be checked using a vacuum gauge.

2 Disconnect the vacuum pipe from the pump, and connect the gauge to the pump union using a suitable length of hose.

3 Start the engine and allow it to idle, then measure the vacuum created by the pump. As a guide, after one minute, a minimum of approximately 500 mm Hg should be recorded. If the vacuum registered is significantly less than this, it is likely that the pump is faulty. However, seek the advice of a Ford dealer before condemning the pump.

4 Overhaul of the vacuum pump is not possible, since no components are available separately. If faulty, the complete pump assembly must be renewed.

Chapter 10
Suspension and steering

Contents

Degrees of difficulty

Easy, suitable for novice with little experience	Fairly easy, suitable for beginner with some experience	Fairly difficult, suitable for competent DIY mechanic	Difficult, suitable for experienced DIY mechanic	Very difficult, suitable for expert DIY or professional

Specifications

Front suspension
Type . . . . Independent, with MacPherson struts incorporating coil springs and telescopic shock absorbers. Anti-roll bar fitted to all models

Rear suspension
Type . . . . Fully-independent, multilink with separate coil springs and hydraulic telescopic shock absorbers. Anti-roll bar fitted to all models

Steering
Type . . . . Electro-hydraulic power-assisted rack and pinion

Wheel alignment and steering angles
Front wheel:
  Hatchback and Saloon models:
    Camber angle:
      Standard chassis . . . . 0.36° to -1°58'
      Sports chassis . . . . 0.25° to -2°0.7'
    Castor angle:
      Standard chassis . . . . 4°13' to 2°09'
      Sports chassis . . . . 4°14' to 2°13'
    Toe setting . . . . 0°06' ± 0°15' toe-in
  Estate models:
    Camber angle . . . . 0°35' to -1°58'
    Caster angle . . . . 4°16' to 2°14'
    Toe setting . . . . 0°06' ± 0°15' toe-in
Rear wheel:
  Camber angle:
    Standard chassis . . . . 0° to -2°35'
    Sports chassis . . . . -0°08' to -2°38'
  Toe setting . . . . 0°38' to 0°08' toe-in

Tyres
Tyre pressures . . . . See sticker on the driver's side door pillar

Torque wrench settings

	Nm	lbf ft
Front suspension		
ABS sensor	10	7
Anti-roll bar clamp bolts*	50	37
Anti-roll bar connecting link nuts*	50	37
Balljoint nut to hub carrier*	70	52
Balljoint-to-control arm bolts	70	52
Brake caliper mounting bracket bolts*	120	89
Control arm to subframe:*		
Rear bolt	115	85
Front bolt	175	129
Driveshaft bolt	See Chapter 8	
Lower balljoint to control arm	70	52
Lower torque rod bolts:		
M10	60	44
M12	80	59
Subframe mounting bolts:*		
Front	120	89
Rear	280	207
Subframe rear mounting brackets	70	52
Suspension strut piston nut*	50	37
Suspension strut to hub carrier*	90	66
Suspension strut upper mounting to body	32	24
Suspension upper mount brace-to-bulkhead nuts	25	18
Rear suspension		
Anti-roll bar link to anti-roll bar (link with balljoints)	70	52
Anti-roll bar link to lower arm (solid link)	25	18
Anti-roll bar link to lower control arms (link with balljoints)	50	37
Anti-roll bar-to-subframe bolts	50	37
Lateral link/hub carrier to body	115	85
Lower control arm to hub carrier	115	85
Lower control arm to subframe	90	66
Rear hub bearing assembly	55	41
Shock absorber lower mounting bolt	115	85
Shock absorber upper mounting nut:*		
Normal suspension	25	18
Self-levelling suspension (Nivomat)	60	45
Shock absorber upper mounting bolts		
Hatchback and Saloon models	25	18
Estate models	115	85
Tie-rod bolts	115	85
Upper control arm to hub carrier/lateral link and subframe	115	85
Steering		
EHPS pump mounting bolts	23	17
Steering column mounting bolts*	25	18
Steering rack mounting bolts	90	66
Steering shaft universal joint pinch-bolt*	28	21
Steering wheel bolt	48	35
Track rod end balljoint nuts*	50	37
Track rod locknuts	62	46
Roadwheels		
Wheel nuts	Refer to Chapter 1	

* Do not re-use

---

1 General information

The independent front suspension is of the MacPherson strut type, incorporating coil springs and integral telescopic shock absorbers. The struts are located by transverse control arms, which are attached to the front subframe via rubber bushes at their inner ends, and incorporate a balljoint at their outer ends. The hub carriers, which carry the hub bearings, brake calipers and the hub/disc assemblies, are bolted to the MacPherson struts, and connected to the control arms through the balljoints. A front anti-roll bar is fitted to all models, and is attached to the subframe and to the MacPherson struts via link arms (see illustration).

The rear suspension is of the fully independent, multilink type, consisting of an upper and lower control arm mounted via rubber bushes, to the lateral link/hub carrier and rear subframe. The lateral link is attached to the vehicle body at the front end

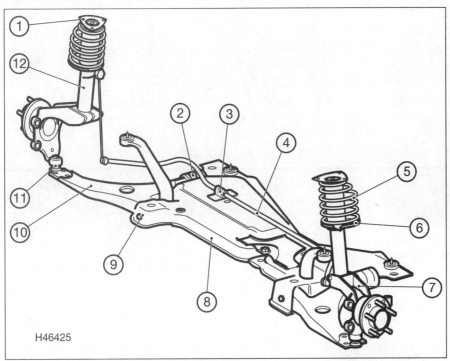

H46425

1.1 Front suspension

1 Upper bearing, mounting and spring seat	4 Anti-roll bar	9 Front bush
	5 Spring	10 Control arm
2 Rear bush	6 Lower spring seat	11 Balljoint
3 Clamp	7 Hub carrier	12 MacPherson strut
	8 Front subframe	

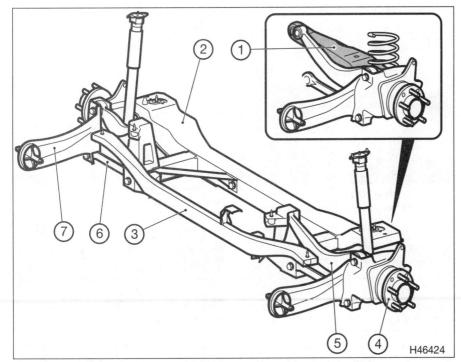

1.2 Rear suspension

1 Lower control arm	3 Anti-roll bar	6 Tie rod
	4 Wheel speed sensor	7 Lateral link/hub carrier
2 Subframe	5 Upper control arm	

and incorporate the hub carrier at the rear. The assembly is located by a tie rod each side. Coil springs are fitted between the lower control arm and the subframe. Separate hydraulic telescopic shock absorbers are fitted between the hub carrier between the lower control arm and the vehicle body **(see illustration)**.

Power assistance for the steering is derived from a hydraulic pump driven by an electric motor, controlled by the Electro-Hydraulic Power Steering module (EHPS).

2 Front hub carrier and bearing – removal and refitting

Note: *The hub bearing is a sealed, pre-adjusted and pre-lubricated, double-row ball type, and is intended to last the car's entire service life without maintenance or attention. The hub flange and bearing are serviced as a complete assembly, and these components cannot be dismantled or renewed individually.*

Removal

1 Loosen the appropriate front wheel nuts, then jack up the front of the car and support it on axle stands (see *Jacking and vehicle support*). Remove the appropriate front roadwheel.

2 Undo the bolt securing the headlight levelling sensor bracket to the right-hand front lower arm (where applicable).

3 Slacken and remove the bolt securing the driveshaft to the hub **(see illustration)**. Have an assistant depress the brake pedal to prevent the hub from rotating. Discard the bolt, a new one must be used.

4 Remove the front brake disc as described in Chapter 9.

5 Disconnect the wiring plug, undo the bolt and remove the ABS wheel sensor from the hub carrier – refer to Chapter 9 if necessary.

6 Undo the retaining nut, then disconnect the steering track rod end balljoint from the hub carrier. If necessary, use a balljoint separator tool **(see illustrations 19.3a and 19.3b)**.

7 Undo the bolt and remove the lower arm balljoint heat shield.

2.3 Slacken the driveshaft bolt (arrowed)

2.8 Use a balljoint separator tool to detach the lower arm balljoint from the hub carrier

2.10 Lever the control arm downwards, pull the hub carrier outwards, and withdraw the end of the driveshaft from the hub flange

2.11a With the bolt removed, spread the hub carrier slightly using a large screwdriver . . .

2.11b . . . then gently tap the hub carrier downwards from the shock absorber

8 Slacken the nut until it is level with the end of the balljoint shank, then using a balljoint separator tool, detach the suspension control arm balljoint from the hub carrier. Use an Allen key in the end of the balljoint shank to prevent it from rotating as the nut is slackened **(see illustration)**.

9 Use a stout bar to lever the control arm downwards and move the hub carrier over the end of the balljoint shank. Take care not to damage the balljoint dust cover during and after disconnection.

10 Swivel the hub carrier assembly outwards, and withdraw the driveshaft CV joint from the hub flange **(see illustration)**.

11 Remove the bolt securing the hub carrier to the shock absorber. Insert a flat-bladed tool into the gap and very slightly spread the hub carrier where it clamps onto the lower end of the shock absorber. Tap the hub carrier downwards from the shock absorber at the same time. Note which way the bolt is inserted – from the front **(see illustrations)**.

12 The hub and bearing must now be removed from the hub carrier as an assembly. Due to the design of the assembly, we found it impossible to press the new hub/bearing into the carrier without using Ford special tool No 204-348 **(see illustrations)**. The bearing will be rendered unserviceable by removal and cannot be re-used.

2.12a Using the Ford special tool to support the hub carrier, press the hub flange and bearing out . . .

2.12b . . . then assembly the special tool around the new bearing/flange assembly . . .

2.12c . . . position the hub carrier over the new bearing, and the special tool in place on the hub carrier . . .

2.12d . . . then press the hub carrier . . .

2.12e . . . fully onto the bearing

3.5a Prise forward the clips (arrowed) . . .

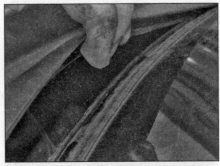

3.5b . . . and pull the scuttle cowl panel upwards from the base of the windscreen

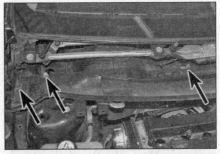

3.6 Undo the bolt at each end (arrowed) and pull the bulkhead extension panel forwards to release it from the clips (arrowed)

Refitting

13 Prior to refitting, remove all traces of metal adhesive, rust, oil and dirt from the splines and threads of the driveshaft outer CV joint and the bearing housing mating surface on the hub carrier.

14 The remainder of refitting is a reversal of removal, but observe the following points:

a) Ensure that the hub and brake disc mating faces are spotlessly clean, and refit the disc with the orientation marks aligned.

b) A new driveshaft retaining bolt should be used.

c) Ensure that the ABS sensor, and the sensor location in the hub carrier, are perfectly clean before refitting.

d) Tighten all nuts and bolts to the specified torque (see Chapter 9 for brake component torque settings).

3 Front suspension strut – removal and refitting

Removal

1 Loosen the appropriate front wheel nuts, then jack up the front of the car and support it on axle stands (see *Jacking and vehicle support*). Remove the appropriate front roadwheel.

2 Remove the plastic cover from the top of the engine (where fitted).

3 Undo the 2 nuts securing the brake fluid remote reservoir (where fitted) to the cowl panel.

4 Remove the wiper arms as described in Chapter 12.

5 Release the 5 clips and remove the scuttle cowl panel **(see illustrations)**.

6 Undo the 2 bolts, release the clips and remove the bulkhead extension panel **(see illustration)**.

7 Undo the nut securing the anti-roll bar link balljoint to the suspension strut. Use an Allen key to counter-hold the balljoint shank **(see illustration)**. A new nut will be required.

8 Unclip the brake hose from the bracket on the suspension strut.

9 Remove the bolt securing the hub carrier to the shock absorber. Insert a flat-bladed tool into

3.7 Use an Allen key to counter-hold the anti-roll bar link balljoint nut

the gap and very slightly spread the hub carrier where it clamps onto the lower end of the shock absorber. Tap the hub carrier downwards from the shock absorber at the same time. Note which way the bolt is inserted – from the front **(see illustrations 2.11a and 2.11b)**. A new bolt will be required.

10 Undo the 3 bolts and 2 nuts, and remove the brace between the suspension top mountings and the bulkhead **(see illustration)**. Have an assistant support the strut assembly.

11 Manoeuvre the strut out from underneath the wheel arch.

Refitting

12 Refitting is a reversal of removal, but observe the following point:

a) Tighten all nuts and bolts to the specified torque, using new nuts/bolts where necessary.

4.2 Hold the strut piston rod with an Allen key, and slacken the retaining nut

3.10 Undo the 3 bolts and 2 nuts, then remove the brace (arrowed)

4 Front suspension strut – dismantling, inspection and reassembly

Warning: Before attempting to dismantle the suspension strut, a suitable tool to hold the coil spring in compression must be obtained. Adjustable coil spring compressors which can be positively secured to the spring coils are readily available, and are recommended for this operation. Any attempt to dismantle the strut without such a tool is likely to result in damage or personal injury.

Dismantling

1 Remove the strut from the car as described in Section 3.

2 Slacken the strut mounting nut 1/2 a turn, while holding the protruding portion of the piston rod with an Allen key **(see illustration)**. Do not remove the nut at this stage.

3 Fit the spring compressors to the coil springs, and tighten the compressors until the load is taken off the spring seats **(see illustration)**.

4 Remove the piston nut, then make alignment marks where the ends of the spring contact the upper and lower seats **(see illustration)**. Discard the nut – a new one must be fitted.

5 Remove the upper mounting/spring seat, bump stop and gaiter followed by the spring **(see illustration)**. Do not attempt to separate the spring seat from the mounting or the bearing balls will fall out.

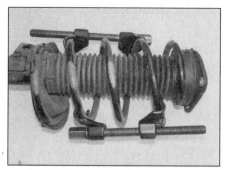

4.3 Fit the compressors to the springs

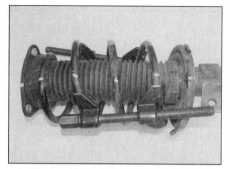

4.4 Make alignment marks between the spring and seats

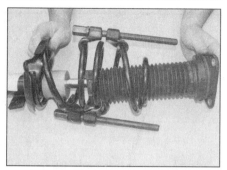

4.5 With the springs fully compressed, remove the mounting/seat/bump stop and gaiter, followed by the spring

4.11a Ensure the spring ends are correctly located in their seats

4.11b Tighten the new piston rod nut to the specified torque

Inspection

6 With the strut assembly now completely dismantled, examine all the components for wear, damage or deformation. Renew any of the components as necessary.

7 Examine the shock absorber for signs of fluid leakage, and check the strut piston for signs of pitting along its entire length. Test the operation of the shock absorber, while holding it in an upright position, by moving the piston through a full stroke and then through short strokes of 50 to 100 mm. In both cases, the resistance felt should be smooth and continuous. If the resistance is jerky, or uneven, or if there is any visible sign of wear or damage, renewal is necessary.

8 If any doubt exists about the condition of the coil spring, gradually release the spring compressor, and check the spring for distortion and signs of cracking. Since no

minimum free length is specified by Ford, the only way to check the tension of the spring is to compare it to a new component. Renew the spring if it is damaged or distorted, or if there is any doubt as to its condition.

9 Inspect all other components for signs of damage or deterioration, and renew any that are suspect.

10 If a new shock absorber is being fitted, hold it vertically and pump the piston a few times to prime it.

Reassembly

11 Reassembly is a reversal of dismantling, but ensure that the spring is fully compressed before fitting. Make sure that the spring ends are correctly located in the upper and lower seats, aligning the marks made on removal, then tighten the new shock absorber piston retaining nut and strut mounting bolts to the specified torque **(see illustrations)**.

5.5a Drill out the 3 rivets . . .

5.5b . . . and pull the balljoint from the control arm

5 Front suspension control arm and balljoint – removal, overhaul and refitting

Balljoint

Removal

1 Loosen the appropriate front wheel nuts. Chock the rear wheels and apply the handbrake, then jack up the front of the vehicle and support it on axle stands (see *Jacking and vehicle support*). Remove the appropriate front roadwheel, then release the fasteners and remove the engine undershield (where fitted).

2 Undo the bolt securing the headlight levelling sensor bracket to the control arm (where fitted).

3 Slacken the nut until it is level with the end of the balljoint shank, then using a balljoint separator tool, detach the suspension control arm balljoint from the hub carrier. Use an Allen key in the end of the balljoint shank to prevent it from rotating as the nut is slackened **(see illustration 2.8)**. Discard the nut – a new one must be fitted.

4 Use a stout bar to lever the control arm downwards and over the end of the balljoint shank. Take care not to damage the balljoint dust cover during and after disconnection.

5 If the original balljoint is being removed, use a drill to remove the 3 balljoint-to-control arm retaining rivets **(see illustrations)**. Pull the balljoint from the control arm.

6 If the balljoint being removed is not the original, undo the 3 bolts and pull the balljoint from the control arm.

Refitting

7 New balljoints may be supplied with suitable retaining bolts. If not, obtain 3 bolts, M10 x 30 mm, and 3 suitable self-locking nuts. Position the new balljoint in the end of the control arm, insert the bolts from underneath, and tighten the nuts to the specified torque. Note that 2 different balljoints may be available. The balljoints are identical apart from the diameter of the taper of the balljoint shank. The shank with the larger diameter taper is identified by a blue band on the gaiter, and the smaller diameter taper by a yellow

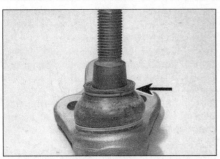

5.7a The colour of the rubber band (arrowed) determines the diameter of the balljoint shank

5.7b Insert the bolts from the underside of the control arm . . .

5.7c . . . and fit the self-locking nuts on the upper side

band **(see illustrations)**. Select the balljoint that matches the one to be renewed.

8 The remainder of refitting is a reversal of removal. Tighten all fasteners to their specified torque, where given.

Control arm

Removal

9 Proceed as described in Paragraphs 1 to 4.
10 Undo the two bolts securing the control arm rear mounting and the single bolt securing the front mounting and manoeuvre the control arm from under the vehicle **(see illustrations)**. Discard the bolts, new ones must be fitted.

Overhaul

11 Thoroughly clean the control arm and the area around the control arm mountings. Inspect the arm for any signs of cracks, damage or distortion, and carefully check the inner pivot bushes for signs of swelling, cracks or deterioration of the rubber.
12 If either bush requires renewal, the work should be entrusted to a Ford dealer or specialist. A hydraulic press and suitable spacers are required to remove and refit the bushes and a setting gauge is needed for accurate positioning of the bushes in the arm.

Refitting

13 Locate the arm in its mountings, and starting at the rear, fit the new mounting bolts finger-tight only. Once all the bolts are in place, tighten the bolts to their specified torque. Do not allow the control arm to move during the tightening procedure.
14 Engage the balljoint shank in the control arm, then tighten the new nut to the specified torque.
15 The remainder of refitting is a reversal of removal. Have the front wheel alignment checked at the earliest opportunity.

---

6 Front anti-roll bar – removal and refitting

Removal

1 Loosen the appropriate front wheel nuts. Chock the rear wheels and apply the handbrake, then jack up the front of the vehicle and support it on axle stands (see *Jacking*

5.10a Control arm rear mounting bolts (arrowed) . . .

and vehicle support). Remove the appropriate front roadwheel, then release the fasteners and remove the engine undershield (where fitted) **(see illustration)**
2 Slacken the nut until it is level with the end of the balljoint shank, then using a balljoint separator tool, detach the suspension control arm balljoint from the hub carrier. Use an Allen key in the end of the balljoint shank to prevent it from rotating as the nut is slackened **(see illustration 2.8)**.
3 Use a stout bar to lever the control arm downwards and over the end of the balljoint shank. Take care not to damage the balljoint dust cover during and after disconnection.
4 Ensure the wheels are in the straight-ahead position, then working under the facia, undo and remove the steering column lower universal joint pinch-bolt **(see illustration 14.8)**. Discard the bolt – a new one must be fitted.
5 Undo the nut each side securing the lower

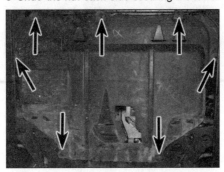

6.1 Undo the fasteners (arrowed) and remove the engine undershield

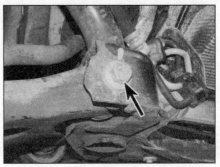

5.10b . . . and front mounting bolt (arrowed)

end of the anti-roll bar links to the bar. Use a Torx bit to counter-hold the nut.
6 Undo the nut and detach the track rod end balljoint from the hub carrier each side, using a balljoint separator tool as described in Section 19.
7 Undo the bolt at the lower rear of the engine securing the lower torque rod to the bracket on the transmission/engine.
8 Attach splints each side of the exhaust flexible section (two wooden strips secured by cable tie will suffice) to prevent excessive bending, then undo the bolts/nuts securing the centre exhaust section to the front section.
9 Unhook the exhaust mounting rubbers at the front.
10 Position a sturdy trolley jack beneath, and in contact with, the rear of the subframe.
11 Undo the bolt each side securing the front of the subframe to the body approximately 6 turns **(see illustration)**. Note that new

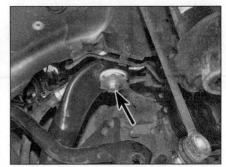

6.11 Slacken the subframe front mounting bolt each side (arrowed) about 6 turns

6.12 Undo the subframe rear mounting bolts (arrowed)

6.14 Anti-roll bar clamp bolts (arrowed)

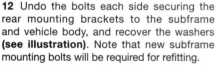

6.15 The anti-roll bar bushes are split to facilitate renewal, and are shaped to fit the bar profile

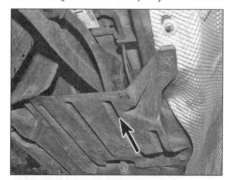

6.18 Align the front subframe by inserting aligning tools (arrowed) through the holes in the subframe into the corresponding holes in the vehicle body

subframe front mounting bolts will be required for refitting.

12 Undo the bolts each side securing the rear mounting brackets to the subframe and vehicle body, and recover the washers **(see illustration)**. Note that new subframe mounting bolts will be required for refitting.

13 Carefully lower the jack and allow the subframe to drop slightly at the rear, so that the anti-roll bar clamp bolts are accessible. Take care not to damage the power steering hoses.

14 Undo the bolts securing the anti-roll bar clamps on each side of the subframe, and manipulate the anti-roll bar out from under the car **(see illustration)**. Discard the bolts, new ones must be fitted.

15 Examine the anti-roll bar for signs of

damage or distortion, and the connecting links and mounting bushes for signs of deterioration of the rubber. The bushes are split along their length and must be fitted in their original positions **(see illustration)**.

Refitting

16 Manipulate the anti-roll bar into position on the subframe. Fit the new clamp bolts and tighten to the specified torque.

17 Raise the subframe at the rear, fit the rear mounting brackets to the body, and tighten the bolts (new where applicable) hand-tight only at this stage.

18 The alignment of the subframe must be checked by inserting round tools can be inserted through the holes in the sidemembers. Ford tools (part No 205-316) may be available.

Alternatively, using two lengths of wooden dowel, 20 mm in diameter, and approximately 150 mm in length **(see illustration)**.

19 With the subframe correctly aligned, fit new front subframe mounting bolts, and tighten all subframe bolts to the specified torque.

20 The remainder of refitting is a reversal of removal. Have the front wheel alignment checked at the earliest opportunity.

7 Rear hub bearings – renewal

1 The rear hub bearings cannot be renewed separately, and are supplied with the rear hub as a complete assembly.

2 Remove the brake disc or drum (as applicable) as described in Chapter 9.

3 Undo the bolt and remove the ABS wheel speed sensor from the hub carrier.

4 Undo the four Torx bolts and withdrawn the bearing assembly from the hub carrier.

5 Fit the new assembly to the hub carrier then insert and tighten the bolts to the specified torque.

6 Refit the ABS wheel speed sensor and brake disc or drum as described in Chapter 9.

8 Rear hub carrier/lateral link – removal and refitting

Removal

1 Remove the rear hub as described in the previous Section. On models with disc brakes, unbolt and remove the disc shield.

2 Undo the bolt securing the handbrake cable retaining clip to the lateral link, then unhook the cable from the connecting sleeve. Pull the cable through the lateral link/hub carrier.

3 Unclip the brake hose from the hub carrier.

4 Unclip the handbrake cable from the hub carrier.

5 Release the ABS wheel speed sensor wiring harness from the clips on the lateral link.

6 Remove the relevant rear coil spring as described in Section 10.

7 Fabricate a spacer, 20 mm in diameter, and 113 mm (Hatchback and Saloon) or 184 mm (Estate) long. Unscrew the suspension bump stop, insert the spacer between the lower control arm and the coil spring upper seat, then raise the lower control arm with a trolley jack until the spacer is lightly trapped **(see illustration)**. Ensure the spacer is vertical.

8 Undo the fasteners and remove the air baffle plate from the relevant side **(see illustration)**.

9 Undo the retaining bolt and withdraw the ABS wheel sensor from hub carrier/lateral link. Do not disconnect the wheel sensor wiring plug.

10 Undo the bolts securing the upper control

Diagram

J46819

8.7 Remove the bump stop (B), and insert the spacer (A) between the lower control arm (D) and the spring upper seat (C)

8.8 Remove the air baffle plate (arrowed)

arm and tie rod to the lateral link/hub carrier (**see illustrations 11.4 and 11.10b**).

11 Undo the bolt and detach the lower control arm from the lateral link/hub carrier (**see illustration 11.14a**).

12 Undo the 2 bolts securing the front mounting to the vehicle body, and withdrawn the lateral link from under the vehicle (**see illustration**).

13 Renewal of the bush at the front of the lateral link requires the use of Ford special tools and a hydraulic press. Therefore it is recommended that this task should be entrusted to a Ford dealer or suitably-equipped specialist.

Refitting

14 Manoeuvre the lateral link into position and tighten the 2 front mounting bolts to the specified torque.

15 Refit the ABS wheel speed sensor wiring harness clips to the link.

16 Position the handbrake cable and refit the cable retaining clip.

17 Refit the upper control arm, lower control arm and tie rod, but don't tighten the bolts yet.

18 Ensure the fabricated spacer (paragraph 7) is still in place between the lower control arm and the spring seat (**see illustration 8.7**).

19 Tighten the upper control arm, lower control arm and tie rod bolts to their specified torque. Remove the spacer, and refit the bump stop.

20 The remainder of refitting is a reversal of removal. Have the rear wheel alignment checked at the earliest opportunity.

8.12 Lateral link/hub carrier front mounting bolts

9 Rear shock absorber – removal and refitting

Removal

1 Slacken the rear roadwheel nuts, then chock the front wheels then jack up the rear of the vehicle and support it on axle stands (see *Jacking and vehicle support*). Remove the rear wheels.

2 Place a trolley jack under the hub carrier and raise the suspension a little to take the load off the shock absorber.

Hatchback and Saloon models

3 Undo the 2 bolts securing the upper end of the shock absorber to the vehicle body (**see illustration**).

4 Undo the lower mounting bolt, and pull

the shock absorber from the hub carrier (**see illustration**).

5 If required, undo the nut and pull the upper mounting from the shock absorber (**see illustration**).

6 Check the condition of the shock absorber and renew as necessary.

Estate models

7 If removing the left-hand shock absorber, unhook the rear silencer from the rubber mountings, undo the fasteners, and remove the exhaust heat shield (**see illustration**).

8 Undo the shock absorber upper mounting nut and remove the bolt (**see illustration**).

9 Undo and remove the shock absorber lower mounting bolt (**see illustration**). Manoeuvre the shock absorber from under the vehicle.

Refitting

10 Refitting is a reversal of removal, tightening all nuts and bolts to the specified torques.

10 Rear coil spring – removal and refitting

Removal

1 Slacken the roadwheel nuts, then chock the front wheels and raise the rear of the vehicle. Support it securely on axle stands (see *Jacking and vehicle support*). Remove the roadwheels.

2 Undo the nut securing the anti-roll bar link to the lower control arm (**see illustration 12.2**).

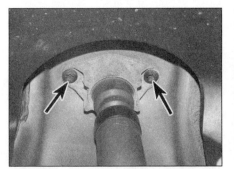

9.3 Shock absorber upper mounting bolts (arrowed)

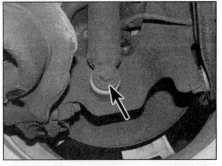

9.4 Shock absorber lower mounting bolt (arrowed)

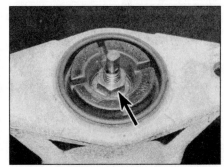

9.5 Undo the shock absorber upper mounting nut (arrowed)

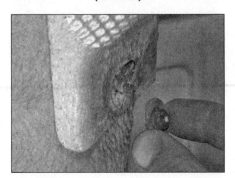

9.7 Undo the nuts securing the heat shield

9.8 Rear shock absorber upper mounting bolt (arrowed)

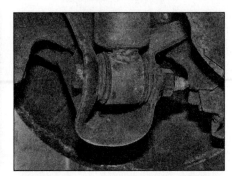

9.9 Rear shock absorber lower mounting bolt

10.5 Remove the rear springs using spring compressors

10.8a The lug (arrowed) on the underside of the seat must locate in the hole in the arm

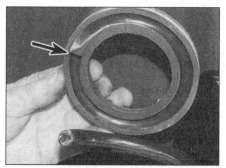

10.8b The end of the spring must fit against the stop in the rubber seat (arrowed)

3 Position a trolley jack under the hub carrier, and take the weight.

4 Remove the shock absorber lower mounting bolt.

5 Attach spring compressors to the spring and compress the spring. Ford specify tools No 204-215 and 204-167. Alternative spring compressors may be available **(see illustration)**.

6 Remove the trolley jack, and remove the spring.

7 Examine all the components for wear or damage, and renew as necessary.

Refitting

8 Refit the rubbers seats to the control arm and spring, ensuring the ends of the spring locate correctly **(see illustrations)**.

9 Refit the compressed spring onto the seat in the lower control arm. Rotate the spring until

the spring engages correctly in the control arm grooves.

10 Raise the control arm by means of the jack, and engage the upper end of the spring in its recess in the body.

11 Refit the shock absorber lower mounting bolt, securing it in place before removing the jack. Tighten all nuts and bolts to the specified torque.

12 Release and remove the spring compressor.

13 Remainder of refitting is a reversal of removal.

11 Rear suspension link arms – removal and refitting

Removal

1 Loosen the rear wheel bolts. Chock the front wheels, then jack up the rear of the vehicle and support it on axle stands (see *Jacking and vehicle support*). Remove the appropriate rear roadwheel(s).

Tie-rod – Hatchback and Saloon models

2 Remove the rear spring as described in Section 10.

3 Fabricate a spacer, 20 mm in diameter, and 113 mm long. Unscrew the suspension bump stop, insert the spacer between the lower control arm and the coil spring upper seat, then raise the lower control arm with a trolley jack until the spacer is lightly trapped

(see illustration 8.7). Ensure the spacer is vertical.

4 Undo the outer and inner bolts, then remove the tie-rod **(see illustration)**. Note that the tie-rod is marked FRONT on one side.

Tie-rod – Estate models

5 Remove the rear spring as described in Section 10.

6 Fabricate a spacer, 20 mm in diameter, and 184 mm long. Insert the spacer between the lower control arm and the coil spring upper seat, then raise the lower control arm with a trolley jack until the spacer is lightly trapped **(see illustration 8.7)**. Ensure the spacer is vertical.

7 Undo the outer and inner bolts, then remove the tie-rod **(see illustration 11.4)**. Note that the tie-rod is marked FRONT on one side.

Upper control arm – Hatchback and Saloon models

8 Remove the rear spring as described in Section 10.

9 Fabricate a spacer, 20 mm in diameter, and 113 mm long. Unscrew the suspension bump stop, insert the spacer between the lower control arm and the coil spring upper seat, then raise the lower control arm with a trolley jack until the spacer is lightly trapped **(see illustration 8.7)**. Ensure the spacer is vertical.

10 Undo the outer and inner bolts, then remove the control arm **(see illustrations)**.

Upper control arm – Estate models

11 Fabricate a spacer, 20 mm in diameter, and 184 mm long. Insert the spacer between the lower control arm and the coil spring upper seat, then raise the lower control arm with a trolley jack until the spacer is lightly trapped **(see illustration 8.7)**. Ensure the spacer is vertical.

12 Undo the outer and inner bolts, then remove the control arm **(see illustrations 11.10a and 11.10b)**.

Lower control arm

13 Remove the coil spring as described in Section 10.

14 Mark the position of the inner bolt eccentric washer in relation to the arm, then undo the inner and outer control arm

11.4 Tie-rod mounting bolts (arrowed)

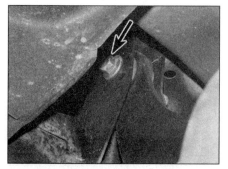

11.10a Upper control arm inner bolt (arrowed) . . .

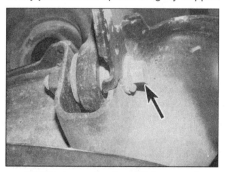

11.10b . . . and outer bolt (arrowed)

bolts, rotate the anti-roll bar approximately 30° and remove the control arm **(see illustrations)**.

15 Examine the condition of the metal-elastic bushes in the control arm. If renewal is necessary, the bushes must be pressed from the arm and new ones pressed into place. This necessitates the use of an hydraulic press. Entrust this task to a Ford dealer or suitably-equipped garage.

Refitting

16 Refitting any of the control arms/tie rods is essentially a reversal of removal, noting the following points:

a) Tighten all fasteners to their specified torque where given, using a little thread-locking compound.

b) Before tightening any control arm/tie rod mounting bolts, ensure the suspension is in the 'normal' position using the fabricated spacers as described in the removal procedures.

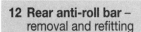

12 Rear anti-roll bar –
removal and refitting

Removal

1 Chock the front wheels, then jack up the rear of the vehicle and support it on axle stands (see *Jacking and vehicle support*).

2 Undo the nuts securing the outer ends of the anti-roll bar to the links **(see illustration)**. Take care not to damage the rubber boots.

3 Undo the bolts securing the anti-roll bar clamps to the subframe, manoeuvre the anti-roll bar from under the vehicle **(see illustration)**.

4 Examine the anti-roll bar for signs of damage or distortion, and the connecting links and mounting bushes for signs of deterioration of the rubber. The bushes are split along their length and must be fitted in their original positions.

Refitting

5 Position the anti-roll bar, then fit and tighten the bolts securing the anti-roll bar clamps to the subframe.

6 Refit the anti-roll bar links and tighten the

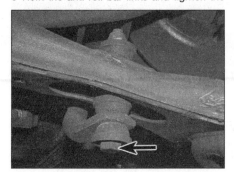

12.2 Rear anti-roll bar-to-control arm bolt (arrowed)

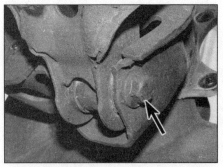

11.14a Undo the lower control arm outer bolt (arrowed) . . .

nuts to the specified torque, using a Torx bit to counterhold the nuts.

7 The remainder of refitting is a reversal of removal.

13 Steering wheel –
removal and refitting

⚠ *Warning: Handle the airbag unit with extreme care as a precaution against personal injury, and always hold it with the cover facing away from the body. If in doubt concerning any proposed work involving the airbag unit or its control circuitry, consult a Ford dealer.*

Removal

1 Drive the car forwards, and park it with the front wheels in the straight-ahead position.

2 Remove the driver's airbag as described in Chapter 12. Secure the rotary contact unit in place using tape to prevent any rotation.

3 Disconnect the wiring plug at the top of the steering wheel aperture.

4 Undo the steering wheel centre retaining bolt **(see illustration)**.

5 On vehicles built up to 01/2005, if a new steering wheel is being fitted, but the original driver's airbag is to be used, undo the bolt and remove the earth spring from the wheel. This must be fitted to the new wheel.

6 Make alignment marks between the steering wheel centre and the column shaft, then lift the steering wheel off the column shaft, and

12.3 Undo the bolts (arrowed) securing the anti-roll bar clamps

11.14b . . . then mark the position of the eccentric washer (arrowed) and remove the bolt

feed the wiring and plastic strip through the hole in the wheel.

Refitting

7 Ensure that the front wheels are still in the straight-ahead position.

8 On vehicles built up to 01/2005, if a new steering wheel is being fitted, but the original driver's airbag is to be used, undo the bolt and remove the earth cable from the new wheel, then attach the old earth spring.

9 Check the airbag rotary contact unit is still aligned. If necessary refer to Chapter 12. Remove the securing tape.

10 Feed the wiring through the hole in the steering wheel, then engage the wheel with the steering column shaft. Ensure that the marks made on removal are aligned, and that the pegs on the contact reel engage with the recesses on the steering wheel hub.

11 Refit the steering wheel retaining bolt, and tighten it to the specified torque.

12 Refit the airbag unit to the steering wheel as described in Chapter 12.

14 Steering column –
removal and refitting

Removal

1 Disconnect the battery negative lead – see Chapter 5.

2 Fully extend the steering column, then on models with an audio control switch fitted to the column shroud, release the locking tang,

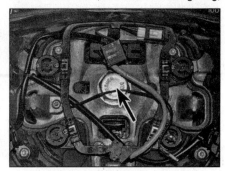

13.4 Steering wheel retaining bolt (arrowed)

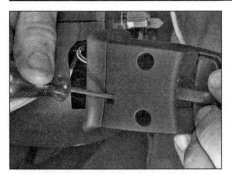

14.2 Release the clip and pull the audio control switch from the column shroud

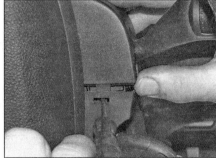

14.4 Release the clip each side securing the column upper shroud to the lower

14.5 Undo the bolts (arrowed) securing the column lower shroud

pull the switch from place and disconnect the wiring plug **(see illustration)**.

3 Undo the fasteners and remove the lower facia panel on the driver's side – see Chapter 11.

4 Turn the steering wheel for access, then release the retaining clips and remove the steering column upper shroud **(see illustration)**. Turn the steering wheel back to the straight-ahead position.

5 Undo the 3 retaining bolts, and remove the steering column lower shroud **(see illustration)**. Release the steering column locking lever to remove the shroud completely.

6 Remove the steering wheel as described in Section 13.

7 Note their fitted positions and routing, then disconnect the various column wiring plugs and release the loom retaining clips.

8 Undo the steering column lower pinch-bolt and pull the joint upwards from the pinion **(see illustration)**. Ensure the column adjustment lever is released before detaching the joint from the pinion. Discard the pinch-bolt, a new one must be fitted.

9 Undo the 4 retaining bolts and manoeuvre the column from the vehicle **(see illustration)**. Discard the bolts, new ones must be fitted.

10 If required, drill out the security bolts, and remove the steering lock from the column **(see illustration)**. No further dismantling of the assembly is recommended.

Refitting

11 Refitting is a reversal of removal, bearing in mind the following points:

a) *Lubricate universal joint splines with grease before engaging the steering column.*

b) *When fitting the new column retaining bolts, the shortest bolts are nearest the bulkhead.*

c) *Use a new universal joint pinch-bolt.*

d) *If refitting the steering lock, tighten the new security bolts until their heads snap off.*

e) *If the steering column has been rotated, or the front wheels turned from straight-ahead, reset the airbag contact reel as described in Chapter 12.*

15 Steering rack – removal and refitting

Removal

1 Drive the car forwards and park it with the steering wheels in the straight-ahead position. Remove the ignition key to lock the steering in this position.

2 Remove the lower facia panel (where fitted) on the driver's side as described in Chapter 11.

3 Remove the steering column lower gaiter (where fitted), then undo the pinch-bolt and pull the joint upwards from the pinion **(see illustration 14.8)**. Ensure the column adjustment lever is released before detaching the joint from the pinion. Discard the pinch-bolt, a new one must be fitted.

4 Loosen the front wheel nuts. Chock the rear wheels then jack up the front of the vehicle

and support it on axle stands (see *Jacking and vehicle support*). Remove both front roadwheels.

5 Undo the fasteners and remove the engine undershield (where fitted) **(see illustration 6.1)**.

6 Undo the bolt securing the headlight levelling sensor bracket to the lower control arm (where applicable)**.**

7 On some models, disconnect the steering angle sensor wiring plug (located at the steering column pinion in the engine compartment).

8 Attach splints each side of the exhaust flexible section (two wooden strips secured by cable tie will suffice) to prevent excessive bending, then undo the bolts/nuts securing the centre exhaust section to the front section.

9 Unhook the exhaust mounting rubbers at the front.

10 Slacken the nut until it is level with the end of the balljoint shank, then using a balljoint separator tool, detach the suspension control arm balljoint from the hub carrier. Use an Allen key in the end of the balljoint shank to prevent it from rotating as the nut is slackened **(see illustration 2.8)**.

11 Use a stout bar to lever the control arm downwards and over the end of the balljoint shank. Take care not to damage the balljoint dust cover during and after disconnection.

12 Undo the nut each side securing the lower end of the anti-roll bar links to the bar. Use a Torx bit to counter-hold the nut.

13 Undo the nut and detach the track rod end balljoint from the hub carrier each side, using a balljoint separator tool as described in Section 19.

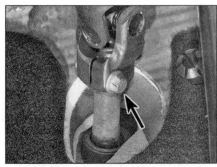

14.8 Steering column lower pinch-bolt (arrowed)

14.9 Steering column upper mounting bolts (arrowed)

14.10 Drill out the security bolt (arrowed) each side

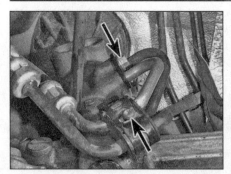

15.15 Steering rack pipes clamp bolts (arrowed)

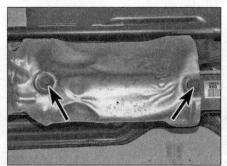

15.21 Steering rack heat shield bolts (arrowed)

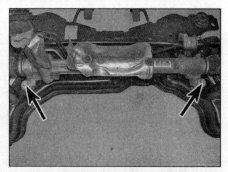

15.22 Steering rack retaining bolts (arrowed)

14 Undo the bolt at the lower rear of the engine securing the lower torque rod to the bracket on the transmission/engine.

15 Remove the bolt, unclip the power steering pipes from the steering rack, then undo the bolt, rotate the clamp plate and disconnect the pipes from the steering rack pinion **(see illustration)**.

16 Position a sturdy trolley jack beneath, and in contact with, the rear of the subframe.

17 Undo the bolt each side securing the front of the subframe **(see illustration 6.11)**. Note that new subframe front mounting bolts will be required for refitting.

18 Undo the bolts each side securing the rear mounting brackets to the subframe and vehicle body, and recover the washers **(see illustration 6.12)**. Note that new subframe mounting bolts will be required for refitting.

19 Carefully lower the jack and subframe. Take care not to damage the power steering hoses.

20 Undo the bolts and remove the anti-roll bar **(see illustration 6.14)**. Discard the bolts – new ones must be fitted.

21 Undo the 3 bolts and remove the steering rack heat shield **(see illustration)**.

22 Undo the retaining bolts, and lift the steering rack from the subframe **(see illustration)**.

Refitting

23 Manipulate the steering rack into position and tighten the bolts to the specified torque.

24 Refit the steering rack heat shield and tighten the bolts securely.

25 Refit the anti-roll bar to the subframe and tighten the new bolts to the specified torque.

26 Ensure the steering rack pinion bulkhead seal is in place, then raise the subframe into position.

27 Fit the subframe rear mounting brackets to the body, then insert the new front and rear subframe mounting bolts. Only hand-tighten them at this stage.

28 The alignment of the subframe must be checked by inserting round tools though the holes in the sidemembers. Ford tools (part No 205-316) may be available. Alternatively, using two lengths of wooden dowel, 20 mm in diameter, and approximately 150 mm in length **(see illustration 6.18)**.

29 With the subframe correctly aligned, tighten all subframe bolts to the specified torque.

30 Engage the steering shaft universal joint with the pinion shaft, and push it fully home.

31 Fit the new universal joint pinch-bolt and tighten it to the specified torque.

32 Refit the fluid pipes to the steering rack using new O-ring seals, and tighten the retaining bolt securely.

33 The remainder of refitting is a reversal of removal, noting the following points:

a) *Tighten all fasteners to their specified torque where given.*

b) *Bleed the power steering system as described in Section 17.*

c) *Have the front wheel alignment checked at the earliest opportunity.*

16 Steering rack gaiters – renewal

1 Remove the track rod end on the side concerned as described in Section 19. Unscrew the locknut from the track rod.

2 Release the two clips and peel off the gaiter. Disconnect the breather hose as the gaiter is withdrawn **(see illustration)**

3 Clean out any dirt and grit from the inner end of the track rod and (when accessible) the rack.

4 Wrap insulating tape around the track rod threads to protect the new gaiter whilst installing.

5 Refit the track rod end locknut.

6 Refit the track rod end as described in Section 19.

17 Steering system – bleeding

1 Remove the right-hand headlight as described in Chapter 12.

2 Wipe clean the area around the reservoir filler neck, and unscrew the filler cap/dipstick from the reservoir.

3 If topping-up is necessary, use clean fluid of the specified type (see *Weekly checks*). Check for leaks if frequent topping-up is required. Do not run the engine without fluid in the reservoir.

4 After component renewal, or if the fluid level has been allowed to fall so low that air has entered the hydraulic system, bleeding must be carried out as follows.

5 Fill the reservoir to the MAX mark as described in *Weekly checks*. Note that the power steering fluid should be cold, and poured slowly into the reservoir to minimise aeration.

6 Raise the front of the vehicle until the tyres are just clear of the ground, then support the vehicle securely on axle stands (see *Jacking and vehicle support*).

7 Start the engine, slowly turn the steering wheel from lock to lock, and add power steering fluid until the fluid level ceases to drop.

8 Switch off the engine and check the fluid level. Top-up if necessary.

9 Start the engine and turn the steering from lock to lock. If excessive noise is still apparent (indicating air in the system), leave the vehicle overnight, then try again.

10 If the steering is still noisy, it may be that the pump is faulty. Consult a Ford dealer or specialist.

11 On completion, stop the engine, lower the vehicle to the ground, and recheck the fluid level.

18 Power steering pump – removal and refitting

Note: *If a new EHPS pump/module is to be fitted, the relevant program code needs to be*

16.2 Steering rack gaiter clips and breather hose (arrowed) – shown with the rack removed for clarity

18.2 Disconnect the wiring plugs from the EHPS module

18.7 Disconnect the fluid return and pressure pipes

extracted and reloaded to the module. Entrust this task to a Ford dealer or suitably-equipped specialist.

Removal

1 Remove the right-hand side headlight as described in Chapter 12.

2 Disconnect the pump wiring plugs **(see illustration)**.

3 Jack up the front of the vehicle and support it securely on axle stands (see *Jacking and vehicle support*).

4 Undo the fasteners and remove splash shield under the radiator and the engine undershield.

5 Undo the Torx bolts and remove the right-hand wheel arch liner.

6 Use a syringe to extract as much fluid as possible from the pump reservoir.

7 Undo the union nut and disconnect the pump pressure pipe **(see illustration)**. Be prepared for fluid spillage. Plug the openings to prevent contamination.

8 Release the clamp and disconnect the fluid return hose from the pump **(see illustration 18.7)**. Be prepared for fluid spillage. Plug the openings to prevent contamination.

9 Undo the 3 bolts and remove the assembly **(see illustration)**.

10 No individual parts are available. If faulty, exchange units are available from Ford.

Refitting

11 Refitting is a reversal of removal, bearing in mind the following points:
  a) *Use a new O-ring on pressure pipe union.*
  b) *Tighten the mounting bolts to the specified torque.*
  c) *If a new EHPS has been fitted, suitable software will need to be downloaded from Ford. Consult your local dealer or specialist.*
  d) *Refill/top-up the fluid reservoir, and bleed the system as described in Section 17.*

19 Track rod end – removal and refitting

Removal

1 Loosen the appropriate front wheel nuts. Chock the rear wheels, then jack up the front of the vehicle and support it on axle stands (see *Jacking and vehicle support*). Remove the appropriate front roadwheel.

2 Counter-hold the track rod, and slacken the track rod end locknut by half a turn **(see illustration)**. If the locknut is now left in this position, it will act as a further guide for refitting.

3 Unscrew the track rod end balljoint nut, using and Allen key to counter-hold the balljoint shank. Separate the balljoint from the steering arm with a proprietary balljoint separator, then remove the nut and disengage the balljoint from the arm **(see illustrations)**.

4 Unscrew the track rod end from the track rod, counting the number of turns needed to remove it. Make a note of the number of turns, so that the tracking can be reset (or at least approximated) on refitting.

Refitting

5 Screw the track rod end onto the track rod by the same number of turns noted during removal.

6 Engage the balljoint in the steering arm.

18.9 EHPS module retaining bolts (arrowed)

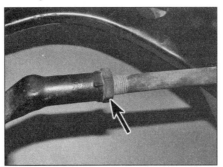

19.2 Slacken the track rod end locknut (arrowed)

19.3a Use an Allen key to counter-hold the track rod end balljoint shank

19.3b Use a separator tool to detach the track rod end from the hub carrier

Fit a new nut and tighten it to the specified torque.

7 Counter-hold the track rod and tighten the locknut.

8 Refit the front wheel, lower the car and tighten the wheel bolts in a diagonal sequence to the specified torque.

9 Have the front wheel toe-in (tracking) checked and adjusted by a Ford dealer or suitably-equipped repairer.

20 Wheel alignment and steering angles – general information

1 A car's steering and suspension geometry is defined in four basic settings – all angles are expressed in degrees (toe settings are also expressed as a measurement); the relevant settings are camber, castor, steering axis inclination, and toe setting **(see illustration)**. On the models covered by this manual, only the front and rear wheel toe settings are adjustable.

2 Camber is the angle at which the front wheels are set from the vertical when viewed from the front or rear of the car. Negative camber is the amount (in degrees) that the wheels are tilted inward at the top from the vertical.

3 The front camber angle is adjusted by slackening the steering knuckle-to-suspension strut mounting bolts and repositioning the hub carrier assemblies as necessary.

4 Castor is the angle between the steering axis and a vertical line when viewed from each side of the car. Positive castor is when the steering axis is inclined rearward at the top.

5 Steering axis inclination is the angle (when viewed from the front of the vehicle) between the vertical and an imaginary line drawn through the front suspension strut upper mounting and the control arm balljoint.

6 Toe setting is the amount by which the distance between the front inside edges of the roadwheels (measured at hub height) differs from the diametrically opposite distance measured between the rear inside edges of the roadwheels. Toe-in is when the roadwheels point inwards, towards each other at the front, while toe-out is when they splay outwards from each other at the front.

7 The front wheel toe setting is adjusted by altering the length of the steering track rods on both sides. This adjustment is normally referred to as the tracking.

8 The rear wheel toe setting is adjusted by rotating the lateral link front mounting bolt in the chassis. The bolt incorporates an eccentric washer, and the pivot point for the link varies as the bolt is rotated.

9 All other suspension and steering angles are set during manufacture, and no adjustment is possible. It can be assumed, therefore, that unless the vehicle has suffered accident damage, all the preset angles will be correct.

10 Special optical measuring equipment is necessary to accurately check and adjust the front and rear toe settings and front camber angles, and this work should be carried out by a Ford dealer or similar expert. Most tyre-fitting centres have the expertise and equipment to carry out at least a front wheel toe setting (tracking) check for a nominal charge.

21 Front subframe – removal and refitting

1 The front subframe removal and refitting is described within the steering rack removal and refitting procedure, as described in Section 15. If the subframe is to be removed as part of another procedure (eg, catalytic converter renewal), the steering rack and anti-roll bar can be left in place on the subframe.

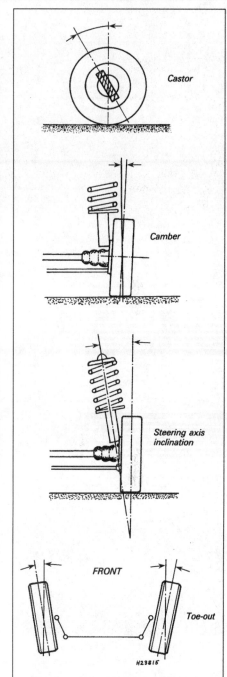

20.1 Front wheel geometry

Notes

Chapter 11
Bodywork and fittings

Contents

Degrees of difficulty

| Easy, suitable for novice with little experience | | Fairly easy, suitable for beginner with some experience | | Fairly difficult, suitable for competent DIY mechanic | | Difficult, suitable for experienced DIY mechanic | | Very difficult, suitable for expert DIY or professional | |

Specifications

Torque wrench settings	Nm	lbf ft
Bumper bar mounting:		
Front bolts	25	18
Rear bolts.	20	15
Front seat mounting bolts	35	26
Passenger's airbag module lower support bracket:		
Bolts.	9	7
Nuts.	7	5
Rear seat backrest catch retaining bolts	23	17
Rear seat hinge	35	26
Seat belt mounting nuts and bolts:		
Front inertia reel bolt.	38	28
Front lower anchorage	38	28
Front seat belt buckle stake.	47	35
Front seat bolts shoulder height adjuster.	35	26
Front upper anchorage.	38	28
Rear centre belt buckle stalk	55	41
Rear centre inertia reel	35	26
Rear centre lower anchorage	55	41
Rear outer inertia reel	40	30
Rear outer lower anchorage.	38	28

1 General information

The bodyshell and underframe on all models feature variable thickness steel. Achieved by laser-welded technology, used to join steel panels of different gauges. This gives a stiffer structure, with mounting points being more rigid, which gives an improved crash performance.

An additional safety crossmember is incorporated between the A-pillars in the upper area of the bulkhead, and the facia and steering column are secured to it. The lower bulkhead area is reinforced by additional systems of members connected to the front of the vehicle. The body side rocker panels (sills) have been divided along the length of the vehicle by internal reinforcement, this functions like a double tube which increases its strength. All doors are reinforced and incorporate side impact protection, which is secured in the door structure. There are additional impact absorbers to the front and rear of the vehicle, behind the bumper assemblies.

All sheet metal surfaces which are prone to corrosion are galvanised. The painting process includes a base colour which closely matches the final topcoat, so that any stone damage is not as noticeable. The front wings are of a bolt-on type to ease their renewal if required.

Automatic seat belts are fitted to all models, and the front seat safety belts are equipped with a pyrotechnic pretension seat belt buckle, which is attached to the seat frame of each front seat. In the event of a serious front impact, the system is triggered and pulls the stalk buckle downwards to tension the seat belt. It is not possible to reset the tensioner once fired, and it must therefore be renewed. The tensioners are fired by an explosive charge similar to that used in the airbag, and are triggered via the airbag control module. The safety belt retractor, which is fitted in the base of the B-pillar, has a device to control the seat belt, if the deceleration force is enough to activate the airbags.

In the UK, central locking is standard on all models. In other countries, it is available on certain models only. Where double-locking is fitted, the lock mechanism is disconnected (when the system is in use) from the interior door handles, making it impossible to open any of the doors or the tailgate/boot lid from inside the vehicle. This means that, even if a thief should break a side window, he will not be able to open the door using the interior handle. In the event of a serious accident, a crash sensor unlocks all doors if they were previously locked.

Many of the procedures in this Chapter require the battery to be disconnected, refer to Chapter 5.

2 Maintenance – bodywork and underframe

The general condition of a vehicle's bodywork is the one thing that significantly affects its value. Maintenance is easy, but needs to be regular. Neglect, particularly after minor damage, can lead quickly to further deterioration and costly repair bills. It is important also to keep watch on those parts of the vehicle not immediately visible, for instance the underside, inside all the wheel arches, and the lower part of the engine compartment.

The basic maintenance routine for the bodywork is washing – preferably with a lot of water, from a hose. This will remove all the loose solids which may have stuck to the vehicle. It is important to flush these off in such a way as to prevent grit from scratching the finish. The wheel arches and underframe need washing in the same way, to remove any accumulated mud, which will retain moisture and tend to encourage rust. Paradoxically enough, the best time to clean the underframe and wheel arches is in wet weather, when the mud is thoroughly wet and soft. In very wet weather, the underframe is usually cleaned of large accumulations automatically, and this is a good time for inspection.

Periodically, except on vehicles with a wax-based underbody protective coating, it is a good idea to have the whole of the underframe of the vehicle steam-cleaned, engine compartment included, so that a thorough inspection can be carried out to see what minor repairs and renovations are necessary. Steam-cleaning is available at many garages, and is necessary for the removal of the accumulation of oily grime, which sometimes is allowed to become thick in certain areas. If steam-cleaning facilities are not available, there are some excellent grease solvents available which can be brush-applied; the dirt can then be simply hosed off. Note that these methods should not be used on vehicles with wax-based underbody protective coating, or the coating will be removed. Such vehicles should be inspected annually, preferably just prior to Winter, when the underbody should be washed down, and any damage to the wax coating repaired. Ideally, a completely fresh coat should be applied. It would also be worth considering the use of such wax-based protection for injection into door panels, sills, box sections, etc, as an additional safeguard against rust damage, where such protection is not provided by the vehicle manufacturer.

After washing paintwork, wipe off with a chamois leather to give an unspotted clear finish. A coat of clear protective wax polish will give added protection against chemical pollutants in the air. If the paintwork sheen has dulled or oxidised, use a cleaner/polisher combination to restore the brilliance of the shine. This requires a little effort, but such dulling is usually caused because regular washing has been neglected. Care needs to be taken with metallic paintwork, as special non-abrasive cleaner/polisher is required to avoid damage to the finish. Always check that the door and ventilator opening drain holes and pipes are completely clear, so that water can be drained out. Brightwork should be treated in the same way as paintwork. Windscreens and windows can be kept clear of the smeary film which often appears, by the use of proprietary glass cleaner. Never use any form of wax or other body or chromium polish on glass.

3 Maintenance – upholstery and carpets

Mats and carpets should be brushed or vacuum-cleaned regularly, to keep them free of grit. If they are badly stained, remove them from the vehicle for scrubbing or sponging, and make quite sure they are dry before refitting. Seats and interior trim panels can be kept clean by wiping with a damp cloth. If they do become stained (which can be more apparent on light-coloured upholstery), use a little liquid detergent and a soft nail brush to scour the grime out of the grain of the material. Do not forget to keep the headlining clean in the same way as the upholstery. When using liquid cleaners inside the vehicle, do not over-wet the surfaces being cleaned. Excessive damp could get into the seams and padded interior, causing stains, offensive odours or even rot.

Caution: If the inside of the vehicle gets wet accidentally, it is worthwhile taking some trouble to dry it out properly, particularly where carpets are involved. Do not leave oil or electric heaters inside the vehicle for this purpose.

4 Minor body damage – repair

Minor scratches in bodywork

If the scratch is very superficial, and does not penetrate to the metal of the bodywork, repair is very simple. Lightly rub the area of the scratch with a paintwork renovator, or a very fine cutting paste, to remove loose paint from the scratch, and to clear the surrounding bodywork of wax polish. Rinse the area with clean water.

Apply touch-up paint to the scratch using a fine paint brush; continue to apply fine layers of paint until the surface of the paint in the scratch is level with the surrounding paintwork. Allow the new paint at least two weeks to harden, then blend it into the surrounding paintwork by rubbing the scratch area with a paintwork renovator or a very fine cutting paste. Finally, apply wax polish.

Where the scratch has penetrated right through to the metal of the bodywork, causing the metal to rust, a different repair technique is required. Remove any loose rust from the bottom of the scratch with a penknife, then apply rust-inhibiting paint to prevent the formation of rust in the future. Using a rubber or nylon applicator, fill the scratch with bodystopper paste. If required, this paste can be mixed with cellulose thinners to provide a very thin paste which is ideal for filling narrow scratches. Before the stopper-paste in the scratch hardens, wrap a piece of smooth cotton rag around the top of a finger. Dip the finger in cellulose thinners, and quickly sweep it across the surface of the stopper-paste in the scratch; this will ensure that the surface of the stopper-paste is slightly hollowed. The scratch can now be painted over as described earlier in this Section.

Dents in bodywork

When deep denting of the vehicle's bodywork has taken place, the first task is to pull the dent out, until the affected bodywork almost attains its original shape. There is little point in trying to restore the original shape completely, as the metal in the damaged area will have stretched on impact, and cannot be reshaped fully to its original contour. It is better to bring the level of the dent up to a point which is about 3 mm below the level of the surrounding bodywork. In cases where the dent is very shallow anyway, it is not worth trying to pull it out at all. If the underside of the dent is accessible, it can be hammered out gently from behind, using a mallet with a wooden or plastic head. Whilst doing this, hold a suitable block of wood firmly against the outside of the panel, to absorb the impact from the hammer blows and thus prevent a large area of the bodywork from being 'belled-out'.

Should the dent be in a section of the bodywork which has a double skin, or some other factor making it inaccessible from behind, a different technique is called for. Drill several small holes through the metal inside the area – particularly in the deeper section. Then screw long self-tapping screws into the holes, just sufficiently for them to gain a good purchase in the metal. Now the dent can be pulled out by pulling on the protruding heads of the screws with a pair of pliers.

The next stage of the repair is the removal of the paint from the damaged area, and from an inch or so of the surrounding 'sound' bodywork. This is accomplished most easily by using a wire brush or abrasive pad on a power drill, although it can be done just as effectively by hand, using sheets of abrasive paper. To complete the preparation for filling, score the surface of the bare metal with a screwdriver or the tang of a file, or alternatively, drill small holes in the affected area. This will provide a really good 'key' for the filler paste.

To complete the repair, see the Section on filling and respraying.

Rust holes or gashes in bodywork

Remove all paint from the affected area, and from an inch or so of the surrounding 'sound' bodywork, using an abrasive pad or a wire brush on a power drill. If these are not available, a few sheets of abrasive paper will do the job most effectively. With the paint removed, you will be able to judge the severity of the corrosion, and therefore decide whether to renew the whole panel (if this is possible) or to repair the affected area. New body panels are not as expensive as most people think, and it is often quicker and more satisfactory to fit a new panel than to attempt to repair large areas of corrosion.

Remove all fittings from the affected area, except those which will act as a guide to the original shape of the damaged bodywork (e.g. headlight shells etc). Then, using tin snips or a hacksaw blade, remove all loose metal and any other metal badly affected by corrosion. Hammer the edges of the hole inwards, in order to create a slight depression for the filler paste.

Wire-brush the affected area to remove the powdery rust from the surface of the remaining metal. Paint the affected area with rust-inhibiting paint, if the back of the rusted area is accessible, treat this also.

Before filling can take place, it will be necessary to block the hole in some way. This can be achieved by the use of aluminium or plastic mesh, or aluminium tape.

Aluminium or plastic mesh, or glass-fibre matting, is probably the best material to use for a large hole. Cut a piece to the approximate size and shape of the hole to be filled, then position it in the hole so that its edges are below the level of the surrounding bodywork. It can be retained in position by several blobs of filler paste around its periphery.

Aluminium tape should be used for small or very narrow holes. Pull a piece off the roll, trim it to the approximate size and shape required, then pull off the backing paper (if used) and stick the tape over the hole; it can be overlapped if the thickness of one piece is insufficient. Burnish down the edges of the tape with the handle of a screwdriver or similar, to ensure that the tape is securely attached to the metal underneath.

Filling and respraying

Before using this Section, see the Sections on dent, deep scratch, rust holes and gash repairs.

Many types of bodyfiller are available, but generally speaking, those proprietary kits which contain a tin of filler paste and a tube of resin hardener are best for this type of repair. A wide, flexible plastic or nylon applicator will be found invaluable for imparting a smooth and well-contoured finish to the surface of the filler.

Mix up a little filler on a clean piece of card or board – measure the hardener carefully (follow the maker's instructions on the pack),

otherwise the filler will set too rapidly or too slowly. Using the applicator, apply the filler paste to the prepared area; draw the applicator across the surface of the filler to achieve the correct contour and to level the surface. As soon as a contour that approximates to the correct one is achieved, stop working the paste – if you carry on too long, the paste will become sticky and begin to 'pick-up' on the applicator. Continue to add thin layers of filler paste at 20-minute intervals, until the level of the filler is just proud of the surrounding bodywork.

Once the filler has hardened, the excess can be removed using a metal plane or file. From then on, progressively-finer grades of abrasive paper should be used, starting with a 40-grade production paper, and finishing with a 400-grade wet-and-dry paper. Always wrap the abrasive paper around a flat rubber, cork, or wooden block – otherwise the surface of the filler will not be completely flat. During the smoothing of the filler surface, the wet-and-dry paper should be periodically rinsed in water. This will ensure that a very smooth finish is imparted to the filler at the final stage.

At this stage, the 'dent' should be surrounded by a ring of bare metal, which in turn should be encircled by the finely 'feathered' edge of the good paintwork. Rinse the repair area with clean water, until all of the dust produced by the rubbing-down operation has gone.

Spray the whole area with a light coat of primer – this will show up any imperfections in the surface of the filler. Repair these imperfections with fresh filler paste or bodystopper, and once more smooth the surface with abrasive paper. Repeat this spray-and-repair procedure until you are satisfied that the surface of the filler, and the feathered edge of the paintwork, are perfect. Clean the repair area with clean water, and allow to dry fully.

The repair area is now ready for final spraying. Paint spraying must be carried out in a warm, dry, windless and dust-free atmosphere. This condition can be created artificially if you have access to a large indoor working area, but if you are forced to work in the open, you will have to pick your day very carefully. If you are working indoors, dousing the floor in the work area with water will help to settle the dust which would otherwise be in the atmosphere. If the repair area is confined to one body panel, mask off the surrounding panels; this will help to minimise the effects of a slight mis-match in paint colours. Bodywork fittings (e.g. chrome strips, door handles etc) will also need to be masked off. Use genuine masking tape, and several thicknesses of newspaper, for the masking operations.

Before commencing to spray, agitate the aerosol can thoroughly, then spray a test area (an old tin, or similar) until the technique is mastered. Cover the repair area with a thick coat of primer; the thickness should be built up using several thin layers of paint, rather than

6.4 Undo the bolt and prise out the scrivet each side of the radiator grille aperture

6.7 Undo the 3 bolts securing the bumper to the wing (arrowed) – viewed from under the wheel arch

one thick one. Using 400-grade wet-and-dry paper, rub down the surface of the primer until it is really smooth. While doing this, the work area should be thoroughly doused with water, and the wet-and-dry paper periodically rinsed in water. Allow to dry before spraying on more paint.

Spray on the top coat, again building up the thickness by using several thin layers of paint. Start spraying at one edge of the repair area, and then, using a side-to-side motion, work until the whole repair area and about 2 inches of the surrounding original paintwork is covered. Remove all masking material 10 to 15 minutes after spraying on the final coat of paint.

Allow the new paint at least two weeks to harden, then, using a paintwork renovator, or a very fine cutting paste, blend the edges of the paint into the existing paintwork. Finally, apply wax polish.

Plastic components

With the use of more and more plastic body components by the vehicle manufacturers (e.g. bumpers. spoilers, and in some cases major body panels), rectification of more serious damage to such items has become a matter of either entrusting repair work to a specialist in this field, or renewing complete components. Repair of such damage by the DIY owner is not really feasible, owing to the cost of the equipment and materials required for effecting such repairs. The basic technique involves making a groove along the line of the crack in the plastic, using a rotary burr in a

power drill. The damaged part is then welded back together, using a hot-air gun to heat up and fuse a plastic filler rod into the groove. Any excess plastic is then removed, and the area rubbed down to a smooth finish. It is important that a filler rod of the correct plastic is used, as body components can be made of a variety of different types (e.g. polycarbonate, ABS, polypropylene).

Damage of a less serious nature (abrasions, minor cracks etc) can be repaired by the DIY owner using a two-part epoxy filler repair material. Once mixed in equal proportions, this is used in similar fashion to the bodywork filler used on metal panels. The filler is usually cured in twenty to thirty minutes, ready for sanding and painting.

If the owner is renewing a complete component himself, or if he has repaired it with epoxy filler, he will be left with the problem of finding a suitable paint for finishing which is compatible with the type of plastic used. At one time, the use of a universal paint was not possible, owing to the complex range of plastics encountered in body component applications. Standard paints, generally speaking, will not bond to plastic or rubber satisfactorily. However, it is now possible to obtain a plastic body parts finishing kit which consists of a pre-primer treatment, a primer and coloured top coat. Full instructions are normally supplied with a kit, but basically, the method of use is to first apply the pre-primer to the component concerned, and allow it to dry for up to 30 minutes. Then the primer is applied, and left to dry for about an hour

before finally applying the special-coloured top coat. The result is a correctly-coloured component, where the paint will flex with the plastic or rubber, a property that standard paint does not normally posses.

5 Major body damage – repair

Where serious damage has occurred, or large areas need renewal due to neglect, it means that complete new panels will need welding-in; this is best left to professionals. If the damage is due to impact, it will also be necessary to check completely the alignment of the bodyshell; this can only be carried out accurately by a Ford dealer, using special jigs. If the body is left misaligned, it is primarily dangerous, as the car will not handle properly, and secondly, uneven stresses will be imposed on the steering, suspension and possibly transmission, causing abnormal wear or complete failure, particularly to items such as the tyres.

6 Bumpers – removal and refitting

Front bumper removal

1 Apply the handbrake, jack up the front of the vehicle and support it on axle stands. Undo the fasteners and remove the engine undershield.

Models up to 12/2007

2 Undo the fasteners and remove the splash shield under the radiator.
3 Remove the radiator grille as described in Section 7.
4 Remove the scrivet each side of the radiator grille aperture (see illustration).
5 Remove both front headlights as described in Chapter 12.
6 Undo the 2 bolts each side securing the wheel arch liner to the bumper.
7 Undo the 3 bolts each side securing the bumper to the underside of the wing (see illustration).
8 Pull the headlight washer jets forwards (where fitted), then release the clips and detach the jet assembly from the pipe.
9 Release the 7 clips at the upper edge, then with the help of an assistant to support one end of the bumper, pull the sides away from the body and withdraw it forwards from the vehicle (see illustrations). Disconnect the foglamp connectors as the bumper is withdrawn.

Models from 12/2007

10 Undo the fasteners and remove the splash shield under the radiator.
11 Remove the front headlights as described in Chapter 12.

6.9a The bumper is retained by 3 clips in the centre (arrowed) . . .

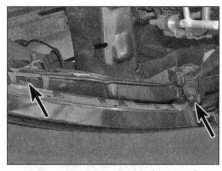

6.9b . . . and 2 each side (arrowed)

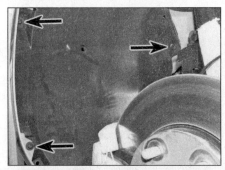

6.12a Undo the bolts at the front of the wheel arch liner (arrowed) . . .

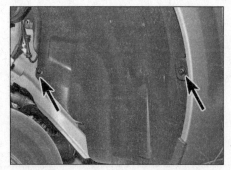

6.12b . . . and at the rear (arrowed)

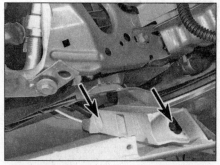

6.13a Undo the 2 bolts securing the bumper to the wing (arrowed)

6.13b Undo the scrivet each side of the radiator grille (arrowed)

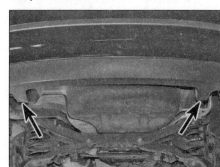

6.16a Squeeze together the sides of the clip securing the wing to the bumper each side (arrowed)

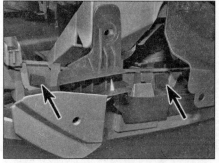

6.16b Release the clips (arrowed) at the top edge of the bumper

12 Undo the bolts securing the wheel arch liners to the front bumper (see illustrations).

13 Undo the 2 bolts each side securing the bumper to the front wing, and the scrivet each side of the radiator grille (see illustrations).

14 Remove the radiator grille as described in Section 7.

15 Pull the headlight washer jets forwards (where fitted), then release the clips and detach the jet assembly from the pipe.

16 Release the clips at the upper and outer edges, then with the help of an assistant to support one end of the bumper, withdraw it forwards from the vehicle (see illustrations). Disconnect the foglamp connectors as the bumper is withdrawn.

Rear bumper removal

Hatchback models up to 12/2007

17 Chock the front wheels, jack up the rear of the vehicle and support it on axle stands (see *Jacking and vehicle support*). Open up the tailgate.

18 Remove the 2 retaining bolts and pull out the plastic expanding rivets from the bumper underside (see illustration).

19 Undo the bolt each side in the tailgate aperture (see illustration). When refitting these bolts, apply a little thread-locking compound.

20 Undo the 2 bolts each side securing the bumper to the wheel arch liner (see illustration).

21 Undo the nut each side in the wheel arch securing the bumper to the wing, and pull the front edges of the bumper outwards to release the guide pin each side (see illustration).

22 Disconnect the wiring plug for the rear foglamp/reversing light/parking assistance sensors (as applicable).

23 With the help of an assistant, pull the bumper rearwards.

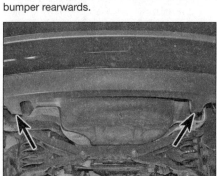

6.18 Undo the bolts and prise out the plastic rivets (arrowed)

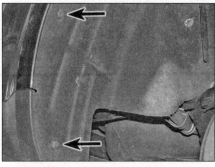

6.20 Wheel arch liner-to-bumper bolts (arrowed)

Hatchback models from 12/2007

24 Chock the front wheels, jack up the rear of the vehicle and support it on axle stands (see *Jacking and vehicle support*). Open up the tailgate.

6.19 Undo the bolt each side in the tailgate aperture

6.21 Undo the nut each side securing the bumper to the wing

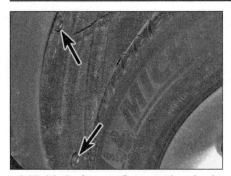

6.25 2 bolts (arrowed) secure the wheel arch liner to the bumper each side

6.27a Undo the bolt in the tailgate aperture . . .

6.27b . . . and the nut securing the bumper to the wing

25 Undo the 2 bolts each side securing the mudlfap/wheel arch liner to the bumper **(see illustration)**.
26 Disconnect the wiring plug for the rear foglamp/reversing light/parking assistance sensors (as applicable).

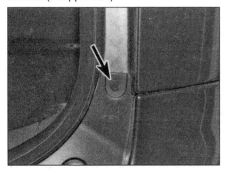

6.32 Undo the bolt (arrowed) in the tailgate aperture

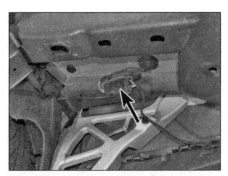

6.34 Disconnect the wiring plug under the right-hand side of the bumper (arrowed)

6.28 Undo the bolt each side (arrowed) on the underside of the bumper

27 The bumper is retained by 1 bolt each side in the tailgate aperture, and a nut each side at its front, inner edge **(see illustrations)**. Remove the bolts and nuts.
28 Undo the bolts on the bumper underside, and prise out the plastic inserts **(see**

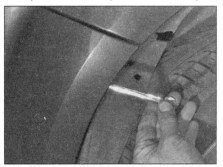

6.33 Undo the nut each side behind the wheel arch liner

6.35 Pull the front edges of the bumper outwards to disengage the locating lugs

illustration). With the help of an assistant, pull the sides away from the body, and withdraw the bumper rearwards.

Estate models up to 12/2007

29 Chock the front wheels, jack up the rear of the vehicle and support it on axle stands (see *Jacking and vehicle support)*.
30 Undo the 2 bolts each side securing the mudlfap/wheel arch liner to the bumper.
31 Remove the 2 retaining bolts and pull out the plastic expanding rivets from the bumper underside **(see illustration 6.28)**.
32 Undo the bolt each side in the tailgate aperture **(see illustration)**.
33 Pull forwards the wheel arch liner, then undo the nut each side securing the bumper **(see illustration)**.
34 Disconnect the wiring plug for the rear foglamp/reversing light/parking assistance sensors (as applicable) **(see illustration)**.
35 With the help of an assistant, pull out the front edges, and manoeuvre the bumper rearwards **(see illustration)**.

Estate models from 12/2007

36 Chock the front wheels, jack up the rear of the vehicle and support it on axle stands (see *Jacking and vehicle support)*.
37 Disconnect the wiring plug for the rear foglamp/reversing light/parking assistance sensors (as applicable).
38 Undo the 2 bolts each side securing the mudlfap/wheel arch liner to the bumper.
39 Remove the 2 retaining bolts and pull out the plastic expanding rivets from the bumper underside **(see illustration 6.28)**.
40 Undo the bolt each side in the tailgate aperture **(see illustration 6.32)**.
41 Undo the nut each side, and release the clip securing the bumper to the rear wings **(see illustration 6.33)**.
42 Disconnect the wiring plug for the rear foglamp/reversing light/parking assistance sensors (as applicable).
43 Release the 3 clips at the top edge of the bumper and, with the help of an assistant, pull the sides away from the body and manoeuvre the bumper rearwards.

Saloon models up to 12/2007

44 Chock the front wheels, jack up the rear of the vehicle and support it on axle stands (see *Jacking and vehicle support)*.
45 Carefully prise out the moulding strip each side of the bumper, and undo the bolt each side **(see illustrations)**.
46 Undo the 2 scrivets on the lower edge of the bumper **(see illustration 6.28)**.
47 Disconnect the wiring plug for the rear foglamp/reversing light/parking assistance sensors (as applicable).
48 Undo the 2 bolts each side securing the mudlfap/wheel arch liner to the bumper.
49 Undo the bolt each side in the boot lid aperture **(see illustration)**.

50 Undo the nut each side, and release the clip securing the bumper to the rear wings **(see illustration)**.

51 Release the 3 clips at the top edge of the bumper and, with the help of an assistant, pull the sides away from the body and manoeuvre the bumper rearwards.

Saloon models from 12/2007

52 Chock the front wheels, jack up the rear of the vehicle and support it on axle stands (see *Jacking and vehicle support*). Open up the boot.

53 Undo the 2 bolts each side securing the mudlfap/wheel arch liner to the bumper.

54 Disconnect the wiring plug for the rear foglamp/reversing light/parking assistance sensors (as applicable).

55 The bumper is retained by 2 bolts each side in the boot lid aperture. Remove the bolts, then with the help of an assistant, pull the sides away from the body, and withdraw the bumper rearwards.

All models

56 If required, the parking distance sensors can be removed from the bumper cover, by depressing the retaining tangs and withdrawing the sensor.

Refitting

57 Refitting is a reversal of the removal procedure. Make sure that, where applicable, the bumper guides are located correctly. Check all electrical components that have been disconnected.

---

7 Radiator grille –
removal and refitting

Removal

1 Support the bonnet in the open position. Undo the 4 scrivets and remove the plastic panel above the radiator grille **(see illustrations)**.

2 Release the 2 clips securing the bonnet lock linkage to the radiator grille **(see illustration)**.

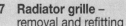

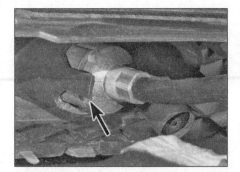

7.2 Prise apart the clip each side (arrowed) to release the bonnet lock linkage

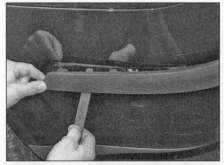

6.45a Prise away the moulding . . .

6.49 Undo the bolt (arrowed) in the boot lid aperture

3 Unscrew the 2 radiator grille upper mounting scrivets **(see illustration)**.

4 Pivot the grille forwards, the undo the 2 lower clips and remove the grille **(see illustration)**.

7.1a Undo the bolt and prise out the scrivets . . .

7.3 Remove the scrivet each side of the radiator grille (arrowed)

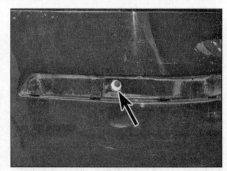

6.45b . . . and undo the bolt (arrowed)

6.50 Undo the nut each side behind the wheel arch liner

Refitting

5 Refitting is a reversal of the removal procedure.

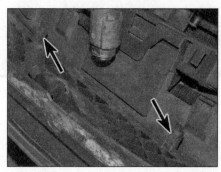

7.1b . . . along the front edge (arrowed) of the air deflector panel

7.4 Radiator grille lower clips (arrowed)

8 Bonnet –
removal, refitting and adjustment

Removal

1 Open the bonnet, and support it in the open position using the stay. Where fitted, release the clips and remove the bonnet insulation panel.
2 Disconnect the windscreen washer hoses from the bottom of the jets, and unclip them from the bonnet.
3 Disconnect the windscreen washer wiring connector from the bottom of the jets, and unclip from the bonnet.
4 To assist in correctly realigning the bonnet when refitting it, mark the outline of the hinges with a soft pencil. Loosen the

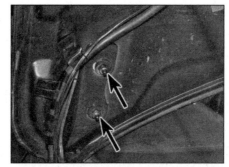

8.4 Bonnet hinge retaining nuts (arrowed)

two hinge retaining nuts on each side **(see illustration)**.
5 With the help of an assistant, unscrew the four nuts, release the stay, and lift the bonnet from the vehicle.

Refitting and adjustment

6 Refitting is a reversal of the removal procedure, noting the following points:
  a) *Position the bonnet hinges within the outline marks made during removal, but if necessary, alter its position to provide a uniform gap all round.*
  b) *Adjust the front height by repositioning the lock (see Section 9) and turning the rubber buffers on the engine compartment front cross panel up or down to support the bonnet.*

9 Bonnet lock –
removal, refitting and adjustment

Removal

1 Undo the 4 bolts, release the 2 clips and remove the air deflector panel over the bonnet lock **(see illustrations 7.1a and 7.1b)**.
2 Make alignment marks between the lock and panel, then undo the 2 bolts securing the lock assembly to the bonnet slam panel **(see illustration)**.
3 Note its fitted position, then detach the bonnet lock key cylinder link rod from the lock assembly **(see illustration)**.
4 Disconnect the wiring connector from the lock assembly, as it is being removed.
5 Push the lock cylinder from the housing, using a screwdriver to unclip it.

Refitting and adjustment

6 Refitting is a reversal of the removal procedure, starting by positioning the lock as noted before removal.
7 If the front of the bonnet is not level with the front wings, the lock may be moved up or down within the mounting holes. After making an adjustment, raise or lower the rubber buffers to support the bonnet correctly.

9.2 Undo the bonnet lock bolts

9.3 Release the clip (arrowed) each side of the link rod

10 Door inner trim panel –
removal and refitting

Removal

1 Disconnect the battery negative (earth) lead (Chapter 5).

Front door

2 Operate the inner door release handle, and carefully pull the bezel from place **(see illustrations)**. Disconnect the keyless entry/ door lock/electric window (as applicable) switch wiring plug as the bezel is withdrawn (where fitted).
3 Insert a blunt, flat-bladed tool under the door grab handle, then twist it to unclip the cover trim. Undo the two bolts from behind the cover inside the door pull handle **(see illustrations)**.
4 If working on the driver's door, disconnect the wiring connector from the window operating switch.

10.2a Starting at the front edge, carefully pull the interior handle bezel from place

10.2b Disconnect the switch wiring plug

10.3a Prise the handle lower cover downwards . . .

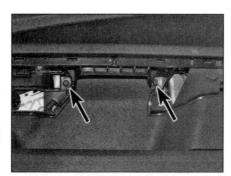

10.3b . . . and undo the 2 bolts in the recess (arrowed)

10.5a Use a forked tool to lever between the door panel retaining clips and their collars (arrowed) – shown with the panel removed for clarity

10.5b With the clips released, remove the panel

5 Working around the outer edge, use a forked trim release tool to release the retaining clips securing the trim panel **(see illustrations)**.

Rear door

6 Operate the inner door release handle, and carefully pull the bezel from place **(see illustration)**. Disconnect the window switch wiring plug as the bezel is withdrawn.

7 On models fitted with manual (ie, non-electric) rear windows, fully shut the window, and note the position of the regulator handle. Release the spring clip by inserting a clean cloth between the handle and the door trim. Using a 'sawing' action, pull the cloth

against the open ends of the clip to release it, at the same time pulling the handle from the regulator shaft splines. Withdraw the handle and the spacer **(see illustrations)**.

8 Carefully prise the cover from the door grab handle. Undo the two bolts from behind the cover inside the door pull handle **(see illustrations)**.

9 Working around the outer edge, use a forked trim release tool to release the retaining clips **(see illustration 10.5a)** securing the trim panel **(see illustration)**. Disconnect the tweeter speaker wiring plug (where fitted) as the panel is withdrawn.

10.6 Carefully pull the handle bezel from place

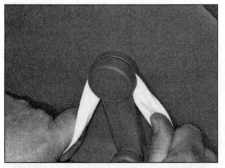

10.7a Use a clean cloth and a sawing motion to release the regulator handle retaining clip

10.7b The edges of the clip (arrowed) must be pushed towards the handle

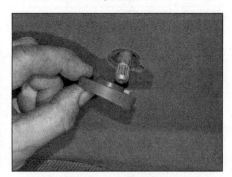

10.7c Recover the handle spacer

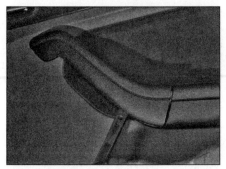

10.8a Prise the cover from the door grab handle . . .

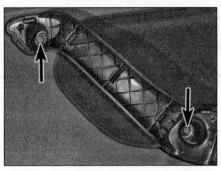

10.8b . . . and undo the 2 bolts (arrowed)

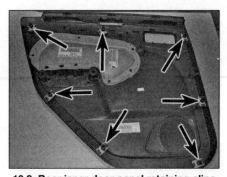

10.9 Rear inner door panel retaining clips (arrowed)

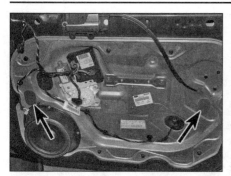

11.2 Prise the rubber grommets (arrowed) from the panel

11.3 Pull the inner weather strip up from the door

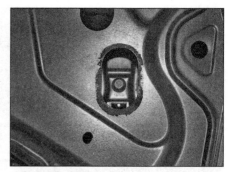

11.5 Align the window clamp bolts with the apertures in the panel

Refitting

10 Refitting is a reversal of the removal procedure. On the rear manual windows, ensure the retaining clip is fitted to the winder handle before refitting the handle to the regulator shaft.

11 Door window glass – removal and refitting

Removal

Front door

1 Remove the door inner trim panel as described in Section 10.
2 Prise the rubber grommet from the front and rear of the door panel to access the window clamps **(see illustration)**.

11.7 Lift the rear of the window and withdraw it from the outside of the door

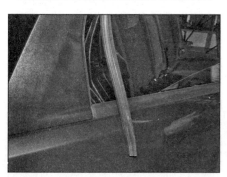

11.9b ... and rear window guide rubbers

3 Carefully prise the rubber inner weather strip from the door **(see illustration)**.
4 Reconnect the door window switch, and reconnect the battery negative lead.
5 Operate the window switch and align the window clamp bolts with the apertures exposed by removing the grommets **(see illustration)**.
6 Slacken each of the window clamp bolts by 2 turns.
7 Lift the window glass from the door while tilting it up at the rear, and withdraw it from the outside of the door frame **(see illustration)**.

Rear door

8 Remove the door window regulator panel as described in Section 12. Note that there is no need to drill out the rivets securing the regulator to the panel.

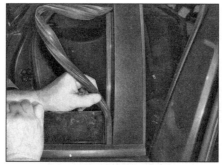

11.9a Prise out the front ...

11.10 Prise up the door inner weather strip

9 Lower the window, then prise out the lower sections of the window guide rubber at the front and rear of the window frame **(see illustrations)**.
10 Carefully prise the rubber inner weather strip from the door **(see illustration)**.
11 Lift the window glass from the door while tilting it up at the rear, and withdraw it from the outside of the door frame **(see illustration)**.

Refitting

12 Refitting is a reversal of the removal procedure, making sure that the glass is correctly located in the clamps.

12 Door window regulator – removal and refitting

Removal

Front door

1 Remove the front door window as described in Section 11.
2 Disconnect the wiring plugs, then undo the 3 bolts and remove the electric window motor **(see illustration)**.
3 Disconnect the cable from the door inner release handle **(see illustration)**.
4 Remove the exterior handle as described in Section 13.

11.11 Tilt it up at the rear, and remove the glass from the door

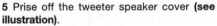

12.2 Window motor retaining bolts (arrowed)

12.3 Push the lock button into the door, then lift the release cable end fitting from the handle

12.5 Prise the 'tweeter' cover from place

5 Prise off the tweeter speaker cover **(see illustration)**.

6 Undo the retaining bolt, pull the exterior mirror trim panel from the door, and lift it from place **(see illustration)**.

7 Disconnect the wiring plug(s) as the panel is withdrawn.

8 Undo the 10 bolts securing the inner panel to the door frame **(see illustration)**.

9 Undo the 5 bolts securing the door lock to the door **(see illustrations)**.

10 Manoeuvre the panel from the door **(see illustration)**.

11 Using a suitable-sized drill bit, remove the 6 (3-door models) or 4 (4/5-door models) rivets securing the window regulator to the door panel **(see illustrations)**.

Rear door

12 Remove the rear door inner trim panel as described in Section 10.

12.6 Undo the bolt (arrowed) and pull the mirror trim panel from the door

13 Prise the foam/rubber grommet from the front and rear of the door panel to access the window clamps **(see illustration)**.

14 On models with manual windows, refit the window winder handle, and fully

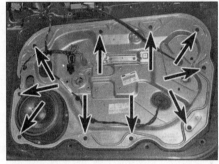

12.8 Inner panel retaining bolts (arrowed)

lower the window. On models with electric windows, reconnect the window switch and the battery negative lead, then fully lower the window.

15 Operate the window switch/handle

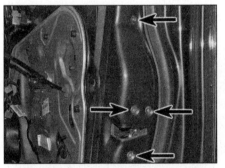

12.9a Undo the 4 bolts (arrowed) at the end of the door . . .

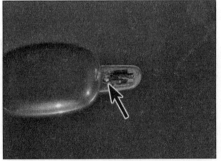

12.9b . . . and the one (arrowed) on the outside of the door

12.10 Manoeuvre the panel from the door

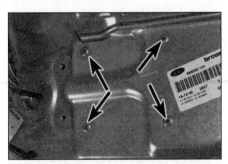

12.11a Drill out the rivets (arrowed) securing the regulator to the panel – 4/5-door model

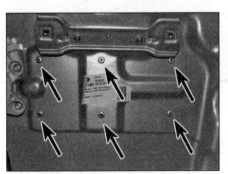

12.11b 3-door model regulator rivets (arrowed)

12.13 Prise out the grommets (arrowed) to access the window clamps

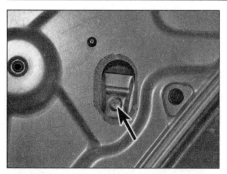

12.15 Raise the window until the clamp bolt is visible (arrowed)

12.17 Undo the bolts and pull the window motor from the panel

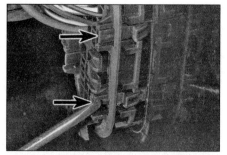

12.19a Release the 2 clips each side of the connector (arrowed) and pull it from the pillar

12.19b Disconnect the door wiring plug

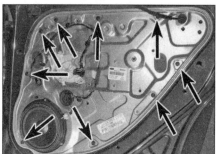
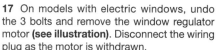

12.21 Rear door panel bolts (arrowed)

and align the window clamp bolts with the apertures exposed by removing the grommets **(see illustration)**.

16 Slacken the clamp bolts two turns, then lift the window to the top of the door and secure it in place using tape.

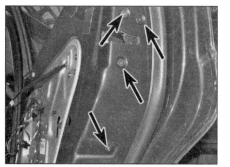

12.22a Undo the 4 bolts at the end of the door (arrowed) . . .

17 On models with electric windows, undo the 3 bolts and remove the window regulator motor **(see illustration)**. Disconnect the wiring plug as the motor is withdrawn.

18 Set the handle in the 'Lock' position, then lift the interior door release handle operating

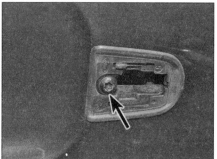

12.22b . . . and one on the outside of the door (arrowed)

cable end fitting upwards, and disconnect it **(see illustration 12.3)**.

19 Close the door, prise away the rubber gaiter, release the 4 clips and pull the connector from the door pillar, then disconnect the door wiring plug **(see illustrations)**. Push the wiring harness into the door.

20 Open the door, and remove the exterior handle as described in Section 13.

21 Undo the 9 bolts securing the inner panel to the door frame **(see illustration)**.

22 Undo the 4 bolts securing the door lock at the rear edge of the door, and the single bolt securing the exterior handle frame to the door **(see illustrations)**. Manoeuvre the panel/regulator from the door.

23 Using a suitable-sized drill bit, remove the 5 rivets (manual windows) or 4 rivets (electric windows) securing the window regulator to the door panel **(see illustration)**.

Refitting

24 Refitting is a reversal of the removal procedure.

12.23 Drill out the rivets (arrowed) securing the regulator to the panel – electric window model

13.1 Prise out the grommet at the end of the door

---

13 Door handle and lock components – removal and refitting

> ⚠ **Warning: before working on any electrical components, disconnect the battery negative (earth) lead (Chapter 5, Section 1).**

Removal

Exterior handle – front

1 Prise out the rubber grommet from the end of the door adjacent to the exterior handle **(see illustration)**.

2 Working through the aperture, slacken the handle retaining bolt approximately 22 turns **(see illustration)**.

3 Carefully pull the trim and lock cylinder from the door **(see illustration)**. On models with the Keyless Entry system, remove the trim at the rear of the handle (where the lock cylinder would be on conventional systems).

4 Pull the exterior handle rearwards, and manoeuvre it from the door. Recover the seals between the handle and the door skin.

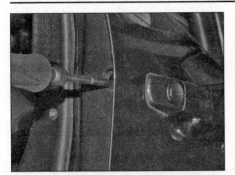

13.2 Slacken the handle retaining bolt approximately 22 turns . . .

5 On models with the Keyless Entry system, gently pull the handle antenna wiring harness until an audible click is heard, and the harness connector is in the horizontal position. Disconnect the wiring plug.

Exterior handle – rear

6 Prise out the rubber grommet from the end of the door adjacent to the exterior handle **(see illustration)**.
7 Working through the aperture, slacken the handle retaining bolt approximately 7 turns **(see illustration)**.
8 Pull the trim at the rear of the handle outwards **(see illustration)**.
9 Pull the exterior handle rearwards, and manoeuvre it from the door. Recover the seals between the handle and the door skin.

Interior handle

10 Remove the door inner trim panel Section 10.
11 Detach the door release handle from the door by undoing the bolt, unclipping the front end, then slide the handle out in a forwards direction **(see illustrations)**.
12 Set the handle in the 'Lock' position, then lift the operating cable end fitting upwards, and disconnect it **(see illustration 12.3)**.

Lock motor/module – front

13 Proceed as described in Paragraphs 1 to 10 of Section 12.
14 Press in the centre pins, prise out the plastic rivets securing the lock and latch retaining bracket to the door panel **(see illustration)**. Disconnect the lock wiring plugs as it's withdrawn.

13.3 . . . until the lock cylinder and trim can be pulled from the door

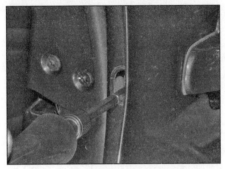

13.7 . . . undo the bolt approximately 7 turns . . .

15 Depress the retaining clips each side of the lock remote control cable outer fitting, and pull it from the support bracket, then rotate the cable end fitting 90° and detach it from the lever on the lock **(see illustration)**.

13.11a Undo the bolt (arrowed) . . .

13.6 Prise out the grommet . . .

13.8 . . . until the trim can be removed

Repeat this procedure on the exterior handle cable.
16 Using a suitable-sized drill bit, remove the rivet securing the lock to the bracket **(see illustration)**.

13.11b . . . and pull the front end of the handle assembly from the door

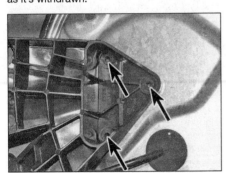

13.14 Push in the centre pins of the 3 rivets (arrowed)

13.15 Depress the clips (arrowed) and pull the fitting from the bracket

13.16 Drill out the rivet (arrowed) securing the lock to the bracket

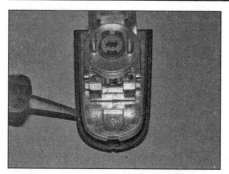

13.19a Release the clip each side . . .

13.19b . . . and detach the cover from the lock cylinder

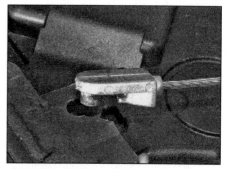

13.21 Rotate the end fitting and detach it from the lever

13.22 Press the centres from the 3 rivets . . .

13.23 . . . and drill out the rivet securing the lock to the bracket (arrowed)

Lock cylinder

17 Prise out the rubber grommet from the end of the door adjacent to the exterior handle **(see illustration 13.1)**.
18 Working through the aperture, slacken the handle retaining bolt approximately 22 turns **(see illustration 13.2)**.
19 Pull the trim and lock cylinder from the door **(see illustration 13.3)**. If required, release the clip each side with a small screwdriver, and separate the lock cylinder from the trim **(see illustrations)**

Lock motor/module – rear

20 Proceed as described in Paragraphs 12 to 22 of Section 12.
21 Depress the retaining clips each side of the lock remote control cable outer fitting, and pull it from the support bracket **(see illustration 13.15)**, then rotate the cable end fitting and detach it from the lever on the lock

(see illustration). Repeat this procedure on the exterior handle cable.
22 Using a suitably-sized rod, drive out the centres of the 3 plastic rivets securing the lock and latch retaining bracket to the door panel **(see illustration)**. Disconnect the lock wiring plugs as it's withdrawn.
23 Using a suitable-sized drill bit, remove the rivet securing the lock to the bracket **(see illustration)**.

Refitting

Handles (exterior and interior)

24 Refitting is a reversal of the removal procedure. When refitting the exterior handle on models with the Keyless Entry system, reconnect the antenna wiring connector and push it into the holder.

Lock cylinder

25 Refitting is a reversal of removal.

Lock motor/modules

26 Refitting is a reversal of the removal procedure, but check that the door lock passes over the striker centrally. If necessary, reposition the striker before fully tightening the mounting bolts.

14 Door – removal and refitting

Removal

1 Disconnect the battery negative (earth) lead (Chapter 5).
2 Using a Torx key, unscrew and remove the check strap mounting bolt from the door pillar **(see illustration)**.
3 Have an assistant support the door, then undo the retaining bolts in the top and bottom hinges **(see illustration)**.
4 Carefully lift the door from the hinges, and support it on a trolley jack or similar.
5 Prise out the rubber gaiter, and disconnect the wiring block connector **(see illustrations 12.19a and 12.19b)**.

Refitting

6 Refitting is a reversal of the removal procedure, but check that the door lock passes over the striker centrally. If necessary, reposition the striker.

15 Exterior mirror and glass – removal and refitting

Removal

Mirror

1 Unclip the trim panel from the front of the window opening over the tweeter speaker and remove it **(see illustration 12.6)**.
2 Undo the retaining bolt, then starting at the top, pull the exterior mirror trim panel from the door, and lift it from place **(see illustration 12.7)**. Disconnect the wiring plug as the panel is withdrawn

14.2 Check strap retaining bolt (arrowed)

14.3 Undo the upper and lower hinge bolts

3 Unscrew the mirror mounting bolts, then release the clip and withdraw the mirror from the outside of the door. Recover the mirror seal as the wiring/cable is being drawn through the rubber grommet **(see illustrations)**.

Mirror glass

4 Pull the outer edge of the glass rearwards, insert a flat-bladed screwdriver and gently prise the glass from place **(see illustrations)**.
5 Withdraw the mirror glass and disconnect the wiring connectors for the heated mirrors.

Refitting

6 Refitting is a reversal of the removal procedure. Take care not to drop the rubber grommet inside the door panel when removing the mirror, as the interior door trim will have to be removed to retrieve it.

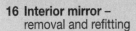

16 Interior mirror –
removal and refitting

Basic mirror

1 Press the retaining clip away from the windscreen, then slide the mirror up from the base **(see illustrations)**.
2 Refitting is a reversal of removal.

Auto-dimming mirror

3 Squeeze together the sides, and slide up the mirror base upper cover **(see illustration)**.
4 Pull apart the top edges and slide down the mirror base lower cover **(see illustration)**.
5 Disconnect the mirror wiring plug (where applicable).
6 Rotate the mirror base 60° anti-clockwise and detach it from the mounting **(see illustration)**.
7 Refitting is the reversal of the removal procedure.

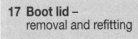

17 Boot lid –
removal and refitting

Removal

1 Disconnect the battery negative (earth) lead (Chapter 5), and open the boot lid.

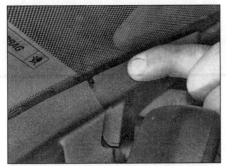

16.3 Squeeze together the sides and slide up the upper cover

15.3a Mirror mounting bolts (arrowed)

15.4a Insert a screwdriver and gently prise the mirror from place

2 Undo the bolts, and prise out the scrivets securing the trim panel to the boot lid **(see illustration)**.

16.1a Push the clip at the base of the mirror rearwards, and slide it up from the windscreen mounting

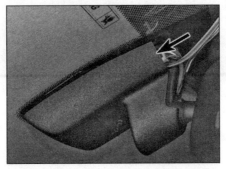

16.4 Pull apart the top edges (arrowed) and slide down the lower cover

15.3b Recover the mirror housing seal

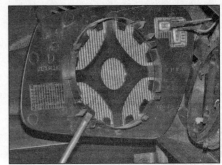

15.4b Insert the screwdriver into the mirror retaining clip as shown

3 Pull down the edge of the boot lid trim panel, and carefully prise the interior grab handle from the lid **(see illustration)**.

16.1b Mirror retaining clip – viewed from the front face of the mirror base

16.6 Rotate the mirror 60° anti-clockwise to release it

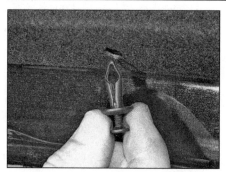

17.2 Undo the bolt and prise out the scrivets

17.3 Pull down the edge of the boot lid trim, and prise the grab handle from the lid

17.5 Pull the rubber grommet from the boot lid

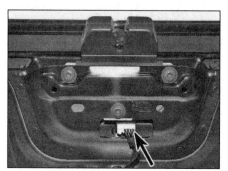

18.3 Boot lid lock wiring plug (arrowed)

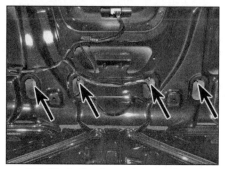

18.5 Undo the 4 nuts (arrowed) and remove the release button assembly

4 Note their fitted positions, then disconnect the various wiring connectors on the inside of the boot lid.

5 Prise the rubber grommet from the left-hand corner of the boot lid, and pull the wiring loom through **(see illustration)**.

6 Mark the position of the hinge arms with a pencil. Place rags beneath each corner of the boot lid, to prevent damage to the paintwork.

7 With the help of an assistant, unscrew the mounting bolts and lift the boot lid from the car.

Refitting

8 Refitting is a reversal of the removal procedure, noting the following points:
  a) *Check that the boot lid is correctly aligned with the surrounding bodywork, with an equal clearance around its edge.*
  b) *Adjustment can be made by loosening*

the hinge bolts, and moving the boot lid within the elongated mounting holes.
  c) *Check that the lock enters the striker centrally when the boot lid is closed.*

18 Boot lid lock components – removal and refitting

Removal

1 Undo the bolts, and prise out the scrivets securing the trim panel to the boot lid **(see illustration 17.2)**.

2 Pull down the edge of the boot lid trim panel, and carefully prise the interior grab handle from the lid **(see illustration 17.3)**.

3 Disconnect the wiring plug from the lock assembly **(see illustration)**.

4 Using a Torx key, unscrew the lock mounting bolts, and withdraw the lock.

5 If required, undo the nuts and remove the boot lid lock release button assembly **(see illustration)**.

Refitting

6 Refitting is a reversal of the removal procedure.

19 Tailgate – removal and refitting

Removal

1 Disconnect the battery negative (earth) lead (Chapter 5).

2 The tailgate may be unbolted from the hinges and the hinges left in position.

3 On models without a rear spoiler, remove the two bolts from the high-level brake light cover, and disconnect the bulbholder wiring and washer pipe **(see illustrations)**. On models with a rear spoiler, undo the bolts, remove the high-level brake light and disconnect the wiring plug, then starting at the front edge, prise out the washer jet and disconnect the hose.

4 Undo the retaining bolts in the handle recesses, then pull trim panel away from the tailgate to release the retaining clips.

5 Carefully unclip the upper central tailgate trim (where fitted), then pull the rear window side trims inwards to release the clips **(see illustrations)**.

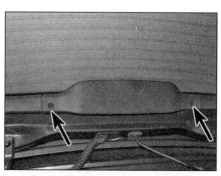

19.3a Undo the 2 bolts (arrowed) and remove the high-level brake light cover

19.3b Disconnect the washer jet pipe

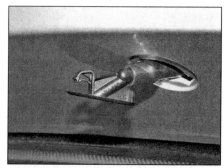

19.3c On models with a rear spoiler, prise out the washer jet and disconnect the pipe

6 Disconnect the wiring loom connectors through the tailgate inner skin aperture including the earth wiring. Attach a strong fine cord to the end of the wiring loom, to act as an aid to guiding the wiring through the tailgate when it is refitted.
7 Prise the rubber grommet from the tailgate aperture, and pull out the wiring loom. Untie the cord, leaving it in position in the tailgate for guiding the wire through on refitting.
8 Have an assistant support the tailgate in its open position.
9 Using a small screwdriver, prise off the clip securing the struts to the tailgate. Pull the sockets from the ball-studs, and move the struts downwards **(see illustration 20.2)**.
10 Unscrew and remove the hinge bolts (two each side) from the tailgate **(see illustration)**. Withdraw the tailgate from the body aperture, taking care not to damage the paintwork.
11 If the hinges are to be removed from the roof panel, remove the D-pillar trim panels as described in Section 28.
12 Carefully pull down the rear edge of the headlining for access to the nuts and bolts. Take care not to damage the headlining.
13 Unscrew the mounting nuts and bolts for the hinges from the rear roof panel.

Refitting

14 Refitting is a reversal of the removal procedure, but check that the tailgate is located centrally in the body aperture, and that the striker enters the lock centrally. If necessary, loosen the mounting nuts and reposition the tailgate as required.

20 Support struts – removal and refitting

Removal

1 Have an assistant support the tailgate, boot or bonnet in its open position.
2 Prise off the upper spring clip securing the strut to the tailgate, boot or bonnet, then pull the socket from the ball-stud **(see illustration)**.
3 Similarly prise off the bottom clip, and pull the socket from the ball-stud. Withdraw the strut.

Refitting

4 Refitting is a reversal of the removal procedure, making sure that the strut is fitted the same way up as when it was removed.

21 Tailgate lock components – removal and refitting

Removal

Estate

1 With the tailgate open, undo the 2 bolts in

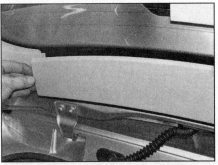

19.5a Pull away the upper, central tailgate trim (models with a rear spoiler)

19.10 Tailgate hinge bolts

the handle recesses and unclip the trim panel from the tailgate **(see illustration)**.
2 Disconnect the electrical connector from the tailgate lock assembly **(see illustration)**.
3 Undo the 3 lock securing bolts and remove the lock assembly.

21.1 Undo the bolt in the tailgate handle recess (arrowed)

21.4 Undo the bolt (arrowed) each side in the handle recess

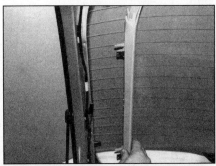

19.5b Pull the window side trims inwards

20.2 Prise the retaining clip from the ends of the strut

Hatchback

4 Undo the 2 bolts at the lower edge, and pull the interior trim panel from the tailgate **(see illustration)**.
5 Disconnect the wiring plug from the lock assembly **(see illustration)**.

21.2 Tailgate lock wiring plug (arrowed)

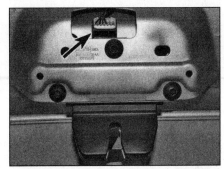

21.5 Tailgate lock wiring plug (arrowed)

21.7 Undo the 6 nuts (arrowed) and remove the release button assembly

6 Using a Torx key, unscrew the lock mounting bolts, and withdraw the lock.

7 To remove the release button assembly, undo the 6 nuts and remove the panel from the tailgate **(see illustration)**. Unclip the button from the panel.

Refitting

8 Refitting is a reversal of the removal procedure.

22 Central locking system
– testing, reprogramming, removal and refitting

Testing/reprogramming

1 Testing of the central locking/alarm system can only be carried out using Ford's WDS diagnostic tester.

2 Prior to reprogramming a remote locking transmitter, ensure the vehicle battery is fully-charged, and the alarm is not armed or triggered. Fasten all seat belts, and close all doors.

3 Turn the ignition switch from position I to position II four times within 6 seconds, then turn it to position 0 (off).

4 A chime will be heard to indicate that the 'learning mode' has begun.

5 Within 10 seconds of the previous step, press any button on the remote transmitter until a further chime is heard. This indicates the process has been successful. Turn the ignition switch to position II to exit the learning mode.

Removal

Generic electronic module (GEM)

Note: *If the GEM is to be renewed, the unit settings must be saved prior to removal, then initialised using the FORD WDS diagnostic tester.*

6 Removal and refitting of the GEM is described in Chapter 12.

Keyless entry system module

Note: *If the module is to be renewed, the unit settings must be saved prior to removal, then initialised using the FORD WDS diagnostic tester.*

7 Disconnect the battery negative lead as described in Chapter 5.

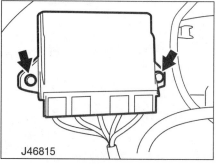

22.9 Keyless entry module retaining bolts (arrowed)

8 Remove the left-hand luggage compartment side panel, C-pillar panel and parcel shelf support as described in Section 28.

9 Undo the 2 retaining bolts, and remove the module **(see illustration)**. Disconnect the wiring plugs as the module is withdrawn.

Door motors

10 The door lock motors are integral with the locks. Refer to Section 13.

Boot lid/tailgate motor

11 The boot lid/tailgate motors are integral with the locks. Refer to Section 18 or 21 as applicable.

Refitting

12 In all cases, refitting is a reversal of the removal procedure.

23 Windscreen and fixed windows –
removal and refitting

1 The windscreen and rear window on all models are bonded in place with special mastic, as are the rear side windows. Special tools are required to cut free the old units and fit new ones; special cleaning solutions and primer are also required. It is therefore recommended that this work is entrusted to a Ford dealer or windscreen specialist.

24 Body side-trim mouldings and adhesive emblems –
removal and refitting

Removal

1 Body side trims and mouldings are attached either by retaining clips or adhesive bonding. On bonded mouldings, insert a length of strong cord (fishing line is ideal) behind the moulding or emblem concerned. With a sawing action, break the adhesive bond between the moulding or emblem and the panel.

2 Thoroughly clean all traces of adhesive from the panel using methylated spirit, and allow the location to dry.

3 On mouldings with retaining clips, unclip the mouldings from the panel, taking care not to damage the paintwork.

Refitting

4 Peel back the protective paper from the rear face of the new moulding or emblem. Carefully fit it into position on the panel concerned, but take care not to touch the adhesive. When in position, apply hand pressure to the moulding/emblem for a short period, to ensure maximum adhesion to the panel.

5 Renew any broken retaining clips before refitting trims or mouldings.

25 Sunroof –
general information and adjustment

Glass panel

1 Slide back the sun blind, and set the glass panel in the closed position.

2 Pull the panel guide arm covers inwards and remove them **(see illustration)**.

3 Undo the 2 retaining bolts each side, then lift the sunroof glass panel out from the vehicle.

4 When refitting, adjust the position of the rear edge of the panel so that it is flush with the roof, then tighten the bolts.

5 The remainder of refitting is a reversal of removal.

Sun blind

6 Remove the glass panel as described in paragraphs 1 to 3.

7 Close the sun blind, then undo the bolts each side securing the blind.

8 Manoeuvre the blind from the vehicle.

9 Refitting is a reversal of removal.

Sunroof mechanism and motor

10 Removal of the sunroof mechanism and/or motor involves removal of the headlining. This is a complex task, which requires patience and dexterity, and is considered to be beyond the scope of a DIYer. Consequently, we recommend this task be entrusted to a Ford dealer or upholstery specialist.

Adjustment

11 The sunroof should operate freely, without sticking or binding, as it is opened and closed. When in the closed position, check that the panel is flush with the surrounding roof panel.

12 If adjustment is required, slide back the sun blind, but leave the glass panel in the closed position.

13 Loosen the rear securing bolts (one each side). Adjust the glass panel up or down, so that it is flush at its back edge with the roof panel.

14 Loosen the front securing bolts (one each side). Adjust the glass panel up or down, so that it is flush at its front edge with the roof panel.

15 Retighten the four securing bolts.

16 Check the roof seal for wind noise and water leaks.

Drain tubes

17 There are four drain tubes, one located in each corner of the sunroof aperture.

18 To remove any obstruction insert a length of suitable nylon wire down through the tubes. If the obstruction cannot be cleared, access the drain tubes as follows:

19 The front drain tubes go down the front A-pillars; remove the lower trim panel to gain access to the drain tube.

20 The rear drain tubes go down the C-(Hatchback and Saloon) or D-pillars (Estate); remove the rear side trims to gain access.

26 Seats – removal and refitting

Removal

Front seat

1 Disconnect the battery negative lead, and position the lead away from the battery (see Chapter 5).

⚠️ **Warning: Before proceeding, wait a minimum of 5 minutes, as a precaution against accidental firing of the airbag unit or seat belt pretensioner. This period ensures that any residual electrical energy is dissipated.**

2 Undo the security bolt and disconnect the wiring plug under the front of the seat **(see illustration)**.

3 Undo the 4 seat retaining bolts and with the help of an assistant, manoeuvre the seat from the vehicle **(see illustration)**. Note that the seat is extremely heavy.

Rear seat cushion

4 On some models, unclip the plastic trim from the hinges at the front of each seat cushion.

5 Unscrew and remove the Torx mounting bolts from the hinges **(see illustration)**, then withdraw the seat cushion from inside the vehicle.

Rear seat backrest

6 Fold the rear seat cushion forwards (if not already removed), and fold the backrest forward.

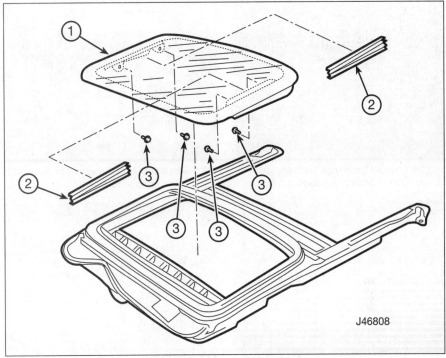

25.2 Sunroof glass panel details

1 *Glass panel*   2 *Guide arm covers*   3 *Retaining bolts*

7 Use a screwdriver to force rearwards the locking catch, and lift the outer end of the backrest from the hinge **(see illustration)**.

8 Pull the backrest from the centre pivot to disengage the mounting pin **(see illustration)**. If necessary, undo the seat belt stalk mounting bolt and manoeuvre the backrest from the vehicle.

26.2 Undo the bolt (arrowed) and disconnect the seat wiring plug

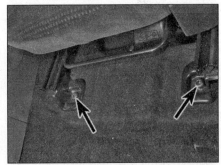

26.3 Seat front retaining bolts (arrowed)

26.5 Undo the bolts securing the rear seat hinges (arrowed)

26.7 Release the catch and lift the outer end of the backrest

26.8 Pull the backrest from the pivot to disengage the mounting pin

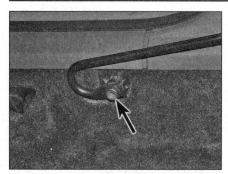

27.2 Lower anchorage bolt (arrowed) – 3-door models

27.5 Front seal belt upper anchorage bolt (arrowed) – 3-door models

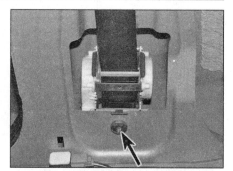

27.6 Seat belt inertia reel bolt (arrowed) – 3-door models

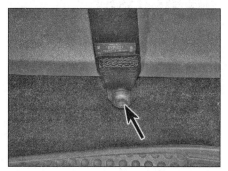

27.7 Front belt lower anchorage bolt (arrowed)

27.9 Front belt upper anchorage bolt (arrowed)

27.10 Inertia seat belt reel mounting bolt (arrowed)

Refitting

9 Refitting is a reversal of the removal procedure, tighten the mounting bolts to the specified torque.

27 Seat belts –
removal and refitting

⚠️ *Warning: Be careful when handling the seat belt tensioning device, it contains a small explosive charge (pyrotechnic device) similar to the one used to deploy the airbag(s). Clearly, injury could be caused if these are released in an uncontrolled fashion. Once fired, the tensioner cannot be reset, and must be renewed. Note also that seat belts and associated components which have been subject to impact loads must be renewed.*

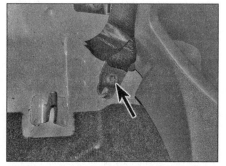

27.11 Rear belt lower anchorage bolt (arrowed)

Removal – front seat belt

1 Disconnect the battery negative lead, and position the lead away from the battery (see Chapter 5).

⚠️ *Warning: Before proceeding, wait a minimum of 5 minutes, as a precaution against accidental firing of the seat belt tensioner. This period ensures that any residual electrical energy is dissipated.*

⚠️ *Warning: There is a potential risk of the seat belt tensioning device firing during removal, so it should be handled carefully. Once removed, treat it with care – do not allow use chemicals on or near it, and do not expose it to high temperatures, or it may detonate.*

3-door models

2 Undo the anchorage rail bolt and slide the

27.12 Unclip the cover over the seat belt reel

belt off **(see illustration)**. Note that the spacer and washer are integral with the bolt.
3 Remove the B-pillar trim panel and rear side panel as described in Section 28.
4 Rotate the seat belt guide loop anti-clockwise and remove it from the B-pillar.
5 Undo the seat belt upper anchorage bolt **(see illustration)**. Note that the spacer and washer are integral with the bolt.
6 Unscrew the mounting bolt, and lift the seat belt reel unit to remove from the base of the pillar **(see illustration)**.

4-door & 5-door models

7 Undo and remove the bolt for the lower seat belt anchorage **(see illustration)**. Note that the spacer and washer are integral with the bolt.
8 Remove the B-pillar trim panel as described in Section 28.
9 Undo the seat belt upper anchorage bolt from the height adjuster **(see illustration)**.
10 Unscrew the mounting bolt, and lift seat belt reel unit to remove from the base of the pillar **(see illustration)**.

Removal – rear side seat belt

3-door & 5-door models

11 Fold the rear seat cushions forward, and unscrew the seat belt lower anchorage bolt **(see illustration)**.
12 Prise up the front edge, and unclip the cover trim from over the seat belt reel **(see illustration)**.
13 Unscrew the mounting bolt securing the seat belt reel unit, and withdraw from the vehicle.

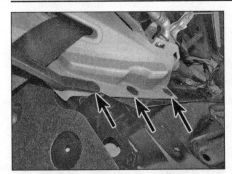

27.16a Prise out the 3 clips (arrowed) . . .

27.16b . . . and remove the panel over the inertia reel

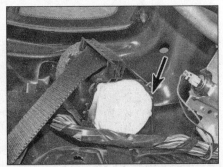

27.17 Undo the inertia reel bolt (arrowed)

Saloon

14 Fold the rear seat cushions forward, and unscrew the seat belt lower anchorage bolt.

15 Remove the C- and D-pillar trim panels as described in Section 28.

16 Fold the rear seat backrest forward, then remove the 3 clips securing the cover trim from over the seat belt reel (**see illustrations**). Feed the seat belt through the cover as it's withdrawn.

17 Unscrew the mounting bolt securing the seat belt reel unit, and withdraw from the vehicle (**see illustration**).

Removal – rear centre seat belt

18 The centre rear seat belt reel is attached to the rear seat backrest. Remove the backrest as described in Section 26.

19 Use a screwdriver to prise up the backrest release button surround trim, releasing the clips (**see illustration**). When refitting the trim, align the notch with the slot (**see illustration**).

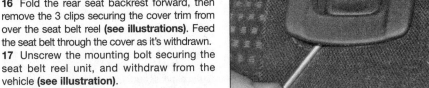

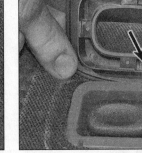

27.19a Prise up the backrest release button surround

27.19b Align the notch with the slot (arrowed)

20 Push down the backrest padding and use a screwdriver to depress the clip on the side of the headrest guide tubes (**see illustrations**). Pull the guide tubes from the backrest.

21 Depress the clips and remove the seat belt guide trim from the top of the backrest

(**see illustration**). Feed the seat belt through the slot in the trim.

22 Gently prise out the beading securing the top half of the backrest seat fabric (**see illustration**).

23 Carefully pull the seat foam padding from the top part of the backrest (**see illustrations**).

27.20a Push in the clip and pull the headrest guide tube from the backrest

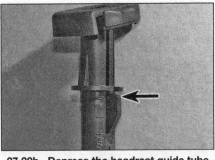

27.20b Depress the headrest guide tube clip (arrowed) – shown with the tube removed

27.21 Depress the clips and remove the belt guide trim

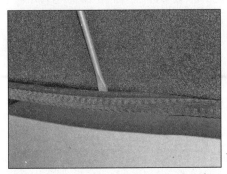

27.22 Prise out the beading securing the top part of the backrest fabric

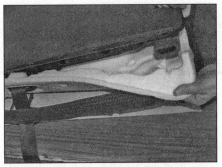

27.23a Pull the foam padding from the top part of the backrest . . .

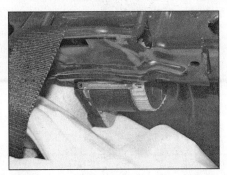

27.23b . . . to access the inertia seat belt reel

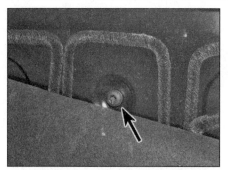

27.24 Peel away the top part of the seat backrest fabric to expose the inertia reel retaining bolt (arrowed)

24 Peel away the top part of the backrest fabric covering, which is glued in place **(see illustration)**.

25 Undo the Torx bolt and manoeuvre the seat belt reel from the seat backrest. Feed the seat belt through the seat backrest bracket as the reel is withdrawn.

Removal – front seat belt stalks

26 The front seat belt stalks are bolted to the seat frame **(see illustration)** and can be removed after removing the front seat as described in Section 26.

27 Note its routing, then unclip the pretensioner wiring harness from the underside of the seat.

28 Unclip the pretensioner wiring plug from the seat frame.

29 Undo the Torx bolt and remove the pretensioner/stalk.

27.26 Seat belt pretensioner retaining bolt (arrowed)

Refitting

30 Refitting is a reversal of the removal procedure, noting the following points:

a) Tighten the mounting nuts and bolts to the specified torque.

b) Make sure the seat belt reel locating dowel is correctly positioned.

c) Refit spacers in their correct position.

d) On 3-door models, make sure the anchor rail is located correctly.

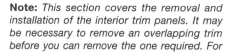

28 Interior trim panels – removal and refitting

Note: This section covers the removal and installation of the interior trim panels. It may be necessary to remove an overlapping trim before you can remove the one required. For more information on trim removal, look at relevant Chapters and Sections, where the trims may need to be removed to carry out any other procedures (eg, to remove the steering column you will need to remove the shrouds).

Sun visor removal

1 Unscrew the mounting bolts and remove the visor **(see illustration)**.

2 Disconnect the wiring for the vanity mirror light, where fitted.

3 Prise up the cover, unscrew the inner bracket mounting bolts, and remove the bracket **(see illustration)**.

Passenger grab handle removal

4 Prise up the covers, then unscrew the mounting bolts and remove the grab handle **(see illustration)**.

A-pillar trim removal

5 Pull the rubber weatherstrip away from the area adjacent to the pillar.

6 Starting at the top, carefully pull the A-pillar trim inwards to release the retaining clips **(see illustration)**. Note that it is quite likely that some of the clips will be damaged during the removal procedure.

B-pillar trim removal

4- and 5-door models

7 Pull the rubber weatherstrip from the rear door aperture adjacent to the B-pillar trim.

8 Prise up the front edge of the rear door sill trim to access the B-pillar trim **(see illustration)**.

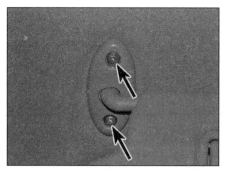

28.1 Sunvisor outer mounting bolts (arrowed)

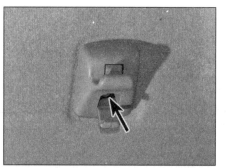

28.3 Prise up the cover to expose the sunvisor inner mounting bolt (arrowed)

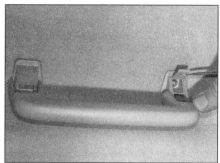

28.4 Prise up the covers to expose the grab handle bolts

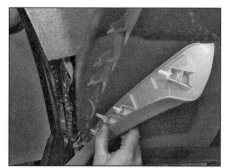

28.6 Pull the A-pillar trim inwards to release the clips

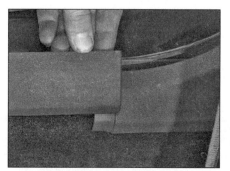

28.8 Prise up the front edge of the rear door sill trim . . .

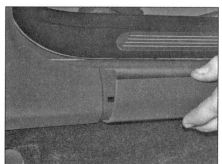

28.9 . . . and the rear edge of the front door sill trim

28.10a Prise out the cover . . .

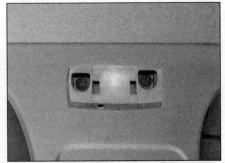

28.10b . . . and undo the 2 retaining bolts

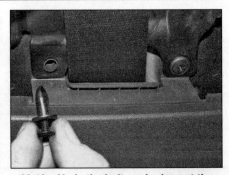

28.13a Undo the bolt, and prise out the scrivets . . .

28.13b . . . then pull the panel from the pillar

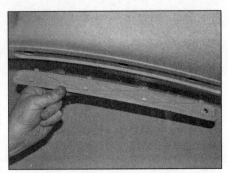

28.16a Prise down the cover . . .

28.16b . . . undo the 3 bolts (arrowed) . . .

9 Pull up the rear edge of the front door sill scuff plate panel (see illustration).
10 Prise out the cover and undo the 2 bolts at the top of the B-pillar trim (see illustrations).
11 If required, unscrew the seat belt mounting bolt from its lower anchorage point.
12 Carefully pull the upper B-pillar trim from the pillar.
13 Slacken the two bolts and prise out the scrivets from the top of the lower trim panel, then unclip it from the B-pillar (see illustrations).

3-door models

14 Undo the bolt securing the lower seat belt anchorage rail (see illustration 27.2).
15 Pull the rubber weatherstrip from the area adjacent to the B-pillar.
16 Carefully prise the cover from the upper window trim, undo the 2 bolts and lower the front end of the trim adjacent to the window (see illustrations).
17 Prise the cover from the top of the B-pillar trim, and undo the 2 bolts (see illustrations).
18 Pull the B-pillar trim inwards to release the retaining clips. Feed the seat belt through the trim as it's withdrawn.

C-pillar trim removal

3-door models

19 Remove the rear parcel shelf
20 Fold the rear seat backrest cushion forwards.
21 Pull the rubber weatherstrip from the tailgate aperture adjacent to the C-pillar.
22 Undo the 2 bolts, and pull the parcel shelf support inwards to release the clips (see

illustration 28.48). Disconnect any wiring plugs as the support is withdrawn.
23 Pull the C-pillar trim downwards/inwards to release the retaining clips (see illustration).

28.16c . . . and pull down the front edge of the window trim

28.17b . . . and undo the 2 bolts

4-door Saloon and 5-door Hatchback models

24 Pull the rubber weatherstrip from the door aperture adjacent to the C-pillar.
25 Starting at the lower edge, prise out the

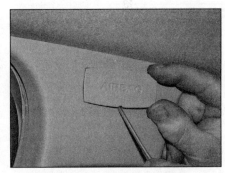

28.17a Prise away the cover . . .

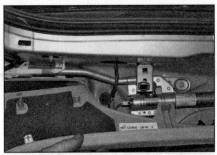

28.23 Pull the C-pillar trim panel forwards and inwards to release the clips – 3-door models

28.25a Prise out the cover . . .

28.25b . . . undo the bolt (arrowed) . . .

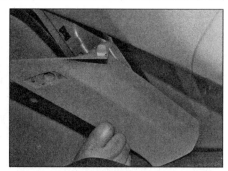

28.26 . . . and pull the C-pillar trim panel from position

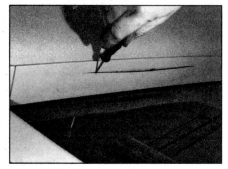

28.27a Prise down the cover . . .

28.27b . . . undo the 3 bolts . . .

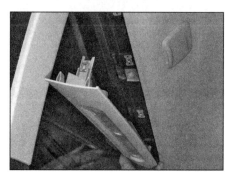

28.27c . . . and pull down the panel

plastic cover at the top of the trim and undo the bolt **(see illustrations)**.

26 Pull the C-pillar trim inwards to release the retaining clips **(see illustration)**.

Estate models

27 Prise down the cover, undo the 3 bolts, then pull down the trim panel at the top of the

rear side window aperture to release the clips **(see illustrations)**.

28 Pull the rubber weatherstrip from the door aperture adjacent to the C-pillar.

29 Starting at the front edge, prise out the plastic cover at the top of the trim and undo the bolt **(see illustrations)**.

30 Pull the C-pillar trim inwards to release the retaining clips **(see illustrations)**.

D-pillar trim removal

4-door Saloon models

31 Remove the parcel shelf and C-pillar trim panel as described in this Section.

32 Prise out the 2 clips at the base of the trim, then pull the rear window glass trim panel inwards to release the retaining clips **(see illustration)**.

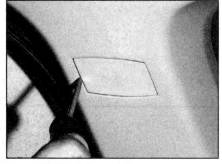

28.29a Prise out the cover . . .

29.29b . . . and undo the bolt

28.30a Release the clip at the front edge . . .

28.30b . . . and pull the C-pillar trim inwards

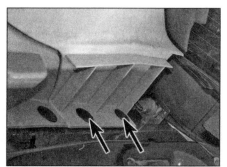

28.32 Prise out the clips (arrowed) at the base of the window trim panel

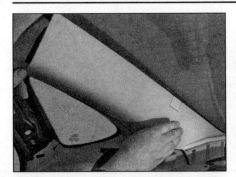

28.33 Starting at the top, pull the D-pillar trim forwards

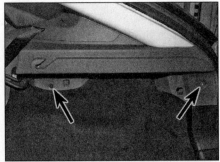

28.36 Parcel shelf support panel bolts (arrowed)

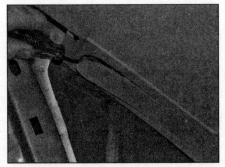

28.37 Prise out the cover to expose the bolts

28.38 Pull the D-pillar trim panel forwards and downwards

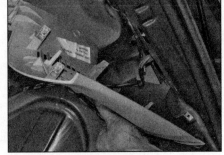

28.41 Pull the D-pillar trim inwards to release the clips

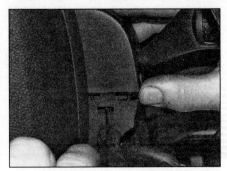

28.42 Rotate the steering wheel 90° and release the upper shroud clips

33 Pull the remaining D-pillar trim forwards to release it **(see illustration).**

5-door Hatchback models

34 Tilt the rear seat backrest forwards, then remove the C-pillar trim as described previously in this Section.

35 Pull the rubber weatherstrip from the tailgate aperture adjacent to the D-pillar

36 Undo the 2 bolts, and pull the parcel shelf support panel inwards to release the retaining clips **(see illustration).**

37 Carefully prise off the cover at the front, upper edge of the D-pillar, and undo the 2 bolts exposed **(see illustration).**

38 Pull the D-pillar trim forwards and downwards to release it **(see illustration).**

Estate models

39 Remove the luggage compartment side panel as described in this Section.

40 Pull the rubber weatherstrip from the tailgate aperture adjacent to the D-pillar.

41 Pull the D-pillar trim inwards to release the retaining clips **(see illustration).**

Steering column shrouds removal

42 To release the upper shroud from the lower shroud, turn the steering wheel 90°, insert a thin screwdriver into a hole at each side of the column **(see illustration)**. Lift the upper shroud from the column and unclip from the bottom of the instrument panel.

43 Using a thin screwdriver unclip the radio control switch from the lower shroud **(see illustration).**

44 Release the steering column height lever. Undo the 2 securing bolts from the lower shroud, and remove from the column **(see illustration).**

Luggage area side panel removal

3-door models

45 Remove the parcel shelf and the luggage compartment floor covering.

46 Tilt the rear seat backrest and cushion forwards.

47 Pull the rubber weatherstrip from the tailgate aperture.

48 Undo the 2 bolts and pull the parcel shelf support inwards to release the retaining clips **(see illustration)**. Disconnect any wiring plugs as the support is withdrawn.

49 Remove the 4 retaining clips and pull

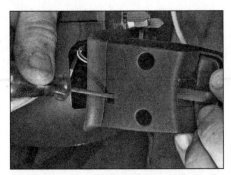

28.43 Depress the clip to release the audio switch from the shroud

28.44 Lower shroud retaining bolts (arrowed)

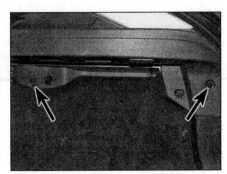

28.48 Undo the 2 parcel shelf support bolts (arrowed)

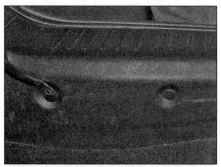

28.49 Prise out the tailgate sill trim clips

28.50 Pull the tailgate aperture corner trim panel inwards to release the clips

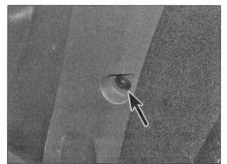

28.51 Prise out the clip (arrowed) at the front edge of the side panel

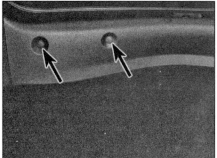

28.57a Prise out the 2 clips (arrowed) each side of the tailgate sill trim front face . . .

28.57b . . . then pull the trim upwards from place

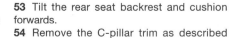

28.58 Pull away the trim panel in the lower corner of the tailgate aperture

the tailgate sill panel upwards to release the retaining clips **(see illustration)**.

50 Pull the trim panel in the lower corner of the tailgate aperture inwards to release the retaining clips **(see illustration)**.

51 Remove the retaining clip at the front

edge of the luggage compartment side panel, then pull the panel inwards to remove it **(see illustration)**.

5-door Hatchback models

52 Remove the parcel shelf and the luggage compartment floor covering.

53 Tilt the rear seat backrest and cushion forwards.

54 Remove the C-pillar trim as described previously in this Section.

55 Pull the rubber weatherstrip from the tailgate aperture.

56 Undo the 2 bolts and pull the parcel shelf support inwards to release the retaining clips **(see illustration 28.36)**.

57 Remove the 4 retaining clips and pull the tailgate sill panel upwards to release the retaining clips **(see illustrations)**.

58 Pull the trim panel in the lower corner of the tailgate aperture inwards to release the retaining clips **(see illustration)**.

59 Remove the retaining clip at the front edge of the luggage compartment side panel, then pull the panel inwards to remove it **(see illustration)**.

Estate models

60 Remove the luggage compartment floor covering.

61 Tilt the rear seat backrest and cushion forwards.

62 Pull the rubber weatherstrip from the tailgate aperture.

63 Prise up and remove the cover over the rear seat belt reel, then undo the 3 bolts and pull the luggage compartment upper side panel inwards to release the clips **(see illustrations)**.

64 Pull the tailgate sill panel upwards to release the retaining clips.

65 Pull the trim panel in the lower corner of the tailgate aperture inwards to release the retaining clips **(see illustration)**.

28.59 Prise out the clip at the front edge of the panel

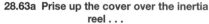
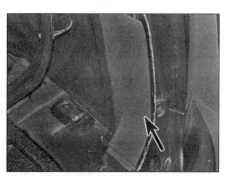

28.63a Prise up the cover over the inertia reel . . .

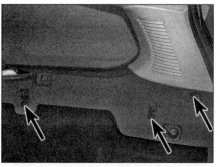

28.63b . . . then undo the 3 bolts (arrowed) at the top of the panel

28.65 Pull the trim panel (arrowed) inwards to release the clips

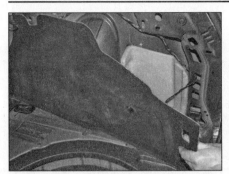

28.66 Pull the luggage compartment side panel inwards

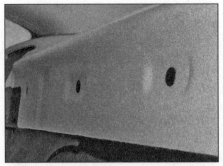

28.68 Prise out the clips at the front edge of the parcel shelf

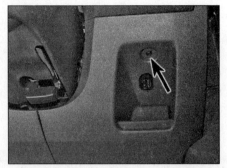

28.69 Undo the lower facia panel bolt (arrowed)

28.70 Unclip the diagnostic socket as the facia panel is removed

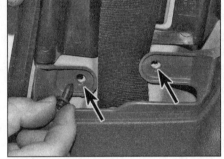

28.72 Undo the bolts and prise out the scrivets (arrowed)

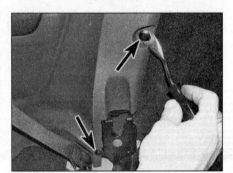

28.74 Prise out the clips (arrowed) at the rear of the side panel

66 Remove the retaining clip securing the side panel/storage compartment lid, then pull the side panel inwards and remove it **(see illustration)**.

Parcel shelf removal

Saloon only

67 Tilt the rear seat backrest forwards.
68 Remove the 4 retaining clips at the front edge, then pull the parcel shelf forwards **(see illustration)**.

Driver's lower facia panel removal

69 Undo the single bolt in the coin recess **(see illustration)**.
70 Pull the panel rearwards to release the clips, then unclip the diagnostic plug as the panel is withdrawn **(see illustration)**.

Rear side panel removal

3-door models

71 Remove the B-pillar trim panel as described previously in this Section.
72 Undo the 2 scrivets at the front upper edge of the panel **(see illustration)**.
73 Fold forwards the rear seat cushion and remove the rear seat backrest as described in Section 26.
74 Prise out the clips at the rear edge of the panel **(see illustration)**.
75 Pull up the rear edge of the door sill trim.
76 Starting at the front pull the rear side panel inwards to release the various push-in clips, and manoeuvre the panel from the vehicle.

Refitting

77 Refitting is a reversal of the removal procedure. Where seat belt fastenings have been disturbed, make sure that they are

tightened to the specified torque. Renew any broken clips as required.

29 Centre console – removal and refitting

Removal

Models up to 03/2007 with an armrest

1 Prise out the covers, and remove the bolts at the front of the console side panels (2 on the left-hand side, and one on the right) **(see illustration)**.
2 Starting at the front edges, pull the console side panels from place **(see illustration)**.
3 Starting at the rear, unclip the gear lever gaiter trim from the surround trim, then unclip the surround trim from the centre console, leaving the gaiter on the gear lever **(see illustrations)**.

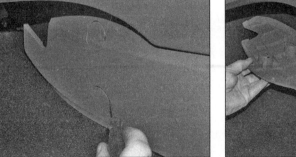

29.1 Prise out the covers, undo the bolts . . .

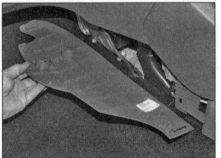

29.2 . . . and remove the console side panels

29.3a Unclip the gaiter trim . . .

29.3b ... and the surround trim

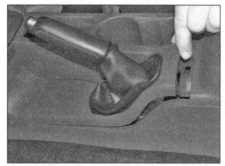

29.4a Unclip the handbrake lever trim ...

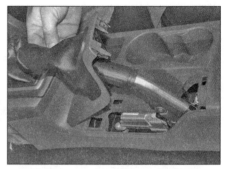

29.4b ... and pull it over the lever

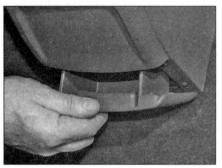

29.5 Lift the storage compartment to release the retaining clips

29.6a Undo the 2 bolts at the front of the gear lever aperture (arrowed) ...

29.6b ... and the 2 (arrowed) in the rear storage compartment aperture

4 Starting at the rear, unclip the handbrake lever surround trim from the centre console and remove it from the handbrake lever **(see illustrations)**.
5 Open the rear storage compartment, then lift it slightly to release the lower retaining

clips, and remove it from the console **(see illustration)**.
6 Undo the bolt each side of the gear lever aperture, and the bolts in the rear storage compartment aperture **(see illustrations)**.
7 Manoeuvre the centre console from

place, disconnecting any wiring plugs as it's withdrawn **(see illustration)**.

Models from 03/2007 with an arm rest

8 Prise up the gear lever surround trim **(see illustration 29.3a and 29.3b)**.
9 Prise out the covers and undo the bolts each side (2 on the left, one on the right-hand side), then remove the console side panels **(see illustrations 29.1 and 29.2)**.
10 Lift the armrest lid, and undo the 2 bolts exposed, then remove the trim panel at the front of the armrest pedestal/handbrake lever trim **(see illustrations)**. Carefully work the gaiter over the handbrake lever as the panel is withdrawn.
11 Lift out the rubber mat from the cup holders, and undo the bolt beneath **(see illustration)**
12 Pull the top half of the console upwards to release the retaining clips **(see illustration)**.

29.7 Manoeuvre the centre console over the gear lever and handbrake lever

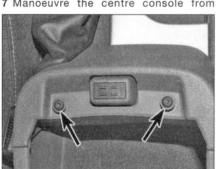

29.10a Undo the 2 bolts (arrowed) ...

29.10b ... and remove the trim panel

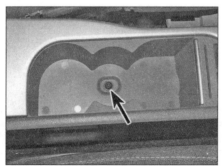

29.11 Undo the bolt (arrowed) under the cupholder mat

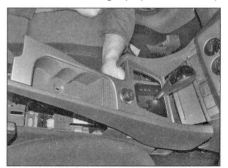

29.12 Pull the top half of the console upwards

29.13a Undo the 2 bolts (arrowed) at the front of the console . . .

29.13b . . . and the bolt each side at the rear

29.15 Prise up the handbrake lever surround trim

Disconnect the power outlet wiring plug as it becomes accessible.

13 Undo the 2 bolts at the front of the console, and the 2 at the rear each side **(see illustrations)**. Lift the console from place, and disconnect any wiring plugs as it's removed.

Models without an armrest

14 Prise up and remove the gear lever surround trim.

15 Starting at the rear, prise up and remove the handbrake lever surround trim **(see illustration)**

16 Prise out the covers and undo the bolts each side (2 on the left, one on the right-hand side), then remove the console side panels **(see illustrations 29.1 and 29.2)**.

17 Prise up the plastic cover in the rear storage box and undo the 2 bolts exposed **(see illustrations)**.

18 Undo the 2 bolts at the front of the gear lever aperture and manoeuvre the console from place **(see illustration 29.13a)**.

Refitting

19 Refitting is a reversal of the removal procedure.

29.17a Prise up the plastic cover . . .

29.17b . . . and undo the 2 bolts

30 Overhead console –
removal and refitting

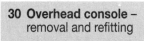

Removal

1 Starting at the front edge, carefully prise the interior light unit from the console **(see illustration)**. Disconnect the wiring plug as the light is removed.

2 On models with an electrically-operated sunroof, remove the sunroof switch (Chapter 12, Section 4).

3 Undo the 2 bolts in the light aperture, then starting at the front edge, prise down the console panel **(see illustration)**. Disconnect any wiring plugs as the console is removed.

Refitting

4 Refitting is a reversal of the removal procedure.

31 Glovebox –
removal and refitting

1 On models with an air conditioned glovebox, undo the fasteners and lower the GEM/fusebox from below the passenger's side of the facia, then reach up to the right-hand side of the glovebox and pull the cool air pipe from the fitting on the side of the box.

2 Open the glovebox lid, undo the 7 retaining bolts and pull the glovebox from place **(see illustration)**. Prise down the covers to access the lower 3 bolts. Take care not to lose the lock striker from the top of the glovebox as it's withdrawn.

3 Disconnect the wiring plugs as the glovebox is withdrawn. If required, the glovebox lid simply pulls from place.

4 Refitting is a reversal of the removal procedure, making sure that the glovebox is located correctly before tightening the bolts.

30.1 Insert a screwdriver, depress the clip, and pull the interior light from the console

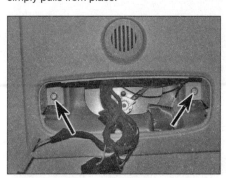

30.3 Console retaining bolts (arrowed)

31.2 Glovebox retaining bolts (arrowed)

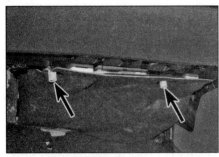

32.4 Release the fasteners (arrowed) securing the cover under the central junction box

32.5 Undo the fasteners (arrowed) and lower the central junction box

32.8 Remove the airbag lower support bracket nuts and bolts (arrowed). Note the earth lead attached to the lower bolt

32.9a Insert screwdrivers into the passenger's side inner air vent . . .

32.9b . . . to release the upper clips . . .

32.9c . . . and pull the vent from the facia

32 Facia – removal and refitting

Removal

1 Disconnect the battery negative (earth) lead (Chapter 5).
2 Remove the centre console as described in Section 29.

Models up to 04/2006

3 Remove the passenger's airbag module as described in Chapter 12.

Models from 04/2006

4 Squeeze together the sides and remove the fasteners, then remove the cover under the central junction box under the facia **(see illustration)**.

5 Rotate the fasteners anti-clockwise and detach the central junction box from the facia crossmember **(see illustration)**.
6 On models with air conditioning, reach up and disconnect the cooling hose from the glovebox.
7 Remove the glovebox as described in Section 31.
8 Undo the passenger's airbag module lower support bracket bolts/nuts and remove the bracket **(see illustration)**.
9 Use thin, flat-bladed screwdrivers (or similar) to release the passenger's side, inner air vent upper retaining clips, then manoeuvre the vent from the facia **(see illustrations)**.
10 Disconnect the passenger's airbag module wiring plug, then undo the module outer retaining bolts **(see illustrations)**.

All models

11 Remove the heater/climate control panel as described in Chapter 3.

12 Remove the instrument panel as described in Chapter 12.
13 Remove the driver's side lower facia panel as described in Section 28.
14 Remove the headlight switch, hazard switch and facia centre console switch panel as described in Chapter 12.
15 Disconnect the passenger cabin temperature sensor wiring plug (where fitted).
16 Release the clips and remove the glovebox light switch **(see illustration)**.
17 Pull the passenger's side facia outer trim rearwards to release the retaining clips **(see illustration)**.
18 Use a thin, flat-bladed screwdriver to release the air vents' retaining clips, then manoeuvre the vents from the facia **(see illustrations 32.9a, 32.9b and 32.9c)**.
19 Disconnect the wiring plug from the rear of the cigar lighter/power outlet and keyless entry module (where fitted).

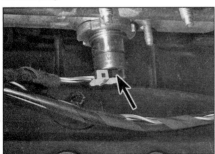

32.10a Squeeze together the clips (arrowed) and disconnect the airbag connector

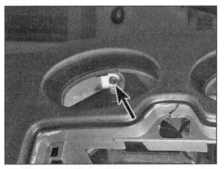

32.10b Undo the airbag bracket inner bolt (arrowed) . . .

32.10c . . . and outer bolt (arrowed)

32.16 Squeeze together the clips (arrowed) and push the glovebox light switch from place

32.17 Pull the passenger's side outer trim rearwards

32.20 Slide the damper from the glovebox lid

20 Detach the glovebox damper from the lid (see illustration).

21 Remove the left-hand steering column switch as described in Chapter 12.

22 Undo the 9 bolts and with the help of an assistant, manoeuvre the facia from the vehicle (see illustrations).

23 With the help of an assistant, pull the facia rearwards to release the extension panel retaining clips, and manoeuvre it from the cabin.

Refitting

24 Refitting is a reversal of the removal procedure. On completion, check the operation of all electrical components.

32.22a Undo the 3 bolts (arrowed) in the facia central aperture . . .

32.22b . . . 2 bolts (arrowed) in the glovebox aperture . . .

33 Wheel arch liner – removal and refitting

Removal

Front

1 Apply the handbrake. If the wheel is to be removed (to improve access), loosen the wheel nuts. Jack up the front of the vehicle and support it on axle stands (see *Jacking and vehicle support*). Remove the front wheel.

2 Unscrew the bolts securing the liner to the inner wheel arch panel.

3 Remove the bolts and clips securing the liner to the outer edge of the wheel arch and bumper. Withdraw the liner from under the vehicle.

Rear

4 Chock the front wheels, and engage 1st gear.

32.22c . . . 1 bolt (arrowed) in the instrument panel aperture . . .

If the wheel is to be removed (to improve access), loosen the wheel nuts. Jack up the rear of the vehicle and support it on axle stands (see *Jacking and vehicle support*). Remove the rear wheel.

5 Undo the bolts securing the liner to the outer edge of the wheel arch and bumper.

6 Remove the clips securing the liner to the

32.22d . . . and 3 bolts (arrowed) under the driver's side of the facia

inner wheel arch, and withdraw the liner from under the vehicle.

Refitting

7 Refitting is a reversal of the removal procedure. If the wheels were removed, tighten the wheel nuts to the specified torque.

Notes

Chapter 12
Body electrical system

Contents

Degrees of difficulty

Easy, suitable for novice with little experience	Fairly easy, suitable for beginner with some experience	Fairly difficult, suitable for competent DIY mechanic	Difficult, suitable for experienced DIY mechanic	Very difficult, suitable for expert DIY or professional

Specifications

System type	12 volt, negative earth

Bulbs — Power rating (watts)

Bulbs	Power rating (watts)
Brake light	21
Brake/tail light	21/5
Direction indicators	21
Direction indicator side repeaters	5 capless
Foglamp:	
Front	35 H8
Rear	21
Headlight:	
Halogen:	
Dipped	55 H7
Main	55 H1
Gas discharge headlights:	
Dipped	35 DS2
Main	55 H1
Glovebox light	3 capless
High-level brake light	5
Interior light	10
Number plate light	5
Luggage compartment light	5 capless
Reading light	5
Reversing light	21
Sidelights	5
Vanity mirror	5

Torque wrench settings	Nm	lbf ft
Airbag control unit nuts	7	5
Crash sensor bolts	6	4

1 General information and precautions

Warning: Before carrying out any work on the electrical system, read through the precautions given in 'Safety first!' at the beginning of this manual, and in Chapter 5.

1 The electrical system is of 12 volt negative earth type. Power for the lights and all electrical accessories is supplied by asilver-calcium type battery which is charged by the alternator.

2 This Chapter covers repair and service procedures for the various electrical components not associated with the engine. Information on the battery, alternator and starter motor can be found in Chapter 5.

3 It should be noted that prior to working on any component in the electrical system, the battery negative terminal should first be disconnected to prevent the possibility of electrical short-circuits and/or fires. **Note:** *If the vehicle has a security-coded radio, check that you have a copy of the code number before disconnecting the battery. Refer to your Ford dealer if in doubt.*

2 Electrical fault finding – general information

Note: *Refer to the precautions given in 'Safety first!' and in Chapter 5 before starting work. The following tests relate to testing of the main electrical circuits, and should not be used to test delicate electronic circuits (such as anti-lock braking systems), particularly where an electronic control unit is used.*
Caution: The Ford Focus electrical system is extremely complex. Many of the ECMs are connected via a 'Databus' system, where they are able to share information from the various sensors, and communicate with each other. Due to the design of the Databus system, it is not advisable to backprobe the ECMs with a multimeter in the traditional manner. Instead, the electrical systems are equipped with a sophisticated self-diagnosis system, which can interrogate the various ECMs to reveal stored fault codes, and help pinpoint faults. In order to access the self-diagnosis system, specialist test equipment (fault code reader/scanner) is required.

General

1 Typically, electrical circuit consists of an electrical component, any switches, relays, motors, fuses, fusible links or circuit breakers related to that component, and the wiring and connectors which link the component to both the battery and the chassis. To help

to pinpoint a problem in an electrical circuit, wiring diagrams are included at the end of this Chapter.

2 Have a good look at the appropriate wiring diagram before attempting to diagnose an electrical fault, to obtain a complete understanding of the components included in the particular circuit concerned. The possible sources of a fault can be narrowed down by noting if other components related to the circuit are operating properly. If several components or circuits fail at one time, the problem is likely to be related to a shared fuse or earth connection.

3 An electrical problem will usually stem from simple cause, such as loose or corroded connections, a faulty earth connection, a blown fuse, a melted fusible link, or a faulty relay (refer to Section 3 for details of testing relays). Visually inspect the condition of all fuses, wires and connections in a problem circuit before testing the components. Use the wiring diagrams to determine which terminal connections will need to be checked in order to pinpoint the trouble-spot.

4 The basic tools required for electrical fault finding include a circuit tester or voltmeter (a 12 volt bulb with a set of test leads can also be used for certain tests); a self-powered test light (sometimes known as a continuity tester); an ohmmeter (to measure resistance); a battery and set of test leads; and a jumper wire, preferably with a circuit breaker or fuse incorporated, which can be used to bypass suspect wires or electrical components. Before attempting to locate a problem with test instruments, use the wiring diagram to determine where to make the connections.

5 Sometimes, an intermittent wiring fault (usually caused to a poor or dirty connection, or damaged wiring insulation) can be pinpointed by performing a wiggle test on the wiring. This involves wiggling the wiring by hand to see if the fault occurs as the wiring is moved. It should be possible to narrow down the source of the fault to a particular section of wiring. This method of testing can be used in conjunction with any of the tests described in the following sub-Sections.

6 Apart from problems due to poor connections, two basic types of fault can occur in an electrical circuit: open-circuit, or short-circuit.

7 Largely, open-circuit faults are caused by a break somewhere in the circuit, which prevents current from flowing. An open-circuit fault will prevent a component from working, but will not cause the relevant circuit fuse to blow.

8 Low resistance or short-circuit faults are caused by a 'short'; a failure point which allows the current flowing in the circuit to 'escape' along an alternative route, somewhere in the circuit. This typically occurs when a positive supply wire touches either an earth wire, or an earthed component such as the bodyshell. Such

faults are normally caused by a breakdown in wiring insulation, A short circuit fault will normally cause the relevant circuit fuse to blow.

9 Fuses are designed to protect a circuit from being overloaded. A blown fuse indicates that there may be problem in that particular circuit and it is important to identify and rectify the problem before renewing the fuse. Always renew a blown fuse with one of the correct current rating; fitting a fuse of a different rating may cause an overloaded circuit to overheat and even catch fire.

Finding an open-circuit

10 One of the most straightforward ways of finding an open-circuit fault is by using a circuit test meter or voltmeter. Connect one lead of the meter to either the negative battery terminal or a known good earth. Connect the other lead to a connector in the circuit being tested, preferably nearest to the battery or fuse. Switch on the circuit, bearing in mind that some circuits are live only when the ignition switch is moved to a particular position. If voltage is present (indicated either by the tester bulb lighting or a voltmeter reading, as applicable), this means that the section of the circuit between the relevant connector and the battery is problem-free. Continue to check the remainder of the circuit in the same fashion. When a point is reached at which no voltage is present, the problem must lie between that point and the previous test point with voltage. Most problems can be traced to a broken, corroded or loose connection.

Warning: Under no circumstances may live measuring instruments such as ohmmeters, voltmeters or a bulb and test lead be used to test any of the airbag circuitry. Any testing of these components must be left to a Ford dealer or specialist, as there is a danger of activating the system if the correct procedures are not followed.

Finding a short-circuit

11 Loading the circuit during testing will produce false results and may damage your test equipment, so all electrical loads must be disconnected from the circuit before it can be checked for short circuits. Loads are the components which draw current from a circuit, such as bulbs, motors, heating elements, etc.

12 Keep both the ignition and the circuit under test switched off, then remove the relevant fuse from the circuit, and connect a circuit test meter or voltmeter to the fuse connections.

13 Switch on the circuit, bearing in mind that some circuits are live only when the ignition switch is moved to a particular position. If voltage is present (indicated either by the tester bulb lighting or a voltmeter reading, as applicable), this means that there is a short-

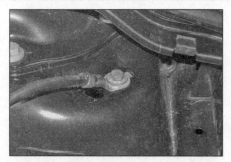

2.14a Earth connection on the left-hand side suspension turret in the engine compartment . . .

2.14b . . . left-hand chassis member in the engine compartment (under the air filter) . . .

2.14c . . . left-hand transmission mounting (under the battery tray) . . .

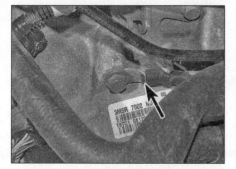

2.14d . . . transmission bellhousing (arrowed) . . .

2.14e . . . right-hand facia support bracket (arrowed) . . .

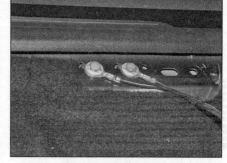

2.14f . . . left- and right-hand front door sills (under the sill trims)

circuit. If no voltage is present, but the fuse still blows with the load(s) connected, this indicates an internal fault in the load(s).

Finding an earth fault

14 The battery negative terminal is connected to 'earth': the metal of the engine/transmission and the car body – and most systems are wired so that they only receive a positive feed, the current returning through the metal of the car body. This means that the component mounting and the body form part of that circuit. Loose or corroded mountings can therefore cause a range of electrical faults, ranging from total failure of a circuit, to a puzzling partial fault. In particular, lights may shine dimly (especially when another circuit sharing the same earth point is in operation), motors (eg, wiper motors or the radiator auxiliary cooling fan motor) may run slowly, and the operation of one circuit may have an

apparently unrelated effect on another. Note that on many vehicles, earth straps are used between certain components, such as the engine/transmission and the body, usually where there is no metal-to-metal contact between components due to flexible rubber mountings, etc **(see illustrations)**.

15 To check whether a component is properly earthed, disconnect the battery and connect one lead of an ohmmeter to a known good earth point. Connect the other lead to the wire or earth connection being tested. The resistance reading should be zero; if not, check the connection as follows.

16 If an earth connection is thought to be faulty, dismantle the connection and clean back to bare metal both the bodyshell and the wire terminal or the component earth connection mating surface. Be careful to remove all traces of dirt and corrosion, then use a knife to trim away any paint, so

that a clean metal-to-metal joint is made. On reassembly, tighten the joint fasteners securely; if a wire terminal is being refitted, use serrated washers between the terminal and the bodyshell to ensure a clean and secure connection. When the connection is remade, prevent the onset of corrosion in the future by applying a coat of petroleum jelly or silicone-based grease or by spraying on (at regular intervals) a proprietary ignition sealer or a water dispersant lubricant.

---

3 Fuses and relays – general information

Main fuses

1 The fuses are located on a single panel under the passenger's side of the facia (also known as the central junction box), and in a fusebox on the left-hand side of the engine compartment (also known as the engine junction box).

2 Access to the passenger cabin fuses is gained by removing the trim panel concealing the fusebox. The panel is secured by 2 fasteners. Undo the fasteners and allow the panel to drop down. Rotate the fusebox fasteners anti-clockwise, lower the fusebox from place, and pull it towards you. Hook the fusebox into the rear part of the bracket **(see illustrations)**.

3 To access the engine compartment fusebox, open the bonnet, pull up on the lever and open the fusebox cover **(see illustration)**.

4 Each fuse is numbered; the fuses' ratings

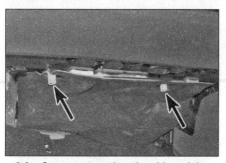

3.2a Squeeze together the sides of the fasteners to release them (arrowed) and lower the panel

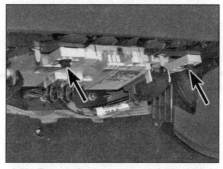

3.2b Rotate the fasteners anti-clockwise (arrowed) . . .

3.2c . . . then pull the fusebox rearwards

3.3 Release the clip at the rear then lift off the engine compartment fusebox cover

and circuits they protect are listed on the rear face of the cover panel. A list of fuses is given with the wiring diagrams.

5 To remove a fuse, first switch off the circuit concerned (or the ignition), then pull the fuse out of its terminals – a pair of tweezers provided specifically for this purpose is fitted on the underside of the engine compartment fusebox cover. The wire within the fuse should be visible; if the fuse is blown the wire will have a break in it, which will be visible through the plastic casing.

6 Always renew a fuse with one of an identical rating; never use a fuse with a different rating from the original or substitute anything else. Never renew a fuse more than once without tracing the source of the trouble. The fuse rating is stamped on top of the fuse; note that the fuses are also colour-coded for easy recognition.

7 If a new fuse blows immediately, find the cause before renewing it again; a short to earth as a result of faulty insulation is most likely. Where a fuse protects more than one circuit, try to isolate the defect by switching on each circuit in turn (if possible) until the fuse blows again. Always carry a supply of spare fuses of each relevant rating on the vehicle, a spare of each rating should be clipped into the base of the fusebox.

8 Note that some circuits are protected by 'maxi' fuses fitted in the engine compartment fusebox. These fuses are physically much bigger than the normal fuses, and have correspondingly higher ratings. Should one of these fuses fail, have the circuit examined a Ford dealer or specialist prior to renewing the fuse.

9 Two fusible links are fitted to the battery positive lead. These are designed to protect the starter motor and alternator wiring harnesses from damage resulting from a major

fault. If either of these two links should fail, do not renew them until the circuit concerned has been examined.

Relays

10 The main relays are located in the and engine compartment fusebox. The location and function of the relays is given on the underside of the fusebox lid.

11 The relays are of sealed construction, and cannot be repaired if faulty. The relays are of the plug-in type, and may be removed by pulling directly from their terminals. In some cases, it will be necessary to prise the two plastic clips outwards before removing the relay.

12 If a circuit or system controlled by a relay develops a fault and the relay is suspect, operate the system; if the relay is functioning, it should be possible to hear it click as it is energised. If this is the case, the fault lies with the components or wiring of the system. If the relay is not being energised, then either the relay is not receiving a main supply or a switching voltage, or the relay itself is faulty. Testing is by the substitution of a known good unit, but be careful; while some relays are identical in appearance and in operation, others look similar but perform different functions.

13 To renew a relay, first ensure that the ignition switch is off. The relay can then simply be pulled out from the socket and the new relay pressed in.

4   Ignition switch –
removal and refitting

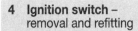

Removal

1 Ensure the battery negative lead has been disconnected as described in Chapter 5, then turn the ignition switch to position I.

2 Using a thin screwdriver, release the locking clip at the front edge, the remove the audio control switch from the steering column (where fitted) **(see illustration)**. Disconnect the wiring plug as the switch is withdrawn.

3 Rotate the steering wheel as necessary to access the column upper shroud retaining clips. Release the clips and remove the shroud **(see illustration)**.

4 Undo the bolts and remove the steering column lower shroud **(see illustration)**. Release the steering column adjustment lever to remove the shroud.

5 Disconnect the wiring plug, then depress the clips and remove the ignition switch **(see illustration)**. Do not turn the lock cylinder (key) from position I whilst the ignition switch is removed.

6 With the key still in position I, insert a thin rod into the hole in the lower part of the cylinder housing and depress spring-loaded locking lug, and pull the cylinder from the housing **(see illustrations)**.

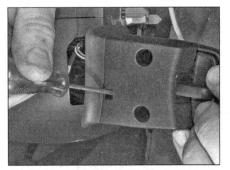

4.2 Depress the clip and remove the audio control switch from the column shroud

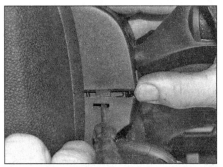

4.3 Rotate the steering wheel and release the upper shroud retaining clip each side

4.4 Lower steering column shroud bolts (arrowed)

4.5 Release the clips (arrowed) and pull the switch from the lock

Refitting

7 Refitting is a reversal of removal. Note that the lock cylinder (key) must be in position I prior to refitting the ignition switch.

5 Switches – removal and refitting

Steering column switches

1 Using a thin screwdriver, release the locking clip at the front edge, then remove the audio control switch from the steering column (where fitted) (**see illustration 4.2**). Disconnect the wiring plug as the switch is withdrawn.

2 Rotate the steering wheel as necessary to access the column upper shroud retaining clips. Release the clips and remove the shroud (**see illustration 4.3**).

3 Undo the 2 bolts and remove the steering column lower shroud (**see illustration 4.4**). Release the steering column adjustment lever to remove the shroud.

4 Undo the bolts and slide the relevant switch from the assembly (**see illustration**).

5 If the multifunction switch/rotary contact carrier is to be removed, begin by removing the steering wheel as described in Chapter 10.

6 Disconnect the wiring plugs, undo the 4 bolts and slide the assembly from the steering column (**see illustrations**).

7 Refitting is a reversal of removal.

4.6a Insert a thin rod into the hole on the underside of the lock to release the locking lug . . .

Light switch

8 Remove the driver's side lower facia panel as described in Chapter 11.

9 Reach up, squeeze together the switch upper and lower retaining clips, and pull the switch from the facia (**see illustration**). Disconnect the wiring plug as the switch is withdrawn.

10 Refitting is a reversal of removal.

Glovebox light switch

11 Remove the glovebox as described in Chapter 11.

12 Disconnect the switch wiring plug.

13 Release the clips and remove the switch (**see illustration**).

14 Refitting is a reversal of removal.

4.6b . . . and pull the lock cylinder from the housing

Door mirror adjuster

15 The door mirror adjusters are integral with the window switch assemblies fitted to the door panels.

16 To remove the switch assemblies, using a flat-bladed, blunt tool, carefully prise away the grab handle recess trim (**see illustration**).

17 Detach the wiring connector, then undo the retaining bolts and pull the switch from the surround (**see illustration**).

18 Refit in the reverse order of removal.

Facia centre panel switches

19 Remove the facia-mounted audio unit as described in Section 18, then on models up to 03/2007, undo the 2 bolts and pull the surround trim from place (**see illustration**).

5.4 Undo the bolts (arrowed) and slide the relevant switch from place

5.6a Undo the bolts (arrowed) on the top . . .

5.6b . . . and the ones underneath (arrowed), then slide the multifunction switch/contact carrier assembly from the column

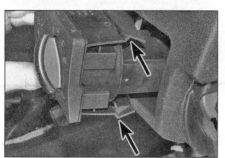

5.9 Reach up behind the facia and squeeze together the light switch clips (arrowed)

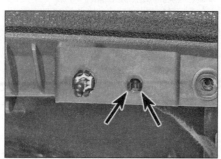

5.13 Squeeze together the clips (arrowed) and pull the glovebox light switch from place

5.16 Carefully prise the grab handle recess trim downwards

5.17 Undo the bolts (arrowed) securing the switch assembly

5.19 Audio unit surround trim bolts (arrowed)

5.20 Switch panel retaining bolts (arrowed)

5.21 Release the clips and pull the switch from the panel

5.26 Prise out the front edge, and remove the handle surround

5.27 Depress the clips (arrowed) and pull the switch from the surround

20 Undo the 2 retaining bolts and pull the switch panel from the facia **(see illustration)**. Disconnect the wiring plugs as the panel is withdrawn.

21 If required, release the clips and pull the relevant switch from the panel **(see illustration)**.

22 Refitting is a reversal of removal.

Sunroof control switch

23 Remove the overhead console as described in Chapter 11.

24 Press-out the retaining clips and pull the switch from the console.

25 Refit in the reverse order of removal.

Central locking switches

26 Prise out the front edge and remove the interior release handle surround **(see illustration)**. Disconnect the switch wiring plug as the surround is removed.

5.34 Handbrake warning switch retaining bolt (arrowed)

27 Disconnect the wiring plug from the switch, then depress the retaining clips and press the switch from the panel **(see illustration)**.

28 Refitting is a reversal of removal.

Window switches

29 To remove the switch assemblies, using a flat-bladed, blunt tool, carefully prise the grab handle recess trim downwards **(see illustration 5.16)**.

30 Detach the wiring connector, then undo the retaining bolts and pull the switch from the surround **(see illustration 5.17)**.

31 Refit in the reverse order of removal.

Courtesy light switches

32 The courtesy lights are controlled by microswitches incorporated into the door locks. The switches are not available separately. If defective, the door lock assembly must be renewed (see Chapter 11).

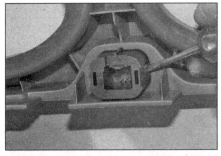

5.41 Depress the clips each side of the hazard warning switch – shown with the facia removed for clarity

Handbrake warning switch

33 Remove the centre console as described in Chapter 11.

34 Undo the single bolt and detach the switch **(see illustration)**.

35 Detach the wiring connector from the switch.

36 Refit in the reverse order of removal.

Brake light switch

37 Refer to Chapter 9.

Headlight control/foglamp/instrument illumination

38 These switches are integral with the light switch module. Removal is described earlier in this Section.

Hazard warning switch

39 Remove the facia-mounted audio unit as described in Section 18. then on models up to 03/2007, undo the 2 bolts and pull the surround trim from place **(see illustration 5.19)**.

40 Disconnect the wiring plug from the switch.

41 Depress the clips and push the switch from position **(see illustration)**.

42 Refitting is a reversal of removal.

Steering wheel switches

43 Remove the driver's airbag as described in Section 22.

44 Undo the bolts and remove the relevant switch pad **(see illustration)**. Disconnect the wiring plug as the switch pad is withdrawn.

45 Refitting is a reversal of removal.

Seat heating switches

46 Remove the facia centre switch panel as described in Paragraph 19 and 20.
47 Release the clips and slide the switch from the panel **(see illustration 5.21)**.

6 Exterior light bulbs – renewal

Note: *This section does not cover bulb renewal on models fitted with gas discharge headlights; refer to Section 9 for renewal details.*
1 Whenever a bulb is renewed, note the following points:
 a) *Remember that if the light has just been in use, the bulb may be extremely hot.*
 b) **Do not** *touch the bulb glass with the fingers, as the small deposits can cause the bulb to cloud over.*
 c) *Always check the bulb contacts and holder, ensuring that there is clean metal-to-metal contact. Clean off any corrosion or dirt before fitting a new bulb.*
 d) *Wherever bayonet-type bulbs are fitted, ensure that the live contacts bear firmly against the bulb contact.*
 e) *Always ensure that the new bulb is of the correct rating and that it is completely clean before fitting it.*

Halogen main beam

2 Remove the headlight unit as described in Section 8.

Models up to 12/2007

3 Push the retaining clips outwards and remove the plastic cover from the rear of the headlight **(see illustrations)**.
4 Pull the wiring plug from the bulb, then release the retaining clip and remove the bulb **(see illustrations)**. If the bulb is to be refitted, do not touch the glass with the fingers. If the glass is accidentally touched, clean it with methylated spirit.
5 Fit the new bulb using a reversal of the removal procedure.

Models from 12/2007

6 Peel away the plastic cap from the rear of the unit.

6.7 Depress the clip (arrowed) and pull the wiring plug from the bulb

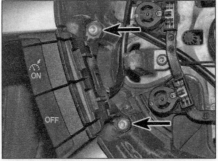

5.44 Steering wheel switch retaining bolts (arrowed)

7 Depress the clip and pull the wiring plug from the bulb **(see illustration)**.
8 Remove the bulb from the reflector **(see illustration)**. If the bulb is to be refitted, do not touch the glass with the fingers. If the glass is

6.4a Disconnect the wiring plug and unhook the clip (arrowed) . . .

6.8 Pull the bulb from the reflector

accidentally touched, clean it with methylated spirit.
9 Fit the new bulb using a reversal of the removal procedure.

Halogen dipped beam

10 Remove the headlight as described in Section 8.

Models up to 12/2007

11 Push the retaining clips outwards and remove the plastic cover from the rear of the headlight **(see illustration 6.3a and 6.3b)**.
12 Disconnect the wiring plug from the rear of the bulb, then release the retaining clip and remove the bulb from the headlight, noting which way around it's fitted **(see illustrations)**. If the bulb is to be refitted, do not touch the glass with the fingers. If the glass is accidentally touched, clean it with methylated spirit.

6.3b . . . and remove the plastic cover from the rear of the headlight

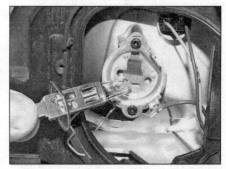

6.4b . . . then pull the bulb from the reflector

6.12a Pull the wiring plug from the bulb . . .

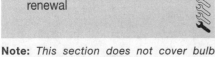

6.3a Release the clips around its edge . . .

6.12b . . . then unhook the bulb retaining clip

6.15 Depress the clip (arrowed) and pull the wiring plug from the bulb

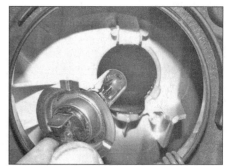

6.16 Pull the bulb from the reflector

13 Fit the new bulb using a reversal of the removal procedure.

Models from 12/2007

14 Peel away the plastic cap from the rear of the unit.
15 Depress the clip and pull the wiring plug from the bulb **(see illustration)**.
16 Remove the bulb from the reflector **(see illustration)**. If the bulb is to be refitted, do not touch the glass with the fingers. If the glass is accidentally touched, clean it with methylated spirit.
17 Fit the new bulb using a reversal of the removal procedure.

Sidelight

Models up to 12/2007

18 Remove the headlight unit as described in Section 8, then remove the cover from the rear of the headlight **(see illustrations 6.3a and 6.3b)**.
19 Squeeze together the clips and pull the bulbholder from the headlight unit **(see illustration)**. Pull only on the bulbholder – not the cable.
20 Pull the wedge-type bulb directly from the bulbholder.
21 Fit the new bulb using a reversal of the removal procedure.

Models from 12/2007

22 Remove the headlight as described in Section 8, then pull the rubber cover from the rear of the sidelight location **(see illustration)**.
23 Rotate the bulbholder clockwise and pull it from the reflector **(see illustration)**.
24 Pull the wedge-type bulb from the holder **(see illustration)**.
25 Fit the new bulb using a reversal of the removal procedure.

Front foglamp

26 Remove the foglamp as described in Section 8.
27 Disconnect the wiring from the bulbholder.
28 Rotate the bulbholder anti-clockwise and pull it from the foglamp **(see illustration)**. Note that the bulb is integral with the bulbholder.
29 Fit the new bulb using a reversal of the removal procedure.

Front direction indicator

30 Remove the headlight as described in Section 8.
31 Rotate the bulbholder anti-clockwise and pull it from the headlight **(see illustration)**.
32 Depress and twist the bulb to remove it from the bulbholder **(see illustration)**.
33 Fit the new bulb using a reversal of the removal procedure.

6.19 Squeeze together the clips (arrowed)

6.22 Pull the rubber cover away to access the sidelight bulb

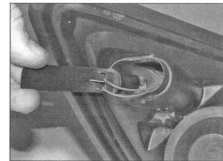

6.23 Rotate the bulbholder clockwise and withdraw it from the headlight

6.24 Pull the wedge-type bulb from the holder

6.28 Rotate the foglamp bulbholder anti-clockwise

6.31 Rotate the bulbholder anti-clockwise

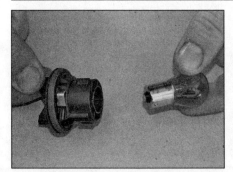

6.32 Depress and twist the bulb

6.34 Push the repeater rearwards and pull the front edge outwards

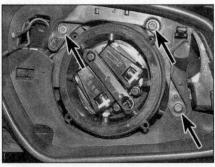

6.39a Undo the 3 bolts (arrowed) . . .

Direction indicator side repeater

In wing

34 Slide the side repeater lens rearwards, the pull the front edge from the wing **(see illustration)**.
35 Holding the bulbholder, twist the lens anti-clockwise and it from the place.
36 Pull the wedge type bulb from the holder.
37 Refitting is a reversal of removal.

In mirror

38 Remove the mirror glass as described in Chapter 11.
39 Undo the 3 bolts, release the 2 clips and remove the plastic trim around the mirror motor **(see illustrations)**
40 Slide forward the cover over the mirror housing.
41 Release the clip and remove the repeater **(see illustration)**.
42 Fold back the rubber sleeve, and pull the

bulbholder from the repeater. Pull the wedge type bulb from the holder.
43 Refitting is a reversal of removal.

Approach light

44 Remove the door mirror glass as described in Chapter 11.
45 Release the clip and manoeuvre the lens from the mirror housing.
46 Pull the wedge-type bulb from the bulb-holder.
47 Fit the new bulb using a reversal of the removal procedure.

Rear combination light

Hatchback models

48 Remove the rear light unit as described in Section 8.
49 Rotate the relevant bulbholder anti-clockwise and pull it from the light **(see illustration 8.15)**.

50 Push and twist the bulb anti-clockwise, and pull it from the bulbholder.
51 Refitting is a reversal of removal.

Saloon models

52 Working in the luggage compartment, rotate the fasteners 90° and remove the appropriate access panel on the relevant side **(see illustration)**.
53 Squeeze the plastic tabs and withdraw the bulbholder from the rear light unit **(see illustration)**.
54 Press and twist the relevant bulb anti-clockwise, and withdraw it from the bulbholder.
55 Fit the new bulb using a reversal of the removal procedure.

Estate models

56 Remove the rear light unit as described in Section 8.
57 Undo the bolts, and remove the bulbholder **(see illustrations)**.

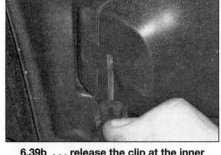

6.39b . . . release the clip at the inner edge . . .

6.39c . . . and the one at the lower, outer edge

6.41 Release the retaining clip

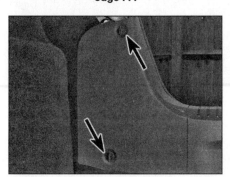

6.52 Rotate the fasteners (arrowed) and remove the panel

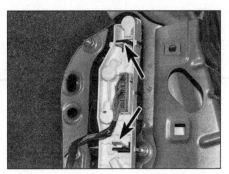

6.53 Squeeze together the plastic tabs (arrowed)

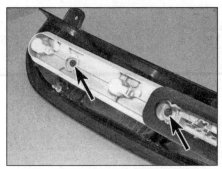

6.57a Undo the 2 bolts (arrowed) . . .

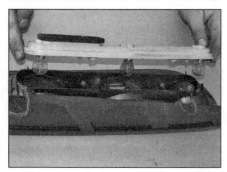

6.57b . . . and withdraw the bulbholder

6.61 Rotate the bulbholder anti-clockwise

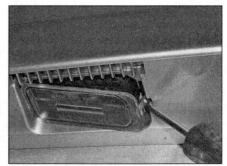

6.64 Release the clip and withdrawn the number plate light

58 Press and twist the relevant bulb anti-clockwise, and withdraw it from the bulbholder.
59 Fit the new bulb using a reversal of the removal procedure.

Rear foglamp/reversing light

60 Remove the relevant light unit as described in Section 8.
61 Rotate the relevant bulbholder anti-clockwise and pull it from the light **(see illustration)**.
62 Push and twist the bulb anti-clockwise, and pull it from the bulbholder.
63 Refitting is a reversal of removal.

Number plate light

64 On some models, undo the retaining bolts, and pull the lens from the tailgate/ boot lid. On other models, using a small, flat-bladed screwdriver, release the clips and carefully prise the lens from the tailgate **(see illustration)**.
65 Pull the festoon-type or wedge-type bulb from the contacts.
66 Fit the new bulb using a reversal of the removal procedure.

High-level brake light

Hatchback and Estate models

67 Undo the bolts and remove the light unit **(see illustration)**. Note that on models with a spoiler the bolts are accessed from the outside of the tailgate, whilst on models without a spoiler, they are accessed from inside.
68 Unclip the bulbholder, and pull the wedge-type bulb from place **(see illustration)**.
69 Fit a new bulb using a reversal of the removal procedure.

Saloon models

70 Starting at the rear edge, unclip the cover over the light unit **(see illustration)**.
71 Release the 2 clips and lower the light unit **(see illustration)**.
72 Disconnect the wiring plug, then unclip the bulbholder **(see illustration)**.
73 Pull the wedge-type bulb from place.
74 Refitting is a reversal of removal.

**7 Interior light bulbs –
renewal**

---

1 Whenever a bulb is renewed, note the following points:
  a) *Remember that if the light has just been in use, the bulb may be extremely hot.*
  b) *Always check the bulb contacts and holder, ensuring that there is clean metal-to-metal contact between the bulb and its live and earth. Clean off any corrosion or dirt before fitting a new bulb.*
  c) *Wherever bayonet-type bulbs are fitted, ensure that the live contact(s) bear firmly against the bulb contact.*
  d) *Always ensure that the new bulb is of the correct rating and that it is completely clean before fitting it.*

Reading lights

2 Inset a small flat-bladed screwdriver into the slot in the front face, depress the clip; and carefully prise the light unit from place **(see illustration)**.

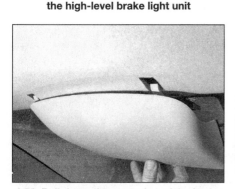

6.67 Undo the bolts (arrowed) and remove the high-level brake light unit

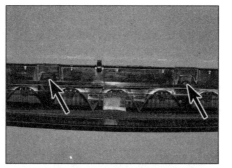

6.68 Release the clips (arrowed) and withdraw the bulbholder

6.70 Pull down the rear edge of the brake light cover

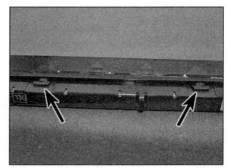

6.71 Release the clips (arrowed) and remove the light unit

6.72 Bulbholder retaining clips (arrowed)

7.2 Depress the clip at the front of the interior light

7.3 Twist the reading light bulbholder anti-clockwise and remove it

7.5a Prise the lens from place . . .

3 Twist the reading light bulbholder anti-clockwise and remove it **(see illustration)**. Pull the wedge type bulb from the holder.

4 Fit a new bulb using a reversal of the removal procedure.

Interior lights

5 Unclip the lens, and pull the interior light festoon type bulb from the contacts **(see illustrations)**.

6 Fit a new bulb using a reversal of the removal procedure.

Glovebox/luggage area light

7 Carefully prise the light unit from place **(see illustration)**.

8 Pull the wedge-type bulb from its holder.

9 Fit the new bulb using a reversal of the removal procedure. Note that the lens will only fit one-way round.

Footwell lights

10 Reach under the facia, and pull the wedge-type capless bulb from the holder **(see illustration)**.

11 Fit the new bulb using a reversal of the removal procedure.

Sunvisor/vanity mirror light

12 Carefully prise the light unit from place **(see illustration)**.

13 Pull the wedge-type bulb from the bulb-holder **(see illustration)**.

14 Fit the new bulb using a reversal of the removal procedure.

Instrument panel bulbs

15 On all models covered by this Manual, it

is not possible to renew the instrument panel bulbs individually as they are of LED design and soldered to a printed circuit board. It is not possible to renew a single LED. Where an LED is not functioning, the complete instrument panel must be renewed.

Switch illumination

16 The switches are illuminated by LEDs, and cannot be renewed separately. Refer to Section 5 and remove the switch.

Heater/air conditioning control panel illumination

17 The control panel is illuminated by non-renewable LEDs. If defective, the control panel may need to be renewed.

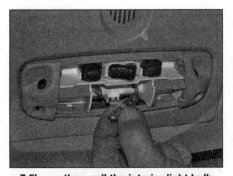

7.5b . . . then pull the interior light bulb from the contacts

7.5c Prise the rear interior light lens from place

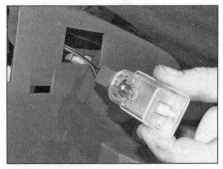

7.7 Prise the luggage compartment light from place

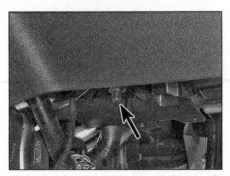

7.10 Pull the footwell light bulb (arrowed) from the holder

7.12 Carefully prise the vanity light lens from place

7.13 Pull the bulb (arrowed) from the holder

8.1 Headlight retaining bolt (arrowed)

8.2 Depress the clips (arrowed) and pull the headlight forwards – shown with the headlight removed for clarity

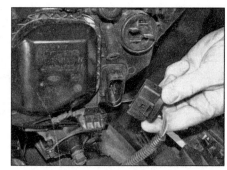

8.3 Disconnect the headlight wiring plug

8 Exterior light units – removal, refitting and beam adjustment

Headlight unit

Removal

Caution: On models equipped with gas discharge headlights, disconnect the battery negative lead as described in Chapter 5, prior to working on the headlights.

1 Open the bonnet, and undo the headlight upper retaining bolt **(see illustration)**.

2 Depress the retaining clips on the rear of the headlight, and pull the unit from place **(see illustration)**.

3 Disconnect the wiring plugs from the rear of the headlight as it's withdrawn **(see illustration)**.

4 If required, the headlight levelling motor can be renewed after the headlight has been removed, as follows: **Note:** *On models after 12/2007, it is not possible to renew the motor separately. If defective, it would appear that the complete headlight assembly must be renewed – check with your local dealer or parts specialist.*

5 Release the clips and remove the plastic cover from the rear of the headlight **(see illustrations 6.3a and 6.3b)**.

6 Disconnect the motor wiring plug, then rotate the motor clockwise (left-hand headlight) or anti-clockwise (right-hand headlight), manoeuvre the motor ball-head from the guide on the reflector and pull it from the headlight **(see illustrations)**.

Refitting

7 Refitting is a reversal of the removal procedure. On completion check for satisfactory operation, and have the headlight beam adjustment checked as soon as possible (see below).

Front foglamp

Removal – models up to 12/2007

8 Carefully prise out the trim above the foglamp, and the foglamp surround trim **(see illustrations)**.

9 Undo the 2 mounting bolts, withdraw the foglamp from the front bumper, and disconnect the wiring **(see illustration)**.

Removal – models from 12/2007

10 Carefully prise out the foglamp surround trim **(see illustration)**.

8.6a Disconnect the levelling motor wiring plug . . .

8.6b . . . then rotate the motor (see text) and disengage the ball-head from the guide on the reflector

8.8a Prise out the trim above the foglamp . . .

8.8b . . . and the trim around the foglamp

8.9 Foglamp mounting bolts (arrowed)

8.10 Prise away the foglamp surround trim

8.11 Foglamp mounting bolts (arrowed)

8.12a Foglamp adjustment screw (arrowed) – pre 12/2007 models . . .

8.12b . . . and post-12/2007 models

11 Undo the 2 mounting bolts, withdraw the foglamp from the front bumper, and disconnect the wiring **(see illustration)**.

Refitting

12 Refitting is a reversal of removal, but have the foglamp beam setting checked at the earliest opportunity. An approximate adjustment can be made by positioning the car 10 metres in front of a wall marked with the centre point of the foglamp lens. Turn the adjustment screw as required **(see illustrations)**. Note that only height adjustment is possible – there is no lateral adjustment.

Direction indicator side repeater

Removal and refitting

13 The procedure is as described for bulb renewal in Section 6.

Rear combination light

Hatchback and Estate models

14 Open the tailgate, and undo the 2 light unit retaining bolts **(see illustration)**.
15 Pull the light unit rearwards, and disconnect the wiring plug **(see illustration)**.
16 Refitting is a reversal of removal.

Saloon models

17 Remove the bulbholder as described in Section 6.
18 Undo the 3 retaining nuts, and remove the light unit **(see illustration)**.
19 Refitting is a reversal of removal. Ensure that the seal is correctly positioned.

Number plate light

20 The procedure is as described for bulb renewal in Section 6.

High-level brake light

Hatchback and Estate models

21 The procedure is as described for bulb renewal in Section 6.

Saloon models

22 Starting at the rear, unclip the plastic cover from the light unit **(see illustration 6.70)**.
23 Release the 2 clips and remove the light unit **(see illustration 6.71)**. Disconnect the wiring plug as the unit is withdrawn.
24 Refitting is a reversal of removal.

Rear foglamp/reversing lights

25 Reach up behind the light unit and release the retaining clips at its edge **(see illustration)**.

8.14 Rear light retaining bolts (arrowed)

26 Pull the light unit rearwards, and disconnect the wiring plug.
27 Refitting is a reversal of removal.

Beam adjustment

Halogen headlights

28 Accurate adjustment of the headlight beam is only possible using optical beam setting equipment, and this work should therefore be carried out by a Ford dealer or suitably-equipped workshop.
29 For reference, the headlights can be adjusted using the adjuster screws, accessible via the top of each light unit **(see illustration)**.
30 Some models are equipped with an electrically-operated headlight beam adjustment system which is controlled through the switch in the facia. On these models, ensure that the switch is set to the basic O position before adjusting the headlight aim.

8.15 Rotate the bulbholders (arrowed) anti-clockwise

8.18 Rear light retaining nuts (arrowed) – Saloon models

8.25 Release the clips (arrowed) at the edge of the rear foglamp/reversing light

8.29 Headlight beam adjustment screws (arrowed)

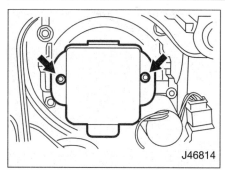

9.8 Undo the bolts (arrowed) and pull the bulb and module rearwards

J46814

31 On vehicles with adaptive front headlights (the headlight reflectors turn in the direction of the steering) it is possible to adjust the headlight beams for driving on the right-hand, or left-hand side of the road. Remove the headlight as described in this Section.

32 Release the clips and remove the cover from the rear of the headlight **(see illustrations 6.3a and 6.3b)**.

33 Press the lever on the side of the reflector upwards for driving on the right, and down for driving on the left.

34 For information on the lighting control module, see Section 9, paragraphs 19 to 21.

9 Xenon gas discharge headlight system – component removal, refitting and adjustment

General information

1 Xenon gas discharge headlights were available as an optional extra on all models covered in this manual. The headlights' dipped beam bulbs produce light by means of an electric arc, rather than by heating a metal filament as in conventional halogen bulbs. An electronically-operated shutter is fitted in front of the bulb which angles the light for dipped beam, then re-angles the light for main beam. A conventional halogen bulb is also fitted to augment the main beam light output. The arc is generated by a control circuit which operates at voltages of above 28 000 volts. The intensity of the emitted

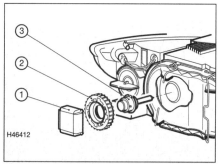

H46412

9.11 Xenon bulb details

1	Ignition module	2	Collar
		3	Bulb

light means that the headlight beam has to be controlled dynamically to avoid dazzling other road users. An electronic control unit monitors the vehicle's pitch and overall ride height by sensors mounted on the front and rear suspension, and adjusts the beam range accordingly, using the range control motors built into the headlight units.

⚠️ **Warning: The discharge bulb starter circuitry operates at extremely high voltages. To avoid the risk of electric shock, ensure that the battery negative cable is disconnected before working on the headlight units (see Chapter 5), then additionally switch the dipped beam on and off to discharge any residual voltage.**

Headlight main beam

2 Remove the headlight as described in Section 8.

3 Push the retaining clips outwards, and remove the plastic cover from the rear of the headlight **(see illustrations 6.3a and 6.3b)**.

4 Disconnect the wiring plug from the rear of the bulb, then release the retaining clip and pull the bulb from the reflector **(see illustrations 6.4a and 6.4b)**. Note how the lugs on the bulb engage with the slots in the reflector. If the bulb is to be refitted, do not touch the glass with the fingers. If the glass is accidentally touched, clean it with methylated spirit.

5 Fit the new bulb using a reversal of the removal procedure.

Headlight dipped beam

Caution: The dipped beam bulb is under gas pressure of at least 10 bars, therefore it is recommended that protective glasses are worn during this procedure.

6 Remove the headlight as described in Section 8.

Models up to 12/2007

7 Release the retaining clips and detach the plastic cover from the rear of the light unit **(see illustrations 6.3a and 6.3b)**.

8 Disconnect the wiring plug, then undo the 2 retaining bolts and pull the bulb and module rearwards **(see illustration)**. If the glass is accidentally touched, clean it with methylated spirit.

9 Fit the new bulb using a reversal of the removal procedure.

Models from 12/2007

10 Remove the plastic cap from the rear of the headlight, then disconnect the bulb module wiring plug.

11 Rotate the bulb locking collar anti-clockwise, and pull the bulb and module from the reflector **(see illustration)**.

12 Slide the locking collar upwards and remove the bulb from the module **(see illustration)**.

13 Fit the new bulb using a reversal of the removal procedure.

Sidelight

14 Remove the headlight unit as described in Section 8.

15 Pull the bulbholder from the headlight unit. Pull only on the bulbholder – not the cable.

16 Pull the wedge-type bulb directly from the bulbholder.

17 Fit the new bulb using a reversal of the removal procedure.

Lighting lamp control module

Note: *If a new module is to be fitted, it must be configured using Ford dedicated diagnostic equipment (WDS). Entrust this task to a Ford dealer or suitably-equipped specialist.*

18 The lighting control module is fitted to vehicles with Xenon high-intensity gas discharge lights, or models with adaptive front lighting system (see Section 8, paragraph 31). The module is located behind the driver's side lower facia.

19 Undo the single bolt, and remove the facia panel beneath the main light control switch. Unclip the diagnostic plug connector as the panel is withdrawn.

20 Disconnect the wiring plug, then release the clip each side and remove the module.

21 Refitting is a reversal of removal.

Front ride height sensor

Removal

22 The sensor is mounted on the lower control arm of the right-hand wheel. Apply the handbrake, then jack up the front of the vehicle and support it on axle stands (see *Jacking and vehicle support*). Remove the wheel.

23 Undo the bolt securing the sensor arm bracket to the control arm.

24 Drill out the 2 rivets securing the sensor bracket to the vehicle body.

25 Disconnect the wiring plus as the sensor is withdrawn.

Refitting

26 Refitting is a reversal of removal. Note that if a new sensor has been fitted, then a calibration procedure must be carried out. This requires access to Ford diagnostic equipment – entrust this task to a Ford dealer or suitably-equipped specialist.

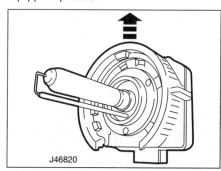

J46820

9.12 Slide the collar upwards

Rear ride height sensor

Removal

27 The sensor is secured to the left-hand lower control arm and the rear subframe. Chock the front wheels, then jack up the rear of the vehicle and support it on axle stands (see *Jacking and vehicle support*).

28 Disconnect the sensor wiring plug, then undo the bolts and remove the sensor, bracket and lever arm assembly.

Refitting

29 Refitting is a reversal of removal. Note that if a new sensor has been fitted, then a calibration procedure must be carried out. This requires access to Ford diagnostic equipment – entrust this task to a Ford dealer or suitably-equipped specialist.

Setting-up for left- or right-hand drive

Note: *This feature is also available on some halogen headlights (see Section 8, paragraphs 31 to 33).*

30 On models equipped with gas discharge headlights, the 'dipping' characteristics of the unit can be set-up for countries who drive on the left or right. Remove the headlight as described in Section 8.

31 Release the clips and remove the plastic cover from the rear of the headlight behind the dipped beam location.

32 Press the lever on the side of the reflector upwards for driving on the right, and down for driving on the left.

Beam adjustment

33 The basic alignment procedure of the headlights is the same as normal halogen headlights (see Section 8). However, before the procedure is attempted, the ride height sensors must be calibrated using dedicated Ford test equipment. Therefore this task should be entrusted to a Ford dealer or suitably-equipped specialist.

Range control positioning motor

34 Remove the headlight as described in Section 8.

35 Remove the cover from the rear of the headlight.

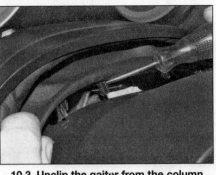

10.3 Unclip the gaiter from the column upper shroud

36 Disconnect the motor wiring plug, then undo the 2 retaining bolts.

37 Disengage the motor ball-head from the guide in the reflector and remove the motor.

38 Refitting is a reversal of removal.

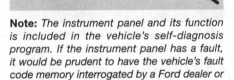

10 Instrument panel – removal and refitting

Note: *The instrument panel and its function is included in the vehicle's self-diagnosis program. If the instrument panel has a fault, it would be prudent to have the vehicle's fault code memory interrogated by a Ford dealer or specialist, prior to removing the panel.*

Note: *If the instrument panel is being substituted with a new or exchange unit, the assistance of a Ford dealer or specialist is required to download necessary software, and initialise/adapt the various instrument panel functions.*

Removal

1 Disconnect the battery negative lead as described in Chapter 5.

2 Fully extend the steering column, and move it to its lowest position.

3 Unclip the rubber gaiter from the steering column upper shroud, then pull the bezel attached to the lower part of the instrument panel rearwards and remove it **(see illustration)**.

4 Undo the 2 retaining bolts on the lower

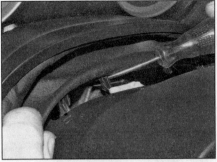

10.4 Undo the bolts at the lower edge (arrowed) the pull the top of the instrument panel rearwards

edge of the instrument panel, then carefully pull the top edge of the panel rearwards and manoeuvre it from place **(see illustration)**.

5 Disconnect the wiring plug(s) as the panel is withdrawn.

Refitting

6 Refitting is a reversal of removal, but see the note at the beginning of this section.

11 Windscreen wiper components – removal and refitting

Wiper blades

1 Refer to *Weekly checks*.

Wiper arms

Removal

2 If the wipers are not in their parked position, switch on the ignition, and allow the motor to automatically park.

3 Before removing an arm, mark its parked position on the glass with a strip of adhesive tape. Prise off the cover and unscrew the spindle nut **(see illustrations)**. Ease the arm from the spindle by rocking it slowly from side-to-side.

Refitting

4 Refitting is a reversal of removal, but before tightening the spindle nuts, position the wiper blades as marked before removal.

11.3a Pull of the rubber cap, undo the nut . . .

11.3b . . . and remove the wiper arm

11.3c Lift the cover to expose the wiper spindle nut – rear wiper

11.6a Prise forwards the clips (arrowed) . . .

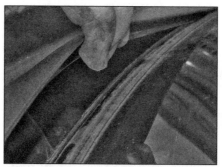

11.6b . . . then pull the scuttle cowling panel upwards from the base of the windscreen

11.7 Undo the bolt at each end (right-hand one arrowed) and pull the bulkhead extension panel forwards

and remove the bulkhead extension panel **(see illustration)**.

8 Undo the 3 bolts securing the motor linkage **(see illustration)**.

9 Move the assembly towards the left-hand side 20 mm to release the rubber mounting lug from the bracket on the bulkhead **(see illustration)**. Disconnect the wiper motor wiring plug as the assembly is withdrawn.

10 Using a screwdriver, carefully prise the linkage arm from the balljoint stud.

11 Undo the 3 bolts and remove the motor.

Refitting

12 When refitting, with the motor/linkage back in place, reconnect the wiring plug then operate the touch-wipe button to set the motor in the rest position. The remainder of refitting is a reversal of removal.

11.8 Undo the 3 bolts and slide the wiper linkage assembly 20 mm to the left . . .

Wiper motor

Removal

5 Remove the wiper arms as described in the previous sub-Section.

11.9 . . . to release the rubber mounting lug from the bracket

6 Remove the clips at the front edge, then pull the scuttle cowling panel upwards to release it from the base of the windscreen **(see illustrations)**. Lift the panel from place.

7 Undo the bolt at each end, release the 4 clips

12 Washer system – general

1 All models are fitted with a windscreen washer system. Estate models also have a tailgate washer, and some models are fitted with headlight washers.

2 The fluid reservoir for the windscreen/headlight washer is located behind the right-hand side inner wing, behind the wheel arch liner. The windscreen washer fluid pump is attached to the side of the reservoir body **(see illustrations)** and where headlight washers are fitted, a lift cylinder/accumulator is located in the supply tube, behind the front

12.2a The washer fluid reservoir is retained by 2 bolts (arrowed) – viewed from under the wheel arch

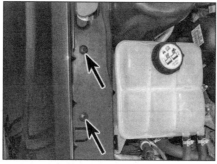

12.2b Remove the scrivets (arrowed) . . .

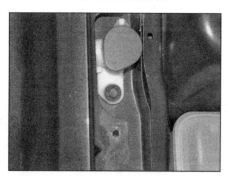

12.2c . . . to access the reservoir upper retaining bolt

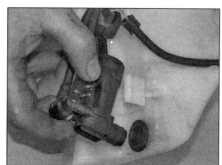

12.2d Pull the pump from the grommet in the reservoir . . .

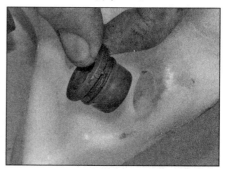

12.2e . . . then pull the grommet from the reservoir

12.2f The grommet incorporates a coarse filter

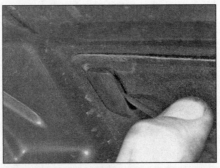

12.6a Prise out the bonnet insulation panel clips

12.6b Disconnect the hose from the underside of the washer jet

bumper. Access to the reservoir, pump and lift cylinder is achieved by removing either the right-hand front wheel arch liner or front bumper, and the plastic panel at the right-hand side of the engine compartment.

3 The tailgate washer is fed by the same reservoir, with a dual output pump.

4 The reservoir fluid level must be regularly topped-up with windscreen washer fluid containing an antifreeze agent, but not cooling system antifreeze – see *Weekly checks*.

5 The supply hoses are attached by rubber couplings to their various connections, and if required, can be detached by simply pulling them free from the appropriate connector.

6 The windscreen washer jets can be adjusted by inserting a pin into the jet and altering the aim as required. To remove a washer jet, open the bonnet, and disconnect the hose from the jet. Note that on some models, the bonnet insulation panel must be unclipped and removed (**see illustrations**).

7 Where applicable, disconnect the wiring plug, then push the jet forwards, and lift the rear edge. Manoeuvre the jet from the bonnet (**see illustration**).

8 The headlight washer jets are best adjusted using the Ford tool, and should therefore be entrusted to a Ford dealer or specialist to set.

9 On models with a rear spoiler, starting at the front edge, carefully prise the jet from place (**see illustration**). Disconnect the hose as the jet is withdrawn.

13 Tailgate wiper motor – removal and refitting

Removal

1 Make sure the tailgate wiper is switched off and in its rest position, then remove the tailgate trim panel as described in Chapter 11.

2 Remove the wiper arm and blade as described in Section 11.

3 Detach the wiring connector from the wiper motor.

4 Undo the 3 wiper motor mounting bolts and remove the wiper motor from the tailgate (**see illustration**). Check the condition of the spindle rubber grommet in the tailgate, and if necessary, renew it.

12.7 Press the jet forwards and lift the rear edge

Refitting

5 Refit in the reverse order of removal. Refit the wiper arm and blade so that the arm is parked correctly.

14 Horns – removal and refitting

Removal

1 The horns are located at the front end of the vehicle. Raise the front of the vehicle and support it securely on axle stands (see *Jacking and vehicle support*).

2 Release the fasteners and remove the splash shield under the radiator.

3 Disconnect the horn wiring plug, undo the mounting bolt and remove the horn from the vehicle (**see illustration**).

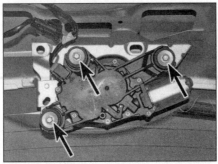

13.4 Tailgate wiper motor bolts (arrowed)

12.9 Carefully prise the front edge of the rear washer jet from place

Refitting

4 Refit in the reverse order of removal. Check for satisfactory operation on completion.

15 Sunroof motor – removal and refitting

Removal of the sunroof motor requires the headlining to be removed. This is an involved task, requiring patience and dexterity. Consequently, we recommend you entrust this task to a Ford dealer or upholstery specialist.

16 Central locking system – general information

1 All models are equipped with a central door

14.3 Horn retaining bolt (arrowed) – viewed from above

17.4 Undo the parking aid module bolts (arrowed)

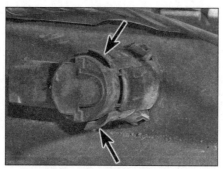

17.7 Press apart the clips (arrowed) and pull the sensor from place

sensor firmly into position until the retaining clips engage.

Speaker

9 The parking aid warning speaker is located adjacent to the right-hand side rear seat belt inertia reel units. To access the speakers, remove the parcel shelf support brackets/ luggage compartment side panels as described in Chapter 11.

10 Undo the 2 retaining bolts, and remove the speaker. Disconnect the wiring plug as the speaker is removed.

18 Audio/DVD units – removal and refitting

Note: *This Section applies only to standard-fit audio equipment.*

Note: *If a new audio unit is to be fitted, it must be configured using Ford diagnostic equipment (WDS). Entrust this task to a Ford dealer or suitably-equipped specialist.*

Removal

1 Disconnect the battery negative lead as described in Chapter 5.

Audio unit – models up to 03/2007

2 Removal of the facia unit requires the use of Ford special tools No GV3301. Equivalent tools may be available from car audio specialist.

3 Insert the 4 tools into the slots in each corner of the audio control panel **(see illustrations)**. Note that the tools must be inserted with the straight-edges to the outside. Pull the audio unit from the facia.

4 Release the clocking catches and disconnect the wiring plug(s) as the unit is withdrawn.

Audio unit – models from 03/2007

5 Starting at the top edge, carefully prise the surround panel from the facia centre **(see illustration)**.

6 Undo the bolt in each corner of the audio unit **(see illustration)**. Pull the audio unit from place, and disconnect the wiring plugs.

Audio unit with DVD player – models up to 01/2008

7 Removal of the facia unit requires the use of

---

locking system, which automatically locks all doors and the rear tailgate/boot lid in unison with the manual locking of the driver's front door. The system is operated electronically with motors/switches incorporated into the door lock assemblies. The system is controlled by the Generic Electronic Module (GEM) and the Keyless Vehicle Module (KVM) – where fitted. The GEM and the KVM communicate with the vehicle's other control modules via an information network known as a Databus. Control modules integral with electric window motors receive signals from the GEM via the databus, and directly control the operation of the door locks. The tailgate/boot lid has its own control module, integral with the lock assembly. If any module is renewed, new software for the unit must be downloaded from Ford. Entrust this task to a Ford dealer or suitably-equipped specialist.

2 The control unit is equipped with a self-diagnosis capability. Should the system develop a fault, have the control unit interrogated by a Ford dealer or suitably-equipped specialist. Once the fault has been established, refer to the relevant Section of Chapter 11 to renew a door module or tailgate/boot lid lock as applicable.

17 Parking aid components – general, removal and refitting

General information

1 The parking aid system is available on all

models. Four ultrasound sensors located in the bumpers measure the distance to the closest object behind or in front the car, and inform the driver using acoustic signals from a buzzer located under the rear luggage compartment trim. The nearer the object, the more frequent the acoustic signals.

2 The system includes a control module and self-diagnosis program, and therefore, in the event of a fault, the vehicle should be taken to a Ford dealer or suitably-equipped specialist who will be able to interrogate the system.

Parking Aid Module (PAM)

Removal

3 The control unit is located behind the right-hand luggage compartment side trim panel. Remove the luggage compartment side panel trim as described in Chapter 11, and remove the foam padding behind the panel.

4 Undo the 2 retaining bolts, and remove the PAM **(see illustration)**. As the unit is removed, disconnect the wiring plugs.

Refitting

5 Refitting is a reversal of removal.

Range/distance sensor

Removal

6 Remove the relevant bumper as described in Chapter 11.

7 Disconnect the sensor wiring plug, then push the retaining clips apart, and pull the sensor from position **(see illustration)**.

Refitting

8 Refitting is a reversal of removal. Press the

18.3a Insert the tools into the slots in the corners the unit

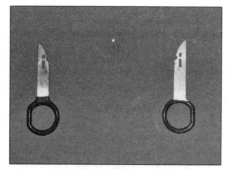

18.3b The tools must be inserted with the straight-edges to the outside

18.5 Carefully prise the top edge of the surround panel from the facia

18.6 Undo the 4 bolts (arrowed) and pull the audio unit from place

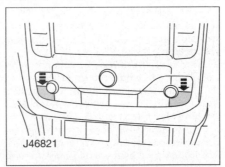

18.11 Prise out the blanking plugs (arrowed)

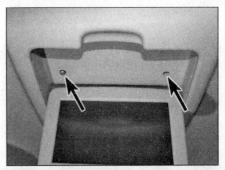

18.16a Fold down the screen and undo the security bolts (arrowed)

Ford special tools No GV3301. Equivalent tools may be available from car audio specialist.

8 Insert the 4 tools into the slots in each corner of the audio control panel **(see illustrations 18.3a and 18.3b)**. Note that the tools are marked 'top left', etc. Pull the audio unit from the facia.

9 Release the clocking catches and disconnect the wiring plug(s) as the unit is withdrawn.

Audio unit with DVD player – models from 01/2008

10 Removal of the facia unit requires the use of Ford special tools No GV3301. Equivalent tools may be available from car audio specialist.

11 Carefully prise out the blanking plates in the lower corners of the control panel **(see illustration)**.

12 Insert the 4 tools into the slots in each corner of the audio control panel **(see illustrations 18.3a and 18.3b)**. Note that the tools are marked 'top left', etc. Pull the audio unit from the facia.

13 Release the clocking catches and disconnect the wiring plug(s) as the unit is withdrawn.

CD autochanger

Note: *If a new autochanger is to be fitted, the new unit must be configured using Ford diagnostic equipment (WDS). Entrust this task to a Ford dealer or suitably-equipped specialist.*

14 Remove the front seat as described in Chapter 11.

15 Undo the 5 retaining bolts and pull the autochanger from place. Disconnect the wiring plug as the unit is withdrawn.

Headlining-mounted DVD player

16 Fold down the DVD screen, and remove the 2 Torx security bolts **(see illustrations)**.

17 Slide the assembly rearwards and lower it from place **(see illustration)**. Disconnect the wiring plug as the assembly is withdrawn. **Note:** *Handle the DVD assembly with care – it's very delicate.*

18 No further dismantling is recommended. When refitting the assembly, position it in line with the front mounting bolt holes, and push it upwards to engage the rear clips.

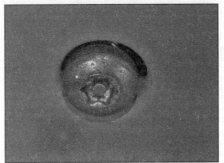

18.16b Note the pin in the centre of the security bolts

Refitting

19 Refitting is a reversal of removal, but if a new unit has been fitted, suitable software must be downloaded from Ford. Entrust this task to a Ford dealer or suitably-equipped specialist.

19 Aerial – removal and refitting

Removal and refitting of the aerial requires the headlining to be removed. This is an involved task, requiring patience and dexterity. Consequently, we recommend you entrust this task to a Ford dealer or upholstery specialist.

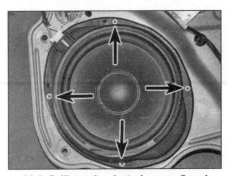

20.2 Drill out the rivets (arrowed) and remove the speaker

18.17 Slide the DVD assembly rearwards

20 Speakers – removal and refitting

Door speakers

1 To remove a door-mounted speaker, remove the appropriate door trim as described in Chapter 11.

2 Drill out the rivets securing the speaker to the door **(see illustration)**.

3 Disconnect the wiring plugs as the speaker is withdrawn.

4 Refit in the reverse order of removal.

Tweeter speaker

5 Pull the trim panel over the door mirror mounting from place **(see illustration)**.

20.5 Pull the mirror mounting trim panel from place

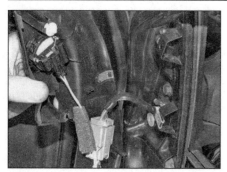

20.6 Undo the bolt and pull the trim panel from the door frame

6 Undo the bolt and pull the trim panel from the door frame **(see illustration)**.

7 Release the retaining clips and remove the speaker. Disconnect the speaker wiring plug as it's withdrawn.

8 Refitting is a reversal of removal.

Rear speakers – 3-door models

9 Remove the rear side panel as described in Chapter 11.

10 Disconnect the wiring plug, undo the 3 bolts and remove the speaker.

11 Refitting is a reversal of removal.

---

21 Airbag system – general information and precautions

 Warning: Before carrying out any operations on the airbag system, disconnect the battery

negative terminal (see Chapter 5). When operations are complete, make sure no one is inside the vehicle when the battery is reconnected.
• *Note that the airbag(s) must not be subjected to temperatures in excess of 90°C. When the airbag is removed, ensure that it is stored the correct way up (pad upwards) to prevent possible inflation.*
• *Do not allow any solvents or cleaning agents to contact the airbag assemblies. They must be cleaned using only a damp cloth.*
• *The airbags and control unit are both sensitive to impact. If either is dropped or damaged they should be renewed.*
• *Disconnect the airbag control unit wiring plug prior to using arc-welding equipment on the vehicle.*

A driver's and passenger's airbag, side airbags (seat mounted) and overhead curtain airbags were fitted as standard equipment to models in the Ford Focus range. The driver's airbag is fitted to the centre of the steering wheel. The passenger's airbag is fitted to the upper surface of the facia, above the glovebox. The airbag system comprises the airbag unit(s) (complete with gas generators), impact sensors, the control unit and a warning light in the instrument panel.

The airbag system is triggered in the event of a direct or offset frontal impact above a predetermined force. The airbag is inflated within milliseconds, and forms a safety cushion between the driver and the steering wheel or (where applicable) the passenger and

the facia. This prevents contact between the upper body and the steering wheel, column and facia, and therefore greatly reduces the risk of injury. The airbag then deflates almost immediately through vents in the side of the airbag. The side airbags and overhead curtain airbags are triggered by side impacts, registered by the sensors fitted to the base of the B-pillars on each side.

Every time the ignition is switched on, the airbag control unit performs a self-test. The self-test takes approximately 7 seconds, and during this time the airbag warning light on the facia is illuminated. After the self-test has been completed, the warning light should go out. If the warning light fails to come on, remains illuminated after the initial 7-second period, or comes on at any time when the vehicle is being driven, there is a fault in the airbag system. The vehicle should then be taken to a Ford dealer or specialist for examination at the earliest possible opportunity.

22 Airbag system components – removal and refitting

Note: *Refer to the warnings in Section 21 before carrying out the following operations.*

1 Disconnect the battery negative terminal (see Chapter 5). Wait at least 5 minutes for any residual electrical energy to dissipate before commencing work. **Note:** *If removing the driver's airbag, turn the steering wheel 90° from straight-ahead before disconnecting the battery, otherwise the steering lock will engage.*

Driver's airbag

2 Set the steering wheel and front wheels in the 'straight-ahead' position.

3 Rotate the steering wheel 90° in each direction to access the steering column upper shroud retaining clips. Release the clips and remove the shroud **(see illustrations 4.2, 4.3 and 4.4)**.

4 Locate the access hole in the reverse side of the steering wheel, and insert a flat-bladed screwdriver into the hole, then push the handle downwards to release the retaining clip **(see illustrations)**. Turn the steering wheel 180° and release the clip on the other side, followed by the clip at the base of the unit.

5 Temporarily touch the striker plate of the front door to discharge any electrostatic electricity. Return the steering wheel to the straight-ahead position, then carefully lift the airbag assembly away from the steering wheel and disconnect the wiring connectors from the rear of the unit **(see illustration)**. Note that the airbag must not be knocked or dropped, and should be stored the correct way up with its padded surface uppermost.

6 On refitting, reconnect the wiring connectors and locate the airbag unit in the steering wheel, making sure the wire does not become trapped, and push the airbag into place to

22.4a Insert a flat-bladed screwdriver and push the handle down to release the airbag clip

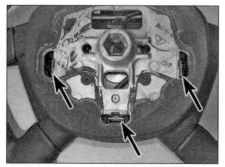

22.4c There are 3 airbag retaining clips (arrowed)

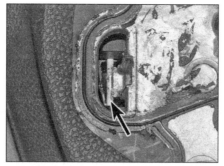

22.4b The airbag clips (arrowed) must be pushed outwards

22.5 Squeeze together the clips (arrowed) and pull the connector from the airbag

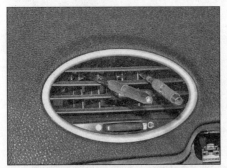

22.8a Insert screwdrivers into the passenger's side inner air vent . . .

22.8b . . . to release the upper clips . . .

22.8c . . . and pull the vent from the facia

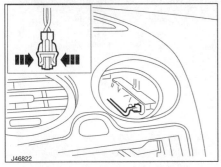

22.9 Squeeze together the sides and disconnect the airbag wiring plug

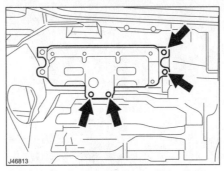

22.11 Undo the remaining airbag bolts (arrowed)

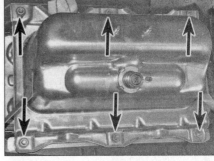

22.14 Passenger's airbag nuts (arrowed)

engage the retaining clips. Reconnect the battery negative lead (see Chapter 5). Ensure no-one is in the vehicle when the battery is reconnected.

Passenger airbag

Models up to 04/2006

7 Remove the passenger's glovebox as described in Chapter 11.

8 Using a small screwdriver, release the upper retaining clips from the passenger's side central facia air vent, the pull the top edge forwards, release the lower clips and remove the vent **(see illustrations)**.

9 Disconnect the airbag wiring plug **(see illustration)**.

10 Undo the airbag module inner retaining bolts.

11 Working underneath the facia, undo the 4 remaining airbag mounting bolts **(see illustration)**. Manoeuvre the airbag from place.

12 Refitting is a reversal of removal. Ensure that the wiring connector is securely reconnected. Ensure that no-one is inside the vehicle. Reconnect the battery negative lead as described in Chapter 5.

Models from 04/2006

13 Remove the facia as described in Chapter 11.

14 Undo the 6 nuts and remove the airbag from the facia **(see illustration)**.

15 Refitting is a reversal of removal. Ensure that the wiring connector is securely reconnected. Ensure that no-one is inside the vehicle. Reconnect the battery negative lead as described in Chapter 5.

Airbag wiring contact unit

16 Remove the steering wheel as described in Chapter 10.

17 Fully extend the steering column, then on models with an audio control switch fitted to the column shroud, release the locking tang, pull the switch from place and disconnect the wiring plug **(see illustration 4.2)**.

18 Undo the fasteners and remove the lower facia panel on the driver's side – see Chapter 11.

19 Release the retaining clips and remove the steering column upper shroud **(see illustration 4.3)**.

20 Undo the retaining bolts, and remove the steering column lower shroud **(see illustration 4.4)**. Release the steering column locking lever to remove the shroud completely.

21 Disconnect the wiring plug from the contact unit and the steering angle sensor (where fitted).

22 If the contact unit is to be refitted, apply tape to lock the unit in position **(see illustration)**. Do not attempt to rotate the unit.

23 Undo the 4 bolts and remove the contact unit **(see illustration)**.

24 If required, release the clips and detach the steering angle sensor from the contact unit.

25 Begin refitting by attaching the steering angle sensor to the contact unit. Ensure the retaining clips fully engage and the sensor locating tangs align with the ones on the contact unit. **Note:** *If a new sensor is being fitted, it must be configured and calibrated using Ford diagnostic equipment. Entrust this task to a Ford dealer or suitably-equipped specialist.*

26 Ensure the front wheels are still in the 'straight-ahead' position, and the directional indicator stalk is in the off position, then fit the contact unit into position. Tighten the retaining bolts.

22.22 Apply tape to secure the rotary contact unit

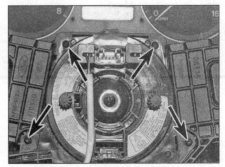

22.23 Contact unit retaining bolts (arrowed)

22.27 Align the marks (arrowed) on the contact unit rotor and cover

22.31 Note the arrow on the top of the RCM must point forwards

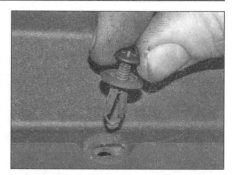

22.35a Undo the bolt and prise out the scrivets . . .

22.35b . . . along the front edge (arrowed) of the air deflector panel

22.40 Side crash sensor (arrowed)

39 Remove the B-pillar (see Chapter 11).
40 Disconnect the sensor wiring plug, then undo the bolt and remove the sensor **(see illustration)**. Take great care not to damage the sensor wiring harness. Note that the sensor must be handled carefully. Do not refit a sensor that has been dropped or knocked.
41 Refitting is a reversal of removal.

23 Anti-theft alarm system – general information

An anti-theft alarm and immobiliser system is fitted as standard equipment. Should the system become faulty, the vehicle should be taken to a Ford dealer or specialist for examination. They will have access to a special diagnostic tester which will quickly trace any fault present in the system.

24 Electronic control modules – removal and refitting

Note: *All of these modules are included in the vehicle's sophisticated self-diagnosis system. Should a fault occur, have the system interrogated using a fault code reader/Ford test equipment, via the diagnostic plug located under the driver's side of the facia, above the pedals (see illustration).*

Removal

1 Disconnect the battery negative lead as described in Chapter 5.

Generic Electronic Module (GEM)

2 The GEM is integral with the passenger compartment fusebox/central junction box. This module is responsible for the management of the following functions:
Current distribution.
Headlights.
Headlight range adjustment.
Foglamps.
Sidelights.
Reversing lights.
High-level brake light.
Interior lights.

27 If there is any doubt as to the position of the contact unit (eg, securing tape missing or disturbed), the unit must be centralised as follows:
  a) *Rotate the contact unit rotor anti-clockwise until a resistance is felt.*
  b) *Rotate the rotor clockwise until the arrow marked on the rotor aligns with the raised V section on the outer cover, at approximately the 7 o'clock position (see illustration).*
  c) *Rotate the rotor 3 turns in a clockwise direction.*
28 The remainder of refitting is a reversal of removal.

Restraint Control Module (RCM)

29 Refer to Chapter 11 and remove the centre console.
30 Release the locking devices and disconnect the wiring plugs for the control unit.

24.0 The diagnostic plug (arrowed) is located under the driver's side of the facia

31 Undo the retaining bolts and remove the control unit **(see illustration)**.
32 Refitting is a reversal of removal, ensuring the module is refitted with the arrow mark on the top pointing forwards. Note that if a new module has been fitted, software for it will need to be downloaded from Ford. Entrust this task to a Ford dealer or suitably-equipped specialist.

Side airbags

33 The side airbags are incorporated into the side of the front and rear seats. Removal of the units requires the seat upholstery to be removed. This is a specialist task, which we recommend should be entrusted to a Ford dealer or specialist.

Head/overhead curtain airbags

34 Renewal of the head airbags/inflatable curtain requires removal of the headlining. This is a specialist task, and should be entrusted to a Ford dealer or specialist.

Crash/lateral acceleration sensors

Front sensor – vehicles up to 05/2005

35 Open the bonnet, undo the 4 scrivets and remove the air deflector panel **(see illustrations)**.
36 Undo the retaining bolt and remove the sensor.
37 Refitting is a reversal of removal.

Side sensors

38 The side sensors are located in the vehicle's B-pillars each side.

25.2 Remove the wheel arch liner

25.3 Undo the bolts (arrowed) securing the filler/breather pipe assembly

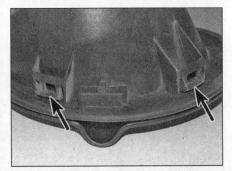

25.4a Reach up and depress the clips (arrowed) . . .

25.4b . . . then manoeuvre the filler flap from the wing

25.5 Depress the clip each side (arrowed) then slide the cover and motor from the flap assembly

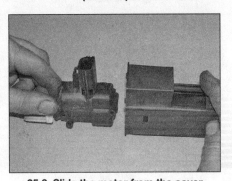

25.6 Slide the motor from the cover

Wipers.
Heated windscreen.
Cruise control.
Central locking.
Anti-theft system.
Handbrake switch.
Brake fluid level monitoring.
Fuel pump.
Battery charging.
Databus communications.

3 Remove the trim panel above the passenger's side footwell **(see illustration 3.2a)**.

4 Undo the 2 fasteners and lift the GEM/junction/fusebox from the mounting bracket **(see illustrations 3.2b and 3.2c)**.

5 Note their fitted positions, and disconnect the wiring plugs as the GEM is withdrawn.

6 If a new GEM is to be fitted, the unit must be configured and initialised using Ford diagnostic equipment (WDS). Entrust this task to a Ford dealer or suitably-equipped specialist.

Lighting control module (LCM)

7 This module is only fitted to vehicles equipped with adaptive front lights (AFS) or Xenon high-intensity gas discharge headlights (HID). On models with AFS it controls the movement of the reflectors as the steering is operated, and on models with HID, it controls the range control as the suspension compresses or extends.

8 Renewal of the module is described in Section 9.

Keyless vehicle module (KVM)

9 Renewal of the KVM is described in Chapter 11.

Climate control module (CCM)

10 Removal of the CCM is described in Chapter 3, Section 10.

Refitting

11 Refitting is a reversal of removal. If a new module has been fitted, software will need to be downloaded from Ford. Entrust this task to a Ford dealer or suitably-equipped specialist.

25 Fuel filler flap motor – removal and refitting

1 Slacken the right-hand rear roadwheel nuts, then raise the rear of the vehicle and support it securely on axle stands (see *Jacking and vehicle support*. Remove the roadwheel.

2 Undo the fasteners and remove the right-hand rear wheel arch liner **(see illustration)**.

3 Undo the bolts securing the filler pipe assembly to the inner wing and chassis member **(see illustration)**.

4 Reach up behind the wheel arch, depress the 2 retaining clips, and manoeuvre the filler flap assembly from place **(see illustrations)**. Disconnect the wiring plug and unclip with harness as the assembly is withdrawn.

5 Release the clip each side and slide the cover and motor from the filler funnel **(see illustration)**.

6 Slide the motor from the cover **(see illustration)**.

7 Refitting is a reversal of removal.

Ford Focus wiring diagrams

Diagram 1

 WARNING: This vehicle is fitted with a supplemental restraint system (SRS) consisting of a combination of driver (and passenger) airbag(s), side impact protection airbags and seatbelt pre-tensioners. The use of electrical test equipment on any SRS wiring systems may cause the seatbelt pre-tensioners to abruptly retract and airbags to explosively deploy, resulting in potentially severe personal injury. Extreme care should be taken to correctly identify any circuits to be tested to avoid choosing any of the SRS wiring in error.
For further information see airbag system precautions in body electrical systems chapter.
Note: The SRS wiring harness can normally be identified by yellow and/or orange harness or harness connectors.

Key to symbols

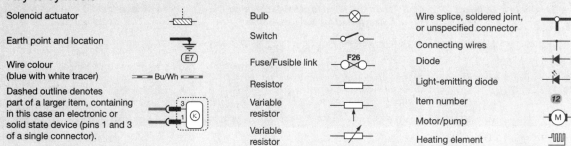

Solenoid actuator	Bulb	Wire splice, soldered joint, or unspecified connector
Earth point and location	Switch	Connecting wires
Wire colour (blue with white tracer)	Fuse/Fusible link	Diode
Dashed outline denotes part of a larger item, containing in this case an electronic or solid state device (pins 1 and 3 of a single connector).	Resistor / Variable resistor / Variable resistor	Light-emitting diode / Item number / Motor/pump / Heating element

Engine fusebox (4)

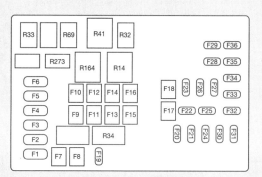

F1	50A	Engine cooling fan
F2	80A	Power steering
F3	60A	Passenger fusebox supply
F4	60A	Passenger fusebox supply
F5	80A	Auxiliary heater
F6	60A	Glow plug (Diesel only)
F7	30A	ABS, stability control pump
F8	20A	ABS, stability control valves
F9	20A	Engine management
F10	30A	Heater blower
F11	20A	Ignition switch
F12	40A	Ignition relay
F13	20A	Starter solenoid
F14	40A	Heated front screen RH
F15	30A	Engine cooling fan relay
F16	40A	Heated front screen LH
F17	30A	Convertible roof
F18	30A	Power inverter
F19	10A	ABS
F20	15A	Horn
F21	20A	Auxiliary heater
F22	10A	Power steering control unit
F23	30A	Headlight washer
F24	15A	Diesel auxiliary heater
F25	10A	Ignition relays
F26	15A	Automatic transmission
F27	10A	Air conditioning clutch
F28	10A	Diesel glow plug monitoring
F29	10A	Climate control
F30	3A	Engine management, auto. transmission
F31	10A	Battery smart charging
F32	10A	Automatic transmission
F33	10A	Heated oxygen sensor
	10A	Intercooler bypass valve
F34	10A	Engine management
F35	10A	Engine management
F36	10A	Engine management

Passenger fusebox (18)

F100	10A	Electronic control units ignition supply
F101	20A	Sunroof, driver's electric seat, convertible roof
F102	10A	Heater control, steering column, Diesel particulate filter, remote control receiver
F103	10A	Lighting
F104	10A	Battery saver, interior lights
F105	25A	Heated rear window
F106	20A	Keyless entry system
F107	10A	Instrument cluster, diagnostics
F108	7.5A	Instrument cluster (audio and navigation unit)
F109	20A	Cigar lighter, rear auxiliary power socket
F110	10A	Daytime running lights, lighting control switch
F111	15A	Fuel pump (petrol)
F112	15A	Audio supply
F113	10A	Daytime running lights (parking lights)
F114	10A	Instrument cluster, engine immobiliser

F115	7.5A	Lighting control
F116	20A	Foglights
F117	7.5A	Number plate lights
F118	20A	LH rear door control unit
F119	15A	Luggage compartment auxiliary power socket
F120	20A	RH rear door control unit
F121	20A	Heated front seats
F122	10A	Airbag
F123	7.5A	Heated mirrors
F124	7.5A	Parking lights, side & tail lights LHS
F125	7.5A	Parking lights, side & tail lights RHS
F126	20A	Keyless entry system
F127	25A	Electric windows
F128	-	Not used
F129	20A	Windscreen wiper

F130	-	Not used
F131	15A	Rear window wiper
F132	15A	Stop lights
F133	25A	Central locking, passenger door control unit
F134	20A	Central locking, driver's door control unit
F135	20A	Daytime running lights
F136	15A	Washer pump, heated washer jets
F137	10A	Battery backup sounder
F138	10A	Engine management, automatic transmission
F139	10A	RH main beam
F140	10A	LH main beam
F141	10A	Reversing light, electric mirrors
F142	15A	RH dip beam
F143	15A	LH dip beam

Earth locations

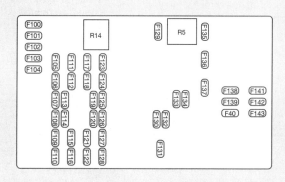

E1	On engine
E2	On engine
E3	In engine bay, behind LH headlight
E4	'A' pillar driver's side
E5	In luggage compartment
E6	LH side of luggage compartment
E7	In engine bay, behind RH headlight
E8	In passenger compartment, front of LH inner sill
E9	In passenger compartment, front of LH inner sill
E10	In engine bay, by LH strut tower
E11	In passenger compartment, front of RH inner sill
E12	In passenger compartment, front of RH inner sill
E13	In passenger compartment, front of RH inner sill
E14	Roof opening panel
E15	Behind centre of dash
E16	In passenger compartment, LH inner sill, below 'B' post

H33944

Colour codes

Wh White   **Og** Orange
Bu Blue   **Rd** Red
Gy Grey   **Pk** Pink
Ye Yellow   **Gn** Green
Bn Brown   **Vt** Violet
Bk Black   **Sr** Silver
Na Natural   **Lg** Light green

Key to items

1 Battery
2 Starter motor
3 Alternator
4 Engine fusebox
   R13 = power hold relay
   R22 = starter relay
   R33 = horn relay
   R212 = glow plug relay

5 Ignition switch
6 Engine cooling fan
7 Air conditioning pressure switch
8 Engine coolant temp. sensor
9 Horn (low tone)
10 Horn (high tone)
11 Steering wheel clock springs
12 Horn switch

13 Glow plug no. 1
14 Glow plug no. 2
15 Glow plug no. 3
16 Glow plug no. 4

Diagram 2

H33945

Typical starting & charging

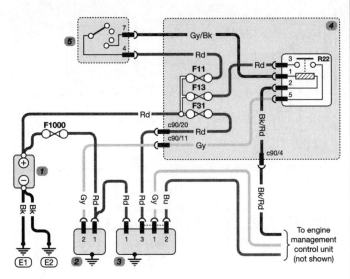

Typical engine cooling fan

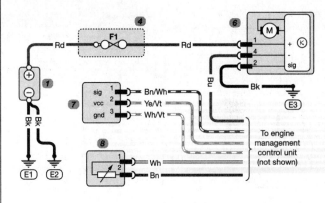

Typical horn

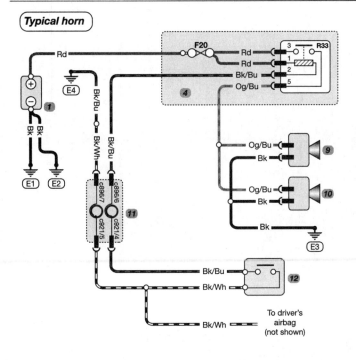

Typical pre-heating system

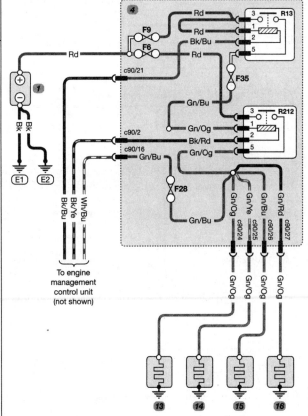

Colour codes

Wh	White	**Og**	Orange
Bu	Blue	**Rd**	Red
Gy	Grey	**Pk**	Pink
Ye	Yellow	**Gn**	Green
Bn	Brown	**Vt**	Violet
Bk	Black	**Sr**	Silver
Na	Natural	**Lg**	Light green

Key to items

1 Battery
4 Engine fusebox
   R41 = ignition relay
5 Ignition switch
18 Passenger fusebox
   a = GEM control unit
   b = autolighting relay
   c = dip beam relay
   d = main beam relay

19 LH rear light
   a = stop/tail light
20 RH rear light
   (as above)
21 Stop light switch
22 Reversing light switch
23 Reversing light
24 High level stop light
25 Number plate light

26 Light switch
   a = park/off/side/head/auto
27 LH headlight
   a = side light
   b = dip beam
   c = main beam
   d = light shade
28 RH headlight
   (as above)

29 Autolighting/rain sensor
30 Multifunction switch
   a = main beam/flasher

Diagram 3

H33946

Typical stop & reversing lights

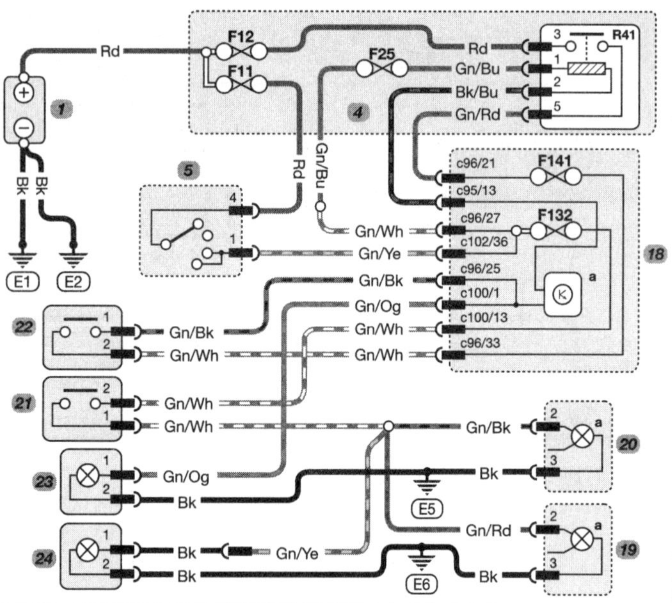

Typical side, tail & number plate lights

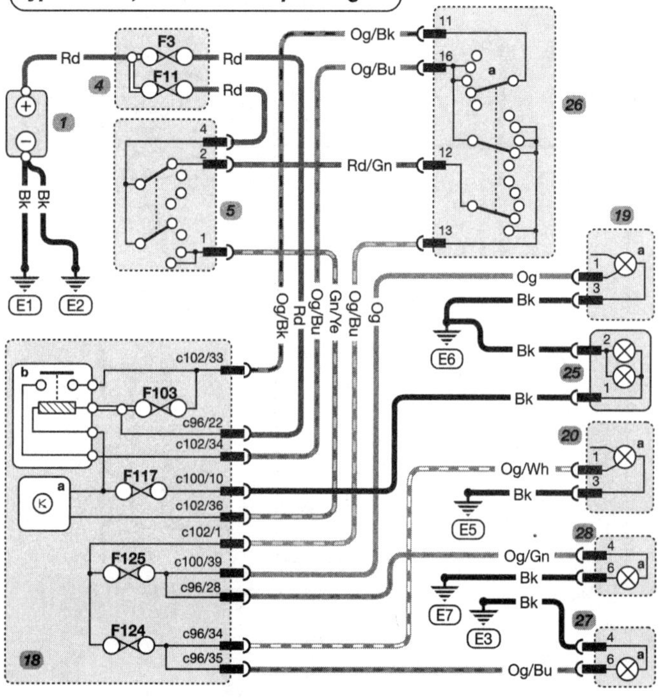

Typical headlights

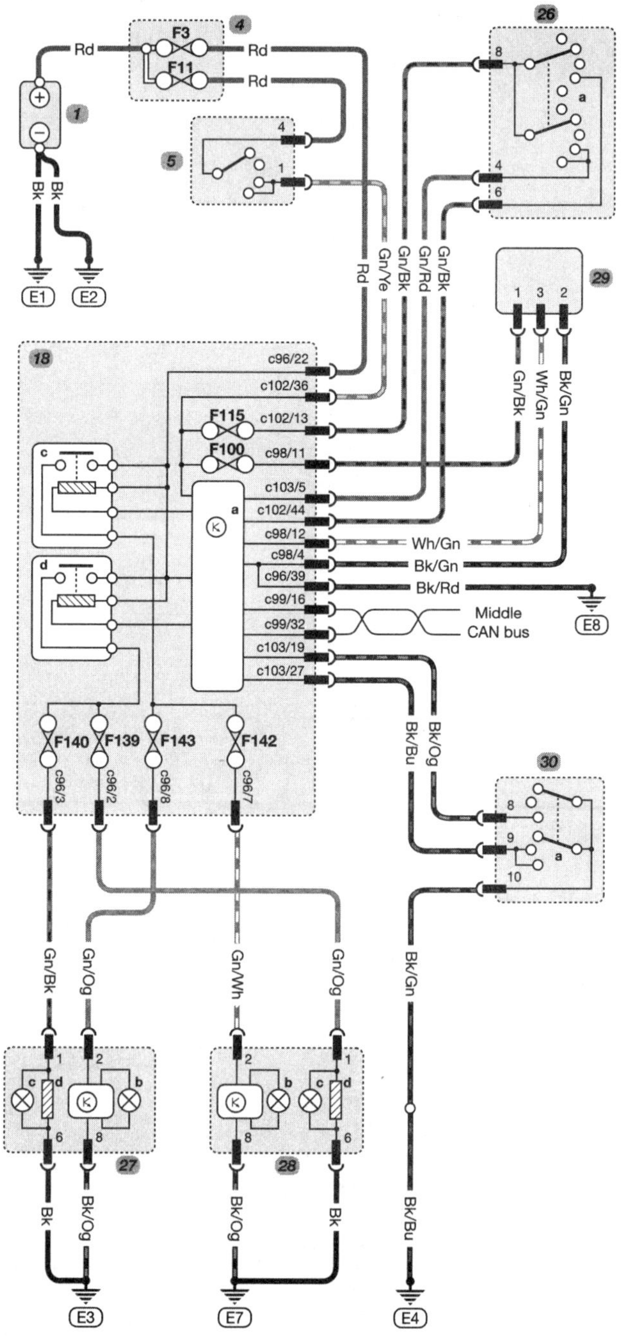

Colour codes

Wh	White	**Og**	Orange
Bu	Blue	**Rd**	Red
Gy	Grey	**Pk**	Pink
Ye	Yellow	**Gn**	Green
Bn	Brown	**Vt**	Violet
Bk	Black	**Sr**	Silver
Na	Natural	**Lg**	Light green

Key to items

1   Battery
4   Engine fusebox
    R41 = ignition relay
5   Ignition switch
18 Passenger fusebox
    a = GEM control unit
19 LH rear light
    b = direction indicator
20 RH rear light
    (as above)

26 Light switch
    b = front/rear foglight
27 LH headlight
    e = direction indicator
28 RH headlight
    (as above)
30 Multifunction switch
    b = direction indicator
33 LH front side repeater
34 RH front side repeater

35 Hazard warning switch
36 LH exterior mirror
    a = indicator side repeater
37 RH exterior mirror
    a = indicator side repeater
38 LH front foglight
39 RH front foglight
40 Rear foglight

Diagram 4

H33947

Typical direction indicators & hazard warning lights

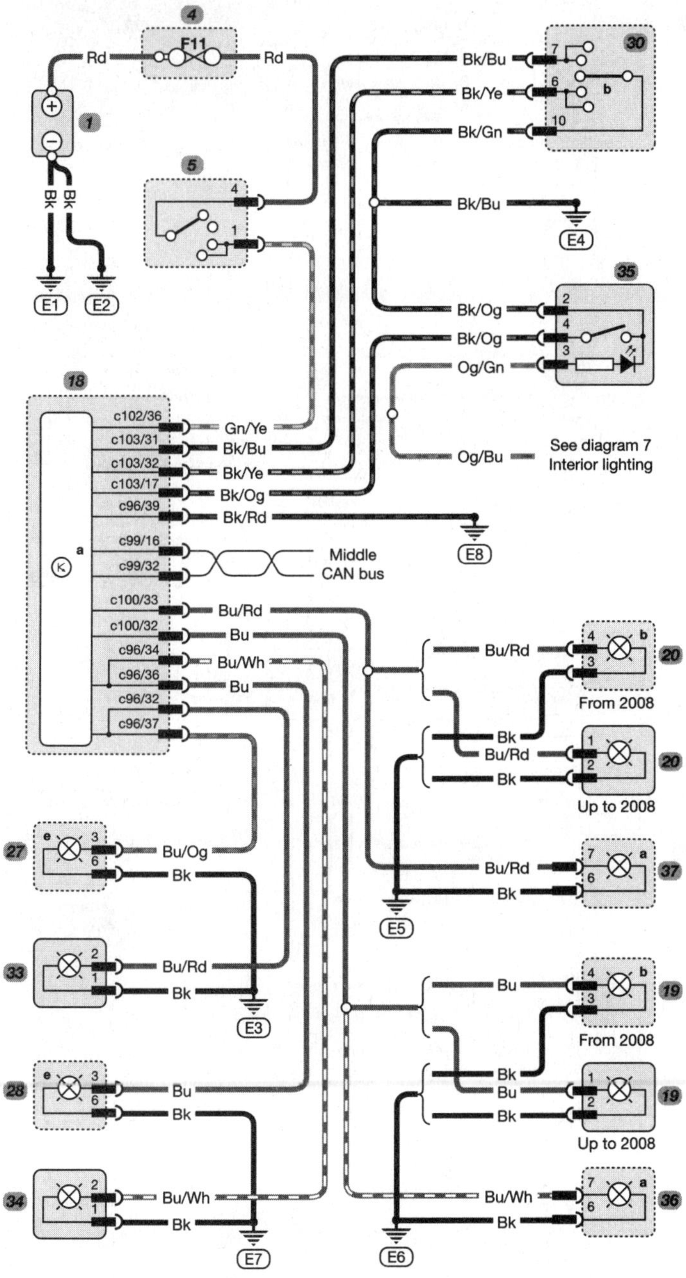

Typical foglights

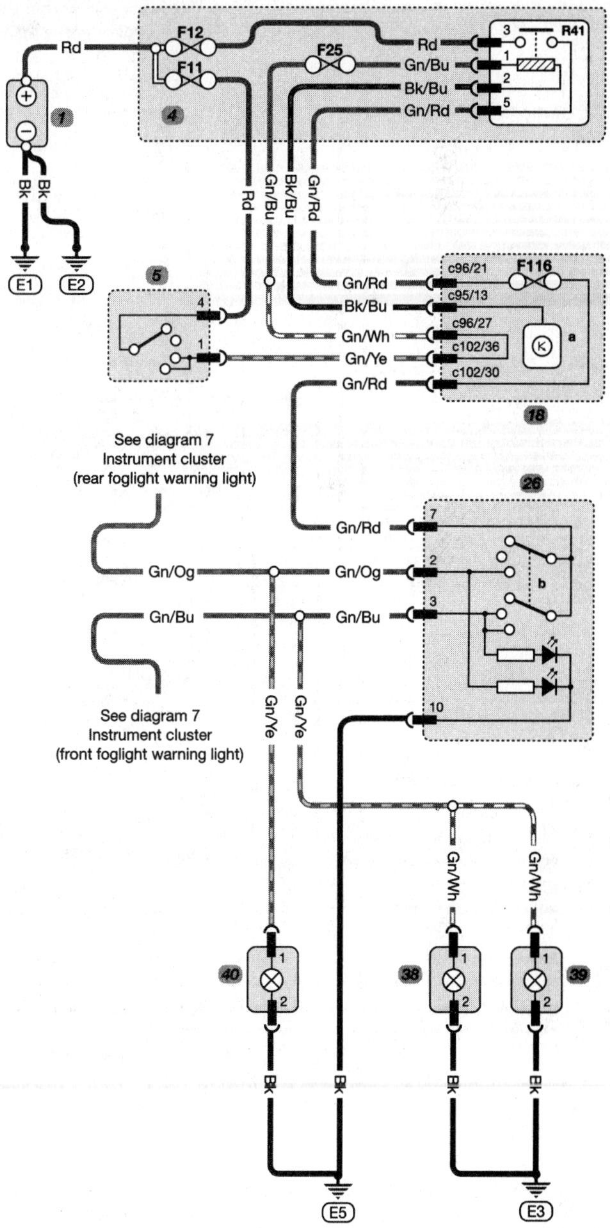

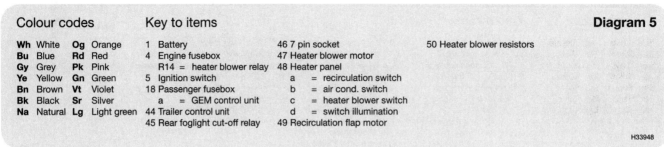

Colour codes

Wh White   **Og** Orange
Bu Blue   **Rd** Red
Gy Grey   **Pk** Pink
Ye Yellow   **Gn** Green
Bn Brown   **Vt** Violet
Bk Black   **Sr** Silver
Na Natural   **Lg** Light green

Key to items

1   Battery
4   Engine fusebox
   R14 = heater blower relay
5   Ignition switch
18   Passenger fusebox
   a = GEM control unit
44   Trailer control unit
45   Rear foglight cut-off relay

46   7 pin socket
47   Heater blower motor
48   Heater panel
   a = recirculation switch
   b = air cond. switch
   c = heater blower switch
   d = switch illumination
49   Recirculation flap motor

50   Heater blower resistors

Diagram 5

H33948

Typical trailer socket

Typical air conditioning

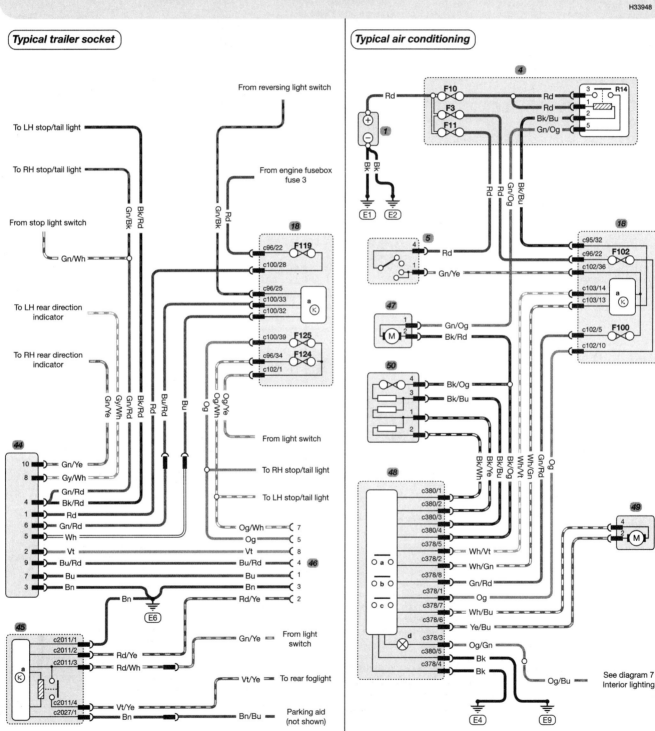

Colour codes

Wh	White	**Og**	Orange
Bu	Blue	**Rd**	Red
Gy	Grey	**Pk**	Pink
Ye	Yellow	**Gn**	Green
Bn	Brown	**Vt**	Violet
Bk	Black	**Sr**	Silver
Na	Natural	**Lg**	Light green

Key to items

1 Battery
4 Engine fusebox
  R34 = headlight cleaning relay
  R41 = ignition relay
5 Ignition switch
18 Passenger fusebox
  a = GEM control unit
  e = rear wiper relay
  f = low speed wiper relay
  g = high speed wiper relay

26 Light switch
  a = park/off/side/head/auto
29 Autolighting/rain sensor
53 Wash/wipe switch
  a = variable wiper control
  b = front wiper switch
  c = rear wash/wipe switch
  d = front washer switch
54 Front wiper motor
55 Rear wipe motor

56 Headlight washer pump
57 LH washer jet heater
58 RH washer jet heater
59 Front/rear washer pump

Diagram 6

H33949

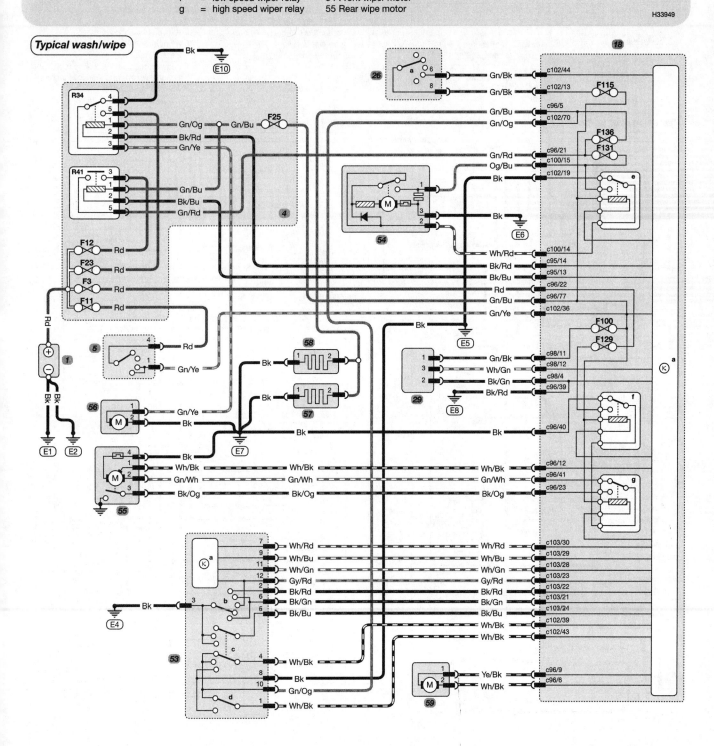

Typical wash/wipe

Colour codes

Wh	White	Og	Orange
Bu	Blue	Rd	Red
Gy	Grey	Pk	Pink
Ye	Yellow	Gn	Green
Bn	Brown	Vt	Violet
Bk	Black	Sr	Silver
Na	Natural	Lg	Light green

Key to items

1 Battery
4 Engine fusebox
5 Ignition switch
18 Passenger fusebox
  a = GEM control unit
  h = battery saver relay
26 Light switch
  a = park/off/side/head/auto
  c = interior lighting dimmer
30 Multifunction switch
  c = display mode
  d = set/reset
60 Instrument cluster
  a = tachometer
  b = coolant temp. gauge
  c = speedometer
  d = alternator warning light

e = low oil pressure warning light
f = shift up warning light
g = MIL warning light
h = speed control warning light
i = check engine warning light
j = preheater warning light
k = ice warning light
l = low brake fluid/handbrake warning light
m = electric power stering warning light
n = seatbelt warning light
o = airbag warning light
p = instrument illumination
q = lights on warning light
r = door ajar warning light
s = LCD display
61 Handbrake switch
62 Outside air temp. sensor

Diagram 7

63 Brake fluid level switch
64 Low washer fluid level switch
65 Fuel gauge sender unit
66 Driver's door lock assy
67 Passenger's door lock assy
68 LH rear door lock assy
69 RH rear door lock assy
70 Glovebox light/switch
71 LH footwell light
72 RH footwell light
73 LH vanity mirror light
74 RH vanity mirror light
75 Front interior light
76 Rear interior light
77 Luggae compartment light (not estate)
78 Luggage compartment light (estate)
79 Tailgate lock unit

H33950

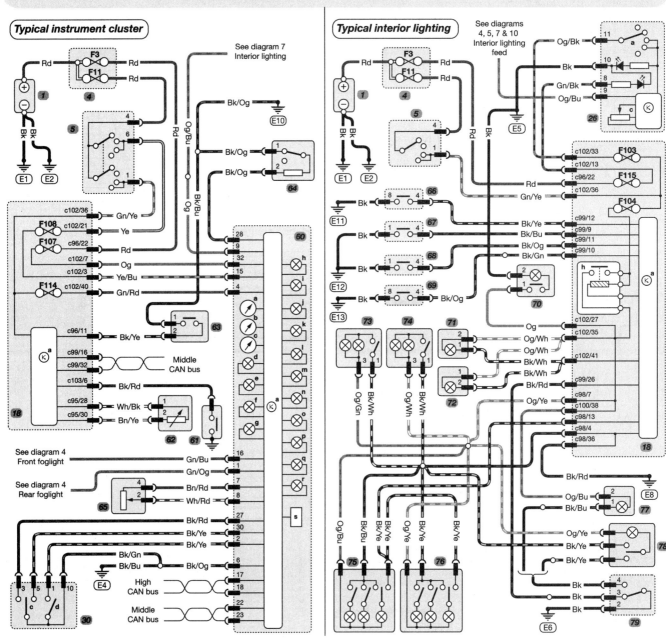

Typical instrument cluster

Typical interior lighting

Colour codes

Wh	White	**Og**	Orange
Bu	Blue	**Rd**	Red
Gy	Grey	**Pk**	Pink
Ye	Yellow	**Gn**	Green
Bn	Brown	**Vt**	Violet
Bk	Black	**Sr**	Silver
Na	Natural	**Lg**	Light green

Key to items

1 Battery
4 Engine fusebox
5 Ignition switch
18 Passenger fusebox
  a = GEM control unit
  h = door lock relay
  i = double locking relay
  j = driver's door lock relay
  k = door unlock relay

64 Driver's door lock unit
65 Passenger's door lock unit
66 LH rear door lock unit
67 RH rear door lock unit
79 Tailgate lock unit
83 Remote control unit
88 Tailgate lock switch
89 Fuel filler lock motor

Diagram 8

H33951

Typical central locking

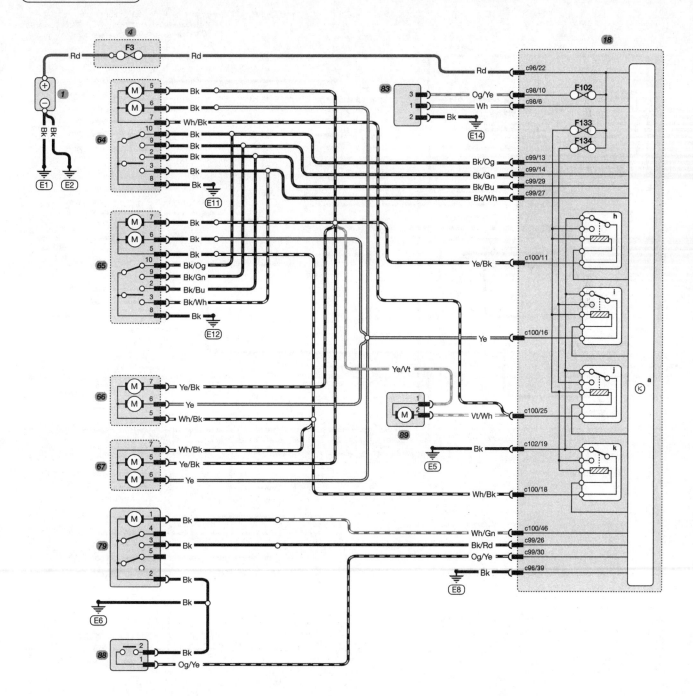

Colour codes

Wh	White	**Og**	Orange
Bu	Blue	**Rd**	Red
Gy	Grey	**Pk**	Pink
Ye	Yellow	**Gn**	Green
Bn	Brown	**Vt**	Violet
Bk	Black	**Sr**	Silver
Na	Natural	**Lg**	Light green

Key to items

1 Battery
4 Engine fusebox
18 Passenger fusebox
36 LH exterior mirror
  b = fold motor
  c = up/down motor
  d = left/right motor
  e = heater element
  f = puddle light

37 RH exterior mirror
  b = fold motor
  c = up/down motor
  d = left/right motor
  e = heater element
  f = puddle light
92 Driver's window/mirror control switch
93 Electric mirror fold control unit
94 Electric mirror fold switch

95 Driver's door control unit
96 Passenger's door control unit

Diagram 9

H33952

Typical electric mirrors

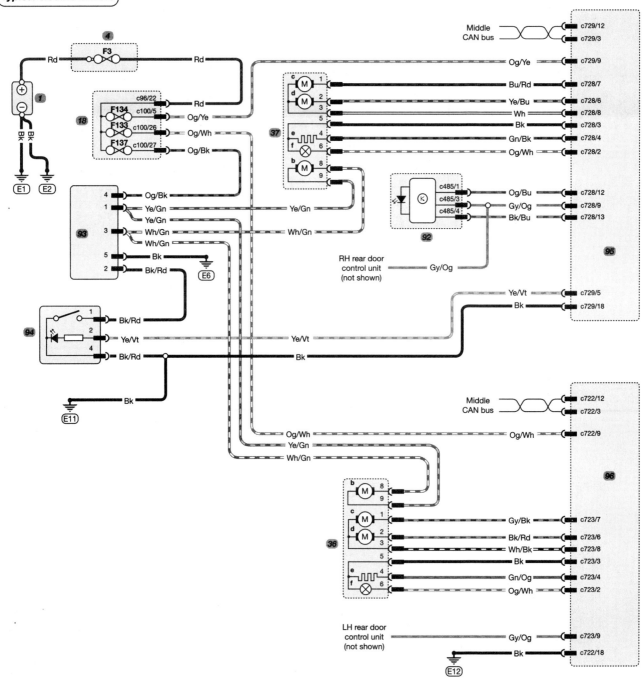

Colour codes

Wh	White	**Og**	Orange
Bu	Blue	**Rd**	Red
Gy	Grey	**Pk**	Pink
Ye	Yellow	**Gn**	Green
Bn	Brown	**Vt**	Violet
Bk	Black	**Sr**	Silver
Na	Natural	**Lg**	Light green

Key to items

1 Battery
4 Engine fusebox
  R41 = ignition relay
5 Ignition switch
18 Passenger fusebox
  a = GEM control unit
92 Driver's window/mirror control switch
98 Passenger's window switch

99 Driver's window motor
100 Passenger's window motor
101 Audio unit
102 CD changer
103 Steering wheel remote control
104 LH front speaker 1
105 LH front speaker 2
106 RH front speaker 1

107 RH front speaker 2
108 LH rear door speaker 1
109 LH rear door speaker 2
110 RH rear door speaker 1
111 RH rear door speaker 2

Diagram 10

H33953

Typical electric windows

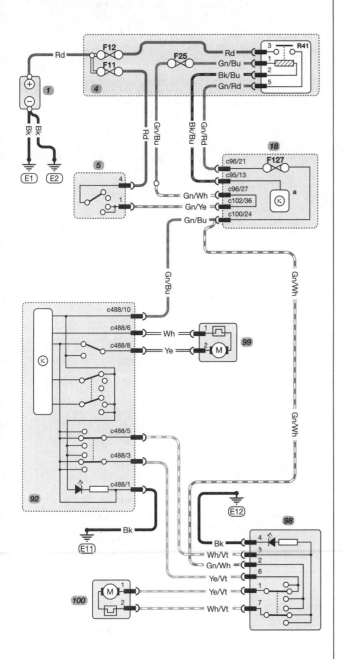

Typical audio system

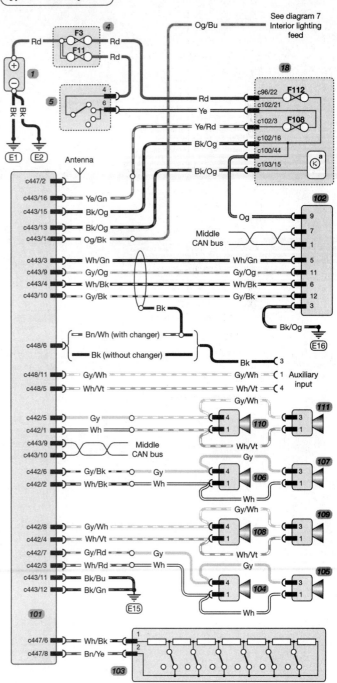

Dimensions and weights

Note: *All figures are approximate, and may vary according to model. Refer to manufacturer's data for exact figures.*

Dimensions

Overall length:
   Hatchback models . . . . 4337 to 4351 mm
   Saloon models . . . . 4481 to 4488 mm
   Estate models. . . . . 4472 to 4494 mm
Overall width (including mirrors). . . . . 1991 to 2020 mm
Wheelbase . . . . 2640 mm
Height (without roof bars):
   Hatchback models . . . . 1458 to 1497 mm
   Saloon models . . . . 1458 to 1497 mm
   Estate . . . . 1459 to 1503 mm

Weights

Gross vehicle weight . . . . See Vehicle Identification Plate
Maximum towing weight . . . . See Vehicle Identification Plate

Fuel economy

Although depreciation is still the biggest part of the cost of motoring for most car owners, the cost of fuel is more immediately noticeable. These pages give some tips on how to get the best fuel economy.

Working it out

Manufacturer's figures

Car manufacturers are required by law to provide fuel consumption information on all new vehicles sold. These 'official' figures are obtained by simulating various driving conditions on a rolling road or a test track. Real life conditions are different, so the fuel consumption actually achieved may not bear much resemblance to the quoted figures.

How to calculate it

Many cars now have trip computers which will

display fuel consumption, both instantaneous and average. Refer to the owner's handbook for details of how to use these.

To calculate consumption yourself (and maybe to check that the trip computer is accurate), proceed as follows.

1. Fill up with fuel and note the mileage, or zero the trip recorder.
2. Drive as usual until you need to fill up again.
3. Note the amount of fuel required to refill the tank, and the mileage covered since the previous fill-up.
4. Divide the mileage by the amount of fuel used to obtain the consumption figure.

For example:

Mileage at first fill-up (a) = 27,903
Mileage at second fill-up (b) = 28,346
Mileage covered (b - a) = 443
Fuel required at second fill-up = 48.6 litres

The half-completed changeover to metric units in the UK means that we buy our fuel

in litres, measure distances in miles and talk about fuel consumption in miles per gallon. There are two ways round this: the first is to convert the litres to gallons before doing the calculation (by dividing by 4.546, or see Table 1). So in the example:

48.6 litres ÷ 4.546 = 10.69 gallons
443 miles ÷ 10.69 gallons = 41.4 mpg

The second way is to calculate the consumption in miles per litre, then multiply that figure by 4.546 (or see Table 2).

So in the example, fuel consumption is:

443 miles ÷ 48.6 litres = 9.1 mpl
9.1 mpl x 4.546 = 41.4 mpg

The rest of Europe expresses fuel consumption in litres of fuel required to travel 100 km (l/100 km). For interest, the conversions are given in Table 3. In practice it doesn't matter what units you use, provided you know what your normal consumption is and can spot if it's getting better or worse.

Table 1: conversion of litres to Imperial gallons

litres	1	2	3	4	5	10	20	30	40	50	60	70
gallons	0.22	0.44	0.66	0.88	1.10	2.24	4.49	6.73	8.98	11.22	13.47	15.71

Table 2: conversion of miles per litre to miles per gallon

miles per litre	5	6	7	8	9	10	11	12	13	14
miles per gallon	23	27	32	36	41	46	50	55	59	64

Table 3: conversion of litres per 100 km to miles per gallon

litres per 100 km	4	4.5	5	5.5	6	6.5	7	8	9	10
miles per gallon	71	63	56	51	47	43	40	35	31	28

Maintenance

A well-maintained car uses less fuel and creates less pollution. In particular:

Filters

Change air and fuel filters at the specified intervals.

Oil

Use a good quality oil of the lowest viscosity specified by the vehicle manufacturer (see *Lubricants and fluids*). Check the level often and be careful not to overfill.

Spark plugs

When applicable, renew at the specified intervals.

Tyres

Check tyre pressures regularly. Under-inflated tyres have an increased rolling resistance. It is generally safe to use the higher pressures specified for full load conditions even when not fully laden, but keep an eye on the centre band of tread for signs of wear due to over-inflation.

When buying new tyres, consider the 'fuel saving' models which most manufacturers include in their ranges.

Driving style

Acceleration

Acceleration uses more fuel than driving at a steady speed. The best technique with modern cars is to accelerate reasonably briskly to the desired speed, changing up through the gears as soon as possible without making the engine labour.

Air conditioning

Air conditioning absorbs quite a bit of energy from the engine – typically 3 kW (4 hp) or so. The effect on fuel consumption is at its worst in slow traffic. Switch it off when not required.

Anticipation

Drive smoothly and try to read the traffic flow so as to avoid unnecessary acceleration and braking.

Automatic transmission

When accelerating in an automatic, avoid depressing the throttle so far as to make the transmission hold onto lower gears at higher speeds. Don't use the 'Sport' setting, if applicable.

When stationary with the engine running, select 'N' or 'P'. When moving, keep your left foot away from the brake.

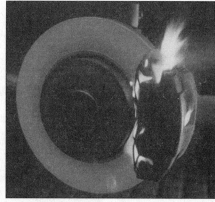

Braking

Braking converts the car's energy of motion into heat – essentially, it is wasted. Obviously some braking is always going to be necessary, but with good anticipation it is surprising how much can be avoided, especially on routes that you know well.

Carshare

Consider sharing lifts to work or to the shops. Even once a week will make a difference.

Electrical loads

Electricity is 'fuel' too; the alternator which charges the battery does so by converting some of the engine's energy of motion into electrical energy. The more electrical accessories are in use, the greater the load on the alternator. Switch off big consumers like the heated rear window when not required.

Freewheeling

Freewheeling (coasting) in neutral with the engine switched off is dangerous. The effort required to operate power-assisted brakes and steering increases when the engine is not running, with a potential lack of control in emergency situations.

In any case, modern fuel injection systems automatically cut off the engine's fuel supply on the overrun (moving and in gear, but with the accelerator pedal released).

Gadgets

Bolt-on devices claiming to save fuel have been around for nearly as long as the motor car itself. Those which worked were rapidly adopted as standard equipment by the vehicle manufacturers. Others worked only in certain situations, or saved fuel only at the expense of unacceptable effects on performance, driveability or the life of engine components.

The most effective fuel saving gadget is the driver's right foot.

Journey planning

Combine (eg) a trip to the supermarket with a visit to the recycling centre and the DIY store, rather than making separate journeys.

When possible choose a travelling time outside rush hours.

Load

The more heavily a car is laden, the greater the energy required to accelerate it to a given speed. Remove heavy items which you don't need to carry.

One load which is often overlooked is the contents of the fuel tank. A tankful of fuel (55 litres / 12 gallons) weighs 45 kg (100 lb) or so. Just half filling it may be worthwhile.

Lost?

At the risk of stating the obvious, if you're going somewhere new, have details of the route to hand. There's not much point in achieving record mpg if you also go miles out of your way.

Parking

If possible, carry out any reversing or turning manoeuvres when you arrive at a parking space so that you can drive straight out when you leave. Manoeuvering when the engine is cold uses a lot more fuel.

Driving around looking for free on-street parking may cost more in fuel than buying a car park ticket.

Premium fuel

Most major oil companies (and some supermarkets) have premium grades of fuel which are several pence a litre dearer than the standard grades. Reports vary, but the consensus seems to be that if these fuels improve economy at all, they do not do so by enough to justify their extra cost.

Roof rack

When loading a roof rack, try to produce a wedge shape with the narrow end at the front. Any cover should be securely fastened – if it flaps it's creating turbulence and absorbing energy.

Remove roof racks and boxes when not in use – they increase air resistance and can create a surprising amount of noise.

Short journeys

The engine is at its least efficient, and wear is highest, during the first few miles after a cold start. Consider walking, cycling or using public transport.

Speed

The engine is at its most efficient when running at a steady speed and load at the rpm where it develops maximum torque. (You can find this figure in the car's handbook.) For most cars this corresponds to between 55 and 65 mph in top gear.

Above the optimum cruising speed, fuel consumption starts to rise quite sharply. A car travelling at 80 mph will typically be using 30% more fuel than at 60 mph.

Supermarket fuel

It may be cheap but is it any good? In the UK all supermarket fuel must meet the relevant British Standard. The major oil companies will say that their branded fuels have better additive packages which may stop carbon and other deposits building up. A reasonable compromise might be to use one tank of branded fuel to three or four from the supermarket.

Switch off when stationary

Switch off the engine if you look like being stationary for more than 30 seconds or so. This is good for the environment as well as for your pocket. Be aware though that frequent restarts are hard on the battery and the starter motor.

Windows

Driving with the windows open increases air turbulence around the vehicle. Closing the windows promotes smooth airflow and

reduced resistance. The faster you go, the more significant this is.

And finally . . .

Driving techniques associated with good fuel economy tend to involve moderate acceleration and low top speeds. Be considerate to the needs of other road users who may need to make brisker progress; even if you do not agree with them this is not an excuse to be obstructive.

Safety must always take precedence over economy, whether it is a question of accelerating hard to complete an overtaking manoeuvre, killing your speed when confronted with a potential hazard or switching the lights on when it starts to get dark.

Length (distance)

Inches (in)	x 25.4	= Millimetres (mm)	x 0.0394	= Inches (in)
Feet (ft)	x 0.305	= Metres (m)	x 3.281	= Feet (ft)
Miles	x 1.609	= Kilometres (km)	x 0.621	= Miles

Volume (capacity)

Cubic inches (cu in; in³)	x 16.387	= Cubic centimetres (cc; cm³)	x 0.061	= Cubic inches (cu in; in³)
Imperial pints (Imp pt)	x 0.568	= Litres (l)	x 1.76	= Imperial pints (Imp pt)
Imperial quarts (Imp qt)	x 1.137	= Litres (l)	x 0.88	= Imperial quarts (Imp qt)
Imperial quarts (Imp qt)	x 1.201	= US quarts (US qt)	x 0.833	= Imperial quarts (Imp qt)
US quarts (US qt)	x 0.946	= Litres (l)	x 1.057	= US quarts (US qt)
Imperial gallons (Imp gal)	x 4.546	= Litres (l)	x 0.22	= Imperial gallons (Imp gal)
Imperial gallons (Imp gal)	x 1.201	= US gallons (US gal)	x 0.833	= Imperial gallons (Imp gal)
US gallons (US gal)	x 3.785	= Litres (l)	x 0.264	= US gallons (US gal)

Mass (weight)

Ounces (oz)	x 28.35	= Grams (g)	x 0.035	= Ounces (oz)
Pounds (lb)	x 0.454	= Kilograms (kg)	x 2.205	= Pounds (lb)

Force

Ounces-force (ozf; oz)	x 0.278	= Newtons (N)	x 3.6	= Ounces-force (ozf; oz)
Pounds-force (lbf; lb)	x 4.448	= Newtons (N)	x 0.225	= Pounds-force (lbf; lb)
Newtons (N)	x 0.1	= Kilograms-force (kgf; kg)	x 9.81	= Newtons (N)

Pressure

Pounds-force per square inch (psi; lbf/in²; lb/in²)	x 0.070	= Kilograms-force per square centimetre (kgf/cm²; kg/cm²)	x 14.223	= Pounds-force per square inch (psi; lbf/in²; lb/in²)
Pounds-force per square inch (psi; lbf/in²; lb/in²)	x 0.068	= Atmospheres (atm)	x 14.696	= Pounds-force per square inch (psi; lbf/in²; lb/in²)
Pounds-force per square inch (psi; lbf/in²; lb/in²)	x 0.069	= Bars	x 14.5	= Pounds-force per square inch (psi; lbf/in²; lb/in²)
Pounds-force per square inch (psi; lbf/in²; lb/in²)	x 6.895	= Kilopascals (kPa)	x 0.145	= Pounds-force per square inch (psi; lbf/in²; lb/in²)
Kilopascals (kPa)	x 0.01	= Kilograms-force per square centimetre (kgf/cm²; kg/cm²)	x 98.1	= Kilopascals (kPa)
Millibar (mbar)	x 100	= Pascals (Pa)	x 0.01	= Millibar (mbar)
Millibar (mbar)	x 0.0145	= Pounds-force per square inch (psi; lbf/in²; lb/in²)	x 68.947	= Millibar (mbar)
Millibar (mbar)	x 0.75	= Millimetres of mercury (mmHg)	x 1.333	= Millibar (mbar)
Millibar (mbar)	x 0.401	= Inches of water (inH₂O)	x 2.491	= Millibar (mbar)
Millimetres of mercury (mmHg)	x 0.535	= Inches of water (inH₂O)	x 1.868	= Millimetres of mercury (mmHg)
Inches of water (inH₂O)	x 0.036	= Pounds-force per square inch (psi; lbf/in²; lb/in²)	x 27.68	= Inches of water (inH₂O)

Torque (moment of force)

Pounds-force inches (lbf in; lb in)	x 1.152	= Kilograms-force centimetre (kgf cm; kg cm)	x 0.868	= Pounds-force inches (lbf in; lb in)
Pounds-force inches (lbf in; lb in)	x 0.113	= Newton metres (Nm)	x 8.85	= Pounds-force inches (lbf in; lb in)
Pounds-force inches (lbf in; lb in)	x 0.083	= Pounds-force feet (lbf ft; lb ft)	x 12	= Pounds-force inches (lbf in; lb in)
Pounds-force feet (lbf ft; lb ft)	x 0.138	= Kilograms-force metres (kgf m; kg m)	x 7.233	= Pounds-force feet (lbf ft; lb ft)
Pounds-force feet (lbf ft; lb ft)	x 1.356	= Newton metres (Nm)	x 0.738	= Pounds-force feet (lbf ft; lb ft)
Newton metres (Nm)	x 0.102	= Kilograms-force metres (kgf m; kg m)	x 9.804	= Newton metres (Nm)

Power

Horsepower (hp)	x 745.7	= Watts (W)	x 0.0013	= Horsepower (hp)

Velocity (speed)

Miles per hour (miles/hr; mph)	x 1.609	= Kilometres per hour (km/hr; kph)	x 0.621	= Miles per hour (miles/hr; mph)

Fuel consumption*

Miles per gallon, Imperial (mpg)	x 0.354	= Kilometres per litre (km/l)	x 2.825	= Miles per gallon, Imperial (mpg)
Miles per gallon, US (mpg)	x 0.425	= Kilometres per litre (km/l)	x 2.352	= Miles per gallon, US (mpg)

Temperature

Degrees Fahrenheit = (°C x 1.8) + 32   Degrees Celsius (Degrees Centigrade; °C) = (°F - 32) x 0.56

It is common practice to convert from miles per gallon (mpg) to litres/100 kilometres (l/100km), where mpg x l/100 km = 282

Spare parts are available from many sources, including maker's appointed garages, accessory shops, and motor factors. To be sure of obtaining the correct parts, it will sometimes be necessary to quote the vehicle identification number. If possible, it can also be useful to take the old parts along for positive identification. Items such as starter motors and alternators may be available under a service exchange scheme – any parts returned should be clean.

Our advice regarding spare parts is as follows.

Officially appointed garages

This is the best source of parts which are peculiar to your car, and which are not otherwise generally available (eg, badges, interior trim, certain body panels, etc). It is also the only place at which you should buy parts if the vehicle is still under warranty.

Accessory shops

These are very good places to buy materials and components needed for the maintenance of your car (oil, air and fuel filters, light bulbs, drivebelts, greases, brake pads, touch-up paint, etc). Components of this nature sold by a reputable shop are usually of the same standard as those used by the car manufacturer.

Besides components, these shops also sell tools and general accessories, usually have convenient opening hours, charge lower prices, and can often be found close to home. Some accessory shops have parts counters where components needed for almost any repair job can be purchased or ordered.

Motor factors

Good factors will stock all the more important components which wear out comparatively quickly, and can sometimes supply individual components needed for the overhaul of a larger assembly (eg, brake seals and hydraulic parts, bearing shells, pistons, valves). They may also handle work such as cylinder block reboring, crankshaft regrinding, etc.

Tyre and exhaust specialists

These outlets may be independent, or members of a local or national chain. They frequently offer competitive prices when compared with a main dealer or local garage, but it will pay to obtain several quotes before making a decision. When researching prices, also ask what extras may be added – for instance fitting a new valve and balancing the wheel are both commonly charged on top of the price of a new tyre.

Other sources

Beware of parts or materials obtained from market stalls, car boot sales or similar outlets. Such items are not invariably sub-standard, but there is little chance of compensation if they do prove unsatisfactory. in the case of safety-critical components such as brake pads, there is the risk not only of financial loss, but also of an accident causing injury or death.

Second-hand components or assemblies obtained from a car breaker can be a good buy in some circumstances, but this sort of purchase is best made by the experienced DIY mechanic.

Vehicle identification

Modifications are a continuing and unpublicised process in vehicle manufacture, quite apart from major model changes. Spare parts manuals and lists are compiled upon a numerical basis, the individual vehicle identification numbers being essential to correct identification of the component concerned.

When ordering spare parts, always give as much information as possible. Quote the car model, year of manufacture, body and engine numbers as appropriate.

The *vehicle identification plate* is situated on the drivers side B-pillar **(see illustration)**. The *vehicle identification number* is also repeated in the form of plate visible through the windscreen on the passenger's side **(see illustration)**.

The engine identification numbers are situated on the front face of the cylinder block, either on a plate, or stamped directly to the centre or side, of the block face. On some models, the engine type is shown on a sticker affixed to the timing belt cover.

Other identification numbers or codes are stamped on major items such as the gearbox, etc.

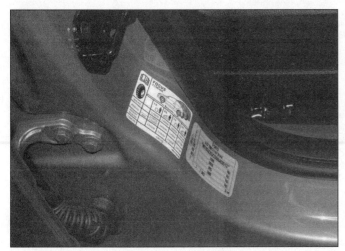

The VIN plate is mounted on the right-hand door pillar . . .

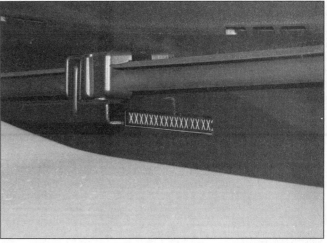

. . . and on a plate on the facia (visible through the windscreen)

Whenever servicing, repair or overhaul work is carried out on the car or its components, observe the following procedures and instructions. This will assist in carrying out the operation efficiently and to a professional standard of workmanship.

Joint mating faces and gaskets

When separating components at their mating faces, never insert screwdrivers or similar implements into the joint between the faces in order to prise them apart. This can cause severe damage which results in oil leaks, coolant leaks, etc upon reassembly. Separation is usually achieved by tapping along the joint with a soft-faced hammer in order to break the seal. However, note that this method may not be suitable where dowels are used for component location.

Where a gasket is used between the mating faces of two components, a new one must be fitted on reassembly; fit it dry unless otherwise stated in the repair procedure. Make sure that the mating faces are clean and dry, with all traces of old gasket removed. When cleaning a joint face, use a tool which is unlikely to score or damage the face, and remove any burrs or nicks with an oilstone or fine file.

Make sure that tapped holes are cleaned with a pipe cleaner, and keep them free of jointing compound, if this is being used, unless specifically instructed otherwise.

Ensure that all orifices, channels or pipes are clear, and blow through them, preferably using compressed air.

Oil seals

Oil seals can be removed by levering them out with a wide flat-bladed screwdriver or similar implement. Alternatively, a number of self-tapping screws may be screwed into the seal, and these used as a purchase for pliers or some similar device in order to pull the seal free.

Whenever an oil seal is removed from its working location, either individually or as part of an assembly, it should be renewed.

The very fine sealing lip of the seal is easily damaged, and will not seal if the surface it contacts is not completely clean and free from scratches, nicks or grooves. If the original sealing surface of the component cannot be restored, and the manufacturer has not made provision for slight relocation of the seal relative to the sealing surface, the component should be renewed.

Protect the lips of the seal from any surface which may damage them in the course of fitting. Use tape or a conical sleeve where possible. Where indicated, lubricate the seal lips with oil before fitting and, on dual-lipped seals, fill the space between the lips with grease.

Unless otherwise stated, oil seals must be fitted with their sealing lips toward the lubricant to be sealed.

Use a tubular drift or block of wood of the appropriate size to install the seal and, if the seal housing is shouldered, drive the seal down to the shoulder. If the seal housing is unshouldered, the seal should be fitted with its face flush with the housing top face (unless otherwise instructed).

Screw threads and fastenings

Seized nuts, bolts and screws are quite a common occurrence where corrosion has set in, and the use of penetrating oil or releasing fluid will often overcome this problem if the offending item is soaked for a while before attempting to release it. The use of an impact driver may also provide a means of releasing such stubborn fastening devices, when used in conjunction with the appropriate screwdriver bit or socket. If none of these methods works, it may be necessary to resort to the careful application of heat, or the use of a hacksaw or nut splitter device. Before resorting to extreme methods, check that you are not dealing with a left-hand thread!

Studs are usually removed by locking two nuts together on the threaded part, and then using a spanner on the lower nut to unscrew the stud. Studs or bolts which have broken off below the surface of the component in which they are mounted can sometimes be removed using a stud extractor.

Always ensure that a blind tapped hole is completely free from oil, grease, water or other fluid before installing the bolt or stud. Failure to do this could cause the housing to crack due to the hydraulic action of the bolt or stud as it is screwed in.

For some screw fastenings, notably cylinder head bolts or nuts, torque wrench settings are no longer specified for the latter stages of tightening, "angle-tightening" being called up instead. Typically, a fairly low torque wrench setting will be applied to the bolts/nuts in the correct sequence, followed by one or more stages of tightening through specified angles.

When checking or retightening a nut or bolt to a specified torque setting, slacken the nut or bolt by a quarter of a turn, and then retighten to the specified setting. However, this should not be attempted where angular tightening has been used.

Locknuts, locktabs and washers

Any fastening which will rotate against a component or housing during tightening should always have a washer between it and the relevant component or housing.

Spring or split washers should always be renewed when they are used to lock a critical component such as a big-end bearing retaining bolt or nut. Locktabs which are folded over to retain a nut or bolt should always be renewed.

Self-locking nuts can be re-used in non-critical areas, providing resistance can be felt when the locking portion passes over the bolt or stud thread. However, it should be noted that self-locking stiffnuts tend to lose their effectiveness after long periods of use, and should then be renewed as a matter of course.

Split pins must always be replaced with new ones of the correct size for the hole.

When thread-locking compound is found on the threads of a fastener which is to be re-used, it should be cleaned off with a wire brush and solvent, and fresh compound applied on reassembly.

Special tools

Some repair procedures in this manual entail the use of special tools such as a press, two or three-legged pullers, spring compressors, etc. Wherever possible, suitable readily-available alternatives to the manufacturer's special tools are described, and are shown in use. In some instances, where no alternative is possible, it has been necessary to resort to the use of a manufacturer's tool, and this has been done for reasons of safety as well as the efficient completion of the repair operation. Unless you are highly-skilled and have a thorough understanding of the procedures described, never attempt to bypass the use of any special tool when the procedure described specifies its use. Not only is there a very great risk of personal injury, but expensive damage could be caused to the components involved.

Environmental considerations

When disposing of used engine oil, brake fluid, antifreeze, etc, give due consideration to any detrimental environmental effects. Do not, for instance, pour any of the above liquids down drains into the general sewage system, or onto the ground to soak away. Many local council refuse tips provide a facility for waste oil disposal, as do some garages. You can find your nearest disposal point by calling the Environment Agency on 08708 506 506 or by visiting www.oilbankline.org.uk.

Note: It is illegal and anti-social to dump oil down the drain. To find the location of your local oil recycling bank, call 08708 506 506 or visit www.oilbankline.org.uk.

The jack supplied with the vehicle tool kit should only be used for changing the roadwheels – see *Wheel changing* at the front of this manual. When carrying out any other kind of work, raise the vehicle using a hydraulic trolley jack, and always supplement the jack with axle stands positioned under the vehicle jacking points.

When using a trolley jack or axle stands, position the jack head or axle stand head adjacent to one of the relevant wheel changing jacking points under the sills **(see illustration)**. Use a block of wood between the jack or axle stand and the sill.

Do not attempt to jack the vehicle under the sump, or any of the suspension components.

The jack supplied with the vehicle locates in the jacking points on the underside of the sills – see *Wheel changing* at the front of this manual. Ensure that the jack head is correctly engaged before attempting to raise the vehicle.

Never work under, around, or near a raised vehicle, unless it is adequately supported in at least two places.

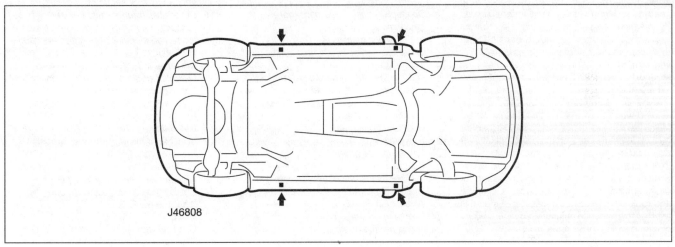

J46808

Use a workshop/trolley jack at the points indicated

Introduction

A selection of good tools is a fundamental requirement for anyone contemplating the maintenance and repair of a motor vehicle. For the owner who does not possess any, their purchase will prove a considerable expense, offsetting some of the savings made by doing-it-yourself. However, provided that the tools purchased meet the relevant national safety standards and are of good quality, they will last for many years and prove an extremely worthwhile investment.

To help the average owner to decide which tools are needed to carry out the various tasks detailed in this manual, we have compiled three lists of tools under the following headings: *Maintenance and minor repair*, *Repair and overhaul*, and *Special*. Newcomers to practical mechanics should start off with the *Maintenance and minor repair* tool kit, and confine themselves to the simpler jobs around the vehicle. Then, as confidence and experience grow, more difficult tasks can be undertaken, with extra tools being purchased as, and when, they are needed. In this way, a *Maintenance and minor repair* tool kit can be built up into a *Repair and overhaul* tool kit over a considerable period of time, without any major cash outlays. The experienced do-it-yourselfer will have a tool kit good enough for most repair and overhaul procedures, and will add tools from the *Special* category when it is felt that the expense is justified by the amount of use to which these tools will be put.

Maintenance and minor repair tool kit

The tools given in this list should be considered as a minimum requirement if routine maintenance, servicing and minor repair operations are to be undertaken. We recommend the purchase of combination spanners (ring one end, open-ended the other); although more expensive than open-ended ones, they do give the advantages of both types of spanner.

☐ *Combination spanners:*
Metric - 8 to 19 mm inclusive
☐ *Adjustable spanner - 35 mm jaw (approx.)*
☐ *Spark plug spanner (with rubber insert) - petrol models*
☐ *Spark plug gap adjustment tool - petrol models*
☐ *Set of feeler gauges*
☐ *Brake bleed nipple spanner*
☐ *Screwdrivers:*
Flat blade - 100 mm long x 6 mm dia
Cross blade - 100 mm long x 6 mm dia
Torx - various sizes (not all vehicles)
☐ *Combination pliers*
☐ *Hacksaw (junior)*
☐ *Tyre pump*
☐ *Tyre pressure gauge*
☐ *Oil can*
☐ *Oil filter removal tool (if applicable)*
☐ *Fine emery cloth*
☐ *Wire brush (small)*
☐ *Funnel (medium size)*
☐ *Sump drain plug key (not all vehicles)*

Repair and overhaul tool kit

These tools are virtually essential for anyone undertaking any major repairs to a motor vehicle, and are additional to those given in the *Maintenance and minor repair* list. Included in this list is a comprehensive set of sockets. Although these are expensive, they will be found invaluable as they are so versatile - particularly if various drives are included in the set. We recommend the half-inch square-drive type, as this can be used with most proprietary torque wrenches.

The tools in this list will sometimes need to be supplemented by tools from the *Special* list:

☐ *Sockets to cover range in previous list (including Torx sockets)*
☐ *Reversible ratchet drive (for use with sockets)*
☐ *Extension piece, 250 mm (for use with sockets)*
☐ *Universal joint (for use with sockets)*
☐ *Flexible handle or sliding T "breaker bar" (for use with sockets)*
☐ *Torque wrench (for use with sockets)*
☐ *Self-locking grips*
☐ *Ball pein hammer*
☐ *Soft-faced mallet (plastic or rubber)*
☐ *Screwdrivers:*
Flat blade - long & sturdy, short (chubby), and narrow (electrician's) types
Cross blade – long & sturdy, and short (chubby) types
☐ *Pliers:*
Long-nosed
Side cutters (electrician's)
Circlip (internal and external)
☐ *Cold chisel - 25 mm*
☐ *Scriber*
☐ *Scraper*
☐ *Centre-punch*
☐ *Pin punch*
☐ *Hacksaw*
☐ *Brake hose clamp*
☐ *Brake/clutch bleeding kit*
☐ *Selection of twist drills*
☐ *Steel rule/straight-edge*
☐ *Allen keys (inc. splined/Torx type)*
☐ *Selection of files*
☐ *Wire brush*
☐ *Axle stands*
☐ *Jack (strong trolley or hydraulic type)*
☐ *Light with extension lead*
☐ *Universal electrical multi-meter*

Sockets and reversible ratchet drive

Brake bleeding kit

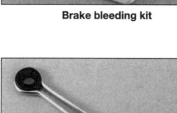

Torx key, socket and bit

Hose clamp

Angular-tightening gauge

Special tools

The tools in this list are those which are not used regularly, are expensive to buy, or which need to be used in accordance with their manufacturers' instructions. Unless relatively difficult mechanical jobs are undertaken frequently, it will not be economic to buy many of these tools. Where this is the case, you could consider clubbing together with friends (or joining a motorists' club) to make a joint purchase, or borrowing the tools against a deposit from a local garage or tool hire specialist.

The following list contains only those tools and instruments freely available to the public, and not those special tools produced by the vehicle manufacturer specifically for its dealer network. You will find occasional references to these manufacturers' special tools in the text of this manual. Generally, an alternative method of doing the job without the vehicle manufacturers' special tool is given. However, sometimes there is no alternative to using them. Where this is the case and the relevant tool cannot be bought or borrowed, you will have to entrust the work to a dealer.

- ☐ *Angular-tightening gauge*
- ☐ *Valve spring compressor*
- ☐ *Valve grinding tool*
- ☐ *Piston ring compressor*
- ☐ *Piston ring removal/installation tool*
- ☐ *Cylinder bore hone*
- ☐ *Balljoint separator*
- ☐ *Coil spring compressors (where applicable)*
- ☐ *Two/three-legged hub and bearing puller*
- ☐ *Impact screwdriver*
- ☐ *Micrometer and/or vernier calipers*
- ☐ *Dial gauge*
- ☐ *Tachometer*
- ☐ *Fault code reader*
- ☐ *Cylinder compression gauge*
- ☐ *Hand-operated vacuum pump and gauge*
- ☐ *Clutch plate alignment set*
- ☐ *Brake shoe steady spring cup removal tool*
- ☐ *Bush and bearing removal/installation set*
- ☐ *Stud extractors*
- ☐ *Tap and die set*
- ☐ *Lifting tackle*

Buying tools

Reputable motor accessory shops and superstores often offer excellent quality tools at discount prices, so it pays to shop around.

Remember, you don't have to buy the most expensive items on the shelf, but it is always advisable to steer clear of the very cheap tools. Beware of 'bargains' offered on market stalls, on-line or at car boot sales. There are plenty of good tools around at reasonable prices, but always aim to purchase items which meet the relevant national safety standards. If in doubt, ask the proprietor or manager of the shop for advice before making a purchase.

Care and maintenance of tools

Having purchased a reasonable tool kit, it is necessary to keep the tools in a clean and serviceable condition. After use, always wipe off any dirt, grease and metal particles using a clean, dry cloth, before putting the tools away. Never leave them lying around after they have been used. A simple tool rack on the garage or workshop wall for items such as screwdrivers and pliers is a good idea. Store all normal spanners and sockets in a metal box. Any measuring instruments, gauges, meters, etc, must be carefully stored where they cannot be damaged or become rusty.

Take a little care when tools are used. Hammer heads inevitably become marked, and screwdrivers lose the keen edge on their blades from time to time. A little timely attention with emery cloth or a file will soon restore items like this to a good finish.

Working facilities

Not to be forgotten when discussing tools is the workshop itself. If anything more than routine maintenance is to be carried out, a suitable working area becomes essential.

It is appreciated that many an owner-mechanic is forced by circumstances to remove an engine or similar item without the benefit of a garage or workshop. Having done this, any repairs should always be done under the cover of a roof.

Wherever possible, any dismantling should be done on a clean, flat workbench or table at a suitable working height.

Any workbench needs a vice; one with a jaw opening of 100 mm is suitable for most jobs. As mentioned previously, some clean dry storage space is also required for tools, as well as for any lubricants, cleaning fluids, touch-up paints etc, which become necessary.

Another item which may be required, and which has a much more general usage, is an electric drill with a chuck capacity of at least 8 mm. This, together with a good range of twist drills, is virtually essential for fitting accessories.

Last, but not least, always keep a supply of old newspapers and clean, lint-free rags available, and try to keep any working area as clean as possible.

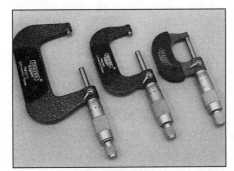
Micrometers

Dial test indicator ("dial gauge")

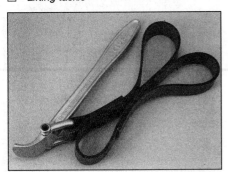
Oil filter removal tool (strap wrench type)

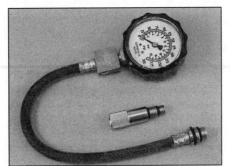
Compression tester

Bearing puller

This is a guide to getting your vehicle through the MOT test. Obviously it will not be possible to examine the vehicle to the same standard as the professional MOT tester. However, working through the following checks will enable you to identify any problem areas before submitting the vehicle for the test.

It has only been possible to summarise the test requirements here, based on the regulations in force at the time of printing. Test standards are becoming increasingly stringent, although there are some exemptions for older vehicles.

An assistant will be needed to help carry out some of these checks.

The checks have been sub-divided into four categories, as follows:

1 Checks carried out **FROM THE DRIVER'S SEAT**

2 Checks carried out **WITH THE VEHICLE ON THE GROUND**

3 Checks carried out **WITH THE VEHICLE RAISED AND THE WHEELS FREE TO TURN**

4 Checks carried out on **YOUR VEHICLE'S EXHAUST EMISSION SYSTEM**

1 Checks carried out **FROM THE DRIVER'S SEAT**

Handbrake (parking brake)

☐ Test the operation of the handbrake. Excessive travel (too many clicks) indicates incorrect brake or cable adjustment.
☐ Check that the handbrake cannot be released by tapping the lever sideways. Check the security of the lever mountings.

☐ If the parking brake is foot-operated, check that the pedal is secure and without excessive travel, and that the release mechanism operates correctly.
☐ Where applicable, test the operation of the electronic handbrake. The brake should engage and disengage without excessive delay. If the warning light does not extinguish when the brake is disengaged, this could indicate a fault which will need further investigation.

Footbrake

☐ Depress the brake pedal and check that it does not creep down to the floor, indicating a master cylinder fault. Release the pedal,

wait a few seconds, then depress it again. If the pedal travels nearly to the floor before firm resistance is felt, brake adjustment or repair is necessary. If the pedal feels spongy, there is air in the hydraulic system which must be removed by bleeding.

☐ Check that the brake pedal is secure and in good condition. Check also for signs of fluid leaks on the pedal, floor or carpets, which would indicate failed seals in the brake master cylinder.
☐ Check the servo unit (when applicable) by operating the brake pedal several times, then keeping the pedal depressed and starting the engine. As the engine starts, the pedal will move down slightly. If not, the vacuum hose or the servo itself may be faulty.

Steering wheel and column

☐ Examine the steering wheel for fractures or looseness of the hub, spokes or rim.
☐ Move the steering wheel from side to side and then up and down. Check that the steering wheel is not loose on the column, indicating wear or a loose retaining nut. Continue moving the steering wheel as before, but also turn it slightly from left to right.

☐ Check that the steering wheel is not loose on the column, and that there is no abnormal movement of the steering wheel, indicating wear in the column support bearings or couplings.
☐ Check that the ignition lock (where fitted) engages and disengages correctly.
☐ Steering column adjustment mechanisms (where fitted) must be able to lock the column securely in place with no play evident.

Windscreen, mirrors and sunvisor

☐ The windscreen must be free of cracks or other significant damage within the driver's field of view. (Small stone chips are acceptable.) Rear view mirrors must be secure, intact, and capable of being adjusted.

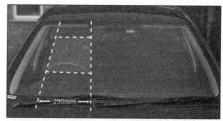

☐ The driver's sunvisor must be capable of being stored in the "up" position.

Seat belts and seats

Note: *The following checks are applicable to all seat belts, front and rear.*

☐ Examine the webbing of all the belts (including rear belts if fitted) for cuts, serious fraying or deterioration. Fasten and unfasten each belt to check the buckles. If applicable, check the retracting mechanism. Check the security of all seat belt mountings accessible from inside the vehicle, ensuring any height adjustable mountings lock securely in place.

☐ Seat belts with pre-tensioners, once activated, have a "flag" or similar showing on the seat belt stalk. This, in itself, is not a reason for test failure.

☐ The front seats themselves must be securely attached and the backrests must lock in the upright position.

Doors

☐ Both front doors must be able to be opened and closed from outside and inside, and must latch securely when closed.

Bonnet and boot/tailgate

☐ The bonnet and boot/tailgate must latch securely when closed.

2 Checks carried out WITH THE VEHICLE ON THE GROUND

Vehicle identification

☐ Number plates must be in good condition, secure and legible, with letters and numbers correctly spaced – spacing at (A) should be 33 mm and at (B) 11 mm. At the front, digits must be black on a white background and at the rear black on a yellow background. Other background designs (such as honeycomb) are not permitted.

☐ The VIN plate and/or homologation plate must be permanently displayed and legible.

Electrical equipment

☐ Switch on the ignition and check the operation of the horn.

☐ Check the windscreen washers and wipers, examining the wiper blades; renew damaged or perished blades. Also check the operation of the stop-lights.

☐ Check the operation of the sidelights and number plate lights. The lenses and reflectors must be secure, clean and undamaged.

☐ Check the operation and alignment of the headlights. The headlight reflectors must not be tarnished and the lenses must be undamaged.

☐ Switch on the ignition and check the operation of the direction indicators (including the instrument panel tell-tale) and the hazard warning lights. Operation of the sidelights and stop-lights must not affect the indicators - if it does, the cause is usually a bad earth at the rear light cluster. Indicators should flash at a rate of between 60 and 120 times per minute – faster or slower than this could indicate a fault with the flasher unit or a bad earth at one of the light units.

☐ Check the operation of the rear foglight(s), including the warning light on the instrument panel or in the switch.

☐ The ABS warning light must illuminate in accordance with the manufacturers' design. For most vehicles, the ABS warning light should illuminate when the ignition is switched on, and (if the system is operating properly) extinguish after a few seconds. Refer to the owner's handbook.

Footbrake

☐ Examine the master cylinder, brake pipes and servo unit for leaks, loose mountings, corrosion or other damage. If ABS is fitted, this unit should also be examined for signs of leaks or corrosion.

☐ The fluid reservoir must be secure and the fluid level must be between the upper (**A**) and lower (**B**) markings.

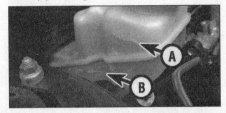

☐ Inspect both front brake flexible hoses for cracks or deterioration of the rubber. Turn the steering from lock to lock, and ensure that the hoses do not contact the wheel, tyre, or any part of the steering or suspension mechanism. With the brake pedal firmly depressed, check the hoses for bulges or leaks under pressure.

Steering and suspension

☐ Have your assistant turn the steering wheel from side to side slightly, up to the point where the steering gear just begins to transmit this movement to the roadwheels. Check for excessive free play between the steering wheel and the steering gear, indicating wear or insecurity of the steering column joints, the column-to-steering gear coupling, or the steering gear itself.

☐ Have your assistant turn the steering wheel more vigorously in each direction, so that the roadwheels just begin to turn. As this is done, examine all the steering joints, linkages, fittings and attachments. Renew any component that shows signs of wear or damage. On vehicles with power steering, check the security and condition of the steering pump, drivebelt and hoses.

☐ Check that the vehicle is standing level, and at approximately the correct ride height.

Shock absorbers

☐ Depress each corner of the vehicle in turn, then release it. The vehicle should rise and then settle in its normal position. If the vehicle continues to rise and fall, the shock absorber is defective. A shock absorber which has seized will also cause the vehicle to fail.

Exhaust system

☐Start the engine. With your assistant holding a rag over the tailpipe, check the entire system for leaks. Repair or renew leaking sections.

3 Checks carried out **WITH THE VEHICLE RAISED AND THE WHEELS FREE TO TURN**

Jack up the front and rear of the vehicle, and securely support it on axle stands. Position the stands clear of the suspension assemblies. Ensure that the wheels are clear of the ground and that the steering can be turned from lock to lock.

Steering mechanism

☐Have your assistant turn the steering from lock to lock. Check that the steering turns smoothly, and that no part of the steering mechanism, including a wheel or tyre, fouls any brake hose or pipe or any part of the body structure.
☐ Examine the steering rack rubber gaiters for damage or insecurity of the retaining clips. If power steering is fitted, check for signs of damage or leakage of the fluid hoses, pipes or connections. Also check for excessive stiffness or binding of the steering, a missing split pin or locking device, or severe corrosion of the body structure within 30 cm of any steering component attachment point.

Front and rear suspension and wheel bearings

☐Starting at the front right-hand side, grasp the roadwheel at the 3 o'clock and 9 o'clock positions and rock gently but firmly. Check for free play or insecurity at the wheel bearings, suspension balljoints, or suspension mount-ings, pivots and attachments.
☐Now grasp the wheel at the 12 o'clock and 6 o'clock positions and repeat the previous inspection. Spin the wheel, and check for roughness or tightness of the front wheel bearing.

☐If excess free play is suspected at a component pivot point, this can be confirmed by using a large screwdriver or similar tool and levering between the mounting and the component attachment. This will confirm whether the wear is in the pivot bush, its retaining bolt, or in the mounting itself (the bolt holes can often become elongated).

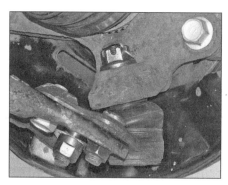

☐Carry out all the above checks at the other front wheel, and then at both rear wheels.

Springs and shock absorbers

☐Examine the suspension struts (when applicable) for serious fluid leakage, corrosion, or damage to the casing. Also check the security of the mounting points.
☐If coil springs are fitted, check that the spring ends locate in their seats, and that the spring is not corroded, cracked or broken.
☐If leaf springs are fitted, check that all leaves are intact, that the axle is securely attached to each spring, and that there is no deterioration of the spring eye mountings, bushes, and shackles.

☐The same general checks apply to vehicles fitted with other suspension types, such as torsion bars, hydraulic displacer units, etc. Ensure that all mountings and attachments are secure, that there are no signs of excessive wear, corrosion or damage, and (on hydraulic types) that there are no fluid leaks or damaged pipes.
☐Inspect the shock absorbers for signs of serious fluid leakage. Check for wear of the mounting bushes or attachments, or damage to the body of the unit.

Driveshafts (fwd vehicles only)

☐Rotate each front wheel in turn and inspect the constant velocity joint gaiters for splits or damage. Also check that each driveshaft is straight and undamaged.

Braking system

☐If possible without dismantling, check brake pad wear and disc condition. Ensure that the friction lining material has not worn excessively, (A) and that the discs are not fractured, pitted, scored or badly worn (B).

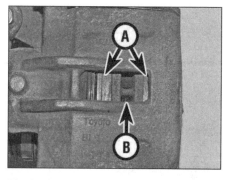

☐Examine all the rigid brake pipes underneath the vehicle, and the flexible hose(s) at the rear. Look for corrosion, chafing or insecurity of the pipes, and for signs of bulging under pressure, chafing, splits or deterioration of the flexible hoses.
☐Look for signs of fluid leaks at the brake calipers or on the brake backplates. Repair or renew leaking components.
☐Slowly spin each wheel, while your assistant depresses and releases the footbrake. Ensure that each brake is operating and does not bind when the pedal is released.

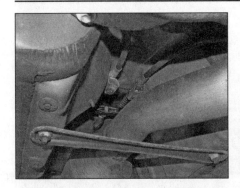

☐ Examine the handbrake mechanism, checking for frayed or broken cables, excessive corrosion, or wear or insecurity of the linkage. Check that the mechanism works on each relevant wheel, and releases fully, without binding.

☐ It is not possible to test brake efficiency without special equipment, but a road test can be carried out later to check that the vehicle pulls up in a straight line.

Fuel and exhaust systems

☐ Inspect the fuel tank (including the filler cap), fuel pipes, hoses and unions. All components must be secure and free from leaks. Locking fuel caps must lock securely and the key must be provided for the MOT test.

☐ Examine the exhaust system over its entire length, checking for any damaged, broken or missing mountings, security of the retaining clamps and rust or corrosion.

Wheels and tyres

☐ Examine the sidewalls and tread area of each tyre in turn. Check for cuts, tears, lumps, bulges, separation of the tread, and exposure of the ply or cord due to wear or damage. Check that the tyre bead is correctly seated on the wheel rim, that the valve is sound and properly seated, and that the wheel is not distorted or damaged.

☐ Check that the tyres are of the correct size for the vehicle, that they are of the same size and type on each axle, and that the pressures are correct.

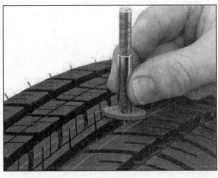

☐ Check the tyre tread depth. The legal minimum at the time of writing is 1.6 mm over the central three-quarters of the tread width. Abnormal tread wear may indicate incorrect front wheel alignment or wear in steering or suspension components.

☐ If the spare wheel is fitted externally or in a separate carrier beneath the vehicle, check that mountings are secure and free of excessive corrosion.

Body corrosion

☐ Check the condition of the entire vehicle structure for signs of corrosion in load-bearing areas. (These include chassis box sections, side sills, cross-members, pillars, and all suspension, steering, braking system and seat belt mountings and anchorages.) Any corrosion which has seriously reduced the thickness of a load-bearing area (or is within 30 cm of safety-related components such as steering or suspension) is likely to cause the vehicle to fail. In this case professional repairs are likely to be needed.

☐ Damage or corrosion which causes sharp or otherwise dangerous edges to be exposed will also cause the vehicle to fail.

Towbars

☐ Check the condition of mounting points (both beneath the vehicle and within boot/hatchback areas) for signs of corrosion, ensuring that all fixings are secure and not worn or damaged. There must be no excessive play in detachable tow ball arms or quick-release mechanisms.

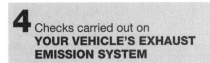

4 Checks carried out on **YOUR VEHICLE'S EXHAUST EMISSION SYSTEM**

Petrol models

☐ The engine should be warmed up, and running well (ignition system in good order, air filter element clean, etc).

☐ Before testing, run the engine at around 2500 rpm for 20 seconds. Let the engine drop to idle, and watch for smoke from the exhaust. If the idle speed is too high, or if dense blue or black smoke emerges for more than 5 seconds, the vehicle will fail. Typically, blue smoke signifies oil burning (engine wear); black smoke means unburnt fuel (dirty air cleaner element, or other fuel system fault).

☐ An exhaust gas analyser for measuring carbon monoxide (CO) and hydrocarbons (HC) is now needed. If one cannot be hired or borrowed, have a local garage perform the check.

CO emissions (mixture)

☐ The MOT tester has access to the CO limits for all vehicles. The CO level is measured at idle speed, and at 'fast idle' (2500 to 3000 rpm). The following limits are given as a general guide:

  At idle speed – Less than 0.5% CO
  At 'fast idle' – Less than 0.3% CO
  Lambda reading – 0.97 to 1.03

☐ If the CO level is too high, this may point to poor maintenance, a fuel injection system problem, faulty lambda (oxygen) sensor or catalytic converter. Try an injector cleaning treatment, and check the vehicle's ECU for fault codes.

HC emissions

☐ The MOT tester has access to HC limits for all vehicles. The HC level is measured at 'fast idle' (2500 to 3000 rpm). The following limits are given as a general guide:

  At 'fast idle' – Less then 200 ppm

☐ Excessive HC emissions are typically caused by oil being burnt (worn engine), or by a blocked crankcase ventilation system ('breather'). If the engine oil is old and thin, an oil change may help. If the engine is running badly, check the vehicle's ECU for fault codes.

Diesel models

☐ The only emission test for diesel engines is measuring exhaust smoke density, using a calibrated smoke meter. The test involves accelerating the engine at least 3 times to its maximum unloaded speed.

Note: *On engines with a timing belt, it is VITAL that the belt is in good condition before the test is carried out.*

☐ With the engine warmed up, it is first purged by running at around 2500 rpm for 20 seconds. A governor check is then carried out, by slowly accelerating the engine to its maximum speed. After this, the smoke meter is connected, and the engine is accelerated quickly to maximum speed three times. If the smoke density is less than the limits given below, the vehicle will pass:

  Non-turbo vehicles: 2.5m-1
  Turbocharged vehicles: 3.0m-1

☐ If excess smoke is produced, try fitting a new air cleaner element, or using an injector cleaning treatment. If the engine is running badly, where applicable, check the vehicle's ECU for fault codes. Also check the vehicle's EGR system, where applicable. At high mileages, the injectors may require professional attention.

Engine

- [ ] Engine fails to rotate when attempting to start
- [ ] Engine rotates, but will not start
- [ ] Engine difficult to start when cold
- [ ] Engine difficult to start when hot
- [ ] Starter motor noisy or excessively-rough in engagement
- [ ] Engine starts, but stops immediately
- [ ] Engine idles erratically
- [ ] Engine misfires at idle speed
- [ ] Engine misfires throughout the driving speed range
- [ ] Engine hesitates on acceleration
- [ ] Engine stalls
- [ ] Engine lacks power
- [ ] Engine backfires
- [ ] Oil pressure warning light illuminated with engine running
- [ ] Engine runs-on after switching off
- [ ] Engine noises

Cooling system

- [ ] Overheating
- [ ] Overcooling
- [ ] External coolant leakage
- [ ] Internal coolant leakage
- [ ] Corrosion

Fuel and exhaust systems

- [ ] Excessive fuel consumption
- [ ] Fuel leakage and/or fuel odour
- [ ] Excessive noise or fumes from exhaust system

Clutch

- [ ] Pedal travels to floor – no pressure or very little resistance
- [ ] Clutch fails to disengage (unable to select gears)
- [ ] Clutch slips (engine speed increases, with no increase in vehicle speed)
- [ ] Judder as clutch is engaged
- [ ] Noise when depressing or releasing clutch pedal

Manual transmission

- [ ] Noisy in neutral with engine running
- [ ] Noisy in one particular gear
- [ ] Difficulty engaging gears
- [ ] Jumps out of gear
- [ ] Vibration
- [ ] Lubricant leaks

Driveshafts

- [ ] Vibration when accelerating or decelerating
- [ ] Clicking or knocking noise on turns (at slow speed on full-lock)

Braking system

- [ ] Vehicle pulls to one side under braking
- [ ] Noise (grinding or high-pitched squeal) when brakes applied
- [ ] Excessive brake pedal travel
- [ ] Brake pedal feels spongy when depressed
- [ ] Excessive brake pedal effort required to stop vehicle
- [ ] Judder felt through brake pedal or steering wheel when braking
- [ ] Pedal pulsates when braking hard
- [ ] Brakes binding
- [ ] Rear wheels locking under normal braking

Steering and suspension

- [ ] Vehicle pulls to one side
- [ ] Wheel wobble and vibration
- [ ] Excessive pitching and/or rolling around corners, or during braking
- [ ] Wandering or general instability
- [ ] Excessively-stiff steering
- [ ] Excessive play in steering
- [ ] Lack of power assistance
- [ ] Tyre wear excessive

Electrical system

- [ ] Battery will not hold a charge for more than a few days
- [ ] Ignition/no-charge warning light remains illuminated with engine running
- [ ] Ignition/no-charge warning light fails to come on
- [ ] Lights inoperative
- [ ] Instrument readings inaccurate or erratic
- [ ] Horn inoperative, or unsatisfactory in operation
- [ ] Windscreen/tailgate wipers inoperative, or unsatisfactory in operation
- [ ] Windscreen washers inoperative, or unsatisfactory in operation
- [ ] Electric windows inoperative, or unsatisfactory in operation

Introduction

The vehicle owner who does his or her own maintenance according to the recommended service schedules should not have to use this section of the manual very often. Modern component reliability is such that, provided those items subject to wear or deterioration are inspected or renewed at the specified intervals, sudden failure is comparatively rare. Faults do not usually just happen as a result of sudden failure, but develop over a period of time. Major mechanical failures in particular are usually preceded by characteristic symptoms over hundreds or even thousands of miles. Those components which do occasionally fail without warning are often small and easily carried in the vehicle.

With any fault-finding, the first step is to decide where to begin investigations. Sometimes this is obvious, but on other occasions, a little detective work will be necessary. The owner who makes half a dozen haphazard adjustments or replacements may be successful in curing a fault (or its symptoms), but will be none the wiser if the fault recurs, and ultimately may have spent more time and money than was necessary. A calm and logical approach will be found to be more satisfactory in the long run. Always take into account any warning signs or abnormalities that may have been noticed in the period preceding the fault – power loss, high or low gauge readings, unusual smells, etc – and remember that failure of components such as fuses or spark plugs may only be pointers to some underlying fault.

The pages which follow provide an easy-reference guide to the more common problems which may occur during the operation of the vehicle. These problems and their possible causes are grouped under headings denoting various components or systems, such as

Engine, Cooling system, etc. The general Chapter which deals with the problem is also shown in brackets; refer to the relevant part of that Chapter for system-specific information. Whatever the fault, certain basic principles apply. These are as follows:

Verify the fault. This is simply a matter of being sure that you know what the symptoms are before starting work. This is particularly important if you are investigating a fault for someone else, who may not have described it very accurately.

Don't overlook the obvious. For example, if the vehicle won't start, is there fuel in the tank? (Don't take anyone else's word on this particular point, and don't trust the fuel gauge either!) If an electrical fault is indicated, look for loose or broken wires before digging out the test gear.

Cure the disease, not the symptom. Substituting a flat battery with a fully-charged one will get you off the hard shoulder, but if the underlying cause is not attended to, the new battery will go the same way.

Don't take anything for granted. Particularly, don't forget that a new component may itself be defective (especially if its been rattling around in the boot for months), and don't leave components out of a fault diagnosis sequence just because they are new or recently-fitted. When you do finally diagnose a difficult fault, you'll probably realise that all the evidence was there from the start.

Diesel fault diagnosis

The majority of starting problems on small diesel engines are electrical in origin. The mechanic who is familiar with petrol engines but less so with diesel may be inclined to view the diesel's injectors and pump in the same light as the spark plugs and distributor, but this is generally a mistake.

When investigating complaints of difficult starting for someone else, make sure that the correct starting procedure is understood and is being followed. Some drivers are unaware of the significance of the preheating warning light – many modern engines are sufficiently forgiving for this not to matter in mild weather, but with the onset of winter, problems begin. Glow plugs in particular are often neglected – just one faulty plug will make cold-weather starting very difficult.

As a rule of thumb, if the engine is difficult to start but runs well when it has finally got going, the problem is electrical (battery, starter motor or preheating system). If poor performance is combined with difficult starting, the problem is likely to be in the fuel system. The low-pressure (supply) side of the fuel system should be checked before suspecting the injectors and high-pressure pump. The most common fuel supply problem is air getting into the system, and any pipe from the fuel tank forwards must be scrutinised if air leakage is suspected.

Engine

Engine fails to rotate when attempting to start

- ☐ Battery terminal connections loose or corroded (see *Weekly checks*).
- ☐ Battery discharged or faulty (Chapter 5).
- ☐ Broken, loose or disconnected wiring in the starting circuit (Chapter 5).
- ☐ Defective starter solenoid or switch (Chapter 5).
- ☐ Defective starter motor (Chapter 5).
- ☐ Starter pinion or flywheel/driveplate ring gear teeth loose or broken (Chapter 2 and 5).
- ☐ Engine earth strap broken or disconnected (Chapter 5 or 12).

Engine rotates, but will not start

- ☐ Fuel tank empty.
- ☐ Battery discharged (engine rotates slowly) (Chapter 5).
- ☐ Battery terminal connections loose or corroded (see *Weekly checks*).
- ☐ Preheating system faulty (Chapter 5).
- ☐ Air in fuel system (Chapter 4).
- ☐ Major mechanical failure (eg, timing belt) (Chapter 2).

Engine difficult to start when cold

- ☐ Battery discharged (Chapter 5).
- ☐ Battery terminal connections loose or corroded (see *Weekly checks*).
- ☐ Preheating system faulty (Chapter 5).
- ☐ Low cylinder compressions (Chapter 2).

Engine difficult to start when hot

- ☐ Air filter element dirty or clogged (Chapter 1).
- ☐ Low cylinder compressions (Chapter 2).

Starter motor noisy or excessively-rough in engagement

- ☐ Starter pinion or flywheel ring gear teeth loose or broken (Chapter 2 and 5).
- ☐ Starter motor mounting bolts loose or missing (Chapter 5).
- ☐ Starter motor internal components worn or damaged (Chapter 5).

Engine idles erratically

- ☐ Air filter element clogged (Chapter 1).
- ☐ Uneven or low cylinder compressions (Chapter 2).
- ☐ Camshaft lobes worn (Chapter 2).
- ☐ Timing belt incorrectly fitted (Chapter 2).
- ☐ Faulty injector(s) (Chapter 4).

Engine misfires at idle speed

- ☐ Faulty injector(s) (Chapter 4).
- ☐ Uneven or low cylinder compressions (Chapter 2).
- ☐ Disconnected, leaking, or perished crankcase ventilation hoses (Chapter 4).

Engine misfires throughout the driving speed range

- ☐ Fuel filter choked (Chapter 1).
- ☐ Fuel tank vent blocked, or fuel pipes restricted (Chapter 4).
- ☐ Faulty injector(s) (Chapter 4).
- ☐ Uneven or low cylinder compressions (Chapter 2).

Engine hesitates on acceleration

- ☐ Faulty injector(s) (Chapter 4).

Engine (continued)

Engine stalls

- ☐ Fuel filter choked (Chapter 1).
- ☐ Fuel tank vent blocked, or fuel pipes restricted (Chapter 4).
- ☐ Faulty injector(s) (Chapter 4).

Engine lacks power

- ☐ Timing belt incorrectly fitted or tensioned (Chapter 2).
- ☐ Fuel filter choked (Chapter 1).
- ☐ Uneven or low cylinder compressions (Chapter 2).
- ☐ Faulty injector(s) (Chapter 4).
- ☐ Brakes binding (Chapter 9).
- ☐ Clutch slipping (Chapter 6).
- ☐ Air filter element clogged (Chapter 1).

Engine backfires

- ☐ Timing belt incorrectly fitted or tensioned (Chapter 2).

Oil pressure warning light illuminated with engine running

- ☐ Low oil level, or incorrect oil grade (*Weekly checks*).
- ☐ Faulty oil pressure switch (Chapter 2).
- ☐ Worn engine bearings and/or oil pump (Chapter 2).
- ☐ High engine operating temperature (Chapter 3).
- ☐ Oil pressure relief valve defective (Chapter 2).
- ☐ Oil pick-up strainer clogged (Chapter 2).

Engine runs-on after switching off

- ☐ Excessive carbon build-up in engine (Chapter 2).
- ☐ High engine operating temperature (Chapter 3).

Engine noises

Pre-ignition (pinking) or knocking during acceleration or under load

- ☐ Excessive carbon build-up in engine (Chapter 2).

Whistling or wheezing noises

- ☐ Leaking exhaust manifold gasket or pipe-to-manifold joint (Chapter 4).
- ☐ Leaking vacuum hose (Chapters 4 and 9).
- ☐ Blowing cylinder head gasket (Chapter 2).

Tapping or rattling noises

- ☐ Worn valve gear or camshaft (Chapter 2).
- ☐ Ancillary component fault (coolant pump, alternator, etc) (Chapters 3, 5, etc).

Knocking or thumping noises

- ☐ Worn big-end bearings (regular heavy knocking, perhaps less under load) (Chapter 2).
- ☐ Worn main bearings (rumbling and knocking, perhaps worsening under load) (Chapter 2).
- ☐ Piston slap (most noticeable when cold) (Chapter 2).
- ☐ Ancillary component fault (coolant pump, alternator, etc) (Chapters 3, 5, etc).

Cooling system

Overheating

- ☐ Insufficient coolant in system (*Weekly checks*).
- ☐ Thermostat faulty (Chapter 3).
- ☐ Radiator core blocked, or grille restricted (Chapter 3).
- ☐ Electric cooling fan or thermostatic switch faulty (Chapter 3).
- ☐ Inaccurate temperature gauge sender unit (Chapter 3).
- ☐ Airlock in cooling system (Chapter 1).
- ☐ Expansion tank pressure cap faulty (Chapter 3).

Overcooling

- ☐ Thermostat faulty (Chapter 3).
- ☐ Inaccurate temperature gauge sender unit (Chapter 3).

External coolant leakage

- ☐ Deteriorated or damaged hoses or hose clips (Chapter 1).
- ☐ Radiator core or heater matrix leaking (Chapter 3).
- ☐ Pressure cap faulty (Chapter 1).
- ☐ Coolant pump internal seal leaking (Chapter 3).
- ☐ Coolant pump-to-housing seal leaking (Chapter 3).
- ☐ Boiling due to overheating (Chapter 3).
- ☐ Core plug leaking (Chapter 2).

Internal coolant leakage

- ☐ Leaking cylinder head gasket (Chapter 2).
- ☐ Cracked cylinder head or cylinder block (Chapter 2).

Corrosion

- ☐ Infrequent draining and flushing (Chapter 1).
- ☐ Incorrect coolant mixture or inappropriate coolant type (see *Weekly checks*).

Fuel and exhaust systems

Excessive fuel consumption

- ☐ Air filter element dirty or clogged (Chapter 1).
- ☐ Faulty injector(s) (Chapter 4).
- ☐ Tyres under-inflated (see *Weekly checks*).

Fuel leakage and/or fuel odour

- ☐ Damaged fuel tank, pipes or connections (Chapter 4).

Excessive noise or fumes from exhaust system

- ☐ Leaking exhaust system or manifold joints (Chapters 1 and 4).
- ☐ Leaking, corroded or damaged silencers or pipe (Chapters 1 and 4).
- ☐ Broken mountings causing body or suspension contact (Chapter 1).

Clutch

Pedal travels to floor – no pressure or very little resistance

☐ Faulty master or slave cylinder (Chapter 6).
☐ Faulty hydraulic release system (Chapter 6).
☐ Broken clutch release bearing or arm (Chapter 6).
☐ Broken diaphragm spring in clutch pressure plate (Chapter 6).

Clutch fails to disengage (unable to select gears)

☐ Faulty master or slave cylinder (Chapter 6).
☐ Faulty hydraulic release system (Chapter 6).
☐ Clutch driven plate sticking on gearbox input shaft splines (Chapter 6).
☐ Clutch driven plate sticking to flywheel or pressure plate (Chapter 6).
☐ Faulty pressure plate assembly (Chapter 6).
☐ Clutch release mechanism worn or incorrectly assembled (Chapter 6).

Clutch slips (engine speed increases, with no increase in vehicle speed)

☐ Faulty hydraulic release system (Chapter 6).
☐ Clutch driven plate linings excessively worn (Chapter 6).
☐ Clutch driven plate linings contaminated with oil or grease (Chapter 6).
☐ Faulty pressure plate or weak diaphragm spring (Chapter 6).

Judder as clutch is engaged

☐ Clutch driven plate linings contaminated with oil or grease (Chapter 6).
☐ Clutch driven plate linings excessively worn (Chapter 6).
☐ Faulty or distorted pressure plate or diaphragm spring (Chapter 6).
☐ Worn or loose engine or gearbox mountings (Chapter 2).
☐ Clutch driven plate hub or gearbox input shaft splines worn (Chapter 6).

Noise when depressing or releasing clutch pedal

☐ Worn clutch release bearing (Chapter 6).
☐ Worn or dry clutch pedal pivot (Chapter 6).
☐ Faulty pressure plate assembly (Chapter 6).
☐ Pressure plate diaphragm spring broken (Chapter 6).
☐ Broken clutch friction plate cushioning springs (Chapter 6).

Manual transmission

Noisy in neutral with engine running

☐ Input shaft bearings worn (noise apparent with clutch pedal released, but not when depressed) (Chapter 7).*
☐ Clutch release bearing worn (noise apparent with clutch pedal depressed, possibly less when released) (Chapter 6).

Noisy in one particular gear

☐ Worn, damaged or chipped gear teeth (Chapter 7).*

Difficulty engaging gears

☐ Clutch fault (Chapter 6).
☐ Worn or damaged gear linkage (Chapter 7).
☐ Worn synchroniser units (Chapter 7).*

Jumps out of gear

☐ Worn or damaged gear linkage (Chapter 7).
☐ Worn synchroniser units (Chapter 7).*
☐ Worn selector forks (Chapter 7).*

Vibration

☐ Lack of oil (Chapter 1).
☐ Worn bearings (Chapter 7).*

Lubricant leaks

☐ Leaking oil seal (Chapter 7).
☐ Leaking housing joint (Chapter 7).*
☐ Leaking input shaft oil seal (Chapter 7).

Although the corrective action necessary to remedy the symptoms described is beyond the scope of the home mechanic, the above information should be helpful in isolating the cause of the condition, so that the owner can communicate clearly with a professional mechanic.

Driveshafts

Vibration when accelerating or decelerating

☐ Worn inner constant velocity joint (Chapter 8).
☐ Bent or distorted driveshaft (Chapter 8).

Clicking or knocking noise on turns (at slow speed on full-lock)

☐ Worn outer constant velocity joint (Chapter 8).
☐ Lack of constant velocity joint lubricant, possibly due to damaged gaiter (Chapter 8).

Braking system

Note: Before assuming that a brake problem exists, make sure that the tyres are in good condition and correctly inflated, that the front wheel alignment is correct, and that the vehicle is not loaded with weight in an unequal manner. Apart from checking the condition of all pipe and hose connections, any faults occurring on the anti-lock braking system should be referred to a Ford dealer for diagnosis.

Vehicle pulls to one side under braking

☐ Worn, defective, damaged or contaminated front or rear brake pads on one side (Chapters 1 and 9).
☐ Seized or partially-seized front or rear brake caliper (Chapter 9).
☐ A mixture of brake pad lining materials fitted between sides (Chapter 9).
☐ Brake caliper mounting bolts loose (Chapter 9).
☐ Worn or damaged steering or suspension components (Chapters 1 and 10).

Noise (grinding or high-pitched squeal) when brakes applied

☐ Brake pad friction lining material worn down to metal backing (Chapters 1 and 9).
☐ Excessive corrosion of brake disc – may be apparent after the vehicle has been standing for some time (Chapters 1 and 9).
☐ Foreign object (stone chipping, etc) trapped between brake disc and shield (Chapters 1 and 9).

Excessive brake pedal travel

☐ Faulty master cylinder (Chapter 9).
☐ Air in hydraulic system (Chapter 9).
☐ Faulty vacuum servo unit (Chapter 9).
☐ Faulty vacuum pump (Chapter 9).

Brake pedal feels spongy when depressed

☐ Air in hydraulic system (Chapter 9).
☐ Deteriorated flexible rubber brake hoses (Chapters 1 and 9).
☐ Master cylinder mountings loose (Chapter 9).
☐ Faulty master cylinder (Chapter 9).

Excessive brake pedal effort required to stop vehicle

☐ Faulty vacuum servo unit (Chapter 9).
☐ Disconnected, damaged or insecure brake servo vacuum hose (Chapters 1 and 9).
☐ Faulty vacuum pump (Chapter 9).
☐ Primary or secondary hydraulic circuit failure (Chapter 9).
☐ Seized brake caliper (Chapter 9).
☐ Brake pads incorrectly fitted (Chapter 9).
☐ Incorrect grade of brake pads fitted (Chapter 9).
☐ Brake pads contaminated (Chapter 9).

Judder felt through brake pedal or steering wheel when braking

☐ Excessive run-out or distortion of brake disc(s) (Chapter 9).
☐ Brake pad linings worn (Chapters 1 and 9).
☐ Brake caliper mounting bolts loose (Chapter 9).
☐ Wear in suspension or steering components or mountings (Chapters 1 and 10).

Pedal pulsates when braking hard

☐ Normal feature of ABS – no fault.

Brakes binding

☐ Seized brake caliper piston(s) (Chapter 9).
☐ Incorrectly-adjusted handbrake mechanism (Chapter 9).
☐ Faulty master cylinder (Chapter 9).

Rear wheels locking under normal braking

☐ Rear brake pad linings contaminated (Chapters 1 and 9).
☐ Rear brake discs warped (Chapters 1 and 9).

Steering and suspension

Note: *Before diagnosing suspension or steering faults, be sure that the trouble is not due to incorrect tyre pressures, mixtures of tyre types, or binding brakes.*

Vehicle pulls to one side

- ☐ Defective tyre (see *Weekly checks*).
- ☐ Excessive wear in suspension or steering components (Chapters 1 and 10).
- ☐ Incorrect front wheel alignment (Chapter 10).
- ☐ Accident damage to steering or suspension components (Chapters 1 and 10).

Wheel wobble and vibration

- ☐ Front roadwheels out of balance (vibration felt mainly through the steering wheel) (Chapter 10).
- ☐ Rear roadwheels out of balance (vibration felt throughout the vehicle) (Chapter 10).
- ☐ Roadwheels damaged or distorted (Chapter 10).
- ☐ Faulty or damaged tyre (*Weekly checks*).
- ☐ Worn steering or suspension joints, bushes or components (Chapters 1 and 10).
- ☐ Wheel nuts loose (Chapter 1 and 10).

Excessive pitching and/or rolling around corners, or during braking

- ☐ Defective shock absorbers (Chapters 1 and 10).
- ☐ Broken or weak coil spring and/or suspension component (Chapters 1 and 10).
- ☐ Worn or damaged anti-roll bar or mountings (Chapter 10).

Wandering or general instability

- ☐ Incorrect front wheel alignment (Chapter 10).
- ☐ Worn steering or suspension joints, bushes or components (Chapters 1 and 10).
- ☐ Roadwheels out of balance (Chapter 10).
- ☐ Faulty or damaged tyre (*Weekly checks*).
- ☐ Wheel nuts loose (Chapter 10).
- ☐ Defective shock absorbers (Chapters 1 and 10).

Excessively-stiff steering

- ☐ Seized track rod end balljoint or suspension balljoint (Chapters 1 and 10).
- ☐ Broken or incorrectly adjusted auxiliary drivebelt (Chapter 1).
- ☐ Incorrect front wheel alignment (Chapter 10).
- ☐ Steering gear damaged (Chapter 10).

Excessive play in steering

- ☐ Worn steering column universal joint(s) (Chapter 10).
- ☐ Worn steering track rod end balljoints (Chapters 1 and 10).
- ☐ Worn steering gear (Chapter 10).
- ☐ Worn steering or suspension joints, bushes or components (Chapters 1 and 10).

Lack of power assistance

- ☐ Broken or incorrectly-adjusted auxiliary drivebelt (Chapter 1).
- ☐ Incorrect power steering fluid level (*Weekly checks*).
- ☐ Restriction in power steering fluid hoses (Chapter 10).
- ☐ Faulty power steering pump (Chapter 10).
- ☐ Faulty steering gear (Chapter 10).

Tyre wear excessive

Tyres worn on inside or outside edges

- ☐ Incorrect camber or castor angles (Chapter 10).
- ☐ Worn steering or suspension joints, bushes or components (Chapters 1 and 10).
- ☐ Excessively-hard cornering.
- ☐ Accident damage.

Tyre treads exhibit feathered edges

- ☐ Incorrect toe setting (Chapter 10).

Tyres worn in centre of tread

- ☐ Tyres over-inflated (*Weekly checks*).

Tyres worn on inside and outside edges

- ☐ Tyres under-inflated (*Weekly checks*).
- ☐ Worn shock absorbers (Chapter 10).

Tyres worn unevenly

- ☐ Tyres/wheels out of balance (*Weekly checks*).
- ☐ Excessive wheel or tyre run-out (Chapter 10).
- ☐ Worn shock absorbers (Chapters 1 and 10).
- ☐ Faulty tyre (*Weekly checks*).

Electrical system

Note: *For problems associated with the starting system, refer to the faults listed under Engine earlier in this Section.*

Battery will not hold a charge more than a few days

- ☐ Battery defective internally (Chapter 5).
- ☐ Battery terminal connections loose or corroded (*Weekly checks*).
- ☐ Auxiliary drivebelt worn – or incorrectly adjusted, where applicable (Chapter 1).
- ☐ Alternator not charging at correct output (Chapter 5).
- ☐ Alternator or voltage regulator faulty (Chapter 5).
- ☐ Short-circuit causing continual battery drain (Chapters 5 and 12).

Ignition/no-charge warning light remains illuminated with engine running

- ☐ Auxiliary drivebelt broken, worn, or incorrectly adjusted (Chapter 1).
- ☐ Internal fault in alternator or voltage regulator (Chapter 5).
- ☐ Broken, disconnected, or loose wiring in charging circuit (Chapter 5).

Ignition/no-charge warning light fails to come on

- ☐ Broken, disconnected, or loose wiring in warning light circuit (Chapter 12).
- ☐ Alternator faulty (Chapter 5).

Electrical system (continued)

Lights inoperative

- ☐ Bulb blown (Chapter 12).
- ☐ Corrosion of bulb or bulbholder contacts (Chapter 12).
- ☐ Blown fuse (Chapter 12).
- ☐ Faulty relay (Chapter 12).
- ☐ Broken, loose, or disconnected wiring (Chapter 12).
- ☐ Faulty switch (Chapter 12).

Instrument readings inaccurate or erratic

Fuel or temperature gauges give no reading

- ☐ Faulty coolant temperature sensor (Chapter 3).
- ☐ Wiring open-circuit (Chapter 12).
- ☐ Faulty gauge (Chapter 12).

Fuel or temperature gauges give continuous maximum reading

- ☐ Faulty coolant temperature sensor (Chapters 3).
- ☐ Wiring short-circuit (Chapter 12).
- ☐ Faulty gauge (Chapter 12).

Horn inoperative, or unsatisfactory in operation

Horn operates all the time

- ☐ Horn contacts permanently bridged or horn push stuck down (Chapter 12).

Horn fails to operate

- ☐ Blown fuse (Chapter 12).
- ☐ Cable or cable connections loose, broken or disconnected (Chapter 12).
- ☐ Faulty horn (Chapter 12).

Horn emits intermittent or unsatisfactory sound

- ☐ Cable connections loose (Chapter 12).
- ☐ Horn mountings loose (Chapter 12).
- ☐ Faulty horn (Chapter 12).

Windscreen/tailgate wipers inoperative, or unsatisfactory in operation

Wipers fail to operate, or operate very slowly

- ☐ Wiper blades stuck to screen, or linkage seized or binding (*Weekly checks* and Chapter 12).
- ☐ Blown fuse (Chapter 12).
- ☐ Cable or cable connections loose, broken or disconnected (Chapter 12).
- ☐ Faulty relay (Chapter 12).
- ☐ Faulty wiper motor (Chapter 12).

Wiper blades sweep over too large or too small an area of the glass

- ☐ Wiper arms incorrectly positioned on spindles (Chapter 12).
- ☐ Excessive wear of wiper linkage (Chapter 12).
- ☐ Wiper motor or linkage mountings loose or insecure (Chapter 12).

Wiper blades fail to clean the glass effectively

- ☐ Wiper blade rubbers worn or perished (*Weekly checks*).
- ☐ Wiper arm tension springs broken, or arm pivots seized (Chapter 12).
- ☐ Insufficient windscreen washer additive to adequately remove road film (*Weekly checks*).

Windscreen washers inoperative, or unsatisfactory in operation

One or more washer jets inoperative

- ☐ Blocked washer jet (Chapter 12).
- ☐ Disconnected, kinked or restricted fluid hose (Chapter 12).
- ☐ Insufficient fluid in washer reservoir (*Weekly checks*).

Washer pump fails to operate

- ☐ Broken or disconnected wiring or connections (Chapter 12).
- ☐ Blown fuse (Chapter 12).
- ☐ Faulty washer switch (Chapter 12).
- ☐ Faulty washer pump (Chapter 12).

Electric windows inoperative, or unsatisfactory in operation

Window glass will only move in one direction

- ☐ Faulty switch (Chapter 12).

Window glass slow to move

- ☐ Regulator seized or damaged, or in need of lubrication (Chapter 11).
- ☐ Door internal components or trim fouling regulator (Chapter 11).
- ☐ Faulty motor (Chapter 11).

Window glass fails to move

- ☐ Blown fuse (Chapter 12).
- ☐ Broken or disconnected wiring or connections (Chapter 12).
- ☐ Faulty motor (Chapter 12).

Central locking system inoperative, or unsatisfactory in operation

Complete system failure

- ☐ Blown fuse (Chapter 12).
- ☐ Faulty ECM (Chapter 12).
- ☐ Broken or disconnected wiring or connections (Chapter 12).

Latch locks but will not unlock, or unlocks but will not lock

- ☐ Faulty switch (Chapter 12).
- ☐ Broken or disconnected latch operating rods or levers (Chapter 11).
- ☐ Faulty ECM (Chapter 12).

One lock fails to operate

- ☐ Broken or disconnected wiring or connections (Chapter 12).
- ☐ Faulty motor (Chapter 11).
- ☐ Broken, binding or disconnected lock operating rods or levers (Chapter 11).
- ☐ Fault in door lock (Chapter 11).

A

ABS (Anti-lock brake system) A system, usually electronically controlled, that senses incipient wheel lockup during braking and relieves hydraulic pressure at wheels that are about to skid.

Air bag An inflatable bag hidden in the steering wheel (driver's side) or the dash or glovebox (passenger side). In a head-on collision, the bags inflate, preventing the driver and front passenger from being thrown forward into the steering wheel or windscreen.

Air cleaner A metal or plastic housing, containing a filter element, which removes dust and dirt from the air being drawn into the engine.

Air filter element The actual filter in an air cleaner system, usually manufactured from pleated paper and requiring renewal at regular intervals.

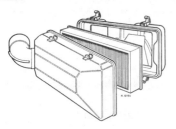

Air filter

Allen key A hexagonal wrench which fits into a recessed hexagonal hole.

Alligator clip A long-nosed spring-loaded metal clip with meshing teeth. Used to make temporary electrical connections.

Alternator A component in the electrical system which converts mechanical energy from a drivebelt into electrical energy to charge the battery and to operate the starting system, ignition system and electrical accessories.

Alternator (exploded view)

Ampere (amp) A unit of measurement for the flow of electric current. One amp is the amount of current produced by one volt acting through a resistance of one ohm.

Anaerobic sealer A substance used to prevent bolts and screws from loosening. Anaerobic means that it does not require oxygen for activation. The Loctite brand is widely used.

Antifreeze A substance (usually ethylene glycol) mixed with water, and added to a vehicle's cooling system, to prevent freezing of the coolant in winter. Antifreeze also contains chemicals to inhibit corrosion and the formation of rust and other deposits that would tend to clog the radiator and coolant passages and reduce cooling efficiency.

Anti-seize compound A coating that reduces the risk of seizing on fasteners that are subjected to high temperatures, such as exhaust manifold bolts and nuts.

Anti-seize compound

Asbestos A natural fibrous mineral with great heat resistance, commonly used in the composition of brake friction materials. Asbestos is a health hazard and the dust created by brake systems should never be inhaled or ingested.

Axle A shaft on which a wheel revolves, or which revolves with a wheel. Also, a solid beam that connects the two wheels at one end of the vehicle. An axle which also transmits power to the wheels is known as a live axle.

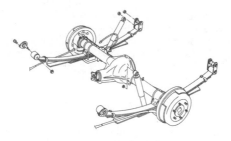

Axle assembly

Axleshaft A single rotating shaft, on either side of the differential, which delivers power from the final drive assembly to the drive wheels. Also called a driveshaft or a halfshaft.

B

Ball bearing An anti-friction bearing consisting of a hardened inner and outer race with hardened steel balls between two races.

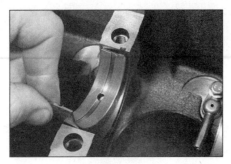

Bearing

Bearing The curved surface on a shaft or in a bore, or the part assembled into either, that permits relative motion between them with minimum wear and friction.

Big-end bearing The bearing in the end of the connecting rod that's attached to the crankshaft.

Bleed nipple A valve on a brake wheel cylinder, caliper or other hydraulic component that is opened to purge the hydraulic system of air. Also called a bleed screw.

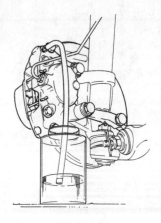

Brake bleeding

Brake bleeding Procedure for removing air from lines of a hydraulic brake system.

Brake disc The component of a disc brake that rotates with the wheels.

Brake drum The component of a drum brake that rotates with the wheels.

Brake linings The friction material which contacts the brake disc or drum to retard the vehicle's speed. The linings are bonded or riveted to the brake pads or shoes.

Brake pads The replaceable friction pads that pinch the brake disc when the brakes are applied. Brake pads consist of a friction material bonded or riveted to a rigid backing plate.

Brake shoe The crescent-shaped carrier to which the brake linings are mounted and which forces the lining against the rotating drum during braking.

Braking systems For more information on braking systems, consult the *Haynes Automotive Brake Manual*.

Breaker bar A long socket wrench handle providing greater leverage.

Bulkhead The insulated partition between the engine and the passenger compartment.

C

Caliper The non-rotating part of a disc-brake assembly that straddles the disc and carries the brake pads. The caliper also contains the hydraulic components that cause the pads to pinch the disc when the brakes are applied. A caliper is also a measuring tool that can be set to measure inside or outside dimensions of an object.

Camshaft A rotating shaft on which a series of cam lobes operate the valve mechanisms. The camshaft may be driven by gears, by sprockets and chain or by sprockets and a belt.

Canister A container in an evaporative emission control system; contains activated charcoal granules to trap vapours from the fuel system.

Canister

Carburettor A device which mixes fuel with air in the proper proportions to provide a desired power output from a spark ignition internal combustion engine.

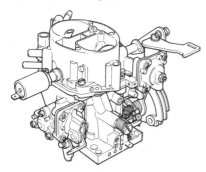

Carburettor

Castellated Resembling the parapets along the top of a castle wall. For example, a castellated balljoint stud nut.

Castellated nut

Castor In wheel alignment, the backward or forward tilt of the steering axis. Castor is positive when the steering axis is inclined rearward at the top.

Catalytic converter A silencer-like device in the exhaust system which converts certain pollutants in the exhaust gases into less harmful substances.

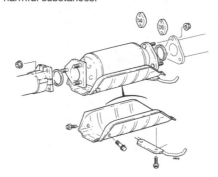

Catalytic converter

Circlip A ring-shaped clip used to prevent endwise movement of cylindrical parts and shafts. An internal circlip is installed in a groove in a housing; an external circlip fits into a groove on the outside of a cylindrical piece such as a shaft.

Clearance The amount of space between two parts. For example, between a piston and a cylinder, between a bearing and a journal, etc.

Coil spring A spiral of elastic steel found in various sizes throughout a vehicle, for example as a springing medium in the suspension and in the valve train.

Compression Reduction in volume, and increase in pressure and temperature, of a gas, caused by squeezing it into a smaller space.

Compression ratio The relationship between cylinder volume when the piston is at top dead centre and cylinder volume when the piston is at bottom dead centre.

Constant velocity (CV) joint A type of universal joint that cancels out vibrations caused by driving power being transmitted through an angle.

Core plug A disc or cup-shaped metal device inserted in a hole in a casting through which core was removed when the casting was formed. Also known as a freeze plug or expansion plug.

Crankcase The lower part of the engine block in which the crankshaft rotates.

Crankshaft The main rotating member, or shaft, running the length of the crankcase, with offset "throws" to which the connecting rods are attached.

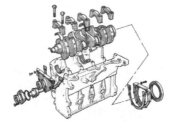

Crankshaft assembly

Crocodile clip See Alligator clip

D

Diagnostic code Code numbers obtained by accessing the diagnostic mode of an engine management computer. This code can be used to determine the area in the system where a malfunction may be located.

Disc brake A brake design incorporating a rotating disc onto which brake pads are squeezed. The resulting friction converts the energy of a moving vehicle into heat.

Double-overhead cam (DOHC) An engine that uses two overhead camshafts, usually one for the intake valves and one for the exhaust valves.

Drivebelt(s) The belt(s) used to drive accessories such as the alternator, water pump, power steering pump, air conditioning compressor, etc. off the crankshaft pulley.

Accessory drivebelts

Driveshaft Any shaft used to transmit motion. Commonly used when referring to the axleshafts on a front wheel drive vehicle.

Driveshaft

Drum brake A type of brake using a drum-shaped metal cylinder attached to the inner surface of the wheel. When the brake pedal is pressed, curved brake shoes with friction linings press against the inside of the drum to slow or stop the vehicle.

Drum brake assembly

E

EGR valve A valve used to introduce exhaust gases into the intake air stream.

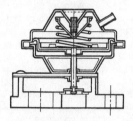

EGR valve

Electronic control unit (ECU) A computer which controls (for instance) ignition and fuel injection systems, or an anti-lock braking system. For more information refer to the *Haynes Automotive Electrical and Electronic Systems Manual*.

Electronic Fuel Injection (EFI) A computer controlled fuel system that distributes fuel through an injector located in each intake port of the engine.

Emergency brake A braking system, independent of the main hydraulic system, that can be used to slow or stop the vehicle if the primary brakes fail, or to hold the vehicle stationary even though the brake pedal isn't depressed. It usually consists of a hand lever that actuates either front or rear brakes mechanically through a series of cables and linkages. Also known as a handbrake or parking brake.

Endfloat The amount of lengthwise movement between two parts. As applied to a crankshaft, the distance that the crankshaft can move forward and back in the cylinder block.

Engine management system (EMS) A computer controlled system which manages the fuel injection and the ignition systems in an integrated fashion.

Exhaust manifold A part with several passages through which exhaust gases leave the engine combustion chambers and enter the exhaust pipe.

Exhaust manifold

F

Fan clutch A viscous (fluid) drive coupling device which permits variable engine fan speeds in relation to engine speeds.

Feeler blade A thin strip or blade of hardened steel, ground to an exact thickness, used to check or measure clearances between parts.

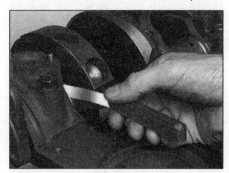

Feeler blade

Firing order The order in which the engine cylinders fire, or deliver their power strokes, beginning with the number one cylinder.

Flywheel A heavy spinning wheel in which energy is absorbed and stored by means of momentum. On cars, the flywheel is attached to the crankshaft to smooth out firing impulses.

Free play The amount of travel before any action takes place. The "looseness" in a linkage, or an assembly of parts, between the initial application of force and actual movement. For example, the distance the brake pedal moves before the pistons in the master cylinder are actuated.

Fuse An electrical device which protects a circuit against accidental overload. The typical fuse contains a soft piece of metal which is calibrated to melt at a predetermined current flow (expressed as amps) and break the circuit.

Fusible link A circuit protection device consisting of a conductor surrounded by heat-resistant insulation. The conductor is smaller than the wire it protects, so it acts as the weakest link in the circuit. Unlike a blown fuse, a failed fusible link must frequently be cut from the wire for replacement.

G

Gap The distance the spark must travel in jumping from the centre electrode to the side

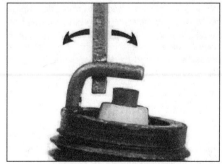

Adjusting spark plug gap

electrode in a spark plug. Also refers to the spacing between the points in a contact breaker assembly in a conventional points-type ignition, or to the distance between the reluctor or rotor and the pickup coil in an electronic ignition.

Gasket Any thin, soft material - usually cork, cardboard, asbestos or soft metal - installed between two metal surfaces to ensure a good seal. For instance, the cylinder head gasket seals the joint between the block and the cylinder head.

Gasket

Gauge An instrument panel display used to monitor engine conditions. A gauge with a movable pointer on a dial or a fixed scale is an analogue gauge. A gauge with a numerical readout is called a digital gauge.

H

Halfshaft A rotating shaft that transmits power from the final drive unit to a drive wheel, usually when referring to a live rear axle.

Harmonic balancer A device designed to reduce torsion or twisting vibration in the crankshaft. May be incorporated in the crankshaft pulley. Also known as a vibration damper.

Hone An abrasive tool for correcting small irregularities or differences in diameter in an engine cylinder, brake cylinder, etc.

Hydraulic tappet A tappet that utilises hydraulic pressure from the engine's lubrication system to maintain zero clearance (constant contact with both camshaft and valve stem). Automatically adjusts to variation in valve stem length. Hydraulic tappets also reduce valve noise.

I

Ignition timing The moment at which the spark plug fires, usually expressed in the number of crankshaft degrees before the piston reaches the top of its stroke.

Inlet manifold A tube or housing with passages through which flows the air-fuel mixture (carburettor vehicles and vehicles with throttle body injection) or air only (port fuel-injected vehicles) to the port openings in the cylinder head.

J

Jump start Starting the engine of a vehicle with a discharged or weak battery by attaching jump leads from the weak battery to a charged or helper battery.

L

Load Sensing Proportioning Valve (LSPV) A brake hydraulic system control valve that works like a proportioning valve, but also takes into consideration the amount of weight carried by the rear axle.

Locknut A nut used to lock an adjustment nut, or other threaded component, in place. For example, a locknut is employed to keep the adjusting nut on the rocker arm in position.

Lockwasher A form of washer designed to prevent an attaching nut from working loose.

M

MacPherson strut A type of front suspension system devised by Earle MacPherson at Ford of England. In its original form, a simple lateral link with the anti-roll bar creates the lower control arm. A long strut - an integral coil spring and shock absorber - is mounted between the body and the steering knuckle. Many modern so-called MacPherson strut systems use a conventional lower A-arm and don't rely on the anti-roll bar for location.

Multimeter An electrical test instrument with the capability to measure voltage, current and resistance.

N

NOx Oxides of Nitrogen. A common toxic pollutant emitted by petrol and diesel engines at higher temperatures.

O

Ohm The unit of electrical resistance. One volt applied to a resistance of one ohm will produce a current of one amp.

Ohmmeter An instrument for measuring electrical resistance.

O-ring A type of sealing ring made of a special rubber-like material; in use, the O-ring is compressed into a groove to provide the sealing action.

O-ring

Overhead cam (ohc) engine An engine with the camshaft(s) located on top of the cylinder head(s).

Overhead valve (ohv) engine An engine with the valves located in the cylinder head, but with the camshaft located in the engine block.

Oxygen sensor A device installed in the engine exhaust manifold, which senses the oxygen content in the exhaust and converts this information into an electric current. Also called a Lambda sensor.

P

Phillips screw A type of screw head having a cross instead of a slot for a corresponding type of screwdriver.

Plastigage A thin strip of plastic thread, available in different sizes, used for measuring clearances. For example, a strip of Plastigage is laid across a bearing journal. The parts are assembled and dismantled; the width of the crushed strip indicates the clearance between journal and bearing.

Plastigage

Propeller shaft The long hollow tube with universal joints at both ends that carries power from the transmission to the differential on front-engined rear wheel drive vehicles.

Proportioning valve A hydraulic control valve which limits the amount of pressure to the rear brakes during panic stops to prevent wheel lock-up.

R

Rack-and-pinion steering A steering system with a pinion gear on the end of the steering shaft that mates with a rack (think of a geared wheel opened up and laid flat). When the steering wheel is turned, the pinion turns, moving the rack to the left or right. This movement is transmitted through the track rods to the steering arms at the wheels.

Radiator A liquid-to-air heat transfer device designed to reduce the temperature of the coolant in an internal combustion engine cooling system.

Refrigerant Any substance used as a heat transfer agent in an air-conditioning system. R-12 has been the principle refrigerant for many years; recently, however, manufacturers have begun using R-134a, a non-CFC substance that is considered less harmful to the ozone in the upper atmosphere.

Rocker arm A lever arm that rocks on a shaft or pivots on a stud. In an overhead valve engine, the rocker arm converts the upward movement of the pushrod into a downward movement to open a valve.

Rotor In a distributor, the rotating device inside the cap that connects the centre electrode and the outer terminals as it turns, distributing the high voltage from the coil secondary winding to the proper spark plug. Also, that part of an alternator which rotates inside the stator. Also, the rotating assembly of a turbocharger, including the compressor wheel, shaft and turbine wheel.

Runout The amount of wobble (in-and-out movement) of a gear or wheel as it's rotated. The amount a shaft rotates "out-of-true." The out-of-round condition of a rotating part.

S

Sealant A liquid or paste used to prevent leakage at a joint. Sometimes used in conjunction with a gasket.

Sealed beam lamp An older headlight design which integrates the reflector, lens and filaments into a hermetically-sealed one-piece unit. When a filament burns out or the lens cracks, the entire unit is simply replaced.

Serpentine drivebelt A single, long, wide accessory drivebelt that's used on some newer vehicles to drive all the accessories, instead of a series of smaller, shorter belts. Serpentine drivebelts are usually tensioned by an automatic tensioner.

Serpentine drivebelt

Shim Thin spacer, commonly used to adjust the clearance or relative positions between two parts. For example, shims inserted into or under bucket tappets control valve clearances. Clearance is adjusted by changing the thickness of the shim.

Slide hammer A special puller that screws into or hooks onto a component such as a shaft or bearing; a heavy sliding handle on the shaft bottoms against the end of the shaft to knock the component free.

Sprocket A tooth or projection on the periphery of a wheel, shaped to engage with a chain or drivebelt. Commonly used to refer to the sprocket wheel itself.

Starter inhibitor switch On vehicles with an automatic transmission, a switch that prevents starting if the vehicle is not in Neutral or Park.

Strut See MacPherson strut.

T

Tappet A cylindrical component which transmits motion from the cam to the valve stem, either directly or via a pushrod and rocker arm. Also called a cam follower.

Thermostat A heat-controlled valve that regulates the flow of coolant between the cylinder block and the radiator, so maintaining optimum engine operating temperature. A thermostat is also used in some air cleaners in which the temperature is regulated.

Thrust bearing The bearing in the clutch assembly that is moved in to the release levers by clutch pedal action to disengage the clutch. Also referred to as a release bearing.

Timing belt A toothed belt which drives the camshaft. Serious engine damage may result if it breaks in service.

Timing chain A chain which drives the camshaft.

Toe-in The amount the front wheels are closer together at the front than at the rear. On rear wheel drive vehicles, a slight amount of toe-in is usually specified to keep the front wheels running parallel on the road by offsetting other forces that tend to spread the wheels apart.

Toe-out The amount the front wheels are closer together at the rear than at the front. On front wheel drive vehicles, a slight amount of toe-out is usually specified.

Tools For full information on choosing and using tools, refer to the *Haynes Automotive Tools Manual*.

Tracer A stripe of a second colour applied to a wire insulator to distinguish that wire from another one with the same colour insulator.

Tune-up A process of accurate and careful adjustments and parts replacement to obtain the best possible engine performance.

Turbocharger A centrifugal device, driven by exhaust gases, that pressurises the intake air. Normally used to increase the power output from a given engine displacement, but can also be used primarily to reduce exhaust emissions (as on VW's "Umwelt" Diesel engine).

U

Universal joint or U-joint A double-pivoted connection for transmitting power from a driving to a driven shaft through an angle. A U-joint consists of two Y-shaped yokes and a cross-shaped member called the spider.

V

Valve A device through which the flow of liquid, gas, vacuum, or loose material in bulk may be started, stopped, or regulated by a movable part that opens, shuts, or partially obstructs one or more ports or passageways. A valve is also the movable part of such a device.

Valve clearance The clearance between the valve tip (the end of the valve stem) and the rocker arm or tappet. The valve clearance is measured when the valve is closed.

Vernier caliper A precision measuring instrument that measures inside and outside dimensions. Not quite as accurate as a micrometer, but more convenient.

Viscosity The thickness of a liquid or its resistance to flow.

Volt A unit for expressing electrical "pressure" in a circuit. One volt that will produce a current of one ampere through a resistance of one ohm.

W

Welding Various processes used to join metal items by heating the areas to be joined to a molten state and fusing them together. For more information refer to the *Haynes Automotive Welding Manual*.

Wiring diagram A drawing portraying the components and wires in a vehicle's electrical system, using standardised symbols. For more information refer to the *Haynes Automotive Electrical and Electronic Systems Manual*.

Note: *References throughout this index are in the form* **"Chapter number"** • **"Page number".** *So, for example, 2C•15 refers to page 15 of Chapter 2C.*

Note: *References throughout this index are in the form* **"Chapter number"** • **"Page number"**. *So, for example, 2C•15 refers to page 15 of Chapter 2C.*

Haynes Manuals – The Complete **UK Car** List

Title	Book No.
ALFA ROMEO Alfasud/Sprint (74 - 88) up to F *	0292
Alfa Romeo Alfetta (73 – 87) up to E *	0531
AUDI 80, 90 & Coupe Petrol (79 – Nov 88) up to F	0605
Audi 80, 90 & Coupe Petrol (Oct 86 – 90) D to H	1491
Audi 100 & A6 Petrol & Diesel (May 91 – May 97) H to P	3504
Audi A3 Petrol & Diesel (96 – May 03) P to 03	4253
Audi A3 Petrol & Diesel (June 03 – Mar 08) 03 to 08	4884
Audi A4 Petrol & Diesel (95 – 00) M to X	3575
Audi A4 Petrol & Diesel (01 – 04) X to 54	4609
Audi A4 Petrol & Diesel (Jan 05 – Feb 08) 54 to 57	4885
AUSTIN A35 & A40 (56 – 67) up to F *	0118
Mini (59 – 69) up to H *	0527
Mini (69 – 01) up to X	0646
Austin Healey 100/6 & 3000 (56 – 68) up to G *	0049
BEDFORD/Vauxhall Rascal & Suzuki Supercarry (86 – Oct 94) C to M	3015
BMW 1-Series 4-cyl Petrol & Diesel (04 – Aug 11) 54 to 11	4918
BMW 316, 320 & 320i (4-cyl)(75 – Feb 83) up to Y *	0276
BMW 3- & 5- Series Petrol (81 – 91) up to J	1948
BMW 3-Series Petrol (Apr 91 – 99) H to V	3210
BMW 3-Series Petrol (Sept 98 – 06) S to 56	4067
BMW 3-Series Petrol & Diesel (05 – Sept 08) 54 to 58	4782
BMW 5-Series 6-cyl Petrol (April 96 – Aug 03) N to 03	4151
BMW 5-Series Diesel (Sept 03 – 10) 53 to 10	4901
BMW 1500, 1502, 1600, 1602, 2000 & 2002 (59 – 77) up to S *	0240
CHRYSLER PT Cruiser Petrol (00-09) W to 09	4058
CITROEN 2CV, Ami & Dyane (67 – 90) up to H	0196
Citroen AX Petrol & Diesel (87- 97) D to P	3014
Citroen Berlingo & Peugeot Partner Petrol & Diesel (96 – 10) P to 60	4281
Citroen C1 Petrol (05 – 11) 05 to 11	4922
Citroen C3 Petrol & Diesel (02 – 09) 51 to 59	4890
Citroen C4 Petrol & Diesel (04 – 10) 54 to 60	5576
Citroen C5 Petrol & Diesel (01 – 08) Y to 08	4745
Citroen C15 Van Petrol & Diesel (89 – Oct 98) F to S	3509
Citroen CX Petrol (75 – 88) up to F	0528
Citroen Saxo Petrol & Diesel (96 – 04) N to 54	3506
Citroen Visa Petrol (79 – 88) up to F	0620
Citroen Xantia Petrol & Diesel (93 – 01) K to Y	3082
Citroen XM Petrol & Diesel (89 – 00) G to X	3451
Citroen Xsara Petrol & Diesel (97 – Sept 00) R to W	3751
Citroen Xsara Picasso Petrol & Diesel (00 – 02) W to 52	3944
Citroen Xsara Picasso (Mar 04 – 08) 04 to 58	4784
Citroen ZX Diesel (91 – 98) J to S	1922
Citroen ZX Petrol (91 – 98) H to S	1881
FIAT 126 (73 – 87) up to E *	0305
Fiat 500 (57 – 73) up to M *	0090
Fiat 500 & Panda (04 – 12) 53 to 61	5558
Fiat Bravo & Brava Petrol (95 – 00) N to W	3572
Fiat Cinquecento (93 – 98) K to R	3501
Fiat Panda (81 – 95) up to M	0793
Fiat Punto Petrol & Diesel (94 – Oct 99) L to V	3251
Fiat Punto Petrol (Oct 99 – July 03) V to 03	4066
Fiat Punto Petrol (03 – 07) 03 to 07	4746

Title	Book No.
Fiat Punto Petrol (Oct 99 – 07) V to 07	5634
Fiat X1/9 (74 – 89) up to G *	0273
FORD Anglia (59 – 68) up to G *	0001
Ford Capri II (& III) 1.6 & 2.0 (74 – 87) up to E *	0283
Ford Capri II (& III) 2.8 & 3.0 V6 (74 – 87) up to E	1309
Ford C-Max Petrol & Diesel (03 – 10) 53 to 60	4900
Ford Escort Mk I 1100 & 1300 (68 – 74) up to N *	0171
Ford Escort Mk I Mexico, RS 1600 & RS 2000 (70 – 74) up to N *	0139
Ford Escort Mk II Mexico, RS 1800 & RS 2000 (75 – 80) up to W *	0735
Ford Escort (75 – Aug 80) up to V *	0280
Ford Escort Petrol (Sept 80 – Sept 90) up to H	0686
Ford Escort & Orion Petrol (Sept 90 – 00) H to X	1737
Ford Escort & Orion Diesel (Sept 90 – 00) H to X	4081
Ford Fiesta Petrol (Feb 89 – Oct 95) F to N	1595
Ford Fiesta Petrol & Diesel (Oct 95 – Mar 02) N to 02	3397
Ford Fiesta Petrol & Diesel (Apr 02 – 08) 02 to 58	4170
Ford Fiesta Petrol & Diesel (08 – 11) 58 to 11	4907
Ford Focus Petrol & Diesel (98 – 01) S to Y	3759
Ford Focus Petrol & Diesel (Oct 01 – 05) 51 to 05	4167
Ford Focus Petrol (05 – 09) 54 to 09	4785
Ford Focus Diesel (05 – 09) 54 to 09	4807
Ford Fusion Petrol & Diesel (02 – 11) 02 to 61	5566
Ford Galaxy Petrol & Diesel (95 – Aug 00) M to W	3984
Ford Galaxy Petrol & Diesel (00 – 06) X to 06	5556
Ford Granada Petrol (Sept 77 – Feb 85) up to B *	0481
Ford Ka (96 – 08) P to 58	5567
Ford Mondeo Petrol (93 – Sept 00) K to X	1923
Ford Mondeo Petrol & Diesel (Oct 00 – Jul 03) X to 03	3990
Ford Mondeo Petrol & Diesel (July 03 – 07) 03 to 56	4619
Ford Mondeo Petrol & Diesel (Apr 07 – 12) 07 to 61	5548
Ford Mondeo Diesel (93 – Sept 00) L to X	3465
Ford Sierra V6 Petrol (82 – 91) up to J	0904
Ford Transit Connect Diesel (02 – 11) 02 to 11	4903
Ford Transit Diesel (Feb 86 – 99) C to T	3019
Ford Transit Diesel (00 – Oct 06) X to 56	4775
Ford 1.6 & 1.8 litre Diesel Engine (84 – 96) A to N	1172
HILLMAN Imp (63 – 76) up to R *	0022
HONDA Civic (Feb 84 – Oct 87) A to E	1226
Honda Civic (Nov 91 – 96) J to N	3199
Honda Civic Petrol (Mar 95 – 00) M to X	4050
Honda Civic Petrol & Diesel (01 – 05) X to 55	4611
Honda CR-V Petrol & Diesel (02 – 06) 51 to 56	4747
Honda Jazz (02 to 08) 51 to 58	4735
JAGUAR E-Type (61 – 72) up to L *	0140
Jaguar Mk I & II, 240 & 340 (55 – 69) up to H *	0098
Jaguar XJ6, XJ & Sovereign, Daimler Sovereign (68 – Oct 86) up to D	0242
Jaguar XJ6 & Sovereign (Oct 86 – Sept 94) D to M	3261
Jaguar XJ12, XJS & Sovereign, Daimler Double Six (72 – 88) up to F	0478
JEEP Cherokee Petrol (93 – 96) K to N	1943
LAND ROVER 90, 110 & Defender Diesel (83 – 07) up to 56	3017
Land Rover Discovery Petrol & Diesel (89 – 98) G to S	3016

Title	Book No.
Land Rover Discovery Diesel (Nov 98 – Jul 04) S to 04	4606
Land Rover Discovery Diesel (Aug 04 – Apr 09) 04 to 09	5562
Land Rover Freelander Petrol & Diesel (97 – Sept 03) R to 53	3929
Land Rover Freelander (97 – Oct 06) R to 56	5571
Land Rover Series II, IIA & III 4-cyl Petrol (58 – 85) up to C	0314
Land Rover Series II, IIA & III Petrol & Diesel (58 – 85) up to C	5568
MAZDA 323 (Mar 81 – Oct 89) up to G	1608
Mazda 323 (Oct 89 – 98) G to R	3455
Mazda B1600, B1800 & B2000 Pick-up Petrol (72 – 88) up to F	0267
Mazda MX-5 (89 – 05) G to 05	5565
Mazda RX-7 (79 – 85) up to C *	0460
MERCEDES-BENZ 190, 190E & 190D Petrol & Diesel (83 – 93) A to L	3450
Mercedes-Benz 200D, 240D, 240TD, 300D & 300TD 123 Series Diesel (Oct 76 – 85) up to C	1114
Mercedes-Benz 250 & 280 (68 – 72) up to L *	0346
Mercedes-Benz 250 & 280 123 Series Petrol (Oct 76 – 84) up to B *	0677
Mercedes-Benz 124 Series Petrol & Diesel (85 – Aug 93) C to K	3253
Mercedes-Benz A-Class Petrol & Diesel (98 – 04) S to 54	4748
Mercedes-Benz C-Class Petrol & Diesel (93 – Aug 00) L to W	3511
Mercedes-Benz C-Class (00 – 07) X to 07	4780
Mercedes-Benz Sprinter Diesel (95 – Apr 06) M to 06	4902
MGA (55 – 62)	0475
MGB (62 – 80) up to W	0111
MGB 1962 to 1980 (special edition) *	4894
MG Midget & Austin-Healey Sprite (58 – 80) up to W *	0265
MINI Petrol (July 01 – 06) Y to 56	4273
MINI Petrol & Diesel (Nov 06 – 13) 56 to 13	4904
MITSUBISHI Shogun & L200 Pick-ups Petrol (83 – 94) up to M	1944
MORRIS Minor 1000 (56 – 71) up to K	0024
NISSAN Almera Petrol (95 – Feb 00) N to V	4053
Nissan Almera & Tino Petrol (Feb 00 – 07) V to 56	4612
Nissan Micra (83 – Jan 93) up to K	0931
Nissan Micra (93 – 02) K to 52	3254
Nissan Micra Petrol (03 – Oct 10) 52 to 60	4734
Nissan Primera Petrol (90 - Aug 99) H to T	1851
Nissan Qashqai Petrol & Diesel (07 – 12) 56 to 62	5610
OPEL Ascona & Manta (B-Series) (Sept 75 – 88) up to F *	0316
Opel Ascona Petrol (81 – 88)	3215
Opel Ascona Petrol (Oct 91 – Feb 98)	3156
Opel Corsa Petrol (83 – Mar 93)	3160
Opel Corsa Petrol (Mar 93 – 97)	3159
Opel Kadett Petrol (Oct 84 – Oct 91)	3196
Opel Omega & Senator Petrol (Nov 86 – 94)	3157
Opel Vectra Petrol (Oct 88 – Oct 95)	3158
PEUGEOT 106 Petrol & Diesel (91 – 04) J to 53)	1882
Peugeot 107 Petrol (05 – 11) 05 to 11	4923
Peugeot 205 Petrol (83 – 97) A to P	0932
Peugeot 206 Petrol & Diesel (98 – 01) S to X	3757

* Classic reprint

Title	Book No.
Peugeot 206 Petrol & Diesel (02 – 06) 51 to 06	4613
Peugeot 207 Petrol & Diesel (06 – July 09) 06 to 09	4787
Peugeot 306 Petrol & Diesel (93 – 02) K to 02	3073
Peugeot 307 Petrol & Diesel (01 – 08) Y to 58	4147
Peugeot 308 Petrol & Diesel (07 – 12) 07 to 12	5561
Peugeot 405 Diesel (88 – 97) E to P	3198
Peugeot 406 Petrol & Diesel (96 – Mar 99) N to T	3394
Peugeot 406 Petrol & Diesel (Mar 99 – 02) T to 52	3982
Peugeot 407 Diesel (04 -11) 53 to 11	5550
PORSCHE 911 (65 – 85) up to C	0264
Porsche 924 & 924 Turbo (76 – 85) up to C	0397
RANGE ROVER V8 Petrol (70 – Oct 92) up to K	0606
RELIANT Robin & Kitten (73 – 83) up to A *	0436
RENAULT 4 (61 – 86) up to D *	0072
Renault 5 Petrol (Feb 85 – 96) B to N	1219
Renault 19 Petrol (89 – 96) F to N	1646
Renault Clio Petrol (91 – May 98) H to R	1853
Renault Clio Petrol & Diesel (May 98 – May 01) R to Y	3906
Renault Clio Petrol & Diesel (June 01 – 05) Y to 55	4168
Renault Clio Petrol & Diesel (Oct 05 – May 09) 55 to 09	4788
Renault Espace Petrol & Diesel (85 – 96) C to N	3197
Renault Laguna Petrol & Diesel (94 – 00) L to W	3252
Renault Laguna Petrol & Diesel (Feb 01 – May 07) X to 07	4283
Renault Megane & Scenic Petrol & Diesel (96 – 99) N to T	3395
Renault Megane & Scenic Petrol & Diesel (Apr 99 – 02) T to 52	3916
Renault Megane Petrol & Diesel (Oct 02 – 08) 52 to 58	4284
Renault Scenic Petrol & Diesel (Sept 03 – 06) 53 to 06	4297
Renault Trafic Diesel (01 – 11) Y to 11	5551
ROVER 216 & 416 Petrol (89 – 96) G to N	1830
Rover 211, 214, 216, 218 & 220 Petrol & Diesel (Dec 95 – 99) N to V	3399
Rover 25 & MG ZR Petrol & Diesel (Oct 99 – 06) V to 06	4145
Rover 414, 416 & 420 Petrol & Diesel (May 95 – 99) M to V	3453
Rover 45 / MG ZS Petrol & Diesel (99 – 05) V to 55	4384
Rover 618, 620 & 623 Petrol (93 – 97) K to P	3257
Rover 75 / MG ZT Petrol & Diesel (99 – 06) S to 06	4292
Rover 820, 825 & 827 Petrol (86 – 95) D to N	1380
Rover 3500 (76 – 87) up to E *	0365
Rover Metro, 111 & 114 Petrol (May 90 – 98) G to S	1711
SAAB 95 & 96 (66 – 76) up to R *	0198
Saab 90, 99 & 900 (79 – Oct 93) up to L	0765
Saab 900 (Oct 93 – 98) L to R	3512
Saab 9000 4-cyl (85 – 98) C to S	1686
Saab 9-3 Petrol & Diesel (98 – Aug 02) R to 02	4614
Saab 9-3 Petrol & Diesel (92 – 07) 52 to 57	4749
Saab 9-3 Petrol & Diesel (07-on) 57 on	5569
Saab 9-5 4-cyl Petrol (97 – 05) R to 55	4156
Saab 9-5 (Sep 05 – Jun 10) 55 to 10	4891
SEAT Ibiza & Cordoba Petrol & Diesel (Oct 93 – Oct 99) L to V	3571
Seat Ibiza & Malaga Petrol (85 – 92) B to K	1609
Seat Ibiza Petrol & Diesel (May 02 – Apr 08) 02 to 08	4889

Title	Book No.
SKODA Fabia Petrol & Diesel (00 – 06) W to 06	4376
Skoda Felicia Petrol & Diesel (95 – 01) M to X	3505
Skoda Octavia Petrol (98 – April 04) R to 04	4285
Skoda Octavia Diesel (May 04 – 12) 04 to 61	5549
SUBARU 1600 & 1800 (Nov 79 – 90) up to H *	0995
SUNBEAM Alpine, Rapier & H120 (68 – 74) up to N *	0051
SUZUKI SJ Series, Samurai & Vitara 4-cyl Petrol (82 – 97) up to P	1942
Suzuki Supercarry & Bedford/Vauxhall Rascal (86 – Oct 94) C to M	3015
TOYOTA Avensis Petrol (98 – Jan 03) R to 52	4264
Toyota Aygo Petrol (05 – 11) 05 to 11	4921
Toyota Carina E Petrol (May 92 – 97) J to P	3256
Toyota Corolla (80 – 85) up to C	0683
Toyota Corolla (Sept 83 – Sept 87) A to E	1024
Toyota Corolla (Sept 87 – Aug 92) E to K	1683
Toyota Corolla Petrol (Aug 92 – 97) K to P	3259
Toyota Corolla Petrol (July 97 0 Feb 02) P to 51	4286
Toyota Corolla Petrol & Diesel (02 – Jan 07) 51 to 56	4791
Toyota Hi-Ace & Hi-Lux Petrol (69 – Oct 83) up to A	0304
Toyota RAV4 Petrol & Diesel (94 – 06) L to 55	4750
Toyota Yaris Petrol (99 – 05) T to 05	4265
TRIUMPH GT6 & Vitesse (62 0 74) up to N *	0112
Triumph Herald (59 – 71) up to K *	0010
Triumph Spitfire (62 – 81) up to X	0113
Triumph Stag (70 – 78) up to T *	0441
Triumph TR2, TR3, TR3A, TR4 & TR4A (52 – 67) up to F *	0028
Triumph TR5 & TR6 (67 – 75) up to P *	0031
Triumph TR7 (75 – 82) up to Y *	0322
VAUXHALL Astra Petrol (Oct 91 – Feb 98) J to R	1832
Vauxhall/Opel Astra & Zafira Petrol (Feb 98 – Apr 04) R to 04	3758
Vauxhall/Opel Astra & Zafira Diesel (Feb 98 – Apr 04) R to 04	3797
Vauxhall/Opel Astra Petrol (04 – 08)	4732
Vauxhall/Opel Astra Diesel (04 – 08)	4733
Vauxhall/Opel Astra Petrol & Diesel (Dec 09 – 13) 59 to 13	5578
Vauxhall/Opel Calibra (90 – 98) G to S	3502
Vauxhall Cavalier Petrol (Oct 88 0 95) F to N	1570
Vauxhall/Opel Corsa Diesel (Mar 93 – Oct 00) K to X	4087
Vauxhall Corsa Petrol (Mar 93 – 97) K to R	1985
Vauxhall/Opel Corsa Petrol (Apr 97 – Oct 00) P to X	3921
Vauxhall/Opel Corsa Petrol & Diesel (Oct 03 – Aug 06) 53 to 06	4617
Vauxhall/Opel Corsa Petrol & Diesel (Sept 06 – 10) 56 to 10	4886
Vauxhall/Opel Corsa Petrol & Diesel (00 – Aug 06) X to 06	5577
Vauxhall/Opel Frontera Petrol & Diesel (91 – Sept 98) J to S	3454
Vauxhall/Opel Insignia Petrol & Diesel (08 – 12) 08 to 61	5563
Vauxhall/Opel Meriva Petrol & Diesel (03 – May 10) 03 to 10	4893
Vauxhall/Opel Omega Petrol (94 – 99) L to T	3510
Vauxhall/Opel Vectra Petrol & Diesel (95 – Feb 99) N to S	3396

Title	Book No
Vauxhall/Opel Vectra Petrol & Diesel (Mar 99 – May 02) T to 02	3930
Vauxhall/Opel Vectra Petrol & Diesel (June 02 – Sept 05) 02 to 55	4618
Vauxhall/Opel Vectra Petrol & Diesel (Oct 05 – Oct 08) 55 to 58	4887
Vauxhall/Opel Vivaro Diesel (01 – 11) Y to 11	5552
Vauxhall/Opel Zafira Petrol & Diesel (05 -09) 05 to 09	4792
Vauxhall/Opel 1.5, 1.6 & 1.7 litre Diesel Engine (82 – 96) up to N	1222
VW Beetle 1200 (54 – 77) up to S	0036
VW Beetle 1300 & 1500 (65 – 75) up to P	0039
VW 1302 & 1302S (70 – 72) up to L *	0110
VW Beetle 1303, 1303S & GT (72 – 75) up to P	0159
VW Beetle Petrol & Diesel (Apr 99 – 07) T to 57	3798
VW Golf & Jetta Mk 1 Petrol 1.1 & 1.3 (74 – 84) up to A	0716
VW Golf, Jetta & Scirocco Mk 1 Petrol 1.5, 1.6 & 1.8 (74 – 84) up to A	0726
VW Golf & Jetta Mk 1 Diesel (78 – 84) up to A	0451
VW Golf & Jetta Mk 2 Petrol (Mar 84 – Feb 92) A to J	1081
VW Golf & Vento Petrol & Diesel (Feb 92 – Mar 98) J to R	3097
VW Golf & Bora Petrol & Diesel (Apr 98 – 00) R to X	3727
VW Golf & Bora 4-cyl Petrol & Diesel (01 – 03) X to 53	4169
VW Golf & Jetta Petrol & Diesel (04 – 09) 53 to 09	4610
VW LT Petrol Vans & Light Trucks (76 – 87) up to E	0637
VW Passat 4-cyl Petrol & Diesel (May 88 – 96) E to P	3498
VW Passat 4-cyl Petrol & Diesel (Dec 96 – Nov 00) P to X	3917
VW Passat Petrol & Diesel (Dec 00 – May 05) X to 05	4279
VW Passat Diesel (June 05 – 10) 05 to 60	4888
VW Polo Petrol (Nov 90 – Aug 94) H to L	3245
VW Polo Hatchback Petrol & Diesel (94 – 99) M to S	3500
VW Polo Hatchback Petrol (00 – Jan 02) V to 51	4150
VW Polo Petrol & Diesel (02 – May 05) 51 to 05	4608
VW Transporter 1600 (68 – 79) up to V	0082
VW Transporter 1700, 1800 & 2000 (72 – 79) up to V *	0226
VW Transporter (air cooled) Petrol (79 – 82) up to Y *	0638
VW Transporter (water cooled) Petrol (82 – 90) up to H	3452
VW Type 3 (63 – 73) up to M *	0084
VOLVO 120 & 130 Series (& P1800) (61 – 73) up to M *	0203
Volvo 142, 144 & 145 (66 – 74) up to N *	0129
Volvo 240 Series Petrol (74 – 93) up to K	0270
Volvo 440, 460 & 480 Petrol (87 – 97) D to P	1691
Volvo 740 & 760 Petrol (82 – 91) up to J	1258
Volvo 850 Petrol (92 – 96) J to P	3260
Volvo 940 Petrol (90 – 98) H to R	3249
Volvo S40 & V40 Petrol (96 – Mar 04) N to 04	3569
Volvo S40 & V50 Petrol & Diesel (Mar 04 – Jun 07) 04 to 07	4731
Volvo S60 Petrol & Diesel (01 – 08) X to 09	4793
Volvo S70, V70 & C70 Petrol (96 – 99) P to V	3573
Volvo V70 / S80 Petrol & Diesel (98 – 07) S to 07	4263
Volvo V70 Diesel (June 07 – 12) 07 to 61	5557
Volvo XV60 / 90 Diesel (03 – 12) 52 to 62	5630

* Classic reprint

CL 27.08.13

Preserving Our Motoring Heritage

< The Model J Duesenberg Derham Tourster. Only eight of these magnificent cars were ever built – this is the only example to be found outside the United States of America

Almost every car you've ever loved, loathed or desired is gathered under one roof at the Haynes Motor Museum. Over 300 immaculately presented cars and motorbikes represent every aspect of our motoring heritage, from elegant reminders of bygone days, such as the superb Model J Duesenberg to curiosities like the bug-eyed BMW Isetta. There are also many old friends and flames. Perhaps you remember the 1959 Ford Popular that you did your courting in? The magnificent 'Red Collection' is a spectacle of classic sports cars including AC, Alfa Romeo, Austin Healey, Ferrari, Lamborghini, Maserati, MG, Riley, Porsche and Triumph.

A Perfect Day Out

Each and every vehicle at the Haynes Motor Museum has played its part in the history and culture of Motoring. Today, they make a wonderful spectacle and a great day out for all the family. Bring the kids, bring Mum and Dad, but above all bring your camera to capture those golden memories for ever. You will also find an impressive array of motoring memorabilia, a comfortable 70 seat video cinema and one of the most extensive transport book shops in Britain. The Pit Stop Cafe serves everything from a cup of tea to wholesome, home-made meals or, if you prefer, you can enjoy the large picnic area nestled in the beautiful rural surroundings of Somerset.

> John Haynes O.B.E., Founder and Chairman of the museum at the wheel of a Haynes Light 12.

< Graham Hill's Lola Cosworth Formula 1 car next to a 1934 Riley Sports.

The Museum is situated on the A359 Yeovil to Frome road at Sparkford, just off the A303 in Somerset. It is about 40 miles south of Bristol, and 25 minutes drive from the M5 intersection at Taunton.

Open 9.30am - 5.30pm (10.00am - 4.00pm Winter) 7 days a week, *except Christmas Day, Boxing Day and New Years Day*

Special rates available for schools, coach parties and outings Charitable Trust No. 292048